HARCOURT

Science

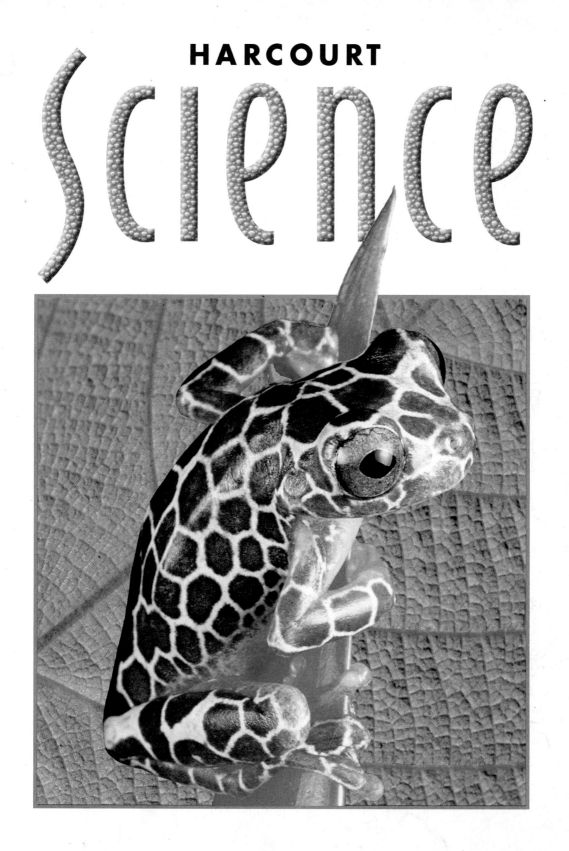

Harcourt School Publishers

Orlando • Boston • Dallas • Chicago • San Diego

www.harcourtschool.com

Cover Image
This frog is a reticulated clown tree frog. It is found in the rainforest surrounding the Amazon river valley in Peru.

Authors

Marjorie Slavick Frank
Former Adjunct Faculty Member at
    Hunter, Brooklyn, and Manhattan
    Colleges
New York, New York

Robert M. Jones
Professor of Education
University of Houston-Clear Lake
Houston, Texas

Gerald H. Krockover
Professor of Earth and Atmospheric
    Science Education
School Mathematics and Science
    Center
Purdue University
West Lafayette, Indiana

Mozell P. Lang
Science Education Consultant
Michigan Department of Education
Lansing, Michigan

Joyce C. McLeod
Visiting Professor
Rollins College
Winter Park, Florida

Carol J. Valenta
Vice President—Education, Exhibits,
    and Programs
St. Louis Science Center
St. Louis, Missouri

Barry A. Van Deman
Science Program Director
Arlington, Virginia

Printed in the United States of America

ISBN 0-15-311208-5

5 6 7 8 9 10 032 2002 2001 2000

UNIT C

EARTH SCIENCE
Processes That Change The Earth

UNIT E

PHYSICAL SCIENCE
Building Blocks of Matter

Using Science Process Skills

When scientists try to find an answer to a question or do an experiment, they use thinking tools called process skills. You use many of the process skills whenever you think, listen, read, and write. Think about how these students used process skills to help them answer questions and do experiments.

Greg is finding leaves for his leaf collection. He carefully **observes** the leaves and **compares** their shapes, sizes, and colors. He **measures** each leaf with a ruler. Then he **classifies** the leaves into groups by their sizes.

Try This Use the process skills of observing, comparing, measuring, and classifying to organize your own collection of nature objects.

Talk About It By what other characteristics could Greg classify the leaves in his collection?

Process Skills

Observe —use the senses to learn about objects and events

Compare —identify characteristics of things or events to find out how they are alike and different

Measure —compare an attribute of an object, such as its mass, length, or volume, to a standard unit such as a gram, a centimeter, or liter

Classify —group or organize objects or events in categories based on specific characteristics

It is a rainy Monday. Pilar wants to know if it will rain during the coming weekend. She **gathers** and **records** data to make a prediction about the weather. She observes the weather each day of the week and records it. She **displays** the data on a chart. On Friday, she **predicts**, based on her observations, that it will rain during the weekend.

Try This Beginning on a Monday, gather data about the temperature at noon. Record your data. Repeat this for four more days. Find a way to display your data. Then predict what the temperature will be at noon on Saturday.

Talk About It Why do you think Pilar predicted it would rain during the weekend?

Process Skills

Gather Data—make observations and use them to make inferences or predictions

Record Data—write down observations

Display Data—make tables, charts, or graphs

Predict—form an idea of an expected outcome based on observations or experience

Kim is interested in knowing how the size of a magnet is related to its strength. He **hypothesizes** that larger magnets are stronger than smaller magnets. He **plans and conducts a simple investigation** to see if his hypothesis is correct. He gathers magnets of different sizes. He finds items of different weights that the magnet will attract. He tests each item on each magnet, and records his findings. His hypothesis is correct until he tests the last item, a toy truck. When the largest horseshoe magnet cannot pick up the truck, but a smaller bar magnet can, he **infers** that the largest magnet is usually the strongest, but not always.

Try This Make a hypothesis about something you are interested in. Plan and conduct an investigation to test your hypothesis.

Talk About It Kim used different shapes of magnets as well as different sizes in his investigation. Do you think this could make a difference in the results? Why or why not?

Process Skills

Hypothesize — make a statement about the expected outcome based on observation, knowledge, and experience

Plan and conduct simple investigations — identify and perform the steps necessary to find the answer to a question, using appropriate tools and recording and analyzing the data collected

Infer — use logical reasoning to explain events and draw conclusions based on observations

Emily sees an ad about food wrap. The people in the ad claim that Tight-Right food wrap seals containers better than other food wraps. She plans a simple investigation to find out if this claim is true.

Emily **identifies and controls the variables** by choosing three bowls that are exactly the same. She labels the bowls A, B, and C. She places the bowls on a tray, and puts exactly 250 mL of water in each bowl. She cuts a 25-cm piece of Tight-Right wrap and places it on top of bowl A. She places 25-cm pieces of other brands of wrap on bowls B and C. She seals the wrap to the top of all three bowls as tightly as she can.

Emily **experiments** with the seals by pulling sharply on the tray. The water sloshes up the sides of the bowls. Water does not leak out the top of bowl A. On bowls B and C, the seals are broken, and water has spilled over onto the tray. From her observations, Emily infers that the claim for Tight-Right wrap is true.

Try This Plan an experiment to test different brands of a product your family uses. Identify the variables that you will control.

Talk About It Why did Emily use the tray in her experiment?

Process Skills

Identify and Control Variables — identify and control factors that affect the outcome of an experiment

Experiment — design ways to collect data to test hypotheses under controlled conditions

You will have many opportunities to practice and apply these and other process skills in *Harcourt Science.* An exciting year of science discoveries lies ahead!

Safety in Science

Doing investigations in science can be fun, but you need to be sure you do them safely. Here are some rules to follow.

① Think ahead. Study the steps of the investigation so you know what to expect. If you have any questions, ask your teacher. Be sure you understand any safety symbols that are shown.

② Be neat. Keep your work area clean. If you have long hair, pull it back so it doesn't get in the way. Roll or push up long sleeves to keep them away from your experiment.

③ Oops! If you should spill or break something, or get cut, tell your teacher right away.

④ Watch your eyes. Wear safety goggles anytime you are directed to do so. If you get anything in your eyes, tell your teacher right away.

⑤ Yuck! Never eat or drink anything during a science activity.

⑥ Don't get shocked. Be especially careful if an electric appliance is used. Be sure that electric cords are in a safe place where you can't trip over them. Don't ever pull a plug out of an outlet by pulling on the cord.

⑦ Keep it clean. Always clean up when you have finished. Put everything away and wipe your work area. Wash your hands.

In some activities you will see these symbols. They are signs for what you need to be safe.

CAUTION
Be especially careful.

CAUTION
Wear safety goggles.

CAUTION
Be careful with sharp objects.

CAUTION
Don't get burned.

CAUTION
Protect your clothes.

CAUTION
Protect your hands with mitts.

CAUTION
Be careful with electricity.

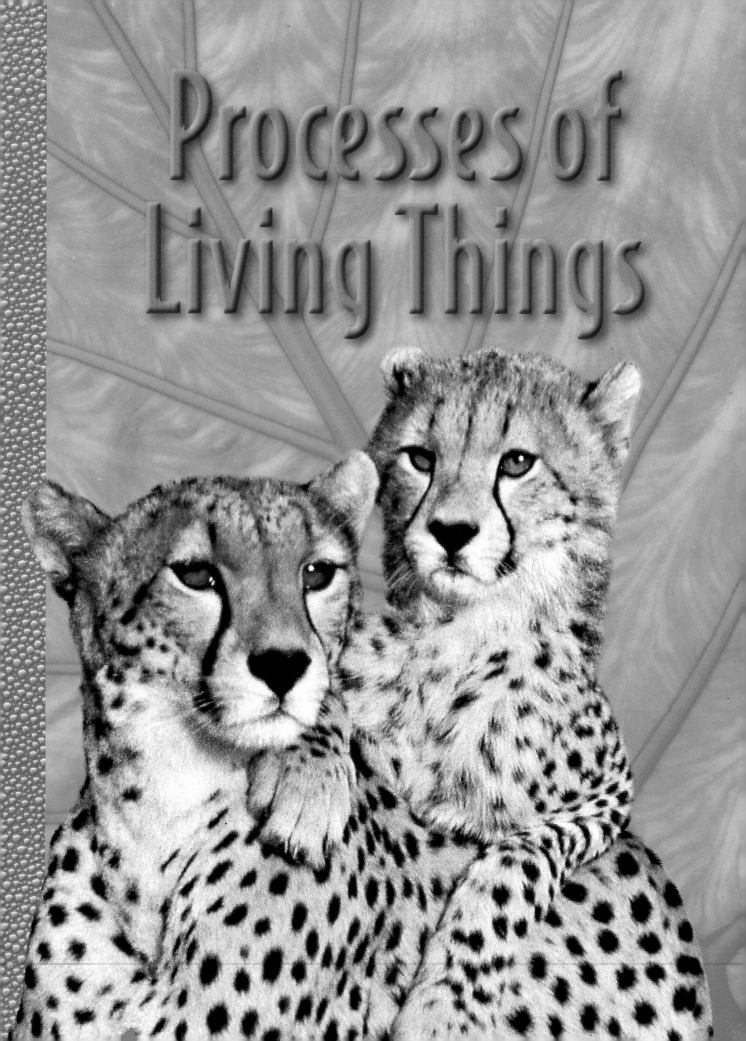

Processes of
Living Things

LIFE SCIENCE

Processes of Living Things

Unit Project

Animal and Plant Fold-Outs

Make fold-outs that show the growth of living things. Choose two plants and two animals to investigate. Fold four large sheets of paper into three parts each. Label the parts of each sheet *Young, Growing and Changing,* and *Mature.* Research how the plants and animals you've chosen grow and change. Draw a picture showing the growth process on each section of the fold-outs. Make notes on the back of the fold-outs that describe your pictures.

From Single Cells to Body Systems

Do you know what a fish, a tree, and a human being have in common? They are all made of tiny cells that carry on the processes of life.

Vocabulary Preview

cell	villi
cell	nephrons
membrane	bone marrow
nucleus	joints
cytoplasm	tendons
diffusion	ligaments
osmosis	neuron
tissue	receptors
organ	
system	
capillaries	
alveoli	

≡FAST FACT

Your body contains about
40,000 miles of blood vessels.
Within the blood vessel shown
here are disk-shaped red
blood cells and round white
blood cells.

A scanning electron microscope (SEM) can magnify objects as much as 900,000 times. This electron micrograph shows human face cells magnified 100,000 times.

A single square inch of human skin has more than 19 million cells.

What Are Cells, and What Do They Do?

In this lesson, you can . . .

INVESTIGATE what cells look like.

LEARN ABOUT cells.

LINK to math, writing, health, and technology.

This microscope allows a person to study a thin slice of material under high magnification.

![INVESTIGATE]

Observing Cells

Activity Purpose If you're looking at a landscape from far away, you might use a telescope to make the details clearer. Suppose you focused the telescope on a distant farm. You can see crates of freshly harvested onions. Now suppose you used a microscope to magnify the scene more and more. What details about an onion might you **observe**? In this investigation you'll observe a thin layer of an onion skin. Then you will observe and **compare** other plant cells and animal cells.

Materials
- Microslide Viewer
- Microslide of cell structure
- colored pencils

Alternate Materials
- slice of onion
- microscope slide
- coverslip
- dropper
- red food coloring
- microscope
- colored pencils

Activity Procedure

1 Insert the Cell Structure Microslide in the slot on the Microslide Viewer. Turn the focus knob until you can see the cells clearly. (Picture A)

2 **Observe** the onion skin cells and the human cheek cells. **Record** your observations by using the colored pencils to make drawings.

3 Now **observe** the green leaf cells and the nerve cells. Again, **record** your observations by making drawings. (Picture B)

4 Now **compare** your drawings. Make a Venn diagram with two large, overlapping circles. Label the circles *Plant Cells* and *Animal Cells*. Label the area where the circles overlap *Both Cells*. Draw the cell parts that you **observed** in the proper circles. Leave enough room to label the parts as you read about them in this lesson.

Picture A

Draw Conclusions

1. **Compare** the outer layers of plant and animal cells.

2. In the centers of most cells are structures that control the cells' activities. How many of these structures are there in each of the cells you **observed**?

3. **Scientists at Work** Scientists often **infer** characteristics of a group of objects by **observing** just a few of the objects. From your observations, what do you infer about the number of controlling structures in a cell?

leaf cells
Picture B

Investigate Further Now that you have **observed** photomicrographs of cells, use the materials in the *Alternate Materials* list to observe living cells from onion skin. Then **compare** your observations with the drawings you made in this investigation. See page R4 for tips on using a microscope.

Process Skill Tip

You can **infer** based on what you **observe**, or based on other information you have about a subject.

Cells

The Discovery of Cells

The Microslide you used in the investigation allowed you to observe parts of plants and animals under magnification. Without magnification, you couldn't have seen the structures you did. A microscope magnifies objects in a similar way. In fact, the photomicrographs you observed were taken through a microscope. The first microscopes were invented in the early 1600s. One scientist who built and used an early microscope was Robert Hooke.

In 1665 Hooke observed a thin slice of cork through a microscope. The tiny walled spaces he saw in the cork reminded him of tiny rooms. So he called them cells. Over the next 200 years, scientists learned more and more about cells. They learned that the **cell** is the basic unit of structure and function of all living things. The time line below shows some important early discoveries about cells.

✓ **Why were cells not observed before the 1600s?**

FIND OUT

- what cells are
- how cells are organized
- what cells do

VOCABULARY

cell
cell membrane
nucleus
cytoplasm
diffusion
osmosis
tissue
organ
system

1665 Robert Hooke records his observations of cork cells.

1838 Matthias Schleiden determines that every plant is made up of cells.

plant cells

1839 Theodor Schwann concludes that animals are also made up of cells.

animal cells

| 1600–1700 | 1700–1800 | 1800–1900 |

Kinds of Cells

Scientists have classified about a million kinds of plants and animals. But as different as those plants and animals seem to be, all of them are made of cells.

The simplest organisms, such as bacteria, are each a single cell. Most plants and animals, however, are made up of many cells. Humans, for example, are made up of *trillions* of cells. An organism with many cells usually has many different kinds of cells. Each kind of cell has a special function for the organism.

The size and shape of a cell depend on its function. Red blood cells, for example, are small and disc-shaped. They can easily fit through the smallest blood vessels. Muscle cells are long and thin. When they contract, or shorten, they produce movement. Nerve cells, which carry signals from the brain to the muscles, are very long.

Plants also have different kinds of cells. Some plant cells take in water from the soil. Others protect the plant. And still others make food.

Cells work together to perform basic life processes that keep organisms alive. These processes include releasing energy from food, getting rid of body wastes, and making new cells for growth and repair. However, every individual cell can perform all of these processes for itself.

✔ **Why might bone cells be different from muscle cells?**

The "skin" cells of this plant's leaves keep it from losing too much water. ▼

The skin cells make a watertight covering of scales that keep this iguana from losing water, too.

Plant and Animal Cells

Although cells are the basic unit of all living organisms, cells contain even smaller structures called *organelles* (awr•guh•NELZ). Each organelle has a particular function in the life processes of a cell.

All cells—except those of bacteria—have similar organelles. For example, every cell is enclosed by a thin covering called the **cell membrane**. The cell membrane holds the parts of the cell together. It also separates the cell from its surroundings.

Most cells have a nucleus (NOO•klee•uhs). The **nucleus** controls the cell's activities. The nucleus is enclosed in its own membrane. One function of the nucleus is cell reproduction. Cells can grow only to a certain size. So in order for plants and animals to grow, the number of cells has to increase.

Inside the nucleus are threadlike structures called *chromosomes* (KROH•muh•sohmz).

THE INSIDE STORY

Comparing Plant and Animal Cells

Plant cells have different shapes and sizes, but they all have the same parts. The diagram shows what you might observe if you could look inside a leaf cell. The organelles you see are working parts of a complete cell. Each organelle has its own specific function.

Plant Cell Structures

Nucleus— ① the organelle that controls all of a plant cell's activities and the production of new cells

Chromosomes— ② threadlike structures that contain information about the characteristics of the plant

Cell membrane— ③ a covering that holds the plant cell together and separates it from its surroundings

Cell wall— ④ a rigid layer that supports and protects the plant cell

Cytoplasm— ⑤ a jellylike substance that contains many chemicals to keep the cell functioning

Chloroplasts— ⑥ organelles that make food for the plant cell

Vacuole— ⑦ an organelle that stores food, water, or wastes

Mitochondria— ⑧ organelles that release energy from food

These contain information about the characteristics of the organism. When a cell reproduces, identical chromosomes go into each new cell.

Between the cell membrane and the nucleus is the cytoplasm (SYT•oh•plaz•uhm). **Cytoplasm** is a jellylike substance containing many chemicals to keep the cell functioning.

There are several kinds of organelles in the cytoplasm. Each is enclosed in a membrane. *Mitochondria* (myt•oh•KAHN•dree•uh)

release energy from food. *Vacuoles* (VAK•yoo•ohlz) are storage organelles. They store food, water, or waste materials.

Two organelles make plant cells different from animal cells. In addition to a cell membrane, a plant cell is surrounded by a rigid *cell wall*, which gives it strength. Plant cells also have *chloroplasts*, which make food.

✓ **How do plant cells and animal cells differ?**

The functions that allow an animal to live and grow are also carried out in its cells. Although the iguana's skin cells are a different shape and size from its blood cells, each cell typically contains the same parts. As you look at the diagram of an animal cell, notice how it differs from the plant cell.

Animal Cell Structures

Nucleus— ❶ the organelle that controls all of an animal cell's activities and the production of new cells

Chromosomes— ❷ threadlike structures that contain information about the characteristics of the animal

Cell membrane— ❸ a covering that holds the animal cell together and separates it from its surroundings

Cytoplasm— ❹ a jellylike substance that contains many chemicals to keep the cell functioning

Vacuoles— ❺ organelles that store food, wastes, or water

Mitochondria— ❻ organelles that release energy from food

Cell Transport

All the activities of a cell require energy. That energy is supplied by the mitochondria. Mitochondria need food, oxygen, and water to produce energy. This process produces carbon dioxide as a waste. How do cells get needed materials like food, water, and oxygen? And how do they get rid of wastes, like carbon dioxide?

Most materials move into and out of cells by diffusion. In the process of **diffusion**, particles of a substance move from an area where there are a lot of particles of the substance to an area where there are fewer particles of the substance.

For example, red blood cells carry oxygen from the lungs to all parts of the body. There is a lot of oxygen in red blood cells and very little in other body cells. So oxygen diffuses out of red blood cells and into body cells. At the same time, there is a lot of carbon dioxide in body cells and very little in the blood. So carbon dioxide diffuses out of body cells and into the blood.

Diffusion of materials into and out of cells takes place through the cell membrane. You might think of a cell membrane as a filter. It allows some particles to pass through, but it keeps other particles out.

Water and materials dissolved in water—such as oxygen or sugar—diffuse easily through cell membranes. Diffusion doesn't need energy from the cell. This energy-free movement of materials through a cell membrane is called *passive transport*.

The movement of water and dissolved materials through cell membranes is so important to living organisms that it is given a special name— **osmosis**. Cells get most of their water by osmosis.

Osmosis keeps plants from wilting. There is usually more water in the soil than in the

When you water a plant, water travels up the roots and stem and into the leaves. When a plant has too little water, it wilts because the concentration of water is higher inside the cells than outside, so water moves out of the cells as shown below.

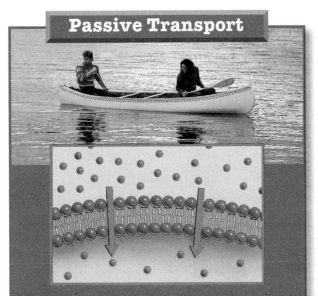

Passive Transport

This diagram of a cell membrane shows how substances enter a cell during passive transport. Notice how water can diffuse through any part of the cell membrane. Passive transport is like traveling downstream in a canoe. The current carries the canoe, and you don't need to use any energy to paddle.

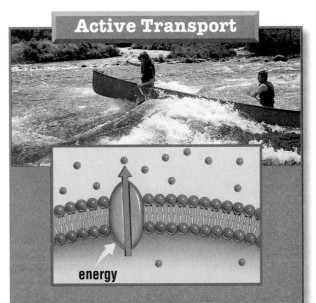

Active Transport

This diagram shows how substances move through a cell membrane during active transport. Cell energy "pushes" the carrier proteins through channels in the cell membrane. Active transport is like traveling upstream in a canoe. You must use energy to paddle the canoe to make it move.

energy

roots of plants. So water flows into plant cells. Water flowing into plant cells fills the vacuoles, which pushes the cytoplasm tightly against the cell walls. This causes plant stems and leaves to stand straight.

If the soil is very dry, there is more water in the plant than in the soil. Water leaves the plant by osmosis. The loss of water from the plant's vacuoles causes cytoplasm to shrink away from cell walls. The plant wilts and may die if it loses too much water.

Not all of the materials a cell needs are small enough to simply diffuse into the cell. And cells often need more of a substance than they can get through diffusion. For example, if a swimmer's muscle cells already have more sugar in them than there is in the blood, sugar won't diffuse into those cells. Mitochondria in the muscle cells might not

be able to produce the energy the swimmer needs.

However, there is another way for cells to get the materials they need. Cells can use a carrier either to transport materials that are too large to pass through the cell membrane or to transport materials against diffusion. This type of transport is called *active transport.*

A carrier transports materials into and out of a cell through a channel in the cell membrane. To do this, the carrier needs energy from the cell. In fact, one-third of the energy made by a cell is used to transport substances through the cell membrane in this way.

✓ **How does active transport differ from passive transport?**

Tissues, Organs, and Systems

In an organism made up of many cells, similar cells work together. Cells that work together to perform a specific function form a **tissue**. There are four kinds of tissues in humans.

Most of the mass of an animal is *muscle tissue*. Muscle tissue is made up of cells that contract when they receive signals from the brain. The contraction and relaxation of muscle tissue move the skeleton. The signals that cause muscle tissue to contract travel through another kind of tissue—*nervous tissue*. The brain and spinal cord, as well as the places where sight, hearing, taste, smell, and touch begin, are all nervous tissue.

Connective tissue is the third kind of tissue. It includes the tissue in bones, cartilage, and tendons. Blood is also a connective tissue.

The final kind of tissue is *epithelial* (ep•ih•THEE•lee•uhl) *tissue*. Epithelial tissue includes the body covering of an animal. It also lines most internal organs.

Just as cells that work together form a tissue, tissues that work together form an **organ**. Each organ in an animal's body is made of several kinds of tissues. Skin, for example, is an organ. It is made of many layers of epithelial tissue, as well as muscle tissue, nervous tissue, and a cushioning layer of connective tissue.

Each organ in an animal's body performs a major function that keeps the animal alive. The heart, for example, is an organ that pumps blood throughout the animal's body.

Organs that work together to perform a function form a **system**. A human has ten

In this diagram, you can see the four levels of organization in the digestive system. ▼

Body Organization

① This is a specialized cell.

② Similar cells form a tissue.

③ This tissue forms part of an organ—the stomach.

④ The stomach is part of a system that digests food, transfers digested food into the blood, and removes wastes.

major body systems. You will learn about some of those systems in the next two lessons.

Plant cells also form tissues, such as the bark of a tree. And plant tissues work together, forming organs, such as roots and leaves. You will learn more about plants in Chapters 3 and 4.

✓ **What kind of tissue gives an organism the ability to move?**

Summary

All living things are made up of one or more cells. Each cell is able to perform the functions that support life. Plant cells differ from animal cells in that they have cell walls and chloroplasts. Cells obtain the materials they need by passive or active transport through the cell membrane. Cells with similar functions form tissues. Tissues that function together make up an organ. Organs working together form a body system.

Review

1. What is the function of a cell's nucleus?
2. How do vacuoles in plant cells help keep the plant upright?
3. What is the difference between diffusion and osmosis?
4. **Critical Thinking** If you stand at one end of a room and spray perfume into the air, a person at the other end of the room will soon smell the perfume. Explain.
5. **Test Prep** One example of a tissue is —
   - **A** heart
   - **B** nucleus
   - **C** muscle
   - **D** mitochondria

LINKS

MATH LINK

Problem Solving Suppose a single cell divides into two cells every 15 min. If each of those also divides into two, and so on, how long will it take for a single cell to produce 500 cells?

WRITING LINK

Informative Writing—Compare and Contrast Write two or three paragraphs for your teacher comparing plant cells and animal cells.

HEALTH LINK

Interview a Doctor Find out how studying cells helps doctors understand the human body. Brainstorm with a family member to come up with questions you can ask your doctor the next time you have an appointment.

TECHNOLOGY LINK

Learn more about cells and body systems by visiting the Harcourt Learning Site.
www.harcourtschool.com

WELCOME TO THE LEARNING SITE

How Are Human Body Systems Organized?

In this lesson, you can . . .

INVESTIGATE cells and tissues.

LEARN ABOUT four human body systems.

LINK to math, writing, social studies, and technology.

◀ The materials your body uses to produce energy must be replaced.

INVESTIGATE

Cells and Tissues

Activity Purpose Your body is made up of cells that are organized into tissues, organs, and systems. Cells are highly specialized for the functions they perform for the body. Even cells that make up similar tissues can differ in many ways. In this investigation you will **observe** and **compare** under magnification several kinds of cells and tissues.

Materials

- Microslide Viewer
- Microslide of animal tissues
- colored pencils

Alternate Materials

- prepared slides of epithelial, connective, and nervous tissues
- microscope

Activity Procedure

1 Insert the Animal Tissues Microslide in the slot of the Microslide Viewer. Turn the focus knob until you can see the cells and tissues clearly. (Picture A)

2 **Observe** the voluntary muscle cells. **Record** your observations by using the colored pencils to make a drawing. Label your drawing with the name of the tissue. Then describe the tissue. You may use the Microslide text folder to help you write your description. (Picture B)

Picture A

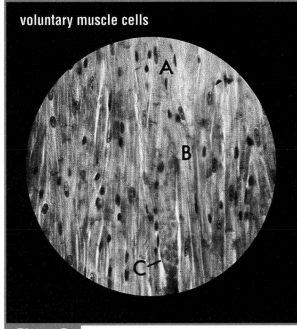

voluntary muscle cells

A

B

C

Picture B

3. Repeat Step 2 for the smooth muscle cells and the heart muscle.

4. **Compare** the three kinds of muscle tissue.

Draw Conclusions

1. How are the three kinds of muscle tissue alike? How are they different?

2. The dark-stained organelles you **observed** in the muscle tissues are mitochondria. Which kind of muscle tissue has the most mitochondria?

3. **Scientists at Work** When scientists **compare** objects, they often **infer** reasons for any differences. What do you infer about why one kind of muscle tissue has more mitochondria than the others?

Investigate Further Now that you have **observed** several kinds of tissues, use the materials in the *Alternate Materials* list to study other kinds of tissue. Observe the tissues under the microscope, and draw what you see. **Compare** these tissues with the muscle tissues you observed. See page R4 for tips on using a microscope.

Process Skill Tip

Making drawings of objects allows you to **compare** them and **infer** reasons for differences between them.

Human Body Systems

From Cells to Systems

FIND OUT

- about the circulatory, respiratory, digestive, and excretory systems

- which organs make up each system

- how the systems work together

VOCABULARY

capillaries
alveoli
villi
nephrons

The tissues you observed in the investigation combine in various ways to form body organs. Certain organs work together to form body systems. Each body system has a specific task that helps keep you alive. But your body systems also work together. On its own, a single body system cannot keep you alive.

The digestive system, for example, breaks down food into nutrients the body needs for energy. But without the circulatory system, the nutrients couldn't travel to the parts of the body that need them. The circulatory system also delivers the oxygen needed to release energy from food. However, without the respiratory system, oxygen couldn't get into the circulatory system. And all body processes produce wastes that must be removed. The excretory and respiratory systems share this function, with transportation provided by the circulatory system.

As you can see, working together is important for living organisms. Cells work together to form tissues. Tissues work together to form organs. Organs work together to form systems. And systems work together to keep you alive.

✔ **How do body systems depend on each other?**

These red blood cells are part of a tissue—blood. ▼

Blood vessels are another kind of tissue in the circulatory system. ▶

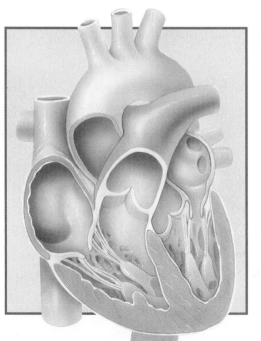

The heart is an organ of the circulatory system. It is made of muscle tissue. ▶

The Circulatory System

The circulatory system transports oxygen, nutrients, and wastes through the body in the blood. The liquid part of blood, called *plasma*, is mostly water. It also contains dissolved nutrients and waste products, such as carbon dioxide. The solid part of blood includes red blood cells and white blood cells. Red blood cells absorb oxygen from air in the lungs and transport it to every cell in the body. White blood cells help the body fight infection. They attack and destroy viruses and bacteria that enter the body.

Blood also contains *platelets*—tiny pieces of blood cells inside membranes. Platelets cause blood to clot when a blood vessel is cut. They also help repair damage to blood vessels.

The heart, an organ made of muscle tissue, pumps blood through blood vessels. The heart has four chambers, or parts. Oxygen-rich blood from the lungs enters one chamber. It moves to the next chamber, from which it is pumped to the body. Oxygen-poor blood from the body enters the third chamber. It moves to the fourth chamber, from which it is pumped to the lungs.

Blood leaves the heart through blood vessels called *arteries*. Arteries lead to capillaries. **Capillaries** are blood vessels so small that blood cells have to move through them in single file. There are capillaries throughout the body, so nutrients and oxygen can reach every cell. Waste products from cells are picked up by plasma in the capillaries. Capillaries lead to larger vessels, called *veins*, which return blood to the heart.

✔ **Why are platelets important?**

Capillaries

▲ Oxygen and nutrients diffuse from the blood into cells through capillary walls. The total length of capillaries in an adult human is more than 80,000 km (about 50,000 mi).

The heart beats all the time, pushing the blood into arteries. You can feel the push as a pulse in the artery in your wrist. ▼

blood

heart

veins

arteries

The Respiratory System

Your body uses a lot of energy. So your cells need a lot of food and oxygen. You get the oxygen your cells need by breathing. When you inhale, several liters of air are pulled into your body. The air is filtered by tiny hairs in your nose and warmed by capillaries that line the nasal passages. Warm, clean air then travels down your *trachea*, or windpipe.

In your chest, the trachea branches into two tubes called *bronchi* (BRAHNG•kee). Each tube leads into a lung. In the lungs, the bronchi divide into smaller and smaller tubes. At the end of the smallest tubes are tiny air sacs called **alveoli** (al•VEE•oh•lee). The walls of the alveoli are only one cell thick and are surrounded by capillaries.

The capillaries surrounding the alveoli get blood from the *pulmonary arteries* coming from the heart. This blood contains a lot of carbon dioxide. Carbon dioxide is a waste produced by the process that releases energy in cells. Carbon dioxide diffuses through the thin walls of the alveoli and into air that will be exhaled. At the same time, oxygen from inhaled air diffuses through the alveoli and into red blood cells in the capillaries. The oxygen-rich blood then flows from the capillaries into the *pulmonary veins* and back to the heart. From the heart, the oxygen-rich blood is pumped to other parts of the body.

✔ **What happens in the alveoli?**

The lungs are the major organs of the respiratory system. ▼

trachea

bronchi

▲ The gas exchange of oxygen and carbon dioxide takes place in the alveoli.

The lungs are on a separate circuit of the circulatory system. The heart pumps oxygen-poor blood through the pulmonary arteries to the lungs. The oxygen-rich blood travels through the pulmonary veins back to the heart. ▼

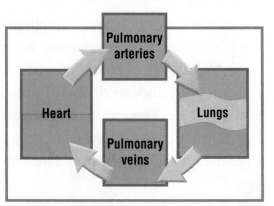

The Digestive System

Your digestive system provides the nutrients your cells need to produce energy. To provide nutrients, the digestive system performs two functions. The first is to break food into nutrients. The second is to get the nutrients into the blood. Then the circulatory system transports them to your cells.

Digestion begins as you chew food, breaking it into smaller pieces so that you can swallow it. Glands in your mouth produce saliva. Saliva moistens food and begins to break down starchy foods, such as pasta, into sugars. (If you chew an unsalted cracker for a while, it will begin to taste sweet.)

When you swallow, food passes through the *esophagus* (ih•SAHF•uh•guhs), a long tube that leads to the stomach. Gastric juice, produced by the stomach, contains acid and chemicals that break down proteins.

After several hours in the stomach, partly digested food moves into the small intestine. Digestion of food into nutrients is completed by chemicals produced in the small intestine. Nutrients diffuse through the **villi**, projections sticking out of the walls of the small intestine, into the blood. From the small intestine, undigested food passes into the large intestine. There, water and minerals diffuse into the blood and wastes are removed from the body.

Two other organs have a role in digestion. The *liver* produces bile, which is stored in the *gallbladder* until it's needed. Bile breaks down fats into smaller particles that can be more easily digested. The *pancreas* produces a fluid that neutralizes stomach acid and chemicals that help finish digestion.

✔ **In what organ of the digestive system do nutrients enter the blood?**

As food passes through the digestive system, chemicals break it down into nutrients the body cells need. ▼

salivary glands

esophagus

liver

gall bladder

stomach

pancreas

small intestine

large intestine

▲ Nutrients diffuse into the blood through the walls of the villi in the small intestine.

The Excretory System

The circulatory system supplies food and oxygen to the body's cells. It carries away waste products from the production of energy. The wastes must then be removed from the blood. This is the function of the excretory system.

Cell wastes include carbon dioxide and ammonia. As you learned, the respiratory system gets rid of carbon dioxide. Ammonia is carried by the blood to the liver, where it is changed to urea.

From the liver, urea is carried by the blood to the kidneys. These organs are located behind the liver and stomach. As blood flows through capillaries in the kidneys, urea and water diffuse into tubes called **nephrons**.

Urine, which is urea and water, flows from the kidneys through tubes called *ureters*. The ureters empty into a muscular organ called the bladder. When the bladder is full, urine leaves the body through a channel called the *urethra*.

The kidneys, ureters, bladder, and urethra make up the excretory system. This system takes wastes from the blood and removes them from the body as urine. ▼

▲ Wastes and water are removed from the capillaries that run through the kidneys. Materials that the body needs are returned to the capillaries.

The excretory system keeps the amount of water in the body fairly constant.

Daily Water Gain and Water Loss in Adults

Water Gain		Water Loss	
From cell activities	400 mL	In solid wastes	100 mL
From eating	900 mL	From skin and lungs	1000 mL
From drinking	1300 mL	As urine	1500 mL
Total	2600 mL	Total	2600 mL

Cell wastes aren't the only wastes the body needs to get rid of. When you exercise, your body gets warm. Excess heat is eliminated by sweating. Sweat is a salty liquid that evaporates from the skin. Evaporation pulls heat from capillaries just below the skin. The blood and the entire body are cooled.

✔ **How do cell wastes get to the kidneys?**

Summary

Body cells are organized into tissues, organs, and systems that work together to keep the body alive. The circulatory system transports materials throughout the body. In the respiratory system, oxygen diffuses into the blood and carbon dioxide diffuses out of the blood. The digestive system breaks down food into nutrients that can be used by cells. The excretory system removes cell wastes from the blood.

Review

1. How do the functions of red blood cells and white blood cells differ?
2. In what way do the respiratory and circulatory systems work together?
3. What does the pancreas do?
4. **Critical Thinking** Between the trachea and the esophagus is a flap of skin called the *epiglottis*. What do you think its function is?
5. **Test Prep** Inhaled oxygen diffuses through the walls of the —
   A ureters
   B bronchioles
   C pulmonary arteries
   D alveoli

LINKS

MATH LINK

Heartbeat Rate Count the number of times your heart beats in 15 sec. Then multiply the number by 4 to find your approximate heart beat rate per minute. At that rate, how many times would your heart beat in one year?

WRITING LINK

Informative Writing—Report Find out more about one of the body systems. Write a brief report for your teacher. Describe in detail the organs of the system. Also explain how the system functions.

SOCIAL STUDIES LINK

Early Physicians Some of the first recorded information about physicians described Imhotep, who lived in Egypt during the Third Dynasty (about 2700–2500 B.C.). Find out about Imhotep and his contributions to ancient medicine.

TECHNOLOGY LINK

Learn more about the functioning of the heart by investigating *One Heart—Two Amazing Pumps* on the **Harcourt Science Explorations CD-ROM.**

How Do Bones, Muscles, and Nerves Work Together?

In this lesson, you can . . .

INVESTIGATE how muscles cause movement.

LEARN ABOUT the skeletal, muscular, and nervous systems.

LINK to math, writing, art, and technology.

INVESTIGATE

How Muscles Cause Movement

Activity Purpose Your respiratory, circulatory, digestive, and excretory systems function automatically, without the need for you to give them directions. Other systems in your body are under your control, at least some of the time. When you run for a bus, for example, you direct your skeleton, muscles, and nerves to work together. In this investigation you'll **observe** what your muscles do when you bend your arm.

Materials

■ tape measure

Activity Procedure

1 Place your left hand on top of your right arm, between the shoulder and elbow. Bend and straighten your right arm at the elbow. **Observe** the movement by feeling the muscles in your right arm. (Picture A)

2 The muscle on the front of the upper arm is called the *biceps.* The muscle on the back of the upper arm is called the *triceps.* **Compare** the biceps and the triceps as you bend and straighten your arm. **Infer** which muscle controls the bending movement and which controls the straightening movement.

◄ In-line skating requires the coordination of your skeletal system, muscular system, and nervous system.

Picture A

Picture B

3 Have a partner use the tape measure to **measure** the distance around your upper arm when it is straight and when it is bent. **Record** the measurements. (Picture B)

4 Repeat Steps 2 and 3, using your right hand and your left arm.

5 **Compare** the sets of measurements.

Draw Conclusions

1. What did you **infer** about the muscles controlling the bending and the straightening of your upper arm?

2. Why are two muscles needed to bend and straighten your arm? Why can't one muscle do it?

3. **Scientists at Work** Scientists often **hypothesize** about things they **observe**. Hypothesize about any differences between the measurements of your right arm and the measurements of your left arm.

Investigate Further Repeat the investigation with different pairs of muscles. Try bending your leg at the knee while **observing** the muscles in your thigh. See if these observations also support your hypothesis.

Process Skill Tip

When you **hypothesize**, you tell what you think will happen based on what you **observe**. A hypothesis can be tested by doing an experiment.

Systems Working Together

Bones and Joints

FIND OUT

- what the structure and function of bones are
- how the skeletal, muscular, and nervous systems work together

VOCABULARY

bone marrow
joints
tendons
ligaments
neuron
receptors

The bones of your body are living organs made up of connective tissues. The tissues include an outer protective membrane, a layer of hard material, and a soft center containing bone marrow. **Bone marrow** is a connective tissue that produces red blood cells and white blood cells.

Bone cells form canals throughout the hard layer. The cells are connected to each other and to blood vessels. Bone cells secrete the rocklike material, made of calcium, that gives bones their strength and hardness. The protective membrane surrounding bones repairs them if they are broken.

Your body contains several kinds of bones. These include long bones in your arms and legs, flat bones in your shoulders and hips, and short bones in your fingers and toes. Other kinds of bones include the irregular bones in your wrists and ankles.

Bones meet at **joints**, where they are attached to each other and to muscles. Different kinds of joints allow different kinds of movement. Hinge joints, for example, allow back-and-forth movement, like the movement of a door hinge. Ball-and-socket joints allow circular motion, like the motion of a joystick. Some joints, such as the ones in your skull, don't allow any movement.

✔ **What kind of tissue are bones made of?**

Bones

long bone

flat bone

short bone

Joints

hinge joint

immovable joint

ball-and-socket joint

The Skeletal System

Bones are organized into a skeleton, which provides support for your body. Your skeleton also protects many of your internal organs. For example, your skull completely encloses your brain.

The outer layer of a bone provides a surface for the attachment of muscles. On each side of a joint, muscles are attached to bones by **tendons**, tough bands of connective tissue. Bones are attached to each other by **ligaments**, bands of connective tissue that hold the skeleton together.

An adult human skeleton has 206 bones. Each hand has 27 bones and each foot has 26 bones. The skull is made up of 23 bones. Not all of the skeleton is bone. Your outer ears and the tip of your nose are *cartilage*— another type of connective tissue. Cartilage also coats the ends of bones where they meet at a joint. This allows smooth movement between bones.

The Muscular System

There are three kinds of muscles—voluntary muscles, smooth muscles, and cardiac muscles. *Voluntary muscles* move bones and hold your skeleton upright. These muscles are made up of groups of muscle tissues bound together by connective tissue. They are generally attached to two or more bones, either directly or through tendons. Where muscles attach to bones at a joint, they work in opposing pairs. As you observed in the investigation, one muscle contracts to bend a joint. Another contracts to straighten it.

Smooth muscles contract slowly and move substances through the organs they surround. These muscles run in bands around the walls of blood vessels and digestive organs.

Cardiac muscles make up the walls of the heart. Their function is to pump blood. Some cardiac muscles work together to set the heartbeat rate. They ensure that all the cardiac muscles beat at the same time.

✔ **How are muscles attached to bones?**

✔ **Why must voluntary muscles work in pairs?**

The bones of the elbow are held together by ligaments.

Long tendons connect the wrist bones with the muscles in the forearm.

The rib cage protects the heart and lungs.

The Nervous System

Your nervous system allows you to experience things and to react to your environment. It connects all the tissues and organs of your body to your brain. The nervous system consists of two parts—the central nervous system and the peripheral nervous system. The central nervous system is made up of the brain and the spinal cord. The spinal cord is a bundle of nerves, about as thick as a pencil. It runs from the base of the brain to the hips.

The peripheral nervous system consists of sensory organs, such as the eyes and ears, and body nerves. Nerves are bundles of nerve cells, or neurons. A **neuron** is a specialized cell that can receive signals and transmit them to other neurons.

Signals traveling along nerves jump the gap between neurons. This gap is called a *synapse.* The signal is carried across the synapse by chemicals produced in the sending neuron.

Sensory organs contain neurons called receptors. **Receptors** are nerve cells that detect conditions in the body's environment. Receptors in the ears detect sound waves. Those in the skin detect heat and cold, pressure, touch, and pain. Receptors in the eyes detect light and color. Those in the mouth and nose detect tastes and smells. Each receptor sends a signal through nerves to the central nervous system.

The central nervous system interprets signals it receives from nerves and determines what response is needed. Signals sent by the brain travel through nerves and direct all of the body's muscles. The brain also controls the body's automatic functions, such as respiration, circulation, and digestion.

Some muscle actions are automatic responses to situations. These are called *reflexes.* For example, when a pain signal from a skin receptor reaches the spinal cord, the nerve carrying the signal transmits it directly to a nerve that controls muscles, as well as to a nerve traveling to the brain. The reflex action of the muscles to avoid the source of pain happens before the signal reaches the brain. In other words, you react to pain before you even feel pain.

✔ **What takes place at a synapse?**

spinal cord

Nerves are clusters of neurons that stretch between the central nervous system—the brain and the spinal cord—and every other part of the body. ▶

Axons make nerve cells the longest cells in the body. A single axon stretches between the spinal cord and the toes. ▼

dendrites

axon

If you accidentally touch a very hot object, your hand pulls back in a reflex action. This happens before the information reaches your brain. The signal from a heat receptor makes a "shortcut," triggering a neuron in the spinal cord that makes the muscles in your arm move your hand out of danger.

Summary

Bones are living organs that make up the skeletal system. Skeletal bones move because of the action of pairs of voluntary muscles. Smooth muscles line the digestive organs and blood vessels. Cardiac muscles make up the walls of the heart. Muscles are controlled by the central nervous system. Nerves are bundles of neurons. They carry signals from sensory organs to the brain and from the brain to the muscles.

Review

1. What is produced in bone marrow?
2. What function do ligaments perform?
3. What kinds of muscles move food through the digestive system?
4. **Critical Thinking** What kind of action is a sneeze caused by pepper in the air? Explain.
5. **Test Prep** Tendons are connective tissue that —
   A makes blood cells
   B carries signals from receptors
   C connects one bone to another
   D connects a bone to a muscle

LINKS

MATH LINK

Comparing Measurements Work with a partner to test your reaction time. Have your partner hold a meterstick vertically so that the lower end is just above the open fingers of your hand. When your partner lets the meterstick go—without warning—catch it between your fingers. Record the measurement where your fingers grasp the stick. Repeat the activity several times. Calculate how much your performance improves with practice.

WRITING LINK

Informative Writing—Description Fill one bowl with ice-cold water, one with hot—but not too hot—water, and one with lukewarm water. Leave one hand in the cold water and one in the hot water for about a minute. Then put both hands into the lukewarm water. Write a paragraph describing the results.

ART LINK

Pointillism Pointillist paintings are composed of small, separate dots of color, like a photograph. The brain interprets the dots as a picture. Try making a pointillist painting of your own.

TECHNOLOGY LINK

Learn more about the benefits of exercise by viewing *The Importance of Exercise* on the **Harcourt Science Newsroom Video.**

DISCOVERING CELLS

In 1665, English scientist Robert Hooke peered through his homemade microscope. Studying cork tissue, he named the little boxes he saw "cells." Hooke didn't realize it at the time, but his discovery of cells would have a great impact on biology.

Plants and Animals

It was nearly 200 years before scientists began to realize that Hooke's cells were a part of all living things. In 1831 scientists observed the nucleus of a cell and named it "little nut." They had no idea how impor-

tant it was to the cell. In 1838 Matthias Schleiden studied a variety of plant tissues and found that every type was made of many cells. A year later Theodor Schwann found that all animal tissues, too, were made of cells. Schleiden and Schwann are considered to have begun the cell theory—which states that cells are the building blocks of life and that cells come from other cells.

Cells and Germs

Developments in the cell theory produced interest in single-celled organisms. In 1857,

The History of Cells

1665
Robert Hooke names the "cell".

1796
A smallpox vaccine is developed.

1866
Mendel writes of "factors" in cells that transmit traits from parents to offspring.

A.D. 1600   A.D. 1700   A.D. 1800   A.D. 1900

1677
An improved microscope allows scientists to view microorganisms.

1953
Scientists discover the structure of DNA.

A28

after researching single-celled organisms, Louis Pasteur showed that some single-celled microorganisms, such as bacteria, can enter into and infect an organism, causing disease. Pasteur's germ theory changed medicine. Disease-causing organisms could now be identified, and methods could be developed to fight them.

Vaccines and Antibiotics

Pasteur's work also contributed to the development of vaccination—a process in which a killed microorganism is used to prevent infection by similar, but deadly, live microoganisms. Pasteur developed the first vaccine against rabies.

By the turn of the century, many other scientists were studying microorganisms and disease. In 1905 the bacteria that causes tuberculosis was identified. By the 1940s, scientists had developed antibiotics, such as penicillin, to fight bacterial infections.

Mysteries of the Cell Unraveled

Cell research wasn't limited to medicine. Scientists were also researching cell parts and their functions, as well as the factors of heredity carried by cells. In 1953 scientists discovered the structure of DNA—the chemical inside the nucleus that contains all the information a cell needs to function and reproduce.

Today scientists research how certain molecules are used by and affect cells. Scientists are also working to alter or control chemical processes in cells that cause diseases or disorders.

THINK ABOUT IT

1. How did Pasteur's research with single-celled organisms improve people's lives?
2. In addition to Hooke's observations of cells, what other scientific evidence led to the development of the cell theory?

A white blood cell (stained purple) surrounds bacteria (stained orange) and destroys them.

1997
Geneticists clone a living organism—a sheep—by implanting the nucleus from a body cell of an adult sheep into a fertilized egg cell.

A.D. 2000

1980
Molecular biologists identify several genes that can cause cancers in humans.

Bernard A. Harris, Jr.

ASTRONAUT, PHYSICIAN

*"What a sight . . .
the Earth below us,
the clouds that look
like they're hugging it.
It's even more incredible
than I imagined."*

When Bernard A. Harris, Jr., opened the hatch of the space shuttle *Discovery* and stepped outside, he became the first African American ever to walk in space. It was an amazing moment for a man who, from the age of 13, had dreamed of becoming an astronaut. His dream had been born as, watching on television, he saw Neil Armstrong take that first step on the moon. Although he kept his goal a secret, Dr. Harris worked constantly toward it, studying biology and medicine.

Dr. Harris's first trip in space was aboard the space shuttle *Columbia* in 1993. He and his crewmates experimented to find out the effects of space travel on the human body. The researchers learned that for every month astronauts spend in space, they lose 22.4–44.5 newtons (5–10 lb) of their body weight. In addition, they lose 20 percent of their blood volume because their bone marrow makes less blood.

While in space, Dr. Harris used sound waves to "see" his own heart and discovered that, under the conditions of near weightlessness, it shrank and shifted in his chest. "I had to listen for it in a slightly different place," he recalls.

Today, Dr. Harris is vice-president of SPACE-HAB, Inc., a company that furnishes payloads and experimental modules for NASA's space shuttles. He also is active in a program called Dare to Dream, which he started in a Houston school district.

THINK ABOUT IT

1. Why did Dr. Harris have to listen for his heart in a different place?
2. What physical effects might astronauts experience if they remain in space for many months?

Medical research in space

Balloon Lungs

How do lungs work?

Materials

- 2 balloons
- plastic soda bottle
- scissors

Procedure

1. Remove the cap and cut the bottom off the bottle.

2. Put one balloon into the bottle. Secure the lip of the balloon to the top of the bottle.

3. Cut the lip off the second balloon. Stretch the large part of the second balloon over the bottom of the bottle.

4. With your fingers, pull down on the second balloon and then release it. Observe what happens to the first balloon.

Draw Conclusions

When you pull on the second balloon, what happens inside the bottle? What part of the respiratory system does each part of your model represent?

Skeletal Systems

What adaptations do skeletons show?

Materials

- butcher paper
- meterstick
- 5 people
- marker

Procedure

1. Measure out about 7 m of butcher paper.

2. Have one person lie in the center of the paper. This person should stretch out his or her arms as shown.

3. Have two other people lie end-to-end on each side of the first person.

4. Use the marker to draw around the first person, including the top edge of his or her outstretched arms and thumbs.

5. To complete the top edge, draw a sloping line the lengths of the people on both sides as shown. Draw the lower edge with four points and four scallops as shown.

Draw Conclusions

While the skeletal systems of all mammals are similar, there are differences due to various adaptations. The skeletons of some mammals show adaptations for flight. If humans could fly, how many times longer than their bodies would their wings need to be? What other skeletal adaptations of mammals can you think of?

A31

Chapter 1 Review and Test Preparation

Vocabulary Review

Use the terms below to complete the sentences. The page numbers in ( ) tell you where to look in the chapter if you need help.

cell (A6)
cell membrane (A8)
nucleus (A8)
cytoplasm (A9)
diffusion (A10)
osmosis (A10)
tissue (A12)
organ (A12)
system (A12)
capillaries (A17)

alveoli (A18)
villi (A19)
nephron (A20)
bone marrow (A24)
joints (A24)
tendons (A25)
ligaments (A25)
neuron (A26)
receptors (A26)

1. The ____ are projections of the inside wall of the small intestine.

2. The smallest blood vessels are the ____.

3. Similar cells work together in a ____, which is part of an ____, which is part of a ____.

4. Cells that detect conditions in the body's environment are ____.

5. The ____ controls cell activities, and the ____ regulates what enters and leaves the cell.

6. Air sacs in the lungs through which oxygen and carbon dioxide diffuse into and out of the blood are the ____.

7. The ____ is the basic unit of structure of all living things.

8. At ____, bones are connected to each other by ____, while ____ connect bones to muscles.

9. A ____ is made up of a cell body, an axon, and several dendrites.

10. The structure in the kidney that filters urea and water from the blood is a ____.

11. Particles move from areas where there are a lot of them to areas where there are fewer of them by ____. Water and materials dissolved in water pass through a membrane by ____.

12. The jellylike substance between the cell membrane and the nucleus is the ____.

13. Blood cells are produced in ____.

Connect Concepts

Complete the chart by filling in terms from the Word Bank.

smooth muscle
oxygen
small intestine
nutrients
cardiac muscle

lungs
esophagus
alveoli
voluntary muscle

Food
travels down the **14.** to the stomach and then to the **15.**, where **16.** diffuse into the blood.

Air
travels down the trachea to the **17.**, where **18.** diffuses into the blood through the walls of the **19.**.

16. and **18.**
are carried by the blood to muscle cells. The energy they produce in **20.** tissue is used to move bones. The energy they produce in **21.** tissue is used to move food through the digestive system. The energy they produce in **22.** tissue is used to move blood through the circulatory system.

Check Understanding

Write the letter of the best choice.

23. The tissue that makes up bones, tendons, and ligaments is —
    A connective tissue
    B epithelial tissue
    C muscle tissue
    D voluntary tissue

24. Bile, produced by the liver, breaks down —
    F muscle tissue
    G fats
    H stomach acid
    J white blood cells

25. The urea and water that make up urine are removed from the blood in the —
    A bladder
    B kidneys
    C pancreas
    D urethra

26. A plant stands up straight because of water pressure against the —
    F cell walls
    G nucleus
    H cellular membrane
    J chloroplasts

27. A neuron transmits signals from its —
    A synapse
    B dendrites
    C cell body
    D axon

28. The liver is an organ of the —
    F digestive system only
    G excretory and digestive systems
    H circulatory system only
    J circulatory and excretory systems

Critical Thinking

29. A nerve can carry signals both to the brain and from the brain. Why can't an individual neuron do this?

30. Platelets in the blood cause clotting. Why is this important?

31. On each side of the heart, a valve allows blood to travel from the upper chamber to the lower chamber. Why is this important?

Process Skills Review

32. If you are **observing** cells under a microscope, what will lead you to **infer** that the cells are animal cells?

33. How would you test the **hypothesis** that there is never a ball-and-socket joint between a hinged joint and the end of a limb of a skeleton?

Performance Assessment

Body Systems

Use colored pencils to draw the organs and vessels of the circulatory system and the respiratory system on the human body outline your teacher gives you. Label each part. Describe how these systems work together to exchange oxygen and carbon dioxide in the body cells and in the lungs.

Chapter 2

Vocabulary Preview

chromosome
mitosis
asexual reproduction
sexual reproduction
meiosis
life cycle
direct development
metamorphosis
inherited trait
dominant trait
recessive trait
gene

A34

Animal Growth and Reproduction

Human children look like their parents. So do the young of many animals, such as this turtle. The young of many other organisms, however, do not look anything like their parents. Many organisms go through big changes as they grow and mature.

⫸FAST FACT

It's sometimes hard to determine how long wild animals live, but we do know how long domesticated animals, like dogs and cats, and zoo animals live. Some can live as long as human beings.

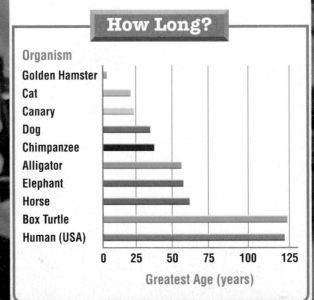

How Long?

Organism: Golden Hamster, Cat, Canary, Dog, Chimpanzee, Alligator, Elephant, Horse, Box Turtle, Human (USA)

Greatest Age (years): 0, 25, 50, 75, 100, 125

About 3 billion of your body's cells die every minute. Thanks to a process called *mitosis,* about the same number of new cells are formed every minute.

Many animals mature quickly. Mice, for example, start having young of their own when they are only four months old. By the time they are a year old, they may already be great-grandparents.

How Do Animals Grow and Reproduce?

In this lesson, you can . . .

INVESTIGATE cell reproduction.

LEARN ABOUT how organisms grow.

LINK to math, writing, language arts, and technology.

◄ The cells that make up the tiger cub will reproduce rapidly as the cub grows into an adult.

INVESTIGATE

Cell Reproduction

Activity Purpose Cells are the basic units of all living things. Cells make up bones, muscles, skin, and blood. They make up leaves, roots, stems, and flowers. Every part of an animal or a plant is made up of cells. As these cells grow and reproduce, the organism grows and develops. In this investigation you will **observe** how plant and animal cells reproduce.

Materials

- Microslide Viewer
- Microslide of plant mitosis
- Microslide of animal mitosis

Alternate Materials

- microscope
- prepared slides of plant cells dividing
- prepared slides of animal cells dividing

Activity Procedure

1 Insert the Plant Mitosis Microslide into the slot in the Microslide Viewer. Turn the focus knob until you can see the cells clearly. (Picture A)

2 **Observe** the plant cells dividing. **Record** what you observe in each stage of cell division. The descriptions on the microslide card may help you. Then draw pictures of what you see at each stage.

3 Now insert the Animal Mitosis Microslide into the slot in the Microslide Viewer. Again turn the focus knob until you can see the cells clearly.

Picture A

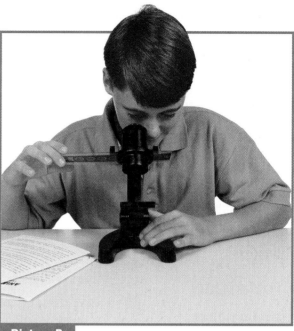

Picture B

4. **Observe** the animal cells dividing. **Record** what you observe in each stage of cell division. Again you may use the descriptions on the Microslide card to help you. Then draw pictures of what you see at each stage. (Picture B)

5. Now **compare** the stages of plant cell division with the stages of animal cell division. How are the stages alike? How are they different? **Record** your observations.

Draw Conclusions

1. What part of the cell changes as cell division occurs? What changes take place?

2. How many new cells does each dividing cell produce?

3. What similarities and differences did you **observe** between the dividing plant cells and the dividing animal cells?

4. **Scientists at Work** Scientists **observe** cells and ask questions based on their observations. What questions do you have about cell division, based on what you observed?

Investigate Further Now that you have observed photomicrographs of plant and animal cells dividing, use the materials on the *Alternate Materials* list to observe other cells dividing. See page R4 for tips on using a microscope.

> **Process Skill Tip**
>
> As you **observe** each slide, make a note of every detail—even if it doesn't seem important. Details will help you track exactly how a dividing cell changes from one stage to the next.

A37

How Organisms Grow

Growth

FIND OUT

- about growth and cell division
- about regeneration
- about mitosis and meiosis

VOCABULARY

chromosome
mitosis
asexual reproduction
sexual reproduction
meiosis

You began life as a single cell. That one cell divided into two cells. The two cells divided into four cells, the four cells into eight cells, and so on. By the time you were born, your body was already made up of billions of cells.

It may be hard to observe, but you're probably a little taller than you were a month ago. In that short time, your bone cells have divided again and again to make more bone tissue. Muscle and skin cells have also been dividing. As cells throughout your body continue dividing, your body will continue growing. By the time you are an adult, your body will have more than 100 trillion cells.

You know that body systems are made up of organs, organs are made of tissues, and tissues are made up of cells. The cells that make up each tissue have specific functions as part of an organ. So when bone cells divide, for example, they must produce cells exactly like themselves. Nearly all body cells produce exact copies of themselves. Producing identical cells enables new cells to perform the same functions as older cells. This allows organs to continue functioning properly as they grow.

✔ **Why do bone cells make exact copies of themselves?**

DAY 1
A chick begins life as an egg—a single cell.

DAY 5
After 5 days the single cell has divided into many cells.

DAY 8
By Day 8, eyes begin to develop.

DAY 14
At 14 days the chick has developed tiny feathers.

DAY 21+
After 21 days the chick is fully developed.

Nucleus

Chromosomes

Cytoplasm

Before a cell divides, the chromosomes shorten, thicken, and become visible.

Cell Division

Every square centimeter of your skin has about 150,000 skin cells. The top layer of skin is damaged by contact with the world around you. Its cells are always dying. Fortunately, skin cells reproduce quickly and replace the dead cells. In fact, the surface layer of your skin will be replaced twice today. Like most cells, skin cells reproduce by dividing in two. But what makes cells divide?

You know that the nucleus controls everything a cell does. So it is the nucleus that "tells" a cell when to divide. Inside the nucleus are threadlike strands. Each strand is called a **chromosome** (KROH•muh•sohm). Chromosomes are made up of a chemical called DNA, which forms a chemical code. This code determines the shape and function of a cell. It also determines when a cell will divide.

Whenever a cell divides, each new cell must get an exact copy of the parent cell's chromosomes. Having an identical set of chromosomes gives each new skin cell, for example, the same DNA code as its parent cell. This ensures that it will look and act like older skin cells.

The process of cell division is called **mitosis** (my•TOH•sihs). The nucleus of a cell prepares for mitosis by making an exact copy of its chromosomes. After the chromosomes have been copied, but before mitosis begins, a cell has enough DNA for two cells. During mitosis each chromosome separates from its copy. The two groups of chromosomes pull apart. Then the cell membrane pinches in at the middle, forming two new cells. Each new cell has the same DNA—and therefore the same shape and function—as its parent cell.

✔ **What happens in the nucleus before a cell divides?**

Mitosis

▲ Before mitosis the chromosomes (made up of DNA) make copies of themselves. Each chromosome and its copy are connected.

▲ As mitosis begins, the chromosomes grow thick and short. The nuclear membrane disappears.

▲ A network of thin tubes, called a spindle, forms. As the spindle gets longer, the attached chromosomes form a straight line in the middle of the cell.

This starfish escaped a hungry predator by dropping one of its arms. When regeneration is complete, the starfish will have a new arm. ▼

Regeneration

At one time or another, you have probably scraped your knee or cut your finger. If you cleaned the wound and kept it clean, after a few days all signs of the wound vanished. As soon as your body is wounded, it begins repairing itself.

Healing is a kind of *regeneration* (rih•jen•uh•RAY•shuhn), or tissue replacement. Skin cells divide, and regenerated skin grows over the cut. In humans, regeneration is pretty much limited to healing wounds.

Plants and some animals, however, can regenerate major body parts. For example, if a large animal grabs a lizard by its tail, the tail may drop off. If this happens, the lizard's remaining tail cells begin rapid mitosis. Before long, the lizard has regenerated a new tail.

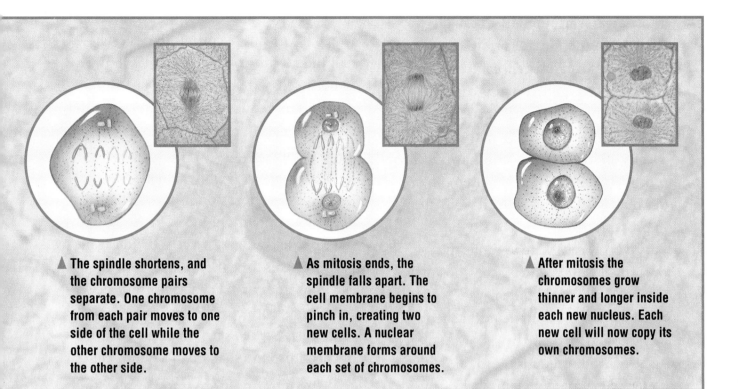

▲ The spindle shortens, and the chromosome pairs separate. One chromosome from each pair moves to one side of the cell while the other chromosome moves to the other side.

▲ As mitosis ends, the spindle falls apart. The cell membrane begins to pinch in, creating two new cells. A nuclear membrane forms around each set of chromosomes.

▲ After mitosis the chromosomes grow thinner and longer inside each new nucleus. Each new cell will now copy its own chromosomes.

Planaria (pluh•NEHR•ee•uh), a type of freshwater flatworm, can regenerate most of its body. If a planarian is cut in two, each piece regenerates the missing parts through mitosis. And chopping a sponge into many pieces is never deadly. The pieces simply regenerate many new, complete sponges.

✔ **How does mitosis help heal a wound?**

Asexual Reproduction

Many one-celled organisms, such as bacteria and protozoa, reproduce by simple cell division, or *fission*. This type of reproduction—without the joining of male and female cells—is called **asexual reproduction**. In fission the parent produces offspring through the process of mitosis.

Yeast—a one-celled fungus—reproduces asexually by a process called *budding*. A tiny

bud forms on the parent cell. Mitosis takes place within the parent cell, and a copy of the parent's chromosomes enters the growing bud. When the bud is fully grown, it separates from the parent cell.

Some plants also reproduce asexually. You will learn about asexual reproduction in plants in the next chapter.

✔ **How many parents are needed in asexual reproduction?**

A paramecium (par•uh•MEE•see•uhm) is a one-celled organism that lives in lakes and ponds. This paramecium is in the process of reproducing asexually. ▶

Sexual Reproduction

Most organisms reproduce sexually. In **sexual reproduction**, cells from two parents unite to form one cell, called a *zygote* (ZY•goht). The zygote contains chromosomes from both the female parent and the male parent.

Nearly all human body cells have 46 chromosomes each. If a body cell has more or fewer than 46 chromosomes, it won't function properly.

If two body cells were to unite, the zygote they formed would have 92 chromosomes. Every body cell would then have 92 chromosomes, instead of 46. In the next generation, the zygote and all the body cells would each have 184 chromosomes, and so on. With each new generation, the number of chromosomes would double.

This never happens, though, because the human body produces reproductive cells, which have only 23 chromosomes each—half the number of chromosomes found in body cells. **Meiosis** (my•OH•sis) is the process that reduces the number of chromosomes in reproductive cells.

In the first stage of meiosis, the cell copies its chromosomes and divides. Both of the new cells have 46 chromosomes. This process is similar to mitosis. In the second stage of meiosis, the two cells divide again. However, this time they do not copy their chromosomes first. Each of the four new cells is a reproductive cell, or *gamete* (GAM•eet). Gametes have half the number of chromosomes that are in a body cell.

✔ **Why must gametes have half the number of chromosomes that are in a body cell?**

Meiosis

The cells at the top of the diagram are body cells. The cells in the center of the diagram are reproductive cells. Because of meiosis, the reproductive cells have half the number of chromosomes that are in body cells. The cell at the bottom of the diagram is a zygote, with the same number of chromosomes as in body cells.

▲ Each of these gametes has half the number of chromosomes of a body cell.

Summary

Organisms grow when their cells divide. Body cells divide through the process of mitosis. Before mitosis, a cell makes copies of its chromosomes. After mitosis each of the new cells has an exact copy of the original cell's chromosomes. Reproductive cells have half the number of chromosomes that are in body cells. Meiosis reduces the number of chromosomes.

Review

1. What are chromosomes? Why are they important to cells?
2. How can some animals regenerate body parts?
3. Why must chromosomes be duplicated before mitosis?
4. What is asexual reproduction?
5. **Critical Thinking** Suppose an organism has 12 chromosomes in its body cells. How many chromosomes do its reproductive cells and zygotes have?
6. **Test Prep** During mitosis, what part of the cell pinches in to make two new cells?
   A the nucleus
   B the chromosomes
   C the DNA
   D the cell membrane

LINKS

MATH LINK

Dividing Chromosomes The list of organisms below shows the numbers of chromosomes in their body cells. Determine how many chromosomes each organism's reproductive cells have.

alligator, 32	housefly, 12
earthworm, 36	chimpanzee, 48
pigeon, 80	lettuce, 18

WRITING LINK

Informative Writing—Explanation Write an article for your school newspaper explaining the importance of meiosis. Briefly describe meiosis, and explain how it enables an organism to keep the same number of chromosomes in its body cells after sexual reproduction.

LANGUAGE ARTS LINK

Sequencing Mitosis Cut a sheet of paper into 10 pieces. On each piece, write something that happens during mitosis—for example, *spindle forms* or *nuclear membrane disappears*. Exchange pieces of paper with a classmate. Challenge each other to put the pieces in order.

TECHNOLOGY LINK

Learn more about cell division and reproduction by visiting this Internet site.
www.scilinks.org/harcourt

SC*i*LINKS™
THE WORLD'S A CLICK AWAY

What Is a Life Cycle?

In this lesson, you can . . .

 INVESTIGATE the stages of a mealworm's life.

LEARN ABOUT the stages of life.

LINK to math, writing, art, and technology.

 INVESTIGATE

The Stages of a Mealworm's Life

Activity Purpose   Many animals change as they grow and develop. The way an animal behaves and looks when it is young may change by the time it is an adult. In this investigation you will **observe** how a mealworm changes as it grows.

Materials
- mealworm culture
- paper plate
- hand lens

Activity Procedure

1 Your teacher will give you a mealworm from the mealworm culture.

2 Put the mealworm on the paper plate. Using the hand lens, **observe** the mealworm closely. Draw what you see. (Picture A)

3 Label these parts on your drawing: head, segment, antenna, outer shell, claw, mouth, and leg.

4 **Observe** the mealworm's movements. Does it move straight forward or from side to side? Does it move quickly or slowly? **Record** your observations.

5 Now your teacher will give you a beetle from the mealworm culture. Repeat Steps 2–4 with the beetle.

◀ This butterfly is about to begin the adult stage of its life cycle.

Picture A

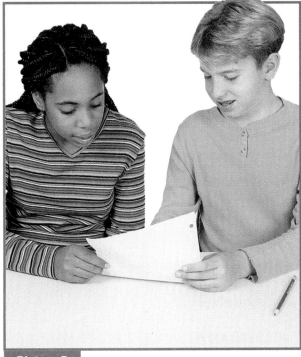

Picture B

6 Finally, **observe** the mealworm culture. Try to find evidence of other stages of a mealworm's life, such as eggs and pupa cases. Draw pictures of what you find.

7 **Compare** your drawings of the eggs and pupa cases with your drawings of the mealworm and the beetle. Form a **hypothesis** about the order of these life stages. Then list the ways in which a mealworm changes as it grows. (Picture B)

Draw Conclusions

1. How are the mealworm and the beetle similar?

2. How is the beetle different from the mealworm?

3. **Scientists at Work** Scientists often **observe** an organism and then **hypothesize** about their observations. What observations enabled you to form your hypothesis about the order of the life stages?

Investigate Further **Plan and conduct a simple investigation** to test your hypothesis about the life stages of a mealworm. Decide what equipment or technology you will need to use to test your hypothesis. Then use the equipment or technology in your investigation.

Process Skill Tip

As you **observe** stages in the life of an organism, you may find it helpful to **hypothesize** about the order in which the stages occur.

The Stages of Life

Life Cycles

Most organisms grow and mature through several distinct stages of life. These stages make up the organism's **life cycle**. All life cycles begin with a young organism struggling to survive in the world. Some organisms are born alive. Others develop in eggs and then hatch. Still others sprout from spores or seeds.

VOCABULARY

life cycle
direct development
metamorphosis

During each stage of life, a person changes physically. ▶

Depending on its type, a young organism spends anywhere from a few minutes to many years growing and developing. When an organism reaches its final form and size, it is an adult. During the adult stage, an organism is able to reproduce. Some organisms reproduce during their entire adult lives. Others stop reproducing as they get older.

Many organisms change a lot as they mature. But the young of some animals are identical to the adults, except in size. These organisms grow larger, but they keep the same body features, such as shape and coloring, all their lives. This kind of growth is called **direct development**. Spiders and earthworms have direct development. A young earthworm looks just like an adult earthworm, except smaller. What other animals can you think of that show this type of development?

These young scorpions are identical to the adult carrying them, except in size and color. ▼

✔ **What is a life cycle?**

A46

Incomplete Metamorphosis

Some animals, especially insects, have one kind of body when they are young and a very different kind of body when they are adults. The changes in the shape or characteristics of an organism's body as it grows and matures are called **metamorphosis** (met•uh•MOR•fuh•sis).

The life cycles of many insects, including beetles, butterflies, and grasshoppers, include metamorphosis. Some insects, such as cockroaches and grasshoppers, go through *incomplete metamorphosis*. These insects have only three stages of development: egg, nymph (NIMF), and adult. At each stage the insect looks different from the way it looks at another stage.

When a cockroach nymph first hatches, it doesn't have wings. After a period of growth, tiny wing buds appear on its body. As the nymph continues growing, wings develop from the wing buds. It takes about three months for a young cockroach to become an adult with fully formed wings.

During late spring and early summer, you may come across tiny, wingless hopping insects that look like grasshoppers. They are, in fact, grasshopper nymphs.

Cockroaches, grasshoppers, and other insects that go through incomplete metamorphosis must shed their outer skeletons as they grow. This process is called *molting*. Each time a grasshopper molts, a larger skeleton forms around its body. This gives the insect room to grow for a while.

✔ **Name the stages of incomplete metamorphosis.**

Incomplete Metamorphosis

The life cycle of a grasshopper includes three stages: egg, nymph, and adult.

The grasshopper nymph hatches from an egg.

The nymph looks like an adult, except that it has no wings.

The adult grasshopper has fully developed wings. Females lay hundreds of eggs.

The lifecycle of a beetle includes four stages: egg, larva, pupa, and adult.

When a pupa has become an adult, a mature beetle emerges.

An adult beetle lays hundreds of eggs.

The pupa changes a larva into an adult.

An egg develops into a larva. The larva, sometimes called a grub, eats plant roots, stems, and leaves.

Complete Metamorphosis

Have you ever been startled by a fuzzy, many-legged caterpillar creeping along a tree trunk? It's hard to imagine, but that same creature may one day be a moth or beautiful butterfly. Animals whose bodies change dramatically during their life cycles go through *complete metamorphosis*. A beetle is another example of an animal that goes through complete metamorphosis.

An insect's life cycle that includes complete metamorphosis has four distinct stages. During the first stage, the insect develops inside an egg. When the insect hatches from the egg, it enters the second stage of development. It is then called a

larva (LAR•vuh). A larva lacks wings and looks very different from an adult. It spends nearly all its time eating and storing energy for the next stage of its life cycle.

During the third stage of complete metamorphosis, insects neither eat nor move. At this stage, an insect is called a *pupa* (PYOO•puh). The pupa's body breaks down the organs and tissues it had as a larva. Most of the pupa's energy goes into developing an adult body. When the stage is complete, the pupa no longer exists and the adult insect emerges. Like all adult insects, the female lays eggs, the beginning of a new life cycle.

✔ **What are the stages of complete metamorphosis in insects?**

▲ This palm beetle lives in the Amazon rain forest.

Summary

All organisms have life cycles. Most organisms begin as young and develop into adults. The life cycles of some organisms show direct development. These organisms change only in size as they mature. Other life cycles include incomplete metamorphosis, with three stages of development. A life cycle that includes complete metamorphosis has four stages of development.

Review

1. What is the last stage in the life cycle of a beetle?
2. In what kind of development do the young look like miniature adults?
3. Why does a grasshopper nymph molt?
4. **Critical Thinking** Why doesn't a developing pupa move around?
5. **Test Prep** During the third stage of complete metamorphosis, the larva becomes—

    A a cocoon

    B a pupa

    C an egg

    D an adult

LINKS

MATH LINK

Feeding Monarch butterflies and June bugs go through complete metamorphosis. A monarch caterpillar (the larva) eats milkweed leaves for about a month before becoming a pupa. A June bug larva feeds underground for about three years. How many times as long as a monarch caterpillar eats does a June bug larva eat?

WRITING LINK

Expressive Writing—Poem Choose an animal, such as a frog, and write a poem for your class about its life cycle.

ART LINK

Mobile Research the complete metamorphosis of the monarch butterfly. Then make a hanging mobile illustrating the four stages of the monarch's life cycle. Share your mobile with your class.

TECHNOLOGY LINK

Learn more about complete metamorphosis of butterflies by visiting the Smithsonian Institution Internet site. **www.si.edu/harcourt/science**

 Smithsonian Institution®

LESSON 3

Why Are Offspring Like Their Parents?

In this lesson, you can . . .

INVESTIGATE
inherited characteristics.

LEARN ABOUT
inherited traits.

LINK to math, writing, social studies, and technology.

◄ This child and parent share obvious traits.

Inherited Characteristics

Activity Purpose What color are your hair and eyes? How long are your eyelashes? Are you right-handed or left-handed? These are just a few of the characteristics you have gotten from your parents. You may have some traits in common with your classmates. In this investigation you will **observe** three inherited traits. Then you will **use numbers** to see how common those traits are among your classmates.

Materials

- mirror

Activity Procedure

1 Make a chart like the one on the next page.

2 **Tongue Rolling** Use the mirror to **observe** what you are doing. Stick out your tongue, and try to roll its edges up toward the center. **Record** your results in the chart. (Picture A)

3 **Ear Lobes** Use the mirror to **observe** the shape of your ear lobes. Are they attached to your cheek, or do they hang free? **Record** your results in the chart.

4 **Folded Hands** Clasp your hands in front of you. **Observe** which of your thumbs falls naturally on top. **Record** your results in the chart. (Picture B)

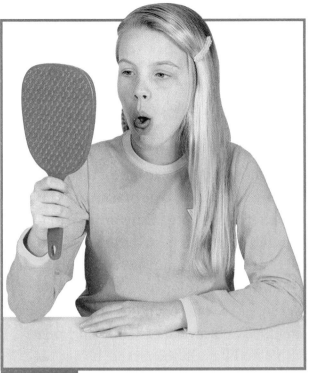

Picture A

Picture B

5 Your teacher will now ask students to report the results of their observations. Tally the results in the chart as students report them. Total the number of students for each characteristic. Then **calculate** what fraction of the class has each characteristic.

Characteristic	Results (Circle one.)		Class Totals
Tongue rolling	Yes	No	
Ear lobes	Attached	Free	
Folded hands	Left	Right	

Draw Conclusions

1. **Infer** whether a person could learn tongue rolling. Explain.

2. What other inherited characteristics could you have **observed**?

3. **Scientists at Work** Scientists often **use numbers** to summarize the data they collect. Which trait in each pair occurred most often in your class?

Investigate Further Do your class results suggest how often these traits occur in other people? Choose one or two of these characteristics. **Predict** whether the results will be the same for another group. Then ask some of your friends, neighbors, and family members to participate in this activity, and **observe** the results. **Record** the results, and share them with your class.

When you **use numbers**, you can summarize the data you collect.

Inherited Traits

From Parent to Offspring

FIND OUT

- how characteristics are inherited

- what genes are

VOCABULARY

inherited trait
dominant trait
recessive trait
gene

You may have friends who look a lot like one of their parents. They might share the same smile, eyes, type of hair, or skin color. Many of the characteristics of organisms are passed to their offspring. A characteristic that is passed from parent to offspring is an **inherited trait**. In many animals, hair color or fur color is an inherited trait. So is eye color.

Sometimes an offspring has a trait that it doesn't seem to have inherited from its parents. Two brown-haired human parents might have a child with blond hair. In the picture below, observe that the mother cat is orange. All but one of her kittens are orange, too. The gray kitten must have inherited its fur color from its parents. But how could orange parents produce a gray kitten?

Some behaviors are also inherited. Most dogs, for example, can swim without having been taught. But this is not an inherited behavior among humans.

✔ **What is an inherited trait?**

Sometimes a trait doesn't seem to have been inherited. ▼

How Characteristics Are Inherited

◀ Gregor Mendel

Gregor Mendel, a monk and a scientist, spent much of his time working with plants in a monastery garden. He observed that some pea plants were tall while others were short. He also observed that some plants produced green peas and others produced yellow peas. He knew the traits were inherited, but he didn't understand how.

In 1857 Mendel began experimenting by crossbreeding different pea plants. He kept detailed records of his results, which were published in 1865.

Mendel first bred a tall pea plant with a short pea plant. All the offspring, the first generation, were tall plants. He then bred two of these tall plants. In the second generation, three-fourths of the offspring were tall and one-fourth were short.

Mendel hypothesized that every trait is controlled by a pair of *factors*. For each trait, an offspring inherits one factor from each parent. The way the factors combine determines which trait appears in the offspring.

Mendel further hypothesized that the first-generation pea plants must have a hidden factor for shortness. Why? In the second generation, one-fourth of the offspring were short.

In peas, tallness is a strong trait, or **dominant trait**. Shortness is a weak trait, or **recessive trait**. Factors for both dominant and recessive traits may occur in an organism's chromosomes. However, recessive traits can be seen only if both parents pass the factor for it to the offspring. If only one parent pea plant, for example, passes a factor for shortness, the factor remains hidden. Then none of the offspring are short.

✔ **How did Mendel know that the tall pea plants in the first generation had a hidden factor for shortness?**

Inherited Factors

The adult rabbits each have a factor for dark brown fur, represented by blue. But each rabbit must also have a factor for light brown fur, represented by red, because one of their offspring is light brown. The light brown rabbit inherited a factor for light brown fur from each of its parents.

The gene for fur color occurs in the same spot on both chromosomes of the pair.

Genes

Today Mendel's factors are called genes. A **gene** contains the DNA codes for all the traits an organism inherits. Genes are on chromosomes. The genes for a particular trait always occupy the same place on a chromosome.

In wild rabbits, dark brown fur is a dominant trait. Light brown fur is a recessive trait. If a rabbit inherits even one gene for dark brown fur, it will have dark brown fur. Mendel's hidden factors were genes for recessive traits. Offspring must inherit two genes for recessive traits—one from each parent—for a recessive trait to be seen.

You can use a chart to calculate the chances that an offspring will inherit a particular combination of genes. The charts below show the chances that the offspring of two rabbits will inherit a particular fur

Dominant Traits

The chart at the left shows that all the offspring have dark brown fur. So the dark brown rabbit had two genes for dark brown fur. The chart at the right shows that half the offspring will have dark brown fur and half will have light brown fur. So the dark brown rabbit had one gene for dark brown fur and one gene for light brown fur.

The dark brown rabbit may have two genes for dark brown fur. Or it may have one gene for dark brown fur and one gene for light brown fur. The light brown rabbit must have two genes for light brown fur. ▼

color. Dark brown fur is a dominant trait. The gene for dark brown fur is highlighted in purple. Any box with a purple-highlighted gene in it stands for an offspring with dark brown fur. Light brown fur is a recessive trait. The gene for light brown fur is highlighted in red. Only a box with two red-highlighted genes stands for an offspring with light brown fur.

✔ **Why must baby rabbits have two genes for light brown fur if they are to have light brown fur?**

Summary

Many traits are inherited by offspring from their parents. Gregor Mendel's experiments with peas led to the discovery of the factors of inheritance. Genes—Mendel's "factors"—are on chromosomes. Each trait is controlled by a pair of genes. Gene combinations determine if traits are seen (dominant traits) or hidden (recessive traits).

Review

1. What are characteristics called that an offspring inherits from its parents?
2. What did Mendel hypothesize about inherited traits?
3. What is a dominant trait?
4. **Critical Thinking** Will an offspring show a recessive trait if only one of its parents has the gene for that trait? Explain.
5. **Test Prep** Mendel's "factors" are now known as —

   A genes
   B chromosomes
   C DNA
   D traits

LINKS

MATH LINK

Probability If you toss a coin 100 times, you might expect it to land heads up 50 times and tails up 50 times. That is, the chance, or probability, of its landing heads up is the same as the probability of its landing tails up. What is the probability that two coins, flipped at the same time, will both land heads up? Make a table with four columns: *Heads/Heads, Heads/Tails, Tails/Heads, Tails/Tails*. Then get two coins from your teacher. Flip them together 100 times. Record your results in the table. What is the probability that two coins will land heads up?

WRITING LINK

Expressive Writing—Song Lyrics Write a song for a friend about one of his or her best traits, such as the color of his or her eyes or hair.

SOCIAL STUDIES LINK

Research Obtain a book about James Watson and Francis Crick, the scientists who helped discover the structure of DNA. Write a paragraph about what they did.

TECHNOLOGY LINK

Learn more about inherited traits by viewing *Better Turkeys* on the **Harcourt Science Newsroom Video.**

Bionic Dog

As dogs grow older, they sometimes develop a painful disorder called hip dysplasia (dihs•PLAY•zhuh). Now veterinarians are able to replace one or both damaged hips with artificial parts.

Why Treat Hip Dysplasia?

Hip dysplasia is an abnormal development and growth of the hip joint, leading to arthritis. It causes pain whenever a dog stands, walks, runs, or jumps. In the early stages of the disorder, medicine can help, but when the pain becomes severe, medication is not enough. Dogs who were once very active no longer want to move. As the disorder progresses, the dog feels pain all the time, even when lying down. A dog may suffer so much that it has to be "put to sleep."

Total Hip Replacement (THR)

A total hip replacement, or THR, can save many dogs with hip dysplasia. In THR the damaged hip is replaced with a steel and plastic joint, often called an implant. Most

Large dogs are more likely than small dogs to have hip dysplasia.

femoral head

acetabular cup

Replacement hip joints are made of plastic and stainless steel.

dogs can walk immediately after surgery. After a recovery period of about two months, they can run, jump, and play as if they had a normal hip. Over 95 percent of all THR surgeries performed on dogs are successful, and the new hip lasts for the rest of the dog's life.

How Does THR Work?

Any dog that is at least 9 months old and weighs at least 30 pounds can be considered for THR. A few days before the surgery, the hair on the dog's leg is shaved and the skin bathed with medicine to prevent infection. During the surgery, which takes 90–120 minutes, the dog is given an anesthetic.

The artificial hip the dog receives consists of three parts. The femoral stem attaches to the femur in the dog's leg. The femoral head replaces the ball of the hip's ball-and-socket joint. A part called the acetabular cup replaces the original socket of the hip joint.

The implants are cemented to healthy bones with surgical cement. Hip implants for dogs are made from the same materials and implanted the same way as those for human hip replacements.

Instead of a THR, a dog can have a femoral head osteotomy, which is removal of the top of the femur of the diseased hip. However, this leaves the dog with less move-

ment than a THR. For a very young dog with hip dysplasia, surgery is done to save as much of the damaged hip as possible.

THINK ABOUT IT

1. Why do you think hip dysplasia usually occurs in bigger dogs rather than smaller dogs?
2. Why do you think a young pup is not given a THR?

WEB LINK:
For science and technology updates, visit The Learning Site.
www.harcourtschool.com

Careers | Veterinary Technician

What They Do
Veterinary technicians, or vet techs, assist veterinarians in private practice and in animal hospitals. Some vet techs assist veterinary surgeons who perform THRs. They may also work as research assistants in pharmaceutical companies.

Education and Training A person wanting to become a vet tech should attend a two-year or four-year college accredited by the American Veterinary Medical Association and major in animal science technology.

Eduardo S. Cantu

GENETICIST

"Physicians are relying more and more on genetics. They realize that many diseases and disorders have a genetic component. It's a very promising, challenging, and exciting field to get into."

Every human baby is born with about 50,000 different genes—and the possibility of more than 3000 genetic disorders. Most of these disorders are very rare, but geneticist Eduardo S. Cantu says that 50 to 100 of them could be considered common. Dr. Cantu, a scientist at the Medical University of South Carolina, studies ways in which genes and chromosomes affect a person's health.

As director of the Medical University's cytogenetic section, Dr. Cantu and his staff run tests that help physicians diagnose genetic disorders. Most of the tests they perform are used to diagnose genetic disorders before birth. The physician collects some of the fluid that surrounds a developing fetus, or unborn child. Then Dr. Cantu and his staff examine the fluid, which contains cells from the fetus, under a microscope. The genes in the cells provide a great deal of information about the unborn child, including whether it is likely to develop certain kinds of cancers and other diseases.

Dr. Cantu, who was born and raised in Texas, began his science education at Pan American University. His interest in genetics began when he was a graduate student. He had intended to study birds, but he found a genetics course so fascinating that he decided to change his course of study. It is a decision that Dr. Cantu is very glad he made.

THINK ABOUT IT

1. What is one kind of information that can be gained by studying the genes in the cells of a fetus?

2. Why do you think genetic research is a growing field of study?

Part of a human chromosome

DNA

How does DNA fit into a cell?

Materials

- sewing thread
- meterstick
- gelatin capsule

Procedure

1. Measure 10 m of thread. The thread stands for the DNA in a cell.

2. Open the gelatin capsule. The gelatin capsule stands for the nucleus of a cell.

3. Put all the thread into the capsule in whatever way you can. Then close the capsule.

Draw Conclusions

How did you get all the thread into the gelatin capsule? How does so much DNA fit into the nucleus of a cell?

Chromosomes

How do chromosome pairs separate?

Materials

- embroidery thread
- meterstick

Procedure

1. Measure 1 m of embroidery thread. The thread represents a chromosome.

2. Starting at one end, separate the thread into two pieces.

3. Again measure 1 m of embroidery thread.

4. Now separate the thread into two pieces, starting in the middle.

Draw Conclusions

Was it easier to separate the thread into two pieces by starting from one end or from the middle? During mitosis, where do chromosome pairs separate?

Chapter 2 Review and Test Preparation

Vocabulary Review

Use the terms below to complete the sentences. The page numbers in ( ) tell you where to look in the chapter if you need help.

chromosomes (A39)

mitosis (A39)

asexual
  reproduction (A41)

sexual
  reproduction (A42)

meiosis (A42)

life cycle (A46)

direct
  development (A46)

metamorphosis (A47)

inherited trait (A52)

dominant trait (A53)

recessive trait (A53)

gene (A54)

1. The term _____ applies to an organism whose body shape, form, or characteristics change during its life cycle.

2. In humans, hair color is an example of an _____.

3. The process which reduces the number of chromosomes in certain cells is called _____.

4. An organism in the adult stage of its _____ is able to reproduce.

5. The offspring of some animals are just like the adults, except for size. This is an example of _____.

6. During _____, duplicated _____ in the cell's nucleus separate, and the cell pinches into two cells.

7. In order for a _____ to be seen, an offspring must receive a factor for the trait from each parent. In order for a _____ to be seen, an offspring needs to receive a factor from only one parent.

8. A _____ carries the DNA code for a particular trait.

9. Reproduction without the joining of cells from the female parent and the male parent is called _____. Reproduction in which cells from two parents unite to form a zygote is called _____.

Connect Concepts

Choose terms from the Word Bank that complete the concept map.

mitosis   recessive

function   nucleus

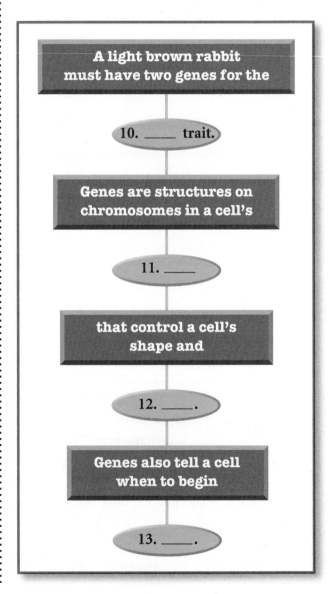

A light brown rabbit must have two genes for the

10. _____ trait.

Genes are structures on chromosomes in a cell's

11. _____

that control a cell's shape and

12. _____.

Genes also tell a cell when to begin

13. _____.

Check Understanding

Write the letter of the best choice.

14. In order for a new cell to function just like its parent cell, it must receive an exact copy of its parent cell's —

  A chromosomes   **C** cell wall

  B gametes   **D** recessive traits

15. Your bones and muscles grow larger as a result of —

  F meiosis   **H** direct

  G metamorphosis   development

                        J mitosis

16. What does **NOT** happen during mitosis?

  A the chromosomes duplicate

  B a spindle fiber forms

  C the number of chromosomes is halved

  D the nuclear membrane disappears

17. All the traits that parents pass to their offspring are called —

  F recessive traits   **H** physical traits

  G dominant traits   **J** inherited traits

18. If an offspring receives two genes, one from each parent, for a particular recessive trait, that trait will —

  A not be seen   **C** be seen halfway

  B be seen   **D** none of the above

19. Which sequence illustrates incomplete metamorphosis?

  F egg, larva, pupa, butterfly

  G kitten, cat

  H egg, nymph, adult

  J young raccoon, adult raccoon

20. When meiosis occurs, the number of chromosomes —

  A is doubled   **C** stays the same

  B is halved   **D** is tripled

Critical Thinking

21. A dark brown rabbit with a gene for light brown fur mates with a light brown rabbit. Out of four offspring, how many are likely to be dark brown?

22. Mitosis is necessary for the individual, but meiosis is necessary for the species. Explain this statement.

Process Skills Review

23. Choose an item in your classroom. It may be living or nonliving. **Observe** the item using as many of your senses as possible. Make at least seven observations about the item's characteristics.

24. **Compare** the life cycle of a grasshopper with that of a butterfly. Which insect's life cycle shows complete metamorphosis?

25. Describe the expected results of a cross between a dark brown rabbit and a light brown rabbit. **Use numbers** to describe the results in the second generation.

Performance Assessment

Charting Traits

Consider two inherited traits, such as tongue rolling and free or attached ear lobes. Choose symbols to represent genes for the dominant traits and genes for the recessive traits. For each trait, make charts showing the possible offspring when one parent has the dominant traits and the other parent has the recessive traits.

Chapter 3

Vocabulary Preview

xylem
phloem
chlorophyll
nonvascular
vascular
spore
gymnosperm
pollen
angiosperm
grain
fiber

Types of Plants and Their Adaptations

While animals can search for food and water, plants must meet these needs rooted in one place. But plants have many adaptations that help them survive.

FAST FACT

Part of a rain forest no larger than a city block may have more than 400 different kinds of trees. Most forests in the United States have no more than 20 different kinds of trees in the same area.

What Are the Functions of Roots, Stems, and Leaves?

In this lesson, you can . . .

INVESTIGATE the parts of plants.

LEARN ABOUT plant parts and their functions.

LINK to math, writing, social studies, and technology.

The silver sword grows only in Hawai'i. ▷

The Parts of a Plant

Activity Purpose Towering oak trees and potted geraniums have many parts in common. Most plants have roots, stems, and leaves. The sizes and shapes of these parts differ, but each part has a function that helps the plant live. In this investigation you will **observe** a potted plant and identify its basic parts.

Materials

- potted plant
- hand lens
- ruler
- newspaper
- plastic knife

Activity Procedure

1 Make a drawing of the plant. List all the parts of the plant that you can name.

2 **Observe** the leaves. What colors are they? Use the ruler to measure the length and width of the leaves. Are they all the same shape and size? Are they wide or narrow? Are they long or short? Do they grow singly or in pairs? Observe them more closely with the hand lens. What more can you say about them? Identify and label the leaves in your drawing. (Picture A)

3 **Observe** the stem. Does it bend? Does it have branches? What more can you say about it? Identify and label the stem in your drawing.

4 Hold the pot upside down over the newspaper. Tap the pot gently until the plant and the soil come out. If the plant won't come out, run the plastic knife around between the soil and the inside of the pot. (Picture B)

Picture A

Picture B

 5 Shake the soil from the roots until you can see them clearly. **Observe** the roots. Is there a single root, or are there many small roots? What shape are the roots? Use the ruler to **measure** the length of the roots. Are they thick or thin? Long or short? Use the hand lens to observe them more closely. What more can you say about them? Identify and label the roots in your drawing.

6 Put the soil and the plant back into the pot. Water the plant lightly to help it recover from being out of the pot.

Draw Conclusions

1. What are the parts of the plant you **observed**?

2. **Compare** the plant parts you identified with the parts of a large tree. How are they the same? How are they different?

3. **Scientists at Work** Scientists learn by making observations. What did you **observe** about each part of the plant?

Investigate Further **Observe** a different type of plant. Then identify its parts. Does it have the same parts as the plant you observed in the activity? Do the parts look the same as the parts you observed in the activity?

Process Skill Tip

When you **observe** something, you should use as many of your senses as you can. Don't just look at the plant. Touch it to see what it feels like and how thick or strong or dry it is. Smell its leaves and roots.

Plant Parts and What They Do

FIND OUT

- how plants grow in different environments
- what roots, stems, and leaves do

VOCABULARY

xylem
phloem
chlorophyll

Common Parts

There are more than half a million types of plants on Earth. They range from tiny desert plants, smaller than a pencil eraser, to giant redwood trees, taller than a 25-story building. No matter how different they appear, most plants have three parts in common—roots, stems, and leaves.

These parts make it possible for plants to live and grow almost everywhere. Plants are found in dry deserts, wet jungles, and cold Arctic plains. Plants are able to live in different environments because their roots, stems, and leaves are adapted to the environments in which they live.

✔ **What parts are common to most plants?**

◀ Some plants are able to grow through the cracks in a city sidewalk.

These crocuses bloom in low temperatures that would kill many other plants. ▼

▲ Mosses are simple plants. They need a lot of water to grow.

Some tall trees have roots that spread out as far as their branches. They help keep the trees from falling over.

A thick mat of fibrous roots allows grasses to take in large amounts of water from the soil. ▶

Dandelions have long taproots. If you try to pull a dandelion out of the ground, part of the root may remain. The dandelion will grow back from the part that is left in the ground. ▶

Roots

The roots of many trees spread as far from the trunk as their branches do. Most plant roots act as anchors. They keep the plant from falling over or blowing away in the wind. Roots also take in water and minerals from the soil through tiny parts called *root hairs*. Some roots also store food for the plant.

Different types of roots are adapted to different environments. Some small desert plants have roots that spread far from the plant but grow close to the surface. These roots are able to take in large amounts of the little rain that falls in the desert.

Forest trees don't need the spreading roots of desert plants because there is more water in the forest soil. These trees need deep roots to anchor them. Some tree roots, called *prop roots,* begin above the ground.

These help keep trees that grow in loose, wet soil from being blown over by the wind.

Many plants have *fibrous* (FY•bruhs) *roots,* which look a little like tree branches. The fibrous roots of some grasses form a thick and tangled mat just under the surface of the soil. Fibrous roots help prevent soil erosion by wind and water because they anchor the soil as well as the plant.

Some plants have a single, thick root that grows straight down. These roots, called *taproots,* can reach water that is deep in the ground. Some taproots store food for the plant as well.

In tropical rain forests there are plants that grow on branches high in the trees. Their roots attach themselves to the trees and take water directly from the moist air.

✔ **What do plant roots do?**

Storage Roots

Some plants store extra food and water to help them survive brief changes in their environments. Most plants cannot make food in the winter. In dry periods they may not be able to get all the water they need from the soil.

In good weather plants produce more food than they need and take in extra water. Some plants store extra food and water in their roots. Others store it in their stems.

Some plants store so much extra food in their roots that people grow them for their own food. You've probably eaten several

◀ This sugar beet root stores food for the plant in the form of sugar. Sugar beets are grown and sold for their sugar.

◀ The sugar cane plant stores sugar in its stems. Sugar cane is also grown and sold for its sugar.

kinds of storage roots. Beets, carrots, sweet potatoes, and turnips are called root vegetables. Because much of the food they store is in the form of sugar and starch, many root vegetables have a sweet taste.

✔ **What do some roots store?**

Stems

Stems do several things for plants. They hold the plant up, and they support the leaves so that they will be in sunlight. Stems also carry water and food to other parts of the plant.

Most plant stems grow upward. The leaves of long-stemmed plants can reach sunlight even in shady places. Some stems even turn during the day. This helps keep the leaves in sunlight, too.

Some plant stems grow sideways, instead of up. Wherever the stem touches the ground, it forms a root from which a new plant grows. Strawberry and spider plants are examples of this type of plant.

Many desert plants have stems that store food and water. The stem of the barrel cactus stores water for the plant. When rain is scarce, the cactus uses water from its stem.

Small plants, such as daisies and dandelions, usually have soft, green, flexible stems. The water inside the stem makes it firm enough to hold the plant up. You might have noticed that a cut flower begins to droop after a few days. Without a root, it can no longer get enough water to keep its stem firm. Most soft-stemmed plants live for just one growing season.

Large plants, such as bushes and trees, need extra support. For this reason, they usually have stiff, woody stems. Woody plants do not die at the end of one growing season but continue to grow year after year. Some woody plants, such as the redwoods of California, may live for hundreds or even thousands of years.

Most plant stems contain narrow tubes that carry water, minerals, and food. The tubes that transport water and minerals are called **xylem** (ZY•luhm). They move water and minerals upward, from the roots to the leaves. The strings you find when you bite into a stalk of celery are xylem tubes.

The tubes that carry food are called **phloem** (FLOH•em). They move the food made in the leaves to other parts of the plant. The food that plants make and store is needed for growth by roots, stems, and leaves.

In plants with flexible stems, xylem and phloem are in bundles scattered all through the stem. In plants with woody stems, the xylem and phloem are arranged in separate rings. The xylem is near the inside of the stem, while the phloem is close to the outside of the stem.

During each growing season, the stem of a woody plant gets thicker as new rings of xylem and phloem form. More xylem than phloem forms each year, so most of the thickness of a tree trunk is xylem. Older rings of xylem no longer transport water. They harden as they become filled with transported materials. This old xylem is the "wood" of a tree. People use the wood of many kinds of trees as lumber to build houses and to make furniture.

✔ **Name the two types of tubes that transport materials in plant stems.**

Each year, trees produce a new layer of xylem, forming a *growth ring.* Counting the growth rings of a cut tree can tell you how many years old the tree was.

xylem

growth ring

phloem

The trunk and branches of a tree are the plant's woody stems. The wood of a tree is old xylem. The bark is old phloem that is pushed outward as the trunk and branches grow thicker. ▶

Leaves

Leaves have many shapes and sizes. Some are smaller than a postage stamp, while others are large enough to cover a school bus. But whether they are big or small, most leaves are thin and flat. This helps them make food.

Leaves are the "food factories" of plants. They use water and minerals from the soil, carbon dioxide from the air, and energy from sunlight to make food. The food-making process also produces oxygen, which the plants release into the air.

A *pigment*, or coloring matter, called **chlorophyll** (KLAWR•uh•fil) helps plants use light energy to produce sugars. Chlorophyll gives leaves their green color. In the fall, as the days get shorter, most leaves stop making chlorophyll. Then other pigments already in the leaves can be seen. So it's not frost but simply a lack of chlorophyll that makes the beautiful fall colors seen throughout most of the country.

A leaf is not as simple as it may appear. Inside are layers of cells containing microscopic *chloroplasts* (KLAWR•uh•plasts), which are full of chlorophyll. The food-making process takes place inside the chloroplasts. There are also veins, or bundles of xylem and phloem, running through a leaf. Veins bring water and minerals to the chloroplasts and take sugars from them.

Carbon dioxide enters a leaf, and oxygen and water leave it, through tiny holes called *stomata* (stoh•MAH•tuh). Stomata open wide during the day, when the plant is making food. They close at night, to conserve water. A waxy outer layer on the top of most leaves helps conserve water during the heat of the day.

The leaves or stems of some plants are adapted as *tendrils*. Tendrils wrap themselves around poles or attach themselves to rough surfaces to help the leaves reach the sunlight they need to make food.

Some leaves "catch" food. The Venus' flytrap grows in places where the soil may not have all the nutrients the plant needs to make food. The plant's traplike leaves are adapted to snap shut when an insect lands on them. The leaves release chemicals that digest the insect and take from it the nutrients the plant needs.

Some leaves also store food. The fleshy layers of an onion bulb—the part we eat—are really leaves.

✓ **What is the main thing leaves do?**

The spines of a cactus (leaves) are an adaptation that protects the plant's food and water from desert animals. ▼

Summary

Each part of a plant has a different function. Roots anchor a plant and take in minerals and water from the soil. A stem supports a plant and moves materials between its parts. Leaves make the plant's food. All of these parts may be adapted to the environment and the needs of the plant.

Review

1. Why are the parts of some plants very different from those of other plants?
2. How are taproots and fibrous roots different?
3. Why do plants store food?
4. **Critical Thinking** What would happen to a green plant if you left it in a dark room for a long time?
5. **Test Prep** Some leaves change color in the fall. This is because —
   A they need to be replaced
   B they stop making chlorophyll
   C there is too much sunlight
   D the trees are dying

LINKS

MATH LINK

Ratio A ratio is a comparison that uses numbers. If a leaf is 6 cm long and 2 cm wide, the ratio of its length to its width is 3 to 1. Use a ruler to measure the length and width of a number of different leaves. Round each measurement to the nearest centimeter and record your measurements. What observations can you make about the ratio of length to width in the leaves you measured?

WRITING LINK

Informative Writing—Description
Suppose there were a world without trees. Write a story describing what such a world would be like. How would the world be different? What products would be missing from people's lives? Share your story with your classmates.

SOCIAL STUDIES LINK

Map Choose a type of plant and find out where in the United States it grows. Use a computer to make a map and identify the places where the plant grows. Then use the computer to make a chart showing the plant type, location, and climate.

TECHNOLOGY LINK

Learn more about plants by visiting the Harcourt Learning Site.
www.harcourtschool.com

WELCOME TO THE LEARNING SITE

LESSON 2

What Are the Two Major Groups of Plants?

In this lesson, you can . . .

INVESTIGATE simple plants.

LEARN ABOUT different types of plants.

LINK to math, writing, language arts, and technology.

INVESTIGATE

Simple Plants

Activity Purpose Scientists group plants by the way they transport water. You read in Lesson 1 that the stems of many plants have xylem that carries water from the roots to other parts of the plant. Now you will **observe** simple plants that have similar-looking parts. You will **infer** what these parts do by **comparing** them to the plant parts you observed in Lesson 1.

Materials
- moss
- liverwort
- hand lens

Activity Procedure

1 **Observe** the moss and the liverwort. **Record** what you see.

2 Now **observe** the plants with a hand lens. Can you see different parts? Do any of the parts you see look like the parts of the potted plant you observed in Lesson 1? (Picture A)

3 **Observe** the plants by touching them with your fingers. Are they soft or firm? Are they dry or moist? What else can you tell by feeling them? Describe what they feel like.

◄ Moss often grows in moist, shady forests. Many tiny plants grow close together to form a mat on tree trunks, rocks, or damp soil.

Picture A

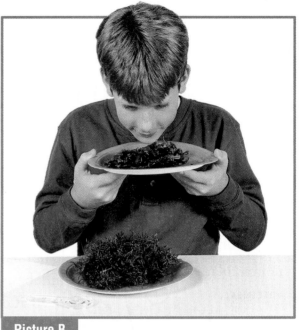

Picture B

4. Touch the plants with a pencil or other object while you **observe** them through the hand lens. Do the parts bend, or are they stiff? Do you see anything new if you push a part of the plant to one side? Describe what you see.

5. **Observe** the plants by smelling them. Do they have any kind of odor? Try to identify the odors. Describe what you smell. (Picture B)

6. Make drawings of the moss and liverwort, identify the parts you observed, and **infer** what each part does.

Draw Conclusions

1. What plant parts did you **observe** on the moss? What parts did you observe on the liverwort?

2. What do you **infer** each part of the plant does?

3. **Scientists at Work** Scientists use observations to **compare** things. Use the observations you made in this investigation to compare the moss and liverwort with the plant you observed in Lesson 1.

Investigate Further **Observe** a fern. How does it **compare** with the moss and the liverwort?

Different Kinds of Plants

Nonvascular Plants

FIND OUT

- what the two major kinds of plants are

- how plants reproduce

VOCABULARY

nonvascular

vascular

spore

gymnosperm

pollen

angiosperm

The spore capsules of moss plants contain hundreds of tiny spores. Each spore can grow into a new plant. ▼

Have you ever seen a green "carpet" growing near a forest stream? Chances are it was one of the plants you observed in the investigation. Mosses and liverworts are simple plants that usually grow in damp places. They need to stay moist because they do not have xylem tubes to transport water. They also lack phloem tubes.

Plants that don't have xylem and phloem are called **nonvascular** (nahn•VAS•kyuh•ler) plants. Nonvascular plants can move water, minerals, and food only from one cell to the next. This is the reason why nonvascular plants are so small. **Vascular** (VAS•kyuh•ler) plants, which have xylem and phloem, can grow much larger.

As you observed in the investigation, nonvascular plants have parts similar to those of vascular plants. Their leaflike parts, for example, have chloroplasts that use sunlight to manufacture food. Their thin, rootlike structures anchor the plants and take in some water and minerals. Their stemlike parts hold the leaflike parts up to the sunlight. However, these parts are not

Nonvascular Reproduction

Male and female cells join, and a spore stalk grows from the female plant.

The stalk releases spores.

Spores grow into new moss plants.

The plants produce male and female cells.

true leaves, roots, or stems, because they do not have xylem and phloem.

Nonvascular plants do not have flowers, so they don't reproduce with seeds. Instead, they reproduce with spores (SPOHRZ). A **spore** is a single reproductive cell that grows into a new plant. During their life cycle, mosses produce male and female reproductive cells on separate plants. A male cell and a female cell unite and produce a stalk that grows out of the female plant. The stalk releases the spores that will grow into new moss plants.

✔ **What are the two major groups of plants, and how are they different?**

Simple Vascular Plants

Simple vascular plants include ferns and horsetails. Many people think of ferns as plants with lacy leaves. In fact, there are more than 11,000 kinds of ferns, with many different kinds of leaves.

About 325 million years ago, vast forests of tall tree ferns covered much of the Earth. Today most ferns are found in the tropics, though some grow in cool forests. A few kinds even grow in the Arctic.

Horsetails are much less common than ferns. There are only about 20 kinds of horsetails. Most are small, and all contain silica, a gritty material like sand. Years ago, people used dried horsetails to scrub pots and pans.

Like mosses and liverworts, simple vascular plants reproduce with spores. Also like nonvascular plants, ferns and horsetails have two different stages in their life cycles.

As is the case with mosses, ferns produce male and female reproductive cells. However, in ferns the united cell, or *zygote*, divides and grows into a separate spore-producing plant.

✔ **How do simple vascular plants reproduce?**

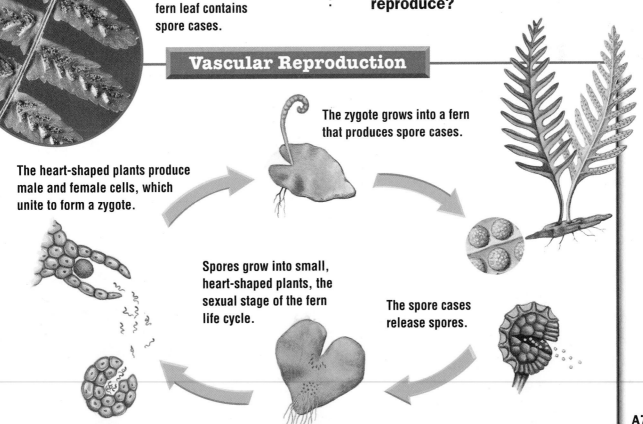

◀ The underside of a fern leaf contains spore cases.

Vascular Reproduction

The heart-shaped plants produce male and female cells, which unite to form a zygote.

The zygote grows into a fern that produces spore cases.

The spore cases release spores.

Spores grow into small, heart-shaped plants, the sexual stage of the fern life cycle.

▲ The cones of spruce trees hang down. The cones of pines grow up.

Conifer trees, such as this Norway spruce, are common in cold northern climates. ▶

Cone-Bearing Vascular Plants

Spore-producing plants make large numbers of spores. This adaptation makes sure that at least some of the spores will grow into new plants. Seed-producing plants make relatively fewer seeds, but a seed has a better chance of growing into a new plant than a spore does. This is because a seed contains a supply of food. This stored food helps the new plant grow until it can begin making its own food. Most vascular plants reproduce with seeds.

There are two kinds of seed-producing vascular plants. One type produces seeds with no protection. The other type produces seeds protected by some kind of fruit.

Plants with unprotected seeds are called **gymnosperms** (JIM•noh•spermz). The most common gymnosperms are the *conifers* (KAHN•uh•ferz), or cone-bearing plants, such as pine trees.

Most conifers produce both male and female cones on the same tree. Male cones produce **pollen**, structures that contain the male reproductive cells.

Female cones vary in size from 2 cm (about $\frac{3}{4}$ in.) to more than 75 cm (about 2 ft). Their shapes vary, too, but most have a kind of stem from which thin, woody plates grow. These plates are called *scales.*

Wind carries pollen from male cones to female cones. There the male and female reproductive cells unite. The resulting zygotes divide and grow into seeds. During dry weather the scales open and the seeds are released.

✔ **What is a gymnosperm?**

▲ Seeds develop between the cone's scales.

Flowering Vascular Plants

Most of the plants you are familiar with are flowering plants, or **angiosperms** (AN•jee•oh•spermz). There are more than 235,000 kinds of angiosperms on Earth. These include grasses, herbs, shrubs, and many trees. Flowering plants are important sources of wood, fiber, and medicine. Nearly all the food that people eat comes directly or indirectly from flowering plants.

Flowers are an adaptation that is important to the success of angiosperms. They help make sure that pollen gets from the male part of a flower to the female part. Unlike gymnosperms, which are pollinated only by the wind, angiosperms are also pollinated by insects and other small animals. The colors, shapes, and odors of flowers attract these

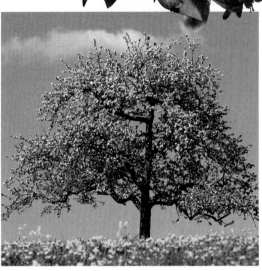

▲ An apple begins as a flower.

◀ There are more than 235,000 kinds of flowering plants. Flowers are important to the success of angiosperms.

▲ The seeds of the apple tree are protected by the fruit. As the fruit rots, it provides extra food for the growth of a new apple tree.

animals, which carry pollen from one flower to another as they move about.

Angiosperm seeds are also an adaptation for success. Unlike the gymnosperms, which produce unprotected seeds, angiosperms produce fruit that protects their seeds. These fruits include apples, oranges, tomatoes, peanuts, and acorns.

A fruit protects the seed or seeds inside it in several ways. It usually keeps birds and other animals from getting at them, even if they eat the outer part of the fruit. A fruit also serves as a covering that protects the seeds from cold weather. In addition, a rotting fruit provides extra food for a new plant when it begins to grow.

✔ **What is an angiosperm?**

Comparing Life Cycles

Both animals and plants go through stages in their lives. A flowering plant sprouts from a seed, grows and matures, flowers, and produces seeds of its own. An animal is born, grows into an adult, and reproduces its own kind. Each organism completes a cycle of life.

Some young animals look very much like their parents. Puppies and kittens are very small when they are born, but you can easily see what they will grow up to become.

Other young animals look very different from their parents. Who would guess that a caterpillar becomes a beautiful butterfly or that a fishlike tadpole becomes a frog?

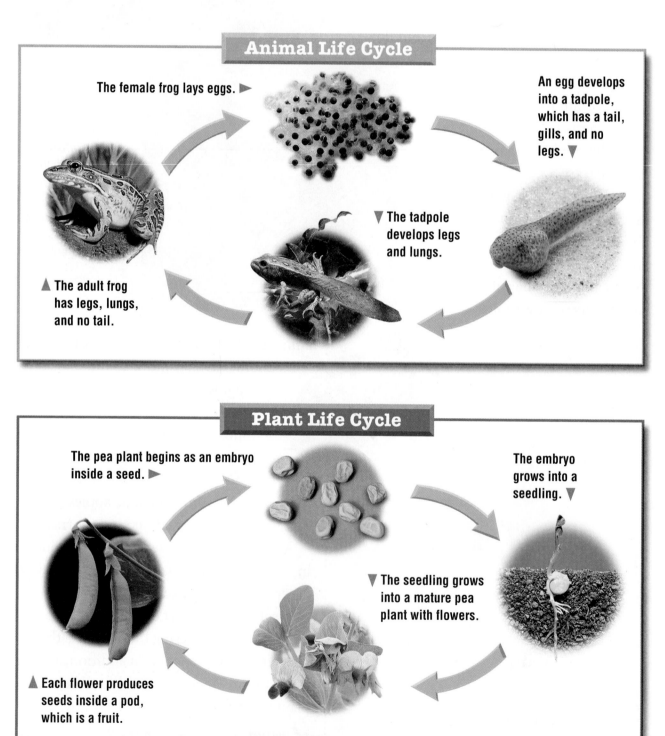

Animal Life Cycle

The female frog lays eggs. ▶

An egg develops into a tadpole, which has a tail, gills, and no legs. ▼

▼ The tadpole develops legs and lungs.

▲ The adult frog has legs, lungs, and no tail.

Plant Life Cycle

The pea plant begins as an embryo inside a seed. ▶

The embryo grows into a seedling. ▼

▼ The seedling grows into a mature pea plant with flowers.

▲ Each flower produces seeds inside a pod, which is a fruit.

In its earliest stages, a flowering plant is also very different from its parent plants. It starts as a tiny plant, called an *embryo,* inside a seed. When the seed sprouts, the embryo grows into a seedling that does not look much like the mature plant. As the plant grows and matures, it looks more and more like the plants it came from.

✓ **How does the life cycle of a flowering plant compare to that of an animal?**

Summary

Vascular plants have xylem and phloem. Nonvascular plants do not have these tubes. Nonvascular plants and simple vascular plants reproduce with spores. Gymnosperms and angiosperms are seed-producing vascular plants. Like animals, plants go through several stages in their life cycles.

Review

1. Why are nonvascular plants so small?
2. How do ferns reproduce?
3. How do conifers produce seeds?
4. **Critical Thinking** Why do you think night-blooming plants have less colorful flowers than day-blooming plants?
5. **Test Prep** The fruit produced by an angiosperm —
   A makes the seeds taste better
   B protects the seeds inside
   C attracts birds and insects
   D is more attractive than the cone of a gymnosperm

LINKS

MATH LINK

What Kind of Flower? Take a look at the plants around you—at home, at school, in parks. Are most of them vascular or nonvascular? Are they gymnosperms or angiosperms? Use a computer graphing program such as *Graph Links* to make a circle graph that compares the percentages of the types of plants you find.

WRITING LINK

Informative Writing—Explanation Write a paragraph explaining how you use plants each day. How many times do you use them? For what purposes? Would it be hard to get through a day without plants? Share your paragraph with your classmates.

LANGUAGE ARTS LINK

Prefixes In the word *nonvascular,* the prefix *non-* means "not." What do you think the words *nonsense, nonbreakable,* and *nonfat* mean? What other *non-* words can you think of? Make a list of words that begin with *non-* and write down what each one means.

TECHNOLOGY LINK

Learn more about flowering plants by visiting the Smithsonian Institution Internet site.
www.si.edu/harcourt/science

Smithsonian Institution®

3

How Do People Use Plants?

In this lesson, you can . . .

 INVESTIGATE how heat and moisture can change popcorn.

LEARN ABOUT the many uses of plants.

LINK to math, writing, music, and technology.

How many uses of plants or plant products do you see here? ▽

Popcorn

Activity Purpose People eat many kinds of seeds as food, but popcorn is probably the most interesting, and the most fun. Popped popcorn is the exploded seeds of a type of corn plant. Popcorn seeds contain water, although you can't see it or feel it. Heating the seeds turns the water quickly to steam. As the steam expands, the popcorn seeds pop. In this investigation you will **predict** and **measure** how popping the seeds affects their volume and mass.

Materials

- large plastic measuring cup
- unpopped popcorn
- balance

Activity Procedure

1 Cover the bottom of the measuring cup with unpopped popcorn seeds.

2 **Estimate** the volume of the unpopped seeds. Put the cup on the balance, and **measure** the mass of the unpopped seeds. (Picture A)

3 **Predict** what will happen to the mass and the volume when the seeds are popped.

Picture A

Picture B

4 Your teacher will help you pop the popcorn. Return the popped seeds to the measuring cup.

5 **Measure** the volume and mass of the cup of popped popcorn. Were your **predictions** correct? (Picture B)

Draw Conclusions

1. How did the volume of the popcorn change?

2. How did the mass change? Explain.

3. **Scientists at Work** One reason why scientists **experiment** is to test predictions. If an experiment doesn't turn out the way they predicted, it may mean that their predictions were wrong. Or it may mean that they did not consider everything that could affect the experiment. Did you predict the volume and mass of the popped popcorn correctly? Explain.

Investigate Further Water turns into a gas when it is heated. What do you **predict** will happen when that gas cools? **Experiment** to test your prediction.

The Uses of Plants

FIND OUT

- how people use plants as food
- how people use plants as medicine

VOCABULARY

grain
fiber

Plants as Food

People use plants more for food than for any other purpose. For example, breakfast cereal is made of **grain**, or the seeds of certain grasses. If you have a sandwich for lunch, you are eating grain again. The bread in the sandwich was made by grinding the seeds of wheat into flour. Does your sandwich have lettuce and tomato on it? Then you're also eating a plant leaf and a fruit. And if the sandwich is seasoned with mustard, you're eating something made from seeds.

People eat many different parts of many different plants. Beans, lentils, corn, and rice, for example, are seeds. Beets, radishes, turnips, and carrots are roots. Bamboo shoots and asparagus are stems. Spinach, lettuce, kale, and cabbage are leaves. Cherries, pears, oranges, and olives are fruits. Artichokes, cauliflower, and broccoli are flowers. And if you like cinnamon in your apple pie, you are eating the bark, the outer part of the stem, of a tree.

✔ **Name the plant parts that people eat.**

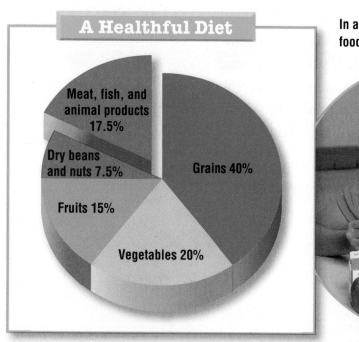

A Healthful Diet

Meat, fish, and animal products 17.5%

Dry beans and nuts 7.5%

Fruits 15%

Vegetables 20%

Grains 40%

In a healthful diet, most of the foods come from plants.

The Food Guide Pyramid

Grains form the largest part of this pyramid because they are the foundation of a healthful diet. The next level is shared by vegetables and fruits. Drinking fruit juice is more healthful than drinking soda, but you should also eat the fruits themselves.

FATS, OILS, SWEETS
Foods in this group are generally not healthful, so don't eat a lot of them.

Meats and dairy products are in a small part of the pyramid because they contain fats. Too much fat can harm your health. Fish and poultry have less fat than other meats. Milk, cheese, and yogurt are good for you, but they also are high in fat. Foods that are very high in fat, oil, or sugar are not healthful.

MILK, YOGURT, CHEESE GROUP
These foods contain fats, so limit yourself to 2–3 servings a day. A cup of milk is one serving.

MEAT, POULTRY, FISH, DRY BEANS, EGGS, NUTS GROUP
Eat 2–3 servings of foods from this group daily. A serving is one egg or about 3 oz of meat.

VEGETABLE GROUP
Eat 3–5 servings of vegetables a day. A half cup of chopped vegetables is one serving.

FRUIT GROUP
Eat 2–4 servings a day. A banana is one serving.

BREAD, CEREAL, RICE, PASTA GROUP
Eat 6–11 servings a day. A slice of bread, for example, is one serving.

The leaves of the aloe plant store food. That food, a jellylike substance, is used in soaps, shampoos, makeup, skin cream, and sunscreens.

This fluffy cotton boll is made of tiny white fibers. The fibers are woven into cotton cloth, which is made into clothing. ▼

Plants as Medicines

Plants contain many substances that can be used to treat illnesses. Native Americans used the leaves and roots of hundreds of plants as medicines. They used them to reduce fevers, relieve pain, calm upset stomachs, and treat other problems.

About 40 percent of the medicines we use today are made from plants. For example, an important heart medicine called digitalis is made from the leaves of the foxglove plant. Foxglove grows in many parts of the United States. Quinine is made from the bark of a tree that grows in the Andes Mountains of South America. Quinine is used to treat malaria.

One of the best-known and most widely used pain medicines is also one of the oldest. Aspirin is a medicine invented in the 1800s. But thousands of years earlier, people took an almost identical medicine by chewing the bark of the willow tree.

✓ **What did some people do for pain before aspirin was invented?**

Other Uses for Plants

Clothing is another important product people get from plants. Blue jeans, for example, are made of fibers from the cotton plant. A **fiber** is any material that can be separated into thread. The dye that gives blue jeans their color was once made from the indigo plant.

Many kinds of trees provide wood for different purposes. Homes are often made of wood, and a lot of the furniture in most homes is wood. Musical instruments, such as guitars, violins, and pianos, are made with wood. And pulp, which is made from wood, is used to make paper.

Soaps and shampoos contain plant substances that can help make skin smooth and hair shiny. Many perfumes are made from flower petals. It takes about 100 kg (220 lb) of rose petals to make 30 mL (about 1 oz) of fragrance. This is one of the reasons why perfumes are expensive.

✓ **Name two products made from trees.**

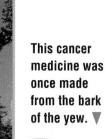

This cancer medicine was once made from the bark of the yew. ▼

Summary

People eat the leaves, stems, roots, seeds, fruits, and flowers of various plants. When they are sick, people often use medicines made from plants. In fact, many things people use every day come from plants.

Review

1. Name three foods that are seeds or are made from seeds.

2. From which food group should you eat the most servings each day?

3. What percentage of the medicines people use come from plants?

4. **Critical Thinking** Nutritionists say people shouldn't eat many French fries. In which food groups do French fries belong? What part of this food may not be healthful?

5. **Test Prep** Aloe is a plant that is used to make —

   A dye

   B skin cream

   C aspirin

   D fiber

LINKS

MATH LINK

How Much Fat? Most people should eat no more than 30 g of fat each day. Food labels list the fat in each serving. Add up the fat in the food you eat in one week. How close to 30 g per day is the amount of fat in your diet?

WRITING LINK

Persuasive Writing—Business Letter Some people think it's healthful to eat only plants. Others think it's important to eat both meat and plants. Write a letter to a health organization requesting information about the reasons for and against both of these diets.

MUSIC LINK

Wooden Instruments Today, some musical instruments are still made of wood. Report to the class on one of them. Explain why it is made of wood instead of some other material. Include a picture of the instrument, and play part of a recording of the instrument.

TECHNOLOGY LINK

Learn more about using plants for food by viewing *Genetic Tomatoes* on the **Harcourt Science Newsroom Video.**

Potato Vaccines

Scientists are using biotechnology to turn common potatoes into vaccines against deadly diseases such as cholera.

Why Potato Vaccines?

Potatoes are an inexpensive, nutritious food that most children like to eat mashed, baked, or French fried. Biologists are using genetic engineering to insert a new gene into potatoes. This gene causes the plants to produce a chemical, called a B-protein, that is a harmless part of cholera toxin, or poison. When children eat a certain amount of these genetically altered potatoes, they become vaccinated against cholera.

What Is Cholera?

Cholera is an infectious disease that affects about 5 million people a year, particularly in poor areas of the world. It's highly contagious, so outbreaks of cholera can easily become epidemics. Cholera toxin causes pores in cells lining the intestines to remain open when they should be closed. Water diffuses from the blood into the intestines and

Potatoes are a good choice for edible vaccines because most people like them.

This white blood cell is attacking *E. coli* bacteria.

then out of the body as diarrhea. People with cholera can lose so much water so quickly that they become very sick and may even die.

How Does the Potato Vaccine Work?

Scientists at the Loma Linda University School of Medicine in California have added the gene that produces the cholera toxin's B-protein to the genes of potato plants. The B-protein attaches to cells in the intestines and triggers the production of antibodies against cholera.

Scientists tested the potato vaccines by feeding genetically altered potatoes to mice. Then they examined tissue from the mice's intestines to see what happened when it was exposed to cholera toxin. They found that only half as much water passed through this tissue compared with tissue from mice that had not eaten the altered potatoes.

People seldom eat potatoes raw, so scientists had to make sure that cooking wouldn't destroy the vaccine. They found that after cooking, the genetically altered potatoes had about half the vaccine they started with. But this is still enough vaccine to be effective. One cooked potato a week for one month provides enough cholera toxin B-protein to protect against the disease for years.

Other uses of the potato vaccine

Toxins produced by the cholera bacteria are nearly identical to toxins produced by another dangerous intestinal bacteria, called *E. coli*. So the potato vaccine that works against cholera may also work against *E. coli* toxins. Scientists are also looking for ways to improve the potato vaccine so that it will help destroy the bacteria directly, not just the toxins the bacteria produce.

THINK ABOUT IT

1. Why do you think potato vaccines would be easier to distribute and give to people than injected vaccines?

2. What would be an advantage of inserting vaccine-producing genes into foods that are eaten raw, such as bananas?

WEB LINK:
For science and technology updates, visit The Learning Site.
www.harcourtschool.com

Careers   Geneticist

What They Do
Geneticists study the ways genes and chromosomes combine to produce variety in plants and animals.

Education and Training People wishing to become geneticists should earn an M.D. degree, specializing in genetics, or a Ph.D. degree in biology, specializing in cell biology.

Alice Eastwood

BOTANIST

"My own destroyed work I do not lament, for it was a joy to me while I did it, and I can still have the same joy in starting it again."

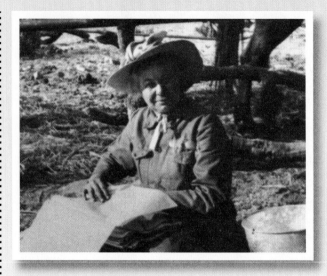

Alice Eastwood might never have become one of the world's greatest botanists if the great San Francisco earthquake and fire of 1906 had not taken place. One of the buildings destroyed in the disaster was the California Academy of Sciences, where Ms. Eastwood had spent more than 12 years building a huge collection of California plants. Although she managed to save nearly 1500 rare plant specimens just minutes before the academy was destroyed by fire, much of her work was lost. However, in the next six years, she produced a collection of more than 340,000 plants that was even better than the one she had lost in the fire.

Overcoming setbacks was nothing new for Ms. Eastwood. Her mother died when she was young, and because the family was poor, she couldn't finish high school with her classmates. After working for a few years, Ms. Eastwood finally graduated at the age of 20 as the top student in her class.

Although she never attended college, Ms. Eastwood continued to educate herself about plants, which had fascinated her from the time she was a young girl. She became known worldwide in the scientific community and at the age of 92 served as honorary president of the Seventh International Botanical Congress in Stockholm, Sweden. Ms. Eastwood died in 1953 at the age of 94.

THINK ABOUT IT

1. How did the San Francisco earthquake help Ms. Eastwood's career?
2. What can you infer about Ms. Eastwood's attitude toward the setbacks of life?

Ms. Eastwood working on her collection

Water in Plants

How does water move through plants?

Materials
- 5 toothpicks
- dropper
- water

Procedure

1 Break the toothpicks in half, but don't separate the parts. The two halves should remain connected.

2 Arrange the toothpicks like the spokes in a wagon wheel.

3 Put several drops of water in the center of the "wheel."

4 Observe any changes to the toothpicks.

Draw Conclusions

What happened to the water you put on the toothpicks? What happened to the toothpicks? Relate this to the way water moves through plants.

Yeast Beasts

What do simple organisms need to live?

Materials
- package of dry yeast
- 250-mL beaker
- 100 mL warm water
- sugar packet
- craft stick
- clock

Procedure

1 Empty the package of dry yeast into the beaker.

2 Add 100 mL of warm water and empty the packet of sugar into the water.

3 Stir the mixture with the craft stick for about 15 seconds. Put the beaker aside for 5 minutes.

4 After 5 minutes, measure the volume of the mixture in the beaker.

Draw Conclusions

What happened to the volume of the yeast, sugar, and warm water mixture? What do simple organisms need to live? Why is yeast used to make bread?

Vocabulary Review

Use the terms below to complete the paragraph. The page numbers in ( ) tell you where to look in the chapter if you need help.

xylem (A69)   **spores** (A75)

phloem (A69)   **gymnosperms** (A76)

chlorophyll (A70)   **pollen** (A76)

nonvascular (A74)   **angiosperms** (A77)

vascular (A74)

A plant that contains tubes for the transport of water and food is called a **1.** plant. The tubes that transport food are **2.** tubes; those that transport water are **3.** tubes. Plants that do not have these tubes are **4.** plants. Whether or not they have transport tubes, all plants have a green pigment called **5.** , which enables them to make their own food. Plants have various means by which they reproduce. Plants will produce either seeds or **6.** , which will grow into a new plant when conditions are favorable. Conifers, or **7.** , produce unprotected seeds in cones. The flowers of **8.** produce protected seeds. In a flower, **9.** contains the male reproductive cells.

Connect Concepts

Write terms from the Word Bank to complete the chart.

angiosperms   **seeds**

gymnosperms   **spores**

nonvascular plants   **vascular plants**

The Two Main Groups of Plants Are
10. _____, which have no xylem or phloem.
11. _____, which have xylem and phloem tubes.

The Two Groups of Vascular Plants Are
12. plants that use _____ to reproduce.
13. plants that use _____ to reproduce.

The Two Groups of Seed-Producing Plants Are
14. _____, which include conifers, such as pines.
15. _____, which include flowering apple trees.

Check Understanding

Write the letter of the best choice.

16. Most leaves are thin and flat because —
    - A they look better that way
    - B this helps them make food
    - C they protect the plant from insects and birds
    - D they absorb water from the air

17. Nonvascular plants are limited in size because —
    - F they must pass water and minerals from one cell to the next
    - G they do not make their own food
    - H birds and other animals like to eat them
    - J they live in shady places

18. Large, colorful flowers are useful for a plant because —
    - A they look pretty
    - B they make food for plants
    - C they attract insects and birds that spread pollen
    - D they collect moisture

19. For a more healthful diet, eat more of foods that are —
    - F near the top of the food guide pyramid
    - G mostly from the milk group
    - H high in sugar
    - J near the bottom of the food guide pyramid

Critical Thinking

20. Could a plant live if all its leaves were cut off? Explain your answer.

21. In what way are fruits better than cones for carrying seeds?

Process Skills Review

22. What can you **observe** about a plant to help you identify the kind of plant it is?

23. **Identify** the products in your classroom that are made from plants or plant parts.

24. **Predict** what would happen if trees did not have fruits or cones.

Performance Assessment

Design a Plant

Choose one condition from each set. Design a plant with roots, stems, and leaves that could live in a place with the conditions you choose.

a lot of rain
some rain
almost no rain

hot temperatures
moderate temperatures
cold temperatures

a lot of light
some light
almost no light

Chapter 4

Plant Processes

Plants depend on their environments. They need light, water, and carbon dioxide to make food. And they need wind or other organisms to help them flower and distribute their seeds.

Vocabulary Preview

epidermis	ovary
palisade layer	embryo
cellular	cotyledons
respiration	germinate
tropism	seedling
gravitropism	grafting
fertilization	tissue
stamens	culture
pistil	
photosynthesis	
phototropism	
vegetative propagation	

FAST FACT

There are about 248,000 different kinds of plants. About 9 out of every 10 of them are flowering plants.

Plant Species

Dicots (angiosperms)
170,000 species

Monocots (angiosperms)
50,000 species

Others
1,300 species

Gymnosperms
529 species

Ferns
10,000 species

Bryophytes
16,600 species

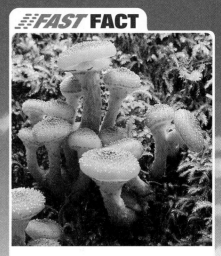

The largest living thing in the world is not a giant sequoia tree or a whale. It is a fungus. The underground part of this fungus, growing in Washington state, covers 1500 acres.

Plants have many ways of attracting animals to help with pollination. Sometimes a plant's shape and colors resemble the insect itself.

How Do Plants Make Food?

In this lesson, you can . . .

INVESTIGATE how plants use leaves.

LEARN ABOUT how plants make and use food.

LINK to math, writing, technology, and other areas.

Plants can be grown anywhere if they get what they need to survive.

INVESTIGATE

How Plants Use Leaves

Activity Purpose What do leaves do for a plant? Why are they important? In this investigation you will **experiment** to determine the importance of leaves. Remember, experimenting involves carefully **controlling variables**.

Materials
- 3 potted plants
- labels
- scissors
- meterstick
- measuring cup

Activity Procedure

1. Label the plants *Normal, Half,* and *None.*

2. Using scissors, carefully cut off all the leaves of the plant labeled *None.* Cut off half the leaves of the plant labeled *Half.* The number of leaves is the variable. (Picture A)

3. Don't do anything to the plant labeled *Normal.* This plant is the control.

4. Use the meterstick to **measure** the height of each plant. **Record** the heights.

5. Put all three plants in a place where they will get plenty of sunlight. Water the plants as needed. Use the measuring cup to ensure they all get the same amount of water.

    What do you **hypothesize** about how the plants will grow?

Picture A

Picture B

6 **Measure** the heights of the plants every day, and **record** your data. Record anything else you **observe** about the plants. Cut off any new leaves that grow on the plants labeled *Half* and *None*. (Picture B)

7 At the end of two weeks, review your data.

Draw Conclusions

1. Which plant grew the most in height? Which plant grew the least? Does the data support your **hypothesis**? What can you conclude about the importance of leaves?

2. Why was making sure the three plants received the same amount of sunlight important in this investigation?

3. **Scientists at Work** Scientists always **control variables** when they **experiment**. Why was watering all the plants with the same amount of water important in your investigation?

Investigate Further Does adding plant food really improve plant growth, as advertisements would have you believe? **Plan and conduct a simple investigation** to find out. Be sure you have a way to **control variables** in your investigation.

Process Skill Tip

When you **control variables**, you are better able to draw valid conclusions about the data you collect as you **experiment**.

How Plants Make Food

Leaf Structure

FIND OUT

- about the structure of leaves

- how plants make and use food

- how energy from food supports different life forms

VOCABULARY

photosynthesis
epidermis
palisade layer
cellular respiration

A cornfield is like a factory, turning raw materials (water and carbon dioxide) into finished products (food and oxygen). ▼

You may remember that plants make their own food by using water, carbon dioxide, chlorophyll, and sunlight. The process by which plants make food is called **photosynthesis** (foh•toh•SIN•thuh•sis). You may already know the two parts of this word. *Photo* means "light" and *synthesis* means "putting together." In photosynthesis, plants put together materials to make food with the energy of sunlight.

Photosynthesis takes place mainly in a plant's leaves. Certain cells in a leaf have most of the leaf's chloroplasts. These structures contain chlorophyll, the pigment that gives plants their green color. During the day, chlorophyll takes in light energy from the sun and changes it into chemical energy needed for photosynthesis.

Most leaves also have a system of xylem and phloem tubes called veins. In addition to carrying water from the roots to the chloroplasts, veins carry food made in the chloroplasts back to the stem and roots. Veins also help keep leaves from wilting. As long as its veins are full of water and food, a leaf will keep its shape.

Photosynthesis takes place mainly near the upper surface of a leaf, where most of the sunlight is, so most leaves are thin and flat. This adaptation provides a large surface area for a leaf to get as much sunlight as possible. The leaves of most plants are not much thicker than the pages in this book.

The upper surface of a leaf has a single layer of cells that protects the inner cells in much the same way your skin protects your inner cells. This layer is called the upper **epidermis** (ep•uh•DER•mis). The epidermis is thin and flat, and sunlight easily passes through it.

Most photosynthesis takes place in the chloroplasts of the palisade cells. A single palisade cell may contain thousands of chloroplasts. Air spaces in the spongy layer connect to the stomata and allow gases to move back and forth between the outside air and the inside of the leaf. ▼

The upper epidermis helps reduce water loss from the surface of a leaf. Sometimes the epidermis has a waxy covering, called a *cuticle* (KYOO•ti•kuhl). The cuticle also protects against water loss.

Directly below the upper epidermis is the **palisade** (pal•uh•SAYD) **layer** of cells. The palisade layer is made up of long, thin, tightly packed cells. Each cell has many chloroplasts. Most photosynthesis takes place in the palisade layer.

The next layer of a leaf is made of loosely packed cells with many air spaces between them. For this reason, this layer is called the *spongy layer.* The air spaces allow carbon dioxide to pass among the cells and get to the chloroplasts. Cells in the spongy layer also have chloroplasts, but not nearly as many as the cells of the palisade layer do.

The bottom layer of a leaf is the lower epidermis. This layer protects the underside of the leaf. There are many openings, or *stomata,* in the lower epidermis. *Guard cells,* which form the edges of stomata, can change shape, depending on the amount of water in them. This causes the stomata to open and close. When the stomata are open, carbon dioxide can enter the leaf. At the same time, some of the oxygen produced during photosynthesis can leave the leaf. When the stomata are closed, at night or when there isn't much water, no photosynthesis takes place.

✔ **How do the materials needed for photosynthesis get to the chloroplasts?**

▲ This photograph of part of a chloroplast shows the layered *grana* where photosynthesis occurs.

How Photosynthesis Works

When sunlight falls on a leaf, the process of photosynthesis begins. Light energy is taken in by chlorophyll in the leaf's chloroplasts. Chlorophyll transforms, or changes, light energy into chemical energy.

This chemical energy starts a series of reactions in the chloroplast. In one reaction, water is split into the two materials that make it up—hydrogen and oxygen. Hydrogen combines with carbon dioxide to make a product called *glucose* (GLOO•kohs). Glucose is a type of sugar. Plants use some of the glucose as food. The rest is stored as starch, which is made up of many glucose particles joined together.

THE INSIDE STORY

Photosynthesis and Cellular Respiration Compared

Photosynthesis

Sunlight is taken in by chlorophyll. Light energy is turned into chemical energy, which is used to split water into hydrogen and oxygen. In a series of reactions, hydrogen combines with the carbon dioxide to form glucose and oxygen.

carbon dioxide and water

+

sunlight and chlorophyll

glucose and oxygen

Oxygen, which was once part of water, is another product of photosynthesis. The plant releases it into the air. Most living things could not survive without the oxygen plants produce. The following word formula summarizes photosynthesis. The formula reads: carbon dioxide and water, using sunlight and chlorophyll, make glucose and oxygen.

carbon dioxide and water + sunlight and chlorophyll → glucose and oxygen

✔ **What are the products of photosynthesis?**

A plant that doesn't get enough light can't make food.

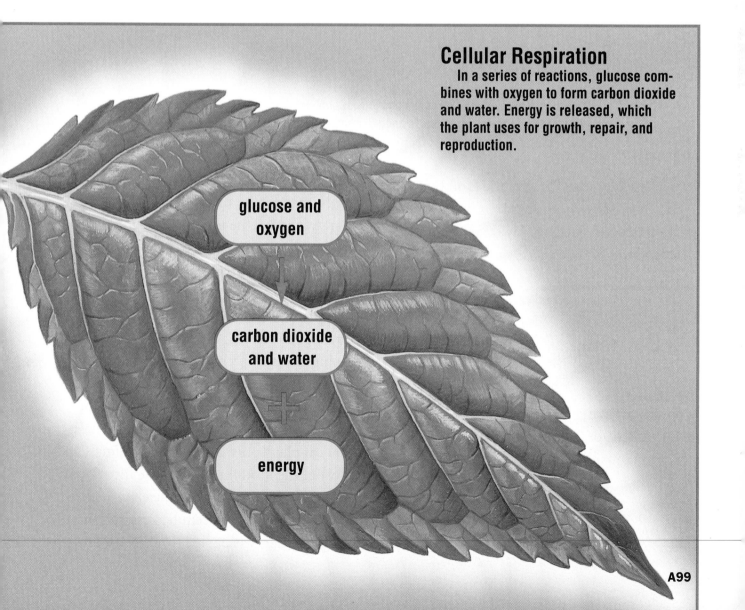

Cellular Respiration

In a series of reactions, glucose combines with oxygen to form carbon dioxide and water. Energy is released, which the plant uses for growth, repair, and reproduction.

glucose and oxygen

↓

carbon dioxide and water

+

energy

A99

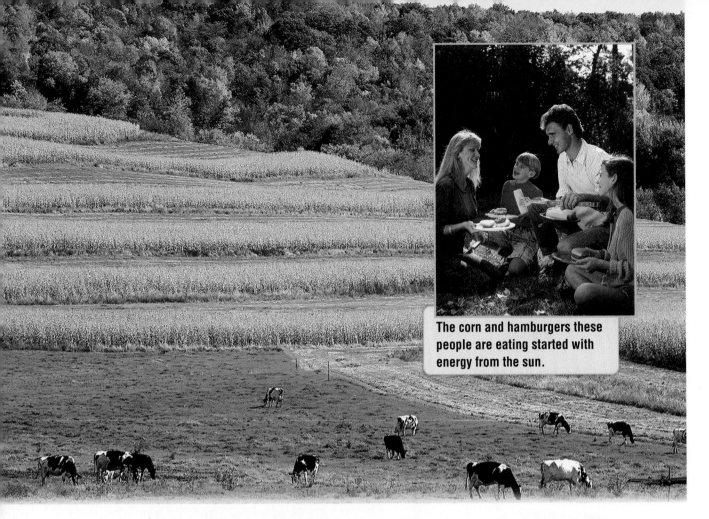

The corn and hamburgers these people are eating started with energy from the sun.

▲ Grass uses the sun's energy to live and grow. Cattle eat grass to live and grow. In this way, the cattle are using the sun's energy, which is stored in the grass.

Food Energy

What do plants do with the food they produce? Most of it is used for the plant's life functions, such as growth, repair, and reproduction. The process by which plants release the energy in food to carry on these life processes is called **cellular respiration**. In the plant's cells, oxygen combines with glucose, forming carbon dioxide and water. During this process a large amount of energy is released. The following word formula summarizes cellular respiration. The formula reads: glucose and oxygen make carbon dioxide and water and energy.

Any extra food is stored in the plant. Different types of plants store food in their roots, their stems, or even their leaves. The stored food will be used whenever the plant is not able to make all the food it needs, such as on cloudy days or during dry periods.

A plant's extra food is usually stored in the form of starch. A potato, for example, is mainly stored starch. When the plant needs food, it turns the starch back into glucose.

Plants use about 90 percent of the food they make. The rest is available to animals that eat plants. Just as plants do, animals use most of the food they eat for life functions. And, as happens in plants, the energy stored in food is released by cellular respiration. In this way, energy is passed from the sun to

A100

the plant and then to the animal. Of all the food an animal eats, about 10 percent is stored in its body. An animal that eats another animal gets energy from the first animal. This energy can also be traced back to the sun.

✓ **How do plants usually store energy?**

Summary

Plants make food by a process called photosynthesis. In plant leaves, chlorophyll uses light energy to combine water and carbon dioxide, forming glucose and oxygen. Plants use most of the food they make. They store the rest. Any extra food is available to animals that eat plants. Plants and animals use food energy, which is released by cellular respiration.

Review

1. In what part of a plant do you find chlorophyll?
2. What three things do plants use to make food?
3. What gas that plants and animals use is a product of photosynthesis?
4. **Critical Thinking** Open stomata allow carbon dioxide, oxygen, and water to pass into and out of leaves. Using this information, explain why photosynthesis takes place early in the morning in many desert plants.
5. **Test Prep** Which cells would you expect to have the most chloroplasts?
   A guard cells
   B palisade cells
   C xylem cells
   D epidermis cells

LINKS

MATH LINK

Calculate If 10 percent of the food an animal eats is stored in its body, how many pounds of corn did a cow eat for every pound of hamburger made from its body?

WRITING LINK

Narrative Writing—Story What would life be like if people could make their own food, as plants do? Write a story for your class about some photosynthesizing friends who have lunch together.

HEALTH LINK

Be Prepared Plants store food for times when they cannot produce it. Humans store food in their bodies for times when they can't get it. Write a short report about how the human body stores food. As you write your report, include answers to the following questions: Why do people need the ability to store food? How can storing excess food be bad for a person's health?

TECHNOLOGY LINK

Learn more about the way plants make food by visiting the National Museum of Natural History Internet site.
www.si.edu/harcourt/science

Smithsonian Institution®

How Do Plants Respond to Light and Gravity?

In this lesson, you can . . .

INVESTIGATE how plants get the light they need.

LEARN ABOUT how tropisms and other responses help plants.

LINK to math, writing, social studies, and technology.

▽ This plant is growing toward the light.

INVESTIGATE

How Plants Get the Light They Need

Activity Purpose You have learned that plants use light as energy for making their own food. You also know that plants can't move from place to place. How then do plants get the light they need for growth? In this investigation you will **compare** plants grown under different conditions to find out.

Materials

- 3 labels
- 2 potted plants
- measuring cup
- water

Activity Procedure

1. Write *Odd days* on one of the labels. Put the label on one side of a pot. Write *Even days* on a second label. Put this label on the other side of the same pot. Write *Don't move* on the third label, and put it on the other pot. (Picture A)

2. Place both potted plants in a sunny area. If you don't have a sunny area, put them under and to one side of a light source, such as a lamp. Make sure both plants are on the same side of and at the same distance from the lamp.

3. Use the measuring cup to give both plants the same amount of water at the same time each day. **Observe** the plants every day, and **record** your observations.

4. Turn the plant labeled *Odd days/Even days* one-half turn every day. If you start the **experiment** on an even-numbered day, place the pot so you

Picture A

Picture B

can see the *Even days* label. If you start on an odd-numbered day, place the pot so that you can see the *Odd days* label. Do not turn the plant labeled *Don't move*. (Picture B)

5 After ten days, write a summary of your **observations** about how the plants have grown. Draw pictures showing how the plants looked at the beginning and at the end of the **experiment**.

Draw Conclusions

1. What did you **observe** about the growth of the plants during the investigation?

2. **Compare** the two plants. What variable were the plants responding to?

3. **Scientists at Work** Scientists often **compare** organisms to help them understand how organisms respond to their environments. In this investigation, how did comparing the way the plants grew help you **draw conclusions** about the way plants respond to light?

Investigate Further **Hypothesize** about all plants needing the same amount of sunlight. Try putting two different plants in a very sunny window. Give both plants the same amount of water. **Observe**, and **record** your observations of the plants for two weeks.

How Tropisms and Other Responses Help Plants

FIND OUT ────

- **how and why plants respond to their environments**
- **how light affects plants**
- **how gravity affects plants**

VOCABULARY

tropism
phototropism
gravitropism

Tropisms

All living things respond, or react, to their environments. For example, if the weather gets cold, you might respond by shivering. This response helps keep your body warm. No organism can survive if it can't respond to major changes in its environment.

A plant doesn't respond to everything in its environment, but many plants respond to certain stimuli (STIM•yoo•ly). A *stimulus* is anything that causes an organism to respond. A plant's response to a stimulus is called a **tropism** (TROH•piz•um).

In the investigation, you learned that plants grow toward light. This response to light is called **phototropism** (FOH•toh•troh•piz•uhm). Phototropism is caused by chemicals that direct the growth of a plant's stem. These chemicals cause cells in the stem on the side away from the light to get longer. Because the cells on the side of the plant toward the light are shorter, the plant bends toward the light.

Different amounts of light may cause different responses in some plants. In Bermuda grass, for example, the stems grow upright in shade. In full sun the stems grow along the ground.

✔ **What causes a plant to grow toward light?**

A plant's response to the stimulus of light can be easy to see. ▶

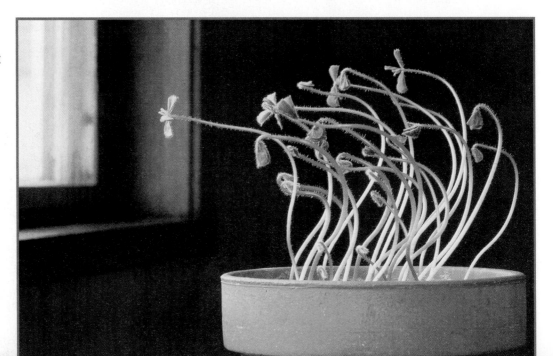

Plants also respond to the force of gravity. This tropism is known as **gravitropism** (GRAV•ih•troh•piz•uhm). Gravitropism is an adaptation that makes sure a plant's roots grow down into the soil and the stems grow up. This is important because roots must hold a plant in place and take in water and minerals from the soil. If plants did not respond to the stimulus of gravity, they would not be able to grow from seeds. Without gravitropism, if a seed landed upside down, its roots might never reach the soil or its leaves might never reach the light.

Gravitropism is caused by the pull of gravity on cells at the ends of roots. This causes growing roots to turn, if necessary, toward the center of the Earth and to grow in that direction. Scientists hypothesize that this may be caused by starch grains that move to the lower side of any root not growing down. In much the same way that cells on the shaded side of a stem are directed to grow longer, these starch grains cause cells on the lower side of a root to grow more slowly.

✔ **How does gravitropism help plants survive?**

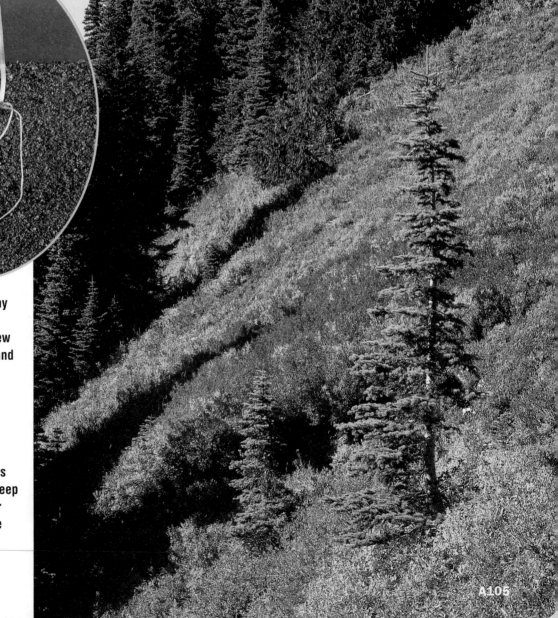

▲ No matter which way this seedling was turned, its roots grew down into the soil and its stem grew up toward the light.

Although these trees are growing on a steep mountainside, their stems and roots are still affected by gravitropism. ▶

Other Responses

Remember the Venus' flytrap that catches insects for food? When the plant's traplike leaves snap shut on an insect that has landed on it, the plant is responding to the stimulus of touch.

The Venus' flytrap isn't the only plant that responds to touch. When an insect lands on a leaf of a sundew and touches one of its sticky hairs, other hairs bend in that direction. Soon the insect is trapped. The bending is caused by cells on one side of the hair growing very rapidly. They grow so fast that a hair pointing in one direction can bend in the opposite direction in less than a minute!

The mimosa, or "sensitive plant," also responds to touch. It has delicate, fernlike leaves. If you touch one leaf, even just a little, all the leaves will curl up tightly. The touch response is an adaptation that protects the mimosa from animals that might eat its leaves.

All plants respond to light, but some respond to certain amounts of light. If they have either too much light or too little light, they won't bloom. These plants usually bloom only during the season that provides them with just the right amount of light.

For example, so-called short-day plants such as the poinsettia need only a few hours of sunlight for blooming. For this reason they bloom during the early spring or in the fall, when days are short. Long-day plants need many hours of sunlight each day to bloom. They usually bloom during the summer, when days are the longest. Plants that bloom no matter how many hours of sunlight they get are called day-neutral plants. The time line below shows how many hours of sunlight each plant needs to bloom.

Although plants need light to grow, the blooming of both long-day plants and short-day plants is actually controlled by the amount of darkness to which they are

Flowering

The poinsettia, a short-day plant, will bloom only if it gets less than 12.5 hours of sunlight a day. ▶

8 hours

The rose is a day-neutral plant that can bloom no matter how many hours of sunlight it gets. ▶

12 hours

Larkspur, a long-day plant, must have nearly 16 hours of sunlight a day to bloom. ▶

16 hours

Hours of Sunlight

exposed. For example, the cocklebur, which needs short days, will not bloom if it gets as little as a minute of light during the night. The fact that plants "measure" darkness has an adaptive advantage. That way, cloudy or rainy days do not keep a plant from blooming.

✓ **What is the difference between long-day plants and short-day plants?**

Summary

Tropisms cause plants to respond to certain stimuli. Phototropism makes plants grow toward light. Gravitropism causes plant roots to grow down and stems to grow up. Some plants respond to touch. Other responses affect when plants will bloom. Responses to stimuli are adaptations that help plants survive.

Review

1. How does phototropism help plants survive?

2. What growing parts of a plant does gravitropism affect?

3. What happens if you touch a mimosa leaf? How does this help the plant?

4. **Critical Thinking** Suppose you put a poinsettia in a dark closet for 18 hours a day during the summer. How might this affect the plant's blooming?

5. **Test Prep** The parts of plants most affected by the number of hours of darkness are their —

   A leaves

   B stems

   C roots

   D flowers

LINKS

MATH LINK

Sunlight Hours The Biloxi soybean must have no more than 14 hours of sunlight each day to bloom. During the growing season, Chicago has an average of 10 percent more hours of sunlight than this, so the Biloxi soybean cannot grow there. How many hours of sunlight does Chicago average during the growing season?

WRITING LINK

Informative Writing—Report Choose a plant to research. Find out what growing conditions the plant needs, especially the number of hours of sunlight it needs to bloom. Write a report for your teacher that includes a picture of the plant and information about the environment in which it grows.

SOCIAL STUDIES LINK

Flowering Sometimes owners of plant nurseries want to make plants bloom for certain holidays, even when it is not their normal flowering season. Find out how nursery owners change conditions to make sure that certain plants bloom at the time they want.

TECHNOLOGY LINK

Learn more about plant responses by viewing *Pitcher Plants* on the **Harcourt Science Newsroom Video.**

How Do Plants Reproduce?

In this lesson, you can . . .

INVESTIGATE
flower parts.

LEARN ABOUT
sexual reproduction in plants.

LINK to math, writing, literature, and technology.

INVESTIGATE

Flower Parts

Activity Purpose Have you ever looked closely at a flower's brightly colored petals? Have you ever wondered why some plants have such beautiful flowers? In this investigation you will find out more about flowers as you **observe** the structures of one.

Materials
- fresh flower
- paper towel
- hand lens
- ruler

Activity Procedure

1 Place a fresh flower on a paper towel.

2 **Observe** the outside of the flower. Notice the green, leaflike parts around the petals. These are called *sepals* (SEE•puhls). How many sepals does the flower have? What shape are the sepals? **Record** your observations. (Picture A)

3 Now **observe** the flower's petals. How many petals does the flower have? What shape are they? What color are they? Do the petals have any patterns, or are they one color? What do the petals feel like? **Record** your observations.

4 **Observe** the flower with your eyes closed. Does it have an odor? How would you describe the odor? What part of the flower do you think the odor is coming from? **Record** your observations about the flower's odor.

◄ As a butterfly drinks sweet nectar from deep inside several flowers, it spreads pollen from one flower to another.

Picture A

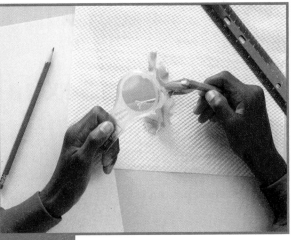

Picture B

5 Using the hand lens, **observe** the inside of the flower. What parts do you see? What are the shapes of these parts? **Measure** these parts. **Record** your observations about the inside of the flower. (Picture B)

6 Now make a drawing of the inside of the flower. As you draw each part, try to **infer** what it does.

Draw Conclusions

1. Colorful markings and strong odors often attract birds and insects to flowers. How might the location of the markings and odors attract birds and insects to the flower?

2. In the very center of a flower is the female reproductive part. Stalks surrounding the center contain male reproductive parts. **Infer** how it might help the plant to have the male parts around the female part.

3. **Scientists at Work** When scientists **infer** a part's function, they sometimes base their inferences on **observing** the part's location. Based on the sepals' location, what could you infer about the function of sepals?

Investigate Further **Observe** the parts of another kind of flower. How does that flower **compare** to the one you observed in this investigation? Does it have the same number of sepals? Are the petals arranged the same way? Do the flower's inner parts look the same? What other questions could you answer by observing the flower?

Process Skill Tip

To **infer** the functions of all the parts of a flower, you might need to cut open some of the smaller parts and use a microscope to **observe** them.

Sexual Reproduction in Plants

VOCABULARY

fertilization
stamens
pistil
ovary

Fertilization and Pollination

Most plants reproduce sexually. In angiosperms and gymnosperms, **fertilization** (fuhr•tul•luh•ZAY•shuhn), the joining of a male reproductive cell with a female reproductive cell, produces seeds. Because of fertilization, a seed has characteristics of both the male parent and the female parent.

Gymnosperms have male and female parts in separate cones. Grains of pollen fall or are carried by the wind from a male cone to a female cone. After fertilization, seeds develop in the female cone.

In angiosperms, both male and female reproductive parts are usually in the same flower. The male parts, called **stamens** (STAY•muhnz), produce pollen. In the pollen grains are the male reproductive cells, or sperm. The female part, called a **pistil** (PIS•tuhl), contains the female reproductive cells, or eggs. Pollen is usually carried by the wind or by insects from the stamens of one flower to the pistil of another flower. Since some flowers can

▼ Male cones are small.

This spruce tree has male and female cones near the ends of its branches. ▼

The red maple tree is a flowering plant. ▼

Female cones are usually larger than male cones. ▼

The stamens of a maple's flower are longer than the petals. The pistil is in the center. ▼

pollinate themselves, fertilization can occur between reproductive cells of the same plant. However, most fertilizations occur between reproductive cells of different plants. After fertilization, seeds and their protective fruit develop in the pistil.

Before a flower blooms, or opens, it is called a *bud*. At that time the petals and reproductive parts are covered by the sepals. Petals can have thousands of shapes and colors, and they are usually pretty and easy to see.

Inside the petals are the reproductive parts. The stamens are long, thin stalks. A flower usually has several stamens. Anthers, small organs at the tops of the stamens, actually produce the pollen.

At the center of the flower is one pistil. Most of the pistil is a long, narrow tube called the *style*. The top of the pistil, the *stigma* (STIG•muh), is a little wider than the style. The stigma is often sticky, which helps it hold pollen grains tightly.

The transfer of pollen from an anther to the stigma is called *pollination*. After a pollen grain lands on the stigma, a tube begins to grow from a cell in the pollen. This pollen tube grows down through the style to an opening in the ovary (OH•vuh•ree), which is at the bottom of the pistil. The **ovary** has the eggs in one or more sections called *ovules* (AHV•yoolz).

Sperm cells move down the pollen tube and into the ovule. Fertilization occurs when a sperm cell joins with an egg to form a zygote.

✔ **What is the difference between pollination and fertilization?**

Flower Details

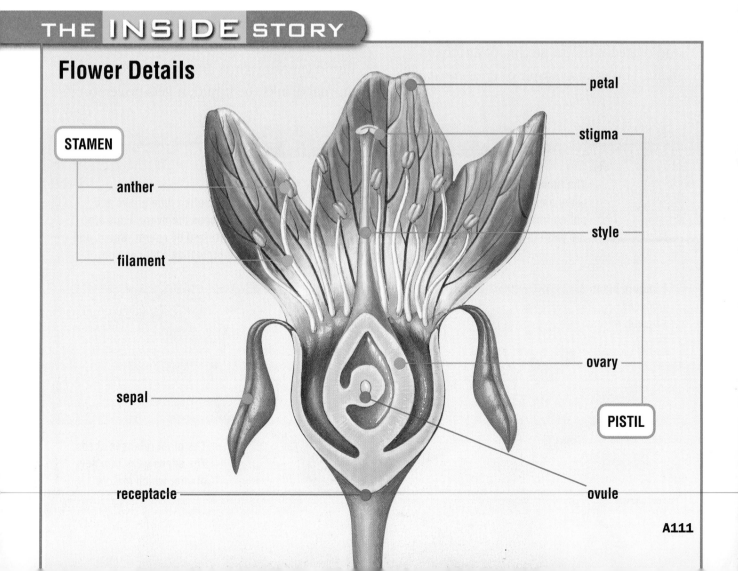

petal

stigma

STAMEN

anther

style

filament

ovary

sepal

PISTIL

receptacle

ovule

◄ Grasses have very small flowers. They depend on the wind for pollination.

◄ The color and the odor of some flowers attract insects. The insects carry pollen from flower to flower.

Methods of Pollination

Plants use many methods to ensure that pollen reaches the stigma. Pollination sometimes takes place inside a single flower. A pollen grain falls or is blown by a gentle breeze from an anther to the stigma. This type of pollination is called *self-pollination*.

Most pollination, however, takes place between different flowers. When Gregor Mendel experimented with pea plants, he took pollen from the anther of one plant and placed it on the stigma of another plant. This is an example of *cross-pollination*.

As the photographs above show, cross-pollination can occur in many ways.

Cross-pollination has adaptive benefits. It allows genetic traits to spread through a population of plants over time. Traits that help the plants survive will be passed to future generations.

Pollination itself is an example of a survival adaptation. Brightly colored petals or sweet odors attract insects and other animals to flowers. Many flowers have nectaries (NEK•tur•eez) that produce a sweet liquid (nectar) some animals seek out. As an animal drinks the liquid, it gets pollen on its

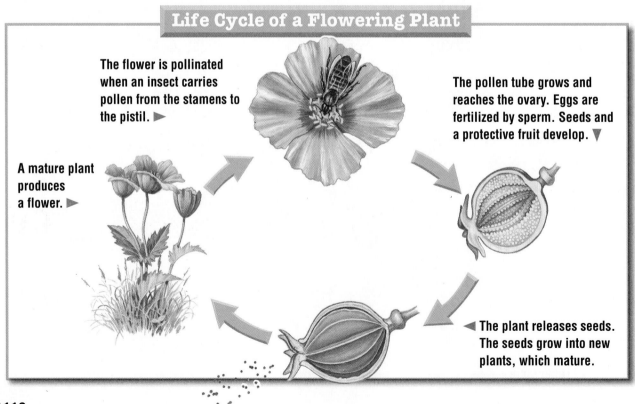

Life Cycle of a Flowering Plant

The flower is pollinated when an insect carries pollen from the stamens to the pistil. ▶

The pollen tube grows and reaches the ovary. Eggs are fertilized by sperm. Seeds and a protective fruit develop. ▼

A mature plant produces a flower. ▶

◄ The plant releases seeds. The seeds grow into new plants, which mature.

◀ Birds and other small animals seek the sweet nectar in some flowers. As this bat drinks, it gets pollen on its face.

body. That pollen may be left on the next flower the animal visits.

✓ **Name two ways in which plants may be cross-pollinated.**

Summary

Most flowers have both male and female reproductive parts. Pollen, which has sperm cells, is produced by stamens. The pistil has the eggs. Pollen is transferred from the stamens to the pistil. After fertilization, eggs develop into seeds. Many flowers attract animals that carry pollen to the pistil. In some plants, pollination depends on the wind.

Review

1. What are the male and female reproductive cells of plants called?
2. Where is pollen produced?
3. What is cross-pollination?
4. **Critical Thinking** Why is wind pollination more useful for grasses than insect pollination?
5. **Test Prep** On what flower part must pollen land for fertilization to occur?
   - **A** stigma
   - **B** ovule
   - **C** style
   - **D** anther

How Do Plants Grow?

In this lesson, you can . . .

INVESTIGATE the parts of a seed.

LEARN ABOUT how plants grow.

LINK to math, writing, health, and technology.

A coconut contains the seed of the coconut tree. This coconut floated onto the beach and began to grow into a new tree. ▽

The Parts of a Seed

Activity Purpose The life cycle of a flowering plant begins with a seed. The seed sprouts and grows into a new plant. How does this happen? What parts do seeds have that allow them to grow? In this investigation you will find out by **observing** the parts of a bean seed.

Materials

- soaked lima beans
- paper towels
- hand lens
- dropper
- iodine solution

CAUTION

Activity Procedure

1. Put a soaked lima bean on a paper towel. **Observe** the seed with the hand lens. **Record** your observations by drawing a picture of what you see.

2. Carefully peel away the outer covering of the bean. This covering is called the *seed coat*. (Picture A)

3. Gently open the bean by splitting it in half. Use the hand lens to **observe** the parts inside the bean. **Record** your observations by drawing a picture of what you see.

4. Using the point of a pencil, carefully remove the part of the bean that looks like a tiny plant. This is called the *embryo*. Look through the hand lens to identify the parts of the embryo that look like leaves, a stem, and a root. (Picture B)

Picture A

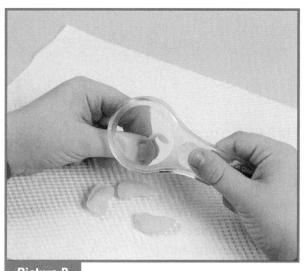

Picture B

5 **CAUTION** **Iodine can stain your hands and clothes.** Carefully put a drop or two of the iodine solution on the other parts of the bean. These parts are called the *cotyledons*. **Observe** what happens. **Record** your observations.

6 Label the seed coat, embryo, and cotyledons on your drawing from Step 3. On the embryo, label the parts that look like leaves, a stem, and a root.

Draw Conclusions

1. What words would you use to describe the seed coat of the bean? What do you **infer** is its function?

2. Iodine turns black in the presence of starch, a kind of food that plants store. Because of this, what do you **infer** is the function of the cotyledons?

3. **Scientists at Work** Scientists **observe** many plant parts. They often **communicate** to other scientists inferences they have made about the functions of certain parts. They use descriptions, data tables, graphs, and drawings. How would you communicate to a classmate your inferences about the function of cotyledons?

Investigate Further **Observe** other seeds that can be easily opened, such as green peas, squash seeds, or watermelon seeds. Examine the seed coats, and then gently split the seeds open. Compare them to the bean seed you studied in this investigation. Draw pictures, and label the parts of the seeds you observe.

How Plants Grow

Seeds

FIND OUT

- **about the parts of seeds**
- **how seeds germinate**
- **how some plants reproduce without seeds**

VOCABULARY

embryo
cotyledons
germinate
seedling
vegetative
    propagation
grafting
tissue culture

A seed is like a package that has nearly everything a new plant needs in order to grow. The seed coat is a kind of "skin" that protects the seed. Inside the seed is an **embryo** (EM•bree•oh), a tiny plant that can grow into a mature plant. The seed also has stored food and some water that will keep the embryo alive until it can sprout and produce its own food.

A seed's food is stored in structures called **cotyledons** (kah•tuh•LEE•duhnz). The seeds of some angiosperms, such as corn, have one cotyledon. These plants are called *monocots*. Other angiosperms, such as beans, roses, and oak trees, have seeds with two cotyledons. They are called *dicots*.

✔ **What is the purpose of the cotyledons?**

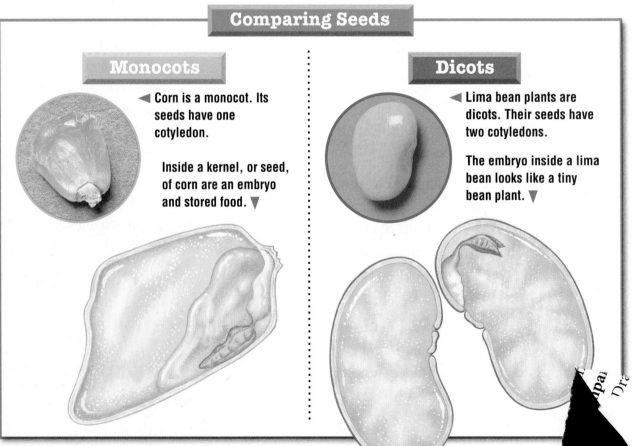

Comparing Seeds

Monocots

◀ Corn is a monocot. Its seeds have one cotyledon.

Inside a kernel, or seed, of corn are an embryo and stored food. ▼

Dicots

◀ Lima bean plants are dicots. Their seeds have two cotyledons.

The embryo inside a lima bean looks like a tiny bean plant. ▼

Seed Dispersal

Once the eggs of a plant have been fertilized and fruits have formed, the plant is ready to release the seeds. If the fruits fall next to the parent plant, the seeds do not have a good chance of growing. But plants are adapted in many ways to disperse, or scatter, fruits and seeds to places far away from the parent plant.

Maple trees, for example, produce wing-shaped fruits that spin as they fall. Spinning slows down their fall and makes it possible for wind to carry the fruit and its attached seed away from the parent tree.

In the Amazon rain forest, the fruits of some trees are dispersed by dropping into the Amazon River. The fruits are carried down the river, where they may wash up on a distant shore. There the seeds may sprout.

Many plants depend on animals to scatter their seeds. Oak trees, for example, produce fruits called acorns. Squirrels eat some acorns when they fall, and bury others to eat during the winter. The seeds inside buried acorns may sprout and grow into new oak trees.

Some seeds are covered by a fruit called a bur. The outside of a bur is usually rough, and it sticks to the fur of any passing animal. When it finally falls off, it may land on the ground and the seed inside may sprout.

✔ **Name two ways in which plants disperse seeds.**

The rough outside of a bur sticks to the fur of a passing animal or to a human's clothes.

Each dandelion seed is attached to a bit of fluff that can be blown by a light wind.

The seeds of this berry will be left in some other place with the bird's droppings.

When an animal eats a fruit, the seed may fall to the ground and sprout.

Seed Germination

A seed survives inside its protective seed coat until conditions are right for it to grow. These conditions usually include fertile soil, warm temperatures, and enough rainfall or moisture. Most seeds can survive for several years, and some seeds have survived for hundreds of years. When conditions are right, a seed will sprout, or **germinate** (JER•mih•nate).

First, the seed takes in water. This makes the seed larger. As the seed swells, the seed coat splits. The embryo then begins to grow and develop the parts it needs to live on its own. The first part to develop is the root, which begins to grow down, toward the center of the Earth.

Next, the stem emerges from the seed and begins to grow up, toward the light. The cotyledons are attached to the stem. At this stage, the growing plant, now called a **seedling**, uses food stored in the cotyledons to grow. Later the first leaves, which have also emerged from the seed, will begin to make food.

As it grows, the seedling produces longer and thicker roots. The stem gets taller and stronger. When the seedling is growing well and its leaves are making all the food the plant needs, the cotyledons drop off. The young, rapidly growing plant can now live on its own.

✔ **What is the first part to emerge from a germinating seed?**

▲ This seed has landed on rain-soaked, fertile soil. It will take in moisture, swell, and germinate.

▲ The first part to emerge from the seed is the root.

▲ As the root gets longer and thicker, a stem begins to emerge.

▲ The seedling now has a well-developed root system, and its first leaves are producing food.

▲ A strawberry plant's runners grow along the ground, putting out roots wherever they touch the soil.

▲ These offspring of the kalanchoe (ka•LAN•choh) plant develop on a leaf of the parent plant.

▲ Potato "eyes" are stem buds that can grow into a new potato plant.

◀ Irises grow from large underground buds, or *bulbs*. Several plants and many flowers may grow from a single bulb.

Vegetative Propagation

Some plants grow in places where there are few animals and little wind to help with pollination. Many of these plants are adapted to reproduce with or without seeds. This asexual reproduction—without seeds—is **vegetative propagation** (VEJ•uh•tay•tiv prah•puh•GAY•shun).

Spider plants, for example, reproduce asexually by growing "babies" at the ends of long stalks. All these young plants are the same as the parent plant. Each develops roots while it is still joined to the stalk, and each will grow into a mature spider plant if it touches the soil.

Strawberry plants have flowers and seeds, but they also reproduce by sending out horizontal stems called *runners*. Like spider plant "babies," strawberry runners grow roots and become exact copies of the parent

plant. Some types of grasses can completely take over lawns because new grass plants grow from a network of runners.

Potato plants have flowers and produce seeds. However, farmers rarely plant potato seeds because the seeds produce plants that have small *tubers*—the part we eat. Instead, farmers grow new plants from pieces of tubers that include a bud, or "eye." The buds are stem buds, not flower buds, that can grow into new plants.

The one disadvantage of vegetative propagation is that asexually produced plants have the same genes as the parent plants. As a result, there are fewer variations within a population of a particular plant. The population has fewer traits that may have adaptive benefits.

✓ **What is vegetative propagation?**

Artificial Reproduction

In the last lesson, you learned that cross-pollination leads to adaptive benefits for plants. It makes it possible for different characteristics to combine in the offspring. By controlling cross-pollination, scientists can artificially produce plants that have the characteristics people find useful. For example, one type of apple might be sweet but small, while another might be sour but large. Through cross-pollination, it's possible to produce a new kind of apple that is both sweet and large.

Grafting is a form of artificial reproduction that can produce desirable characteristics in woody plants. A stem or branch is slit open, and a stem or branch from a different plant is joined to it. When the "wound" heals, the two plants grow together. Grafting is often used to improve fruit trees. For example, black walnut trees have strong roots, but their nuts are not often eaten. English walnut trees have weak roots, but their nuts are prized as food. The branches of English walnut trees are often grafted onto the roots of black walnut trees.

It is also possible to grow a new plant from a piece of a plant. If the top of a pineapple is cut from the fruit and placed in

water or soil, the cutting will grow into a new pineapple plant. Some other plants can be grown from root cuttings or leaf cuttings.

Another method uses plant chemicals that speed up growth. If these chemicals are put on plant tissues, the cells may divide and become new plants. This process is known as **tissue culture**.

✔ **Why do scientists use artificial reproduction with plants?**

◄ The plants in this flask were grown from tissue cultures. Growth chemicals caused the cells to divide and specialize.

The small cactus was grafted onto the larger one. The plants grew together, and the two plants have become one plant. ►

A120

◄ This "multi-fruit" tree is the result of grafting branches from several kinds of fruit trees. The close-up shows how the stems are grafted together.

Summary

Seeds contain embryo plants and stored food. Under the right conditions, seeds germinate. Seedlings are young plants that grow from the embryos. Some plants may reproduce asexually through vegetative propagation. Scientists and farmers use grafting and other types of artificial reproduction to grow useful plants.

Review

1. What does the seed coat do?

2. What is a seedling?

3. What are two characteristics of seeds dispersed by the wind?

4. **Critical Thinking** Some seeds have large cotyledons. Others have small ones. What does the size of cotyledons tell you about the time it takes for a seedling to begin making food?

5. **Test Prep** Which of these is **NOT** a type of vegetative propagation?
   A producing runners
   B growth from cuttings
   C grafting
   D cross-pollination

LINKS

MATH LINK

Counting Seeds Cut an apple into quarters, remove all the seeds, and count them. Your teacher will ask each student how many seeds he or she counted. Then use a calculator to find the average number of seeds in an apple.

WRITING LINK

Expressive Writing—Friendly Letter
You have learned several ways in which plants and animals disperse seeds. Write a letter to a friend. Describe how and where some seeds are dispersed by plants and how animals help with seed dispersal.

HEALTH LINK

Seeds as Food The food that seeds store for growing embryos is good for people too. In fact, health experts say people should eat more seeds—especially grains—than any other kind of food. List all the seeds people eat. Find out what vitamins and other healthful things are in these seeds.

TECHNOLOGY LINK

Learn more about artificial reproduction in plants by visiting this Internet site.
www.scilinks.org/harcourt

Corn Cards and Super Slurpers

Chemists and agricultural scientists are working together to find new ways to use plants. Their goal is to make useful products that won't cause pollution.

Why Use Plants to Make Plastic?

Products made from plastics make life simpler, but plastics can cause problems, too. Most plastics are made from petroleum, and when you throw them away, they aren't really gone. Petroleum-based plastics don't decompose (break down) in the environment. Each year people throw away almost 20 mil-lion tons of plastics. That's a lot of trash. Now scientists who work with plants have discovered how to use corn to produce plastics that do decompose. In a landfill or a backyard compost pile, these plastics break down into hydrogen, oxygen, and small bits of organic matter called humus. Humus helps enrich the soil.

Corn is one of America's most commonly grown crops.

Packaging "peanuts" and phone cards can be made from corn.

Diapers? Not As Corny As It Sounds

What are corn-based plastics good for? Plenty! Companies use these environmentally friendly materials to make products ranging from disposable diapers to prepaid telephone calling cards.

Packaging "peanuts" made from cornstarch protect fragile products. After they have been exposed to moisture and sunlight for a few months, they fall apart.

Chemists at a U.S. Department of Agriculture laboratory discovered a way to use cornstarch to make a material they called hydrosorb. Its nickname is "Super Slurper." Why? Because it can soak up more than 300 times its own weight in water. Diapers containing hydrosorb help keep babies dry. Super Slurper filters remove water from fuels such as gasoline and heating oil. When mixed with soil, hydrosorb holds moisture near the roots of plants, helping them grow with less irrigation.

PLA Plastics

Other scientists have found ways to recombine the hydrogen, oxygen, and carbon in corn to make a material called polylactic acid resin, or PLA. Plastics made from PLA can be used just like petroleum-based plastics to make toys, TV sets, and other products.

Nebraska farmers grow nearly 30 million tons of corn each year. Scientists at the University of Nebraska say that they haven't found anything made with petroleum-based plastic that can't also be made from the PLA plastic that comes from corn.

THINK ABOUT IT

1. What other products could Super Slurpers be used for?
2. What are some advantages and disadvantages of corn-based plastics?

WEB LINK:
For science and technology updates, visit The Learning Site.
www.harcourtschool.com

Careers   Agronomist

What They Do
Agronomists study soils and plants to develop better ways to grow crops and to keep agricultural land productive.

Education and Training People wishing to become agronomists study plant biology and soil chemistry in college and graduate school.

Shirley Mah Kooyman

BOTANIST

"Our food, many of the things we wear, and even some parts of our homes come from plants. People also get enjoyment from looking at plants."

Because we depend on plants for so many things, the health of plants is important to our survival. Shirley Mah Kooyman feels that plants are sometimes taken for granted—that people forget they are living things. Ms. Kooyman is a botanist, or plant scientist, in Chanhassen, Minnesota. An important part of her work is discovering what makes plants grow. The knowledge that she gains is used by other scientists, who work to find ways to grow healthier plants that produce larger crops.

In her work, Ms. Kooyman seeks to better understand some of the growth processes of plants. She knows that in addition to light energy, water, proper temperature, and rich soil, plants need certain hormones. Hormones are chemical "messengers" that "tell" plants to grow. Plant hormones are produced in stems and roots. From there they travel to other parts of the plant.

Today scientists are able to make artificial plant hormones. Artificial hormones placed on a root tip make the root grow, just as natural hormones do. The advantage of artificial hormones is that they can be produced in greater amounts than natural hormones. Farmers can use artificial hormones to speed up plant growth and produce larger crops. This will make plant products more affordable. In addition to working with plant hormones in a laboratory and in the field, Ms. Kooyman teaches people about plants and the joys of gardening.

THINK ABOUT IT

1. Why is it important to understand what makes plants grow?
2. How might artificial hormones be used to produce a large crop of tomatoes?

Ms. Kooyman teaching a young gardener

Leaf Casts

How can you observe stomata?

Materials
- potted plant
- clear fingernail polish
- microscope slide
- microscope

Procedure

1. Paint a 2-cm square of fingernail polish on the underside of one leaf. Let the polish dry.

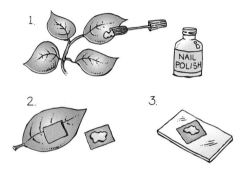

2. Add another layer of polish and let it dry. Repeat until you have 6 layers of polish.

3. Once the last layer of polish is dry, peel it off the leaf.

4. Put the polish, which contains a cast of the leaf epidermis, on a microscope slide.

5. Observe the slide by using the microscope.

Draw Conclusions

You should observe two types of cells. Compare the cells. Explain any differences between them. How do the guard cells form the stomata?

Seed Gravitropism

How do seeds respond to gravity?

Materials
- paper towel
- plastic sandwich bag
- water
- 4 lima beans

Procedure

1. Fold the paper towel to fit inside the plastic sandwich bag.

2. Add water to the bag until the paper towel is completely wet.

3. Put the lima beans facing in very different directions on the paper towel. Then lean the bag against something, as shown.

4. Observe the seeds as they germinate.

Draw Conclusions

What happens to the new roots as the seeds germinate? What force affects the growth of plant roots?

Vocabulary Review

Use the terms below to complete the sentences. The page numbers in ( ) tell you where to look in the chapter if you need help.

photosynthesis (A96)
epidermis (A96)
palisade layer (A97)
cellular respiration (A100)
tropism (A104)
phototropism (A104)
gravitropism (A105)
fertilization (A110)
stamens (A110)
pistil (A110)
ovary (A111)
embryo (A116)
cotyledons (A116)
germinate (A118)
seedling (A118)
vegetative propagation (A119)
grafting (A120)
tissue culture (A120)

1. ____ is the process plants use to make their own food.

2. Growing toward the light is an example of ____.

3. There may be many ovules in a flower's ____.

4. Planting a potato tuber with an "eye" is a form of ____.

5. The male reproductive parts of a flower are the ____.

6. A seed will not ____ unless it has enough water.

7. An embryo plant whose root and stem have started growing is called a ____.

8. A plant's response to a stimulus is called a ____.

9. The joining of an egg and a sperm cell is called ____.

10. The ____ is the part of the seed that will become the plant.

11. Most photosynthesis takes place in the ____ of cells.

12. Making stems from two different plants grow together is called ____.

13. The ____ is the female reproductive part of a flower.

14. ____ contain stored food that helps an embryo plant grow.

15. ____ causes roots to grow down.

16. The process by which organisms release energy stored in food is ____.

17. Growing new plants from plant tissues is called ____.

18. The upper layer of cells in a leaf is the ____.

Connect Concepts

Write the letter of the plant part that best fits each description.

____ 19. Produce pollen

____ 20. Bends toward light

____ 21. Exchange of gases

____ 22. Usually brightly colored

____ 23. Most photosynthesis occurs here

____ 24. Grows toward center of Earth

____ 25. Produces nectar

Check Understanding

Write the letter of the best choice.

26. Phototropism changes the growth of cells in the plant's —
    A roots
    B leaves
    C stem
    D flowers

27. The ovary is part of a flower's —
    F stamens
    G pistil
    H style
    J sepals

28. Nectaries and colorful petals attract insects and other animals that help in —
    A pollination
    B germination
    C grafting
    D dispersal

29. Embryo plants grow by using the food stored in —
    F tubers
    G stems
    H cotyledons
    J seed coats

30. In order to germinate, seeds have to absorb —
    A carbon dioxide
    B water
    C nectar
    D starch

Critical Thinking

31. The leaves of some plants have edges that are sharp enough to cut your finger. How would this be an adaptive benefit to the plant?

32. A weed is sometimes defined as "any plant growing where it is not wanted." Why do farmers and gardeners try to get rid of weeds?

Process Skills Review

33. Do bean seeds need warm temperatures to germinate? **Plan and carry out an experiment** to find out.

34. **Compare** cross-pollination and self-pollination. Which do you think has more adaptive benefits?

Performance Assessment

Design a Flower

Work with a partner to design a flower. Your flower may be as unusual as you wish, but it must contain all the flower parts you learned about in this chapter. Draw a picture or make a model of your flower. Label its parts. Describe how the flower is pollinated.

Unit Project Wrap Up

Here are some ideas for ways to wrap up your unit project.

Display at a Science Fair

Display the fold-outs in a school science fair. You may want to include photographs of the living things you showed in your project.

Write a Disclaimer

Think of an ad for a service that claims to improve your health, such as for a fitness center. Write a paragraph, called a disclaimer, that explains why some people might not get the results described in the ad.

Draw a Cartoon

Use a computer and drawing software to make a cartoon showing a person moving in some way. Explain how the bones, muscles, and nerves work together to enable him or her to move.

Investigate Further

How could you make your project better? What other questions do you have about animals and plants? Plan ways to find answers to your questions. Use the Science Handbook on pages R2-R9 for help.

Systems and Interactions in Nature

LIFE SCIENCE

Systems and Interactions in Nature

Unit Project ## Park Plans

Draw plans for a nature park in your area. Consider the interactions of the living and non-living things in the park, and the needs of the organisms. Write a report about the environment of the park, natural changes that will probably take place in the park, and how the environment can be protected and preserved.

Chapter 1

Cycles in Nature

The water you washed with this morning has been around for millions of years. It has been rain, snow, sleet, and hail. It has flowed over thousands of waterfalls and been frozen in hundreds of glaciers. Dinosaurs might have drunk it. But it has always returned to the ground, the ocean, or the air again and again.

Vocabulary Preview

nitrogen cycle
carbon dioxide-oxygen cycle
water cycle
evaporation
condensation
precipitation
transpiration

 FAST FACT

Waterfalls move. Niagara Falls is moving toward Lake Erie as it slowly wears away the rock at its top. It will reach the lake in about 23,000 years.

About 70 percent of Earth's surface is covered by salt water. Most of it is in Earth's four oceans.

Earth's Oceans

Ocean	Surface Area (millions of km^2)	Volume (millions of km^3)
Pacific	166.0	723.7
Atlantic	82.0	321.9
Indian	73.6	292.1
Arctic	12.2	13.5

FAST FACT

If all of Earth's glaciers and ice caps were to melt, the oceans would rise about 60 meters (200 feet), covering thousands of large coastal cities, such as Venice, Italy.

How Does Nature Reuse Materials?

In this lesson, you can . . .

INVESTIGATE how plants use carbon dioxide.

LEARN ABOUT how materials are reused in nature.

LINK to math, writing, social studies, and technology.

∨ Every cell in this bison's body uses oxygen and produces carbon dioxide.

INVESTIGATE

How Plants Use Carbon Dioxide

Activity Purpose Remember that every time you inhale, or take a breath, your lungs take in oxygen. That oxygen then goes to your blood cells, which carry it to every other cell in your body. Body cells use oxygen for their life functions, or activities. Cell functions produce carbon dioxide, which the blood carries back to the lungs. When you exhale, or breathe out, carbon dioxide leaves your body. In this investigation you will **observe** how plants use carbon dioxide.

Materials

- safety goggles
- 2 beakers, 250 mL
- water
- dropper
- bromothymol blue (BTB), an indicator
- plastic straw
- elodea
- 2 test tubes with caps
- funnel
- clock

Activity Procedure

1 **CAUTION** Put on safety goggles, and leave them on until you complete Step 4. Fill one beaker about two-thirds full of water. Use the dropper to add BTB to the water until you have a blue solution. BTB is an indicator. It changes color when carbon dioxide is present.

2 **CAUTION** Don't suck on the straw. If you do accidentally, don't swallow the solution. Spit it out, and rinse your mouth with water. Put the plastic straw in the solution, and blow into it. What do you **observe**? **Record** your observations. (Picture A)

3 Put the elodea into one test tube, and use the funnel to fill the tube with BTB solution from the beaker. Fill the other test tube with the BTB solution only.

4 Seal the test tubes with the caps. Carefully turn the test tubes upside down, and place them in the empty beaker. (Picture B)

5 Put the beaker containing the two test tubes in a sunny window for 1 hour. **Predict** what changes will occur in the test tubes. After 1 hour, **observe** both test tubes, and **record** your observations.

Picture A

Draw Conclusions

1. What changes did you **observe** in the BTB solution when you blew into it through the straw? Explain.

2. What changes did you **observe** in the test tube of BTB solution after the elodea had been in it for 1 hour?

3. **Compare** the color of the BTB solution in the test tube that had the elodea with the color of the BTB in the test tube that did not have the elodea. Describe any differences.

4. **Scientists at Work** Scientists **observe** changes that happen during experiments. Then they **infer** what caused the changes. What can you infer about any changes that took place in the test tubes?

Investigate Further What is the importance of sunlight in this investigation? **Hypothesize** about the importance of sunlight. Then **plan and conduct a simple investigation** to test your hypothesis.

Picture B

Process Skill Tip

When you **infer** the cause of something, you try to explain why it happened. Your inference is based on what you **observe**.

How Natural Materials Are Reused

Natural Cycles

FIND OUT

- how materials are reused in nature
- about the nitrogen and carbon dioxide–oxygen cycles
- how people can upset nature's recycling

VOCABULARY

nitrogen cycle
carbon dioxide–
    oxygen cycle

Many materials on Earth are used and then reused by living organisms. Earth also stores some materials for later use. The air, for example, stores large amounts of oxygen, nitrogen, and carbon dioxide. Materials such as iron, copper, magnesium, and calcium are stored in rocks.

Running water slowly wears away rocks, releasing stored materials. The materials dissolve in rivers and lakes or become part of the soil. When an animal drinks water, it gets some of the materials it needs. Animals also get materials they need by eating. Animals release some of these materials into the environment in their wastes.

Plants get the materials they need from the soil and from the air. Plants release some of these materials to the environment during photosynthesis. When plants and animals die, their bodies decay. This releases more materials into the environment. The cycle continues as new plants and animals use these materials.

✔ **Where do animals and plants get the materials they need?**

Animals get the materials they need by eating and by drinking water. ▼

Lightning "fixes" a small amount of nitrogen.

Most nitrogen gas is fixed by bacteria in the soil or in nodules on some plant roots.

Plants use nitrogen in the soil to make proteins.

Animals get nitrogen by eating plants and other animals.

Animal wastes and decaying plants and animals return nitrates and ammonia to the soil.

The Nitrogen Cycle

All living organisms need nitrogen (NY•truh•juhn). Plants make proteins from nitrogen in the soil. Animals get the nitrogen they need to make proteins when they eat plants or other animals that eat plants.

Earth's atmosphere is about 78 percent nitrogen. But most organisms can't use nitrogen in this form. In the **nitrogen cycle**, nitrogen gas is *fixed*, or changed, into forms of nitrogen that plants can use. These forms are nitrates and ammonia (uh•MOHN•yuh).

Bacteria in the soil and in nodules (NAHJ•ools), or small lumps, on the roots of certain plants fix most of the nitrogen gas.

A small amount of nitrogen gas is also fixed by lightning. Most fixed nitrogen remains fixed—only a small amount changes back into nitrogen gas.

Nitrates and ammonia are returned to the soil in two ways. First, they are returned through animal wastes. Solid waste from animals contains nitrates. The liquid waste, or urine, that animals produce contains ammonia. Second, when animals and plants die, bacteria release nitrates and ammonia from decaying protein.

✔ **What are two forms of fixed nitrogen?**

Farmers spread animal wastes on their fields to return nitrates to the soil.

The Carbon Dioxide–Oxygen Cycle

In the carbon dioxide–oxygen cycle, carbon and oxygen move among plants, animals, and the environment. All life on Earth is involved in this cycle.

Carbon On Earth

Living animals and plants 3%

Atmosphere 1%

Dead and decaying matter 3%

Fossil fuels 22%

Oceans 71%

FOSSIL FUELS Over millions of years, the carbon in some decaying ocean organisms turned into petroleum.

PHOTOSYNTHESIS Microscopic plantlike organisms make their own food by photosynthesis. These organisms take in carbon dioxide from ocean water. Oceans contain so many of these organisms that almost 90 percent of the oxygen in the atmosphere comes from photosynthesis in the oceans.

RESPIRATION All ocean organisms use oxygen and release carbon dioxide during respiration.

RESPIRATION All plants and animals use oxygen in respiration. Plants and animals release carbon dioxide as a product of respiration.

SOLAR ENERGY
Sunlight provides the energy for photosynthesis in plants.

COMBUSTION is the burning of fossil fuels. Oxygen is used in the burning of fossil fuels. Carbon dioxide is a byproduct of combustion.

FOSSIL FUELS Dense forests once covered large parts of Earth. As these forests died, carbon in the plants became coal.

DECAY Some carbon is stored for a while in the bodies of dead organisms. Bacteria and fungi break down the tissues of dead animals and plants and use some of the carbon as food. The rest is released into the atmosphere as carbon dioxide.

PHOTOSYNTHESIS Plants use sunlight, water, and carbon dioxide in photosynthesis. Plants release oxygen into the atmosphere as a byproduct of photosynthesis.

Changing the Balance

For hundreds of millions of years, the carbon dioxide–oxygen cycle stayed in balance, mostly by the processes of photosynthesis and respiration. However, since the beginning of the Industrial Revolution, about 200 years ago, human activity has started to change the balance.

During the Industrial Revolution, humans began to use machines fueled by wood and coal. Factories needed huge amounts of these fuels. Large areas of forests were cut for timber, and deep mines were dug to remove coal from inside the Earth. The burning of wood and coal put tons of carbon dioxide into the air each year.

Slowly, new methods made it possible to replace wood and some coal with fossil fuels such as natural gas and petroleum. Factories, energy stations, heating systems, and cars, trucks, and airplanes all use fossil fuels. Burning these fuels adds even more carbon dioxide to the air.

Adding carbon dioxide to the air is a problem, because excess carbon dioxide is poisonous to animals. Although many people no longer use wood for fuel, large numbers of trees are still cut down for forest products, such as paper and lumber. Sometimes new trees are planted to replace the ones that are cut. But the total size of Earth's forests is less each year.

Forests are also cut to make room for other human needs, such as new farms and homes and growing cities. With forests becoming smaller, there are fewer trees to

Forests use large amounts of carbon dioxide. Smaller forests mean fewer trees to use the excess carbon dioxide in the air.

use the added carbon dioxide in the air. As a result, carbon dioxide continues to build up in the air. And too much carbon dioxide is poisonous to animals and humans.

✔ **How do trees and other plants help keep the carbon dioxide–oxygen cycle balanced?**

Summary

Most of the materials that organisms need are cycled through nature. Bacteria and lightning fix nitrogen gas into forms that plants can use to make proteins. Animal wastes and decaying organisms return nitrates and ammonia to the soil. Plants and animals cycle oxygen and carbon dioxide through the processes of photosynthesis and respiration. But human activities, such as burning fossil fuels and cutting down forests, upset the balance of the carbon dioxide–oxygen cycle.

Review

1. Name two places where carbon is stored.
2. Where do bacteria fix nitrogen gas?
3. How do photosynthesis and respiration affect the carbon dioxide–oxygen cycle?
4. **Critical Thinking** How might building a shopping mall on land where there is now a park affect the amount of carbon dioxide in the air?
5. **Test Prep** Which human activity does **NOT** increase the amount of carbon dioxide in the air?

   A cutting down trees
   B heating buildings with coal
   C driving cars
   D planting corn

LINKS

MATH LINK

Calculate Each year human activity adds more than 7 billion tons of carbon dioxide to the air. This amount increases by 5 percent each year. If people add 7 billion tons of carbon dioxide to the air in the year 2000, how much will they add in 2001? In 2002?

WRITING LINK

Narrative Writing—Story Write a story for your family from the point of view of a material such as tin, copper, or iron. Begin your story inside a rock. Then describe what happens as you begin to dissolve in water and enter a natural cycle.

SOCIAL STUDIES LINK

Transportation Before the early 1900s, people didn't use cars to travel. Find out how people got around without cars. Write a report or make a poster showing methods of transportation people used before cars were invented.

TECHNOLOGY LINK

Learn more about cycles in nature by visiting this Internet site.
www.scilinks.org/harcourt

SCLINKS
THE WORLD'S A CLICK AWAY

Why Is the Water Cycle Important?

In this lesson, you can . . .

INVESTIGATE how water moves through air.

LEARN ABOUT the water cycle.

LINK to math, writing, literature, and technology.

INVESTIGATE

Water, Water Everywhere

Activity Purpose Every day, you have some contact with water. You drink it, you bathe in it, and maybe you watch it fall from the sky. But have you ever wondered where water comes from, where it goes, or why we never run out of it? In this activity you will **observe** how water is recycled.

Materials
- graduate
- water
- small plastic cup
- zip-top plastic bag

Activity Procedure

1. Using the graduate, **measure** and pour 100 mL of water into the cup. (Picture A)

2. Open the plastic bag, and carefully put the cup inside. Then seal the bag. Be careful not to spill any water from the cup.

3. Place the sealed bag near a sunny window. **Predict** what will happen to the water in the cup. (Picture B)

◀ The warmth of the sun will change the snow into liquid water.

Picture A

Picture B

④ Leave the bag near a window for 3 to 4 days. **Observe** the cup and the bag each day. **Record** what you see.

⑤ Remove the cup from the bag. **Measure** the amount of water in the cup by pouring it back into the graduate. **Calculate** any difference in the amount of water you poured into the cup and the amount of water you removed from the cup.

Draw Conclusions

1. What did you **observe** during the time the cup was inside the bag?

2. Where do you infer the water in the bag came from? Explain.

3. **Scientists at Work** Scientists often **infer** the cause of something they **observe**. What can you infer about the amount of water in the bag?

Investigate Further How could you find out if the amount of water in the bag is the same as the amount of water missing from the cup? Decide what equipment you would need to use. Then **plan and conduct a simple investigation** that would help you answer the question.

Process Skill Tip

If you carefully **observe** the results of an experiment, you can often **infer** what caused those results.

Why the Water Cycle Is Important

FIND OUT

- how water moves through the environment on Earth
- how human activity can affect the water cycle

VOCABULARY

water cycle
evaporation
condensation
precipitation
transpiration

The Water Cycle

As seen from space, Earth looks like a big blue marble. Seas, oceans, lakes, and rivers cover about 75 percent of Earth's surface. Earth's water moves through the environment in what is called the **water cycle**. In the investigation, you inferred that liquid water in the cup became water vapor in the air. The water vapor then became liquid water in the plastic bag.

The heat of the sun changes water on Earth's surface into water vapor. This process is called **evaporation** (ee•vap•uh•RAY•shuhn). The temperature of the air high above the Earth is cold. There water vapor changes back into liquid water through a process called **condensation** (kahn•duhn•SAY•shuhn). Tiny droplets of water appear, forming

If all of Earth's water could be held in a 1-liter bottle, the contents would be divided up like this:

Salt water: 972 mL

Fresh water: 28 mL

a cloud. After a lot of water vapor condenses, the water may fall back to the Earth as rain. If the air temperature is very cold, the water droplets may freeze and fall as snow or hail. Any form of water that falls from clouds is called **precipitation** (pree•sip•uh•TAY•shuhn).

All living organisms need water to survive. In fact, living organisms are made up of mostly water. About 70 percent of the human body is water. Living organisms get the water they need in different ways. Plants use their roots to take in water that seeps into the soil. Most animals get the water

they need by drinking from lakes or streams. Some animals get all the water they need from the food they eat.

Plants and animals also put water back into the environment. Plants give off water through their stomata. This process is called **transpiration** (tran•spuh•RAY•shuhn). Animals give off water vapor from their lungs when they exhale. And most of the urine animals produce is water.

✔ **What are the main processes in the water cycle?**

All the water on Earth keeps recycling. The heat of the sun evaporates water from the ocean's surface. High in the air, water condenses into tiny droplets to form clouds. Winds sweep clouds over the land. When clouds rise over a mountain, water falls as precipitation. Some rainwater runs off the land and returns to the ocean or to lakes. Some rainwater seeps into the Earth and becomes groundwater.

The 28 mL of fresh water is divided up like this:

Ice caps: 22 mL
Glaciers: 1.5 mL

Groundwater: 4 mL

Lakes and rivers: 2 drops

Water in soil and air: 1 drop

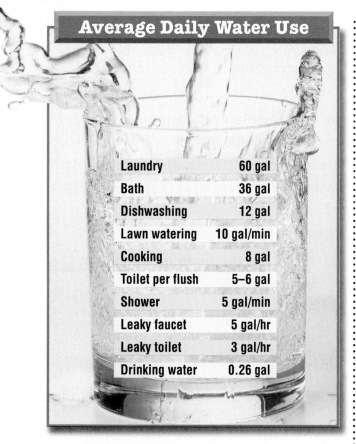

Laundry	60 gal
Bath	36 gal
Dishwashing	12 gal
Lawn watering	10 gal/min
Cooking	8 gal
Toilet per flush	5–6 gal
Shower	5 gal/min
Leaky faucet	5 gal/hr
Leaky toilet	3 gal/hr
Drinking water	0.26 gal

Humans and the Water Cycle

All the water on Earth today is the same water that was here billions of years ago. Yet every year the need for water grows. In addition to drinking, bathing, cooking, and waste removal, people use water to grow crops, feed livestock, and make materials, such as plastic, aluminum, and paper.

Less than 1 percent of the Earth's fresh water can be used because most of it is frozen in ice caps and glaciers. Yet the limited sources of fresh water are sometimes affected by human activity. Rainwater running off the land washes harmful chemicals such as oil

Although trash is more visible, this stream also carries harmful chemicals, such as pesticides, motor oil, and gasoline. ▶

and road salt into lakes and rivers. Expensive forms of water treatment must be used to make lakes and rivers safe for human use.

Rainwater seeping into the soil carries harmful chemicals such as fertilizers and pesticides into groundwater supplies. It stays there for thousands of years. Groundwater supplies provide many people with water for use in their homes. Farmers also use underground supplies to water their crops.

There are ways to conserve water and to improve water quality. For example, in

Some landscaping in west Texas uses native desert plants instead of grass and trees. ▼

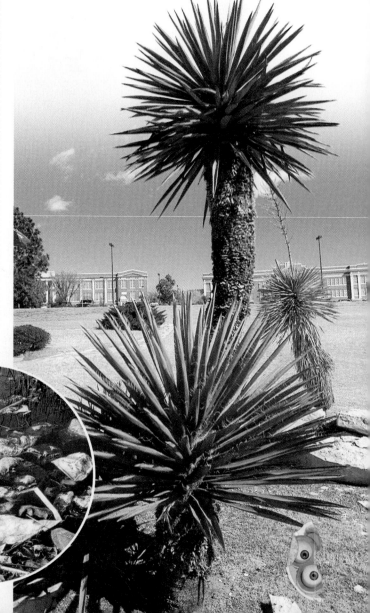

many states, factories must remove harmful chemicals from their waste water. In some places, used motor oil is recycled into new products. And people everywhere can conserve water by using washers and toilets that don't need much water. People in arid places can also landscape with native plants instead of grasses and trees that need a lot of water.

✓ **How do harmful chemicals on the land get into groundwater?**

Summary

In the water cycle, water on Earth's surface evaporates into the atmosphere. There it condenses into cloud droplets and then falls back to Earth as precipitation. Plants and animals return water to the environment through transpiration and respiration. Fresh water is a limited resource that people need to conserve and keep clean.

Review

1. What is the process by which liquid water becomes water vapor?
2. What is the process by which water vapor becomes cloud droplets?
3. Where is most of Earth's fresh water?
4. **Critical Thinking** What do you think causes dew to form on plant leaves during a cool night?
5. **Test Prep** About how much of all the fresh water on Earth can be used by people and other land organisms?
   A less than 1 percent
   B more than 10 percent
   C more than 97 percent
   D 100 percent

LINKS

MATH LINK

Water Use An average person uses about 60 gallons of water a day. Calculate how much water a person uses in a month (30 days) and in a year (365 days). How much would a family of four people use in a year?

WRITING LINK

Informative Writing—Business Letter The United States government has passed laws to improve the quality of the nation's water. Find out about the Clean Drinking Water Act or other laws that protect surface water and groundwater. Draft a letter to the Environmental Protection Agency or to your representative to Congress, asking for information about these laws.

LITERATURE LINK

A Drop of Water Check out either of these two books about water: *A Drop of Water* by Walter Wick (Scholastic, 1998) or *Squishy, Misty, Damp and Muddy: The In-Between World of Wetlands* by Molly Cone (Sierra, 1997). Learn about the importance of water and wetlands.

TECHNOLOGY LINK

Learn more about the water cycle and water treatment by viewing *Natural Water Treatment* on the **Harcourt Science Newsroom Video.**

WETLANDS WITH A PURPOSE

Wetlands are among the most productive ecosystems on Earth. Many kinds of organisms—fish, birds, reptiles, amphibians, insects, and mammals—find food and shelter in wetlands.

What Wetlands Do

In addition to providing habitats for wildlife, wetlands improve water quality. Aquatic plants and microorganisms that live on the plants filter waste materials and pollutants from the water.

Scientists are combining technology with ecology to build artificial wetlands to treat wastewater. An artificial wetland is a wetland with a purpose. Over 500 communities in the United States have already built artificial wetlands to treat sewage effluent (wastewater) and storm runoff.

Technology Imitates Nature

Artificial wetlands are designed to do what natural wetland ecosystems do. The processes are carried out by water, plants, animals, microorganisms, sun, soil, and air working together. What happens is that microorganisms, such as the bacteria and fungi in the soil and on the plants, change organic wastes into nutrients that plants can use. The plants take in materials such as nitrogen and phosphorus from the wastewater.

The Show Low wetland in northeastern Arizona was one of the first artificial wetlands in the country. In 1979 the U.S. Forest Service, the Arizona Fish and Game Commission, and Show Low city officials teamed up to build the wetland. Wastewater was

An artificial wetland

Great blue herons

pumped into a natural low area, making Pintail Lake. Then 14 small islands were built in the lake to attract water birds. The islands and the shoreline were seeded with wetland plants, such as cattails, water grass, duckweed, and bulrushes. In the following years, several more marshes and lakes were made. Now the wetlands complex covers about 81 hectares (200 acres) and receives 5.37 million liters (about 1.42 million gallons) of wastewater daily. Instead of being released into a nearby river, the water stays in the treatment area until it evaporates.

Why Build Wetlands?

Artificial wetlands are very efficient at removing pollutants from municipal,

agricultural, and industrial wastewater at little or no cost. It takes less energy, fewer supplies, and far fewer people to run an artificial wetland than it does to run a conventional water treatment plant.

Artificial wetlands are an example of human technology working with natural processes. In addition to treating wastewater, artificial wetlands provide habitats for wildlife and an environment in which people can enjoy and explore nature.

THINK ABOUT IT

1. For what purposes are artificial wetlands built?

2. How do artificial wetlands combine technology with natural processes?

WEB LINK:
For science and technology updates, visit The Learning Site.
www.harcourtschool.com

Careers — Heavy-Machine Operator

What They Do Heavy-machine operators drive earth-moving and construction machines, such as road scrapers, cranes, forklifts, bulldozers, and front-end loaders.

Education and Training People wishing to become heavy-machine operators may attend special trade schools to learn the basics of how to drive and operate the machinery. They also need on-the-job training and experience.

Marjory Stoneman Douglas

CONSERVATIONIST

"There are no other Everglades in the world. It is a river of grass."

While others saw in the Everglades nothing but a marshy wasteland, Marjory Stoneman Douglas saw "the simplicity, the diversity, the related harmony of the forms of life they enclose." Ms. Douglas began observing the Everglades as a reporter for the *Miami Herald* in 1919. At that time most people believed that the Everglades were a problem to be overcome in the path of development. Ms. Douglas, however, discovered a thriving ecosystem in the Everglades, a vast, shallow "river of grass" that flows south from Florida's Lake Okeechobee to the Gulf of Mexico.

Ms. Douglas became a leader among those working to save the Everglades. She wanted the government to establish an Everglades National Park. That dream was realized in 1947, the same year Ms. Douglas's book The *Everglades: River*

of Grass was published. In 1970 Ms. Douglas founded an organization called Friends of the Everglades, which includes research scientists, engineers, and other citizens. This group was able to prevent the construction of an airport in the Everglades.

Following Ms. Douglas's death in 1998 at the age of 108, John Flicker, president of the National Audubon Society, said, "Marjory Stoneman Douglas showed us that the pen is truly mightier than the sword, and the bulldozer, and the excavator. She introduced the nation and the world to the wonder of an environment overlooked and misunderstood, [and she] stood against formidable forces intent upon destroying this irreplaceable national treasure. She showed us that one person can change the world."

THINK ABOUT IT

1. Why do you think people considered the Everglades a problem to be overcome?
2. Why was action to save the Everglades necessary?

Everglades National Park

The Carbon Cycle

Where can you find carbon?

Materials

- candle
- match
- aluminum pie pan
- white paper
- charcoal
- pencil
- hand lens

Procedure

1 Your teacher or another adult will light the candle and hold it under the aluminum pie pan for a few seconds.

2 Observe the black soot that forms on the pan.

3 After the pan cools, use your finger to scrape off some of the soot. Wipe your finger on the white paper.

4 Now rub the charcoal on the paper. Then make several marks on the paper with the pencil.

5 Using the hand lens, compare the materials on the paper.

Draw Conclusions

What material is in the soot, the charcoal, and the pencil? How did this material become part of each? Where else can you find this material?

The Water Cycle

What are the parts of the water cycle?

Materials

- safety goggles
- 500-mL beaker
- water
- hot plate
- hot pad
- tongs
- glass plate

Procedure

1 **CAUTION** Put on the safety goggles. Put about 400 mL of water in the beaker.

2 Heat the beaker on the hot plate until the water starts to boil.

3 Using the hot pad and the tongs, your teacher or another adult will hold the glass plate above the beaker to catch the steam.

4 Observe the water drops that form on the glass plate and fall back into the beaker.

Draw Conclusions

Where in the model were evaporation, condensation, and precipitation taking place? Heat from the hot plate caused the water to boil. What heat source causes evaporation in nature?

Chapter ① Review and Test Preparation

Vocabulary Review

Use the terms below to complete the sentences. The page numbers in ( ) tell you where to look in the chapter if you need help.

nitrogen cycle (B7)

carbon dioxide–oxygen cycle (B8)

water cycle (B14)

evaporation (B14)

condensation (B14)

precipitation (B15)

transpiration (B15)

1. Plants give off water from their stomata in a process called ____.

2. Ammonia is a usable form of an atmospheric gas that bacteria in the soil fix as part of the ____.

3. ____ such as rain, snow, and sleet is part of the ____.

4. As part of the ____, plants use carbon dioxide and give off oxygen into the atmosphere.

5. Cold temperatures high in the atmosphere cause the ____ of water vapor.

6. After the ____ of liquid water on Earth's surface, water vapor rises into the atmosphere.

Connect Concepts

Fill in the concept map using terms from the Word Bank.

condense   evaporate

precipitation   water vapor

clouds

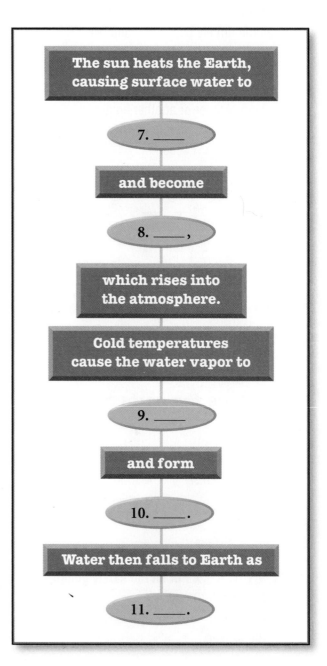

The sun heats the Earth, causing surface water to

7. ____

and become

8. ____,

which rises into the atmosphere.

Cold temperatures cause the water vapor to

9. ____

and form

10. ____.

Water then falls to Earth as

11. ____.

Check Understanding

Write the letter of the best choice.

12. The environment stores many materials. The atmosphere stores a lot of —
    A nitrogen gas   C water vapor
    B oxygen   D carbon dioxide

13. When nitrogen is fixed, it is —
    F dissolved in water
    G removed from lightning
    H changed into a usable form
    J made into a protein

14. Most of the oxygen in the air comes from photosynthesis in —
    A rain forests   C the soil
    B the oceans   D lakes and rivers

15. Fossil fuels contain mostly —
    F fixed nitrogen   H bacteria
    G carbon   J gases

16. What human activity does **NOT** cause an increase in the amount of carbon dioxide in the atmosphere?
    A cutting down trees
    B burning fossil fuels
    C planting trees
    D none of the above

17. Where is most of the fresh water on Earth?
    F lakes   H rivers
    G glaciers   J oceans

18. Plants give off water during —
    A transpiration   C condensation
    B respiration   D evaporation

19. Most nitrogen is fixed by —
    F lightning   H bacteria
    G rocks   J water

Critical Thinking

20. If a region's forests are cut down, do you think the amount of rainfall in that region will increase or decrease? Explain your answer.

21. Explain how buying a car that gets good gas mileage might reduce the amount of carbon dioxide that is added to the atmosphere.

22. How might solar-powered buildings and cars reduce the amount of carbon dioxide that is added to the atmosphere?

Process Skills Review

23. You know that materials such as water, nitrogen, carbon dioxide, and oxygen cycle through the environment. Based on what you know, what can you **predict** about supplies of fossil fuels in the future? Are fossil fuels cycled like water and nitrogen, and therefore unlimited in supply, or is their supply limited?

24. How can you **infer** that some rainwater evaporates after a storm?

Performance Assessment

Water Cycle Art

Make a mural or poster that traces a drop of water through the water cycle. Include how long the drop of water stays in each stage of the cycle. For example, it might stay 10 years in a lake, 12 days in a cloud, and so on. Label each part of the cycle.

Chapter 2

Living Things Interact

When poet John Donne wrote "No man is an island," he was talking about how people need and depend on other people. In fact, almost every living thing on Earth needs and depends on other living things. We are all part of the biosphere, Earth's life zone.

Vocabulary Preview

individual	energy
population	pyramid
community	competition
ecosystem	symbiosis
habitat	instinct
niche	learned
producer	behavior
consumer	exotic
food chain	extinct
decomposer	endangered
food web	threatened

FAST FACT

There are more than 750 endangered species of plants and animals, like this manatee, in the United States.

Endangered Species

Type	Number
Mammals	55
Birds	74
Fish	65
Other animals	126
Plants	434

In 1859 a settler released a few rabbits in Australia. Within a few years, millions of rabbits were competing for food with native birds and mammals. Although the rabbits have done well, some of these native Australian animals are now extinct.

Most islands would have no plants or animals if they didn't arrive from other places. For example, the islands of Hawai'i are the most isolated islands on Earth. The native plants and animals that live there somehow reached the islands from the mainland of Central America.

1

What Are Ecosystems?

In this lesson, you can . . .

INVESTIGATE a local environment.

LEARN ABOUT how organisms live together in an ecosystem.

LINK to math, writing, literature, and technology.

Prairie dogs live in large groups, called colonies. They feed on prairie plants.

INVESTIGATE

The Local Environment

Activity Purpose All living organisms interact with one another and with their environment. The environment includes all the nonliving things in an area, such as weather, soil, and water. In this investigation you will **observe** a local environment and note the interactions that occur in that environment.

Materials

- garden gloves
- meterstick
- 4 wooden stakes
- string
- hand lens
- aluminum pan
- wet paper towels
- garden trowel
- toothpick

CAUTION

Activity Procedure

1 **CAUTION** **Wear garden gloves to protect your hands**. Your teacher will send you to a grassy or lightly wooded area near your school. Once you are there, use the meterstick to **measure** an area of ground that is 1 m² (1 m × 1 m). Push a stake into each corner of the plot. Tie the string around the stakes. (Picture A)

2 Before observing the plot, **predict** what living organisms and nonliving things you might find in this environment. **Record** your prediction.

3 **Observe** the plot carefully. Use the hand lens to look for small things in the plot. **Record** your observations by making lists of the living organisms and the nonliving things in this environment.

4 Sit back and continue to **observe** the plot for a while. Look for living organisms, such as insects, interacting with other organisms or with the environment. Describe and **record** any interactions you observe.

5 Put wet paper towels in the aluminum pan, and use the garden trowel to scoop some soil onto them. Use a toothpick to sift through the soil. Be careful not to injure any living organisms with the toothpick. (Picture B)

6 **Record** what you **observe**, especially any interactions. Then return the soil to the plot of ground.

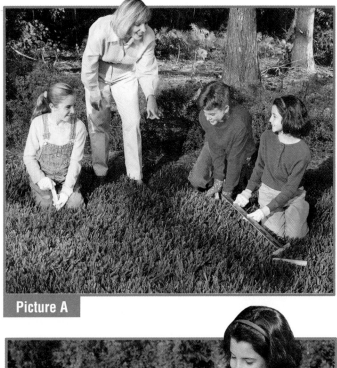

Picture A

Draw Conclusions

1. How did what you **predicted** compare with what you **observed**?

2. What did you **observe** that showed living organisms interacting with one another or with the environment?

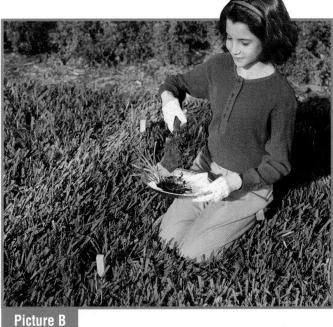

Picture B

3. **Scientists at Work** Scientists often use prior knowledge to **predict** what they might find or what might happen. What prior knowledge did you use to predict what you would find in the plot of ground?

Investigate Further Sometimes you can **infer** what interactions are occurring in an environment by **observing** what's in that environment. Choose an environment near your home or school. Observe what kinds of organisms live there, and infer how they interact with one another and with the environment.

Process Skill Tip

Scientists use what they already know to **predict** what they might find or what might happen. Careful observation also helps make a prediction more than a guess.

Ecosystems

Organisms and Their Environment

FIND OUT

- about the parts of an ecosystem
- how the environment affects living organisms in an ecosystem

VOCABULARY

individual
population
community
ecosystem
habitat
niche

The living organisms you observed in the investigation may stay in that small plot of land as long as the physical environment provides everything they need to survive. The physical environment includes all the nonliving things in an area, such as soil, weather, landforms, air, and water.

A single organism in an environment is called an **individual**. One grasshopper in a field is an individual. Individuals of the same kind living in the same environment make up a **population**. All the grasshoppers in a field are the grasshopper population. All the populations of organisms living together in an environment make up a **community**. A community may include many different populations. Each community interacts with its physical environment. Together, a community and its physical environment make up an **ecosystem**.

✔ **What are the two parts of an ecosystem?**

An individual caribou (KAR•uh•boo) (left) is part of a caribou population (right). Many plant and animal populations make up a community. The community interacts with the environment to make an ecosystem.

Habitats and Niches

Every population has a place where it lives in an ecosystem. This is its **habitat**. Think of a habitat as a neighborhood, and think of a community as the residents of that neighborhood. You might spot a golden eagle on a rocky mountain slope or near an open field that has tall trees around it. These areas are part of the golden eagle's habitat.

Many different populations can share a habitat. But each population has a certain role, or **niche** (NICH), in its habitat. For example, during the day eagles soar high above open ground, hunting for small animals such as mice. Great horned owls share the golden eagle's habitat, and they also hunt mice. But owls hunt at night. Because of their different hunting habits, golden eagles and great horned owls have different niches in the same habitat.

In a healthy ecosystem, populations are interdependent. That is, they depend on each other for survival. For example, great horned owls eat mice, which may eat the seeds of one type of plant. Since eagles help keep the mouse population from getting too large, the plant population never dies out. In a similar way, the mice control the size of the owl population. If there are too many owls and not enough mice for them to eat, some of the owls will die.

In addition, the interactions of plants and animals help keep the balance of carbon dioxide and oxygen in the atmosphere. Plants and animals also give off water. This is an important part of the water cycle.

✔ **What is a niche?**

Red fox

Ground squirrel

Limiting Factors

The environment largely determines what type of ecosystem will develop in an area. Soil conditions, temperature, and rainfall help determine what plants will grow. Cactus plants, for example, have adaptations for living in desert conditions. A desert environment has very little rain, and much of it drains away quickly in the sandy soil. But the shallow roots of cactus plants take in water quickly when it is available.

The kinds and numbers of plants in an ecosystem determine what animals will live there. Where there are only a few plants, the populations of animals that depend on plants for food are small.

Caribou, for example, graze on the few plants that grow in the cold Arctic ecosystems. Caribou must space themselves out, moving in small herds, or groups, from place to place to find enough food.

The amount of food—or any limited resource—in an ecosystem affects the size of

Sandy desert soil has few nutrients and doesn't hold water. High temperatures and little rainfall mean that relatively few plants live in deserts. ▼

▲ The soil of eastern forests has a lot of organic matter. This type of soil holds water well and supports many organisms. Moderate temperatures and plenty of rain allow a variety of plants to grow.

a population. For example, one area may have enough food to support 100 caribou. Another area of the same size but with fewer plants may be able to support only 50 caribou. The *population density,* or number of animals in a certain area, is greater for the first area than it is for the second.

✓ **What is population density?**

Summary

Individuals of the same species make up a population. Populations of different organisms live together in a community. Communities of organisms together with the physical environment make up an ecosystem. Each organism in a habitat has its own niche. Limiting factors, such as the amount of food, affect population density.

Review

1. What is the relationship of a population to a community?

2. What is an ecosystem?

3. Use the data on page B30. How much warmer is it in June in the southern Arizona desert ecosystem than it is in the forest ecosystem of southern Vermont?

4. **Critical Thinking** The environment determines the ecosystem of an area. What things in the environment where you live determine your local ecosystem?

5. **Test Prep** Nonliving things that affect the organisms living in an ecosystem include weather, landforms, and —

   A habitat
   B niche
   C soil
   D population

LINKS

MATH LINK

Population Density A scientist studied the habitat of a certain spider. She counted the number of spiders living in a field. On one hectare of a sunny, open section, she found 80 spiders. On one hectare of a shady, heavily wooded section, she found 10 spiders. How many times as great was the population density of spiders in the open area compared with the shady area?

WRITING LINK

Informative Writing—Narration Write a narration for a nature video about an ecosystem with which you are familiar. Before you begin your narration, make an outline of the living and nonliving things in the ecosystem.

LITERATURE LINK

What's a Penguin Doing in a Place Like This? by Miriam Schlein (Millbrook, 1998) tells how these interesting animals have adapted to a tropical ecosystem, which is very different from that of Antarctica. Read the book and share with your classmates how penguins came to live in this ecosystem.

TECHNOLOGY LINK

Learn more about ecosystems by visiting the Harcourt Learning Site. **www.harcourtschool.com**

WELCOME TO THE LEARNING SITE

2

How Does Energy Flow Through an Ecosystem?

In this lesson, you can . . .

INVESTIGATE what eats what in ecosystems.

LEARN ABOUT how energy is transferred in an ecosystem.

LINK to math, writing, literature, and technology.

A hawk gets the energy it needs from eating this field mouse. ▽

INVESTIGATE

What Eats What In Ecosystems

Activity Purpose All animals must eat to survive. The energy from food is needed for all life processes. Some animals eat plants, and some eat other animals. Any food energy that isn't used by an animal is stored in its body tissue. When an animal is eaten, this stored energy is passed on to the animal that eats it. In this investigation you will **classify** and **order** organisms to see what eats what in a prairie ecosystem.

Materials

- index cards
- markers
- pushpins
- bulletin board
- yarn

Activity Procedure

1 Your teacher will assign you an organism from a prairie ecosystem. Use an encyclopedia to find out what your organism eats. Then **classify** your organism into one of the following groups:
   - plants
   - plant-eating animals
   - meat-eating animals
   - animals that eat both plants and meat
   - animals that eat dead organisms

2 Use markers to draw your organism or write its name on an index card.

Picture A

Picture B

3 Your teacher will now assign you to a class team. Each team will have at least one organism from each group listed in Step 1. With your teammates, **order** your team's cards to show what eats what in a prairie ecosystem. (Picture A)

4 When your team's cards are in order, pin them in a line on the bulletin board. Connect the cards with yarn to show what eats what—both within your team's group of organisms and between those of other teams. (Picture B)

Draw Conclusions

1. When your team put its cards in **order**, what kind of organism was first?

2. How would you **classify** the organism that came right after the first organism?

3. **Scientists at Work** When scientists **classify** things that happen in a particular order, it helps them understand how something works. Look again at your team's cards on the bulletin board. Could you classify or order them in any other way to explain what eats what in an ecosystem?

Investigate Further Find out what eats what in another ecosystem. Then make a drawing to show the flow of energy in that ecosystem. Share your drawing with the class.

How Energy Is Transferred in an Ecosystem

Living Things Need Energy

FIND OUT

- how living things get the energy they need
- why energy is lost in the transfer between organisms

VOCABULARY

producer
consumer
food chain
decomposer
food web
energy pyramid

Cells get the energy they need from food. In the investigation you saw that animals eat plants or other organisms to get energy. The sun provides the energy for almost every ecosystem on Earth. Plants, or **producers**, use sunlight to make the food they need from carbon dioxide and water.

As all other organisms do, plants use food energy to grow and reproduce. Any energy not needed is stored in roots, stems, and leaves. All life in an ecosystem depends on producers to capture the energy of the sun, change it into living tissue, and pass it on to other organisms. All other organisms in an ecosystem community must eat to get the energy they need. So the animals in a community are **consumers**.

✓ **Why do all animals in a community depend on producers?**

Food Chain
The organisms in this prairie ecosystem are lined up in the order of what eats what. This is called a *food chain*.

Prairie grasses and wildflowers are the ecosystem's producers.

Grasshoppers eat producers. Grasshoppers are first-level consumers.

Food Chains

Energy is passed through communities by way of food chains. A **food chain** shows how the consumers in an ecosystem are connected to one another according to what they eat. A food chain has several levels. At the base of every food chain are the producers—usually plants. Consumers make up all the other levels. First-level consumers, called *herbivores,* eat the producers. Second-level consumers, called *carnivores,* eat first-level consumers. Third-level consumers eat second-level consumers, and so on. Each level of consumer eats organisms from the level below it.

Identifying the organisms and their levels in a food chain can help you understand how energy moves through an ecosystem. For example, energy stored in a grass plant may become part of a grasshopper's body.

The grasshopper uses some of this energy and stores the rest.

If a snake eats the grasshopper, it consumes, or uses up, the energy stored in the grasshopper's body. In this way energy moves up through each level of the food chain, from producer to first-level consumer, to second-level consumer, and so on.

Decomposers, such as mushrooms and bacteria, are consumers that break down the tissues of dead organisms. They use some nutrients from the dead tissue as food. What decomposers don't use becomes part of the soil. Soil that has a lot of nutrients helps the ecosystem's producers grow. In this way decomposers connect both ends of a food chain.

✔ **What kind of food does a first-level consumer eat?**

Snakes eat grasshoppers. Snakes are second-level consumers.

Hawks eat snakes. This makes hawks third-level consumers.

Decomposers, such as these mushrooms, get energy from dead organisms.

A Prairie Food Web

A food web shows the relationships between many different food chains in a single ecosystem. Prairie grass, for example, is a producer in several food chains. In one, bison eat the grass. Since few bison are eaten by carnivores, the food chain is short. But prairie grass is also eaten by mice, which in turn are eaten by snakes. And the snakes may be eaten by hawks. A food web shows how organisms may be part of several food chains at the same time. What food chains could you make from these prairie organisms?

1. Needle-and-thread grass
2. Purple coneflower
3. Bison
4. White prairie clover
5. Side-oats grama grass
6. Swainson's hawk
7. Black-eyed Susan
8. Painted lady butterfly
9. Fairy ring mushroom
10. Buffalo grass
11. Thirteen-lined ground squirrel
12. Grass spider
13. Dung fly
14. Bullsnake
15. Field cricket
16. Western harvest mouse
17. Two-striped grasshopper

Energy Pyramids

In the food chains of most ecosystems, there are many more producers than there are consumers. Producers use about 90 percent of the food energy they make during photosynthesis for their life processes. Only 10 percent of the energy is stored in plant tissue. When a consumer eats the plant tissue, it uses about 90 percent of the plant's stored food energy to stay alive. It stores the other 10 percent in its body tissue. This huge loss of stored food energy occurs at each level in a food chain. An energy pyramid shows the amount of energy available to pass from one level of a food chain to the next.

Remember, only 10 percent of the energy at any level of a food chain is passed on to the next higher level. Since less energy is available to organisms higher up the food chain, there are usually fewer organisms at these levels. High-level consumers, such as wolves, have relatively small populations. There is not enough energy available to support a large population of wolves.

The size of each level of an energy pyramid is related to the sizes of the populations at that level. The producer population is usually the largest, since it provides energy for all consumer levels in the pyramid.

✔ **How much of the food energy that is taken in by an organism is used for its own life processes?**

Energy Pyramid

◀ **Third-level consumers** Hawks are at the top of this energy pyramid. They eat snakes. There are few hawks because most of the energy has been used at lower levels of the pyramid.

hawk

◀ **Second-level consumers** There are far fewer snakes than grasshoppers. This is because grasshoppers use 90 percent of the food energy they get for their own life processes.

snakes

◀ **First-level consumers** Since plants use 90 percent of the food energy they produce, there are fewer grasshoppers than there are grasses and other plants.

grasshoppers

◀ **Producers** Producers, such as grasses and other plants, form the base of an energy pyramid.

grass

▲ Vultures are called *scavengers*. They feed on the bodies of dead animals.

Summary

Producers use sunlight to make their own food energy. Consumers eat other organisms to get energy. A food chain may have several levels of consumers. Food webs show feeding relationships among several food chains. All organisms use most of the food energy they take in for themselves. Only 10 percent of the energy is passed on to organisms in the next higher level of an energy pyramid.

Review

1. In most ecosystems, what kinds of organisms are producers?
2. What benefit do decomposers provide for an ecosystem?
3. What is any organism that eats another organism called?
4. **Critical Thinking** Think of three things you like to eat. What level consumer are you for each of the foods you chose?
5. **Test Prep** Organisms at the bottom of an energy pyramid are always —
   A plant eaters
   B producers
   C hunters
   D scavengers

LINKS

MATH LINK

Percents Only 10 percent of the total energy at one level in a food chain is available to organisms in the next higher level. How much of the energy in grass is available to a snake that eats an insect that eats the grass?

WRITING LINK

Persuasive Writing—Opinion Some scientists suggest that if humans ate more producers and fewer consumers, more food could be produced for less money. Write a paragraph in which you support this opinion with facts you learned in this lesson. Then share your paragraph with your classmates.

LITERATURE LINK

Who Eats What? Food Chains and Food Webs by Patricia Lauber (Harper-Collins, 1996) describes the interactions of plants and animals in different kinds of ecosystems. Read it to add to what you've learned in this lesson.

TECHNOLOGY LINK

Learn more about the flow of energy in an ecosystem by investigating *Prairie Dog Town* on the **Harcourt Science Explorations CD-ROM.**

How Do Organisms Compete and Survive in an Ecosystem?

In this lesson, you can . . .

 INVESTIGATE how body color helps animals survive.

LEARN ABOUT the ways in which organisms compete.

LINK to math, writing, literature, and technology.

INVESTIGATE

Body Color

Activity Purpose An animal's physical characteristics, such as its body color, may give it a better chance of survival. For example, the body colors of many animals blend with their background. A green grasshopper in a grassy field may be nearly invisible to hungry snakes. In this investigation you will **gather data** and then **infer** how body color can help animals survive.

Materials

- colored acetate sheets: red, blue, green, yellow
- hole punch
- large green cloth
- clock with second hand

Activity Procedure

1. Copy the table on page B41. Use the hole punch to make 50 pieces from each of the acetate sheets. These colored acetate pieces will stand for insects that a bird is hunting. (Picture A)

2. **Predict** which color would be the easiest to find in grass. Predict which would be the hardest to find. **Record** your predictions.

3. Spread the cloth on the floor. Your teacher will randomly scatter the acetate "insects" over the cloth.

◀ Rattlesnakes eat kangaroo rats, limiting the size of the rat population in this desert ecosystem.

Number of Insects Found

	Red	Blue	Green	Yellow
Hunt 1				
Hunt 2				
Hunt 3				
Total				

Picture A

4 Each member of the group should kneel at the edge of the cloth. You will each try to pick up as many colored acetate "insects" as you can in 15 seconds. You must pick them up one at a time. (Picture B)

5 Total the number of acetate pieces of each color your group collected. **Record** the data in the table.

6 Put aside the "insects" you collected. Repeat Step 4 two more times. After each 15-second "hunt," **record** the number of acetate pieces of each color your group collected. After the third hunt, total each column.

Picture B

Draw Conclusions

1. Look at the data you **recorded** for each hunt. What color of acetate was collected least? Were the results of each hunt the same, or were they different? Explain.

2. **Compare** the results with what you **predicted**. Do the results match your prediction? Explain.

3. **Scientists at Work** Scientists often **gather data** before they **infer** a relationship between things. Based on the data you gathered, what can you infer about the survival chances of brown-colored insects in areas where grasses and leaves turn brown in the fall?

Investigate Further Many insects have a body shape that allows them to blend in with their background. **Hypothesize** about what body shape might help an insect hide in a dead tree. Then **plan and conduct a simple investigation** to test your hypothesis.

Process Skill Tip

You can better **infer** relationships between things after you **gather data**. When scientists infer a relationship, they often conduct another experiment to gather more data.

Ways in Which Organisms Compete

Competition for Limited Resources

Food is a resource, and animals have different ways of getting resources. Because most ecosystems have limited supplies of resources, there may be **competition**, or a contest, among organisms for these resources.

All organisms in a community compete in some way for resources. In the investigation you saw that body color may help some animals survive by making them nearly invisible to *predators*—animals that hunt them. Other animals use patterns of body color, or *camouflage* (KAM•uh•flahzh), to sneak up on *prey*—animals they hunt. Camouflage helps these animals compete for limited food resources. Animals also compete for water and shelter. Plants compete for water and sunlight.

Deer compete with each other for food, especially in winter.

In dry months, fish compete for water in a swamp "gator hole."

Moray eels compete for shelter— a hole in a coral reef.

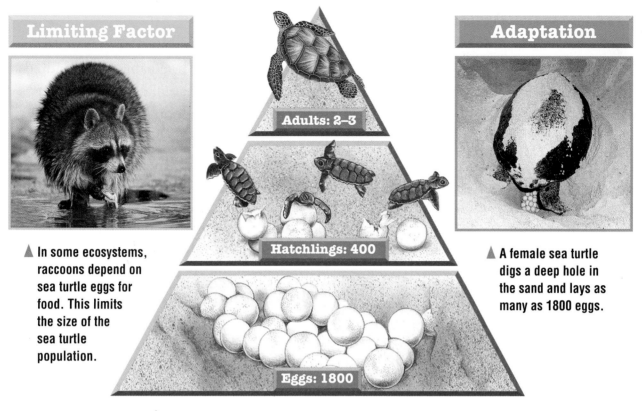

Adults: 2–3

Hatchlings: 400

Eggs: 1800

▲ In some ecosystems, raccoons depend on sea turtle eggs for food. This limits the size of the sea turtle population.

▲ A female sea turtle digs a deep hole in the sand and lays as many as 1800 eggs.

▲ For every 1800 sea turtle eggs that are laid, only 400 will hatch. Only 2 or 3 of the hatchlings will live to become adults.

Every organism has adaptations that help it compete for resources. For example, a cheetah's speed allows it to hunt and capture prey such as zebras and antelopes. Yet cheetahs, too, are limited by competition. Hyenas hunt prey in large packs. A pack of hyenas may chase away a single cheetah feeding on a zebra and then eat the zebra themselves. This adaptation—hunting in packs—helps hyenas compete with cheetahs.

If an organism competes successfully for resources, it is more likely to survive and reproduce. However, a balance usually exists between competing organisms, such as cheetahs and hyenas. Both compete for the same food resource, but each animal wins the contest often enough to survive.

✓ **What are two resources that organisms may compete for?**

Sharing Resources

Sea turtle eggs provide food for raccoons, while newly hatched sea turtles provide food for shorebirds. Although they share a resource, raccoons and shorebirds have different niches in the community.

In some communities animals live together and share resources. For example, many different herbivores eat the plants growing on the African plains. Giraffes eat from the higher branches of trees, antelopes eat from the middle branches, and rhinos eat from the lower branches.

At the same time, zebras and several other kinds of animals graze on the grasses. The reason the animals can all feed together is that they do not directly compete with each other. During a drought, when food is scarce, some animals will have to find other food supplies, or many will die.

Some trees provide food for several kinds of birds. All the birds eat insects, but in different parts of the tree.

The Blackburnian warbler spends more than half its feeding time eating insects at the top of the tree.

The bay-breasted warbler eats insects from the middle of the tree.

Myrtle warblers also eat insects. But they feed near the bottom of the tree.

Resources are shared in many ecosystems, including those in your own neighborhood. A single tree may be a habitat for hundreds of animals. Some animals, such as insects, may eat the leaves or bark of the tree, or they may lay their eggs in or on the tree. Birds may nest near the middle of the tree and eat the insects.

The tree at the left has three different kinds of warblers. Although the birds all feed on insects, they don't compete with each other for food. One kind of warbler feeds only in the top of the tree, while another feeds mainly in the middle branches. The third warbler feeds in the lower branches and along the tree's trunk.

In addition to the warblers, many other animals may find niches in the tree. Owls may sleep all day in the tree's upper branches and then sit on those same branches at night to watch for prey in a nearby field. Woodpeckers looking for insects may make holes in the tree's trunk. Then a squirrel may fill the holes with seeds or pine cones as part of its winter food supply. All of these animals share one resource, the tree, which provides them with food and shelter.

✔ **Why don't warblers compete for food, even though they all eat insects in the same tree?**

Ants herd aphids to fresh leaves where the aphids can feed and the ants can defend them against predators. When an ant rubs an aphid with its antennae, the aphid gives off a sweet juice that the ant eats. ▶

Symbiosis

Different kinds of organisms often live closely together for most or all of their lives. A long-term relationship between different kinds of organisms is called **symbiosis** (sim•be•OH•sis).

Symbiosis may benefit both organisms, or it may benefit one organism but not the other. A relationship where both organisms benefit is called *mutualism.* For example, a small fish called a cleaner fish picks bits of food from between sharks' teeth. The benefit is mutual. The cleaner fish get food, and the sharks get their teeth cleaned.

The relationship between flowers and bees is also an example of mutualism. Flowers produce nectar that bees eat. While the bees feed on the nectar, they pollinate the flowers.

One kind of African tree is protected by a mutual relationship with stinging ants. The ants live in the tree's large, hollow thorns and eat a sweet liquid the tree produces. Whenever another animal lands on or brushes up against the tree, the ants attack and sting the invader to death. The tree provides the ants with food and shelter, while the ants protect the tree.

✔ **What is symbiosis?**

◀ Sea anemones use long tentacles filled with poison to capture prey. Clown fish, however, are not harmed by the poison, so they can live among the anemone's tentacles. The fish attracts prey to the anemone, while the tentacles shelter the clown fish.

▲ Some spiders build webs. Building webs is an instinct. Webs trap insects that the spider eats. Without this instinct, some spiders could not survive.

Instincts and Learned Behaviors

If you have a pet, you're probably familiar with animal behavior. Maybe your dog can "shake hands" or your parrot can say a few words. Wild animals have certain behaviors, too. Most behaviors help animals survive in their communities.

Some behaviors are inherited and some are learned. An **instinct** is a behavior that an organism inherits. An instinct isn't unique to an individual. Instead, it is a behavior shared by an entire population, or by all the males or all the females of a population. Herding aphids, for example, is an instinct for certain populations of ants.

Behaviors for building shelters, finding mates, and hunting prey are usually instinc-

tive. Canada geese, for example, fly south for the winter, mate for life, and eat grains and water plants. These behaviors are instinctive. Squirrels instinctively bury acorns and other seeds for their winter food. And birds instinctively build nests. But the nests are not all alike. Some birds weave their nests from twigs, while others hollow out holes in tree trunks. Knowing what kind of nest to build is not an instinct. It is learned.

Many animals show **learned behaviors,** which are behaviors they have learned from their parents, not inherited from them. Lions, for example, are born with the instinct to kill and eat other animals. To survive, however, young lions must learn hunting skills from adult lions. Both the instinct to hunt and the learned behavior, skillful hunting, help the lion survive.

✔ **What is the difference between an instinct and a learned behavior?**

This peregrine falcon is living on the ledge of a tall skyscraper in the middle of New York City. The falcon has learned to survive in the city, and it will teach its young how to survive in this habitat. ▼

Summary

Organisms may compete for limited resources in an ecosystem. The sizes of certain populations are limited by the amount of resources available. Sometimes organisms share resources, and sometimes they form relationships with other organisms. Instincts, which are inherited, and learned behaviors help organisms survive.

Review

1. Why does a female sea turtle lay more than a thousand eggs at a time?

2. How might the number of oak trees in a park affect the number of squirrels that can live there?

3. What resources are sometimes shared by squirrels and certain birds?

4. **Critical Thinking** Think of an animal that lives in your area. What behaviors does it have for survival?

5. **Test Prep** Which of the following is **NOT** a survival instinct for birds?

   A building nests

   B migrating

   C eating insects

   D learning to talk

LINKS

MATH LINK

Interpreting Tables Look at the table. By how much did the population grow between 1650 and 1850? By how much will it grow between 1850 and 2050?

Year	Human Population
1650	0.5 billion
1850	1 billion
1930	2 billion
1980	4.5 billion
2050	14 billion (projected)

WRITING LINK

Expressive Writing—Poem Choose an animal you are familiar with, and write a poem about it for your class. Moving from head to tail, begin each line of the poem with the name of a body part of that animal. Then describe how the part helps the animal survive.

LITERATURE LINK

What Do You Do When Something Wants to Eat You? by Steven Jenkins (Houghton Mifflin, 1998) describes how behaviors help animals survive. Read and share what you learn with your class.

TECHNOLOGY LINK

Learn more about animal relationships by visiting the Harcourt Learning Site.

www.harcourtschool.com

What Is Extinction and What Are Its Causes?

In this lesson, you can . . .

INVESTIGATE
vanishing habitats.

LEARN ABOUT
extinction and its causes.

LINK to math, writing, literature, and technology.

B48

INVESTIGATE

Vanishing Habitats

Activity Purpose Changing conditions in an ecosystem may cause problems for plants and animals. Populations may decline, or become smaller. They may even disappear. In this investigation you will **use numbers** to **infer** how loss of habitat could lead to the decline of animal populations in a South American rain forest.

Materials
- globe or world map
- calculator
- graph paper
- graphing calculator or computer (optional)

Rain Forest Area and Human Population in Ecuador				
Year	1961	1971	1981	1991
Rain Forest (square km)	173,000	153,000	No data	112,000
Population (in millions)	5.162	7.035	No data	10.782

Activity Procedure

1. Locate Ecuador, a country in South America, on the globe or world map. (Picture A)

2. Study the table above. It shows the size of Ecuador's rain forests and the size of its human population between 1961 and 1991.

3. **Calculate** and **record** the changes in rain-forest area for each of the periods shown (1961–1971 and 1971–1991). Then calculate and record the changes in the population size for the same periods.

◄ Hunting and habitat destruction have almost caused the extinction of wolves in the United States.

Picture A

Picture B

④ Using graph paper and a pencil, a graphing calculator, or a computer, make a double-bar graph that shows changes in forest area and population size for these periods. (Picture B)

Draw Conclusions

1. **Compare** the two sets of data in the double-bar graph. What relationship, if any, do you **observe** between the growth of the human population and the amount of rain forest in Ecuador?

2. Based on the **data collected**, what can you **infer** about the size of Ecuador's human population and the area of its rain forests in 1981?

3. According to the data, what do you **predict** the size of the rain forests in Ecuador will be in 2001 if the human population increases at the same rate as it has in the past?

4. **Scientists at Work** Scientists often **interpret data** to help them **infer** what may happen. If the size of the rain-forest habitat keeps getting smaller, what can you infer about the populations of animals that live there?

Investigate Further Research the changes in the size of the human population over several decades in your area. Then make a graph of the changes. **Infer** how these changes in the human population might have affected animal populations in your area.

Extinction and Its Causes

Population Decline

FIND OUT

- how changes in the environment may lead to the decline or extinction of populations
- how humans can help endangered populations

VOCABULARY

exotic
extinct
endangered
threatened

You observed in the investigation how an increase in human population may be related to a decrease in the size of an ecosystem. Loss of habitat causes a decline in population numbers of many organisms in a community.

Most declines in populations are caused by human activity. In the United States, hunting led to declines in the populations of bison, alligators, and wolves. Importing nonnative, or **exotic,** organisms into the country has brought in diseases that kill native populations. Building new roads, homes, and businesses also reduces the size of natural habitats, causing declines in many populations.

Natural events that change the environment—such as floods, fires, or droughts—also cause populations to decline. An erupting volcano or a strong hurricane may destroy habitats. A drought may kill producers in a food chain, which then causes consumer populations to decline. However, most natural changes are temporary, and healthy populations usually survive. But that is often not the case with changes caused by human activity.

✔ **Give two reasons why populations decline.**

Ivory is prized in many parts of the world. Even though selling ivory is illegal in every country, some people still kill elephants for their ivory tusks, shown at the right. ▼

Extinction Is Forever

A population of organisms can survive only if there are enough individuals to produce healthy offspring. If there are fewer than 50 individuals, the population is not likely to survive. As a result, some organisms become **extinct**. That is, the last individual in the population dies, and the organism is gone forever.

A number of natural processes cause extinction. Through all of Earth's history, disasters have resulted in the extinction of organisms. The extinction of dinosaurs is probably the best-known example. Natural processes usually cause the extinction of several species every thousand years or so. Today, however, habitat destruction causes the rate of extinction to be about 1000 times faster than normal. Scientists know of at least 50 kinds of birds and 75 kinds of mammals that have become extinct in the past 200 years.

Island organisms are especially in danger of extinction. If an organism lives only on one island, any change to its habitat may cause the organism to die out.

Organisms that have populations spread out over several areas have a better chance of avoiding extinction. Because of the islands' distance from other land areas, more species have become extinct in Hawai'i than in any other state.

For decades people in the United States have been working to reduce extinction. In 1973 Congress passed the Endangered Species Act. The act lists organisms according to how small their populations are.

Organisms listed as **endangered** have populations so small that they are likely to become extinct if steps to save them aren't taken right away. Places like state and national wildlife refuges protect endangered birds, mammals, reptiles, coral reefs, and plants.

Organisms listed as **threatened** are likely to become endangered if they are not protected. Threatened organisms, such as alligators, are protected by strict hunting laws. And some threatened organisms, such as bison, have been brought back into areas where there were once large populations.

✔ **What is the biggest cause of extinction today?**

Extinct, Endangered, and Threatened Animals of the United States

Extinct	Endangered	Threatened
Caribbean monk seal	Jaguarundi	American alligator
Mexican grizzly bear	Ridley's sea turtle	Bald eagle
Passenger pigeon	Florida manatee	California sea otter
Steller's sea cow	Mexican wolf	Peregrine falcon
Carolina parakeet	Whooping crane	Brown pelican
Tacoma pocket gopher	Florida panther	American bison
Arizona cotton rat	American crocodile	Spotted owl
Kansas bog lemming	California condor	Sandhill crane

In the 1800s there were billions of passenger pigeons in the United States. On September 1, 1914, the last one, named Martha, died at the Cincinnati Zoo in Ohio. ▶

B51

Success Stories

During the 1940s people began using a poison called DDT to kill insects. It had many harmful effects on the environment that lasted a long time. One effect was the weakening of bald eagles' eggshells. Fewer and fewer offspring hatched, and the bald eagle population began to decline. Bald eagles were listed as endangered in the 1960s. In 1972 the Environmental Protection Agency made the use of DDT illegal. Scientists began raising bald eagles in captivity and releasing them back into the wild. Others worked to save and improve the habitats of bald eagles. Slowly, over many years, the bald eagle population has increased. Although still threatened, the bird that is our national symbol is no longer endangered.

In 1998 another endangered bird, the peregrine falcon, was removed from the endangered list. Like the bald eagle, the peregrine falcon population also declined as a result of DDT use. The falcon was listed as endangered in 1970. By 1975 there were only 324 pairs in the entire country. A program of saving and restoring habitats began. Today there are more than 1600 pairs of peregrine falcons in the wild.

A species that may or may not escape extinction is the California condor. The condor is a large scavenger whose natural habitat is open, hilly areas of southern California. In 1982, when scientists began breeding condors in captivity, only 30 birds were known to exist in the wild. Captive breeding is difficult, but some chicks hatched, grew to adulthood, and were released into the wild. Scientists still aren't sure if the California condor population will recover in its few remaining habitats near the crowded cities of Los Angeles and San Diego.

✓ **What two birds were successfully removed from the endangered list?**

◄ California condor chicks are cared for with a hand puppet that looks like a condor. This helps chicks learn to recognize and trust their own kind instead of humans.

◀ California condors weigh as much as 45 kg (about 100 lb) and have wingspans of about 3 m (10 ft).

Summary

When the last individual dies, an organism is extinct. Extinction occurs naturally, but certain human activities result in a high rate of extinction among the world's plants and animals. An organism is endangered or threatened when its population is too small. People have saved some organisms from extinction.

Review

1. Name a natural cause of decline in a population.
2. How is a threatened organism different from an endangered one?
3. How many living individuals are there in a population that is extinct?
4. **Critical Thinking** Think of an animal or plant in your state. What changes in the environment could cause it to become threatened or endangered? Give specific examples.
5. **Test Prep** It is impossible for an endangered organism to recover if —
   A its habitat is restored
   B its population is too small
   C hunting is stopped
   D it is bred in captivity

LINKS

MATH LINK

Estimate When peregrine falcons were first listed as endangered in 1975, there were about 325 pairs in the United States. When the birds were removed from the endangered list in 1998, there were about 1600 pairs. Estimate how many times more peregrine falcon breeding pairs there were in 1998 than in 1975.

WRITING LINK

Persuasive Writing—Opinion Should endangered organisms be protected? Are some organisms more important than others? Write an essay giving your opinion on this subject.

LITERATURE LINK

There's Still Time: The Success of the Endangered Species Act by Mark Galan (National Geographic, 1998) and *Back to the Wild* by Dorothy H. Patent (Gulliver, 1998) are two interesting and informative books about endangered organisms. Read one of these books. Then tell your classmates about it.

TECHNOLOGY LINK

Learn more about saving endangered animals by viewing *Yellowstone Wolves* on the **Harcourt Science Newsroom Video.**

CNN
Turner
Le@rning

THE NEW ZOOS

What if you were well fed and had a comfortable home but had nothing to do all day? At first you might really enjoy it, but pretty soon you would get bored. Zoo animals get bored, too, and often they show it. The big cats pace back and forth, and the chimps just loaf around, picking at their food and watching the people.

"Natural" Environments

Zoo animals need enriched environments that not only imitate their natural habitats but also give them the chance to behave as they would in the wild. Animal experts have come up with some clever ideas for keeping zoo animals happier and, as a result, healthier.

In the wild, chimpanzees use twigs to pry termites out of mounds. So the Lowry Park Zoo in Tampa, Florida, built their chimps some artificial termite mounds and filled them with honey and jelly. The chimps spend hours using twigs to scoop out their treats.

On African savannas, giraffes walk many miles each day to find baobab leaves to eat. At Disney's Animal Kingdom in Orlando, Florida, an imaginative system of mechanical baobab trees keeps the animals

This chimp is using a twig as a tool to get insects out of this tree.

This polar bear needs a big pool to stay healthy.

moving. Artificial branches with leaves spring out of a tree trunk, and the giraffes walk to them to eat. An hour later a branch pops out of another tree some distance away, and the giraffes are on the move again.

Since lions are hunters, the Animal Kingdom freezes large chunks of meat inside blocks of ice. When a lion pounces on its "prey," the slippery ice block shoots away, and the lion has to chase it down.

Enriched Play

At the Central Park Zoo in New York, Gus the polar bear now swims in a bigger pool. Zoo officials also added some big plastic floats that look like icebergs for Gus to climb on. The floats are always moving because Gus makes waves when he swims, so the bear's environment keeps changing, too.

Orangutans at the National Zoo in Washington, D.C., travel hand over hand just as they do through the trees in the rain forest. Surprisingly, they swing directly over visitors' heads on thick cables 13.5 m (about 45 ft) up in the air. The apes are free to come and go as they please from the Ape House. They cross the open space above a visitors'

walkway on their way to a new play center called the Think Tank.

In the enriched environments of these zoos, animals behave more as they would in the wild. Experts hope that more zoos will develop ways to enrich their environments to keep their animals alert, healthy, and happy.

THINK ABOUT IT

1. How do the new zoo environments help meet animals' needs?
2. Suppose you ran a zoo. Make a list of some ways you would keep the animals happy and healthy. Be creative!

WEB LINK:
For science and technology updates, visit The Learning Site.
www.harcourtschool.com

Careers   Zoo Guide

What They Do Zoo guides take visitors on tours and may also work in school outreach programs. Some guides may also help in the gift shop or with animal care and grounds work.

Education and Training People wishing to be zoo guides need at least a high school diploma and should have taken courses in biology and other sciences. Zoos provide more training in working with the animals, leading tours, and keeping visitors safe.

Dorothy McClendon
MICROBIOLOGIST

Dorothy McClendon works for the U.S. Army Tank Automotive Command (TACOM) in Warren, Michigan. She's not a soldier, however. She's a microbiologist. A microbiologist studies microorganisms—living things too small to be seen without a microscope—such as fungi and bacteria.

Microorganisms are important. For example, they are found in the digestive systems of most animals, including humans. People have learned how to make microorganisms work for them in many ways, such as in making cheese and in cleaning up oil spills. However, microorganisms can also be harmful to humans. Some cause disease. Others cause foods to spoil and materials to decay.

Ms. McClendon is a specialist known as an industrial microbiologist. She is in charge of research on microorganisms for the army. Her job is to develop ways to keep microorganisms from breaking down fuel oil and other materials the army stores. She is now working on the

development of a new fungicide, a chemical that will kill fungi. It must do the job without being harmful to people.

Ms. McClendon was born in Louisiana and moved to Detroit, Michigan, where she became interested in science as a student in high school. She went on to major in biology in college and took advanced science courses at several universities. Before becoming a microbiologist, she was a teacher in Arizona and Arkansas.

THINK ABOUT IT

1. How are some microorganisms harmful to humans?

2. Why might it be difficult to develop a chemical that kills fungi but doesn't harm humans?

A microscopic fungus

Feast on This!

How does an animal's diet affect the environment?

Materials

- sanitized owl pellet
- forceps
- toothpicks
- hand lens
- black paper
- glue

Procedure

1 Use the forceps and toothpicks to separate the materials in the owl pellet.

2 Sort the materials. Group together bones that look the same.

3 Reconstruct the skeletons on the black paper. When you are satisfied that all the bones are arranged correctly, glue the skeletons to the paper.

Draw Conclusions

How many skeletons did you find in the pellet? If an owl throws up one pellet a day, how many animals does the owl eat in a year? If all the owls were removed from an ecosystem, what would happen to the population of prey animals?

Pyramids

Is lunch like an energy pyramid?

Materials

- food-guide pyramid
- energy pyramid

Procedure

1 Put the food-guide pyramid next to the energy pyramid. Compare them.

2 Look at today's menu from the school cafeteria. See if it also makes a pyramid according to the recommendations of the food-guide pyramid.

Draw Conclusions

How are the energy pyramid and the food-guide pyramid alike? Does the cafeteria menu meet the recommendations of the food-guide pyramid? What level consumers are people?

Chapter 2 Review and Test Preparation

Vocabulary Review

Use the terms below to complete the sentences. The page numbers in ( ) tell you where to look in the chapter if you need help.

individual (B28)   **food web** (B36)
population (B28)   **energy pyramid** (B38)
community (B28)   **competition** (B42)
ecosystem (B28)   **symbiosis** (B45)
habitat (B29)   **instinct** (B46)
niche (B29)   **learned behavior** (B46)
producers (B34)   **exotic** (B50)
consumers (B35)   **extinct** (B51)
food chain (B35)   **endangered** (B51)
decomposers (B35)   **threatened** (B51)

1. "Shaking hands" and "playing dead" are examples of ____ in dogs.

2. Green plants are ____, or organisms that make their own food.

3. A ____ is the role a population has in its habitat.

4. Dead organisms are broken down by ____.

5. An ____ is a single member of a ____.

6. A population that begins to decline may be listed as ____.

7. An organism is ____ when all individuals are dead.

8. A ____ consists of all the populations of organisms in an ____.

9. A ____ shows the feeding relationships among food chains.

10. Organisms take part in ____ for the limited amount of resources in an ecosystem.

11. An ____ shows the amount of energy available at each level of a food chain.

12. Different kinds of organisms sharing a long-term, close relationship is called ____.

13. A non-native organism brought into a country is called an ____.

14. Organisms that eat other living things to survive are called ____.

15. Migrating south for the winter is an ____ for Canada geese.

16. Producers will always be the first organisms in any ____.

17. An ____ organism, such as a California condor, is at risk of becoming extinct.

18. The prairie is a ____ for animals such as snakes, hawks, bison, and mice.

Connect Concepts

Put the letter of each organism in the correct level of the Energy Pyramid.

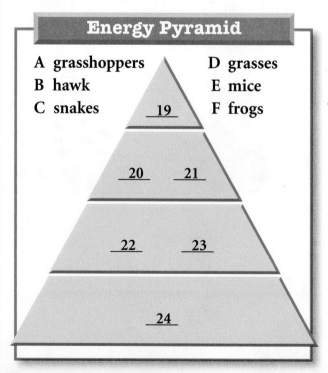

Energy Pyramid

A grasshoppers   D grasses
B hawk   E mice
C snakes   F frogs

19   20   21   22   23   24

Check Understanding

25. When a large volcano erupts, tons of dark ash often stay in the sky for months. If the ash blocks enough sunlight, producers will not be able to —
    A decompose dead organisms
    B perform photosynthesis
    C prey on consumers
    D none of the above

26. Habitat destruction is a major cause of —
    F extinction   H instinct
    G competition   J symbiosis

27. Organisms at the top of a food chain are predators and —
    A producers   C first-level consumers
    B herbivores   D carnivores

28. The oxpecker bird stands on the back of an ox and eats insects off the ox's back. Both the bird and the ox benefit. This relationship is called —
    F competition
    G learned behavior
    H parasitism
    J mutualism

29. If humans do not help endangered populations, the organisms are likely to become —
    A instinct   C threatened
    B extinct   D communities

Critical Thinking

30. Some people place bird feeders in their yards. What effect do you think this has on the bird populations of the local ecosystem?

31. What would be the effect of destroying most or all of the plants in an ecosystem?

32. Birds such as nightingales and mockingbirds imitate the songs of other birds in their environment. Is this behavior an instinct, or is it learned? Explain.

Process Skills Review

33. Wildlife experts know that wolves hunt and eat elk. What would wildlife experts **predict** about the elk population of Yellowstone National Park if all the wolves were killed? Explain.

34. Terns are shorebirds. When one tern's nest is attacked, all the terns in the area gather together and fight the predator. What can you **infer** about how this behavior helps terns survive?

35. A sundew is a green plant that traps and digests live insects. Do you think scientists would **classify** this plant as a consumer or as a producer? Explain.

Performance Assessment

Lunch Line

Choose one kind of food you like to eat, for example, cheeseburgers or pizza. On a sheet of paper, trace each ingredient in the food back to its source. Then make a poster that shows where the ingredients come from.

Chapter 3

Biomes

You probably know that part of this country is desert, part is grassland, and part is forest. And you probably know that these areas normally aren't mixed together. Each area developed where favorable conditions for it existed.

Vocabulary Preview

biome
climate zone
intertidal zone
near-shore zone
open-ocean zone
estuary

FAST FACT

Wheat is the most important food crop of the grasslands. If all the wheat produced in the world were put into freight cars, the train would be more than 160,900 km (about 100,000 mi) long.

FAST FACT

A doubling of the human population requires a doubling of food production. It took 80 years for the human population to double from 1 billion to 2 billion. It took 45 years for the population to double from 2 billion to 4 billion. From the table, when do you infer the population will reach 8 billion?

Earth's Population

Year	Number of People
10,000 B.C.	3,000,000
8000 B.C.	5,000,000
A.D. 1	200,000,000
1650	500,000,000
1850	1,000,000,000
1930	2,000,000,000
1975	4,000,000,000
2000	6,000,000,000

FAST FACT

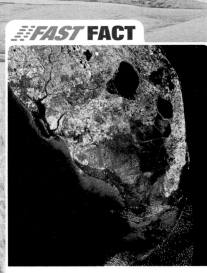

Landsat satellites are used to make maps like this one of south Florida. Scanners on these satellites measure wavelengths of reflected sunlight. This helps scientists identify water, soil, rock, and plants in the area mapped. Landsat maps also help people decide the best way to use the mapped land.

1

What Are Land Biomes?

In this lesson, you can . . .

INVESTIGATE
biomes and climates.

LEARN ABOUT
Earth's biomes.

LINK to math, writing, technology, and other areas.

Biosphere 2, near Tucson, Arizona, is a research center in which scientists have modeled several North American biomes. ▽

INVESTIGATE

Biomes and Climates

Activity Purpose The plants and animals where you live are adapted to live there. In North America there are six large-scale ecosystems called *biomes*. Each biome has characteristic plants and animals adapted to conditions there. In this investigation you will prepare one map of North American biomes and one of North American *climate zones*.

Climate zones are areas in which the long-term weather patterns are similar. Then you will **compare** the maps and **draw conclusions** about relationships between biomes and climate zones.

Materials

- map of North American climate zones
- map of North American biomes
- markers or colored pencils

Activity Procedure

1 On the map of North American climate zones, color the different climates as shown in the first chart on page B63. (Picture A)

2 On the map of North American biomes, color the biomes as shown in the second chart on page B63.

3 **Compare** the green areas on the two maps. How does the area with a warm, wet climate compare to the area of tropical rain forest? Compare other biomes and climate zones that are colored alike.

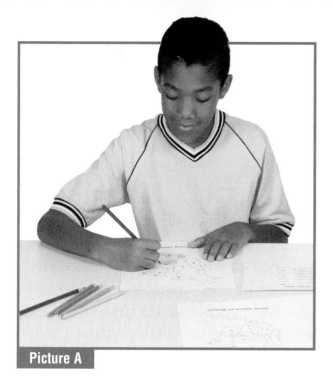

Picture A

North American Climate Zones

Area	Climate	Color
1	More than 250 cm rain; warm all year	green
2	75–250 cm rain or snow; warm summer, cold winter	purple
3	20–60 cm rain or snow; cool summer, cold winter	blue
4	10–40 cm rain or snow; warm summer, cold winter	orange
5	Less than 10 cm rain; hot summer, cool winter	yellow
6	250 cm snow (25 cm rain); cold all year	brown

Draw Conclusions

1. How do areas on the climate map **compare** to areas shown in the same color on the biome map?

2. **Observe** the maps. If an area is too wet to be a desert but too dry to be a forest, what biome would you expect to find there?

3. **Order** the biomes from wettest to driest.

4. **Scientists at Work** When scientists **compare** sets of data, they can **draw conclusions** about relationships between the data sets. Conifers are the dominant plants of the taiga. Broad-leaved trees are the dominant plants of the deciduous forest. What conclusions can you draw about the water needs of conifers compared to those of broad-leaved trees?

Investigate Further Use a computer to make a chart showing the climates of the six biomes and a map combining climate zones and biomes.

North American Biomes

Area	Biome	Color
A	Tropical rain forest	green
B	Deciduous forest	purple
C	Taiga	blue
D	Grassland	orange
E	Desert	yellow
F	Tundra	brown

Process Skill Tip

When scientists **compare** two different sets of data, they can sometimes find relationships between the data sets.

Land Biomes

Earth's Biomes

FIND OUT

- about the Earth's biomes
- what determines the organisms of a biome
- how plants and animals are adapted to living in a biome

VOCABULARY

biome
climate zone

Suppose you suddenly found yourself in a region far from your home. The first thing you would probably be aware of is the weather. Is it hotter or colder than where you live? Is it wetter or drier? Later you might be aware of the plant and animal life. How is it different from the plant and animal life in your region?

You would be in a new biome. A **biome** is a large-scale ecosystem. Its climate and the plants and animals adapted to living in that climate are what make it different from other biomes. As you saw in the investigation, biomes roughly match up with climate zones. A **climate zone** is a region in which yearly patterns of temperature, rainfall, and the amount of sunlight are

The photographs show a little bit of each biome.

Deciduous forest in New England

Rain forest in Costa Rica

World Biomes

ARCTIC OCEAN

NORTH AMERICA

ATLANTIC OCEAN

PACIFIC OCEAN

SOUTH AMERICA

ATLANTIC OCEAN

- Tundra
- Taiga
- Grassland
- Deciduous forest
- Desert
- Tropical rain forest

similar throughout. Wind patterns, land-forms, and closeness to large bodies of water help determine climate zones.

Earth has six major types of biomes: tropical rain forest, deciduous forest, grassland, desert, taiga (TY•guh), and tundra. Each type of biome occurs in several places on Earth. For example, North America, South America, Africa, Asia, and Australia all have desert biomes. All plants and animals that live in deserts have adaptations for living in dry climates. However, a certain organism may live only in a particular desert biome. For instance, lizards live in both Australian and North American deserts. But the collared lizard lives only in North America, while the frilled lizard lives only in Australia.

Differences also occur within biomes. All the plants and animals living in a biome may have similar adaptations for the climate of that biome. But different areas of the biome may have different plants and animals. One reason for these differences is that climate is not the only factor that affects what lives in a certain place. The type of soil, for example, helps determine which plants will grow well. The plant life, in turn, helps determine the kinds of animals that can live there.

✔ **What biome do you live in?**

Taiga in Finland

Tundra in Russia

Desert in Australia

Grassland in South Africa

Tropical Rain Forests

You can get an idea of what it feels like to be in a tropical rain forest by walking through a greenhouse. Tropical rain forests are found near the equator. There, Earth receives direct sunlight most of the year, so temperatures are always warm. The climate of tropical rain forests is also very wet. It rains almost every day.

The strong sunlight and warm, wet climate provide ideal growing conditions for a variety of plants. Tropical rain forests have about half of all the different kinds of plants on Earth. This amazing diversity, or variety, of life is one of the characteristics of tropical rain forests.

Producers in a rain forest are found in three layers. The tallest trees form the upper layer. Slightly lower, a second layer of trees forms a canopy, or roof, of leaves and tree branches. Under the canopy are a few shorter trees and many vines, orchids, and ferns. Very few plants live on the rain-forest floor because very little sunlight gets down through the thick canopy.

A tropical rain forest's animal life is just as diverse as its plant life. Many animals spend most of their lives in the branches of the canopy. Reptiles, amphibians, mammals, insects, fish, and birds all do well in a rain forest. The food webs they form are the most varied and complicated of all of the biomes.

Tucanette

✓ **What factors contribute to the diversity of plant and animal life in a tropical rain forest?**

In North America, tropical rain forests occur from southern Mexico through Panama, on many of the islands in the Caribbean Sea, and in Hawai'i.

Deciduous Forests

The forests of New England are famous for their autumn colors. The leaves of many trees turn red, orange, and yellow before they drop. These broad-leaved trees are deciduous—they shed their leaves each year. They are the dominant plants in deciduous forests. This biome occurs where there are moderate temperatures and moderate amounts of rainfall. Every continent except Africa and Antarctica has deciduous forests.

The varying amounts of sunlight Earth's surface receives at different times of the year cause changes of seasons in deciduous forests. The seasonal changes, in turn, cause a yearly cycle of plant growth. Warm temperatures in the spring and summer allow plants to grow and bloom. During the winter, temperatures often fall below freezing. The growing season in deciduous forests lasts about six months.

Several layers of plants can be found in deciduous forests. The tallest trees—oaks, maples, and hickories—form a thin canopy of leaves. Unlike the tropical rain forest, the deciduous forest lets enough sunlight get through the canopy to allow a layer of small trees and shrubs. Mosses, lichens, and ferns grow beneath the shrubs.

The different layers of plants provide a variety of habitats for animals. Many species of insects and birds live in the canopy. Rabbits, skunks, deer, and chipmunks are plant eaters of the forest floor. Toads, salamanders, and snakes also live on the forest floor. Foxes, coyotes, hawks, and a few other small carnivores prey on the herbivores.

✓ **What characteristic of deciduous forest trees is most obvious?**

Whitetail deer

Deciduous forests in North America occur mostly from southeastern Canada through the mountains of northern Georgia and west to the Mississippi River.

Grasslands

Imagine a sea of grass rippling in the wind like ocean waves. No matter which way you turn, you see tall grasses stretching away to the horizon. This is what you might see in the prairies, or grasslands, of North America. The temperatures are moderate, rainfall is light, and various grasses are the dominant plants. Grasslands are found on all continents except Antarctica.

Grasses have several adaptations that help them live without much rain. Their long, slender leaves allow little water loss. Their roots grow just below the surface of the soil, and they spread out to take in much of the rain that does fall. The few trees that grow in grasslands are usually found along streams and rivers, where they can get more water.

A number of small animals, such as rabbits, prairie dogs, gophers, badgers, rats, mice, snakes, and insects, live in grasslands. Herds of larger herbivores, such as deer, pronghorn, and bison, are also found in North American grasslands.

Grasslands play a major role in world agriculture. Thousands of farmers grow wheat, corn, rice, and other grains, all of which are types of grass. These grasses are used to make animal feed, bread, flour, and cereal. North American grasslands produce so much food that they are sometimes called the breadbasket of the world. Grasslands are also used to graze herds of livestock, such as cattle and sheep, which provide most of the animal products people eat.

✔ **How are grasses adapted to the grassland climate?**

Burrowing owl

North American grasslands stretch from central Canada through Texas and into Mexico.

Deserts

If you ever watch old westerns on TV, you know what a desert looks like. And if you visit the Sonoran Desert in Arizona, you will find that it's just as it looks in movies. The sun is always shining, it doesn't rain very often, and the soil and air are both very dry. Because deserts have little or no water, only a few kinds of plants can grow there.

Most deserts are very hot on summer days, but temperatures can drop below freezing on winter nights. Some deserts have no water at all. In others, streams or lakes form after a few heavy rainstorms, but they don't last long. All desert organisms have adaptations to extremes in temperature and very little water.

Desert plants have adaptations that help them conserve water. The cactus plants of North American deserts store water in their thick leaves or stems. Their roots lie close to the surface of the soil, so they can quickly absorb water from the occasional rains. Unlike the cactus, desert bushes such as the mesquite (mes•KEET) and the creosote (KREE•uh•soht) don't store water. Instead, their roots grow up to 15 m (about 50 ft) long to reach underground water.

Desert animals are also adapted to a dry climate. Reptiles, such as snakes and lizards, have tough, scaly skins that help prevent water loss. Some small mammals get all the water they need from the plants they eat. Most desert animals hide during the heat of the day. They come out to hunt for food at night, when it is cooler.

✔ **How are desert organisms adapted to a dry climate?**

Jackrabbit

Deserts in North America reach from the interior of southwestern Canada through northern Mexico.

Canada lynx

The taiga in North America stretches from Alaska across central Canada to the Atlantic Ocean.

Taiga

You can travel for miles in the taiga and see nothing but evergreen trees. The taiga is a forest of needle-leaved evergreens that extends in a broad belt across Eurasia and North America. Taiga winters are too long for most deciduous trees to survive. A few deciduous trees do grow in the taiga, but only around lakes and streams.

Evergreens, which include pines, firs, spruces, and hemlocks, are adapted to the taiga. The most important adaptation is their needlelike leaves. A waxy covering protects needles from the cold and limits the amount of water loss. And evergreens don't shed their needles all at once, so they can make food all year.

Unlike deciduous forests, the taiga has only two layers. The trees form an almost solid canopy. The forest floor is always covered with a thick mat of dead, dry needles. Even during a heavy rain, most water is caught and held in the canopy. Mosses and lichens are usually the only plants that grow below the canopy, either on the forest floor or on the trunks of the trees.

Insects, mammals, and birds all live in the taiga. The diversity of life, however, changes from season to season. Mosquito and fly populations increase during the summer months, and insect-eating birds return from the south. Owls, warblers, and woodpeckers live in the taiga year-round. Snowshoe hares, porcupines, and mice also live there year-round. Lynxes, weasels, and wolves prey on these other mammals. Bears may also live in the forest, eating nuts, leaves, and small animals.

✔ **Name two differences between deciduous forests and the taiga.**

Tundra

The tundra is a rolling plain that spreads across Greenland and the most northern areas of Eurasia and North America. It also covers the southern tip of South America and a small part of Antarctica.

Low temperatures and long winters in the tundra prevent trees from growing. Only smaller plants that send out roots in dense, shallow mats are able to survive on the tundra. Permafrost, a layer of permanently frozen soil just below the surface, is the reason larger plants cannot survive. In the spring, the surface of the ground above the permafrost begins to thaw. A few small plants grow in this layer of muddy, thawed ground. They grow low to the ground, away from the strong, drying winds.

The tundra is a region of dramatic seasonal changes. Because of its distance from the equator, the sun is rarely seen in the fall and winter. In most of the tundra, it disappears below the horizon in the fall and does not rise again for several months. Many animals, such as birds, caribou, and musk ox, migrate into the taiga for the winter. Animals that remain, like the arctic fox and arctic hare, have thick white coats that help them blend in with the snowy landscape.

In contrast, the sun shines all the time in summer. The constant light allows the tundra plants to sprout, grow, and bloom in only a few weeks. Herds of caribou and musk ox return to graze, and birds come back to their summer nesting grounds.

✔ **How are tundra plants adapted to the cold climate?**

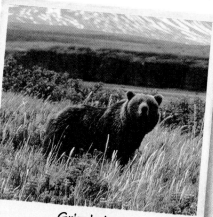

Grizzly bear

In North America the tundra is limited to northern Alaska and Canada, and to the higher peaks of the Rocky Mountains.

Comparing Biomes

Starting at the poles, as you move toward the equator, biomes occur in this order: tundra, taiga, deciduous forest, grassland or desert, and tropical rain forest.

Biomes are in this order because the corresponding climate zones occur in this order. At the equator the sun is directly overhead most of the year, and the number of hours of daylight varies only a little. Because the climate zone near the equator receives more solar energy than other zones, it is warmer. It is also wetter, so it provides a climate in which tropical rain forests can grow.

As you move from the equator toward the poles, each climate zone receives a little less energy from the sun. Near the poles, sunlight reaches Earth at a sharp angle during the summer. No sunlight reaches those areas during the winter. Since little solar energy is available in these cold climate zones, tundra develops.

In temperate climate zones, there are different biomes, depending on the amount of water available. Temperate zones near oceans or other large bodies of water may have enough moisture for deciduous forests, while temperate zones farther from water may have only enough moisture for grasslands.

Variations in landforms also affect climate. High elevations, such as the Rocky Mountains, have local climates that result in taiga on their slopes and tundra on their peaks. When the wind forces moist air up over a mountain, the air cools, and any moisture condenses into clouds. The moisture then falls to Earth as rain or snow. By the time the air reaches the side of the

Waialeale in Hawai'i is the world's wettest place, receiving about 1150 cm (about 450 in.) of rain a year. ▼

The Atacama Desert in northern Chile is the world's driest place. Some areas receive no rain for as long as 20 years at a time. ▼

Amount of Rainfall	
Biome	**Yearly Precipitation**
Tropical rain forests	250 cm (about 100 in.)
Deserts	10 cm (about 4 in.)
Grasslands	10–40 cm (about 4–16 in.)
Deciduous forests	75–250 cm (about 30–100 in.)
Taiga	20–60 cm (about 8–24 in.)
Tundra	25 cm (about 10 in.)

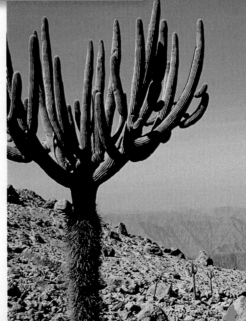

mountain away from the wind, it is very dry. This dry area is called a *rain shadow*. Many deserts occur in the rain shadows of large mountain ranges.

✓ **Why does a certain type of biome occur only within a certain climate zone?**

Summary

The major land biomes are tropical rain forest, deciduous forest, grassland, desert, tundra, and taiga. The climate of each biome is unlike that of any other biome. Climate is affected by the amount of sunlight received, the amount of moisture, and the kinds of landforms. The coldest climate zones are near the poles, and the warmest zone is near the equator. Plants and animals show adaptations to the climate of their particular biome.

Review

1. In what order do biomes occur, from the poles to the equator?
2. How are areas within the same biome alike? How might they differ?
3. How is a tropical rain forest different from the taiga?
4. **Critical Thinking** The map of Earth's major biomes shows sharp borders between different biomes. Would you find this to be true if you traveled from one biome to another? Explain.
5. **Test Prep** The biome with the greatest diversity of plants and animals is the —
   A desert
   B tropical rain forest
   C deciduous forest
   D taiga

LINKS

MATH LINK

Calculate Large areas of the world's tropical rain forests are cut down each year. In Brazil alone, about 13,820 km^2 were cut down in 1990. At that rate, how much will have been cut from 1991 through 2000?

WRITING LINK

Informative Writing—Friendly Letter Write a letter to a relative who lives in a different biome. Describe the biome of your area, and ask the person to describe the biome of his or her area.

SOCIAL STUDIES LINK

Read Maps Work alone or with a partner. Write down one set of coordinates (latitude and longitude). Then locate those coordinates on a map or globe. Write down the name of the continent and the country or the ocean. Then find out what the climate is like and which biome occurs there.

TECHNOLOGY LINK

Learn more about the variety of life in a tropical rain forest by viewing *Rainforest Diversity* on the **Harcourt Science Newsroom Video.**

What Are Water Ecosystems?

In this lesson, you can . . .

 INVESTIGATE life in a pond community.

 LEARN ABOUT three different water ecosystems.

LINK to math, writing, social studies, and technology.

The green heron is a consumer in several freshwater ecosystems. ∨

INVESTIGATE

Life in a Pond Community

Activity Purpose Lakes, rivers, ponds, and oceans are all water ecosystems. In Lesson 1 you learned about the producers and consumers in each land biome. In this investigation you will **observe** some organisms in a pond community and **infer** whether they are producers or consumers.

Materials

- Microslide Viewer
- Microslide set of pond life
- Microslide set of ocean life

Alternate Materials

- pond water
- hand lens
- dropper
- slide
- coverslip
- microscope

Activity Procedure

1 Put the "Pond Life" Microslide in the Microslide Viewer. **Observe** the first photograph, which shows the fish and plants found in a pond. **Record** your observations by making a drawing and writing a short description of these organisms. You may use the information on the Microslide card to help you with your description. (Picture A)

2 The other photographs in the set show microscopic life in a pond. **Observe** each of the organisms. Then **record** your observations by making a drawing and writing a short description of each organism. (Picture B)

3 **Classify** each of the organisms as producer or consumer. **Record** this information on your drawings and in your descriptions.

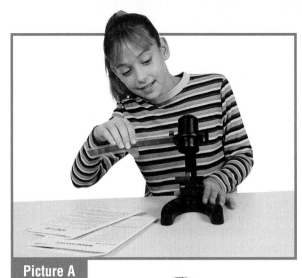

Picture A

4 Now put the "Marine Biology" Microslide in the Microslide Viewer. **Observe** each of the organisms, but don't read the information on the Microslide card yet. **Predict** which of the organisms are producers and which are consumers.

5 Now read the information on the Microslide card to see if your predictions were correct.

Picture B

Draw Conclusions

1. **Compare** the two sets of organisms. Which pond organism was similar to the coral polyp? Which marine organisms were similar to the algae?

2. In what way were all the producers alike?

3. **Scientists at Work** Scientists often **infer** relationships between organisms after they **observe** them in their natural habitats. Think about your observations of pond life and ocean life. What organisms in a pond community have the same position in a pond food chain as zooplankton has in an ocean food chain?

Investigate Further Now that you have observed photographs of pond organisms, use the materials in the *Alternate Materials* list to **observe** a drop of water from a pond or other water ecosystem. Then **classify** as producers and consumers the organisms you observe. See page R4 for tips on using a microscope.

Process Skill Tip

Before you can **infer** a relationship between two organisms, you need to carefully **observe** the organisms in their natural habitats.

Water Ecosystems

FIND OUT

- about three types of water ecosystems
- about adaptations of plants and animals to the ecosystems in which they live

VOCABULARY

intertidal zone
near-shore zone
open-ocean zone
estuary

Life in Water

Living things are found in almost every body of water on Earth. Although there are many water ecosystems, they can be classified into three main types. Saltwater ecosystems include oceans and seas. Freshwater ecosystems include streams, rivers, lakes, and ponds. There are also *brackish*-water ecosystems—where salt water and fresh water mix.

Just as organisms of the various land biomes are adapted to conditions in their particular ecosystems, so are organisms living in water. Sunlight, for example, can reach to a depth of only about 200 m (about 650 ft). So plants can't grow below this depth. The amount of oxygen in the water is another limiting factor. Oxygen gets into water from the water's contact with air at its surface. In deep water, organisms must have adaptations that allow them to survive with less oxygen.

✔ **What are the three types of water ecosystems?**

Intertidal Zone

Near-shore Zone

Saltwater Ecosystems

Varieties of saltwater ecosystems exist because of differences in sunlight, nutrients in the water, the temperature of the water, and the movement of the water. Organisms in the ocean have adaptations to help them survive in their ecosystems.

At the ocean's edge, waves constantly lap at the shore and tides rise and fall each day. In this area, called the **intertidal zone**, the tide and the churning waves provide a constant supply of oxygen and nutrients that living organisms need. Animals of the intertidal zone, such as starfish, sea urchins, clams, and crabs, can live both in water and in moist sand.

Beyond the breaking waves, the **near-shore zone** extends out to waters that are about 180 m (about 600 ft) deep. Rivers that empty into the ocean provide most of the nutrients for this zone. The water is calm in this zone, and the temperature doesn't change much. Schools of fish, including anchovies, cod, and mackerel, feed on the large numbers of algae growing there. Organisms such as oysters and worms, which live on the ocean floor in this zone, rely on the steady "rain" of dead organisms from above for their food. This is because producers can live only as far down as sunlight reaches.

The **open-ocean zone** includes most of the ocean waters. In this zone the water is very deep, but most organisms live near the surface. Trillions of microscopic algae make up *phytoplankton* (FY•toh•plangk•tuhn), the beginning of the open-ocean food chain. Tiny herbivores, which make up *zooplankton* (ZOH•oh•plangk•tuhn), graze on the algae. Small fish eat the zooplankton and, in turn, are eaten by larger carnivores, such as sharks.

✔ **Name the three ocean zones.**

Open-ocean Zone

Few organisms live in the depths of the open-ocean zone, where it is dark and cold. Note: Diagram not to scale.

0 m–30 m

30 m–200 m

deeper than 200 m

Freshwater Ecosystems

Lakes, ponds, streams, rivers, some marshes, and swamps are all freshwater ecosystems. The plants and animals in these ecosystems are adapted to life in fresh water only. They can't survive in salt water. Freshwater plants include duckweed, waterlilies, cattails, and many different grasses. There are also many kinds of algae in fresh water. Trout, bass, catfish, frogs, crayfish, and turtles are a few of the more common freshwater animals.

THE INSIDE STORY

Life in a Pond

On a hot summer day, a pond is a busy world of plants and animals that make up many complex food webs.

1. The roots of water plants are in the bottom of the pond.
2. When frogs are tadpoles, they feed on tiny pond plants, but as adults they catch insects.
3. Water striders, whirligig beetles, and mosquito larvae live at the surface of the water.
4. Turtles and small fish, such as bluegills, swim through the pond and feed on minnows and insects.
5. Bottom feeders and burrowing animals, such as snails, worms, and insect larvae, live in the bottom mud.
6. Birds may not live in the pond, but they go there to nest or to find food and water.
7. Microscopic organisms feed on the plants.

Water temperature and the speed at which the water moves, if it moves at all, determine the kinds of organisms that live in a freshwater ecosystem. In streams and rivers, the water moves fast. Fewer plants and animals live in fast-moving water than in still water such as lakes and ponds. The plants and animals that do live in rivers often have adaptations for anchoring themselves to the bottom. Algae attach themselves to rocks. Insects and crayfish often live under rocks.

✔ **What two factors determine the kinds of organisms living in freshwater ecosystems?**

Estuaries

Brackish water is a mixture of fresh water and salt water. Brackish water is usually found in an **estuary**, a place where a fresh-water river empties into an ocean. At the mouth of the river, the water contains huge amounts of nutrients and organic matter. They make estuaries the most productive ecosystems on Earth. Salt marshes and man-grove swamps are two types of estuaries.

All estuaries have changing water condi-tions. At high tide, salty ocean water flows into the estuary. At low tide, estuaries are filled with fresh water or they become exposed, muddy flats. Organisms in estuar-ies have adaptations that allow them to sur-vive in both fresh water and salt water.

Except for the slow rise and fall of tides, estuary waters are calm and still. The water is always fairly shallow, and sunlight easily reaches the bottom. These factors, along with the large amounts of nutrients, make estuaries ideal habitats for many plants and animals. Two-thirds of all the fish and shell-fish harvested along the east coast of the United States depend on estuaries for their

▲ Mangroves grow along the coasts of Florida, Mexico, Central America, and other tropical areas.

survival. Oysters, mussels, and shrimp feed on plants and decaying plant matter. They then become food for fish and birds.

The young of many fish and shellfish also start their lives in the calm, sunlit waters of estuaries. There is plenty of food, and the young animals are safe from large predators that can't live in brackish water.

The importance of estuaries wasn't noticed for many years. Besides their role as a water habitat, they also help prevent

Tall grasses are the main plants in salt marshes. These plants are able to live in brackish water because they get rid of salt through pores in their leaves. ▼

coastal flooding and the erosion of shore-lines. Now that people recognize both their beauty and their importance, the remaining estuaries may be saved from fill-and-build practices that have destroyed many of these remarkable ecosystems.

✓ **What adaptations must all estuary organisms have?**

Summary

Water ecosystems occur in fresh water, salt water, and brackish water. Water organisms have adaptations to help them survive in their particular ecosystems. Saltwater ecosystems are the intertidal zone, the near-shore zone, and the open-ocean zone. Freshwater ecosystems occur in rivers, ponds, lakes, streams, some marshes, and swamps. Estuaries are brackish-water ecosystems where rivers empty into oceans.

Review

1. What factors determine the kinds of organisms that can live in a saltwater ecosystem?
2. What might be one adaptation of an organism that lives in a river?
3. Where do many shellfish and ocean fish spend the first part of their lives?
4. **Critical Thinking** Why are estuaries critical to both land and sea?
5. **Test Prep** The ocean zone that is the deepest is the —
   A near-shore zone
   B intertidal zone
   C open-ocean zone
   D estuary

LINKS

MATH LINK

Circle Graphs Use a computer to make a circle graph based on the information below. It shows how much of Earth's water is salt water, ice water, and fresh water.

97 percent—salt water (oceans)
 2 percent—ice (glaciers and icecaps).
 1 percent—fresh water

WRITING LINK

Narrative Writing—Story Write a story about what life might be like in a coastal town. Describe the role that the ocean plays in your life and the lives of the townspeople. Then read your finished story to your classmates.

SOCIAL STUDIES LINK

Mangroves Perhaps the greatest value of mangrove swamps is their role as coastal protectors. But in some parts of the world, people cut mangroves and use the wood for fuel. Find out where mangroves are being destroyed and what is being done to protect them.

TECHNOLOGY LINK

Learn more about ocean ecosystems by visiting the National Museum of Natural History Internet site.
www.si.edu/harcourt/science

 Smithsonian Institution®

"SEE" FOOD

Scientists are now using a satellite to study ocean food chains. Images from this satellite provide valuable information about microscopic organisms that are the key to life in the oceans.

Links in a Chain

Life in the oceans—like life on land—depends on organisms that use energy from sunlight to produce food. These producers are the first link in the food chains that connect all living things.

In the ocean, the primary producers are floating algae called phytoplankton. In Greek, *phyto* means "plant" and *plankton* means "drifting." Phytoplankton are no bigger than a pinhead. Tiny consumers called zooplankton (drifting animals) eat the phytoplankton. Larger animals, such as shrimp and small fish, eat the zooplankton, adding another link to the ocean food chain. Larger fish eat the smaller ones, and the chain gets longer. The last link includes the ocean's largest predators, such as sharks and killer whales. It also

A SeaWiFs image

Phytoplankton

SeaWiFS surveys the entire planet every 48 hours. It can scan an entire ocean in less than one hour. "What SeaWiFS can see in one minute would take a decade to measure using ships," says a scientist who helped develop the satellite.

SeaWiFS helps scientists keep track of Earth's ocean "gardens." This allows them to help people plan to take advantage of the oceans' living resources without upsetting the balance that keeps them healthy and productive.

THINK ABOUT IT

1. Why are phytoplankton important?
2. How do satellites make it easier to observe ocean resources?

WEB LINK:
For science and technology updates, visit The Learning Site.
www.harcourtschool.com

includes humans looking for seafood dinners. But all these meat eaters would go hungry without the phytoplankton.

Phytoplankton grow in the warm, sunlit upper layers of the ocean. Changes in wind and weather can change the ocean's currents. The warm waters where phytoplankton grow best can shift location by hundreds of kilometers. When this happens, the animals—including humans who want to find the ocean's best fishing spots—must move.

An Eye in the Sky

Scientists have a new tool to help them find the places where phytoplankton are growing. It's a satellite called SeaWiFS, which stands for Sea-viewing Wide Field Sensor. SeaWiFS orbits more than 640 km (about 400 mi) above Earth. It senses the color of ocean water. Ocean water with a healthy growth of phytoplankton is greener than surrounding water. Images from SeaWiFS can also show where pollution is damaging the ocean's food chains.

Careers   Ecologist

What They Do
Ecologists study the relationships between living things, such as phytoplankton, and their environments.

Education and Training People wishing to become ecologists should study subjects such as botany, zoology, and chemistry in college. They should also do a lot of research outdoors, where they can see how plants and animals react to changes in their environment.

Alissa J. Arp

ECOLOGICAL PHYSIOLOGIST

"Although the average person may not think that what happens at the bottom of the ocean or in the stinky environment of a mud flat is of particular importance, clearly there are some very unique and unusual animals in these habitats."

How can tube worms live in a zone of crushing pressure 7000 meters (about 23,000 ft) below sea level? How do clams live in the untreated sewage released into the ocean by some coastal cities? Why doesn't sulfur, a chemical normally poisonous to animals, kill black abalone? These are questions that Alissa J. Arp tries to answer.

Dr. Arp is an ecological physiologist. She studies marine animals that live under harsh conditions. She tries to learn how these animals can live in toxic chemicals, extremely cold tempera-

tures, and total darkness. Her research takes her from polluted mud flats along the coast to cracks in the crust of the ocean floor. To reach these sea vents, where sulfurous water bubbles out into the near-freezing blackness, she dove in the U.S. Navy's deep-sea submarine, *Sea Cliff*.

Some of Dr. Arp's research may be important for humans. For example, animals who live in toxic chemicals have adaptations to get rid of the poisons. Humans may be able to use some of these animals to clean up polluted environments.

Currently Dr. Arp is a professor of biology and director of the Romberg Tiburon Center for Environmental Studies at San Francisco State University. Dr. Arp uses her position as a professor and research director to inspire young women to consider careers in science.

THINK ABOUT IT

1. How are the animals that Dr. Arp studies able to survive in toxic chemicals?
2. How might Dr. Arp's research be used to help humans living in industrial areas?

Deep-sea vent

Land Biomes

What adaptations do animals from land biomes show?

Materials

- terrarium
- bedding
- water bottle
- food
- small animal: hamster, mouse, snake, or lizard

Procedure

1. Set up the terrarium to meet the needs of the animal.

2. Observe the animal in this environment for several days.

Draw Conclusions

What needs did you provide for the animal? What adaptations does the animal have for living in a land biome? What is the natural environment of the animal? How does the terrarium compare to the natural environment?

Water Ecosystems

What interactions occur in water ecosystems?

Materials

- bucket
- collecting net
- large jar or aquarium
- air pump

Procedure

1. With an adult, visit a stream or pond in your community.

2. Use the bucket and the collecting net to scoop up sand, water, water plants, and water animals.

3. Transfer the materials and organisms to the jar or aquarium.

4. Set up the air pump, and observe the water ecosystem.

Draw Conclusions

List all the living and nonliving things in the ecosystem. How do the living things interact with each other? How do the living things and nonliving things interact?

Vocabulary Review

Use the terms below to complete the sentences. The page numbers in ( ) tell you where to look in the chapter if you need help.

biome (B64)
climate zone (B64)
intertidal zone (B77)
near-shore zone (B77)
open-ocean zone (B77)
estuaries (B80)

1. The _____ extends out into the ocean to a depth of about 180 m (600 ft).

2. A _____ is defined by its climate and the plants and animals that are adapted to that climate.

3. Most animals that live in the _____ can live both in water and in moist sand.

4. The deepest part of the ocean is the _____.

5. A _____ is a region with similar yearly patterns of temperature, rainfall, and sunlight.

6. _____ occur where fresh water and salt water mix.

Connect Concepts

Complete the chart using the choices below.

- Rivers and streams
- Near-shore zone
- Organisms are adapted to live in rapidly moving water.
- Intertidal zone
- Brackish water
- Estuaries such as saltwater marshes and mangrove swamps
- Many organisms can live both in water and in moist sand.
- In deep water, the lack of oxygen can be a factor.
- Open-ocean zone

Water Ecosystems	Characteristics
Fresh water	
7. _____	8. _____
Lakes and ponds	9. _____
Salt water	
10. _____	11. _____
12. _____	Light reaches much of this zone, allowing plants to grow.
13. _____	Most organisms live close to the surface, where light reaches.
14. _____	Areas where salt water mixes with fresh water
15. _____	Organisms can survive in salt water and fresh water.

Check Understanding

Write the letter of the best choice.

16. The biome that has a frozen layer of ground year-round is the —

    A taiga   **C** tundra

    B deciduous forest   **D** polar region

17. A biome is **NOT** characterized by —

    F its plants   **H** its climate

    G its animals   **J** its location

18. The biome where you would find the greatest number of tree species is the —

    A deciduous forest   **C** desert

    B tropical rain forest **D** grasslands

19. A water ecosystem that has brackish water is —

    F the near-shore zone

    G a river

    H the open-ocean zone

    J a mangrove swamp

20. An example of a freshwater biome is —

    A an estuary   **C** a pond

    B a taiga   **D** a tundra

21. Factors that affect water ecosystems include —

    F the amount of sunlight

    G the amount of oxygen

    H the temperature

    J all of the above

Critical Thinking

22. Since the Aswan Dam was built on the Nile River in Egypt, the waters of the Nile no longer reach the sea. How do you think that has affected the estuary at the river's mouth?

23. Deciduous beech and oak trees grow in the lowest regions of the Alps, a moun-tain range in Europe. Higher up, only conifers such as fir and pine grow. Even higher, tundra is found. What do you think causes this series of biomes?

Process Skills Review

24. Explain what you would need to **observe** in an area to determine which biome it is part of.

25. Write a brief paragraph in which you **compare** the climate and plant and animal life found in a desert and in a tropical rain forest.

Performance Assessment

Biome Mystery

Cut a sheet of paper into about 10 or more pieces. On each piece, write a biome clue or a water ecosystem clue. Write the name of the biome or water ecosystem on the back. Clues might be the name of a plant or animal that lives only in that biome or ecosystem, where on Earth the biome is found, the name of one water ecosystem, and so on. A list of clues might include the following: blue whale (ocean), pond (fresh-water ecosystem), biome near the equator (tropical rain forest), and so on. Exchange your collection of clues with a classmate and challenge each other to guess the answers.

Protecting and Preserving Ecosystems

The eastern third of the United States was once covered with forests. Today it is covered with cities. Large parts of the western United States are deserts. But many of the deserts are now green with lawns and golf courses. Ecosystems change—especially when humans live there. Luckily there are places where natural ecosystems still exist.

FAST FACT

Yellowstone National Park was the world's first national park. In the United States, about 10.5 percent of the land is protected in parks and wilderness areas. But some countries have even larger percentages of protected land.

Protected Lands

Country	Percentage
Venezuela	22.2
Bhutan	19.8
Chile	19.8
Botswana	17.4
Panama	16.9
Namibia	12.7

Vocabulary Preview

succession
pioneer plants
climax community
pollution
acid rain
conserving
reduce
reuse
recycle
reclamation
wetlands

Between 25,000 years ago and 10,000 years ago, huge glaciers covered the northern half of North America. As the ice melted, it left deposits of large rocks and thousands of lakes.

≡FAST FACT

Every year about 60,000 km² (23,000 mi²) of Earth becomes desert. That's an area about the size of West Virginia.

How Do Ecosystems Change Naturally?

In this lesson, you can . . .

INVESTIGATE how a pond changes over time.

LEARN ABOUT how ecosystems change.

LINK to math, writing, art, and technology.

This lone plant growing in a crack in the lava is a pioneer for a new ecosystem. ▽

How a Pond Changes

Activity Purpose In any ecosystem small changes occur every day. Those small changes sometimes lead to big changes over time. In this investigation you will **make a model** of a pond ecosystem. You will **observe** some of the changes that occur in a pond ecosystem over time.

Materials

- plastic dishpan
- potting soil
- water
- duckweed
- birdseed
- camera (optional)

Activity Procedure

1 Spread a layer of potting soil about 5 cm deep in the dishpan. Now bank the soil about 10 cm high around the edges of the dishpan. Leave a low spot, with about 1 cm of soil, in the center of the pan. (Picture A)

2 Slowly pour water into the low area of the pan until the water is about 4 cm deep. You may have to add more water as some of it soaks into the soil. Place some duckweed on the "pond."

3 Sprinkle birdseed over the surface of the soil. Don't worry if some of the seed falls into the water. Do not water the seed. Take a photograph or draw a picture to **record** how your pond looks. Put your pond model in a sunny window. (Picture B)

Picture A

Picture B

4 After three or four days, **measure** and **record** the depth of the water. Take another photograph or draw another picture. Then sprinkle more birdseed over the soil. Water the soil lightly.

5 After three or four more days, **observe** how your pond has changed. **Measure** and **record** the depth of the water. **Compare** your observations with the photographs you took or the pictures you drew.

Draw Conclusions

1. Describe any changes in the pond during the week. How did the depth of the water change?

2. **Compare** the changes in your model with those in a real pond. How are they the same? How are they different?

3. **Scientists at Work** By **observing** the changes that occur when they **use models**, scientists can **infer** changes that might occur in nature. From what you observed in your model, what do you infer might happen to a real pond over time?

Investigate Further An actual pond ecosystem has a greater diversity of plants and animals than your model. **Make a model** that includes a greater variety of living things.

Natural Succession

Primary Succession

In the investigation you observed the changes that occur in a pond ecosystem. All ecosystems—both water and land—change constantly. Small changes in climate, in soil conditions, or in plant and animal populations can change an ecosystem. Gradual change in an ecosystem—sometimes occurring over thousands of years—is called **succession**.

There are two types of succession. The first is *primary succession*. This type of succession occurs on bare, newly formed land. New land forms in a number of ways. Volcanic islands emerge from the sea. Glaciers melt, uncovering new land. **Pioneer plants** are the first plants to invade a bare area. Their sprouting and growth begins the process of succession. At the edge of a pond, for example, the roots of duckweed trap tiny bits of soil. As the duckweed dies and decays, more matter is added to the soil. Eventually, there is enough soil for a second community of plants, such as reeds and cattails, to take over. Over time the pond ecosystem grows smaller, and a land ecosystem takes its place.

FIND OUT

- what happens in the stages of succession
- what happens to an ecosystem after a natural disaster

VOCABULARY

succession
pioneer plants
climax community

As a glacier melts, rock that was covered with ice for thousands of years is exposed. ▼

Lichens, shown at the right, and small plants such as fireweed are common pioneer plants on glacier soil.

Glacier Bay, Alaska, is like a giant outdoor laboratory for studying primary succession. For the past 250 years, the glaciers have been melting and receding northward—leaving behind deposits of rock. The rock nearest the glaciers has been exposed for only a few days. Walking south—away from the glaciers and toward the bay—is like walking through time. As you walk, you pass through older stages of succession.

The first stage is the pioneer-plant stage. Pioneer organisms such as lichens—combinations of algae and fungi—grow nearest the glacier. As they die, their decaying matter adds nutrients to the ground. After a few years, a thin layer of soil forms and mosses take over. This is the second stage of succession, the *mossy stage*. Bits of organic matter and bird droppings become trapped in the dense moss. They add more nutrients to the slowly deepening soil.

Farther south, soil conditions have continued to improve. Grasses and flowering plants have taken root. A *grassy stage* is the third stage of succession. Farther still, the soil has become deep enough and rich enough to support the growth of alder and willow trees. Alders and willows gradually make the soil more acidic—producing favorable conditions for spruce trees to grow. The tall spruce trees begin to crowd out the alders as you continue south.

A spruce and hemlock forest makes up the **climax community**, the last stage of succession. If there are no disasters, such as volcanoes or fires, a climax community may stay the same for thousands of years. In the northeastern United States, the climax community is a deciduous forest. A prairie is the climax community in areas of the Midwest.

✔ **What are the first and last stages of primary succession?**

Grasses, shrubs, and small trees form transitional communities between a pioneer community and a climax community.

After 250 years, a climax community of spruce and hemlock has developed.

Secondary Succession

On May 18, 1980, Mount St. Helens erupted in Washington state. The eruption was one of the most violent ever recorded in North America. It blanketed the surrounding land with a thick layer of ash and mud. However, *secondary succession,* the return of a damaged ecosystem to its natural climax community, soon began.

Under the ash and the mud were seeds and living roots. Rains washed away some of the ash, allowing the seeds and roots to sprout. Winds blew in more seeds, some of which sprouted and grew. By the summer of 1981, the slopes of the once-barren mountain blazed with pink fireweed flowers. In the fall, the dying fireweed helped to enrich the soil. As soil conditions improved, shrubs began to grow. Today a community of shrubs dominates the area. This community will probably last at least 20 more years. However, fir trees have already started to grow. They are a sign that a climax community of fir and hemlock trees is returning.

Forest fires burned much of Yellowstone National Park in 1988. Fires are another type of natural disaster that changes ecosystems. However, unlike volcanic eruptions, fires actually speed up the process of secondary succession.

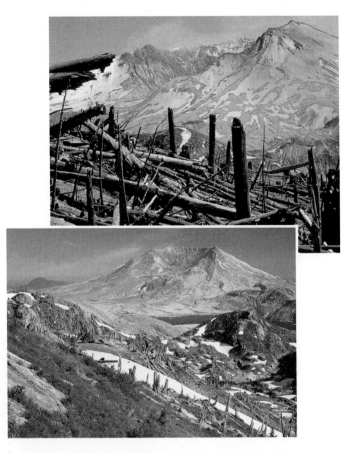

▲ Shock waves from the 1980 eruption leveled the fir trees near Mount St. Helens. Secondary succession is already well underway.

Because of fires in Yellowstone National Park, a patchwork of new meadows and a mix of old and young forests exists. This mixture of plant life provides habitats for a variety of animals. ▼

The Yellowstone fires quickly burned the dead leaves and branches on the forest floor, releasing nutrients into the soil. After the fire, meadows of grasses sprouted in the rich soil. After a few years, a forest of lodgepole pines began growing, blocking out sunlight and gradually replacing the meadows. In the shade of the lodgepoles, a new climax community of spruce and fir has already started growing.

✔ **How are some forest fires helpful?**

Summary

The slow change of an ecosystem is called succession. Primary succession occurs on new, barren land. First, hardy pioneer plants grow. Eventually, most ecosystems reach a stable stage, called the climax community. Secondary succession occurs after a natural disaster has damaged an ecosystem.

Review

1. Describe the four stages of succession that occur after a glacier recedes.
2. What might you expect to find on Mount St. Helens 20 years from now?
3. Where would you find the pioneer stage of succession around a pond?
4. **Critical Thinking** How does a community of pioneer plants produce changes that cause its own destruction?
5. **Test Prep** The most stable stage of succession is the —
   A grassy community
   B pioneer stage
   C climax community
   D mossy stage

LINKS

MATH LINK

Succession Time Line After a glacier recedes, it takes 50 years for thick stands of alders to appear. It takes 120 more years for a dense forest of spruce to replace the alders, and another 80 years for the climax community, a spruce-hemlock forest, to appear. Make a time line, beginning in 1750, of these stages of succession. Include historical events on your time line.

WRITING LINK

Persuasive Writing—Request Some people believe that forest fires in national parks should be put out to save the natural beauty of the parks. Others believe that fires should be allowed to burn because they benefit the natural ecosystems. Write a letter to the head ranger of a nearby national or state park. Ask the ranger to send you information about the fire policy in that park.

ART LINK

Succession Draw a series of pictures showing the stages of succession of abandoned fields in your area. Include in your drawings the plants and animals associated with each stage.

TECHNOLOGY LINK

Learn more about succession by visiting this Internet site.
www.scilinks.org/harcourt

SCI LINKS
THE WORLD'S A CLICK AWAY

How Do People Change Ecosystems?

In this lesson, you can . . .

INVESTIGATE how chemical fertilizers can affect an ecosystem.

LEARN ABOUT how some human activities affect ecosystems.

LINK to math, writing, art, and technology.

INVESTIGATE

How Chemical Fertilizer Affects a Pond

Activity Purpose Many people use chemical fertilizers on their fields, gardens, and lawns to help plants grow. However, not all of the fertilizer stays where it is put. Rain washes some of it into ponds, lakes, rivers, and streams. In this investigation you will **observe** what happens to pond water when fertilizer is added to it.

Materials

- marker
- 4 jars or cups with lids
- pond water
- liquid fertilizer
- dropper

Activity Procedure

1 Use the marker to label the jars 1, 2, 3, and 4. (Picture A)

2 Fill the jars with pond water.

3 Put 10 drops of liquid fertilizer in Jar 1, 20 drops in Jar 2, and 40 drops in Jar 3. Don't put any fertilizer in Jar 4. (Picture B)

◀ Trash that isn't disposed of properly can be harmful to wildlife.

Picture A

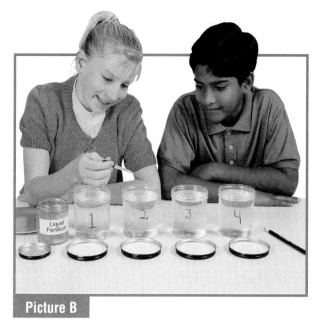

Picture B

4 Put the lids on the jars. Then place the jars in a sunny window.

5 **Observe** the jars every day for two weeks. **Record** your observations.

Draw Conclusions

1. What differences did you **observe** among the jars? Which jar had the most plant growth? Which had the least plant growth? How could you tell?

2. As organisms die and decay, they use up the oxygen in the water. Which cup do you **infer** will eventually have the least oxygen?

3. When water ecosystems are contaminated by fertilizer, fish and other animal populations begin to die off. Why do you think this happens?

4. **Scientists at Work** When scientists **identify and control variables**, they can **observe** the effects of one variable at a time. What variable were you observing the effect of in this investigation? What variables did you control?

Investigate Further Some fertilizers contain additional chemicals that are supposed to kill weeds. **Predict** the effects of using these chemicals on a lawn. Then **plan and conduct a simple investigation** to test your prediction.

> **Process Skill Tip**
>
> When you **identify and control variables**, you can **observe** the effects of one variable at a time.

How People Change Ecosystems

Damaging Ecosystems

FIND OUT

- how human activity changes ecosystems
- where pollution comes from and how it affects ecosystems

VOCABULARY

pollution
acid rain

In the investigation you observed the way one human activity—using chemical fertilizers—can change an ecosystem. There are other ways in which people change ecosystems. For example, some of the richest soil in the world is in the midwestern United States and Canada, where there were once grassland ecosystems. At one time there were several kinds of grasses and many different kinds of wildflowers. They supported a large variety of animal populations, including bison, deer, antelope, and prairie chickens. Now fields of corn, wheat, barley, and oats have replaced most of the natural producers. The diversity, or variety, of life has been greatly reduced.

Farming is vital to human survival. People have cultivated fields for thousands of years. But a growing human population increases the demand for food. This demand results in methods of agriculture that include the use of many different chemicals. In addition to fertilizers, pesticides and herbicides are used to

Chemical pesticides are sprayed on crops to kill insects. These pesticides may harm surrounding ecosystems. ▼

This thick green blanket of algae, called an *algal bloom*, was caused by chemical fertilizers running off nearby farmland. ▽

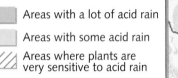

Areas with a lot of acid rain

Areas with some acid rain

Areas where plants are very sensitive to acid rain

▲ Winds can cause acid rain to fall far from the source of the pollution.

▲ This forest has been killed by acid rain.

kill a wide variety of unwanted plant and animal pests. The use of these chemicals can damage ecosystems.

In addition to farming, other human activities damage natural ecosystems. In growing human communities, for example, people build new roads, homes, schools, and shopping centers. New construction damages and often destroys natural habitats.

Getting natural resources to make things also damages ecosystems. Many things people use today are made of wood or paper. To make wood and paper products, people cut down trees. Cutting entire forests damages ecosystems and destroys habitats.

Making things also produces wastes. And many wastes are harmful and difficult to get rid of. Some waste products damage

ecosystems by killing organisms and breaking food chains. Any waste product that damages an ecosystem is called **pollution**.

Burning fossil fuels produces some of the most damaging pollution—air pollution and acid rain. Energy stations, some factories, and motor vehicles give off gases that include nitrogen oxides and sulfur dioxide. When water vapor in the air mixes with these gases, nitric acid and sulfuric acid form. The acids condense into clouds and fall to Earth as **acid rain**.

Many trees are damaged by acid rain, and some die from it. Acid rain also damages crops and destroys soil. Runoff from acid rain can kill plants and animals in lakes. Scientists estimate that about 4 percent of the lakes in North America are too acidic for fish to live in.

If ecosystems are not damaged too severely, some of them can slowly recover. A cut forest, for example, can become a forest ecosystem again through succession.

✔ **How does the making of things damage ecosystems?**

Catastrophic Changes

Some human activities can cause catastrophic (kat•uh•STRAHF•ik) changes to an ecosystem—changes so great that the ecosystem cannot recover. For example, one way to get rock and mineral resources from the ground is by strip mining. In this process, all the topsoil and overlying rock layers are removed until the resource is reached. Strip mining destroys all the communities and many of the nonliving parts of an ecosystem, such as streams and ponds.

Since 1977, however, the United States has required that all strip-mined areas be restored to their original condition. In most cases the soil is replaced, and forests or grasslands are replanted. In other cases the mine pits are turned into lakes. However, many older strip-mined areas have not been restored.

Catastrophic changes can also occur when highways, subdivisions, and shopping malls are built on small or fragile ecosystems. Large-scale construction projects often destroy habitats completely. Even when they don't, they often change conditions so much that natural communities can't survive. Some kinds of ecosystems, such as wetlands, are in danger of disappearing completely.

It is impossible for humans to be part of an ecosystem and not affect it. But people can live in ways that do less damage to natural ecosystems. You will find out more about some of those ways in Lesson 3.

✔ **What is a catastrophic change to an ecosystem?**

The Kennicott copper mine in Utah is the largest strip mine in the world. ▼

▲ In many areas people drain wetlands to build subdivisions and shopping centers.

Summary

Human activity has a huge effect on natural ecosystems. People need land for homes and natural resources to make things. These activities can damage ecosystems and cause pollution. Damaged ecosystems sometimes recover slowly, but catastrophic changes often destroy them.

Review

1. What human activities damage ecosystems?

2. What is acid rain?

3. Why is it difficult to recover land that has been strip-mined?

4. **Critical Thinking** Why do you think desert ecosystems are rarely affected by catastrophic changes?

5. **Test Prep** Acid rain is **NOT** caused by —
   A cars
   B energy stations
   C factories
   D farming

LINKS

MATH LINK

Ordering Acidity is measured on a scale called a pH scale, with 0 being the most acidic and 14 being the least acidic. Each whole unit of the scale stands for an increase or decrease of ten times in acidity. Order the items in the list below from least acidic to most acidic.

lemon juice	2.3	vinegar	3.3
distilled water	7.0	acid rain	4.3
human blood	7.4	sea water	8.0

WRITING LINK

Informative Writing—Compare and Contrast Think of an ecosystem that has been changed by human activity. Write a paragraph in which you compare and contrast the appearance of the ecosystem before and after the change.

ART LINK

Collage Make a collage of items that you think symbolize our modern lifestyle. Cut photographs out of old magazines, or draw pictures of the items. Include pictures of ecosystems that might be changed to produce the items.

TECHNOLOGY LINK

Learn more about damage to forest ecosystems by visiting the National Air and Space Museum Internet site.
www.si.edu/harcourt/science

 Smithsonian Institution®

How Can People Treat Ecosystems More Wisely?

In this lesson, you can . . .

INVESTIGATE what happens to trash in a landfill.

LEARN ABOUT using resources wisely.

LINK to math, writing, social studies, and technology.

KEEP OFF DUNES

Using beach crossovers is an easy way to treat a fragile ecosystem wisely. ▽

INVESTIGATE

What Happens in a Landfill

Activity Purpose Do you know what happens to your trash once it's picked up? Most of it is taken to a landfill. There it is combined with the trash of everyone else in your community. In this investigation you will **make a model** of a landfill to find out what happens to trash.

Materials

- plastic gloves
- newspaper
- small pieces of trash, such as aluminum foil, tissues, plastic bags, Styrofoam cups, potato peels, bones, and apple cores
- shoe box
- plastic wrap
- potting soil
- tray
- measuring cup
- water
- watering can

CAUTION

Activity Procedure

1. Make a chart listing ten different items of trash. Allow space in your chart to **record** observations you will make later.

2. **CAUTION** **Put on the plastic gloves.** Spread newspaper on your work surface. Choose the ten items of trash listed on your chart to put in the model landfill. Lay the trash on the newspaper. (Picture A)

3. Now prepare the model landfill. First, line the shoe box with plastic wrap. Then put a layer of potting soil on the bottom of the box.

Picture A

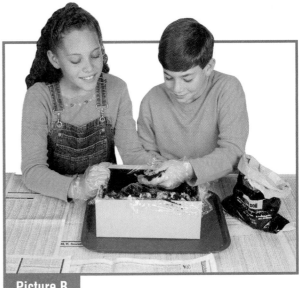

Picture B

4 Take the pieces of trash from the newspaper, and place them on top of the soil. Then cover the trash completely with another layer of soil. (Picture B)

5 Set the model landfill on the tray. Use the watering can to sprinkle the soil each day with 50 mL of water.

6 After two weeks, put on plastic gloves and remove the top layer of soil. **Observe** the items of trash, and **record** your observations.

Draw Conclusions

1. Did you **observe** anything starting to decay? What items decayed the most? What items decayed the least?

2. Things that decay are said to be *biodegradable*. What items in your trash are biodegradable?

3. What do you **infer** might eventually happen to trash that is *not* biodegradable?

4. **Scientists at Work** Scientists often **draw conclusions** based on observations made while **using a model**. From your observations of a model landfill, what conclusions can you draw about using paper trash bags instead of plastic trash bags?

Investigate Further In many places, items that are not biodegradable are removed from trash before it is collected. **Predict** how quickly trash in landfills would decay if it were all biodegradable. **Make a model** to test your prediction.

Process Skill Tip

Observations made while **using a model** can help you **draw conclusions** about real-world situations.

Using Resources Wisely

FIND OUT

- how to reduce your use of resources and how to recycle or reuse resources
- what landfills are

VOCABULARY

conserving
reduce
reuse
recycle

Reduce, Reuse, and Recycle

To help people treat ecosystems more wisely, scientists research and plan ways to protect ecosystems from catastrophic changes. To support these plans, governments pass laws to prevent strip mining, pollution, and overdevelopment. All new cars, for example, must have *catalytic converters,* devices that change some of the poisonous exhaust gases into carbon dioxide and water. New cars must also be more efficient—that is, they need to be able to go farther on less gasoline.

Changing human habits that damage ecosystems is just as important as passing new laws. Everyone can help protect ecosystems by saving, or **conserving**, resources. The three *Rs*— *reduce, reuse,* and *recycle*—are ways of conserving resources.

Reduce means to cut down on the use of resources. For example, appliances like clothes dryers, water heaters, and air

Reducing, reusing, and recycling are three ways to conserve resources and protect ecosystems. ▼

Recycle

Reduce

Reuse

conditioners use huge amounts of electricity. Using them wisely reduces the need for energy resources such as coal. Reducing the need for coal saves ecosystems from being destroyed by strip mining. Using appliances wisely also protects ecosystems by reducing air pollution. The burning of coal to make electricity is one of the main causes of acid rain.

Reuse means not to throw away items that can be used again. For example, cups and plates that can be washed and used again produce less waste than disposable ones. Reusing items also saves the resources needed to make new products.

Reusing also means using items for different purposes. For example, you can wash out milk cartons and juice bottles and use them as planters or bird feeders. You can also give to a resale shop toys or clothes you have outgrown. Buying used items saves resources, reduces pollution, and protects ecosystems.

Recycle means to recover a resource from an item and to use the recovered resource to make a new item. Many resources can be conserved by recycling. Aluminum, glass, and paper can be ground up or melted down and then used over and over again. Recycling saves energy as well as resources. It takes less energy to make an item out of recycled material than it does to make the same item out of raw resources. Like reducing and reusing, recycling protects ecosystems from damage or destruction.

✔ **What are the three ways of conserving resources and protecting ecosystems?**

Today anyone can help protect ecosystems.

Landfills

What can't be recycled or reused usually goes to a landfill. Years ago, trash was either burned or dumped into a huge hole in the ground. These open dumps attracted birds, rats, and insects. When it rained, water filtered through the trash, carrying harmful chemicals into the groundwater. Today most open dumps have been replaced by landfills like the one shown here.

A landfill starts as a large hole in the ground. Unlike an open dump, the bottom and sides of a landfill are layered with heavy clay soil or plastic sheets. This helps keep harmful liquids from getting into groundwater.

Large trucks haul in the trash. Each layer of trash is flattened. Then it is covered with at least 15 cm (about 6 in.) of soil. This helps keep away insects and other animals.

Summary

Governments have passed many laws to reduce pollution and to protect ecosystems. However, people can also do things to protect ecosystems. For example, they can conserve resources using the three *R*s. That is, people can reduce the use of resources, reuse as many items as possible, and recycle. What cannot be reused or recycled should go to landfills.

Review

1. Explain the three *R*s of conserving resources.
2. What is a landfill?
3. How have cars become less harmful to ecosystems?
4. **Critical Thinking** What can people do to reduce the amount of coal burned to produce electricity?
5. **Test Prep** Catalytic converters —
   A reduce the air pollution from factory smokestacks
   B change some exhaust gases into carbon dioxide and water
   C reduce the amount of carbon dioxide in the air
   D change water into oxygen and carbon dioxide

LINKS

MATH LINK

Calculate The average American family throws away about 6.5 kg (14.3 lb) of trash each day. That's 4.5 billion kg (about 10 billion lb) of trash per week for all Americans. How many kilograms of trash does the average family produce each year? How many kilograms of trash are produced by all Americans?

WRITING LINK

Informative Writing—Report Research an environmental "tradeoff," a choice between two actions. For example, which is better for the environment, using disposable baby diapers or using cloth diapers? Cloth diapers don't fill up landfills, but cleaning them uses more water and energy. Report your findings to your class.

SOCIAL STUDIES LINK

Earth Day The first Earth Day was observed in 1970. Interview a parent, an older neighbor, or a teacher to find out how your community has changed since then. Use a tape recorder or video camera to record the interview. Then write a report.

TECHNOLOGY LINK

Learn more about trash disposal by visiting the Harcourt Learning Site. **www.harcourtschool.com**

WELCOME TO
THE
LEARNING
SITE

LESSON 4

How Can People Help Restore Damaged Ecosystems?

In this lesson, you can . . .

INVESTIGATE how waste water can be cleaned.

LEARN ABOUT restoring damaged ecosystems.

LINK to math, writing, social studies, and technology.

How Waste Water Can Be Cleaned

Activity Purpose Fifty years ago, most waste water was dumped directly into rivers, lakes, or other large bodies of water. But waste water can cause great damage to ecosystems. It contains pollutants such as harmful organisms and poisonous chemicals. Now waste water from homes and factories is treated before it is released into the environment. Treatment removes pollutants from the water. In this investigation you will **experiment** with a process that filters pollutants from waste water.

Materials

- plastic jar with lid
- spoon
- soil
- water
- paper clip
- 6 paper cups
- marker
- ruler
- gravel
- sand
- charcoal

Activity Procedure

1 Put several spoonfuls of soil in the jar. Then fill the jar with water and put the lid on. (Picture A)

2 Shake the jar for 15 sec. Then put the jar aside for about 5 min. A process called *sedimentation* is taking place in the jar. It is the first step in waste-water treatment. **Observe** the water in the jar. **Record** your observations.

3 Unbend the paper clip. Use it to punch 10 small holes each in the bottoms of 3 paper cups. Using the marker, label the cups *A*, *B*, and *C*.

◄ A simple way to help restore damaged ecosystems is to provide food for some of the animal populations.

Picture A

Picture B

4 Using the spoon, put a 2.5-cm layer of gravel in Cup A. Put a 2.5-cm layer of sand and then a 2.5-cm layer of gravel in Cup B. Put a 2.5-cm layer of charcoal, then a 2.5-cm layer of sand, and finally a 2.5-cm layer of gravel in Cup C. (Picture B)

5 Put each cup with holes inside a cup without holes. Label the outer cups *A, B,* and *C* to match the inner cups. Then carefully pour equal amounts of water from the jar into the inner cups. Try not to shake the jar as you pour. A process called *filtering* is taking place in the cups. It is the second step in waste-water treatment.

6 Separate each set of cups, allowing all the water to drain into the outer cups. **Observe** the water in the outer cups. **Record** your observations.

Draw Conclusions

1. What did you **observe** happening during sedimentation?

2. What combination of materials did the best job of filtering the water?

3. What materials do you **infer** might not be filtered out of waste water?

4. **Scientists at Work** Scientists must **identify and control variables** when they **experiment**. In a real waste-water treatment plant, what variables might affect the filtering process?

Investigate Further **Plan and conduct a simple investigation**, using water that is "polluted" with food coloring. Decide what equipment you will need. Test several different kinds of filters.

> **Process Skill Tip**
>
> You can **identify and control variables** more easily when you **experiment** with a model of a large or complex system.

Restoring Ecosystems

Rivers

FIND OUT

- how ecosystems are being reclaimed
- what you can do to help restore natural ecosystems

VOCABULARY

reclamation
wetlands

In the investigation you experimented with the best way to filter muddy water. By experimenting on a larger scale, scientists have developed more effective ways to treat waste water. This has helped to restore water ecosystems that had been polluted. In the 1960s, for example, the Hudson River, which flows from the Adirondack Mountains to New York Harbor, was dangerously polluted. Today, all waste water must be treated before being released into the river. The river is much cleaner now, and fish and wildlife populations have increased in size. The Hudson River ecosystem has been restored.

The process of restoring a damaged ecosystem is called **reclamation** (rek•luh•MAY•shuhn). Within the past 20 years, reclamation has occurred in many places. However, restoring most ecosystems takes a long time and a tremendous amount of work. For example, in many freshwater ecosystems, the bodies of fish contain high levels of poisons called PCBs. When carnivores eat these fish, PCBs enter their bodies. And when the fish die and decompose, the PCBs reenter the water. In this way poisons can remain in an ecosystem for many years, passing from one organism to another.

This wetland in California was built to filter waste water. ▼

Sometimes it isn't practical to restore natural ecosystems. The park at the right and the fountain above were once landfills. The lands have been adapted to new useful purposes.

Wetlands

Scientists have only recently learned the importance of saltwater marshes, mangrove swamps, and mud flats. These water ecosystems, called **wetlands**, provide habitats for marine organisms. They also act as natural filters that purify water. But 80 percent of the wetlands in the United States are already gone.

Scientists are now working on ways to protect the remaining wetlands and to restore damaged water ecosystems. The Florida Everglades, a mixture of marshes and mangrove swamps, once covered more than 1.6 million hectares (about 4 million acres). It covers only half that much area today. Since 1983 scientists have been working with the state of Florida and the Save Our Everglades program to help preserve the remaining ecosystem. They have also

started buying farmland that was once part of the Everglades. They plan to restore that land to its original condition.

Scientists are also experimenting with ways to replace ecosystems that have already been destroyed. In 1986 the city of Arcata, California, completed construction of an artificial wetland. The wetland is used in the city's waste-water treatment.

Arcata's waste water is treated first by sedimentation and filtration. Then the water flows into two treatment marshes. The marshes contain plants that filter out most of the remaining pollutants. Only after this final filtering does the city's waste water flow into the ocean. Many wetland animals now live in the marshes, making this artificial environment a complete ecosystem.

✔ **Why are wetlands such important ecosystems?**

Your Own Back Yard

Local governments and civic organizations across the country are helping to restore natural ecosystems in schoolyards, public parks, and back yards. In midwestern states, for example, many people are replacing their lawns with grasses and flowers found in the area's original prairie ecosystem. Traditional lawns require the use of fertilizers and pesticides. As you have learned, fertilizers can get into groundwater, and pesticides can kill birds and other animals. Prairie lawns need little attention once they are established. And unlike traditional lawns, prairie lawns attract a wide variety of birds, butterflies, and other wildlife.

What was the natural ecosystem like in the area where you live? Have parts of it been saved or reclaimed? Reclaiming an ecosystem takes a lot of research, money, and time. The first steps in the process of reclamation are to learn about the causes of habitat loss and to investigate ways to restore native plants.

The bluebonnet, a prairie wildflower, is the state flower of Texas. In the spring, the bright-blue blossoms cover large areas of the Texas prairie. ▼

Members of the Lady Bird Johnson Wildflower Center, in Texas, conduct research on native plants.

But there are many little things that people can do to attract wildlife to an area. Planting a variety of wildflowers and native shrubs will provide food and shelter for birds, butterflies, and other small animals. Building a small pond will attract wildlife searching for water. The pond will also provide a habitat for frogs and insects.

✔ **How can people help to restore ecosystems in their own back yards?**

Summary

Reclamation is the restoring of a damaged ecosystem. Complete reclamation takes years of research and effort. The ecosystems that are still left must first be saved from destruction. Experimenting with new ways to restore ecosystems is also important. Reclaiming ecosystems takes the efforts of many people in an area.

Review

1. Name three types of wetlands.
2. How can research help to restore ecosystems?
3. What can people do to help restore ecosystems?
4. **Critical Thinking** Explain why government action may be needed to save or restore ecosystems.
5. **Test Prep** The recovery of natural ecosystems that have been damaged by human activity is called —

   A restoration
   B reclamation
   C recovery
   D reinstatement

LINKS

MATH LINK

Graphing Design and conduct a survey to determine people's interest in restoring a natural ecosystem in your area. Find out what people know about the original ecosystem and whether or not they are interested in restoring it. Also ask how much time they would be willing to commit each week. Compile the results of your survey, and summarize those results in a bar graph. You may want to use a computer program such as *Graph Links* to make your graph.

WRITING LINK

Expressive Writing—Poem Write a poem about the reclamation of a damaged ecosystem. Describe how the area looks, smells, feels, and sounds. Then read your poem to your class.

SOCIAL STUDIES LINK

National Park System Since 1872 the National Park Service has established more than 330 parks. Find out how the park system tries to meet people's needs while preserving the environment. Report your findings to your class.

TECHNOLOGY LINK

Learn more about restoring natural ecosystems by viewing *Prairie Restoration* on the **Harcourt Science Newsroom Video.**

Major Events in Environmental Awareness

The Industrial Revolution, which began in England in the 1700s and then spread to Europe and the United States, resulted in dramatic changes to the natural environment. Air, water, and land became more and more polluted, and Earth's natural resources were used much more rapidly. With these changes, some people began to develop a greater sense of responsibility for the environment.

Environmental Awareness Begins

In 1789 Englishman Gilbert White, often called the "father of ecology," wrote what is considered to be the first ecology book. In his book, White described the plants and animals of the English countryside.

By the mid-1800s the Industrial Revolution was in full swing on the east coast of the United States. At the same time, westward expansion of the country threatened to destroy the remaining wilderness areas. In 1872 President Ulysses S. Grant established the world's first national park— Yellowstone National Park.

A Book Sparks a Movement

Through the first half of the 1900s, the United States became more urban and more industrialized. Manufacturing plants dumped many kinds of pollutants into the environment. Farmers used large amounts of chemicals to kill insect pests and weeds. In 1962 Rachel Carson published *Silent Spring*, in which she told that the use of

The History of Environmental Awareness

1872
The first national park is established.

1908
The Grand Canyon becomes a national monument.

100 B.C.   A.D. 1700   A.D. 1800   A.D. 1900

100 B.C.
The Chinese develop a natural insecticide made from dried flower parts.

1789
Gilbert White publishes the first ecology book, *The Natural History and Antiquities of Selborne.*

1962
Rachel Carson publishes *Silent Spring.*

DDT—a pesticide—was also killing birds, particularly the bald eagle. She also wrote that poisons in the environment can affect all living things, including people.

Laws that Protect

Largely because of Rachel Carson's work, the government and people of the United States began taking pollution seriously. Many laws were passed to control it. In 1972 Congress passed a law banning the use of DDT. In 1973 the Endangered Species Act was passed. This law helped save threatened and endangered wild plants and animals from extinction. Since then many more environmental laws have been passed, both in the United States and in countries around the world.

Many environmental problems affect the whole planet and require the cooperation of all nations to solve them. For example, in the late 1970s, scientists found that chemicals used in refrigerators and air conditioners destroy the atmosphere's protective ozone layer. Scientists from many nations met to find ways to help stop ozone destruction. The result was the development of new chemicals for refrigeration that do not destroy ozone.

Today the major environmental concern is global warming. Many scientists hypothesize that excess carbon dioxide, released into the air by the burning of fossil fuels, is raising the temperature of the atmosphere. If this hypothesis is correct, the world faces a great challenge, since modern societies depend on the burning of fossil fuels for industry and transportation.

THINK ABOUT IT

1. What started people thinking about ways to save the environment?
2. Why is environmental protection a worldwide problem?

The bald eagle, America's national bird, was saved from extinction when Congress banned the use of DDT in 1972.

1970
The first Earth Day is held, and Congress passes the Clean Water Act.

1987
Twenty-four nations sign the Montreal Protocol, which states that nations must stop using chemicals that destroy ozone.

A.D. 2000

1976
Congress passes the Recycling Act.

1998
Representatives from many nations meet in Argentina to find ways to reduce excess carbon dioxide.

Raman Sukumar

CONSERVATIONIST

"Many species are claimed to be flagships for conservation. But no species can make stronger claim to this than the Asian elephant. If the tiger is the spirit of the jungle, the elephant is its body."

Raman Sukumar is deputy chairperson of the Asian Elephant Specialist Group of the World Conservation Union. He is one of the world's leading authorities on Asian elephants. His work involves planning conservation strategies and finding ways to resolve conflicts between human and elephant use of the same land. He knows that unless these conflicts can be resolved, Asian elephants will not survive in the wild.

Mr. Sukumar believes deeply in the importance of protecting the Asian elephant. "Elephants are beloved locally and globally," he says. Mr. Sukumar stresses that the protection of the elephant will also help to preserve other species living in the elephant's habitat. "Elephants prosper in large forests that are home to a great number of plant and animal species," he says.

Mr. Sukumar first became interested in a career in conservation when he was in high school. It wasn't until college, however, that he began to study elephants. Since that time Mr. Sukumar has spent nearly two decades observing elephants in the wild to better understand their way of life.

Mr. Sukumar currently lives in India with his wife and daughters. Like many scientists, he uses the Internet to stay connected with colleagues around the world.

THINK ABOUT IT

1. What will happen to Asian elephants if conflicts over land use are not resolved?
2. Why will Mr. Sukumar's work help to preserve many other organisms in the Asian elephant's habitat?

Asian elephant at work

Acid Rain

How does acid rain affect art objects?

Materials
- chalk
- paper clip
- modeling clay
- vinegar
- dropper

Procedure
1. Using the paper clip as a tool, carve the piece of chalk into a sculpture.

2. Place your sculpture on a base of clay.

3. Using the dropper, drop vinegar onto your sculpture and observe what happens.

Draw Conclusions
What effect does the vinegar, an acid, have on your sculpture? Chalk is similar to the limestone and marble of real art objects. What do you infer is happening to art objects around the world because of acid rain?

Powerful Plants

How can plants reclaim a damaged ecosystem?

Materials
- 2 small clay pots
- potting soil
- 6 bean seeds
- water
- flour

Procedure
1. Fill both pots half-full of soil. Plant three bean seeds in each pot, and water them with equal amounts of water.

2. Mix the flour and water until it forms a thick batter.

3. Pour the batter into one pot, covering the soil and completely filling the space between the soil and the top of the pot.

4. Place both pots in a warm, sunny place. Water the soil of the uncovered pot when it feels dry.

5. Observe the pots every day for two weeks.

Draw Conclusions
Which pot is the control? What do you observe about the plants in the experimental pot? Where have you noticed plants growing in similar conditions in your neighborhood? How do plants help reclaim damaged ecosystems?

Vocabulary Review

Use the terms below to complete the sentences. The page numbers in ( ) tell you where to look in the chapter if you need help.

succession (B92)   **conserving** (B104)

pioneer plants (B92)   **reduce** (B104)

climax   **reuse** (B105)

   community (B93)   **recycle** (B105)

pollution (B99)   **reclamation** (B110)

acid rain (B99)   **wetlands** (B111)

1. When you ____, you recover a resource from an item and use the resource to make a new item.

2. A spruce and hemlock forest is a final stage of succession, or a ____.

3. Reducing, reusing, and recycling are three ways of ____ resources.

4. If you cut down on the resources you use, you ____. If you ____ items, you use them for new purposes.

5. Primary ____ occurs on new, barren land, such as the land exposed by a receding glacier.

6. When pollutants such as nitrogen oxides and sulfur dioxide combine with water vapor and condense, ____ results.

7. Plants that grow during the first stage of succession are called ____.

8. The ____ of the Hudson River ecosystem has brought life back to the river, but it is not yet complete.

9. Untreated waste water, PCBs, and fertilizers form ____ that damages ecosystems.

10. Mangrove swamps, mud flats, and saltwater marshes are all types of ____.

Connect Concepts

Choose items from the list below to fill in the spaces in the concept map.

   A an increase in population   **E** researching ways to restore habitats

   B following the three *R*s   **F** pollution and acid rain

   C catastrophic changes   **G** passing laws that punish polluters

   D succession after a glacier, fire, or volcanic eruption

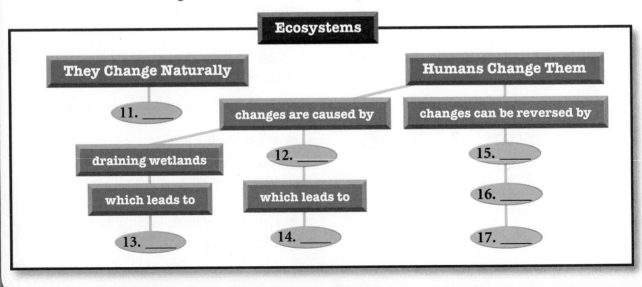

Ecosystems

They Change Naturally

Humans Change Them

11. ____

changes are caused by

changes can be reversed by

draining wetlands

12. ____

15. ____

which leads to

which leads to

16. ____

13. ____

14. ____

17. ____

Check Understanding

Write the letter of the best choice.

18. The last stage of succession is called —
   A the pioneer stage
   B the climax community
   C the third stage
   D the full-forest stage

19. An example of a pioneer plant is the —
   F hemlock tree   **H** fireweed
   G willow tree   **J** spruce tree

20. The causes of acid rain do **NOT** include —
   A pollution from cars
   B pollution from factories
   C pollution from energy stations
   D pollution from waste water

21. The three *R*s are —
   F refuse, reduce, and recycle
   G replace, recycle, and reuse
   H reduce, reuse, and recycle
   J reward, refuse, and reduce

22. The reclamation of ecosystems does **NOT** include —
   A passing laws like the Clean Water Act
   B civic projects like the Save Our Everglades program
   C research to find new ways to restore ecosystems
   D misusing resources

Critical Thinking

23. A pond is dug in an area where a deciduous forest is the climax community. If the pond is left alone, how will it change?

24. In what ways do you think your actions might affect an ecosystem?

25. Explain how reducing the amount of hot water you use could help to save an ecosystem.

Process Skills Review

26. Suppose you are sent to a river to find out whether it is polluted or not. How would you make your observations? Would you use any instruments to help you **observe**? What would you look for?

27. In Lesson 1 you made a pond model to study succession in a pond ecosystem. Suppose you wanted to find out whether the same thing happens in a river ecosystem. Describe how you could **make a model** of a river ecosystem.

28. Describe how you could **experiment** to test how well a certain fertilizer works in sandy soil, in red clay soil, and in black potting soil. What other **variables** would you need to **identify and control**? What problems might you encounter?

Performance Assessment

Algae Growth

In one jar, fertilizer was added to distilled water. The same amount of fertilizer was added to pond water in another jar. The jars were then put in a sunny spot and left undisturbed for two weeks. What variable was changed in this experiment? What variables were controlled? Predict which jar will have more growth. Explain. Then observe the two jars and draw conclusions.

Unit Project Wrap Up

Here are some ideas for ways to wrap up your unit project.

Construct a Model

Make a 3-D model of your nature park. You might want to use clay, paper, and wood as construction materials. Write a guide to the ecosystem you modeled.

Make a Directory

Use a computer and database software to develop a directory listing the parks in your state. Tell about the features of each park, and the plants and animals that might be found there.

Make a Diagram

Make a diagram that shows a cycle in nature.

Investigate Further

How could you make your project better? What other questions do you have about ecosystems? Plan ways to find answers to your questions. Use the Science Handbook on pages R2-R9 for help.

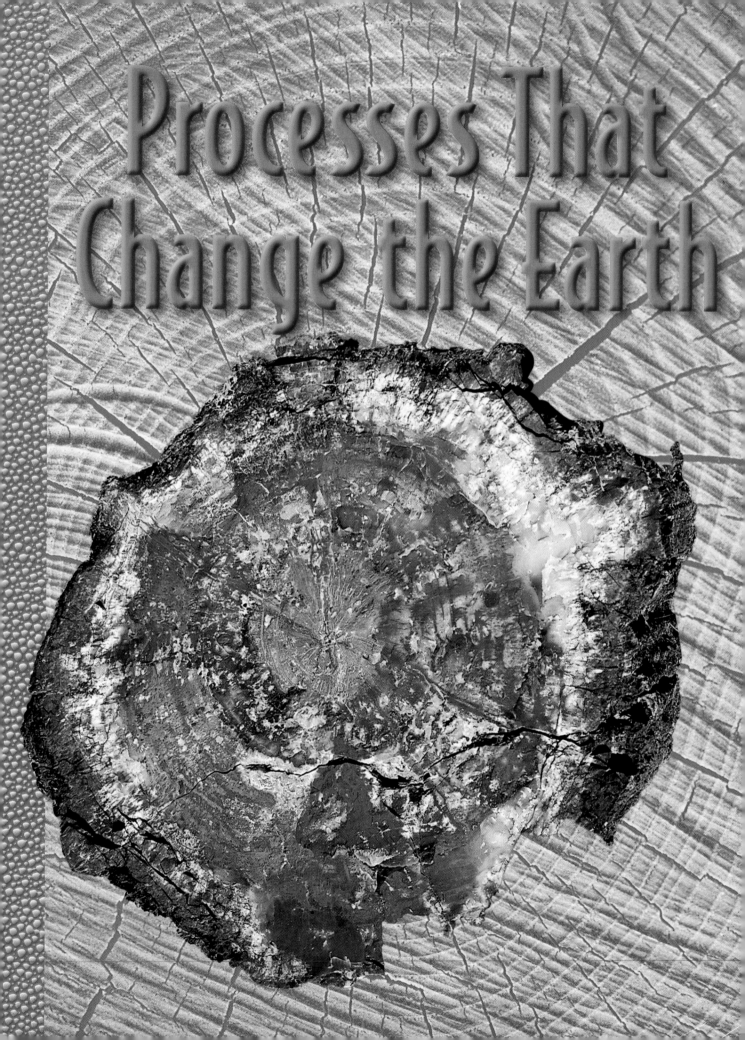

Processes That Change the Earth

EARTH SCIENCE

Processes that Change the Earth

Unit Project

Earth Surface Scrapbook

Cut from magazines and newspapers pictures of processes that change the surface of Earth. Organize your pictures into a scrapbook. Identify the process that is or was taking place in each picture, and describe how the surface of Earth was changed.

Chapter

Changes to Earth's Surface

The expression "on solid ground" means that you are certain about something. But there is really no such thing as solid ground— the ground we stand on is always moving.

Vocabulary Preview

landform
weathering
erosion
deposition
mass movement
crust
mantle
core
plate
magma
volcano
earthquake
fault
continental drift
Pangea
fossil

☰ *FAST* FACT

In May 1980 Mount St. Helens, a volcano in Washington State, erupted. Ash from the eruption covered an area of more than 22,000 square miles.

There are more than half a million earthquakes every year. Most occur at the bottom of the ocean and are too small to be felt. Only about 1000 earthquakes a year cause any damage.

FAST FACT

Mauna Kea, a dormant volcano on the island of Hawai'i, is one of the tallest mountains in the world. From the floor of the Pacific Ocean it rises 9750 m (about 32,000 ft) to sea level and 4205 m (13,796 ft) above sea level, for a total height of nearly 14,000 m (about 46,000 ft). By comparison, Mount Everest is 8848 m (about 29,000 ft) high.

What Processes Change Landforms?

In this lesson, you can . . .

INVESTIGATE how water cuts through sand.

LEARN ABOUT how wind, water, and ice shape landforms.

LINK to math, writing, social studies, and technology.

▽ Sand carried by wind can carve desert rock into unusual shapes.

How Water Changes Earth's Surface

Activity Purpose Moving water is the most powerful force there is for changing Earth's surface. It can move soil, make cliffs fall down, and carve canyons in solid rock. In this investigation, you will **use a model**—a stream table—to **observe** how moving water can cut through sand.

Materials

- stream table
- sand
- 2 lengths of plastic tubing
- 2 plastic pails
- 3 wood blocks
- water

Activity Procedure

1. Place the stream table on a classroom table. Make sure the front end of the stream table is even with the edge of the table. Put the stream-table support under the back end of the stream table. (Picture A)

2. Fill the stream table with sand.

3. Using two fingers, make a path, or channel, down the middle of the sand.

4. Connect one end of one length of tubing to the front of the stream table. Let the other end of the tubing hang over the edge of the table. Place an empty pail on the floor under the hanging end of the tubing. (Picture B)

Picture A

Picture B

5 Place the other pail on two wood blocks near the raised end of the stream-table channel. Fill this pail $\frac{3}{4}$ full of water.

6 Put the second length of tubing into the pail, and fill it with water.

7 Start the water flowing through the tube from the pail to the stream table by lowering one end of the filled tube.

8 **Observe** any changes the water makes to the sand in the stream table. **Record** your observations.

9 Place the third wood block on top of the support under the stream table. Repeat Steps 7 and 8.

Draw Conclusions

1. In which setup was the speed of the water greater?

2. In which setup did you **observe** greater movement of sand from the channel?

3. **Scientists at Work** Scientists learn by **observing**. What did you learn about the way water can change the land by observing the channel in the stream table?

Investigate Further **Hypothesize** what would happen if you replaced the sand with soil. **Experiment** to test your hypothesis.

Process Skill Tip

When you use your eyes to notice how the sand looks before and after water flows through it, you **observe** a change. Careful observations are important in science.

Changes to Earth's Surface

Changing Landforms

VOCABULARY

landforms
weathering
erosion
deposition
mass movement

Earth's surface is changing all around you. Rivers wear away rock and produce deep canyons. Waves eat away at sea cliffs, turning them into beach sand. Glaciers scrape away the tops of mountains, and winds carrying sand grind away desert rock. Earth's **landforms**, physical features on its surface, might seem as if they never change, but they do.

In the investigation, you saw how the force of flowing water can move sand. Forces such as flowing water, waves, wind, ice, and even movements inside the Earth are constantly changing landforms. Sometimes the changes happen fast enough for you to observe. For example, a volcano might erupt suddenly and blow away a mountaintop, or a powerful hurricane might sweep away a sandy beach. But most changes to Earth's landforms happen so slowly that you cannot observe them directly. Sometimes you can see only the results of past changes.

✔ **What are some of the forces that change landforms?**

◀ Thousands of years of rain and wind shaped these landforms in Utah's Monument Valley.

Flowing water cuts into riverbanks and carries away soil. ▼

◀ The pounding of ocean waves slowly wears away rocky cliffs.

This satellite photo shows the delta the Mississippi River has built in the Gulf of Mexico. ▶

Water

Much of Earth's surface is made of rock. The shaping of landforms starts when weathering wears away rock. **Weathering** is the process of breaking rock into soil, sand, and other tiny pieces, or particles, called *sediment*. Water is an important agent, or cause, of weathering.

Water weathers rock in several ways. Fast-flowing rivers can carve deep canyons in rock. Arizona's Grand Canyon, carved by the action of the Colorado River, is 1.6 km (about 1 mi) deep. Also, ocean waves can weather cliffs and cause them to fall into the sea. Water can weather rock in other ways, too. When it rains, water seeps into tiny holes, or pores, and cracks in rock. If this water freezes, it expands, breaking the rock. Rain that becomes acidic because of pollution can dissolve rock. And flowing water tumbles rocks against each other, breaking them into smaller pieces and smoothing their edges.

After weathering has broken rock into sediment, erosion and deposition move the sediment around and leave it in new places. **Erosion** (ee•ROH•zhuhn) is the process of moving sediment from one place to another. **Deposition** (dep•uh•ZISH•uhn) is the process of dropping, or depositing, sediment in a new location.

Water is not only an important agent of weathering but also the chief agent of erosion. Water can erode great amounts of sediment. At the shore, sediment from weathered cliffs is eroded by waves and deposited as new sand on beaches. Rainfall

TOP
Deltas form as rivers slow down and deposit sediment at their mouths.

CENTER
As the delta builds, the river separates into smaller channels.

BOTTOM
The number of channels continues to increase. Each one becomes a place where sediment is deposited.

erodes sediment and carries it into rivers and streams. Rivers pick up the sediment and move it downstream. Most rivers deposit sediment in flat areas along their banks. These *flood plains*, as they are called, can become rich agricultural areas. Some rivers deposit sediment in broad areas at their mouths. These areas of new land are called *deltas*. The Mississippi River delta is one of the largest in the world.

✔ **What is the difference between weathering and erosion?**

C7

Wind

Wind is another agent of weathering and erosion. Have you ever seen a machine called a sandblaster? It uses a powerful jet of air containing sand to clean building surfaces. In a similar way, wind can carry bits of rock and sand that weather rock surfaces. Wind also moves sediment from place to place. If the wind blows hard, it can erode a lot of sediment.

In dry areas like the American Southwest, wind erosion has shaped some of the world's most unusual landforms—rocks that look like tables, arches, or columns. Wind erodes dry sediment more easily than it erodes particles of soil or damp rock. And there is little plant life in dry areas to hold sediment in place.

Wind erosion can also blow sand into large mounds called *dunes*. Huge dunes as much as 100 m (about 325 ft) high form in some deserts. Many sandy beaches have long lines of dunes on their land side. Beach dunes are built by the constantly blowing sea breezes. They help protect the land behind them during storms.

✔ **How does wind erosion change landforms?**

Ice

Ice in the form of glaciers can also change landforms. *Glaciers* are thick sheets of ice, formed in areas where more snow falls during the winter than melts during the summer. Glaciers seem to stand still, but they actually move. Because of a glacier's great size and weight, it erodes everything under it. Glaciers erode sediment from one place and deposit it in another.

There are two kinds of glaciers. *Valley glaciers* are found in high mountain valleys. They flow slowly down mountainsides, eroding the mountain under them and forming U-shaped valleys. Only a few valley glaciers remain in North America. And even those are melting rapidly.

Continental glaciers are ice sheets that cover large areas of Earth. They cover almost all of Greenland and Antarctica today. But thousands of years ago, when the climate was colder, continental glaciers covered Europe, Canada, and the northern United States.

✔ **What are glaciers?**

The Athabasca Glacier recedes about 13 m (43 ft) each year. During the past 100 years, it has receded about 1.6 km (1 mi). ▶

Dunes form where an obstacle, such as a plant or a rock, causes wind to slow and deposit the sand it is carrying. ▼

Sinkhole

◀ The Winter Park sinkhole was large
enough to swallow cars and buildings.

▲ Acid rainwater easily dissolves
soft rock, such as limestone.

Mass Movement

During the winter of 1997–1998, heavy rains fell on much of the California coast. One night, families living in a small canyon heard a loud noise. When they went outside to see what had happened, they discovered that a mound of mud had slid down the steep sides of the canyon, covering part of a house. This mudslide occurred when a mass of soil that was full of water moved rapidly downhill.

A mudslide is one type of mass movement. **Mass movement** is the downhill movement of rock and soil because of gravity. Mass movements, such as mudslides and landslides, can change landforms quickly. Mudslides move wet soil. Landslides move dry soil. Landslides occur when gravity becomes stronger than the friction that holds soil in place on a hill. The soil falls suddenly to the bottom of the hill.

Another type of mass movement—one that occurs slowly, as you might guess from its name—is called *creep*. Creep occurs when soil moves slowly downhill because of gravity. Creep is so slow that changes in landforms are hard to observe directly. The land may move only a few centimeters each year. But over time, creep can move fences, utility poles, roads, and railroad tracks.

One day in 1981, in the city of Winter Park, Florida, an area of land suddenly collapsed, or fell in on itself. The hole swallowed houses, swimming pools, and businesses, including a car dealership. Today there is a lake where there was once dry land. The process that led to the formation of the Winter Park sinkhole is different from that of other types of mass movement.

A sinkhole is a large hole in the ground that opens suddenly. Sinkholes form after rock under the surface has dissolved or become weak. Sinkholes often appear in areas of limestone rock, because limestone dissolves easily. Rain seeping into the ground combines with carbon dioxide from the air to form a weak acid called *carbonic acid*. Carbonic acid dissolves limestone, forming huge holes. When enough rock has dissolved, land over the weakened area collapses.

✔ **What is mass movement?**

New Landforms

Erosion and deposition can change landforms or produce new ones. Rivers can deposit sediment that builds deltas. They can also change their path, or course, producing new lakes on wide flood plains.

Glaciers are major forces for forming new landforms. As the glaciers of the last Ice Age moved forward, they pushed mounds of rock and soil in front of them. When the glaciers melted, they left behind at their lower ends long ridges of soil and rock, called *terminal moraines*. Long Island and Cape Cod are terminal moraines. They mark the leading edge of the glacier that covered much of North America.

New islands can be formed by volcanic eruptions. Underwater volcanoes increase their height by depositing melted rock and ash. In time, they break through the sea surface as islands. The Hawaiian Islands formed in this way. Almost constant eruptions of Kilauea add daily to the size of the island of Hawai'i. Another volcano, now growing slowly on the ocean floor east of Hawai'i, will one day become the island of Hohonu.

✔ **What new landforms are created by erosion and deposition?**

Old, slow-moving rivers form broad loops. ▼

The loops can become so broad that they meet. ▼

Because the river follows the shortest route, its flow cuts off the loop. The old loop forms a crescent-shaped body of water called an *oxbow lake*. ▼

Mississippi River, south of Memphis, Tennessee ▼

Summary

Weathering breaks down the rock of Earth's surface into soil, sand, and other small particles. Agents of erosion, such as water, wind, and ice, change Earth's landforms by moving rock and soil. Water can carve canyons and deposit sediment to form deltas. Wind can form sand dunes. Ice can carve U-shaped valleys and leave landforms such as terminal moraines. Even forces within the Earth, such as volcanoes, can produce new landforms.

Review

1. What is erosion?
2. What is deposition?
3. What forces cause erosion and deposition?
4. **Critical Thinking** Why is weathering so important to life on land?
5. **Test Prep** A type of mass movement is a —

   A glacier
   B delta
   C mudslide
   D terminal moraine

LINKS

MATH LINK

Glacier Size The Aletsch Glacier in Europe is 80 km^2. Malaspina Glacier in Alaska measures 1344 km^2. The Grinnell Glacier in Montana is about 2 km^2. Use a computer, if possible, to make a bar graph that compares these glaciers.

WRITING LINK

Informative Writing—Description During the 1930s huge dust storms eroded large areas of the Great Plains of the United States. Find out what caused the Dust Bowl, as the eroded region was called, and what problems it led to. Write a story for your teacher describing the Dust Bowl from the point of view of someone who lived there.

SOCIAL STUDIES LINK

Topographic Maps Topographic maps use symbols and colors to represent landforms. These maps can tell you how the land looks—if you know how to read them. At the library, look for a topographic map of the area where you live. What kinds of symbols are used to show water, wetlands, and deserts?

TECHNOLOGY LINK

Learn more about landscapes and erosion by visiting this Internet site.
www.scilinks.org/harcourt

SCLINKS
THE WORLD'S A CLICK AWAY

LESSON 2

What Causes Mountains, Volcanoes, and Earthquakes?

In this lesson, you can . . .

INVESTIGATE the structure of Earth.

LEARN ABOUT what forms mountains and volcanoes.

LINK to math, writing, literature, and technology.

Volcanoes release melted rock from deep inside Earth. ▽

Journey to the Center of Earth

Activity Purpose If you could slice Earth in half, you would see that it has several layers. Of course, you can't slice Earth in half, but you can make a model of it. In this investigation you will **make a model** that shows Earth's layers.

Materials

- 2 graham crackers
- 1 small plastic bag
- disposable plastic gloves
- 1 spoon
- 1 jar peanut butter
- 1 hazelnut or other round nut
- freezer
- plastic knife

Activity Procedure

1 Put the graham crackers in the plastic bag. Close the bag and use your hands to crush the crackers into crumbs. Then set the bag aside.

2 Put on the plastic gloves. Use the spoon to scoop a glob of peanut butter from the jar and put it in your gloved hand. Place the nut in the center of the peanut butter. Cover the nut with more peanut butter until there is about 2.5 cm of peanut butter all around the nut. Using both hands, roll the glob of peanut butter with the nut at its center into a ball. (Picture A)

Picture A

Picture B

3 Open the bag of crushed graham crackers, and roll the peanut butter ball in the graham cracker crumbs until the outside of the ball is completely coated.

4 Put the ball in the freezer for about 15 minutes. Remove the ball and cut into your model with the plastic knife. **Observe** the layers inside. You might want to take a photograph of your model for later review. (Picture B)

Draw Conclusions

1. The peanut butter ball is a model of Earth's layers. How many layers does Earth have in this model?

2. Which layer of Earth do the crushed graham crackers represent? Why do you think your model has a thick layer of peanut butter but a thin layer of graham cracker crumbs?

3. **Scientists at Work** Scientists can see and understand complex structures better by **making models** of them. What does the model show about Earth's layers? What doesn't the model show about Earth's layers?

Investigate Further Some geologists, scientists who study the Earth, say that Earth's center is divided into a soft outer part and a hard inner part. How could you **make a model** to show this?

You cannot see Earth's layers. So **making a model** helps you understand how they look in relation to each other. In this activity, you need to cut open the model to see the layers.

Mountains, Volcanoes, and Earthquakes

FIND OUT

- how mountains form
- what causes volcanoes and earthquakes

VOCABULARY

crust
mantle
core
plate
magma
volcano
earthquake
fault

Earth's Interior

As the model you made in the investigation showed, Earth is not a solid ball of rock. It has three distinct layers. We live on Earth's crust. The **crust** is the outer layer, and it is made of rock. Earth's crust is very thin compared to the other layers. If Earth were the size of a chicken's egg, the crust would be thinner than the egg's shell.

The **mantle** is the layer of rock beneath Earth's crust. Just under the crust, the rock of the mantle is solid. But the mantle is very hot. This makes part of the mantle soft, like melted candy. No one has ever been to the mantle, but soft, hot rock from the mantle sometimes reaches Earth's surface through volcanoes.

The **core** is the center layer of Earth. It is Earth's hottest layer. The core can be divided into two parts: an outer core of liquid, or *molten,* iron and an inner core of solid iron. Even though the core is very hot, great pressure at the center of Earth keeps the inner core solid.

✓ **What parts of Earth are solid rock?**

Separating plates

Crust

Mantle

Core

Earth's Crust Moves

Earth's surface is not a single piece of rock. Instead, it is made up of many plates. **Plates** are rigid blocks of crust and upper mantle rock. Most of North America, Greenland, and the western half of the North Atlantic Ocean are on the North American plate. Part of California and most of the Pacific Ocean make up the Pacific plate. There are 12 major plates in all. Earth's plates fit together like the pieces of a jigsaw puzzle.

Although these plates are enormous, they actually float on the soft rock of the mantle. Pressure and heat within the Earth produce currents in the soft rock of the mantle. As the mantle moves, the plates floating on it move, too.

Plate movement is very slow—only a few centimeters each year. But because plates are right next to each other, the movement of one plate affects other plates. Some plates push together. Some pull apart. Other plates slide past each other. As plates move around, they cause great changes in Earth's landforms.

Where plates collide, energy is released, and new landforms are produced. On land, mountains rise and volcanoes erupt. South America's Andes Mountains are a result of the Nazca and South American plates colliding. On the ocean floor, deep trenches form.

As plates pull apart on land, valleys dotted with volcanoes develop. Africa's Great Rift Valley was formed by the African and Arabian plates pulling apart. The rift, or crack, will one day result in a complete separation of part of eastern Africa from the rest of the continent. Where plates pull apart under the sea, ridges and volcanoes form. This spreading forms new sea floor at the ridges.

When plates scrape and slide past each other, they shake Earth's surface. Along the San Andreas (an•DRAY•uhs) fault in California, the Pacific plate is moving past the North American plate. The plates rub and shake as they grind past each other, causing earthquakes.

✔ **What are Earth's plates?**

Colliding ocean plates

Colliding continental plates

The Himalayas formed as the Indian plate pushed into the Eurasian plate. The plates are still pushing together, and the mountains are still getting taller.

Mountain Formation

Mountains are Earth's highest landforms. They form as the crust folds, cracks, and bends upward because of the movements of Earth's plates.

Most of the highest mountains form where continental plates collide. As the plates push together, their edges crumple and fold into mountains. The Himalayas (him•uh•LAY•uhz), Earth's highest mountain range, formed this way.

At some places, continental and oceanic plates collide. Because continental rock is lighter than seafloor rock, the continental plate moves up and over the oceanic plate. The Cascade Mountains, near the Pacific Ocean, formed this way.

Mountains do not form only at the edges, or boundaries, of plates. Some mountains form where pressure from movement at the boundaries pushes a block of rock upward. The Grand Tetons (TEE•tahnz) of Wyoming rise straight up from the flat land around them.

Plates that pull apart leave gaps between them. Magma bubbles up between the plates. **Magma** is hot, soft rock from Earth's mantle. Magma builds up along the cracks, forming long chains of mountains under the ocean. These mountains are called *mid-ocean ridges.* The Mid-Atlantic Ridge is Earth's longest mountain range. It separates the North American and Eurasian plates in the North Atlantic and the South American and African plates in the South Atlantic.

✔ **How do most of the highest mountains form?**

Volcanoes

You have read that most volcanoes form at plate boundaries. A **volcano** is a mountain formed by lava and ash. *Lava* is magma that reaches Earth's surface. *Ash* is small pieces of hardened lava.

Chains of volcanoes form where a continental plate and an oceanic plate collide. The edge of the oceanic plate pushes under the edge of the continental plate. The leading edge of the oceanic plate melts as it sinks deep into the mantle. The melted rock becomes magma that forces its way up between the plates. The volcanoes of the Cascades, such as Mount St. Helens, formed this way.

Sometimes volcanoes form in the middle of plates, over unusually hot columns of magma. The magma melts a hole in the plate and rises through the hole, causing a volcanic eruption. The Hawaiian Islands are the tops of a chain of volcanoes that formed in the middle of the Pacific plate. As the Pacific plate continues moving over this hot spot, new volcanoes and new islands form. The big island of Hawai'i, with its active volcano, Kilauea, is the youngest island in the chain. Kure Atoll, an extinct volcano 2617 km (about 1625 mi) to the northwest, is the oldest.

✔ **What is a volcano?**

▲ Many volcanoes are located at plate boundaries around the Pacific plate. That's why this area is called the Ring of Fire.

THE INSIDE STORY

Volcanoes

Volcanoes take on their characteristic shapes as lava and ash build up around their openings, or *vents*.

Shield volcanoes **are broad volcanoes with gentle slopes. They are mostly lava.**

Cinder cone volcanoes **are tall and narrow, with steep slopes. They are mostly ash.**

Composite volcanoes **are wide and have fairly steep slopes. They are lava and ash.**

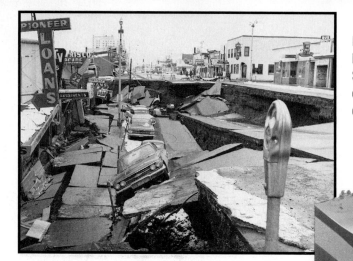

In 1964 a large earthquake hit Anchorage, Alaska. Streets split open, bridges collapsed, and houses slid downhill toward the sea.

Earthquake center, or *focus*

Fault

Earthquakes

On March 27, 1964, thousands of people in Anchorage, Alaska, were shaken as the ground rocked under them. A strong earthquake, possibly the most powerful one ever recorded, knocked down houses, broke up roads, and cut water, gas, and power lines all over the area.

An **earthquake** is a shaking of the ground caused by the sudden release of energy in Earth's crust. The energy released as plates crush together, scrape past each other, or bend along jagged boundaries can cause great damage. Earthquakes are very

Major Earthquakes		
Magnitude	**Year**	**Location**
9.1	1964	Alaska
8.9	1933	Japan
8.4	1946	Japan
8.2	1976	China
8.1	1979	Indonesia
8.1	1985	Mexico
6.9	1989	California
6.8	1994	California

▲ The Richter scale is used to measure relative strengths, or *magnitudes,* of earthquakes. On this scale an earthquake with a magnitude of 7.5, for example, is 32 times more powerful than an earthquake with a magnitude of 6.5.

common. More than a million of them occur each year. However, most are too small to be felt or to cause damage.

Many earthquakes occur along the boundaries of the Pacific plate. Earthquakes also occur along faults in the crust. You have read that Earth's crust can bend or break in the middle of a plate as forces press in on it. These breaks can form **faults**, or places where pieces of the crust move.

An earthquake sends out energy in the form of *seismic* (SYZ•mik) *waves.* Seismic waves are like ripples that form on a pond when a stone is tossed in. Scientists measure and record seismic waves on an instrument called a *seismograph* (SYZ•muh•graf). These measurements can then be used to compare the relative strengths of earthquakes.

✓ **What is an earthquake?**

◄ Sudden movement along a fault can cause an earthquake.

Summary

Earth has three layers: the crust, the mantle, and the core. Rock of the crust and upper mantle makes up plates that fit together like puzzle pieces. Earth's plates collide, pull apart, and slide past each other. Most mountains and volcanoes form at plate boundaries. Many earthquakes also occur at plate boundaries.

Review

1. Describe three ways in which Earth's plates interact.

2. What is magma and where does it come from?

3. How do volcanoes form where oceanic and continental plates collide?

4. **Critical Thinking** Assume that the overall size of Earth's crust stays the same. If one plate is pushing away from the plate next to it on one side, what must be happening at the boundary with another plate on the opposite side?

5. **Test Prep** Many strong earthquakes are caused by —
   A plates sliding past each other
   B lava flowing down the side of a volcano
   C plates spreading apart
   D hot magma

LINKS

MATH LINK

Earthquake Magnitudes Each whole number on the Richter scale represents a force 32 times as strong as the next lower number. An earthquake of magnitude 7 is 32 times as strong as one of magnitude 6. How many times as strong is an earthquake of magnitude 8 compared with an earthquake of magnitude 5?

WRITING LINK

Informative Writing—Explanation The 1980 explosion of Mount St. Helens was a very powerful volcanic eruption. Find pictures in books and magazines of Mount St. Helens before, during, and after the eruption. Write captions for the pictures to explain what happened. Share your photo essay with your class.

LITERATURE LINK

Eruption: Volcano: The Eruption and Healing of Mount St. Helens by Patricia Lauber (Bradbury Press, 1986) explains how and why Mount St. Helens erupted. It also describes the destruction the eruption caused, and how the land has since recovered.

TECHNOLOGY LINK

Learn more about volcanoes by viewing *Ring of Fire* and *Volcano Hunters* on the **Harcourt Science Newsroom Video.**

How Has Earth's Surface Changed?

In this lesson, you can . . .

INVESTIGATE the movement of continents.

LEARN ABOUT how Earth's surface has changed over time.

LINK to math, writing, fine arts, and technology.

< Over millions of years, these trees have turned to stone.

INVESTIGATE

Movement of the Continents

Activity Purpose Earth's surface 100 million years ago probably looked much different than it does today. In the last lesson, you read that Earth's surface is made up of plates that move. In this investigation, you will **make a model** to find out how Earth's surface might have looked before these plates moved to their present locations.

Materials

- 3 copies of a world map
- scissors
- 3 sheets of construction paper
- glue
- globe or world map

Activity Procedure

1 Cut out the continents from one copy of the world map.

2 Arrange the continents into one large "supercontinent" on a sheet of construction paper. As you would with a jigsaw puzzle, arrange them so their edges fit together as closely as possible. (Picture A)

3 Label the pieces with the names of their present continents, and glue them onto the paper.

4 Use a globe or world map to locate the following mountains: Cascades, Andes, Atlas, Himalayas, Alps. Then draw these mountains on the supercontinent.

Picture A

Picture B

5 Use your textbook to locate volcanoes and places where earthquakes have occurred. Put a *V* in places where you know there are volcanoes, such as the Cascades. Put an *E* in places where you know that earthquakes have occurred, such as western North America.

6 Repeat Steps 1–5 with the second copy of the world map, but before gluing the continents to the construction paper, separate them by about 2.5 cm. That is, leave about 2.5 cm of space between North America and Eurasia, between South America and Africa, and so on. (Picture B)

7 Glue the third world map copy onto a sheet of construction paper. Then place the three versions of the world map in order from the oldest to the youngest.

Draw Conclusions

1. Where do the continents fit together the best?

2. Where are most of the mountains, volcanoes, and earthquake sites in relation to the present continents? Why do you think they are there?

3. **Scientists at Work** Scientists **use models**, such as maps, to better understand complex structures and processes. How did your models of Earth's continents help you **draw conclusions** about Earth's past? What limitations did your models have?

Investigate Further **Hypothesize** about the fact that the continents do not fit together exactly. Then **plan and conduct a simple investigation** to test your hypothesis.

Process Skill Tip

It is impossible to actually see Earth's surface as it looked millions of years ago. But by **using a model**, you can **draw conclusions** about how it may have looked.

How Earth's Surface Has Changed

Continental Drift

From evidence like the models you used in the investigation, scientists infer that Earth's surface has not always looked the way it does today. The surface is constantly changing because of continental drift. **Continental drift** is the theory of how Earth's continents move over its surface.

According to the theory, about 225 million years ago, all of the land on Earth was joined together in one "supercontinent" called **Pangea** (pan•JEE•uh). Evidence suggests that about 200 million years ago, Pangea broke into two big continents. The southern one, Gondwana, contained all the land that is now in the Southern Hemisphere. The northern continent, Laurasia, contained land that would become North America and Eurasia. Finally, Gondwana and Laurasia broke into smaller land masses, forming the continents we know today.

Since the continents are still moving, you might infer that the surface of Earth will be very different 200 million years from now. The Atlantic Ocean is getting wider, pushing Europe and North America apart. The Pacific Ocean is getting smaller. And Australia is moving north.

✔ **What is the theory of continental drift?**

FIND OUT

- how Earth's surface features have changed over millions of years
- how fossils help scientists to learn about plants and animals of the past

VOCABULARY

continental drift
Pangea
fossil

Continental Drift

200 million years ago
Pangea begins to break apart.

100 million years ago
Gondwana breaks into smaller continents earlier than Laurasia does.

Today
Earth's surface may look even different in the future.

C22

The Rock Record

If you were floating down the Colorado River through the deepest part of the Grand Canyon, shown at the right, you would be looking up at layers of sedimentary rock nearly 2 billion years old! *Sedimentary rock* is rock formed from sediments that have cemented together. The Grand Canyon is a mile-deep slice into Earth's history, cutting through 20 different layers of sediment.

The sedimentary rocks of the canyon contain a fossil record of organisms from Earth's earliest history. **Fossils** are the remains or traces of past life found in sedimentary rock. Scientists study fossils to find out how life on Earth has changed.

Scientists also depend on the fact that some things will always be the same. Processes that produced features like the Grand Canyon are still occurring today. Running water still erodes sedimentary rock layers, and new layers of sedimentary rock are still forming.

From the position of sedimentary rock layers, scientists can infer the relative ages of the rocks. Younger rock layers are found on top of older rock layers. Some of the oldest rock layers on Earth are near the bottom of the Grand Canyon.

The walls of the Grand Canyon contain rock from only the earliest stages of Earth's history. Erosion has worn away more recent rock. If you stand on the canyon's north rim, you are standing on rock that is about 250 million years old.

✔ **Why is looking at the Grand Canyon like looking at Earth's history?**

The youngest rocks are at the top of the canyon walls.

The oldest rocks are at the bottom of the canyon.

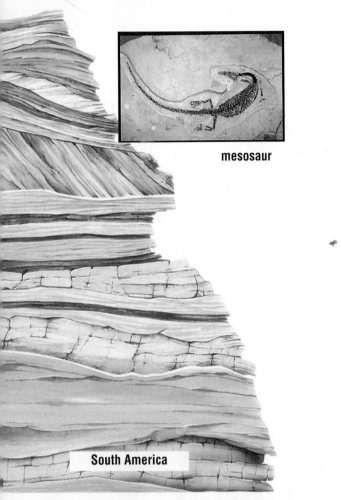

mesosaur

South America

Similar rock layers and similar fossils have been found in both South America and Africa. This provides evidence that the continents may once have been joined together.

mesosaur

Africa

How Fossils Show Changes

Fossils show us that life on Earth has not always been the same as it is now. Dinosaurs once roamed Earth, as did large, elephantlike animals called *woolly mammoths*. Scientists have drawn conclusions about these creatures from what they left behind—whole mammoths frozen in ice and fossilized bones and teeth of dinosaurs.

Most fossils, however, are not the actual remains of once-living organisms. Instead, they are traces left behind when dead plants and animals decayed or dissolved. When sediment buries an organism, it can produce a mold or cast as the sediment hardens into rock. A mold forms when underground water dissolves the organism, leaving only its shape behind in the rock. If minerals fill the empty space and harden, the fossil becomes a cast—like a dinosaur egg.

In addition to showing what kinds of organisms lived on Earth long ago, fossils also show that Earth's surface was different than it is today. Scientists have found fossils of sea organisms in rock at the tops of high mountains. They infer that those areas were once under water.

Scientists use fossil evidence to support the theory of continental drift. Fossils of similar plants and animals have been found in Africa, South America, India, and Australia. This means that these widely separated continents must have been joined at one time.

✓ **How are fossils used to show changes?**

Scientists called *paleontologists* study fossils to learn about life of the past.

Summary

Earth's continents once were joined to form a supercontinent called Pangea. Pangea broke apart and, over millions of years, the continents drifted to their present locations. Fossils, the remains and traces of dead organisms, show what Earth's life was like in the past. They also show that Earth's surface has changed.

Review

1. What was Pangea?
2. How old are the oldest rocks of the Grand Canyon?
3. How do we know that Earth's life was different in the past?
4. **Critical Thinking** Why is the Grand Canyon important to scientists studying Earth's past?
5. **Test Prep** The Southern continent that existed 200 million years ago was called —

   A Gondwana   **C** Laurasia
   B Precambria   **D** Eurasia

LINKS

MATH LINK

Geologic Time Scale Research Earth's history. Then make a chart showing the relative lengths of the various eras and periods. Your chart should show how long each era and period lasted and how long ago each occurred. Draw the chart to scale. For example, if an era lasted for half the time of Earth's history, it should cover half the chart.

WRITING LINK

Informative Writing—Compare and Contrast You learned that Earth's continents were once in different places. Where will they be in the future? Research what a map of the world might look like 100 million years from now. Then compare and contrast this map with a current map in a report for your teacher.

ART LINK

Past Life Look for illustrations of what Earth's surface might have looked like thousands, or even millions, of years ago. Compare what you find with the way Earth's surface looks today.

TECHNOLOGY LINK

Learn more about changes to Earth's surface by visiting the National Air and Space Museum Internet site.
www.si.edu/harcourt/science

 Smithsonian Institution®

Exploring Earth's Surface from Space

Newly released satellite images of the ocean floor are making scientists question old theories about the processes that change Earth's surface.

Satellite Secrets

Until recently, information collected by a U.S. government Geosat satellite was top secret. Now data gathered by this satellite has been released, and geologists are excited. However, they say it will take about ten years to analyze the satellite's images of Earth's geologic processes.

If you've ever sailed on the ocean, you probably couldn't tell that the water bulges up in certain places. It does this because of gravity. Rock on the ocean floor has a gravitational pull for the water around it. The more rock, the stronger the pull. The stronger the pull, the more the water bulges up. A 2000-m (about 6562-ft) underwater volcano causes a water bulge of about 2 m (6.6 ft).

Many of the volcanoes under the Pacific Ocean were discovered by gravity imaging.

This drawing shows a Geosat circling Earth.

Sensitive equipment on board a Geosat can measure these bulges from space. By measuring the surface of the ocean very precisely, the satellite produces clear gravity images of volcanoes, mountain ranges, plains, and other "landforms" on the ocean floor.

New Data Shakes Up Old Theories

Many areas of the ocean floor had never been surveyed before. About half of the underwater volcanoes shown by the Geosat's gravity imaging had not been known to exist. Gravity images of water bulges are also making scientists question old theories about how volcanic island chains form.

The old theory, called the "hot spot" model, said that there are hot areas in Earth's mantle. As Earth's plates pass slowly over a hot spot, a long line of volcanoes forms. Each new volcano in the line is younger than the one just before it.

But the hot spot model can't explain some of the newly discovered volcano chains. For

example, the Pukapuka Ridges, which extend for thousands of kilometers east of Tahiti, seem to have erupted all at the same time. Rock samples from different parts of the chain are all the same age.

Scientists are arguing about what these new discoveries mean in terms of the old theories about hot spots being correct. Many agree that the hot spot model may be wrong. All agree that there is much work ahead to develop more accurate theories based on this Geosat data.

THINK ABOUT IT

1. How does gravity imaging work?
2. Why do you think oil companies might be interested in gravity images?

WEB LINK:
For science and technology updates, visit The Learning Site.
www.harcourtschool.com

Careers — Satellite Technician

What They Do
Satellite technicians work as part of a team that plans, constructs, launches, and operates satellites. They may also work at control stations to receive and monitor data transmissions from satellites.

Education and Training A person wishing to become a satellite technician needs training in electronics, computer sciences, and communications systems.

Kia K. Baptist

GEOSCIENTIST

"A key to being a scientist is to be unafraid to ask questions and unafraid that there may not be answers."

Kia Baptist can see what lies below Earth's surface. She is a geoscientist who works for an oil company. Her job is to help find oil and natural gas resources by finding clues in different kinds of data.

Ms. Baptist collects seismic data by creating small "earthquakes" in rock. Then she analyzes the sound signals that return and uses them to map the rock formations and structures underground.

Ms. Baptist also analyzes geochemical data to learn the chemical nature of the rock. This tells her what kind of rock it is, how old it is, and whether there is oil present. This information, along with computer technology, allows her to give advice to the oil companies on specific locations where oil and natural gas may be found.

Looking for clues is natural for Ms. Baptist. As a child growing up in Baltimore, Maryland, she was a mystery solver. She decided she wanted to help solve the mysteries of space by becoming an astronaut. Several times she worked as an intern at NASA, learning all she could about astronomy and physics. She took courses in many areas of science, believing that knowing about all branches of science would help her do her best work in one. When she began to study geology and chemistry, she realized her true interest lay in those areas. She hasn't stopped studying the Earth since then.

Ms. Baptist gives good advice to young scientists. She says, "Part of the process of science is attacking a problem and trying to find answers, but don't be intimidated if you don't find answers right away. Just keep learning."

THINK ABOUT IT

1. How could analyzing seismic data give clues about where oil is located?
2. Why is it important to know the specific location of oil?

Sedimentary rock layers

Model Earth

How can you model Earth's layers?

Materials

- rounded objects, such as

an apple	a tennis ball
an avocado	an orange
a peach	a plum
a hard-boiled egg	plain chocolates, or
a nectarine	chocolate-covered peanuts

Procedure

1. Make two columns on a sheet of paper.

2. Label one column "Does Model Earth's Layers." Label the other column "Does Not Model Earth's Layers."

3. Decide what characteristics an object must have to model Earth's layers.

4. Examine each object. Then write the name of the object in the appropriate column.

Draw Conclusions

What characteristics must an object have to model Earth's layers? Which parts of the objects in the "Does Model Earth's Layers" column represent Earth's layers? What other objects can you think of that model Earth's layers?

Featuring Earth

How do landforms change?

Materials

- apple
- tape measure
- pan
- hotpad
- oven

Procedure

1. Measure the circumference of the apple.

2. Place the apple in a pan and, using the hot pad, put the pan in the oven and bake it for one hour at 300°F.

300° OVEN

3. Your teacher or another adult will remove the apple from the oven. Allow it to cool, and measure it again.

4. Observe the features of the baked apple.

Draw Conclusions

In some ways, baked apples are a good model of how Earth's landforms change. Compare the circumference of the apple before and after you baked it. What happened to the peel as the apple cooled? What layer of Earth does the peel represent? What "landforms" can you identify on the apple peel? In what ways is the apple *not* a good model of Earth's changing landforms?

Vocabulary Review

Use the terms below to complete the sentences. The page numbers in ( ) tell you where to look in the chapter if you need help.

√landform (C6)   magma (C16)
√weathering (C7)   √volcano (C16)
erosion (C7)   earthquake (C18)
deposition (C7)   fault (C18)
mass movement (C9)   continental
√crust (C14)   drift (C22)
mantle (C14)   Pangea (C22)
√core (C14)   fossils (C23)
√plate (C15)

1. An ____ is a sudden release of energy in Earth's ____, causing the ground to shake.

2. A rigid block of Earth's crust and upper mantle rock is a ____.

3. A ____ is a physical feature on Earth's surface, such as a mountain or valley.

4. The remains or traces of past life found in Earth's crust are called ____.

5. Hot, soft rock from Earth's mantle is ____.

6. A ____ is a break in Earth's crust, along which pieces of the crust move.

7. ____ is the process of breaking rock into soil, sand, and other particles called sediment.

8. Lava is magma that reaches Earth's surface through an opening, called a ____, in Earth's crust.

9. The downhill movement of rock and soil because of gravity is ____.

10. The ____ is the layer of rock beneath Earth's crust.

11. The theory that the continents move over Earth's surface is ____.

12. ____ is the supercontinent that held all of Earth's land 225 million years ago.

13. ____ is the process of moving sediment from one place to another, and ____ is the process of dropping, or depositing, sediment in a new location.

14. The ____ is the center of Earth.

Connect Concepts

Use the Word Bank to complete the sentences.

√deltas   √beaches   tables   √sinkholes   terminal moraines
√arches   √canyons   √dunes   √floodplains

Erosion and Deposition

15. Wind erodes rock and deposits sediments to form ____.

17. Water erodes rock and deposits sediments to form ____.

16. Ice erodes rock and deposits sediments to form ____.

Check Understanding

Write the letter of the best choice.

18. Beginning with the outermost layer, Earth's layers are the —

    A crust, magma, and core

    B crust, mantle, and core

    C core, mantle, and crust

    D core, magma, and crust

19. Gondwana and Laurasia were formed by —

    F continental drift

    G erosion

    H deposition

    J earthquakes

20. Which of the following was **NOT** an ancient continent?

    A Pangea

    B Laurasia

    C Gondwana

    D Cenozoa

Critical Thinking

21. Explain why water erodes Earth's surface more than wind does.

22. If the mantle were solid rock, what feature would not form on Earth's surface? Explain.

23. Scientists have found many fossils of past life. Are fossils still being formed today? Explain.

Process Skills Review

24. What can you **observe** about these pieces of rock that shows you which one has been weathered and moved by water?

25. How might you **make a model** of a volcano?

Performance Assessment

Plate Boundaries

Identify the three types of plate boundaries at A, B, and C in the illustration below. Explain what is happening at each boundary.

Chapter 2

Renewable and Nonrenewable Resources

Can you picture what life would be like if there were no oil or coal? How would people drive their cars or make electricity? Coal and oil are natural resources that people use for energy.

≣FAST FACT

More than three-fourths of the energy we use comes from fossil fuels (natural gas, coal, and petroleum). Less than four percent comes from inexhaustible energy sources, such as the sun, the wind, or the ocean tides.

Energy Sources

Natural gas   Coal   Petroleum

Nuclear energy

Water power   All others

C32

What Are Natural Resources?

In this lesson, you can . . .

INVESTIGATE the properties of minerals.

LEARN ABOUT Earth's natural resources.

LINK to math, writing, technology, and other areas.

Color is just one of the physical properties of minerals. ▽

/ Quartz
▽ Pyrite

INVESTIGATE

Properties of Minerals

Activity Purpose Minerals have physical properties, or characteristics. Minerals can be hard or soft. Some are magnetic. Minerals such as quartz can form beautiful crystals. The properties of minerals make them useful to people for various purposes. In this investigation you will **observe** minerals. Then you will **make predictions** about their properties.

Materials

- 6 mineral samples (talc, pyrite, quartz, fluorite, magnetite, graphite)
- tile
- magnet

Activity Procedure

1. Make a copy of the chart below. List the names of the minerals your teacher gives you.

2. **Observe** each mineral. **Predict** which one will be the hardest. Then rub the minerals against each other to test their hardness. A harder mineral will scratch a softer one. Under *Hardness* on the chart, write a number from 1 to 6 for the hardness of each mineral. Use 1 for the softest mineral and 6 for the hardest mineral.

Mineral	Hardness	Shine	Streak	Magnetic
talc				
pyrite				
quartz				
fluorite				
magnetite				
graphite				

Picture A

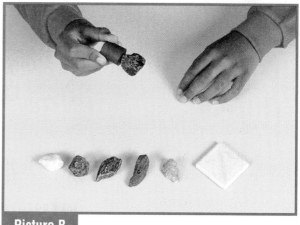

Picture B

3 **Observe** each mineral, and decide whether or not it is shiny. Write *yes* next to the name of the mineral if it is shiny. Write *no* if it is not.

4 Now **predict** the color of the streak each mineral will make. A streak is the colored line a mineral makes when it is rubbed on a tile. Then rub each mineral on the tile. If the mineral makes a streak, write the color of the streak next to the mineral's name. Write *none* if the mineral does not make a streak. (Picture A)

5 Finally, **predict** which minerals will be attracted to a magnet. Test each mineral with a magnet. Write *yes* next to the names of minerals that stick to the magnet. Write *no* next to the names of those that do not. (Picture B)

Draw Conclusions

1. Which mineral is the softest? **Compare** your test results with your predictions.

2. Which minerals make streaks? **Compare** your test results with your color predictions.

3. Which minerals are magnetic? **Compare** your test results with your predictions.

4. **Scientists at Work** Scientists often **predict** what might happen. How did careful observations of the mineral samples help you make better predictions about their properties?

Investigate Further Use the information you gathered on each mineral's properties to **infer** its uses.

> **Process Skill Tip**
>
> Before you **predict,** make careful observations. This makes your prediction better than a simple guess.

Natural Resources

FIND OUT

- what natural resources are

- why some natural resources might get used up

VOCABULARY

natural resource
nonrenewable
   resource
renewable resource
reusable resource

Nonrenewable Resources

In the investigation you learned that minerals have many physical properties. Properties such as hardness and shine make minerals useful for different purposes. Useful minerals and other materials that people take from the Earth are called **natural resources**.

In the past hundred years, people have been using natural resources at a faster rate than ever before. That has made scientists wonder whether some natural resources may one day be completely used up. A resource that cannot be replaced once it is used up is called a **nonrenewable resource**. Nonrenewable resources take thousands of years to form. Once they are used up, they are, as a practical matter, gone.

Rock and mineral resources are nonrenewable. We use rock resources to construct buildings and roads. The silicon chips that make a computer work come from minerals. So does the "lead," or graphite, in a pencil. Other mineral resources are

The aluminum in the basketball backboard comes from the mineral bauxite. ▶

Our bodies need mineral resources. Foods such as fruits and vegetables take minerals from the soil.

ARCTIC OCEAN

ARCTIC OCEAN

NORTH AMERICA

ATLANTIC OCEAN

PACIFIC OCEAN

EURASIA

AFRICA

PACIFIC OCEAN

SOUTH AMERICA

ATLANTIC OCEAN

INDIAN OCEAN

AUSTRALIA

ANTARCTICA

▢ Emerald

▽ Diamond

◉ Ruby

▲ Gems are rare and valuable minerals. Some parts of the world have large deposits of certain gems.

▲ Many buildings are made of granite. Granite is used for buildings because it is hard, and its surface can be polished.

▲ Limestone is also an important building material. It is used to make the concrete for this basketball court.

necessary for the production of metals such as aluminum, iron, copper, silver, and gold. And gems—such as diamonds, rubies, and emeralds—are minerals, too.

Any rock containing a large amount of a mineral is called a *mineral deposit*. Mineral deposits form in several ways. Some minerals dissolve in hot water. As the hot mineral solution flows through cracks in cooler rocks, some minerals fall out of solution and form deposits called *veins*. Gold, copper, and silver are found in veins.

Mineral deposits can also form in magma. As magma cools, heavy minerals sink, forming deposits rich in metals such as iron and nickel.

Mineral deposits are distributed unevenly in the Earth. Some nations have many mineral resources, while other nations have few. Nations usually trade with each other to get the resources they need.

Soil is another nonrenewable resource. All the Earth's forests and food crops take minerals out of the soil as they grow. Minerals go back into the soil when plants and animals die and decay. But people can destroy soil by overusing it, or by putting certain chemicals on it. Overusing soil removes more minerals than decay can put back. And some chemicals can poison soil so that nothing will grow. Losing soil is a major problem, because it takes thousands of years for even a few centimeters of soil to be replaced.

✓ **What are nonrenewable resources?**

Renewable and Reusable Resources

The Earth produces new amounts of some natural resources at the same rate as they are used. A **renewable resource** is a resource that is replaced as it is used.

Most forests, for example, are renewable resources, but only if enough new trees are allowed to grow. Important products, such as lumber, paper, cardboard, tar, and turpentine, come from forests. When humans cut down trees, new ones can grow in their place. If large areas of an old forest are cut at one time, however, the new forest may have different kinds of plants and animals than the old forest did. Some animals need the plants of the old forest for food or shelter. Without those plants the animals might not survive.

Resources such as water and air are not renewable, but they can be used over and over. A **reusable resource** is a natural resource that can be used more than once. Reusable resources are sometimes called *inexhaustible resources*. Natural cycles renew the Earth's reusable resources. The water cycle, for example, allows Earth's limited supply of fresh water to be used over and over again. Heat from the sun evaporates water from the Earth's surface—mainly from the oceans—into the atmosphere. As air cools, water vapor condenses, forming clouds. Water then falls back to Earth from clouds as rain or snow.

Although reusable resources cannot be used up, they can be polluted. During evaporation, water loses any pollution it may have picked up. However, rain and snow pick up any pollution in the air. Acid rain, for example, falls where cloud drops mix with certain chemical pollutants in the air.

✓ **What is a renewable resource?**

Some resources—air, forests, and water—can last forever if they are used carefully.

Summary

Natural resources are useful materials that people take from the Earth. Resources such as soil, rocks, and minerals are nonrenewable. Once they are used up, they cannot be replaced. Some resources—such as forests, water, and air—are renewable or reusable.

Review

1. What is a renewable resource?
2. What is a reusable resource?
3. List two types of nonrenewable resources.
4. **Critical Thinking** What would happen if resources such as air and water could not be reused?
5. **Test Prep** Which of the following is a reusable resource?
   A quartz
   B water
   C a tree
   D iron

LINKS

MATH LINK

Recycling It takes about 100 recycled aluminum cans to make 90 new cans. If your school has a party, and 375 aluminum cans are returned for recycling, how many new cans can be made?

WRITING LINK

Informative Writing—Compare and Contrast Write a paragraph for a younger student explaining the differences between renewable, nonrenewable, and inexhaustible resources. Use examples in your explanation.

SOCIAL STUDIES LINK

Resource Map Choose a mineral resource that is found in the United States, such as copper or iron. Make a map of the United States showing where this resource is found.

PHYSICAL EDUCATION LINK

PE Resources How many products made from natural resources are used during PE class? Look around during the class, and then make a list.

TECHNOLOGY LINK

Learn more about mineral resources by viewing *River of Gold* on the **Harcourt Science Newsroom Video.**

How Do Fossil Fuels Form?

In this lesson, you can . . .

INVESTIGATE storage rocks.

LEARN ABOUT how fossil fuels form.

LINK to math, writing, technology, and other areas.

This tower separates petroleum into products such as asphalt, heating oil, and gasoline. ▼

INVESTIGATE

What Kinds of Rocks Store Petroleum

Activity Purpose Petroleum is one of the most important fuel resources in the United States. The petroleum that people use today came from the decay of ancient sea life. The remains of microscopic organisms settled to the sea floor and became part of the ocean sediments. In time, the sediments changed to rock. It was within this *source rock* that the decaying organisms slowly changed into petroleum. The pressure of additional sediments squeezed the petroleum out of the source rock and into layers called *storage rock*. In this investigation you will **use numbers** to **compare** rocks and determine which is the best storage rock.

Materials

- limestone
- sandstone
- shale
- paper plates
- dropper
- mineral oil
- clock

Activity Procedure

1. Place the rock samples on separate paper plates. **Observe** each rock. **Predict** which will be the best storage rock.

2. Fill the dropper with mineral oil. Put 5 drops of oil on the limestone sample. (Picture A)

Picture A

Picture B

3 **Observe** and **record** the time it takes for the 5 drops of oil to soak into the limestone.

4 Continue adding oil, counting the drops, until the limestone will hold no more oil. **Record** the number of drops it takes. (Picture B)

5 Repeat Steps 2–4 with the other rock samples.

Draw Conclusions

1. Which rock soaked up the oil the fastest? What was the time?

2. Which rock soaked up the most oil? What was the number of drops?

3. Which rock is the best storage rock? Explain.

4. **Scientists at Work** Scientists often **use numbers** to **compare** things. How did you use numbers to compare the oil-storing ability of the rocks?

Investigate Further How could you determine which of the rocks is a source rock for petroleum? **Plan a simple investigation** to answer this question. Then decide what equipment you would need to carry out this investigation.

Process Skill Tip

You can **use numbers** to do many things. You can solve math problems, count objects, put things in order, or **compare** one thing with another. In this activity you compared the oil-storing ability of certain rocks.

How Fossil Fuels Form

Fossil Fuels

FIND OUT

- the types of fossil fuels
- how fossil fuels form

VOCABULARY

fossil fuels
natural gas
peat
lignite
bitumen
anthracite

Coal, natural gas, and petroleum are valuable resources known as **fossil fuels.** They are called *fossil* fuels because they formed from the remains of once-living organisms. Fossil fuels are nonrenewable resources.

Burning a fossil fuel releases large amounts of energy. That's one reason why people use fossil fuels more than any other energy source on Earth. Another reason is that fossil fuels are found in many places. In the last hundred years, the technology for finding fossil fuels has improved. This has increased the use of fossil fuels.

Fossil fuels are also important resources for making other products. For example, coal is used to make steel. And many chemicals, called petrochemicals, are made from petroleum. Petrochemicals are used to produce medicines, makeup, paints, and plastics.

✔ **What are fossil fuels?**

Many energy stations burn coal to produce electricity. ▼

A lot of the items you use every day are made of chemicals that come from petroleum. ▼

Almost all cars, trucks, and buses run on fuel made from petroleum. ▼

Energy from the Sun

Burning fossil fuels releases energy that came from the sun. The energy was stored in the bodies of ancient organisms that were buried in sediments millions of years ago. So coal, natural gas, and petroleum are found in layers of sedimentary rock.

Petroleum is the world's most widely used fossil fuel. It produces a lot of heat when it is burned. Petroleum is used mainly for transportation, because it is easier to store and transport than coal and natural gas.

The petroleum used today formed when microorganisms died and fell to the bottoms of ancient seas. Over many years, layer upon layer of sediment covered them. Deep within the Earth, where there is a lot of heat and pressure, the organic matter of their decayed bodies slowly turned into petroleum and natural gas.

Natural gas is mostly a gas called *methane*. It is usually found with petroleum. Natural gas is used mostly for heating and cooking.

Coal is the most common fossil fuel. Much of the coal used today comes from

coal

Miners travel deep into the Earth to dig coal from underground layers, or seams. ▶

plants that lived in swamps millions of years ago. As these plants died, they sank to the bottoms of the swamps. Mud and other sediments covered their remains, and slowly the plants changed into coal.

The United States has large deposits of fossil fuels, especially coal and natural gas. But the United States uses so much petroleum that some is imported from places such as Saudi Arabia and Nigeria.

Electric energy stations use most of the coal mined in the United States. Years ago, burning coal produced clouds of black smoke. Today, stations that burn coal have ways to control pollution.

The world is slowly running out of fossil fuels. To conserve fuel resources, many nations are trying to cut down on their use of these fuels. They are beginning to use energy sources that are inexhaustible— wind, solar, and hydroelectric energy.

✔ **Where did the energy in fossil fuels come from originally?**

Fossil Fuel Deposits

NORTH
AMERICA

ATLANTIC
OCEAN

N
W E
S

Coal
Natural gas
Petroleum

Coal Formation

As coal forms, it goes through four steps, or stages. At each stage the amount of carbon it contains increases. The first stage is the formation of peat. **Peat** is a soft, brown material made up of partly decayed plants. It forms as dead plants build up in swamps. Today some swamps and bogs, which are areas of wet and spongy ground, have deep layers of peat.

The second stage of coal formation produces lignite. **Lignite** (LIG•nyt) is a soft, brown rock. It forms as layers of sand and mud cover peat. As the layers build up, the pressure of their weight squeezes moisture out of the peat, turning it into a soft rock.

THE INSIDE STORY

Coal Formation

Peat can be found in marshy areas in Great Britain, Russia, and Ukraine. Some people dig out the peat and use it for heating and cooking. Burning peat produces a lot of smoke and pollutants. ▼

Most lignite mines are in eastern European countries. Lignite produces a lot of smoke when it is burned, but it doesn't provide much heat. ▼

Peat

Lignite

Over millions of years, this pressure, along with heat from inside the Earth, turns peat into lignite.

Bitumen is the third stage of coal formation. **Bitumen** (bih•TOO•muhn) is a fairly hard, dark brown or black rock. Millions of years of heat and the weight of even more layers of sediment turn lignite into bitumen.

Bitumen is the most common type of coal mined and used today.

In the fourth stage, bitumen becomes anthracite. **Anthracite** (AN•thruh•syt) is a hard, black rock. Anthracite forms under great heat and pressure. It is almost pure carbon.

✔ **What are the four stages of coal formation?**

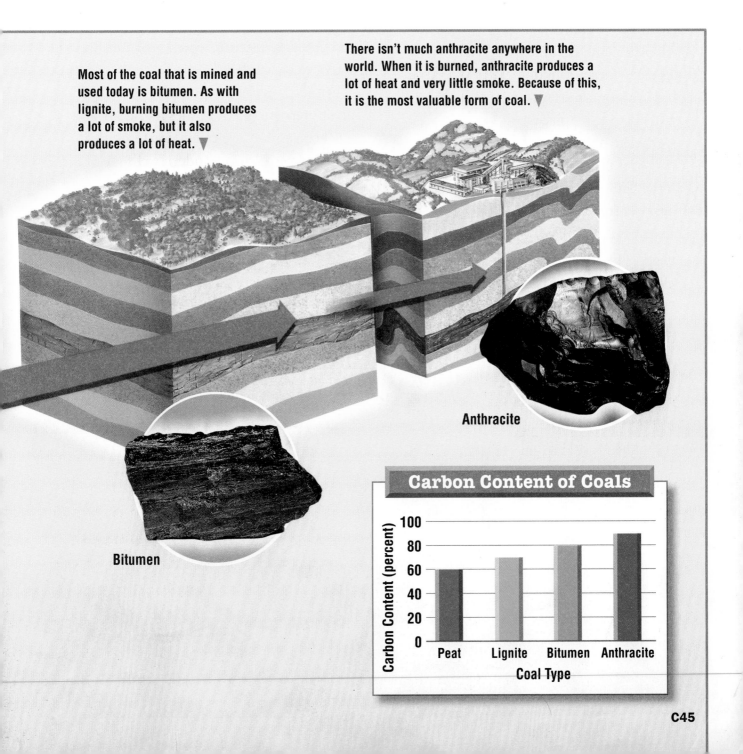

Most of the coal that is mined and used today is bitumen. As with lignite, burning bitumen produces a lot of smoke, but it also produces a lot of heat. ▼

There isn't much anthracite anywhere in the world. When it is burned, anthracite produces a lot of heat and very little smoke. Because of this, it is the most valuable form of coal. ▼

Anthracite

Bitumen

Carbon Content of Coals

Carbon Content (percent)

100
80
60
40
20
0

Peat   Lignite   Bitumen   Anthracite

Coal Type

Petroleum and Natural Gas

Petroleum and natural gas are found only in sedimentary rock. Almost 60 percent of the world's supply is in sandstone. The rest is in limestone and other porous rocks. Geologists can identify rock structures that are likely to hold petroleum and natural gas, so they know where to look for these resources.

Since the microorganisms that formed them lived in seas, many petroleum and natural gas deposits are found under water. Underwater drilling takes place from huge platforms built over the water. In the United States these platforms are located in the Gulf of Mexico and off the California coast.

Some deposits of petroleum and natural gas are under land, in places that were once shallow seas. Drilling for these deposits occurs in California, Texas, Alaska, and other states.

When a drill locates a deposit of petroleum or natural gas, the petroleum has to be pumped from the ground. Natural gas comes out by itself. If there is not enough petroleum in one area to be pumped out directly, hot water or steam is forced into the deposit through a nearby well. This forces the petroleum, which is lighter than water, to the surface.

Sometimes the petroleum is under such great pressure that it gushes to the surface. Gushers, as they are called, waste a lot of valuable petroleum. Modern wells are capped to keep this from happening.

✔ **How are petroleum and natural gas taken from the ground?**

◀ **Drills sink deep into a pocket of petroleum. The petroleum is then pumped to the surface.**

Summary

Coal, oil, and natural gas are fossil fuels. Fossil fuels formed over millions of years from the decayed remains of organisms. Coal formation occurs in four stages, producing peat, lignite, bitumen, and anthracite. Petroleum and natural gas formed from microorganisms buried under ancient seas.

Review

1. List two products that contain petrochemicals made from petroleum.
2. What is most coal used for in the United States?
3. How did Earth's deposits of coal form?
4. **Critical Thinking** As coal forms, how does its carbon content change? How might this change affect its ability to heat?
5. **Test Prep** Which of these is **NOT** a stage in the formation of petroleum?

   A Microorganisms sink to the bottom of shallow seas.

   B Layers of mud pile on top of the remains.

   C Organisms in mud produce new microorganisms.

   D The remains slowly turn into petroleum.

LINKS

MATH LINK

Petroleum Reserves Use a computer and a graphing program such as *Graph Links* to make a graph showing the world's top five producers of petroleum. How does the amount of petroleum the United States produces compare to that of other nations?

WRITING LINK

Informative Writing—Report As you watch TV commercials, look for those that show fossil fuels being used. Then write a commercial that shows ways fossil fuels could be conserved. Present your commercial to your class.

SOCIAL STUDIES LINK

History of Petroleum When was petroleum first discovered? How was it first used? Write a short report on the early history of petroleum.

TECHNOLOGY LINK

Learn more about the formation of fossil fuels by visiting this Internet site.
www.scilinks.org/harcourt

How Are Natural Resources Conserved?

In this lesson, you can . . .

INVESTIGATE how people use natural resources.

LEARN ABOUT how people can conserve natural resources.

LINK to math, writing, social studies, and technology.

This Earth Day costume is made of old cans, paper, and bottles. ▽

INVESTIGATE

How People Use Natural Resources

Activity Purpose Suppose you're on a hike. You started out with three pieces of fruit and you have one piece left. You want to eat it, but you're not sure how long it will be before you can get more food. So you decide to save the fruit. You have reached an important conclusion—it is not always best to use everything right away, because the supply may run out. In this investigation you will **hypothesize** about how people can use resources without using them up too quickly.

Materials
- small bowl of paper clips
- 3 generation cards (parents, children, grandchildren)

Activity Procedure

1 Work in a group of three. Place your group's generation cards face down on a table. The bowl of paper clips stands for Earth's supply of a certain resource, such as iron.

2 Each person in the group now takes a generation card. Hold up your card so the other people in your group can see it. The card tells you your generation. It also tells you how many people are in your generation. (Picture A)

3 Each generation will now get paper clips from the bowl. The person from the parents' generation goes first. He or she takes five clips from the bowl for each person in his or her generation. (Picture B)

4 Next, the person from the children's generation takes five clips for each person in his or her generation.

5 Finally, the person from the grandchildren's generation takes five clips for each person in his or her generation.

Picture A

Draw Conclusions

1. Did everyone get the same number of clips?

2. Where did a problem occur?

3. What could be done to avoid the problem?

Picture B

4. **Scientists at Work** Scientists **hypothesize** what the results of an investigation might be. Hypothesize what will happen if each person from a generation gets only three or four clips, instead of five.

Investigate Further With the members of your group, list the products people use that are made from a natural resource, such as a certain metal. Describe several things people could do to make sure that in the future there will be enough of this resource. Then **plan and conduct a simple investigation** using technology to simulate your plan.

Process Skill Tip

When you **hypothesize,** you make a sensible guess about what might happen under certain conditions. You should base your hypothesis on observations, the results of previous experiments, or what you already know.

Conserving Natural Resources

Making Choices

FIND OUT

- why conserving natural resources is necessary

- how reusing and recycling can conserve resources

VOCABULARY

recycling

What would happen if one day there were no iron or petroleum or lumber? In the investigation you found out that using too much of a resource quickly can cause it to run out. The choices people make today about using natural resources can make the difference between having them in the future or not.

Earth's human population is growing, but the amounts of most natural resources are not. More people will demand more iron, oil, lumber, and other resources. Thinking about future demands for resources helps people plan ways to conserve them now. Conserving natural resources often involves choices. When you pour a glass of lemonade, do you use a disposable paper cup or a washable glass? Using a glass saves paper, but using a paper cup saves water.

Each decision has only a small effect on natural resources. But the choices of many people over time have a big effect. The photograph below shows land that was once a strip mine. The choices for this mined land were to leave it as it was after the coal was removed or to try to restore it to the way it had been before the coal was mined. Because people chose to restore the land, many will enjoy it in the future.

✔ **What does conserving resources often involve?**

The top layers of soil and rock were removed to mine coal. Soil, plants, and wildlife were destroyed. ▼

This mined land was partially restored by replacing the soil and planting grass and trees. Reclaimed land is a future resource.

▲ Instead of cutting down all the trees, people can do selective cutting, taking some trees and leaving others. The trees that are left help replace the cut trees by producing seeds.

◄ People can replant trees where they have been cut down.

Changing Behaviors

The simplest way to conserve natural resources is to use fewer resources. Using fewer aluminum cans, for example, means that less bauxite—aluminum ore—will have to be mined. Driving less or driving cars that are more fuel-efficient means that less petroleum will be needed. This works for nonrenewable resources. However, conserving renewable and reusable resources means saving them from damage and protecting them from overuse.

Saving resources from damage includes keeping them free of pollution. For many years, few people realized how dangerous pollution was to natural resources. Many people thought the supply of Earth's reusable resources was so large that nothing could damage it.

Now people realize that water pollution can kill fish and oxygen-producing microorganisms. People also know that air pollution can kill trees and make people sick. And garbage and rusting cars are just plain ugly. Most scientists agree that preventing pollution is an important part of conserving natural resources.

Renewable resources need protection from overuse. For example, in the early 1900s the hunting of whales was a big business. So many countries hunted whales that the population of blue whales, the largest whale species, was almost completely destroyed. In 1965 it became illegal to hunt blue whales in the Southern Hemisphere. This allowed the population to increase to the point that blue whales are now unlikely to become extinct. Today only Japan, Norway, and Russia hunt blue whales.

Forests are another renewable resource that needs protection from overuse. Forests are not just trees. They also provide habitats for many kinds of animals. Loss of habitat is the biggest threat to wildlife. Reasonable limits on the number of trees that can be cut allow forests to renew themselves. Selective cutting helps protect habitats for wildlife.

✔ **How can reusable and renewable resources be conserved?**

Reduce, Reuse, Recycle

People in the United States use more resources per person than most other people in the world. It takes 500,000 trees each week just to make the paper for Sunday newspapers. Every year, Americans throw away 28 billion glass bottles and jars. The average American uses about 90 kg (200 lb) of plastic each year—most of it in packaging that is thrown away.

One way to conserve resources is to reduce the amounts that are used. Using less energy conserves fossil fuels. Using less paper conserves forests. And using fewer bottles and cans conserves minerals.

Another way to conserve resources is to reuse things. Paper or plastic grocery bags can be reused by taking them back to the store, or they can be used as garbage bags or lunch bags.

Many things that can't be reused can be recycled. **Recycling** is the process of taking back a resource used to make a product. That resource is then made into a new product. Many communities have programs for collecting newspaper, glass, aluminum, and plastic. Trucks carry these materials to recycling centers where they are broken down into raw materials to make new products. In some states or communities, recycling is not just a good idea—it's the law.

Sometimes people choose disposable items because they are less expensive or easier to use. But if the materials can't be reused or recycled, the resources used in them will be lost. Recycling saves other resources, too. Recycling aluminum cans, for example, saves both minerals and fuel. The process of making new cans from recycled aluminum uses much less energy than making cans from bauxite does.

✔ **What is recycling?**

◀ The glass blower uses natural resources such as sand and limestone to make glass.

Long-life fluorescent light bulbs last longer, *reducing* the number of bulbs that have to be made. They use less energy, too. ▼

Glass bottles can be *recycled*. The glass is melted at high temperatures and formed into new products. ▼

A glass bottle can be *reused* for other things.

Although silica sand, used to make glass, seems to be inexhaustible, it is a nonrenewable resource.

Recycling Totals

Percentage Recycled

100
75
50
25
0

Aluminum cans | Glass containers | Newspapers

Materials

▲ Americans recycle almost 67 percent of their aluminum cans, 63 percent of their newspapers, and 38 percent of their glass containers.

Summary

Earth has a limited supply of natural resources. They must be conserved so that they will last as long as possible. Protecting resources from damage and overuse is a part of conservation. Reusing and recycling products saves resources needed to make new products.

Review

1. How does pollution harm natural resources?
2. What changes result from cutting down an old forest?
3. How does reusing products help conserve natural resources?
4. **Critical Thinking** How does using less electricity save natural resources?
5. **Test Prep** Which resource is **NOT** a type of natural resource?

   A reusable resource

   B renewable resource

   C remarkable resource

   D nonrenewable resource

LINKS

MATH LINK

Recycled Content Look for packaging that has *recycled* or *post-consumer content* on the label. Make a list of all the items you find, what each is made of, and how much of the material in each is recycled. Then make a circle graph for all the recycled packaging. The parts of the graph should show the percentages of recycled paper, plastic, aluminum, and glass in the packaging you find.

WRITING LINK

Informative Writing—How-To Make a poster for a school recycling program. Explain the recycling laws or policies in your community.

SOCIAL STUDIES LINK

Conservation Make a list of everything you used this morning. Did you use any recycled or reusable products? How did you conserve resources? How could you have conserved more? Share your ideas with a classmate.

TECHNOLOGY LINK

Learn more about conserving natural resources by visiting this Smithsonian Institution Internet site.
www.si.edu/harcourt/science

 Smithsonian Institution®

Getting More Oil from Wells

Scientists and petroleum engineers are using water, gas, heat, and soap to help keep oil flowing from thousands of old oil wells.

Pumped Up

The petroleum, or oil, that people use is deposited in layers of rock. In some deposits, the oil forms large, flat pools between rock layers. In others it fills a net-work of tiny cracks within the rock. In still others, the oil is mixed with sand, the way sea water is mixed with sand at the beach.

If an oil deposit is deep below the surface, the weight of the rock above produces pressure on it. This makes it easy to get the oil out. Companies drill down to the deposit, and the oil rushes up to the surface. This pressure also keeps the oil flowing out of the well. When the pressure is too low to push the oil up through the well pipe, a pump can often pull it up. The use of this combination of natural pressure and pumping is known as primary oil production.

This photograph from the early 1900s shows an oil gusher in a California oil field. Gushers waste a lot of valuable oil.

Natural gas is burned off so the oil can be pumped from this offshore well.

However, primary production doesn't work on shallow deposits, and it won't get all the oil out of deep deposits. In fact, most deep wells are abandoned when only about one-third of the oil has been removed. Getting the rest of the oil out is too difficult or too expensive.

Wishing for Better Wells

Oil companies have usually looked for new places to drill for oil that is easy to recover. However, oil company geologists and engineers are now also working on ways to get the oil that primary production can't recover. The use of these new methods of getting more oil out of old wells is called secondary recovery or enhanced recovery.

One method used in secondary recovery is injection. Water or gas is pumped down into the ground near an oil well. This produces pressure that forces the oil into the well pipe. In some wells this method makes it possible to pump out about half the oil left after primary production. Injection can also be used to get oil from some shallow deposits.

Scientists at the U. S. Department of Energy are working on other secondary recovery methods, too. One, called thermal extraction, uses heat. Steam is pumped into the deposit. Heat from the steam makes the oil thinner, so it flows more easily. The steam also increases pressure.

Scientists are also mixing detergents with the water injected into wells. The soapy liquid makes the oil flow more easily. Other scientists are experimenting with microorganisms that "eat" oil. When these organisms digest some of the oil in a deposit, they produce gas (like millions of little burps!) that increases pressure in the well.

THINK ABOUT IT

1. What is a name for the use of methods of getting more oil out of old wells?
2. How does thermal extraction work?

WEB LINK:
For science and technology updates, visit The Learning Site.
www.harcourtschool.com

Careers   Oil Rig Worker

What They Do Oil rig workers help drill new wells and help keep old wells productive.

Education and Training Most oil rig workers train on the job. They start by handling pipe and learn to work with complicated drilling machinery.

Paul D. MacCready

ENGINEER

"If you have the enthusiasm to charge ahead, you can do all sorts of things. People can do so much more than they realize."

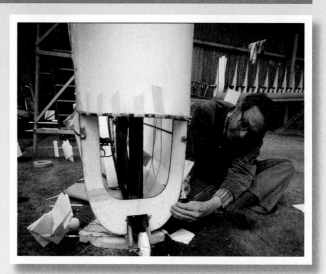

Paul MacCready is best known as the inventor of the *Gossamer Condor,* the world's first successful human-powered flying machine. Yet this remarkable invention is only one of many accomplishments of this creative engineer. Dr. MacCready has won the U.S. soaring championship four times in his gliders, which are aircraft without engines. He was also the first American to win the world soaring championship. His second human-powered vehicle, the *Gossamer Albatross,* was the first human-powered aircraft to cross the English Channel. A third invention, the *Bionic Bat,* set a record for human-powered speed.

Dr. MacCready has done more than invent human-powered aircraft. He has also worked to develop environmentally friendly forms of transportation. In 1987 he built a solar-powered car, the Sunraycer, which competed in a race across

Australia. In 1990 he worked with General Motors to develop the Impact, an electric car.

Today Dr. MacCready is working for AeroVironment, a company he founded in 1971 in Monrovia, California. He and his partners help businesses learn about environmental issues and wind power. They also design remote-controlled electric airplanes, which are used by the Department of Defense to gather information.

THINK ABOUT IT

1. How has Dr. MacCready combined his interests in soaring, engineering, and business?
2. How might the use of Dr. MacCready's vehicles help the environment?

The *Centurion,* an atmospheric research aircraft

Minerals

How can you identify minerals from their crystals?

Materials

- talcum powder
- hand lens
- table salt
- microscope slides
- chalk
- microscope
- black construction paper

Procedure

1. Put a little talcum powder, chalk, and table salt on a sheet of black construction paper. Observe each substance with the hand lens.

2. Put a little of each substance on a microscope slide. Observe under low power of the microscope.

3. Now mix the three substances together on a microscope slide. Observe the mixture under low power.

4. Try to identify each substance in the mixture.

Draw Conclusions

Talc, salt, and chalk are all minerals. Some minerals form crystals with regular shapes. What shape are the salt crystals? How are the talc and chalk different from the salt? How could you separate a mixture of the three minerals?

The 3 *R*s

What objects could be reduced, reused, or recycled?

Materials

- paper
- pencil

Procedure

1. Fold the paper into three columns.

2. Label the columns "Reduce," "Reuse," and "Recycle."

3. As you go through your day at school, write in the appropriate column each object you use that could be reduced in amount, reused in another way, or recycled to make a new object.

Draw Conclusions

How many objects did you list in each column? Compare your lists with those of your classmates. Then every day for a week, choose an object from one column and for that day, reduce the amount you use, reuse the object in a different way, or recycle the object.

Chapter 2 Review and Test Preparation

Vocabulary Review

Use the terms below to complete the sentences. The page numbers in ( ) tell you where to look in the chapter if you need help.

natural resource (C36)

nonrenewable resource (C36)

fossil fuel (C42)

renewable resource (C38)

reusable resource (C38)

natural gas (C43)

peat (C44)

lignite (C44)

bitumen (C45)

anthracite (C45)

recycling (C52)

1. A _____ is a resource that can be replaced as it is used.

2. A hard, black form of coal is _____.

3. A soft, brown material made up of partly decayed plants is _____.

4. _____ is the process of taking a resource back from a product.

5. A _____ is a useful mineral or other material that people take from the Earth.

6. _____ is a gas made up mostly of methane.

7. A soft, brown form of coal is _____.

8. A _____ is a resource that cannot be replaced once it is used.

9. A _____ is a resource that can be used more than once.

10. _____ is a fairly hard, dark brown or black form of coal.

11. A _____ is a fuel such as coal, petroleum, and natural gas that formed in the Earth from decayed organisms.

Connect Concepts

Use the Word Bank to complete the chart. List the three main categories of natural resources on the top lines. Then list an example of each type of resource on the lines below.

minerals/rocks	soil	forests
nonrenewable	coal	fossil
renewable	water	reusable
natural gas	air	petroleum

Three Categories of Natural Resources

12. _____	18. _____	21. _____
13. _____	19. _____	22. _____
14. _____ fuels		
Three types of the resource in #14:	20. _____	23. _____
15. _____		
16. _____		
17. _____		

Check Understanding

Write the letter of the best choice.

24. All natural resources are —
  A useful materials that can be replaced
  B useful materials that cannot be replaced
  C useful materials that are used for fuel
  D useful materials that people take from the Earth

25. Fossil fuels are important to us because —

  F they produce heat when burned

  G they are reusable resources

  H they are the only fuels used to make electricity

  J they are renewable resources

26. Conservation of natural resources could include —

  A the use of more renewable sources of energy

  B cutting down on the use of fossil fuels

  C replacing soil and planting trees

  D all of the above

27. Fossil fuels include —

  F jet fuel, graphite, and lead

  G bauxite, oil, and coal

  H natural gas, oil, and coal

  J coal, oil, and peat

28. The stages of coal formation, in order, are —

  A peat, lignite, bitumen, anthracite

  B bitumen, anthracite, peat, lignite

  C anthracite, peat, lignite, bitumen

  D lignite, bitumen, anthracite, peat

Critical Thinking

29. How would your life be different if water were a nonrenewable resource?

30. Most electricity is produced using fossil fuels. Some people think electricity should be produced using resources such as wind, water, and solar energy. Why might people have this opinion?

31. How does recycling plastic conserve fossil fuels?

Process Skills Review

32. **Predict** what might happen to non-renewable resources as the population increases.

33. Assume that the recycling rate for aluminum cans is 66 percent and that the recycling rate for all other aluminum is 38 percent. **Use numbers** to **infer** the recycling rate of aluminum foil and building materials.

34. Wildlife is a renewable resource. **Predict** what would happen if the number of animals born to a species were less than the number killed by hunters. How could conservation change this?

Performance Assessment

Identifying Resources

Classify the resources needed for each of the following objects or activities as *nonrenewable, renewable, or reusable:* a cotton T-shirt; water used to bathe; a ride on a school bus; a pencil; this book; a glass bottle; and electricity produced by wind energy.

Chapter 3

Weather and Climate

Does weather begin or end? Or does it just keep moving from place to place? Many things contribute to making weather and to changing it.

Vocabulary Preview

atmosphere
air pressure
humidity
precipitation
evaporation
condensation
local winds
prevailing winds
climate
microclimate
El Niño
greenhouse effect
global warming

≣FAST FACT

The United States is a country of many weather extremes. Below are some record-breaking weather measurements.

Heavy Weather		
What	Where	How Much
Highest Temperature	Death Valley, CA	134°F
Lowest Temperature	Prospect Creek, AK	⁻79.8°F
Heaviest Snowfall	Mount Shasta, CA	189 in.
Most Snow in a Year	Mount Rainier, WA	1,224.5 in.
Strongest Wind	Mount Washington, NH	231 mi/hr
Most Rain in a Year	Kukui, HI	739 in.

C61

How Can You Observe and Measure Weather Conditions?

In this lesson, you can . . .

INVESTIGATE and measure weather conditions.

LEARN ABOUT Earth's weather systems.

LINK to math, writing, art, and technology.

◀ A Midwest tornado

INVESTIGATE

Measuring Weather Conditions

Activity Purpose   People have always been affected by the weather. But it wasn't until fairly recently that scientists have been able to predict the weather accurately. Today's weather scientists use many instruments to **measure** and **collect data** about weather conditions. Then they use the data to help **predict** what the weather will be like today, tomorrow, or next weekend. In this investigation you will measure and collect data about weather conditions in your area.

Materials
■ weather station

Activity Procedure

1 Make a copy of the Weather Station Daily Record table. You will use it to **record** the date, the time, the temperature, the amount of rain or snow, the wind direction and speed, and the cloud conditions each day for five days. Try to **record** the weather conditions at the same time each day.

2 Place the weather station in a shady spot, 1 m above the ground. **Record** the temperature. (Picture A)

3 Be sure the rain gauge will not collect runoff from any buildings or trees. **Record** the amount of rain or snow (if any).

Weather Station Daily Record

Date				
Time				
Temperature				
Rainfall or snowfall				
Wind direction and speed				
Cloud conditions				

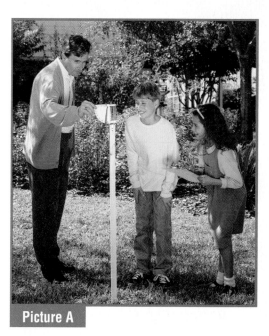

Picture A

4 Be sure the wind vane is located where wind from any direction will reach it. **Record** the wind direction and speed. Winds are labeled with the direction from which they blow. (Picture B)

5 Describe and **record** the cloud conditions by noting how much of the sky is covered by clouds. Draw a circle and shade in the part of the circle that equals the amount of sky covered with clouds.

6 Use the temperature data to make a line graph showing how the temperature changes from day to day.

Draw Conclusions

1. Use your Weather Station Daily Record to **compare** the weather conditions on two different days. Which conditions were about the same? Which conditions changed the most?

2. From the **data** you **gathered** in this activity, how might scientists use weather data to **predict** the weather?

3. **Scientists at Work** Scientists learn about the weather by **measuring** weather conditions and **gathering data.** What did you learn by measuring the amount of rain your area received during the week of your observations?

Investigate Further Find a newspaper weather page, and note the temperatures in various cities throughout the United States. Why are there different temperatures in different cities? **Plan and conduct a simple investigation** using technology to find out.

Picture B

Process Skill Tip

Measurements are a kind of observation. You **measure** when you use a tool, such as a thermometer or rain gauge, to **gather data** about something.

Weather Systems

Where Weather Occurs

FIND OUT

- where most weather occurs
- how weather conditions are measured
- how clouds form

VOCABULARY

atmosphere
air pressure
humidity
precipitation
evaporation
condensation

Almost all weather occurs in the lowest layer of air, or **atmosphere**, that surrounds Earth. The atmosphere stretches about 1000 km (620 mi) from the Earth's surface to outer space. The lowest layer of the atmosphere, called the *troposphere*, is where most water is found and where most clouds form. The troposphere is about 15 km (9 mi) thick at the equator.

Very little weather occurs above the troposphere. There is a little water in the *stratosphere*, the next higher layer, so a few clouds form there. But more important is the stratosphere's ozone layer, about 22.5 km (14 mi) above the Earth's surface. Ozone protects life on Earth by absorbing some of the sun's harmful rays. From the stratosphere to the edge of space, there is no water and too little air for any weather to occur.

✔ **In what layer of the atmosphere does most of Earth's weather occur?**

Blizzards, at the left, and hurricanes at the right, are among the largest and most powerful weather systems of Earth's troposphere, shown below.

A *thermometer* measures air temperature. ▼

Air pressure is the weight of the atmosphere. A *barometer* measures air pressure. ▼

A *rain gauge* measures the amount of precipitation. ▼

◄ Water in the air is called humidity. A *hygrometer* (hy·GRAHM·uht·er) measures humidity.

A *wind vane* measures the direction from which the wind is blowing. An *anemometer* (an·uh·MAHM·uht·er) measures wind speed. ►

Measuring Atmospheric Conditions

The weather changes because the atmosphere is constantly changing. Sometimes the air is cold and sometimes it's warm. As air warms, its weight, or **air pressure**, lessens. And warm air holds more water, or can have more **humidity**, than cold air. These and other conditions of the atmosphere can be observed and measured.

The weather instruments shown on this page can be used to measure atmospheric conditions—air temperature, air pressure, **precipitation** (rain or snow), humidity, wind direction, and wind speed. Other atmospheric conditions, such as cloud type, are observed directly.

Why do people measure atmospheric conditions? One reason is to predict what the weather will be. For example, a change in air pressure or cloud type often means there will be a change in the weather.

✓ **What are some atmospheric conditions that can be measured?**

Air Pressure

You probably don't feel the atmosphere weighing you down. But air does have weight. The atmosphere pushes on you all the time, and this weight is air pressure.

There are several types of barometers for measuring air pressure. A mercury barometer, like the ones shown at the right, consists of a glass tube about 1 m (3 ft) long. Air is removed from the tube, and the glass is sealed at the top. Then the tube is turned upside down, and the open end is placed in a dish of mercury. The weight of the air pushing down on the mercury in the dish pushes mercury up into the glass tube. The mercury rises in the tube until its weight exactly balances the weight of the air pushing down on the mercury in the dish. The height of the mercury in the tube is a measure of air pressure. This measure is compared to a standard, or average, air pressure of about 76 cm (30 in.) of mercury.

Recall that warm air weighs less than cold air. A mass of cold air, called a *high-pressure area,* will measure more than 76 cm of mercury. A mass of warm air, called a *low-pressure area,* will measure less than 76 cm of mercury.

Weather changes because high- and low-pressure areas move. In the winter, areas of high pressure often move from northwestern Canada toward the southeastern United States, bringing cool, dry weather conditions. In the summer, areas of low pressure often move from the Gulf of Mexico to the northeastern United States, bringing warm, wet weather conditions.

As these high-pressure and low-pressure areas move, barometer readings in their paths change. Therefore, changing

HIGH AIR PRESSURE

The mercury in this barometer is high. Areas of high pressure usually have fair weather.

LOW AIR PRESSURE

The mercury in this barometer is low. Areas of low pressure often have stormy weather.

barometer readings can be used to predict changes in weather. If the barometer is rising, the weather will probably become fair. If the barometer is falling, stormy weather is probably coming.

✔ **How can changing air pressure be used to predict changing weather conditions?**

Water in the Air

In addition to temperature and air pressure, humidity, or the amount of water in the air, is an important factor in describing weather conditions. But how does water get into the air?

Earth's oceans are the biggest source of water. As the sun heats the oceans, liquid water changes into an invisible gas called *water vapor,* which rises into the air. The process of liquid water changing to water vapor is called **evaporation**. High up in the atmosphere, where the air is cooler, water vapor turns back into liquid drops of water, forming clouds. This process is called **condensation**.

When cloud drops come together, gravity returns the water to the Earth's surface as precipitation—usually rain. If the temperature in the clouds is below freezing, the precipitation is sleet, hail, or snow. This transferring of water from the Earth's surface to the atmosphere and back is called the *water cycle.*

THE INSIDE STORY

The Water Cycle

Water falls to Earth as precipitation when cloud drops come together.

Water vapor condenses into cloud drops.

Precipitation that sinks into the ground is called *ground water.*

When water evaporates from soil, plants, lakes, and rivers, solids and any pollutants are left behind.

Precipitation that runs off Earth's surface into rivers, lakes, and oceans is called *runoff.*

When water evaporates from the oceans, salt is left behind.

On clear nights, when the surface of the Earth cools quickly, water vapor may condense to form a cloud near the ground. This low cloud is called *fog*. If you have ever walked through fog, you know what the inside of a cloud is like.

Whether a cloud forms near the ground or high in the atmosphere, it forms in the same way. Water vapor condenses onto dust and other tiny particles in the air when it rises and cools. Another way in which air cools enough for water vapor to condense is by moving from a warm place to a colder place. For example, moist air that moves from over a warm body of water to over cooler land forms clouds or fog.

Even though all clouds form by condensation, different weather conditions produce different types of clouds. Weather scientists, or *meteorologists* (meet•ee•uhr•AHL•uh•juhsts),

Types of Clouds

Height

14 km
12 km
10 km
8 km
6 km
4 km
2 km
0

Cirrus clouds are high clouds made mostly of ice crystals. They look thin and wispy. *Cirrus* means "curl of hair." Cirrus clouds are usually associated with fair weather, but they may mean that a change in weather conditions is coming. ▶

Cumulus clouds form when large bubbles of warm air rise rapidly into the atmosphere. They look piled up and puffy. *Cumulus* means "heap." Cumulus clouds usually mean fair weather, but they can produce light rain or snow showers. ▶

Stratus clouds form as a mass of warm air is slowly pushed upward over a mass of colder air or over a mountain. *Stratus* means "layer," and these clouds form layers. Stratus clouds near the ground are called *fog*. Stratus clouds often produce rain or snow. ▶

▲ *Cumulonimbus* (kyoo•myoo•loh•NIM•buhs) clouds are a type of cumulus cloud. Cumulonimbus clouds are tall and bring thundershowers and sometimes hail. These clouds are also called thunderheads or thunderclouds.

give clouds three basic names—cirrus (SEER•uhs), cumulus (KYOO•myoo•luhs), and stratus. Along with other information, the types of clouds in the atmosphere can be used to help predict weather changes. Some basic types of clouds and their descriptions are shown on page C68.

✔ **How do clouds form?**

Summary

Most of Earth's weather takes place in the troposphere, the lowest layer of the atmosphere. Weather conditions such as temperature, air pressure, humidity, wind speed and direction, and the amount of precipitation can be observed and measured. Certain weather conditions, such as changing air pressure and types of clouds, can be used to predict changes in the weather.

Review

1. How do weather scientists **observe** and **measure** weather conditions?
2. How is water recycled in the water cycle?
3. What causes clouds to form?
4. **Critical Thinking** It is a gray, cloudy day, and a light rain is falling. What type of clouds would you expect to see? Explain your answer.
5. **Test Prep** The process by which water vapor turns into liquid water drops is known as —
   A condensation
   B evaporation
   C precipitation
   D the water cycle

LINKS

MATH LINK

Measurement Many meteorologists in the United States measure air pressure in units called *millibars*. At sea level, standard air pressure is 1013.2 millibars. If 1013.2 millibars equals 76 cm of mercury, what would a barometer reading of 75 cm of mercury equal in millibars?

WRITING LINK

Informative Writing—Report Suppose that you are a meteorologist who has just spotted a large cumulonimbus cloud moving toward a city. Write a weather report for the city's residents.

ART LINK

Stormy Weather Make a drawing that includes one or more of the cloud types shown on page C68. Show the weather conditions that are associated with those cloud types.

TECHNOLOGY LINK

Learn more about Earth's atmosphere by visiting the Harcourt Learning Site.
www.harcourtschool.com

WELCOME TO
THE
LEARNING
SITE

What Causes Wind?

In this lesson, you can . . .

INVESTIGATE the rates at which water and soil absorb and release heat.

LEARN ABOUT uneven heating of the Earth's surface as the cause of wind.

LINK to math, writing, music, and technology.

◄ Energy to fly this kite starts with the sun.

INVESTIGATE

The Sun's Energy Heats Unevenly

Activity Purpose If you've ever walked barefoot from pavement to grass on a sunny day, you know that different materials absorb heat differently. On a larger scale, uneven heating like this is what produces wind. In this investigation you will **predict** which material heats up and cools off faster—water or soil. Then you will test your predictions.

Materials

- 2 tin cans (lids removed)
- water
- dry soil
- spoon
- 2 thermometers

Activity Procedure

1. Fill one can about $\frac{3}{4}$ full of water and the other can about $\frac{3}{4}$ full of soil. (Picture A)

2. Place one thermometer in the can of water and the other in the can of soil. Put the cans in a shady place outside. Wait for 10 minutes, and then **record** the temperatures of the water and the soil.

3. Put both cans in sunlight. **Predict** which of the cans will show the faster rise in temperature. **Record** the temperature of each can every 10 minutes for 30 minutes. In which can does the temperature rise faster? Which material—soil or water—heats up faster? (Picture B)

Picture A

4. Now put the cans back in the shade. **Predict** in which of the cans the temperature will drop faster. Again **record** the temperature of each can every 10 minutes for 30 minutes. In which can does the temperature drop faster? Which material—soil or water—cools off faster?

5. Make line graphs to show how the temperatures of both materials changed as they heated up and cooled off.

Draw Conclusions

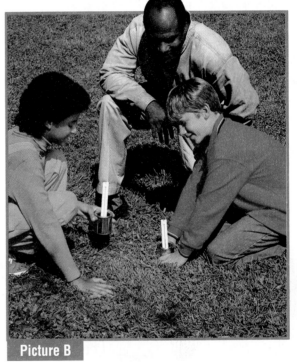

Picture B

1. How did your results match your predictions? Which material—water or soil—heated up faster? Which cooled off faster?

2. From the results you **observed** in this investigation, which would you **predict** heats up faster—oceans or land? Which would you predict cools off faster? Explain.

3. **Scientists at Work** Scientists learn by **predicting** and then testing their predictions. How did you test your predictions about water and soil?

Investigate Further **Predict** how fast other materials, such as moist soil, sand, and salt water, heat up and cool off. **Plan and conduct a simple investigation** to test your predictions.

The Causes of Wind

FIND OUT

- what causes the wind
- about Earth's wind patterns

VOCABULARY

local winds
prevailing winds

Uneven Heating

The illustration below shows how the sun's rays strike the Earth's surface and the atmosphere. The atmosphere absorbs some of the sun's energy and reflects some of it back into space. Some of the energy that reaches the Earth's surface is reflected back into the atmosphere. However, much of the sun's energy is absorbed by the Earth's surface.

In the investigation you discovered that soil heats up faster and cools off faster than water. In the same way, when the sun's rays strike the Earth's surface, land absorbs the sun's energy more quickly and heats up faster than bodies of water, such as lakes, rivers, and oceans. And land releases heat and cools off faster when the sun goes down than bodies of water do.

✔ **What happens to the energy from the sun's rays that reach Earth?**

The atmosphere absorbs energy directly from the sun and from energy reflected from the Earth's surface. ▼

25% absorbed and reflected by clouds

20% absorbed and reflected by air

50% absorbed by Earth's surface

5% reflected by Earth's surface

Local Winds

Because the Earth's surface is heated unevenly, the air above it is in constant motion. Cold air is heavier than warm air, so it sinks, forcing lighter, warm air to rise. The upward movement of warm air in the atmosphere produces *updrafts*. You may have seen birds soaring on updrafts.

At the surface, two places can often have differences in temperature and, therefore, differences in air pressure. These differences cause air to move from the area of higher pressure to the area of lower pressure. This horizontal movement of air is called *wind*. Winds can be local, affecting small areas, or global, affecting large parts of the Earth.

Local winds depend on local changes in temperature. The illustrations below show an example of local winds at the seashore. During the day, the land heats up more quickly than the water does, so the breezes blow from the sea to the land. But at night, air over the water is warmer than air over the land, so the breezes blow from the land to the sea.

✔ What causes local winds?

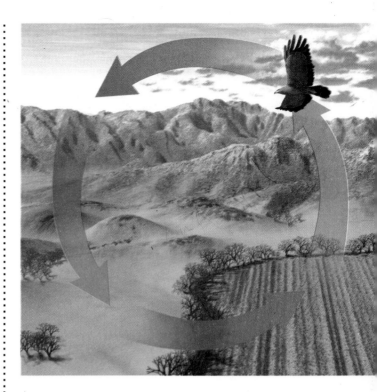

▲ Uneven heating of the Earth's surface produces air masses of different temperatures. Cold air sinks, forcing warm air to rise.

Prevailing Winds

In the age of sailing ships, sailors relied on prevailing winds to carry them across the oceans. **Prevailing winds** are global winds that blow constantly from the same direction. Prevailing winds are caused by the uneven heating of large parts of Earth's atmosphere and by Earth's rotation.

To understand prevailing winds, first suppose an Earth that doesn't rotate. The sun warms the air over the equator, while air over the North and South Poles is very cold. The cold, heavy polar air flows toward the equator, forcing an upward movement of the warmed air at the equator. This air then flows north and south toward the poles. Far from the equator, the warm air cools and sinks at the poles, where it once again flows toward the equator. This flow from the equator to the poles and then back again is continuous.

◀ During the day, the land heats up faster than the sea. Cooler sea air moves toward the land. This is called a sea breeze.

◀ At night, the land loses heat faster than the sea. Cooler air over the land moves toward the sea. This is called a land breeze.

Global Winds

The global winds that blow over most of the United States are the prevailing westerlies.

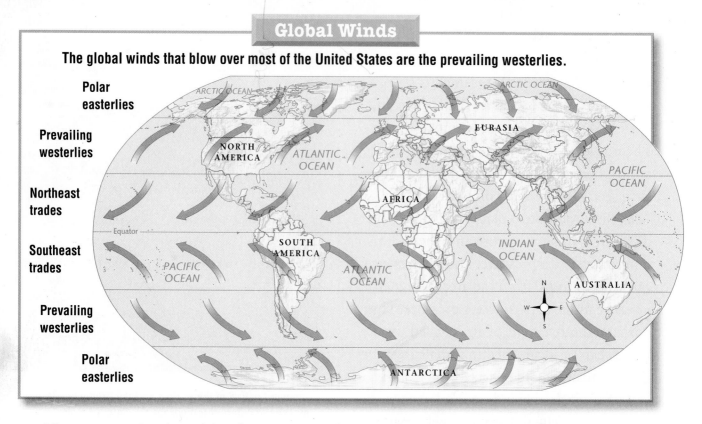

Polar easterlies

Prevailing westerlies

Northeast trades

Southeast trades

Prevailing westerlies

Polar easterlies

Now suppose Earth rotating from west to east. This rotation makes north and south winds curve. You can see this by placing a sheet of paper on a turntable. As the paper spins, try drawing a straight line from the center of the turntable to its edge.

Winds that blow toward the poles curve east. Winds that blow toward the equator curve west. In most of the United States, the prevailing winds curve to the east, producing west winds, or *westerlies*.

The prevailing westerlies cause most weather systems in the United States to move from west to east. Weather conditions on the West Coast today often move to the middle of the country tomorrow and from there to the East Coast the next day.

Weather Map

Weather in the United States usually moves from the west to the east. What kind of weather do you think Atlanta will have in the next day or so? Explain. ▶

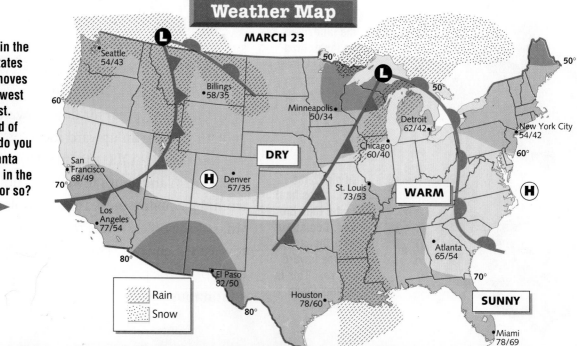

MARCH 23

Seattle 54/43
Billings 58/35
Minneapolis 50/34
Detroit 62/42
New York City 54/42
Chicago 60/40
San Francisco 68/49
Denver 57/35
St. Louis 73/53
WARM
Los Angeles 77/54
DRY
Atlanta 65/54
El Paso 82/50
Houston 78/60
SUNNY
Miami 78/69

Rain
Snow

Look at the weather map at the bottom of page C74. Weather forecasters use maps to show how weather systems move. Forecasters also use maps to help predict weather changes.

✓ **What causes weather systems to move from west to east?**

Summary

Changes in air pressure, from uneven heating of Earth's surface and the air above it, cause the wind to blow. Local winds depend on local changes in temperature. Prevailing, or global, winds are caused by the sun's uneven heating of large parts of the atmosphere and by Earth's rotation on its axis. Prevailing winds in the United States are from the west, so weather systems tend to move from west to east.

Review

1. How does uneven heating of Earth's surface produce wind?
2. Suppose you're at the seashore on a sunny summer day. In which direction is the wind blowing? Why?
3. How do the prevailing winds affect weather systems in the United States?
4. **Critical Thinking** Shortly after daybreak at the seashore, the air temperature over sea and land is about the same. What sort of wind, if any, is blowing? Explain.
5. **Test Prep** A weather map can be used to show —
   - **A** precipitation only
   - **B** how and where weather systems move
   - **C** local winds
   - **D** prevailing winds

LINKS

MATH LINK

Calculate About 35 percent of the sun's rays that reach the Earth are reflected back into space. Another 15 percent are absorbed or reflected by the atmosphere. What percentage of the sun's rays reach the Earth's surface?

WRITING LINK

Expressive Writing—Friendly Letter Suppose you are on vacation. Write a postcard describing the weather to a friend. Include temperature, wind speed, and wind direction.

MUSIC LINK

Weather Songs Many songs are about the weather or compare something to the weather. Some examples are "You Are My Sunshine," "The Itsy Bitsy Spider," and "Sunny Day." Work with a partner to see how many weather songs you can list.

TECHNOLOGY LINK

Learn more about weather conditions and predictions by investigating *Umbrella or Not?* on the **Harcourt Science Explorations CD-ROM.**

LESSON 3

What Is Climate and How Does It Change?

In this lesson, you can . . .

INVESTIGATE local weather conditions.

LEARN ABOUT climates and how they change.

LINK to math, writing, literature, and technology.

Local Weather Conditions

Activity Purpose Why does the temperature change as you go from the city to the country? Why is a city park cooler than nearby streets and sidewalks? You know that different parts of the country often have different weather conditions. In this investigation you'll find out if places very close to each other can have different weather conditions, too.

Materials

- 4 metersticks
- 4 weather stations

Activity Procedure

1 Make a table like the one shown on page C77.

2 Choose four locations near your school to study. Select different kinds of locations, such as a shady parkway, a sunny playground, a parking lot on the south side of your school, and a ball field on the north side. For the same time on any given day, **predict** whether the temperature, wind direction, and wind speed will be the same or different at the different locations.

3 At the chosen time, four people should each take a meterstick and a weather station to a different one of the selected locations. Use the meterstick to locate a point 1 m above the ground. **Measure** and **record** the temperature at that point. Use the weather station to determine the wind direction and speed, too. Record the data in your table. (Pictures A and B)

SCHOOL BUS

26

1031

Picture A

Picture B

4 Make a double-bar graph to show the temperatures and wind speeds recorded at all the locations. Write the wind direction at each location on the appropriate wind-speed bar.

Draw Conclusions

Local Weather Conditions				
	1	2	3	4
Location				
Temperature				
Wind Direction				
Wind Speed				

1. Use your table to **compare** the temperature, wind direction, and wind speed at the different locations. What differences, if any, did you find? What conditions were the same?

2. Local weather conditions affect the organisms that live in a location. Do you think wind speed or temperature is more likely to affect living organisms? Explain.

3. Based on your investigation, how would you define the phrase *local weather conditions*?

4. **Scientists at Work** Scientists learn about local weather conditions by **comparing** weather data from different locations. **Draw conclusions** about local weather conditions, based on the locations you studied.

Investigate Further What other factors, in addition to temperature, wind direction, and wind speed, might affect local weather conditions? **Hypothesize** about a factor that might affect local weather conditions. Then **plan and conduct a simple investigation** to test your hypothesis.

> **Process Skill Tip**
>
> You **compare** before you **draw conclusions** about what is the same and what is different about weather conditions in different locations.

Climates and How They Change

Climate

FIND OUT

- what determines a climate
- how human activity can affect climate

VOCABULARY

climate
microclimate
El Niño
greenhouse effect
global warming

The weather in your area probably changes from day to day and from season to season. Yet year after year many of the same weather conditions are repeated. These repeating conditions, or patterns, make up your area's climate. **Climate** is the average of all weather conditions through all seasons over a period of time. Temperature and precipitation are the major factors that determine climate. Wind speed and direction are also factors.

Temperature is also a major factor of microclimates. A **microclimate** is the climate of a very small area. You probably pass several microclimates on your way to school each day. If you live in a city, you may know that a wooded park has a cooler, wetter climate than a parking lot has. Observing microclimates, as you did in the investigation, is a good way to learn about climates.

These photos of Mount Wheeler, in New Mexico, show different climates on the slope of a high mountain. Notice that, in addition to certain weather conditions, each climate has its own typical plants and animals adapted to living in that climate.

✔ **What is climate?**

At the top of the mountain, you will find a cold, dry climate with few trees or animals. ▼

▲ On the sides of the mountain, the climate is cool and moist, and there are tall trees and forest animals.

▲ At the base of the mountain, the climate is warm and dry. Desert animals and plants such as sagebrush live there.

The coast of northern Maine is covered with snow in the winter. The average daily temperature is in the 20s.

On the Outer Banks of North Carolina, winter temperatures may reach the 40s or 50s.

ATLANTIC OCEAN

Gulf of Mexico

In Florida the average daily temperature in winter is in the 60s or 70s.

Climate and Latitude

The United States has many different climates. There is the cold, *polar* climate of northern Alaska and the hot, *tropical* climate of Hawai'i and Puerto Rico. Most of the country has more moderate, or *temperate*, climates. But among temperate climates, there are big differences in average temperature and precipitation. Along the East Coast of the United States, for example, average temperatures vary quite a bit—from Florida, in the south, to Maine, in the north. These temperature differences are determined by *latitude*, or the distance a place is from the equator.

Most areas near the equator have tropical climates. There the sun is directly overhead nearly all year, which causes intense heating of the Earth's surface. Farther from the equator, in temperate climates, the sun is directly overhead only part of the year, causing less heating of the Earth's surface. These temperate climates have warm summers but cold winters. Near the poles the sun is never directly overhead. The decreased heating of the Earth's surface at latitudes far from the equator results in cold, polar climates.

In addition to latitude, precipitation causes differences among temperate climates. Most of the East Coast receives a lot of precipitation, allowing thick forests to grow. Farther west there is less precipitation. There are fewer trees and more grasslands, which require less water. Still farther west the grasslands give way to even drier, more desertlike climates that receive very little precipitation.

✔ **Why does Florida have a warmer average temperature than Maine?**

Polar Zone
Cold all year; light precipitation

Mountain Zone
Cold winters, cool summers; moderate to heavy precipitation

Temperate Zone
Cold winters, warm summers; moderate precipitation

Tropical Zone
Hot all year; moderate to heavy precipitation

Desert Zone
Hot summers, cool winters; light precipitation

World Climates

So many factors affect an area's climate that no two places on Earth have exactly the same climate. Anything that affects temperature or precipitation affects climate.

Climate is also affected by prevailing winds. In the United States, the prevailing westerlies help to moderate the hot summer climate by pushing cooling air masses across the country.

Ocean currents can affect climate, too. On the West Coast, the cold California Current flows south from the North Pacific. It keeps the summers cool along the coastal areas of Washington, Oregon, and northern California.

Yet another factor that affects climate is the shape of the land itself. A mountain can have a wet climate on the side facing the prevailing winds and a dry climate on the other side.

Although no two places on Earth have exactly the same climate, Earth's climates can be grouped into five major zones—polar, mountain, temperate, tropical, and desert. Each zone has its own weather patterns and its own typical kinds of life. For example, a polar climate supports small plants and animals like the polar bear. A tropical climate supports lush forests and animals such as monkeys.

✔ **What are the five climate zones?**

Climate Changes

Have you ever heard an older relative say, "When I was young, the winters were much colder than they are now. Why, some days the snow was piled up to the windows."

Your relative may be right. Climate does change over time. Scientists have been measuring the Earth's winds, temperatures, and precipitation for many years. Based on this data and other evidence, they know that Earth's climate is slowly warming. As recently as 50 or 60 years ago, average temperatures in parts of the United States were a degree or two cooler than they are now.

Earth's climate hasn't always been warming up. About 20,000 years ago, Earth was in the middle of an Ice Age. When the climate cools enough, large areas of Earth are covered by sheets of ice, or *glaciers*. Earth has gone through many Ice Ages. During the most recent one, glaciers covered 30 percent of Earth's surface. Evidence of this period can still be seen in the glaciers of Greenland and the Canadian Rockies.

At other times, Earth has had a warmer climate than it does today. Look at the graph to see how Earth's temperature has increased and decreased over time.

▲ One effect of El Niño's heavy rains is mudslides.

▲ During most winters, the weather in California is mild and cool, with only moderate precipitation.

Sometimes Earth's climate changes for just a year or so. The **El Niño** (EL NEEN•yoh) effect is a short-term climate change. Every two to ten years, weather conditions around the Pacific Ocean change dramatically because of changing ocean currents. The normally wet countries of Southeast Asia become dry, while heavy rains fall on the normally dry western coasts of Mexico and California. The photographs above show California during a normal winter and during a winter of heavy El Niño rains.

✓ **What evidence is there that Earth's climate is constantly changing?**

Changes in Earth's temperature might be caused by a change in the size or shape of Earth's orbit or a change in the tilt of Earth's axis.

To determine which areas of North America were once covered by ice, scientists look for evidence of glacial erosion and deposition.

Ice Age

Warmer
Less Ice

Cooler
More Ice

500 400 300 200 100 Today
Thousands of Years Ago

Ice cover 18,000 years ago

Ice cover 10,000 years ago

Ice cover today

Ice Age coastline

Humans Affect Climate

You know that a city is warmer than the surrounding countryside. In fact, city temperatures may be as much as 8°C (15°F) warmer than surrounding areas. Cities are warmer for several reasons. Buildings, roads, and sidewalks hold heat longer than trees and grass. Cars, buses, and trucks increase city temperatures. Large buildings block winds that might otherwise blow warm air away. All of these factors combine to make a city an area of warm air surrounded by cooler air, or a *heat island.*

Warm air also results from an effect of the burning of fossil fuels such as gasoline. Fossil fuels give off carbon dioxide when burned. Carbon dioxide in the atmosphere absorbs some of the heat given off by Earth. This process, commonly called the **greenhouse effect**, is necessary for life. Without carbon dioxide and other gases in the atmosphere, all of Earth's heat would go off into space, leaving the planet too cold for life. However, too much carbon dioxide in the air may cause climate changes.

Many scientists hypothesize that excess carbon dioxide will lead to **global warming**,

an abnormally rapid rise in Earth's average temperature. If Earth's average temperature rises just a few more degrees, the polar ice-caps will begin to melt. The melting ice will raise the sea level around the world, flooding many coastal cities.

▲ The level of carbon dioxide (CO_2) in the atmosphere has increased over the past century.

▼ Earth's average temperature over the past century has increased at about the same rate.

Cities have microclimates that are affected by humans. One reason is that a city has buildings, roads, and vehicles that hold or produce heat.

To reduce this possibility, many countries have agreed to try to reduce the amount of carbon dioxide released into the atmosphere. One way to do this is to burn less fossil fuel.

✔ **What are some ways in which humans affect climate?**

Summary

Climate is the average of all weather conditions through all seasons over a period of time. Temperature and precipitation are the major factors that determine climate. Earth's climate has changed over time as average temperatures have risen and fallen. Human activities, such as burning fossil fuels, can affect climate.

Review

1. What is the difference between climate and microclimate?
2. List four factors that affect climate.
3. What causes an Ice Age?
4. **Critical Thinking** During an Ice Age, what is likely to happen to the levels of oceans around the world?
5. **Test Prep** Burning fossil fuels affects climate by —
   A reducing the number of trees
   B decreasing the amount of sunlight that reaches Earth's surface
   C raising Earth's average temperature
   D changing the prevailing winds

LINKS

MATH LINK

Estimation Look at the graph on page C82 showing global temperature variations. Find the highest and lowest values. Estimate how much Earth's average temperature has varied over the last 100 years.

WRITING LINK

Persuasive Writing—Request Do you think the recent measurements of Earth's temperatures are really evidence of global warming? Write a persuasive letter to the editor of a newspaper, requesting that your point of view be printed. Be sure to include facts to support your point of view.

LITERATURE LINK

Earthmaker's Tales Read *Earthmaker's Tales: North American Indian Stories About Earth Happenings* by Gretchen Will Mayo. Earth and its atmosphere are the subjects of this collection of Native American legends about the origins of thunder, tornadoes, and other weather features.

TECHNOLOGY LINK

Learn more about changes in climate by viewing *El Niño Erosion* and *Global Warming* on the **Harcourt Science Newsroom Video.**

Major Events in Weather Forecasting

In ancient times, weather predictions were based on superstitions. It seemed to make sense that good weather depended on the happiness of the gods. Yet as early as the year 100, Egyptian scientists showed that air expanded when it was heated. This early discovery led to other advances in meteorology, the study of weather.

Observing Weather Systems

In 1735 scientists observed that the sun heated areas near the equator more strongly than areas north or south of the equator. They also discovered that as air above the equator expands, it moves toward the cooler latitudes. This movement results in a global wind pattern, which causes a global weather pattern.

This discovery was followed by the discovery of the "trade winds" north and south of the equator and other wind zones in the Northern Hemisphere. In 1835 French physicist Gustave Coriolis described the movement of air masses north and south of the equator. He showed how winds north or south of the equator curve in different directions. Coriolis realized that these curved air routes were caused by the rotation of Earth.

Modern Forecasting

Wind vanes had long been used to determine wind direction, but it wasn't until the 1600s that instruments were invented that could accurately measure other weather conditions. In 1644 the first barometer was

The History of Weather Forecasting

350 B.C.
Aristotle writes *Meteorologica,* a book about weather observations.

1835
Coriolis discovers what is later called the "Coriolis Effect."

1902
Scientists discover that the atmosphere has layers. The troposphere and stratosphere are identified.

400 B.C.   A.D. 1600   A.D. 1700   A.D. 1800

1600
Early weather instruments are invented.

1849
The first weather report sent by telegraph is received by Joseph Henry, secretary of the Smithsonian Institution.

1890
Congress forms an agency called the Weather Bureau, later renamed the National Weather Service.

made. In 1754 G. D. Fahrenheit made the first mercury thermometer.

At least 100 years ago, scientists knew that they could improve their forecasts if they had measurements from enough weather stations around the world. Today there are tens of thousands of weather stations. Each station takes many measurements—temperature, humidity, cloud cover, wind speed and direction, and barometric pressure. Modern communication systems allow scientists to share this information almost instantly. This allows warnings to be issued to people who might be affected by severe weather events.

Weather satellites, first launched in the 1960s, provide the most important data for modern weather forecasting. Satellite data helps scientists understand the global forces that cause local weather conditions. Today countries around the world share satellite weather data.

THINK ABOUT IT

1. What causes winds to curve?
2. What is the most important instrument for weather forecasters today? Explain.

Jacob Bjerknes discovered the warm current, called El Niño, that sometimes produces severe weather along the Pacific coast.

1950s
Bjerknes makes the connection between the El Niño current and certain reversed weather patterns.

1980s
Doppler radar is first used.

A.D. 1900 — A.D. 2000

1960s
The first weather satellites are launched.

NIMBUS SPACECRAFT

1990s
International cooperation and the use of satellites increases understanding of worldwide weather patterns.

Carolyn Kloth

METEOROLOGIST

"A lot of people tend to think that you need to be able to look out of a window to assess the weather. With the use of radar, weather satellites, and all of the other weather data available, you can do the job almost anywhere."

From the time she was in elementary school, Carolyn Kloth knew what she wanted to do—fly airplanes and chase storms. Today Ms. Kloth is doing both of these things as a pilot and a meteorologist at the National Severe Storms Forecast Center in Kansas City, Missouri. She specializes in tracking severe thunderstorms and giving information about them to airplane pilots.

At the severe storms center, Ms. Kloth receives weather data every hour from across North America. The data includes images of cloud patterns, locations of fronts, and the number of lightning strikes. She also studies measurements of air pressure, humidity, precipitation, and temperature, both at the ground and at various levels in the atmosphere. Once all the data has come in, Ms. Kloth uses computers to analyze it. Then she predicts where severe thunderstorms are likely to form across the continent and over nearby coastal waters.

Ms. Kloth issues severe storm warnings to pilots for any storm that has winds of more than 26 m/s, hail larger than 19 mm in diameter, or clouds that may form tornadoes. She finds that about 1 percent of all thunderstorms fit into one or more of those categories. The warnings that Ms. Kloth issues help pilots avoid thunderstorms and result in safer and more comfortable flights.

THINK ABOUT IT

1. How can Ms. Kloth gather weather data without looking out a window?
2. How do you think Ms. Kloth's experience as a pilot helps her in her job at the National Severe Storms Forecast Center?

A large storm system

Air Pressure

How strong is air pressure?

Materials

- plastic sandwich bag
- drinking straw
- tape
- heavy book

Procedure

1. Put one end of the straw in the plastic bag. Then seal the bag shut with tape.

2. Put the plastic bag on a table and lay the book on part of the bag as shown.

3. Blow through the straw into the bag, and observe what happens.

Draw Conclusions

Describe what happened to the bag and the book. Explain what happened. Try to think of a situation where air pressure could be used like this.

Sidewalk Graph

How does sunlight speed up evaporation?

Materials

- sunny sidewalk
- 500 mL water
- chalk
- clock

Procedure

1. Pour about 500 mL of water onto a sidewalk that is in full sunlight.

2. Draw a line around the outside of the puddle with the chalk.

3. Draw a new line around the puddle every 5 min for 20 min.

4. Repeat the experiment on a sidewalk in the shade.

Draw Conclusions

Compare the sizes of the puddles at each 5-min interval. Based on your observations, predict how long it would take for each puddle to evaporate.

Chapter 3 Review and Test Preparation

Vocabulary Review

Use the terms below to complete the sentences. The page numbers in ( ) tell you where to look in the chapter if you need help.

atmosphere (C64) **prevailing winds** (C73)
air pressure (C65) **climate** (C78)
humidity (C65) **microclimate** (C78)
precipitation (C65) **El Niño** (C81)
evaporation (C67) **greenhouse effect** (C82)
condensation (C67) **global warming** (C82)
local winds (C73)

1. Liquid water changes to water vapor through the process of ____. Water vapor turns back into liquid drops of water through the process of ____.

2. Almost all weather occurs in the lowest layer of the ____.

3. Rain or snow is called ____.

4. Water in the air is called ____.

5. The weight of air is known as ____.

6. Global winds that blow constantly from the same direction are known as ____.

7. Winds that depend on local changes in temperature are called ____.

8. The climate of a small area is called a ____.

9. The average of an area's weather conditions through all seasons over a period of time is called ____.

10. Excess carbon dioxide in the atmosphere may lead to ____.

11. The process by which carbon dioxide in the atmosphere absorbs some of the heat given off by Earth is called the ____.

12. One example of a short-term climate change is ____.

Connect Concepts

Copy and complete the idea clusters below, which describe weather and climate.

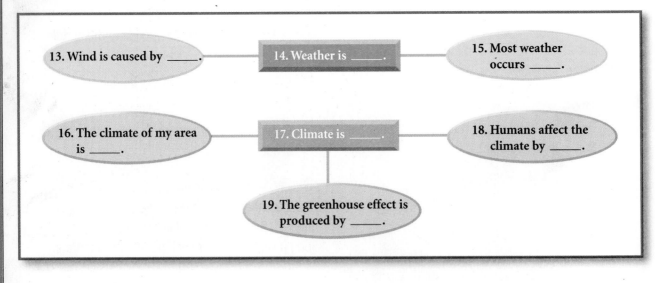

13. Wind is caused by ____.

14. Weather is ____.

15. Most weather occurs ____.

16. The climate of my area is ____.

17. Climate is ____.

18. Humans affect the climate by ____.

19. The greenhouse effect is produced by ____.

Check Understanding

Write the letter of the best choice.

20. As air warms, —

    A air pressure increases

    B air pressure decreases

    C temperature decreases

    D humidity changes

21. A wind vane indicates —

    F air pressure   **H** humidity

    G wind speed   **J** wind direction

22. Wind is caused when air —

    A moves from the land to the sea

    B moves from the sea to the land

    C moves from an area of higher pressure to an area of lower pressure

    D moves from an area of lower pressure to an area of higher pressure

23. Prevailing winds are caused by the uneven heating of Earth's atmosphere and by —

    F local winds   **H** Earth's rotation

    G air pressure   **J** temperature

24. Florida has a warmer climate than Maine because Florida —

    A is closer to the South Pole

    B is closer to the equator

    C is nearer to the Atlantic Ocean

    D receives more precipitation

25. Most of the eastern United States and the West Coast have a climate that is —

    F mountain   **H** desert

    G polar   **J** temperate

Critical Thinking

26. How does the location of Hawai'i, near the equator, affect its climate?

27. Suppose you live in the middle of the United States and are looking at a weather map. To the north and east of your location, it is raining. To the west and south, the weather is clear. What sort of weather can you expect tomorrow? Explain.

Process Skills Review

28. A thermometer measures air temperature. A barometer measures air pressure. A hygrometer measures humidity, and a rain gauge measures precipitation. Which two of these instruments are most useful for the **measurements** that determine a region's climate? Explain.

29. Which would you **predict** would heat up faster on a sunny day—a pond or a meadow? Explain.

30. **Compare** weather and climate.

Performance Assessment

Your Weather and Climate

Look at a map of the United States. Explain where weather in your area comes from. Describe any local conditions that affect the weather. Then identify the climate zone in which you are located—polar, tropical, temperate, desert, or mountain. Explain what determines your climate zone.

4

Exploring the Oceans

If you've ever been to the beach, it may have seemed to you that the water always moves toward the shore. But the movement of ocean water is more complex than that. In addition to causing waves, winds make ocean waters move in great loops around the world.

FAST FACT

In 1947 Thor Heyerdahl crossed the Pacific Ocean on a raft he named *Kon-Tiki*. He wanted to prove that natives of South America could have traveled thousands of miles to the islands of Polynesia by riding on ocean currents.

Vocabulary Preview

wave
current
tide
shore
estuary
headland
tide pool
jetty
scuba
submersible
sonar
desalination

How Do Ocean Waters Move?

In this lesson, you can . . .

INVESTIGATE waves.

LEARN ABOUT the movement of ocean waters.

LINK to math, writing, language arts, and technology.

Waves

Activity Purpose Have you ever stood on a beach and watched the ocean? If so, you probably noticed that the water is always moving in waves. Waves can also move across a lake or a pond. You can even **observe** very small waves, called ripples, on a puddle. What causes waves? In the investigation, you will **use a model** of the ocean to find out.

Materials
- rectangular pan
- water
- straw

Activity Procedure

1 **Make a model** of the ocean by half-filling the pan with water. (Picture A)

2 Place your straw near one side of the pan, and gently blow across the surface of the water. What happens? (Picture B)

◀ Wind and waves work together to make windsurfing an exciting sport.

Picture A

Picture B

3 **Observe** the height and speed of the waves you make. **Record** your observations.

4 Repeat Step 2 several times, blowing a little harder each time. What do you **observe** about the waves you make? **Record** your observations.

Draw Conclusions

1. Use your observations to describe the relationship between how hard you blow and the height and speed of the waves.

2. From what you observed in this activity, what can you **infer** about the cause of waves on oceans and other bodies of water?

3. **Scientists at Work** Scientists often **use models** to learn about things they cannot **observe** directly. What did your model help you observe about waves?

Investigate Further **Predict** how high the waves on a pond, a lake, or the ocean will be on a calm day and on a stormy day. Then test your predictions by **using a model**.

Process Skill Tip

Observing is the most basic science skill. You **observe** when you use your senses to note the properties of an object or event, such as the effect of moving air on water.

How Ocean Waters Move

Wind and Waves

VOCABULARY

wave
current
tide

The waters of the ocean never stop moving. Most of the movement of water on the ocean's surface is due to waves. A **wave** is the up-and-down movement of surface water.

In the investigation you observed that wind produces waves. In fact, most waves are caused by wind. When wind blows over the surface of a body of water, it causes the surface of the water to move with it. Because water moves more slowly than air, the water piles up, forming a ripple. The wind then pushes on the side of the ripple, making it grow in height, and turning the ripple into a wave.

In the investigation you also observed that the height of a wave is related to how hard the wind blows. On a calm day, ocean waves may be less than 1.5 m (about 5 ft) high. But during a storm, waves can reach heights of 30 m (about 100 ft). That's as high as a ten-story building!

Even though the water in a wave may rise and fall by as much as 30 m, very little of the water moves forward. What moves across the ocean's surface is energy. Think about this: When you shake a rope, the rope moves up and down or side to side as waves travel to the

Water in a wave moves in circles, returning to about the place where it started.

end of the rope. But the rope itself doesn't move forward. This motion is similar to what happens to water in the ocean. The waves move across the surface of the water, but the water stays in almost the same place.

✓ **What causes most waves in water?**

Other Kinds of Waves

Most ocean waves are caused by wind. But some waves can be caused by earthquakes and volcanoes, extremely low air pressure, or several things acting together.

Some of the biggest waves in the oceans are caused by earthquakes and volcanoes. These giant waves are called *tsunamis* (soo•NAH•meez). In the deep ocean, a tsunami may be more than 100 km (about 62 mi) long but less than 1 m (about 3 ft) high. These waves pass under ships without being noticed. But when a tsunami reaches a shore, friction with the ocean bottom slows the wave. This causes the wave to grow to as much as 25 m (about 82 ft), destroying everything in its path.

During hurricanes and tropical storms, large domes of water called *storm surges*

Hurricane winds produce huge waves that East Coast surfers enjoy before the storm arrives.

form. Low air pressure at the storm's center causes ocean water to rise. Strong winds form huge waves on top of the storm surge, and they push this high water ahead of the storm. If the storm is moving toward land, it may send a wall of water up to 10 m (about 33 ft) high crashing onto the beach.

Another kind of wave is called a rogue (ROHG) wave. This is a huge wave, much higher than the waves around it. Many rogue waves form when large storm waves join together.

✓ **Name three different kinds of waves, and tell what causes them.**

Tsunamis, such as the one that hit Hilo, Hawai'i, in 1946, cause great damage to buildings along the shore. ▼

Even large boats can be sunk by rogue waves. ▼

Currents

Although waves are the most easily seen kind of ocean movement, currents move much more water. An ocean **current** is a stream of water that flows like a river through the ocean. Unlike waves, currents actually move water forward, sometimes for long distances.

Large ocean currents, known as *surface currents*, flow across the surface of the oceans. Surface currents are usually caused by prevailing winds. As a prevailing wind blows across the surface of the ocean, the water begins to move as a stream. Some surface currents can be hundreds of kilometers wide and hundreds of meters deep. A single one of these "ocean rivers" can move more water than the Amazon, the largest river in the world.

A surface current can carry cold water to warm regions. It can also carry warm water to cold regions. One surface current is the Gulf Stream. This warm current flows northeast from the Caribbean Sea, past the East Coast of the United States, and across the North Atlantic. Even after its long trip across the cold Atlantic, there is enough warm water in this current to warm the climate of Great Britain and northern Europe. That's why palm trees can grow along the southern coast of England.

The warm waters of the Gulf Stream are shown in orange and red in this satellite photograph. Colder waters are shown in green and blue. ▼

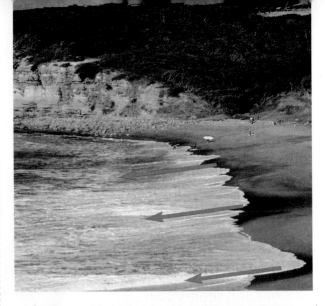

▲ Rip currents (red arrows) may flow away from a beach at 8 km/h (about 5 mi/h). If you get caught in a rip current, swim parallel to the shore until you move out of the current. The water on both sides of the rip current flows toward the beach.

Surface currents aren't the only currents flowing through the oceans. *Shoreline currents* are local currents that run along the coast. Local winds and shifting beach materials may cause shoreline currents to change from day to day.

A *rip current* is a shoreline current that flows away from the beach. A rip current is often caused by a sand spit, a long ridge of sand that forms offshore near a beach. Ocean waves flow over the sand spit and toward the beach. But water from the waves can't flow back over the sand spit. The water piles up, trapped by the sand spit, until a small break opens up in the sand spit. The water then flows rapidly out through the opening, producing a strong current.

When waves strike a shore at an angle, they move water forward along the shore. This movement of water parallel to the beach produces another type of shoreline current, called a longshore current. Longshore currents carry large amounts of beach materials from one place to another.

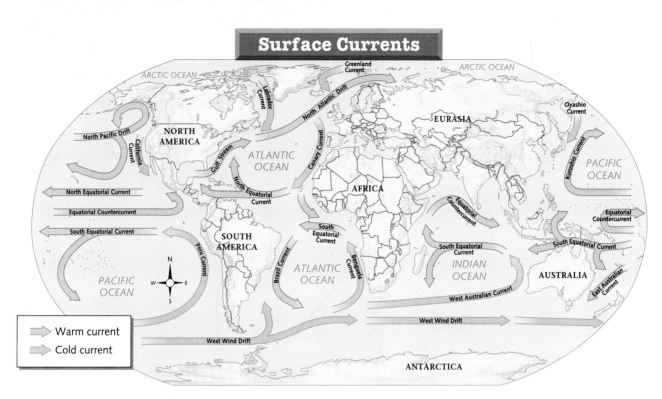

Surface Currents

This diagram shows how surface currents move. The red arrows show warm water, and the blue arrows show cold water.

Although wind blowing across the surface of an ocean can produce currents, these currents don't continue moving in the same direction as the wind. Earth's rotation causes ocean currents to bend to the right in the Northern Hemisphere and to the left in the Southern Hemisphere. The currents start moving in giant circles.

Not all ocean currents are caused by wind. Deep-ocean currents are caused by differences in water temperature. Cold water is heavier than warm water, so it sinks. The cold water then flows along the bottom of the ocean.

✓ **What causes ocean currents?**

▲ As a deep-ocean current rises to the surface, it carries nutrients that can support large amounts of sea life.

Cold deep-ocean currents move 3 to 4 km (about 2 to 3 mi) beneath the surface. As this cold water flows, some of it warms slowly and is pushed to the surface by even colder water underneath. ▶

C97

Tides

Once or twice each day, ocean water rises and falls at every beach around the world. This repeated rise and fall in the level of the ocean is called the **tide**. Tides are caused by the pull of gravity of the sun and the moon on Earth's waters. Since the moon is closer to Earth than the sun, it has a greater effect on tides than the sun does.

The pull of the moon combines with Earth's rotation to produce traveling bulges of water. The moon's pull on the oceans is strongest on the side of Earth facing the moon. This causes Earth's shape to become slightly oval. Solid parts of Earth change very little. But the oceans bulge out on the side of Earth nearest the moon and on the side farthest from the moon. As Earth rotates, it pulls these bulges along.

The bulges of water on either side of Earth are called *high tides*. Low-water levels

▲ Very high tides occur every 14 days when the moon and sun line up. Weaker tides occur when the moon, the sun, and the Earth form a right angle.

between high tides are called *low tides*. Most coastal areas have one or two low tides and one or two high tides every 24 hours. Low and high tides occur at regular times, which can be predicted. The table shows high and

In the Bay of Fundy, between Maine and Nova Scotia, the difference between high and low tides can be as much as 20 m (about 66 ft)!

Tides for the Bay of Fundy

Date	Time	Ht.	Time	Ht.	Time	Ht.	Time	Ht.
1/15/1999	0354	5.4	1003	24.7	1623	3.8	2232	23.6
1/16/1999	0437	4.8	1045	25.2	1705	3.3	2313	24.1
1/17/1999	0519	4.4	1126	25.6	1746	2.8	2354	24.5
1/18/1999	0600	4.0	1206	25.9	1826	2.4		
1/19/1999	0034	24.8	0642	3.7	1247	26.0	1908	2.2
1/20/1999	0115	25.0	0725	3.5	1329	26.0	1950	2.2
1/21/1999	0158	25.1	0810	3.5	1414	25.7	2035	2.4

low tides during one week in Canada's Bay of Fundy. The Bay of Fundy is famous for its extremely high and low tides, so knowing when tides will occur is very important for boaters.

✓ **What causes tides?**

Summary

The ocean is in constant motion. Ocean waters move as waves, currents, and tides. Most waves are caused by wind. Currents are streams of water caused by winds or differences in water temperature. Tides are caused by the gravitational pull of the moon and sun on Earth's oceans.

Review

1. How does the water in an ocean wave move?

2. Compare the causes of surface currents with those of deep-ocean currents.

3. How do the moon's gravity and Earth's rotation affect tides?

4. **Critical Thinking** For a science fair project, a student dissolves food coloring in a cup of cold water. Then the student pours the cold, colored water into a glass of warm water. **Predict** what will happen to the colored water. Explain your prediction.

5. **Test Prep** Tides are caused by —

   A ocean currents

   B waves and the prevailing winds

   C the gravitational pull of the moon and sun on the oceans

   D hurricanes and other tropical storms

LINKS

MATH LINK

Calculate Look at the tide table on page C98. Find the tides for January 20. At what times will high tide occur on that day? About how many hours apart are the two high tides?

WRITING LINK

Narrative Writing—Story Do some research about an ocean current. Where does the current begin? Where does it go? What does the current carry? How does the current affect the lands it touches? Then write a short story for your teacher about the current.

LANGUAGE ARTS LINK

Editing After you finish the first draft of your story about an ocean current, trade stories with a classmate for comments and corrections. Mark any errors in spelling or grammar. Then look for parts of the story that you like. Look also for parts that could be more exciting or that need to be explained better. Write any comments on the manuscript and give it back to your classmate.

TECHNOLOGY LINK

Learn more about the effects of waves and currents by visiting this Smithsonian Institution Internet site. **www.si.edu/harcourt/science**

Smithsonian Institution®

How Do Oceans Interact with the Land?

In this lesson, you can . . .

INVESTIGATE the effect of waves on a beach.

LEARN ABOUT how the oceans affect the shoreline.

LINK to math, writing, technology, and other areas.

INVESTIGATE

The Effect of Waves on a Beach

Activity Purpose Every day ocean waves keep pounding against the shore. How do waves change a shore? In this activity you will **make a model** so you can **observe** the effect of waves on a beach.

Materials
- stream table
- sand
- water

Activity Procedure

1 Use sand to **make a model** of a beach at one end of the stream table. The beach should have a gentle slope. (Picture A)

2 Slowly add water to the stream table until it is about half full. Try not to disturb the beach.

 Ocean waves will soon destroy this sand castle.

Picture A

Picture B

3 Make a wave by lifting the sand end of the stream table about 2 cm above the tabletop and then dropping it. What do you **observe** about the beach and the water? Repeat this several times. **Record** your observations.

4 Repeat Steps 1–3, but this time build a beach that is much steeper than the first one. **Record** your observations. (Picture B)

Draw Conclusions

1. Use your observations to explain how waves affect a beach.

2. Does the slope of the beach matter? Explain.

3. **Scientists at Work** Scientists often **make a model** to study how natural processes work. How did your model help you **observe** how waves affect a beach? What couldn't you observe about wave action with your model?

Investigate Further If possible, study the shore of a pond, a lake, or an ocean in your area. What do you **observe** about the shore? What questions do you have about how waves affect the shore? **Plan and conduct a simple investigation** to help you answer your questions. Decide what equipment you will need to use in your investigation.

Process Skill Tip

Not everyone can **observe** firsthand the effect of waves. But you can **make a model** to help you understand just how waves affect a beach.

C101

How Ocean Waters Shape the Shore

FIND OUT

- how ocean waves and currents shape the shore

- how human activities can change the shore

VOCABULARY

shore
estuary
headland
tide pool
jetty

At the Shore

The area from where waves begin to break to the highest place they reach on the beach is called the shore. The **shore** is the area where the ocean and land meet and interact. Anyone who has lived near the ocean knows that the shore is a place of constant change.

As you saw in the investigation, waves change the shore in several ways. One is by grinding pebbles and rocks against the shore. This action erodes the bottoms of cliffs, causing them to break apart and fall into the ocean. Another way waves change the shore is through water pressure. Each breaking wave hurls tons of water at the shore. This water pressure loosens pebbles and small rocks, which the outgoing waves carry into the ocean. Finally, because seawater is a weak acid, it slowly dissolves rock along the shore.

Sandpipers, sea gulls, and sand crabs look for food in beach materials deposited by waves and currents.

An **estuary** forms at the mouth of a river. Estuaries are usually rich in animal and plant life. These mangrove tree roots provide food and shelter for fish, shrimp, and crabs.

A sand spit forms where beach material is pulled sideways by waves and currents.

Where a shore is made of both soft rock and hard rock, erosion is uneven. Soft rock erodes faster than hard rock. Wave action may destroy the soft rock, forming small bays like those shown below. As the soft rock is washed away, the hard rock may be left as a rocky point, or **headland**. Sometimes the ocean cuts sea caves into a headland. If waves continue to erode the sea caves, a sea arch may form.

Currents also change a shore. If you've ever been swimming in the ocean, you may have noticed that when you came out of the water, you had to walk up and along the beach to the place where you left your towel. A longshore current carried you down the beach.

Longshore currents also move sand, pebbles, and shells along the shore. In places where the shore changes direction, a longshore current slows down and deposits beach materials. A new beach is formed, or the existing beach receives new sand and pebbles.

✔ **How do waves and currents change the shore?**

A **tide pool** is a pool of seawater found along a rocky shoreline. At high tide the pool is under water. This tide pool in California provides a habitat for a great variety of plants and animals.

Two sea caves have further eroded to form a sea arch like this one on Anacapa Island, in Channel Islands National Park, California.

Human Activities Affect the Shore

Human activities also change the shore. People in coastal communities often build structures to protect their beaches from erosion. These structures can block longshore currents and change the natural processes that erode and build up a shore.

At Cape Hatteras, along the coast of North Carolina, the Atlantic Ocean has eroded the beach so much that the lighthouse there was in danger of falling into the sea. The Cape Hatteras Lighthouse is one of the most famous lighthouses in the United States. To save the lighthouse, three jetties were built along the water's edge to catch sand and build up the beach. A **jetty** is a wall-like structure made of rocks that sticks out into the ocean.

A jetty protects a beach by trapping sand and pebbles that normally flow down the coast with the longshore current. But jetties can also harm beaches. Although the beach the jetty protects receives extra sand,

These jetties were built to protect this beach from erosion. ▼

The Cape Hatteras Lighthouse was built in 1870 after many ships had sunk in the so-called Graveyard of the Atlantic. ▼

This was the Cape Hatteras Lighthouse in 1998. On parts of Hatteras Island, ocean waves wash away 4.3 m (about 15 ft) of beach each year. ▶

beaches down the shore may lose their supply of sand and actually erode faster.

Cape Hatteras Lighthouse is safe for now. The lighthouse was moved farther from the ocean in 1999.

✔ **How do human activities affect the shore?**

Summary

The shore is changed by waves, currents, and human activities. Waves erode beaches and cliffs. Longshore currents deposit beach materials such as sand, pebbles, and shells along the shore. Jetties and other structures can affect the natural processes of shore change.

Review

1. How do waves erode beaches and cliffs?
2. How does a longshore current affect the shore?
3. What are two ways in which a jetty can affect a shore?
4. **Critical Thinking** A pier is built sticking out into the ocean. After a few years, sand builds up along one side of the pier. Explain why.
5. **Test Prep** An estuary is an area rich in plant and animal life that forms —
   A along a sandbar
   B along a jetty
   C at a headland
   D at the mouth of a river

Padre Island, Texas, is a wide, beautiful barrier island. A barrier island is a long ridge of sand in the ocean running parallel to the shore. A barrier island gets its name from the fact that it blocks ocean waves and storm surges, protecting the low coastal mainland.

LINKS

MATH LINK

Estimation The Atlantic Ocean is eroding parts of Hatteras Island at the rate of 4.3 m per year. Estimate how many years it will take for 30 m of the island to be eroded.

WRITING LINK

Persuasive Writing—Opinion Take a stand for or against building jetties to save a beach. Prepare notes for a short speech explaining your point of view. Be sure to include facts and drawings or photographs to support your position. Present your speech to your classmates.

ART LINK

Shore Diagram Draw a picture showing how the ocean both erodes and builds up beaches.

SOCIAL STUDIES LINK

Shore Map Find a shore in your state to map. If you don't live near an ocean, map a large lake. Show natural features such as bays, estuaries, and beaches.

TECHNOLOGY LINK

Learn more about the interactions of the ocean and the shore by visiting this Smithsonian Institution Internet site. **www.si.edu/harcourt/science**

 Smithsonian Institution®

LESSON 3

How Do People Explore the Oceans and Use Ocean Resources?

In this lesson, you can . . .

 INVESTIGATE how scientists measure ocean depths.

 LEARN ABOUT how people explore the oceans and use ocean resources.

LINK to math, writing, literature, and technology.

This copper diving helmet was first used in about 1819. ▷

C106

How Scientists Measure Ocean Depths

Activity Purpose In 1521 Portuguese explorer Ferdinand Magellan tried to measure the depth of the Pacific Ocean. He dropped 730 m (about 2400 ft) of weighted rope over the side of his ship. But this wasn't nearly enough rope to reach the bottom of the ocean. Today's scientists use *sonar*, or sound wave devices, to determine how deep the ocean is. In this activity you will learn about two ways to **measure** the depth of water—Magellan's way and a more modern way.

Materials

- shoe box
- sand, pebbles, small rocks
- construction paper
- ruler
- string
- weight
- calculator

Activity Procedure

1 **Make a model** of the ocean floor by pouring sand and pebbles into the shoe box. Then scatter a few small rocks on top of the sand. (Picture A)

2 Cut a piece of construction paper large enough to cover the top of the box. This will stand for the sea surface.

3 With a pencil and ruler, draw a grid on the paper 4 squares wide by 8 squares long. Number the squares 1 through 32, and tape the lid onto the box. Tie the weight to a piece of string about twice as long as the box is deep.

4 Make a hole in the first square in any row and lower the weighted end of the string until the weight just touches the ocean floor. (Picture A)

5 Hold the string at sea level. **Measure** the length of string you pinched off to find the depth of the ocean. **Record** your measurement. Repeat Steps 4 and 5 for the remaining squares in that row.

6 Now copy the Sonar Data table. The "Time" is the number of seconds it takes for a sound to travel from a boat to the bottom of the ocean and back to the boat.

7 Use a calculator to multiply the Location 1 time by 1500 m/s (the speed of sound in water). Then divide the product by 2. This number is the depth of the water in meters at Location 1. This one has been done for you.

8 Repeat Step 7 for each location in the table. Then make a line graph of the depths. The graph will be a profile of the ocean floor.

Picture A

Sonar Data

Location	Time (s)	Depth (m)
1	1.8	1350
2	2.0	
3	3.6	
4	4.5	
5	5.3	
6	2.3	
7	3.1	
8	4.6	
9	5.0	
10	5.2	

Draw Conclusions

1. Why do you think scientists today use sonar rather than weighted ropes to **measure** the depth of the ocean?

2. When using sonar, why must you divide each product by 2 to calculate the depth of the water?

3. **Scientists at Work** How could a scientist use sonar to **measure** the size of large objects on the ocean floor?

Investigate Further How could you find the depth of a pond, lake, or river? **Plan and conduct a simple investigation** to find out. Select the equipment you would need to use.

Process Skill Tip

You **measure** when you use a tool to find how deep the water is.

Exploring the Oceans and Using Ocean Resources

Exploring the Ocean

FIND OUT

- about ocean exploration
- about *Alvin,* the submersible that helped find RMS *Titanic*
- how people use ocean resources

VOCABULARY

scuba
submersible
sonar
desalination

Did you know that more than 70 percent of Earth is covered with water? Viewed from space, the continents we live on seem like big islands with oceans around them. People have been exploring the oceans for thousands of years. Early peoples took trips in small boats to search for food, to move to new homes, and to find better trade routes. Some went just for adventure. The time line below shows some of the ways in which people have explored the oceans in the past 600 years.

Scientists and explorers have been studying the oceans for hundreds of years. People designed diving suits as early as the

The voyage of HMS *Challenger* in 1872 started the modern science of oceanography (oh•shuhn•AWG•ruh•fee) —the scientific study of the oceans.

| 1400s | 1500s | 1600s | 1700s | 1800s |

This diving suit was designed in the 1400s.

Sir Edmond Halley, an English astronomer, built this diving bell in 1690. Air was sent down to the bell using barrels and leather tubes. The bell shape trapped air for the divers to use.

1400s, and by 1690, divers could use Sir Edmond Halley's diving bell to explore to a depth of 18 m (about 60 ft) below sea level.

Detailed studies of the oceans began in 1872 with the voyage of the British ship HMS *Challenger*. Led by C. Wyville Thomson, six scientists spent more than three years at sea. They took thousands of samples and measurements of the oceans. They studied the chemistry of sea water and collected ocean plants, animals, and minerals.

With simple methods like you used in the investigation, Thomson and his staff achieved many firsts. Using a weighted line and a steam engine, they measured a water depth of 8185 m (about 26,850 ft) in the western Pacific. They also captured and classified 4717 new species of marine life. The scientific reports of their expedition filled 50 books.

Today's scientists use many different technologies to explore the oceans. They dive beneath the water wearing **scuba** equipment. (The letters *s-c-u-b-a* stand for *self-contained underwater breathing apparatus.*) They travel in small, underwater vehicles called **submersibles**. Satellites are used to study ocean currents from space, and **sonar** (a device that uses sound waves) is used to map the ocean floor.

✔ **What technologies do scientists use to explore the oceans?**

In 1960 Jacques Piccard and Donald Walsh went down in the *Trieste II* to the deepest place in the Pacific Ocean. They reached a depth of 10,920 m (about 35,800 ft). At this depth the top of Mount Everest would still be about 1525 m (5000 ft) below the ocean's surface.

Today, satellites can measure an ocean's salt content, temperature, wave heights, and current flows from thousands of kilometers in space. Sensors can even show where tiny organisms called plankton are found in ocean waters.

1900–1935   **1935–1960**   **1960–2000**

The Aqua-lung, an early form of scuba, was invented in 1942 by French explorer Jacques Cousteau. With scuba gear, a diver can move freely about underwater to a depth of about 60 m (200 ft).

The submersible *Alvin* has played an important role in exploring ocean depths. To reach the *Titanic* in 1986, it had to travel nearly 4000 m (about 13,000 ft) beneath the ocean's surface.

Submersibles

One of the best-known submersibles is *Alvin*, named in honor of ocean scientist Allyn Vine. In 1956 Vine convinced the United States government that scientists needed deep-diving vessels that could hold small crews. By the 1960s *Alvin* was exploring the oceans.

In 1977 scientists in *Alvin* discovered underwater vents along the Mid-Atlantic Ridge. In 1986 *Alvin* was used to explore the wreckage of the sunken ship RMS *Titanic*.

Alvin may have been the first submersible to explore *Titanic*, but it wasn't the last.

During the 1990s a team of French and American explorers used a newer submersible, *Nautile*, to continue the job *Alvin* started.

Nautile first visited the *Titanic* wreck in 1987, bringing up some objects from the site. In the 1990s even more objects were brought up, including a large part of the sunken ship itself.

> Remote-controlled underwater robot called *Jason Jr.*, or *J.J.*

THE INSIDE STORY

Alvin

◄ *Alvin* is launched from a surface ship. The submersible has made thousands of dives, each lasting about nine hours.

In 1977, scientists in *Alvin* discovered hot springs deep under the ocean. The springs come from vents in the ocean floor over volcanically active areas. ▼

> Portholes—for crew to see out

> Still camera and bright strobe light

> Moving arm with lights, and still and video cameras

> Low-light black-and-white TV camera—to see forward

With space for crews of three—one pilot and two scientists each—*Alvin* and *Nautile* can work inside sea caves, shipwrecks, and other small spaces.

Crewed submersibles allow scientists to observe underwater objects up close. They have been able to make important scientific discoveries, as well as explore sunken ships.

But in the future, underwater exploration may be done with small, crewless submersibles. These underwater robots can fit into places too small for *Alvin* or *Nautile*. And they can dive deeper and stay longer on the ocean floor.

✔ **What kinds of places have scientists used submersibles to explore?**

Hatch door—for crew to enter and exit

In 1986 a team of scientists led by Dr. Robert Ballard used *Alvin* to go down to the wreck of the *Titanic.* They explored the remains of the sunken ocean liner and took the first photographs of the ship since it sank in 1912. ▼

Sphere made of titanium— can hold a crew of three

This photograph shows a chandelier before the *Titanic*'s first—and only— voyage. In 1912 the *Titanic* struck an iceberg in the North Atlantic and sank to the bottom of the ocean. ▶

Low-light black-and-white TV camera— to see down

The same chandelier was filmed nearly 75 years later by a remote-controlled robot named *J.J.* The robot is attached to *Alvin* by a 61-m (about 200-ft) cable. With *J.J.,* scientists can "see" places too small or too dangerous for *Alvin* to enter. ▶

Using Ocean Resources

The importance of the oceans is not just in the discoveries they hold for scientists. The oceans contain huge amounts of natural resources. Ocean waters are filled with plants and animals. The ocean floor contains many minerals. Gas and oil are buried deep beneath the ocean floor. And in some places, sea water itself has become an important resource.

Among the ocean's most important resources are its fish and shellfish. Millions of people around the world feed their families by fishing from small boats. Others fish for large companies on factory ships—huge boats where fish can be cleaned, processed, and canned or frozen right on board.

Sea plants are another ocean resource. People eat some kinds of seaweed as food. Carrageenin (kar•uh•JEE•nuhn), a product made from seaweed, is used in foods, toothpaste, hand creams, and fertilizer.

As resources on land become scarce, people are beginning to mine underwater mineral deposits. Sand, gravel, and shells are easily obtained near the shore. Hundreds of millions of tons are dredged from the sea each year and used for road construction and building materials. Minerals containing iron, copper, manganese, nickel, and cobalt can be taken from lumps, or nodules, lying on the sea floor. These deep-sea nodules are difficult to mine, however, since they are located at depths of 4000 m (about 13,125 ft) or more.

Petroleum and natural gas are pumped from beneath the ocean floor using huge offshore drilling rigs. Almost a quarter of the world's petroleum and natural gas now comes from under the ocean.

Another useful resource, salt, is dissolved in the sea water itself. Since ancient times people have used the process of evaporation to remove salt from sea water. Much of the world's salt is still obtained using this natural process.

There is still another valuable ocean resource—water. In some parts of the world, freshwater supplies are so limited that water is taken from the ocean. The salt is removed from sea water by **desalination**. In one method, sea water is evaporated, leaving the minerals behind. The water vapor is then cooled and condensed back into fresh water. In another desalination method, sea water is passed through a plastic film that allows pure water, but not the dissolved salts, to go through.

✔ **What resources do people take from the ocean?**

Offshore drilling rigs like this one may stand in water as deep as 300 m (about 1000 ft). ▶

▲ Desalination plants like this one provide water for drinking or industry. Right now the cost is usually too high to use desalinated water for farm irrigation.

Summary

Ocean exploration has a long history. Today's ocean scientists have a wide range of technology that they can use, including scuba equipment, submersibles, satellites, and sonar. The oceans also contain valuable natural resources such as fish, petroleum, minerals, and sea water itself.

Review

1. What did the crew of the *Challenger* study?
2. Why are submersibles such as *Alvin* valuable to ocean scientists?
3. What mineral resources are found in or beneath the ocean?
4. **Critical Thinking** The deeper you go in the ocean, the greater the water pressure. Use logical reasoning to **infer** why.
5. **Test Prep** Which word does NOT belong with the others?

   A seaweed

   B salt

   C manganese

   D iron

LINKS

why oh why

MATH LINK

Calculate A typical dive with *Alvin* lasts about 9 hours. Of these 9 hours, 30 minutes are spent launching the craft. Another 30 minutes are spent recovering it from the water. The descent to the ocean floor takes $2\frac{1}{2}$ hours, and the ascent back to the surface takes another $2\frac{1}{2}$ hours. How long do the scientists have for research?

WRITING LINK

Narrative Writing—Story Choose an ocean resource to research. Find out more about this resource, including how it is obtained and how it is used. Then write a science fiction story for your class that describes a world where that resource has become scarce.

LITERATURE LINK

Exploring the Titanic The complete story of the *Titanic* expedition is told in this book by Robert D. Ballard. In 1985 Ballard and his team discovered the remains of the *Titanic* on the ocean floor. A year later the team returned to explore the ship in the submersible *Alvin*.

TECHNOLOGY LINK

Learn more about ocean exploration by viewing *Jacques Cousteau* on the **Harcourt Science Newsroom Video.**

Saltwater Agriculture

Who would grow crops in a desert? Scientists would, and they are using saltwater to do it.

By the Sea

The first major use of salt water for growing crops was in Israel. At the end of World War II, Hugo and Elisabeth Boyko decided to live there. Elisabeth was a horticulturist, an expert in growing certain plants, and Hugo was an ecologist.

The Boykos used their skills to landscape a town near the Red Sea. They wanted to make it prettier so that more people would move there. Growing plants in the seaside town was a challenge. Most plants need rich soil and fresh water to grow, but here the land was sandy and the only water was from the sea. They pumped salt water from the sea to irrigate, or water, their plants. Many plants are killed by salt water, but the Boykos noticed that some plants survived in spite of the salt.

Since then other scientists have continued the Boykos' work. Some have teamed up with desert farmers in Mexico, India, and

This photograph shows a landscaped town along the Red Sea.

Glasswort is a halophyte. It can grow in salty soil.

other countries to build experimental farms that practice saltwater agriculture.

A Growing Challenge

Why grow crops in a desert? And why use salty seawater instead of fresh water from rivers or lakes? There are some very important reasons.

The world's population is increasing, so there are more and more people to feed. But Earth's supplies of good farmland and fresh water are shrinking. Every year it gets harder to raise enough food for everyone. Where could farmers find additional land and water? Areas of desert near an ocean seem like an excellent choice.

Saltwater Crops

Corn, wheat, rice, potatoes, and soybeans are the main crops that people eat. Salt water kills them all. What else is there? Halophytes. Halophytes are plants that grow in the wild and survive in salty soil. In fact, halophytes absorb salt and store it inside themselves. That's why some of them taste so salty.

One halophyte that could be used for food is called glasswort. This leafless plant can be fed to livestock. Its seeds contain protein and oil, and the oil has a nutlike taste. However, glasswort isn't the perfect crop—yet. Glasswort is so salty that it makes livestock thirsty. They have to drink more water than usual which is not a good way to save fresh water, especially in a desert. Can scientists develop a less salty glasswort? Agronomists are trying.

THINK ABOUT IT

1. Why would it be useful to farm deserts near oceans?
2. What advantages and disadvantages are there to growing halophytes?

WEB LINK:
For science and technology updates, visit The Learning Site.
www.harcourtschool.com

Careers   Hydrologist

What They Do   Hydrologists test drinking water, issue flood warnings, check underground water supplies, and protect water in other ways. Many work in government agencies, city or state offices, consulting firms, and waste-treatment plants.

Education and Training   A person wishing to become a hydrologist needs to study physical or natural science or engineering and take courses in soils, marine biology, or other scientific fields. Math and computer skills are also helpful.

Robert D. Ballard

UNDERSEA EXPLORER

"Captain Nemo in Twenty Thousand Leagues Under the Sea by Jules Verne is who I always wanted to be. Absolutely no doubt about it."

Undersea explorer Robert D. Ballard made headlines around the world when he and his crew located the wreck of the R.M.S. *Titanic.* Although most people know of Dr. Ballard for making this discovery, his fellow scientists know him for discovering deep-ocean life forms and geologic processes never seen before.

Although geologists had hypothesized that thermal vents existed, no one had predicted that there would be so many kinds of organisms there. Dr. Ballard observed huge blood-red worms without eyes or mouths, clusters of giant clams, blind crabs, and other strange animals. These animals depend on bacteria, not on plants, for food.

Dr. Ballard's team is also recognized for discovering that all the water of the oceans is recycled over time through Earth's crust. This discovery has helped scientists explain why sea water is full of minerals.

Interested in becoming an undersea explorer from the time he was a boy, Dr. Ballard is thankful to the many people who taught and encouraged him throughout his career. "You need to pick out certain people you have great respect for and listen to them," he says. "At every critical point in my life, when I was ready to quit, I can point to someone who said, 'Keep it up.'"

THINK ABOUT IT

1. Why was discovering that all the water of the oceans is recycled through Earth's crust important?

2. Why is working as part of a team important to scientists?

Inside the submersible *Alvin*

Water World

What happens when waters meet?

Materials

- water
- 200-mL beaker
- food coloring
- hot plate
- tongs
- water-filled aquarium

Procedure

1. Fill the beaker half-full of water. Add food coloring to the water.

2. Using the hot plate, gently warm the water in the beaker.

3. Your teacher or another adult will use the tongs to lower the beaker straight down into the aquarium filled with cold water.

4. Observe the hot, colored water as it leaves the beaker.

Draw Conclusions

Describe what you observed. From your observations, what conclusions can you draw about areas in the ocean where warm currents flow through cooler waters?

Oil and Water

Why did ancient sailors use oil to calm the seas near their ships?

Materials

- glass bread pan
- water
- food coloring
- drinking straw
- cooking oil

Procedure

1. Fill the glass pan about half-full of water.

2. Add several drops of food coloring to the water.

3. Using the straw, gently blow across the surface of the water.

4. Now slowly pour oil into the water until it forms a layer of oil about 1 cm thick on top of the water.

5. Using the straw, blow gently across the surface again.

Draw Conclusions

Compare the waves produced in Step 3 with those produced in Step 5. What do you conclude to be the cause of any differences in the waves? Why would sailors pour oil on the water during rough weather?

Chapter (4) Review and Test Preparation

Vocabulary Review

Use the terms below to complete the sentences. The page numbers in ( ) tell you where to look in the chapter if you need help.

wave (C94)　　　　headland (C103)
current (C96)　　　jetty (C104)
tide (C98)　　　　 scuba (C109)
estuary (C102)　　 submersible (C109)
shore (C102)　　　 sonar (C109)
tide pool (C103)　　desalination (C112)

1. The ___, which is the repeated rise and fall in the level of the ocean, is caused by the pull of gravity of the moon and the sun.

2. The area where the ocean and the land meet and interact is the ___.

3. Scientists can use self-contained underwater breathing apparatus, or ___, equipment to dive beneath the water.

4. In an ocean ___, a stream of water moves through the ocean like a river, but in a ___, water moves up and down in a circular motion.

5. A ___ is a small underwater vehicle used to explore the ocean.

6. A body of water at the mouth of a river is an ___.

7. Scientists can use ___ to map the ocean floor.

8. A pool of sea water found along a rocky shore is called a ___.

9. A ___ is a rocky point that juts out into the ocean.

10. A ___ is a wall-like structure made of rocks that sticks out into the ocean.

11. The process of ___ removes the salt from sea water.

Connect Concepts

Use terms from the Word Bank to complete the concept map below.

wave　　　tide　　　submersible
scuba　　 shore

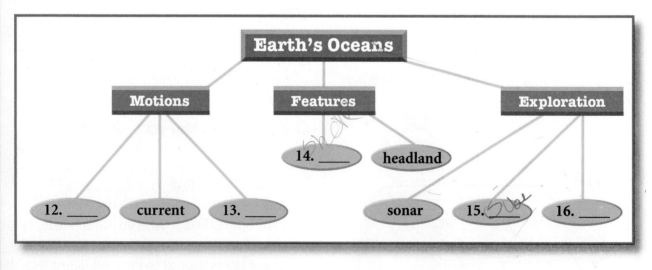

Earth's Oceans

Motions　　　Features　　　Exploration

12. ___　current　13. ___

14. ___　headland

sonar　15. ___　16. ___

Check Understanding

Write the letter of the best choice.

17. A tsunami is a wave caused by —

    A an earthquake   **C** a storm surge

    B a high tide   **D** an ocean current

18. The main cause of tides is —

    F ocean waves

    G the moon's gravity

    H the sun's energy

    J longshore currents

19. Deep-ocean currents are caused by —

    A volcanoes deep under water

    B prevailing winds

    C the Earth's rotation

    D differences in water temperature

20. Shoreline currents are caused by —

    F local winds and conditions

    G prevailing winds

    H the saltiness of the water

    J sandspits

21. Most erosion at the shore is caused by —

    A currents   **C** waves

    B deposition   **D** tides

22. Detailed study of the oceans began with —

    F the discovery of the *Titanic*

    G the invention of scuba gear

    H the voyage of the *Challenger*

    J the scientists of the *Trieste*

23. Scientists explore the oceans with —

    A satellites   **C** sonar

    B scuba   **D** all of the above

24. *Alvin* is a _____ that scientists used to discover hot springs deep under the ocean.

    F sailboat   **H** satellite

    G submersible   **J** robot

Critical Thinking

25. Suppose you drop a ball into the ocean in a place where there is no current. Will waves move the ball quickly away, or will it bob in place? Explain.

26. Suppose you have the choice of buying one of two houses. Both houses are built near the beach. One is 50 m from the ocean. The other is 100 m from the ocean. Which house would you choose? Explain.

27. Suppose you are an ocean miner. Tell how you might obtain a mineral that is on the ocean bottom, 1000 m below the surface.

Process Skills Review

28. How can you **make a model** of a tide pool?

29. Which method of **measuring** works better to determine the depth of the ocean—sonar or weighted ropes? Explain.

Performance Assessment

Waves

Using construction paper, glue, and two pieces of string, make a model to compare the way *energy* in waves travels with the way *water* in waves travels.

Unit Project Wrap Up

Here are some ideas for ways to wrap up your unit project.

Graph Earthquakes

Research the magnitude of the last five earthquakes reported in the United States. Make a graph to show your data. You can use a computer and graphing software to make your graph.

Invent Weather Instruments

Design instruments that will help you measure weather conditions. Write directions that will help others use your instruments.

Make a Map

Investigate the route of an explorer who traveled on an ocean. Make a map to show the explorer's route.

Investigate Further

How could you make your project better? What other questions do you have about Earth's surface? Plan ways to find answers to your questions. Use the Science Handbook on pages R2-R9 for help.

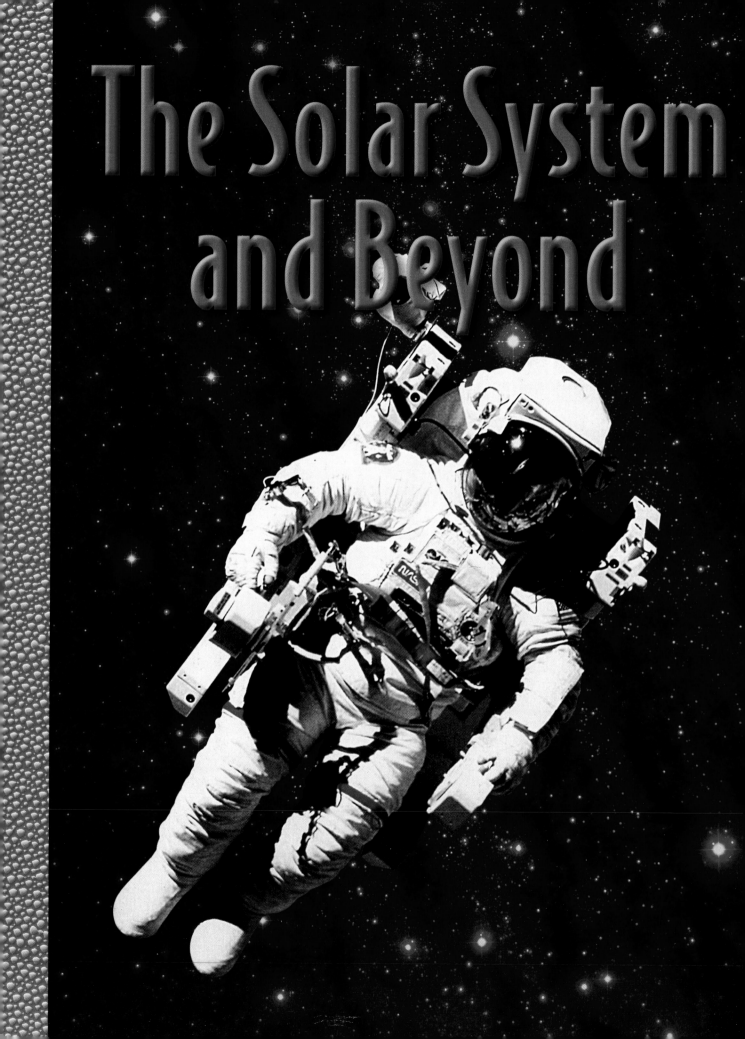

The Solar System and Beyond

EARTH SCIENCE

The Solar System and Beyond

Unit Project

Space Station

Design a space station. Where in space would your station be positioned? What sorts of experiments might be done in your space station? What would the crew need to live in space? Use scrap materials to build a model of your space station.

Earth, Moon, and Beyond

Although Earth moves through space very rapidly, it doesn't *seem* to move at all. That's why the sun and the moon both seem to move around Earth. It took astronomers a long time to realize that Earth actually moves around the sun.

Vocabulary Preview

revolve
orbit
rotate
axis
eclipse
telescope
satellite
space probe

FAST FACT

Observatories located near growing cities are no longer very useful. The city lights and the pollution in the air make it impossible to see the stars clearly. But on the summit of Mauna Kea in Hawai'i, many miles from city lights and pollution, scientists can see the stars quite clearly.

It takes Earth 365.26 days to travel once around the sun. An adjustment to the calendar is made for the 0.26 day by adding a February 29 every four years. These longer years are called leap years.

Once Around the Sun

Planet	Earth Days
Mercury	88
Venus	224.7
Earth	365.26
Mars	687
Jupiter	4,332.6
Saturn	10,759.2
Uranus	30,685.4
Neptune	60,189
Pluto	90,777.6

FAST FACT

The next total solar eclipse in the United States will not take place until August 21, 2017. It will move across the country from Oregon to South Carolina. You can safely view a solar eclipse the way the photograph shows.

How Do Earth and the Moon Compare?

In this lesson, you can . . .

INVESTIGATE how Earth, the moon, and the sun move through space.

LEARN ABOUT Earth and its moon.

LINK to math, writing, music, and technology.

Earth, from the surface of the moon ▼

How Earth, the Moon, and the Sun Move Through Space

Activity Purpose You may not feel as if you're moving right now, but you're actually speeding through space. Earth makes a complete spin once every 24 hours. So if you stand on the equator, you're moving at about 1730 km/hr (1075 mi/hr)! Earth also moves around the sun at about 107,000 km/hr (66,489 mi/hr). At the same time, the moon, which also spins, moves around Earth at about 3700 km/hr (2300 mi/hr). In the investigation you will **make a model** of Earth, the moon, and the sun to **compare** how they move through space.

Materials
- beach ball
- baseball
- Ping Pong ball

Activity Procedure

1 You will work in a group of four to **make a model** of the sun, Earth, and the moon in space. One person should stand in the center of a large open area and hold the beach ball over his or her head. The beach ball stands for the sun. A second person should stand far from the "sun" and hold the baseball overhead. The baseball stands for Earth. The third person should hold the Ping Pong ball near "Earth". The Ping Pong ball stands for the moon. The fourth person should **observe** and **record** what happens.

2 The real Earth moves around the sun in a path like a circle that has been pulled a little at both

ends. This shape, called an *ellipse* (ee•LIPS), is shown here. For the model, Earth should move around the sun in an ellipse-shaped path. Earth should also spin slowly as it moves around the sun. The observer should **record** this motion. (Picture A)

ellipse

Picture A

3 While Earth spins and moves around the sun, the moon should move around Earth in another ellipse-shaped path. The moon should spin once as it moves around Earth. The same side of the moon should always face Earth. That is, the moon should spin once for each complete path it takes around Earth. The observer should **record** these motions. (Picture B)

Picture B

Draw Conclusions

1. Your model shows three periods of time—a year, a month, and a day. Think about the time it takes Earth to spin once, the moon to move around Earth once, and Earth to move around the sun once. Which period of time does each movement stand for?

2. **Compare** the movements of the moon to the movements of Earth.

3. **Scientists at Work** Scientists often **make models** to show **time and space relationships** in the natural world. However, models can't always show these relationships exactly. How was your model of Earth, the moon, and the sun limited in what it showed?

Investigate Further You could **make a model** to show how the sun shines on Earth. **Plan and conduct a simple investigation** to show how the amount of sunlight reaching Earth changes as Earth moves around the sun.

Process Skill Tip

Making a model of the sun-Earth-moon system allowed you to **use time and space relationships** to learn how objects in space move and interact.

How Earth and the Moon Compare

Earth and the Moon in Space

The moon is the brightest object in the night sky and Earth's nearest neighbor in space. Together, Earth and the moon are part of the sun's planetary system. Pulled by the sun's gravity, the Earth-moon system **revolves**, or travels in a closed path, around

FIND OUT

- about the Earth-moon system
- what causes lunar and solar eclipses
- how Earth and the moon are alike and different

VOCABULARY

revolve
orbit
rotate
axis
eclipse

4 WAXING GIBBOUS
The word *gibbous* (GIB•uhs) comes from a word meaning "hump."

3 FIRST QUARTER
About one week after a new moon, the moon looks like a half-circle. This phase is called the first quarter because the moon is a quarter of the way around Earth.

5 FULL MOON
About two weeks after a new moon, we see the entire sunlit half.

6 WANING GIBBOUS
A waning moon appears to get smaller.

7 LAST QUARTER
About three weeks after a new moon, the moon is three-fourths of the way around Earth.

D6

the sun. The path Earth takes as it revolves is called its **orbit**. Earth's orbit is an ellipse, a shape that is not quite circular.

As Earth orbits the sun, it **rotates**, or spins on its axis. The **axis** is an imaginary line that passes through Earth's center and its North and South Poles. Earth's rotation results in day and night. When a location on Earth faces the sun, it is day in that place. When that location faces away from the sun, it is night.

Pulled by Earth's gravity, the moon revolves around Earth in an ellipse-shaped orbit. When the moon is closest to Earth, it is about 356,400 km (221,463 mi) away.

Like Earth, the moon rotates on its axis. However, the moon takes 27.3 Earth days to complete one rotation. This makes a cycle

on the moon of one day and one night that is 27.3 Earth days long.

Even though the moon rotates, the same side of the moon always faces Earth. This is because the moon orbits Earth in 27.3 days—exactly the same amount of time it takes to rotate once on its axis.

Although the moon shines brightly at night, it does not give off its own light. We see the moon from Earth because sunlight is reflected off its surface. As the moon orbits Earth, its position in the sky changes. This produces the different shapes, or phases, of the moon we see each month. The phases of the moon, as seen from Earth, are shown in the photographs below and on page D6.

✔ **How do Earth and the moon move through space?**

2 WAXING CRESCENT
The moon's sunlit surface first appears as a growing crescent. A waxing moon seems to grow larger.

1 NEW MOON
The moon is between Earth and the sun. The moon can't be seen because the part the sun is shining on isn't visible from Earth.

8 WANING CRESCENT
The moon's sunlit part is about to disappear from Earth's view.

▲ **Solar eclipse** A total solar eclipse lasts no more than 7.5 minutes. That's how long it takes for a point on Earth to rotate through the shadow of the moon.

▲ **Lunar eclipse** A total lunar eclipse lasts more than two hours. It may be seen from any place on Earth that is facing the moon.

Solar and Lunar Eclipses

All bodies in the solar system produce shadows in space. An **eclipse** (ee•KLIPS) occurs when one object passes through the shadow of another. A solar eclipse or a lunar eclipse may occur during a new moon or full moon, when Earth, the sun, and the moon line up.

A solar eclipse occurs when Earth passes through a new moon's shadow. During a total solar eclipse, the moon completely covers the sun. The sky darkens, and only the sun's outer atmosphere is visible. It can be seen glowing as a bright circle around the moon. A partial solar eclipse occurs when Earth passes through part of the moon's shadow.

A lunar eclipse occurs when the full moon passes through Earth's shadow. When Earth passes between the sun and the moon, it blocks the sun's light. However, Earth's atmosphere bends certain colors of light, especially red. This makes the eclipsed moon look like a dim red circle.

You may wonder why eclipses do not occur twice each month—at every new moon and full moon. This is because the moon's shadow usually passes above or below Earth, or the moon passes above or below Earth's shadow. Only seven eclipses—two lunar eclipses and five solar eclipses—occur in a single year. And most of those are partial eclipses.

✔ **How does a solar eclipse differ from a lunar eclipse?**

EARTH SCIENCE

UNIT D
The Solar System and Beyond

Unit Project   ## Space Station

Design a space station. Where in space would your station be positioned? What sorts of experiments might be done in your space station? What would the crew need to live in space? Use scrap materials to build a model of your space station.

s surface
ce cooled,
k at the
n see three
lands, and

ge. Tycho
km
rs are so
ld fit on

reas known
maria
s people
the moon
maria are

c dome
ray

Maria formed when hot, molten rock flowed from the interior through cracks in the moon's surface. This molten rock over-flowed some craters and spread across the moon's surface. It then cooled to form a dark rock called *basalt*. The largest mare (MAH•ray) is 1248 km (about 775 mi) across. The illustration below shows craters and other landforms on the moon's surface.

✔ **What are some landforms found on the moon's surface?**

rilles

highlands

ray crater

crater

Comparing Earth's and the Moon's Features

Earth and its moon are alike in several ways. Both are rocky and fairly dense. The same materials that make up Earth—calcium, aluminum, oxygen, silicon, and iron—are found on the moon. Craters occur on both, although there are many more craters on the moon than on Earth.

There are also important differences between Earth and the moon. Unlike Earth, the moon has no atmosphere and no liquid water. Because of this, the moon's landscape has not been eroded by wind and water. The moon's surface weathers very slowly, staying the same for millions of years.

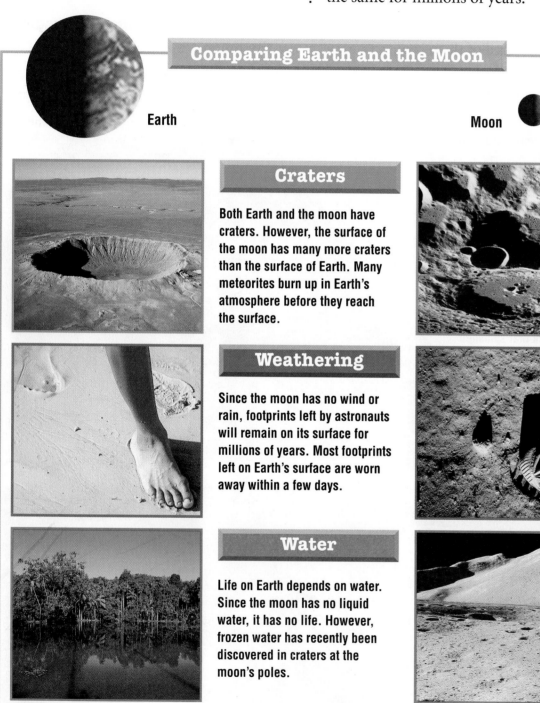

Comparing Earth and the Moon

Earth

Moon

Craters

Both Earth and the moon have craters. However, the surface of the moon has many more craters than the surface of Earth. Many meteorites burn up in Earth's atmosphere before they reach the surface.

Weathering

Since the moon has no wind or rain, footprints left by astronauts will remain on its surface for millions of years. Most footprints left on Earth's surface are worn away within a few days.

Water

Life on Earth depends on water. Since the moon has no liquid water, it has no life. However, frozen water has recently been discovered in craters at the moon's poles.

Earth, Moon, and Beyond

Although Earth moves through space very rapidly, it doesn't *seem* to move at all. That's why the sun and the moon both seem to move around Earth. It took astronomers a long time to realize that Earth actually moves around the sun.

FAST FACT

Observatories located near growing cities are no longer very useful. The city lights and the pollution in the air make it impossible to see the stars clearly. But on the summit of Mauna Kea in Hawai'i, many miles from city lights and pollution, scientists can see the stars quite clearly.

Look at the photographs on page D10 to compare features of the moon and Earth. The photographs on the right were taken on the moon. Those on the left were taken on Earth.

✓ **Compare and contrast features of Earth and the moon.**

Summary

The moon revolves around Earth, while the Earth-moon system orbits the sun. Both Earth and the moon rotate on axes and have day-night cycles. As Earth, the moon, and the sun travel through space, they sometimes line up to produce eclipses. Many of the features on Earth and the moon are different, although some landforms occur on both.

Review

1. Why does the same side of the moon always face Earth?
2. Describe a lunar eclipse.
3. How does a mare differ from a crater?
4. **Critical Thinking** Lunar rocks are very old and do not look as if they were eroded by water. Also, no rocks have been found that contain water combined with minerals, as are found on Earth. What can you **infer** about how long the moon has been without water?
5. **Test Prep** The path that Earth takes around the sun is called its —
   A axis
   B orbit
   C cycle
   D rotation

LINKS

MATH LINK

Moon Fractions During a full moon, we see half of the moon's surface. During a first or third quarter, what fraction of the moon's surface do we see?

WRITING LINK

Narrative Writing—Story Some early people were afraid of solar eclipses. They believed that the sun might not return. They made up stories and myths to explain eclipses. For example, a myth might say that a dragon or wolf ate the sun and then spit it out again. Write a story or myth for your class explaining what happens during a solar eclipse.

MUSIC LINK

Moon Music The moon has given people many ideas for songs. Work with a group to list ideas for as many new titles of songs about the moon as you can think of. Then write a song about the moon. You may find it easier to write words to a tune you already know.

TECHNOLOGY LINK

Learn more about the discovery of ice near the moon's poles by viewing *Ice on the Moon* on the **Harcourt Science Newsroom Video.**

How Have People Explored the Solar System?

In this lesson, you can . . .

INVESTIGATE how the moon's craters were formed.

LEARN ABOUT how people explore the solar system.

LINK to math, writing, art, and technology.

Astronaut working in space ▼

D12

INVESTIGATE

The Moon's Craters

Activity Purpose As Earth's nearest neighbor in space, the moon was the first object in the solar system that people studied. People **observed** that the moon's surface was very different from the Earth's surface. One difference was the large number of craters on the moon. In the investigation you will **make a model** of the moon's surface to **infer** how the craters formed.

Materials

- newspaper
- aluminum pan
- large spoon
- water
- flour
- safety goggles
- apron
- marble
- meterstick

CAUTION

Activity Procedure

1 Copy the table below.

Trial	Height	Width of Craters
1	20 cm	
2	40 cm	
3	80 cm	
4	100 cm	

2 Put the newspaper on the floor. Place the pan in the center of the newspaper.

3 Use a large spoon to mix the water and flour in the aluminum pan. The look and feel of the mixture should be like thick cake batter. Now lightly cover the surface of the mixture with dry flour. (Picture A)

4 **CAUTION** **Put on the safety goggles and apron** to protect your eyes and clothes from flour dust. Drop the marble into the pan from a height of 20 cm. (Picture B)

5 Carefully remove the marble and **measure** the width of the crater. **Record** the measurement in the table. Repeat Steps 4 and 5 two more times.

6 Now drop the marble three times each from heights of 40 cm, 80 cm, and 100 cm. **Measure** the craters and **record** the measurements after each drop.

Picture A

Draw Conclusions

1. **Compare** the height from which each marble was dropped to the size of the crater it made. How does height affect crater size?

2. The Copernicus (koh•PER•nih•kuhs) crater on the moon is 91 km across. Based on your model, what can you **infer** about the object that formed this crater?

3. **Scientists at Work** Most of the moon's craters were formed millions of years ago. Scientists **use models** to **infer** events that occurred too long ago to **observe** directly. What did you infer from the model about how the moon's craters formed?

Picture B

Investigate Further **Hypothesize** how using larger or smaller marbles would affect the size and shape of the craters. **Plan and conduct a simple investigation** to test your hypothesis.

> **Process Skill Tip**
>
> You can **use a model** to **infer** how something happened a long time ago, such as how the moon's craters formed.

Space Exploration

FIND OUT

- about the history of space exploration
- how spacesuits work

VOCABULARY

telescope
satellite
space probe

Exploring the Solar System

Thousands of years ago, people observed the night sky and recorded their observations in cave paintings and rock art. These early observations were made without telescopes or other devices. About the only things early people could see were the phases of the moon and some of the moon's larger features. They could also see some of the planets and many stars. Then, about 400 years ago, the telescope was invented. It allowed people to observe objects in space in much greater detail.

In 1609 Galileo used this telescope to observe the sun, moon, and planets. His telescope had two curved pieces of glass, or lenses, one at each end of a long tube.

 900–1200 | 1200–1500 | 1500–1800

The Mayas, in Central America, built many *observatories*, or places for viewing the stars and planets. This one at Chichén Itzá, in Mexico, was built about 900.

This telescope was designed by English scientist Sir Isaac Newton in 1668. It used two mirrors and one lens to produce sharper images than Galileo's telescope could.

In 1609 the Italian scientist Galileo (gal•uh•LEE•oh) was possibly the first person to use a new invention—the telescope—to observe the sky. A **telescope** is an instrument that magnifies, or makes larger, distant objects. With this telescope Galileo observed the moon and saw mountains, valleys, and craters that had never been seen before. He also observed the phases of Venus and four moons orbiting Jupiter. About fifty years later, English scientist Sir Isaac Newton used an even better telescope to observe other objects in space.

The modern age of space exploration began in 1957, when the Soviet Union launched *Sputnik I*, an artificial satellite. A **satellite** is any natural body, like the moon, or artificial object that orbits another object. *Sputnik,* which was about twice the size of a soccer ball, carried instruments to measure the density and temperature of Earth's upper atmosphere. The United States launched its own satellite the next year. Soon both countries were launching humans into space.

✔ **How did the telescope help people learn more about objects in space?**

Launched in 1957, *Sputnik I* circled the globe once every 95 minutes for more than a year before it fell back to Earth. The word *sputnik* means "traveling companion" in Russian.

In 1961 the Mercury program sent the first Americans into space.

The first radio telescope, built in 1936, detected radio waves coming from objects in space.

| 1930–1940 | 1940–1950 | 1950–1960 | 1960–1970 |

In 1969 the United States landed the first person on the moon.

To the Moon and Beyond

One of the best-known American space programs was Project Apollo. The Apollo missions landed 12 humans on the moon between 1969 and 1972. These astronauts set up experiments and brought back samples of rock. Their work helped scientists learn more about the moon.

In 1977 the *Voyager 1* and *Voyager 2* space probes were launched. A **space probe** is a robot vehicle used to explore deep space. The Voyager space probes have sent back pictures of Jupiter, Saturn, Uranus, and Neptune. Both Voyagers are still traveling through space beyond the solar system.

Other early space probes included *Viking I* and *Viking II*, which landed on Mars in 1976, and the Pioneer probes, which used instruments to "see" through thick clouds that cover Venus. Today's scientists use the Hubble Space Telescope, satellites, and space probes to better understand Earth, the solar system, and what lies beyond.

✔ **What was Project Apollo?**

Space shuttles, which have been in use since 1981, have many uses. They lift heavy cargoes into orbit and provide labs for carrying out scientific research in space. They also provide a place to launch, bring back, and repair satellites.

1970–1980	1980–1990

Two Viking spacecraft landed on Mars in 1976. They photographed their landing sites and sent back data about the planet's soil and atmosphere.

The Hubble Space Telescope, launched in 1990 produces images five times as sharp as those from any telescope on Earth.

Spacesuits

The Apollo spacesuit below, once worn by Neil Armstrong, is a $10 million outfit made to protect an astronaut from the moon's hostile environment. The spacesuit must keep an astronaut from "cooking" in direct sunlight or freezing in cold shadows. It must provide the person who wears it with air, water, and waste removal for a moonwalk that may last up to eight hours. The spacesuit must also be flexible enough for an astronaut to walk, twist, turn, bend over, and pick up objects in the reduced gravity on the moon. Flightsuits, such as the one at the right, are much less bulky.

The visor reflects the sun's intense light.

▲ A shuttle flightsuit

A drinking bag is located inside the helmet.

Communications gear allows astronauts to talk with each other, with other astronauts in orbit, and with scientists at Mission Control.

Medical monitors check heart beat rate and body temperature.

The spacesuit protects against extreme heat and cold and against tiny objects speeding through space.

Stretchy mesh, liquid-cooled underwear is worn under the spacesuit.

Gloves allow as much flexibility as possible.

Boots are made for walking on the moon's surface.

Space Exploration in the Future

The launch of the first modules of the International Space Station in 1998 marked the beginning of a new era in space exploration. As many as seven scientists at a time will be able to live and work in space. When completed, the station will be nearly 80 m (about 260 ft) long and have a mass of more than 455,000 kg. In the future, larger stations could have room for a thousand people or more.

Settlements may one day be built on the moon, or even on Mars. Although there are as yet no plans to build bases on the moon, they could be possible by 2020.

A moon base could be used as a research station, like those in Antarctica. To save money, some materials needed to build and run the base could come from the moon itself. For example, some of the moon's rocks contain oxygen. This oxygen could be taken from the rocks and used by people living on the moon. Recently a probe discovered enough ice at the poles to supply a moon base with water. For electricity the base could use solar energy. And some minerals could be mined from the moon and sent back to Earth for processing.

✔ **How could people live on the moon?**

Living in space for long periods is now a reality with the International Space Station, shown here as a model.

1990–2000

2000–

Summary

People have observed and studied the moon and other objects in space since ancient times. The invention of the telescope allowed people to see features and objects that had never been seen before. Today scientists use telescopes, satellites, and space probes to study objects in the solar system and beyond. In the future, people may live and work on space stations and moon bases.

Review

1. What event marked the start of the space age?

2. What are space shuttles used for?

3. What problems have to be solved to build a permanent research station on the moon?

4. **Critical Thinking** A spacesuit weighs more than most astronauts. How can astronauts wear an outfit that is heavier than they are?

5. **Test Prep** The Apollo missions landed humans on —
   A Mercury
   B Venus
   C Mars
   D the moon

LINKS

MATH LINK

Calculation Earth spins once every 24 hours. A person standing still on the equator is moving with Earth's rotation at more than 1730 km/hr. How far does he or she move in a 24-hour day?

WRITING LINK

Persuasive Writing—Request Suppose that you have been invited to enter an essay contest. The winner will be the first student astronaut in space. Write a one-page essay to the judges requesting that they choose you. Explain why you are the best candidate.

ART LINK

Space Art Design a permanent space station or moon base. Draw a picture to show what it will look like. Label all the major parts, explaining how they will help people live and work in space or on the moon.

TECHNOLOGY LINK

Learn more about the solar system by investigating *Planet Hopping* on the **Harcourt Science Explorations CD-ROM.**

The History of Rockets and Spaceflight

As with many inventions, it is likely that the first rockets were produced partly by accident. Trying to scare off evil forces, the ancient Chinese lit bamboo tubes filled with a combination of charcoal, saltpeter, and sulfur. Perfectly sealed tubes produced loud explosions.

But once in a while an imperfectly sealed tube would shoot off into the air. At some point the Chinese began to produce these tubes, which they called "fire arrows," as weapons.

Rockets of War

Through the centuries, knowledge of how to make rockets spread through Asia, the Middle East, Europe, and the Americas. The "rockets' red glare" that Francis Scott Key wrote about in "The Star-Spangled Banner" were fired by British troops on Fort McHenry near Baltimore, Maryland, during the War of 1812.

The first liquid-fuel rockets were developed during the 1920s by American scientist Robert H. Goddard. These powerful rockets were a great advance in rocket technology. During World War II, a team of German scientists started the Space Age with the launch of the A4 rocket. It traveled 193 km (about 120 mi). Although it was designed to be a weapon of war, the A4 was the first modern rocket, a guided missile. After the war many German rockets were redesigned to collect data from Earth's upper atmosphere.

The History of Rockets and Spaceflight

300 B.C.
The Chinese use simple rockets as weapons.

1920s
Robert Goddard develops rockets powered by liquid fuel.

1950s
The two-stage rocket is developed.

1962
John Glenn, in a Mercury capsule launched by an Atlas rocket, becomes the first American to orbit Earth.

300 B.C. | A.D. 1700 | A.D. 1800 | A.D. 1900

1700s
Sir William Congreve develops more powerful rockets for war.

1947
The first supersonic (faster than sound) flight is made aboard a rocket-powered airplane, the X-I.

1969
Neil Armstrong becomes the first person to walk on the moon.

The Race to Space

In 1957 the Soviet Union used a German-designed rocket to launch *Sputnik,* the first Earth-orbiting satellite. The next year NASA (National Aeronautics and Space Administration) launched the first American satellite, *Explorer I,* and the space race was on. In 1961 a Soviet cosmonaut became the first person in space. Then President Kennedy promised that an American astronaut would be the first person to land on the moon. Competition between the Soviet Union and the United States was fierce. National pride was at stake. In 1964 the United States sent a space probe to Mars. In 1965 a Soviet cosmonaut became the first person to "walk" in space. In 1968 three American astronauts orbited the moon. Finally, in July 1969, the *Eagle* lander of *Apollo 11* touched down on the moon. Neil Armstrong became the first person to walk on another body in space.

Cooperation in Space

The space race ended with the flight of *Apollo 11.* Soon cooperation, not competition, became the key to space exploration. In 1988 Japan, Canada, the United States, Russia, and nine members of the European Space Agency agreed to construct the International Space Station. Many parts have already been built, and the process of launching them on American space shuttles and Russian rockets is underway. Once in orbit the parts are joined by astronauts from several countries.

Rockets began as weapons of war and were improved as sources of national pride. But they have become cargo carriers and transports for scientific research in space.

THINK ABOUT IT

1. Why do you think rockets were first used as weapons?
2. Why do you think the space race ended with *Apollo 11*?

The Mir space station

1981
The first space shuttle, *Columbia,* is launched.

A.D. 2000

1986
The Soviet Union launches the Mir space station.

1998
Russia and the United States launch the first parts of the International Space Station.

Harrison Schmitt
GEOLOGIST, ASTRONAUT

Harrison (Jack) Schmitt is a geologist. He was also the first scientist to fly in space and the only scientist to do research on the moon. In 1971 he was the lunar module pilot for *Apollo 17*. The spacecraft landed in the Taurus-Littrow region of the moon. This area is noted for volcanic cinder cones and steep-walled valleys. At this location Dr. Schmitt collected samples of both young volcanic rock and older mountain rock.

Dr. Schmitt's involvement with the space program began at the United States Geological Survey's Astrogeology Center in Flagstaff, Arizona. There he developed geologic field techniques that were used by all Apollo crews. In 1965 Dr. Schmitt became an astronaut. As the only geologist-astronaut, he trained Apollo astronauts in geology observations. He also studied lunar rock samples and documented the geologic findings of each Apollo flight.

Following his resignation from NASA in 1975, Dr. Schmitt was elected to the United States

Senate and served six years as senator from New Mexico. Today Dr. Schmitt is a consultant on issues concerning business, geology, space, and public safety.

THINK ABOUT IT

1. Why was it important for Apollo crew members to have a knowledge of geology?
2. What kinds of information do you think might be gained from samples of lunar rock?

Taking a ride on the moon

Paper Moon

How can the moon be used to make a calendar?

Materials
- clock
- 28 white paper plates
- scissors

Procedure
1 Observe the moon at the same time each night for 4 weeks.

2 Cut one paper plate each night to represent the shape of the moon as you observed it.

3 Hang the paper-plate moons on a wall to make a record of your observations.

Draw Conclusions

How did the shape of the moon change over the length of your observations? What pattern do you notice about the changing shape of the moon? An Earth calendar has 12 months. How many months (moon cycles) would there be in a moon calendar?

Solar-System Distances

How far is it to Pluto?

Materials
- table of planets' distances from the sun
- roll of toilet paper
- wood dowel
- marker

Procedure
1 Round off all distances on the table to the nearest million kilometers.

2 Use one square of toilet paper to represent the distance from the sun to Mercury.

3 Divide the distance from the sun to Mercury into all the other distances. The quotient for each problem will be how many toilet-paper squares each planet is from the sun.

4 Put the dowel into the toilet-paper roll. Unroll the paper, count the squares of paper, and label the position for each planet.

Draw Conclusions

How many squares of toilet paper does it take to show the location of Pluto? How much farther from the sun is Pluto than Mercury? Distances in the solar system are huge. The toilet-paper model helps you visualize those distances. What kind of model could you make to show the sizes of the planets?

Chapter 1 Review and Test Preparation

Vocabulary Review

Use the terms below to complete the sentences. The page numbers in ( ) tell you where to look in the chapter if you need help.

revolves (D6)   **eclipse** (D8)
orbit (D7)   **telescope** (D15)
rotate (D7)   **satellite** (D15)
axis (D7)   **space probe** (D16)

1. Any natural or artificial object that orbits another object is called a ____.

2. Both Earth and the moon have day-night cycles because they each ____, or spin on an ____.

3. The path the moon takes around Earth is its ____.

4. Galileo used a ____ to observe four of Jupiter's moons.

5. A ____ is a vehicle that is used to explore deep space.

6. As a planet travels around the sun, the planet ____.

7. During an ____, one object in space passes through the shadow of another object.

Connect Concepts

Write terms and phrases from the Word Bank below where they belong in the Venn diagram.

revolve   weathering
rotate   almost no weathering
life   craters
no known life   rocky
liquid water   atmosphere
no liquid water   no atmosphere

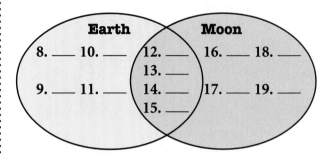

Earth   Moon

8. ____ 10. ____   12. ____   16. ____ 18. ____
                   13. ____
9. ____ 11. ____   14. ____   17. ____ 19. ____
                   15. ____

Check Understanding

Write the letter of the best choice.

20. The diagram below shows Earth's —

A orbit   C revolution
B rotation   D moon

21. During the new-moon phase, a person on Earth cannot see the moon because the sun is shining —

F on the far side of the moon
G on the Earth
H on the moon's axis
J from behind and below the moon

22. The diagram below shows a —

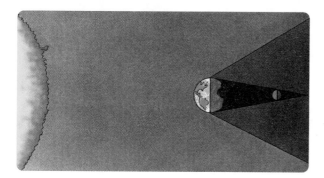

A solar eclipse C full moon

B lunar eclipse D new moon

23. The Apollo flights gave scientists first-hand knowledge of —

F the moon

G Earth's atmosphere

H Mars

J the sun

24. Which of the following must a spacesuit provide for an astronaut?

A life support, including air

B protection from intense heat and cold

C a means to orbit the Earth

D both A and B

Critical Thinking

25. Why does the moon appear to wax, or grow larger, and then wane, or get smaller?

26. The moon has many craters that are millions of years old. Although Earth was hit by large objects from space, just as the moon was, it has few such craters today. Explain why.

27. On Earth the moon appears to rise and set. If you could look at Earth from the moon, would Earth appear to rise and set? Explain why or why not.

Process Skills Review

28. How can you **use a model** to learn more about the moon?

29. You want to **compare** the moon's landforms with landforms on Earth. What processes will you consider? What tools can you use to **observe** the moon's landforms?

30. On the moon, the sun might rise on July 1 and not set until July 14. **Infer** the effects of such a long day on people living on a moon base.

Performance Assessment

On the Moon

Work with a partner to write a dialogue between an astronaut on the moon and Mission Control on Earth. From the astronaut's point of view, describe the moon's landforms and environment. Include a few details about your spacesuit, too.

The Sun and Other Stars

Have you ever looked up at night and seen the Milky Way Galaxy? It's hard to miss because it's the *only* thing you can see. All of the stars and planets visible to your eyes—including Earth—are part of it. Beyond the Milky Way Galaxy are hundreds of billions of other galaxies.

Vocabulary Preview

photosphere
corona
sunspot
solar flare
solar wind
magnitude
main sequence
universe
galaxy
light-year

FAST FACT

On a clear night you can see more than 2000 stars without using a telescope. However, there are 50,000,000 times as many stars in the Milky Way Galaxy alone.

░FAST FACT

In 1989 the *Magellan* spacecraft was launched to Venus from a space shuttle. If you ever get to spend a day on Venus, take plenty of clean clothes. It takes just over 243 Earth days for Venus to rotate once on its axis.

Long Days, Short Days

Planet	Day
Jupiter	9 hr 50 min
Saturn	10 hr 39 min
Neptune	16 hr 3 min
Uranus	17 hr 14 min
Earth	23 hr 56 min
Mars	24 hr 37 min
Pluto	153 hr 18 min
Mercury	1392 hr 30 min
Venus	5832 hr 32 min

░FAST FACT

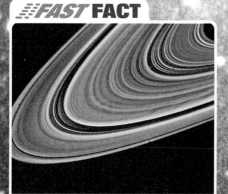

Saturn's rings are made up of chunks of ice, some of which are bigger than most houses. The Voyager space probes showed that Jupiter, Uranus, and Neptune also have rings.

What Are the Features of the Sun?

In this lesson, you can . . .

INVESTIGATE sunspots.

LEARN ABOUT the sun's structure and features.

LINK to math, writing, and technology.

∨ The surface of the sun

INVESTIGATE

Sunspots

Activity Purpose The sun always seems the same from Earth. But is it always the same? What changes take place on the sun? You can find out about some of them as you **observe** sunspots in this investigation.

Materials
- white paper
- clipboard
- tape
- small telescope
- large piece of cardboard
- scissors

◆ CAUTION ◆

Activity Procedure

1. **CAUTION** **Never look directly at the sun. You can cause permanent damage to your eyes.** Fasten the white paper to the clipboard. Tape the edges down to keep the wind from blowing them.

2. Center the eyepiece of the telescope on the cardboard, and trace around the eyepiece.

3. Cut out the circle, and fit the eyepiece into the hole. The cardboard will help block some of the light and make a shadow on the paper.

4. Point the telescope at the sun, and focus the sun's image on the white paper. **Observe** the image of the sun on the paper. (Picture A)

5. On the paper, outline the image of the sun. Shade in any dark spots you see. The dark spots are called *sunspots*. **Record** the date and time on the paper. **Predict** what will happen to the sunspots in the next

Picture A

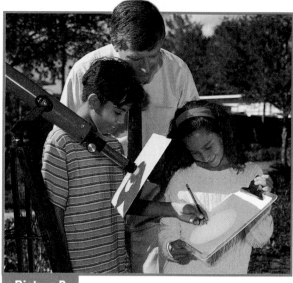

Picture B

day or two. *Note:* Since the image of the sun on the paper is reversed, any movement you **observe** will also be reversed. For example, movement from east to west, or from right to left on the image, represents movement from west to east on the sun.

 Repeat Step 5 each sunny day for several days. **Record** the date, the time, and the positions of the sunspots each day. (Picture B)

Draw Conclusions

1. How did the positions of the sunspots change over several days?

2. What can you **infer** from the movement of sunspots?

3. **Scientists at Work** Scientists **draw conclusions** from what they **observe**. Galileo was the first scientist to observe that it takes a sunspot about two weeks to cross from the left side of the sun's surface to the right side. Two weeks later, the sunspot appears on the left side of the sun's surface again. From this information, what conclusions can you draw about the time it takes the sun to make one complete rotation?

Investigate Further Does the sun always have the same number of spots? Do sunspots change in size? **Plan and conduct a simple investigation** to find answers to these and any other questions you might have about sunspots.

Process Skill Tip

You need to use logical reasoning to **draw conclusions** based on what you **observe**.

The Sun

Energy from the Sun

VOCABULARY

photosphere
corona
sunspot
solar flare
solar wind

◀ The sun is the source of most energy on Earth.

The sun is Earth's "local star"—the star at the center of the solar system. It has no permanent features, like Earth's mountains and oceans, because the sun is a huge ball of very hot gases.

The sun is the source of almost all energy on Earth. Plants are the link between the sun's energy and people. Plants take the sun's energy and change it to food energy. When an animal eats plants—or eats animals that have eaten plants—it gets food energy that comes from the sun.

When organisms die, they decay. Some organisms that died long ago became fossil fuels. So the energy that lights homes and runs cars comes from the sun.

The sun's energy is also the source of wind and other weather on Earth. Recall that when the sun's rays strike Earth's surface, land heats up faster than water. This uneven heating causes weather by producing differences in air pressure.

The sun is the source of most energy on Earth, but where does the sun's energy come from? On Earth, energy often comes from fuel. For example, burning gas or coal produces energy. But the sun's energy doesn't come from burning fuels. It comes from the fusing, or combining, of small particles to form larger ones.

Like all stars, the sun is a huge ball of gases, mostly hydrogen and helium. The temperature at the center of the sun is about

Solar energy from the sun travels as waves. Some of these waves can be seen as light, while others can be felt as heat. ▼

15 million °C (27 million °F). At that temperature, and under enormous pressure, particles of hydrogen smash into each other and produce helium. Every time this happens, the sun releases energy as light and heat.

This process is called *fusion* because hydrogen particles fuse, or join together, to produce helium. The fusion of an amount of hydrogen the size of a pinhead releases more energy than the burning of 1000 metric tons of coal. And the sun fuses about 600 million metric tons of hydrogen every second.

Energy from the sun travels in waves, as shown in the illustration below. There are several kinds of waves. Each kind carries a different amount of energy. We see some of the waves as visible light. We feel infrared waves as heat, and ultraviolet waves tan or burn the skin. The sun even produces radio waves, which we hear as radio or TV static. Some of the sun's energy, such as X rays, is harmful to life on Earth. But the atmosphere keeps most of the harmful energy from reaching Earth's surface.

✔ **How does the sun affect life on Earth?**

▲ Solar energy produces differences in air pressure, causing storms, such as hurricanes and blizzards. This photograph is a satellite image of a large winter storm.

Sometimes particles from the sun stream into space. When these particles reach Earth's atmosphere, they can produce colorful bands of light such as the *aurora borealis,* or northern lights. ▶

Through the process of photosynthesis, plants convert solar energy into food energy. ▼

Exploring the Sun

The sun's diameter is 1.4 million km (about 870,000 mi)—more than 100 times that of Earth. The sun is large enough to hold 1 million Earths. Since the sun is so much closer to Earth than other stars are, astronomers study it to understand stars. They have discovered that the sun has several layers of gases. The layers don't have definite boundaries. Instead, each layer blends into the next.

The layer at the center of the sun is the *core*. As you can see in the illustration, the core is small in comparison with the entire sun. However, most of the sun's mass is in its core.

The Sun's Structure

▲ The sun's *corona*, or atmosphere, is visible only during an eclipse. Streams of tiny particles, called the *solar wind*, travel outward from the corona through the solar system.

▲ The photosphere has a grainy look. Its surface is made up of hot, bright areas, called *granules*, surrounded by cooler, darker areas. A *solar flare*, at the far right, is a brief burst of energy from the sun's photosphere

A *sunspot* is a dark area on the photosphere. Sunspots appear dark because they are cooler than the rest of the sun. Many sunspots are larger than Earth. ▼

As energy from the sun's core moves outward, it passes through the *radiation zone*. Energy from the core heats this layer as a radiator heats the air in a room. From there it moves to the sun's outer layer, the *convection zone*. In the convection zone, energy moves to the surface by a process called convection. In convection, cooler particles are pulled down by gravity, pushing warmer particles up. This is the same way bubbles move energy to the surface of boiling water.

The surface of the sun is known as the **photosphere**, or "sphere of light." This is the surface of the sun we see. Above the photosphere is the sun's atmosphere, the **corona**. This area of hot gases extends 1 million km (about 600,000 mi) from the photosphere.

✔ **What are the layers of the sun?**

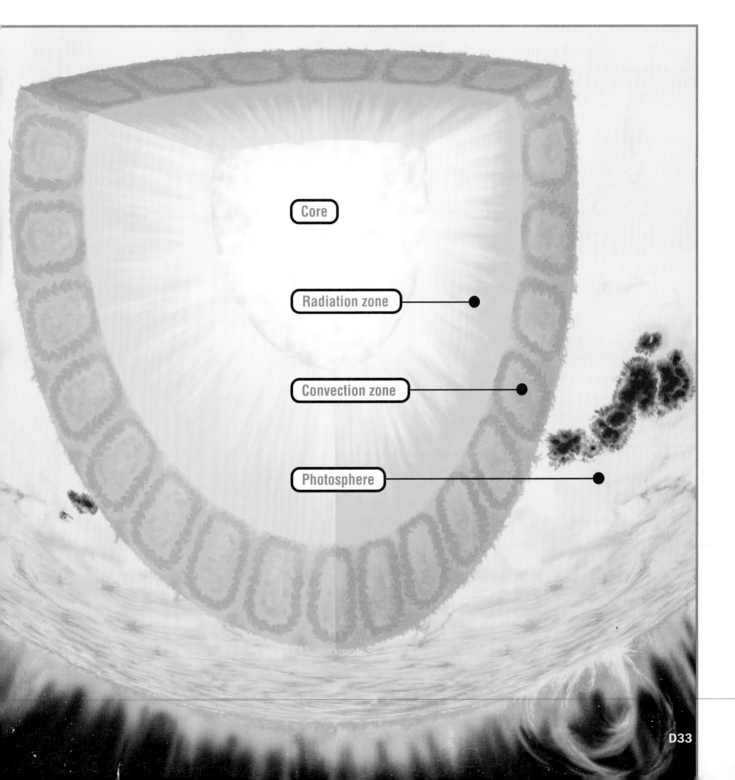

Core

Radiation zone

Convection zone

Photosphere

Solar Features

The sun has several features visible at different times at or near its surface. Bright spots on the photosphere are called *granules*. Granules are the tops of columns of rising gases in the convection layer. Darker areas between granules contain cooler gases.

Dark spots, called **sunspots**, are the most obvious features. Sunspots look dark because they are cooler than the rest of the photosphere. If you could see them by themselves, they would actually look very bright.

Scientists have observed sunspots for thousands of years. In the past few hundred years, they have recorded the number of sunspots observed each year. Scientists noticed that the number of sunspots increases and decreases over a period of about 11 years. This is called a sunspot cycle. The graph below shows sunspot cycles over a period of 300 years.

Sunspots can produce **solar flares**. These are brief bursts of energy from the photosphere. Much of a solar flare's energy is

ultraviolet waves, radio waves, and X rays. As the energy is released, a fast-moving stream of particles is thrown into space. These particles are called the **solar wind**. When the solar wind reaches Earth, the particles can cause magnetic storms. These storms disturb compasses and energy and communication systems. They also produce auroras in the northern skies.

As the sun rotates, groups of sunspots seem to move across its surface. After a few days, the same spots are seen in a different location on the sun's surface, as you saw in the investigation. ▶

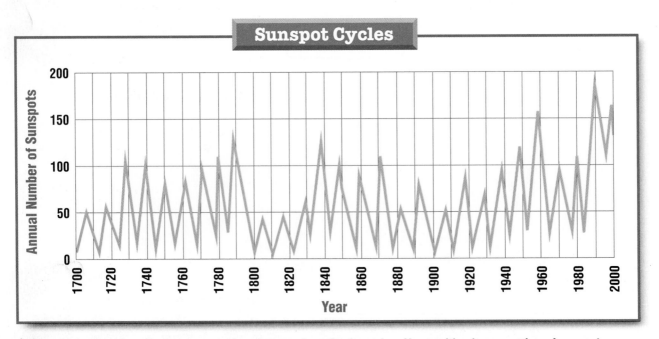

Sunspot Cycles

▲ The graph shows how the average number of sunspots varies in cycles. Years with a large number of sunspots are called *sunspot maximums*. Years with a low number of sunspots are called *sunspot minimums*.

A sun feature similar to a solar flare is called a *solar prominence.* A solar prominence is a bright loop or sheet of gas in the corona. It may hover there for days. Or it may explode and disappear in minutes. The photo on page D28 shows a spectacular solar prominence.

✓ **Compare sunspots, solar flares, and solar wind.**

Summary

The sun is a huge mass of hot gases that produces huge amounts of energy. It is the source of most of the energy on Earth. The sun has several layers: the core, the radiation zone, the convection zone, the photosphere, and the corona. Some of the visible features of the sun are solar prominences, solar flares, granules, and sunspots.

Review

1. How does life on Earth depend on the sun?

2. How is energy produced by the sun?

3. Draw a diagram of the sun, showing each layer.

4. **Critical Thinking** Suppose an astronomer observes a huge solar flare. Predict its effect on Earth in the next day or so.

5. **Test Prep** Solar prominences are loops of gas in the sun's —

   A corona

   B radiation zone

   C core

   D photosphere

LINKS

MATH LINK

Far Out Because distances in the solar system are so large, astronomers use a unit of measure called an astronomical unit, or AU. An AU is the distance between Earth and the sun, about 150 million km. At this distance, energy from the sun reaches Earth in about 8 minutes. Copy the table below, and complete it to show how long it takes the sun's energy to reach each planet.

Planet	Distance (AU)	Time (min)
Mercury	0.4	
Venus	0.7	
Earth	1.0	8
Mars	1.5	
Jupiter	5.2	
Saturn	9.5	
Uranus	19.2	
Neptune	30.0	
Pluto	39.5	

WRITING LINK

Informative Writing—Description Suppose scientists built a space probe that could withstand the sun's high temperatures. Write a description for your teacher of the information the probe might send back as it descends through the sun's layers to its core.

TECHNOLOGY LINK

Learn more about the sun by visiting this Internet site.
www.scilinks.org/harcourt

SCI**LINKS**™
THE WORLD'S A CLICK AWAY

2

How Are Stars Classified?

In this lesson, you can . . .

INVESTIGATE the brightness of stars.

LEARN ABOUT how stars are classified.

LINK to math, writing, technology, and other areas.

Anyone can make discoveries in space using a simple telescope. ▽

The Brightness of Stars

Activity Purpose Think about the last time you looked at a clear night sky. You probably saw millions of stars. Most stars are hot, bright balls of gas, like the sun. Yet some stars appear bright and some appear dim. Why? In this investigation you can **experiment** to find out.

Materials

- lamp with 40-watt bulb
- lamp with 60-watt bulb

Activity Procedure

1. Place the two lamps near the middle of a darkened hall. Turn the lamps on. (Picture A)

2. **Observe** the lamps from one end of the hall. **Compare** how bright they look. **Record** your observations.

3. Move the lamp with the 60-watt bulb to one end of the hall. **Observe** and **compare** how bright the two lamps look from the other end of the hall. **Record** your observations. (Picture B)

Picture A

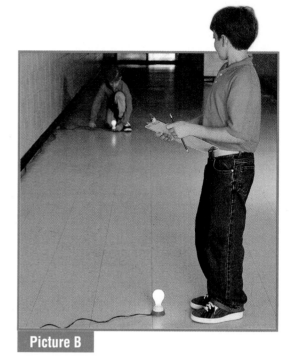

Picture B

4. Now place the lamps side by side at one end of the hall. Again **observe** and **compare** how bright the two lamps look from the other end of the hall. **Record** your observations.

5. **Predict** the distances at which the two lamps seem to be equally bright. **Experiment** by placing the lamps at various places in the hall. **Observe** and **compare** how bright the two lamps look from a variety of distances. **Record** your observations.

Draw Conclusions

1. What two variables did you test in this experiment?

2. From what you **observed**, what two factors affect how bright a light appears to an observer?

3. **Scientists at Work** Scientists often **draw conclusions** when **experimenting**. Use the results of your experiment to draw conclusions about how distance and actual brightness affect how bright stars appear to observers on Earth.

Investigate Further Why can't you see stars during the day? Use the lamps and a brightly lighted room. **Plan and conduct a simple investigation** to show how the sun can make it seem that stars don't shine during the day.

Process Skill Tip

Drawing conclusions should be based on the results obtained while **experimenting** as well as any other information you have.

How Stars Are Classified

Star Magnitude

At night we can see thousands of stars, but during the day we see only one: the sun. The sun is so near that its brightness keeps us from seeing any other stars. As you learned in the investigation, how bright a star looks depends on two factors: its **magnitude**, or brightness, and its distance from Earth.

Suppose two stars that produce the same amount of light are different distances from Earth. They seem to have different magnitudes. The more distant star looks less bright when viewed from Earth, so its *apparent magnitude,* or how bright it seems to be, is less than its *absolute magnitude,* or how bright it really is.

✔ **Why do stars have different apparent magnitudes when viewed from Earth?**

FIND OUT

- about star magnitude
- about the types of stars
- how stars change

VOCABULARY

magnitude
main sequence

◀ This star has a greater apparent magnitude than the star below because it is closer to Earth.

◀ This star has a greater absolute magnitude than the star above. However, since it is farther from Earth, it looks less bright.

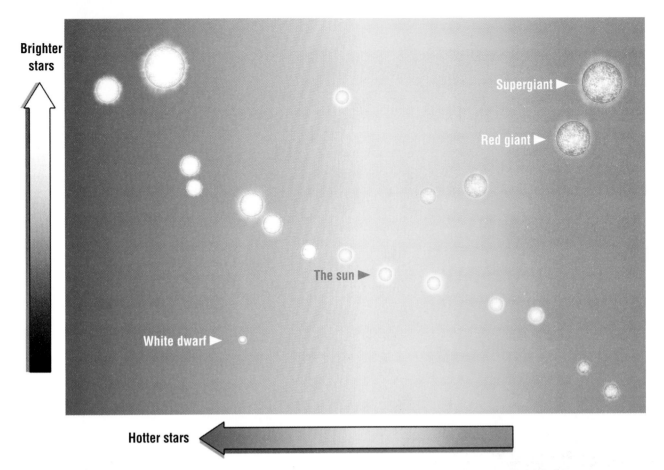

Brighter stars

Hotter stars

▲ This diagram shows relationships between color, size, magnitude, and temperature of stars.

Types of Stars

On a clear, dark night, you can see that although most stars are white, some are blue and others look red. The color of a star is a clue to its surface temperature. Blue stars have the hottest surface temperatures. Red stars have the coolest. Astronomers use surface temperatures and absolute magnitudes to classify stars.

In the early 1900s, two astronomers—Ejnar Hertzsprung, a Dane, and Henry Russell, an American—classified stars. They used a diagram similar to the one above. The diagram shows the relationships between size, magnitude, temperature, and color.

The absolute magnitudes of stars are plotted from bottom to top. The brightest stars are at the top. The surface temperatures of stars are plotted from right to left.

The hottest stars are on the left. The color of a star is shown by its background color. The size of each star is shown by its relative size on the diagram.

Most stars are in a band that runs from the top left of the diagram to the bottom right. This band is called the **main sequence**. Look at the diagram. At the top left are bright, hot, blue stars. In the middle of the main sequence are less bright, cooler stars, such as the sun. These stars shine with a yellow-white light. At the lower right in the main sequence are dim, cool, red stars. About 95 percent of the stars scientists have observed can be classified as main-sequence stars.

✔ **What does a star's position in the main sequence tell you about that star?**

D39

How Stars Change

A star like the sun shines for about 10 billion years. A star with a mass greater than the sun's fuses hydrogen faster. It shines brighter, but for a shorter time. Most of the stars in the main sequence go through the changes shown here.

A typical star begins as a nebula (NEB•yuh•luh). Particles clump together to form a protostar. When the particles become hot enough, the star begins to release energy. It shines steadily for billions of years. Then it begins to run out of hydrogen. The star expands, becoming a red giant. Then its corona expands even more, becoming a planetary nebula. All that remains of the star is a tiny white dwarf.

❶ NEBULA
A star begins within a huge cloud of hydrogen, helium, and tiny particles of dust.

❼ WHITE DWARF
The star continues to shine dimly for billions of years as it slowly cools.

A red giant is a very old star. When the sun becomes a red giant, it will expand until it consumes both Mercury and Venus. Earth will remain, but the planet will become too hot for life. ▼

❻ PLANETARY NEBULA
The red giant's atmosphere expands a million times. It forms a planetary nebula. At the center of the nebula, what is left of the star becomes a white dwarf.

A protostar begins as a gas and dust cloud, billions of kilometers wide. Gravity shrinks that mass into a body 100 million km (about 62 million mi) in diameter. ▶

② PROTOSTAR
After millions of years, the particles begin to squeeze together, attracted to each other by gravity. As the protostar grows in mass, its temperature rises until it begins to glow.

③ MAIN-SEQUENCE STAR
After several million years, the temperature at the center of the protostar reaches about 15 million °C (27 million °F), hot enough for various kinds of energy to be released.

④ EXPANDING STAR
A star with the mass of the sun shines for billions of years before its hydrogen runs low. Then it begins to expand.

⑤ RED GIANT
The star may expand to 100 times its former size. It becomes a red giant.

Observing Stars

As you read in Lesson 1, energy from the sun travels in waves. The same is true of the energy of all stars. Scientists learn about stars by studying the energy they send into space. Each kind of wave carries a different amount of energy. The waves range from high-energy X rays to low-energy radio waves. Astronomers use different kinds of telescopes to detect each kind of wave.

To detect visible light waves, astronomers need only their eyes. But telescopes can gather much more light than human eyes can.

The larger the telescope, the more light it can gather, and the farther into space it can "see." A large telescope, such as the Keck telescope in Hawai'i, can detect stars 2 million times too far for the human eye to see. The Keck telescope has enough light-gathering power to spot a candle on the moon, and it sees twice as far into space as any other telescope on Earth.

Other kinds of telescopes and instruments are used to gather X rays, radio waves, and other waves of energy.

◀ Satellites such as the RXTE are used to detect and measure X rays that stars release into space.

The Keck telescope in Hawai'i is the world's largest reflecting telescope. It has a mirror 10 m (about 33 ft) across for gathering light from distant stars. ▶

The Very Large Array, a group of radio telescopes in New Mexico, is used to detect radio waves. The observatory has 27 antennas, which are like satellite dishes, that move at the same time. Scientists use computers to combine the 27 signals to produce one image of a star.

Each wave of energy gives scientists information about the object it came from. For example, the kinds of waves absorbed or given off by a star can tell what it's made of. This is how scientists know that the sun and most other stars are mostly hydrogen and helium.

✓ **How do scientists learn about stars?**

Summary

Scientists classify stars by absolute magnitude, surface temperature, size, and color. Most stars are in the main sequence. Stars undergo a series of changes from nebula to protostar to main-sequence star to expanding star to red giant to planetary nebula and white dwarf. Scientists learn about stars by using telescopes and other instruments to study the energy that stars release into space.

Review

1. What is the difference between absolute magnitude and apparent magnitude?
2. How will the sun's cycle end?
3. Why does a star begin shining?
4. **Critical Thinking** Most of the stars in the main sequence are to the lower right of the sun. What can you **conclude** about the brightness of these stars and their temperatures?
5. **Test Prep** A star's apparent magnitude depends on —
   A brightness and size
   B absolute magnitude and distance from Earth
   C size and distance from Earth
   D absolute magnitude and size

LINKS

MATH LINK

Neighbors Other than the sun, Proxima Centauri is the star closest to Earth. It is about 4.2 light-years away. A light-year is the distance light travels in one Earth year—about 9.5 trillion km. How far from Earth is Proxima Centauri?

WRITING LINK

Expressive Writing—Poem Write a poem about the stars for your classmates. Use what you have learned in this lesson about stars' magnitudes, temperatures, sizes, and colors.

LANGUAGE ARTS LINK

Star Questions Write a list of five questions you have about stars or other objects in space. If possible, find an astronomer at a local college or an amateur astronomy club. Ask the astronomer your questions.

ART LINK

Star Chart Make a diagram or a drawing to show the difference between absolute magnitude and apparent magnitude.

TECHNOLOGY LINK

Learn more about stars by visiting the Harcourt Learning Site. **www.harcourtschool.com**

WELCOME TO
THE
LEARNING
SITE

What Are Galaxies?

In this lesson, you can . . .

INVESTIGATE the location of the sun in the Milky Way Galaxy.

LEARN ABOUT different types of galaxies.

LINK to math, writing, art, and technology.

These star tracks were made with time-lapse photography. ▽

INVESTIGATE

The Sun's Location in the Milky Way Galaxy

Activity Purpose The sun is in a large grouping of stars called the Milky Way Galaxy. But where in this grouping is the sun? In this investigation you can **make a model** of the Milky Way Galaxy. You can **use the model** to help you find out where the sun is in the galaxy.

Materials
■ scrap paper

Activity Procedure

1 Make about 70 small balls from scrap paper. These will be your "stars."

2 On a table, **make a model** of the Milky Way Galaxy. Arrange the paper stars in a spiral with six arms. Pile extra stars in the center of the spiral. Use fewer stars along the arms. (Picture A)

3 Look down at the model. Draw what you **observe**.

4 Position your eyes at table level. Look across the surface of the table at the model. Again, draw what you **observe**. (Picture B)

5 Look at the photographs at the bottom of page D47. One is of a spiral galaxy viewed from the edge. The other shows the galaxy viewed from the "top." **Compare** the pictures you drew in Steps 3 and 4 with the photographs of a spiral galaxy. Then look at page D46. **Observe** the photograph of a ribbon of stars. This is our view of the Milky Way Galaxy from Earth. Using your drawings and the photographs, **infer** where in the Milky Way Galaxy the sun is.

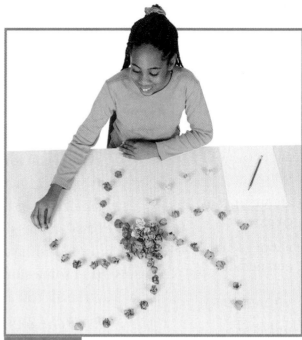
Picture A

Draw Conclusions

1. Suppose the sun is located "above" the Milky Way Galaxy. What view of the galaxy might we see from Earth?

2. If the sun is in one of the arms, what view might we see of the galaxy then?

Picture B

3. From your drawings and the photographs of a spiral galaxy, where in the Milky Way Galaxy do you **infer** the sun is?

4. Scientists at Work Scientists often **infer** when **using models** like the one you made. How did your model of the Milky Way Galaxy help you infer the sun's location in the galaxy?

Investigate Further **Observe** the Milky Way Galaxy in the night sky. You will need a clear, dark night, far away from city lights. Binoculars or a telescope will help you see some of the fainter stars.

Process Skill Tip

When you **infer** while **using models**, you base your inferences on everything you observe about the model. It's important to keep in mind that models are limited in how they show real-world situations.

Galaxies

The Milky Way Galaxy

VOCABULARY

universe
galaxy
light-year

When you look at the sky on a clear, dark night, away from city lights, you can see millions of stars. But you are seeing only a small part of the universe. The **universe** is everything that exists—planets, stars, dust, gases, and energy. Although it seems crowded with stars, most of the universe is empty.

On some summer nights, you may see a bright ribbon of stars overhead. You are looking toward the center of Earth's galaxy. A **galaxy** is a group of stars, gas, and dust. Many galaxies rotate around a core. Most stars are part of galaxies, and the universe contains about a hundred billion galaxies.

Earth's galaxy is called the Milky Way Galaxy. It includes more than 100 billion stars, and it is one of the largest galaxies in the universe. It is so large that the light of a star on one side of the galaxy takes more than 100,000 light-years to reach the other side. As the Milky Way Galaxy rotates, the sun makes one complete turn around the center every 200–250 million Earth years.

✔ **What is a galaxy?**

This photograph of the Milky Way Galaxy was taken from Earth.

D46

| Spiral galaxy | Barred galaxy | Elliptical galaxy | Irregular galaxy |

These drawings show the four types of galaxies. ▶

Types of Galaxies

Galaxies are classified by shape. There are four basic types: spiral, barred spiral, elliptical, and irregular.

The Milky Way Galaxy is a spiral galaxy. A spiral galaxy has a bright bulge of stars in the center and rotating arms. Earth's solar system is in one of the Milky Way Galaxy's spiral arms, about 30,000 light-years from the center of the galaxy. A **light-year** is the distance light travels in one Earth year, about 9.5 trillion km.

A spiral galaxy's arms contain young stars, protostars, dust, and gas. The thick bulge at the center contains older stars.

A barred spiral galaxy is similar to a spiral galaxy. The difference is that the spirals extend from a bar of stars that stretches from the center.

About half of all galaxies are elliptical. The shapes of elliptical galaxies range from almost a sphere, like a basketball, to a shape like a flattened football. Unlike spiral galaxies, elliptical galaxies don't seem to rotate. Irregular galaxies are groups of stars with no obvious shape.

✔ **What are the four basic shapes of galaxies?**

From the side a spiral galaxy looks like a thin rod with a center bulge. A spiral galaxy, seen from the "top," looks like a giant pinwheel spinning through space. The arms wind around the center as it turns, giving the galaxy its spiral appearance.

The Horsehead Nebula in Orion is a dark, dense swirl of dust. Behind the nebula, bright young stars flood the background with light.

Galactic Clusters and Nebulae

Have you ever seen a faint smudge or a misty patch of stars in the night sky? You may have been looking at a galactic cluster or a nebula.

A *galactic cluster* is a group of galaxies. The Milky Way Galaxy is one of about 30 galaxies in a cluster called the Local Group. The Milky Way Galaxy is one of the larger galaxies in this cluster. Most of the galaxies in the Local Group are small and elliptical or irregular.

Beyond the Local Group are other galactic clusters. Some of these are huge, with thousands of galaxies. One of the clusters closest to the Local Group is the Virgo Cluster, which is about 50 million light-years away.

You read about nebulae in Lesson 2. Astronomers hypothesize that stars form in nebulae. Unlike a galactic cluster, a nebula has no

◀ The Virgo Cluster contains more than 100,000 galaxies. At its center are three giant elliptical galaxies. One of these galaxies is about the same size as the entire Local Group.

light of its own. But if there is a hot star within a few light-years, the gases in the nebula shine. This is because hot stars emit a lot of ultraviolet waves. The energy of these waves is absorbed by the gases in the nebula. The gases then glow in different colors. The colors tell what gases are in the nebula. For example, hydrogen glows red, while oxygen and helium glow green. Different combinations of gases and dust create different effects, as in the Horsehead Nebula shown on page D48.

✔ **What is the difference between a galactic cluster and a nebula?**

Summary

A galaxy is a group of stars, gas, and dust. Many galaxies rotate around a central core. The sun is in the Milky Way Galaxy. The Milky Way Galaxy is part of a galactic cluster called the Local Group. Also visible in the night sky are nebulae, which are clouds of gas and dust in which stars form.

Review

1. What is the Local Group?
2. Describe the four basic shapes of galaxies.
3. What is a nebula?
4. **Critical Thinking** The Horsehead Nebula doesn't glow like some nebulae. Why not?
5. **Test Prep** The Virgo Cluster is a —
   A giant elliptical galaxy
   B nebula
   C Local Group
   D galactic cluster

LINKS

MATH LINK

A Long Way It takes the sun about 250 million Earth years to travel around the center of the Milky Way Galaxy. If the sun is about 5 billion Earth years old, how many trips has it made?

WRITING LINK

Expressive Writing—Friendly Letter Suppose there are intelligent life forms in another galaxy. Write a letter to these life forms. Explain where you are in the Milky Way Galaxy, and tell the other life forms about life on Earth.

ART LINK

Galaxies on Stage Choose some of the information in this lesson. Rewrite it as a play. Present the play to other fifth-grade students in your school. Use dialogue, movement, and props in your play.

TECHNOLOGY LINK

Learn more about galaxies and how they move through space by viewing *Colliding Galaxies* on the **Harcourt Science Newsroom Video.**

MAGNETARS

Some people say "there's nothing new under the sun." Astronomers might laugh at this! They are always finding new things in the universe. One exciting discovery is a different kind of star. Stars of this kind spin rapidly and send out gigantic bursts of energy. They might also be the most powerful magnets in the universe. Astronomers call them magnetars.

Surprise in the Sky

The first data about magnetars came from spy satellites. The U.S. government wanted to know when certain countries were testing nuclear weapons. So it launched a series of satellites to detect radiation from nuclear explosions. To government scientists' amazement, the satellites picked up radiation coming from outer space! Bursts of gamma rays seemed to be coming from everywhere in the universe. Government scientists communicated with civilian astronomers about this mysterious energy from space. Using satellites and radio telescopes, astronomers began measuring the energy bursts. Some of the larger bursts released as much energy in one second as the sun does in 1000 years!

Radio telescopes are also used to identify unknown energy sources from space.

This drawing of a magnetar shows its magnetic force field.

A few astronomers hypothesized that these stars have solid crusts and magnetic fields so strong that they cause the crusts to crack, releasing radiation. So magnetars may have starquakes, just as Earth has earthquakes.

A Giant Magnet

What's so different about this new kind of star? For one thing, if you were close enough, a magnetar's huge magnetic field would rearrange the atoms in your body. You wouldn't be you anymore! Think of this star as a giant magnet. Even if it were as far away as the sun, it could pull metal objects, such as paper clips, out of your pockets. The pull of gravity on its surface would flatten you like a pancake. And a magnetar spins very, very fast! While Earth takes 24 hours to complete one rotation, some magnetars take less than 6 seconds.

Luckily for us, the closest magnetars are thousands of light-years away. Astronomers have identified several of them and hypothe-

size that there are millions of others. From studying magnetars, scientists can learn more about magnetism, gravity, and other forces. And, since magnetars seem to have formed after massive stars exploded, they might help scientists learn more about how stars develop and change.

THINK ABOUT IT

1. How are magnetars different from other stars?
2. Why would it be dangerous for a space-craft to fly near a magnetar?

WEB LINK:
For science and technology updates, visit The Learning Site.
www.harcourtschool.com

Careers   Astrophysicist

What They Do
Astrophysicists work in space agencies, universities, or observatories. They study the stars and galaxies to find out more about radiation, magnetism, and other processes in the universe.

Education and Training A person wishing to become an astrophysicist needs to study math, physics, and chemistry. He or she also needs training in using equipment such as radar and telescopes. Some astrophysicists learn how to use satellites to get data from distant stars.

Julio Navarro

ASTRONOMER

"If you look at a galaxy far away, you're seeing the galaxy as it was many years ago. You're looking at the universe as it was when it was young."

Julio Navarro is a theoretical astronomer who studies galaxies. Instead of looking through telescopes, Dr. Navarro works with numerical data from the Hubble Space Telescope and from ground-based telescopes. He uses this data in computer models that help him study the formation of galaxies and other bodies in the universe.

Dr. Navarro explains that the light from distant galaxies can take billions of years to reach our telescopes. So we're not seeing those galaxies as they appear now, but as they appeared billions of years ago.

When he was growing up in Argentina, no one would have guessed that Dr. Navarro would become an astronomer. He was more interested in music. However, an essay assignment in high school changed everything. "I was looking through a lot of books, and I became interested in astronomy," says Dr. Navarro. He kept reading, and his interest grew.

Dr. Navarro earned a bachelor's degree and a Ph.D. in astronomy before leaving Argentina to work and study in North America and Europe. Today Dr. Navarro is at the University of Victoria, in British Columbia, Canada, where he teaches astronomy and does research on the formation of galaxies.

THINK ABOUT IT

1. Why does Dr. Navarro study distant galaxies?
2. How does Dr. Navarro gather data for his studies?

Looking into the past

A Model Sun

What are some sun features?

Materials
- yellow construction paper
- ruler
- scissors
- markers
- black construction paper
- glue
- white legal-sized paper

Procedure

1 Cut a 20-cm circle from the yellow paper to represent the photosphere. Using markers, make sunspots on the photosphere.

2 Cut a 20-cm circle from the black paper to represent the moon during a solar eclipse.

3 Glue the yellow circle to the white paper.

4 Using the markers, color jagged shapes around the sun to represent the sun's corona.

5 Use your black "moon" to eclipse the sun's photosphere to study its corona.

Draw Conclusions

Why did you cut out the moon for the total eclipse the same size as the sun? Scientists learn a great deal about the sun during total eclipses. Why is this an important time to study the sun? What benefits are there to blocking out the sun's photosphere?

Astrolabe

How do people navigate by the stars?

Materials
- 15-cm cardboard square
- protractor
- pencil
- drinking straw
- tape
- 20-cm piece of string
- metal washer

Procedure

1 Using the protractor, and starting in one corner of the cardboard square, draw a line at an angle of 5°. Draw additional lines at 10°, 15°, and so on.

2 Tape the straw to the cardboard as shown.

3 At the point where all the lines meet, make a hole in the cardboard. Push the string through the hole and tie a knot to keep it from pulling through the hole. Tie the washer to the other end of the string.

4 Look at the North Star through the straw. Measure the angle of the North star by noting the angle of the string.

Draw Conclusions

The angle of the North Star tells you your latitude on the Earth. What is the angle of the North Star where you live? What is the latitude where you live?

Chapter ② Review and Test Preparation

Vocabulary Review

Use the terms below to complete the sentences. The page numbers in ( ) tell you where to look in the chapter if you need help.

photosphere (D33)

corona (D33)

sunspot (D34)

solar flare (D34)

solar wind (D34)

magnitude (D38)

main sequence (D39)

universe (D46)

galaxy (D46)

light-year (D47)

1. The sun's atmosphere is the ____.

2. A dark area on the sun that is caused by twists and loops in the sun's magnetic field is a ____.

3. A ____ is a brief burst of energy that occurs above a sunspot.

4. The ____ is a fast-moving stream of particles ejected into space.

5. Two stars the same distance from Earth that give off the same amount of light will appear to have the same ____.

6. The sun's ____ is the layer we see.

7. The classification group to which most stars belong is the ____.

8. The ____ is everything that exists.

9. A group of stars, gas, and dust is a ____.

10. A ____ is the distance light travels in one Earth year.

Connect Concepts

Use the terms in the Word Bank below to complete the chart of Your Place in Space.

solar system   universe   Earth
Local Group   Milky Way Galaxy

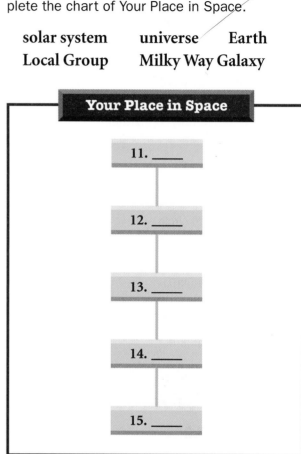

Your Place in Space

11. ____

12. ____

13. ____

14. ____

15. ____

Check Understanding

Write the letter of the best choice.

16. At the center of the solar system is a —
    A galaxy   C planet
    B moon   D star

17. The surface of the sun is the part we can see. It is called the —
    F core   H chromosphere
    G photosphere   J corona

18. Sunspots can cause brief bursts of energy known as solar —
    A flares   C auroras
    B prominences   D fusion

19. The sun is a huge mass of —

F metals   H gases
G light   J liquids

20. The hottest stars in the main sequence are also the —

A brightest   C largest
B least bright   D smallest

21. The Milky Way Galaxy is located in the Local Group, a —

F universe   H nebula
G galactic cluster   J main sequence

22. What type of galaxy is shown in the illustration?

A elliptical   C spiral
B irregular   D spiral barred

Critical Thinking

23. Infrared telescopes have detected new stars forming in the Orion Nebula. Why can't we see these stars forming?

24. Galaxies contain millions of stars. Yet they look faint to people on Earth. Explain why galaxies look so faint to observers on Earth.

25. A light-year is the distance light travels in one Earth year. Suppose you look at a star that is 100,000 light-years away. Explain why you are looking into the past.

Process Skills Review

26. Sunspots appear and disappear in cycles that average about 11 years. As the cycle starts, the number of sun spots increases for 5 to 6 years. Then it decreases for 5 to 6 years. Using what you know about the relationship between solar flares and sunspots, **hypothesize** when solar flares are most frequent.

27. Scientists believe that time spent in the main sequence is one of the stages of a star's "life." Most known stars are main-sequence stars. From this information, what can you **infer** about the amount of time a typical star spends in this stage?

28. How could you **model** changes in the apparent magnitude of stars?

Performance Assessment

Star Light, Star Bright

Make up a star. Draw a picture of your star, showing its color and its type—main sequence, red giant, white dwarf, or nebula. Label the drawing with the type of star. Draw another picture, showing the location of your star in a spiral galaxy as viewed from "above." From your drawing, infer the direction in which the galaxy rotates. Draw an arrow to show the direction.

Unit Project Wrap Up

Here are some ideas for ways to wrap up your unit project.

Contact NASA

Write to NASA asking for information about the International Space Station that is being built. Compare their plans to your plans.

Make a Table

Use a computer and spreadsheet software to make a table that shows the distances from planets in our solar system to the sun.

Display at a Science Fair

Display the results of your project in a school science fair. Prepare a written report describing how you researched and designed the space station.

Investigate Further

How could you make your project better? What other questions do you have about the solar system? Plan ways to find answers to your questions. Use the Science Handbook on pages R2-R9 for help.

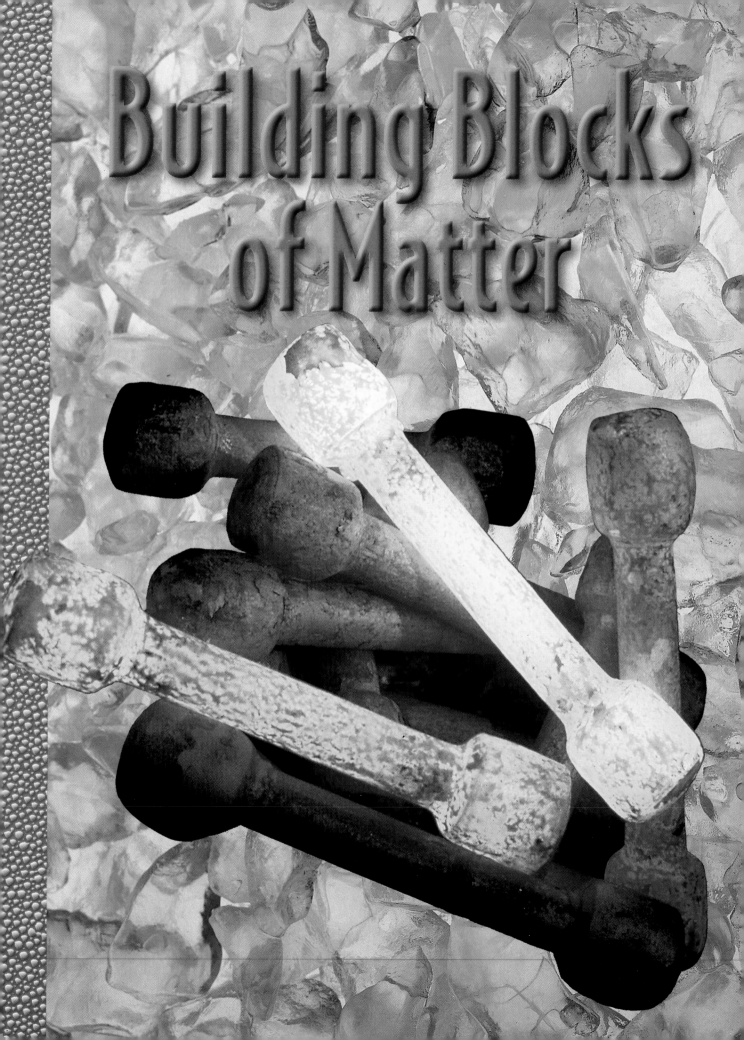

Building Blocks
of Matter

UNIT E

PHYSICAL SCIENCE

Building Blocks of Matter

Unit Project

Let's Cook!

Suppose you are a cook in a restaurant. Develop a menu of foods that could demonstrate ways matter can change. Prepare the items, keeping records of the changes that take place. Identify physical and chemical changes. Invite others to predict whether the changes are reversible, and let them test their predictions. Then, look for advertisements for foods. Find an ad that makes a claim you can test. For example, one cereal manufacturer says their cereal stays crisp longer in milk. Plan and conduct a simple investigation to test the claim.

Chapter 1

Matter and Its Properties

Do you know why water, a liquid, can also be a solid (ice) and a gas (water vapor)? Actually, *every* substance can be a solid, a liquid, and a gas. The form a substance takes depends on its temperature and how fast particles of the substance move.

Water expands as it freezes. Water freezing in tiny cracks in rocks makes the cracks bigger. Over millions of years, this process can turn a mountain into a pile of sand.

Vocabulary Preview

matter
physical properties
mass
weight
volume
density
solubility
solid
liquid
gas
evaporation
condensation
reactivity
combustibility

E2

People used to think that glass was a liquid, not a solid, because old glass windows are thicker at the bottom than at the top. However, at normal temperatures, glass is still more like a solid than it is like a liquid.

How cold can it get? There is a lowest possible temperature, called absolute zero. At this temperature the particles that make up a substance stop moving.

Hot and Cold Temperatures

Temperature	Celsius	Fahrenheit
Absolute zero	−273.15°	−459.67°
Water freezes	0.0°	32.0°
Human body	37.0°	98.6°
Water boils	100.0°	212.0°

How Can Physical Properties Be Used to Identify Matter?

In this lesson, you can . . .

INVESTIGATE physical properties.

LEARN ABOUT how to measure and use physical properties.

LINK to math, writing, physical education, and technology.

Even apples have different physical properties.

INVESTIGATE

Using Physical Properties to Identify Objects

Activity Purpose Some objects, such as a tree and a rock, are so easy to identify that you almost don't have to think about it. But how do you identify two different trees? You have to **observe** their properties, or characteristics, more closely. In this investigation you will use properties to identify objects that are very similar.

Materials

- apples
- balance
- ruler
- string

Activity Procedure

1 Carefully **observe** the apple your teacher gave you. What properties of your apple can you discover just by observing it? **Record** all the properties you observe.

2 Use the balance, ruler, and string to **measure** some properties of your apple. **Record** the properties you measure. (Picture A)

3 Put your apple in the pile of apples on your teacher's desk. Don't watch while your teacher mixes up the apples.

Picture A

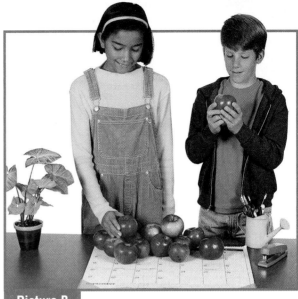

Picture B

4 Using the properties that you recorded, try to identify your apple in the pile. (Picture B)

5 Using the balance, ruler, and string, **measure** this apple. **Compare** the measurements to those you recorded earlier. Then decide whether the apple you chose from the pile is yours. If someone else chose the same apple, comparing measurements should help you decide whose apple it really is.

Draw Conclusions

1. **Compare** your apple with a classmate's apple. How are the two apples alike? How are they different?

2. Why was it helpful to **measure** some properties of your apple in addition to **observing** it?

3. How did you use the string to **measure** the apple?

4. **Scientists at Work** Scientists use both observations and measurements to identify substances. Which is faster, **observing** or **measuring**? Which provides more exact information?

Investigate Further **Compare** the list of your apple's properties with a classmate's list. Then, using your classmate's list, try to find his or her apple. Talk with your classmate about how he or she made the list. Did you and your classmate do things the same way?

Some properties can only be observed. When you **observe**, you use only your senses. Some properties can be measured with instruments. Being able to **measure** something you are studying will help you identify it.

The Importance of Physical Properties

Matter and Physical Properties

FIND OUT

- what physical properties are

- how to measure some physical properties

- examples of physical properties that can be used to identify substances

VOCABULARY

matter
physical properties
mass
weight
volume
density
solubility

The objects you used in the investigation were all alike—they were all apples. But would you believe that apples, parrots, candy, computers, humans, and even the air around you are all alike in one way? They are all made of matter. **Matter** is anything that has mass and takes up space.

Objects made of matter can be very different from each other. Each object has its own set of characteristics, or *properties*. For example, one property of a piece of candy is its color. Another is its taste.

Color, hardness, and taste are examples of physical properties. An object's ability to conduct heat, sound, or electricity or to become a magnet are also physical properties. **Physical properties** are characteristics of a substance that can be observed or measured without changing the substance into something else.

Some physical properties, such as color, can be observed directly. Other physical properties, such as length, must be measured. Measurements are especially useful in science because they provide more exact descriptions of matter than direct observations do.

✔ **What are some examples of physical properties?**

◀ You can tell these balls apart by examining the physical properties of size, mass, and color.

Mass and Weight

One physical property that can be measured is mass. **Mass** is the amount of matter in an object. The mass of an 18-wheel truck is greater than the mass of a small car, because the truck has more matter. In this example you can easily see the difference in the amount of matter. Sometimes the difference in the amount of matter between two objects is very small. In fact, some matter may have so little mass that it is difficult to measure. But all matter has some mass.

It's easy to confuse mass with another physical property—weight. Weight depends on the amount of matter in an object. However, weight also depends on the force of gravity. So **weight** is a measure of the pull of gravity on an object. While the mass of an object is always the same, the weight of an object is not. For example, a car that weighs 12,000 newtons (about 2698 lb) on Earth would weigh only 2000 newtons (about 450 lb) on the moon! This is because the force of gravity is 6 times greater on Earth than it is on the moon. Because weight can vary,

The mass of the foam, on the balance, will be the same no matter what shape it is given. The mass of the gel, in the container at the left, will also stay the same, even though it takes the shape of its container.

mass is a better measurement of the amount of matter in an object.

Different equipment is used to measure weight and mass. Weight is measured on a spring scale. How much the spring in the scale is squeezed or stretched depends on the pull of gravity and the mass of the object being weighed. Mass is measured on a balance to avoid also measuring the pull of gravity. On a balance the mass of an object is compared to a known mass.

✔ **How are mass and weight alike? How are they different?**

An astronaut weighs less on the moon than on Earth. However, the astronaut has the same mass on the moon as on Earth. ▶

Volume

Matter not only has mass but also takes up space. **Volume** is the amount of space that an object takes up. Volume can be measured in several ways.

The volume of a liquid can be measured using a graduated cylinder. A *graduated cylinder* is a clear tube that is marked in milliliters. When liquids are poured into a graduated cylinder, they stick slightly to the tube, forming a curved surface. To measure the volume of a liquid accurately, you need to read the volume at the bottom of this curve.

The volume of some solids can be calculated. First, measure the length, width, and height of the object. Then multiply as shown in this formula:

Volume = length × width × height

For example, the volume of a box 38 cm long, 21 cm wide, and 13 cm high is calculated as follows:

Volume = 38 cm × 21 cm × 13 cm = 10,374 cm³

The volume of the rock is equal to the difference in the volume of the water before and after the rock is placed in it.

Although most solids do not have regular shapes, their volumes can still be measured. One way to do this is to measure the amount of liquid, such as water, that the solid *displaces*, or takes the place of. To do this, partially fill a measuring container with water and place the solid in the liquid. You will observe that the level of the liquid rises. The volume of the water and solid together is greater than the volume of the water alone. The volume of the solid is the difference between these two volumes.

✔ **What are two ways to measure the volume of a solid?**

◀ **The 250 mL (about 8 oz) of juice in the box can be measured in a graduated cylinder. Notice that the volume of a liquid does not depend on the shape of the container.**

Density

Mass and volume are physical properties that can be measured. By themselves, neither can be used to identify unknown objects or substances. However, if you have measured the mass and the volume of an object, you can calculate its density. You can then use this property to identify some objects.

Density is the concentration of matter in an object. It is the amount of matter in a certain volume. Density is calculated by using the following formula:

Density = mass ÷ volume

For example, the density of a substance with a mass of 10 g and a volume of 2 cm³ is calculated as follows:

Density = 10 g ÷ 2 cm³
= 5 g/cm³

Pure substances always have the same density when measured under the same conditions. The density of diamond, for example, is always 3.51 g/cm³ (2.03 oz/in.³).

The Density of Copper			
Mass	8.96 g	89.6 g	134.4 g
Volume	1 cm³	10 cm³	15 cm³
Density	8.96 g/cm³	8.96 g/cm³	8.96 g/cm³

▲ No matter how large or how small a copper ball is, its density is always the same.

▲ The copper cube, made with the densest matter, has the greatest mass. The aluminum cube is less dense than the copper cube. The wooden cube is the same size but is made with the least-dense matter. It has the smallest mass.

Because density is always the same for a pure substance, this property can be used for identification. Suppose you were given a gemstone and didn't know whether it was a diamond or a zircon—a mineral that looks like a diamond but is much less valuable. If you had instruments that were exact enough, you could measure the gemstone's mass on a balance and find out its volume by the amount of water it displaced. Then you could calculate its density. If the density is 4.7 g/cm³ (2.72 oz/in.³), you have a zircon. If the density is 3.51 g/cm³ (2.03 oz/in.³), you have a diamond!

✔ **Will different volumes of the same substance have the same density or different densities?**

Mixtures and Solutions

Most of the objects around us are not pure substances. Instead, they are mixtures. A *mixture* is a combination of two or more different kinds of matter, each of which keeps its own physical properties.

In some mixtures it's easy to tell that each type of matter keeps its physical properties, because you can still see the parts of the mixture. If sugar and iron filings are mixed together, for example, you can still see the individual sugar grains and the iron filings.

Mixtures can be separated into the substances that make them up. The method used to separate a mixture depends on the physical properties of the substances in the mixture. In a mixture of iron filings and sugar, the iron filings keep their physical property of magnetism. Since sugar doesn't have this property, you can separate the mixture with a magnet.

If sugar is mixed with water, it's not easy to tell what is in the mixture. The sugar seems to disappear. But if you taste the mixture, you will find that the water is sweet. The sugar has kept its physical property of taste. In a mixture of sugar and water, the sugar dissolves in the water. When one substance dissolves in another, the two form a solution. A *solution* is a type of mixture in which particles of the two substances are evenly mixed. Solutions cannot be easily separated.

The **solubility** (sahl•yoo•BIL•uh•tee) of substances, or their ability to be dissolved, can be used to help identify them. Sugar, for example, is soluble in water, but ground black pepper is not.

The air in the diver's tank is a mixture of mostly nitrogen and oxygen ▶

Sea water is a mixture of salts and water. The salts in sea water can be separated from the water by evaporation.

Gases in Air

Other gases 1%

Oxygen 21%

Nitrogen 78%

Sand is a mixture of solids. You can still see the different types of solids after they are mixed together.

In the sugar and water solution, a solid is mixed with a liquid. Rubbing alcohol is a solution of two liquids: water and alcohol. But solutions don't have to include a liquid. Mixtures of metals are solutions of solids. Brass is a solution of zinc and copper. It is made by melting the two metals together. Gases can form solutions, too. Air is a solution of several gases, as the circle graph on page E10 shows.

✔ **What is an example of a mixture?**

Summary

Matter is anything that has mass and takes up space. Physical properties can be used to identify different types of objects and substances. Some physical properties (such as mass, volume, and density) can be measured. Physical properties such as density and solubility help scientists identify different substances.

Review

1. How can physical properties be used to identify objects and substances?

2. Does an object on Earth have the same mass as it does on the moon? Explain.

3. What physical properties are used to calculate the density of an object?

4. **Critical Thinking** Are all solutions mixtures? Are all mixtures solutions? Explain with examples.

5. **Test Prep** All of these are physical properties except —

   A mass

   B volume

   C density

   D time

LINKS

MATH LINK

The International System of Units (SI)
SI uses prefixes to tell you how many times to multiply or divide by 10. Put these measurements in order from shortest to longest: 2 dam, 4 m, 60 dm, 500 cm, 10,000 mm.

Prefix	Abbreviation	Multiply By
kilo	k	1000
hecto	h	100
deca	da	10
deci	d	$\frac{1}{10}$
centi	c	$\frac{1}{100}$
milli	m	$\frac{1}{1000}$

WRITING LINK

Informative Writing—Description Suppose you find an unknown substance growing out of the sidewalk in front of your home. Decide on its physical properties, and write a paragraph for your science teacher describing them.

PHYSICAL EDUCATION LINK

Swimming Research to find the dimensions of an Olympic-sized pool. Then figure out the volume of water it can hold.

TECHNOLOGY LINK

Learn more about the physical properties of matter by visiting this Internet site.
www.scilinks.org/harcourt

How Does Matter Change from One State to Another?

In this lesson, you can . . .

INVESTIGATE changes in states of matter.

LEARN ABOUT three states of matter.

LINK to math, writing, physical education, and technology.

Ice (water) changes state from a solid to a liquid when it is warmed by the heat of a human hand. ▽

INVESTIGATE

Changing States of Matter

Activity Purpose Liquid water, ice, and water vapor are all the same substance, but they have different physical properties. That's because they are all different states, or forms, of the same substance. In this investigation you will **observe** and **infer** changing states of matter.

Materials

- 5 ice cubes
- zip-top plastic bag
- balance
- thermometer
- glass beaker
- safety goggles
- hot plate

CAUTION

Activity Procedure

1 Place five ice cubes in a zip-top plastic bag. Be sure to seal the bag. Use the balance to **measure** the mass of the ice cubes and the bag. **Observe** the shape of the ice cubes. **Record** your observations and measurements. (Picture A)

2 Set the bag of ice cubes in a warm place. **Observe** what happens to the shape of the ice cubes. Use the balance to **measure** the mass of the melted ice cubes and the bag. Unzip the bag slightly and insert the thermometer. Measure the temperature of the water. **Record** your observations and measurements. Use your observations to **infer** that a change of state is occurring.

Picture A

Picture B

3 After the ice has completely melted, pour the water into a glass beaker. Put the thermometer in the beaker. **Observe** what happens to the water's shape, and **record** the water's temperature. (Picture B)

4 CAUTION **Put on the safety goggles.** Your teacher will use a hot plate to heat the water in the beaker until it boils. **Observe** what happens to the water when it boils. **Record** the temperature of the boiling water. Use your observations to **infer** that another change of state has occurred.

Draw Conclusions

1. Identify the different states of water at different points in this investigation.

2. **Compare** the mass of the ice to the mass of water after it melted. What does this show about changes in state?

3. What temperatures did you **record** as the water changed states?

4. **Scientists at Work** After scientists use their senses to **observe** the properties of substances, they can **infer** whether a change in state has taken place. What did you observe in this investigation? What did you infer about a change of state from each observation?

Investigate Further The physical change that happens to water when it is boiled produces water vapor—an invisible gas. **Plan and conduct a simple investigation** to test the hypothesis that the mass of the water vapor is the same as the mass of the liquid water.

Process Skill Tip

When you **observe** the physical properties of a substance, you can use your observations to **infer** a change in its state.

E13

Changes in State

Three States of Matter

FIND OUT

- what three states of matter are
- how substances change state

VOCABULARY

solid
liquid
gas
evaporation
condensation

In the investigation you learned that water exists in three states—solid, liquid, and gas. Most matter exists in one or more of these states. Which state it is in depends on the conditions at the time, such as temperature and pressure. A **solid** has a definite shape and a definite volume. A **liquid** has a definite volume but no definite shape. For example, when you pour orange juice, a liquid, from a jug into a glass, the shape of the juice changes to fit the container. The volume of juice, however, doesn't change. A **gas** does not have a definite shape or volume. If you put air into a tire, for example, it takes the same shape as the tire. But even when the tire seems full, you can put more air into it.

✔ **What are three states of matter?**

Two states of water are shown in this picture. A third can be inferred. The snow is solid water. Melted snow and ice are liquid water. Water vapor released into the air by the geysers (GY•zerz) is a gas. However, the steam that can be seen near the geysers is liquid water, not water vapor.

Particles of Matter

Why does a solid keep its shape? Why does a liquid flow? Why can the volume of a gas change? You can better understand the differences between states of matter if you think of matter as particles in motion.

In a solid the particles are very close together. Because there is very little space between particles, they can't be squeezed any closer together. This gives a solid a definite volume and shape. It also keeps particles in a solid from moving very much. In fact, they are packed together so tightly that each particle stays in the same place and just vibrates.

Particles are not packed together as tightly in a liquid, so they move more freely than they do in a solid. This allows a liquid to flow and take the shape of its container. You can see the motion of particles in a liquid by placing a drop of dye in a glass of water. As the particles bump into one another, the dye slowly spreads through the water.

The particles in a gas are packed together the least. Because the particles are freer to move around in gases than in solids or liquids, gas particles move the fastest. Like a liquid, a gas flows and takes the shape of its container. But the density of particles in a gas is so low that an increase in pressure can move the particles closer together. If the pressure is high enough, a gas becomes a liquid.

✔ **In which state of matter are the particles closest together? Farthest apart?**

A solid feels firm when you touch it because the particles that make it up are packed tightly together. A solid can be used to make gear that protects you, like this bicycle helmet.

The particles in a liquid move freely enough to slide past one another. This allows liquids to change shape, as the milk has done in this splash.

The particles in a gas are the farthest apart and move the fastest. Bubbles of carbon dioxide gas are lighter than the liquid in this glass, so they float to the top and escape into the air.

Changes Between States

You may be used to seeing many substances in only one state. Nitrogen is usually a gas, for example, and aluminum is usually a solid. But all substances can change states. Liquid nitrogen is used to cool other materials to very low temperatures. Liquid aluminum can be poured into molds to make objects.

You may have seen puddles freeze and turn to ice when it gets cold. *Freezing* changes a substance from a liquid to a solid.

When the sun comes out and warms the ice, it melts. *Melting* is a change in state from a solid to a liquid.

In the investigation you saw water boiling on a hot plate. *Boiling* changes a substance from a liquid to a gas. Even when the temperature of a liquid has not yet reached its boiling point, some of the particles near the surface may be moving fast enough to evaporate. **Evaporation** occurs when particles escape from a nonboiling liquid and become a gas.

THE INSIDE STORY

Changing States

When enough heat is removed from a liquid, it freezes. The particles slow down and move closer together. They become tightly packed and a solid is formed. ▼

When a solid melts, the addition of heat makes the particles move faster. ▼

Melting

Freezing

◄ This is the solid state of sulfur.

4 Add a dropper of vinegar to the test tube labeled *vinegar*. **Observe** and **record** what happens this time. (Picture A)

5 Add a dropper of iodine solution to the test tube labeled *iodine*. **CAUTION** **Iodine is poisonous if swallowed and can cause stains. Be careful not to spill or touch the iodine solution. Wash your hands if you get iodine on them.** **Observe** and **record** what happens.

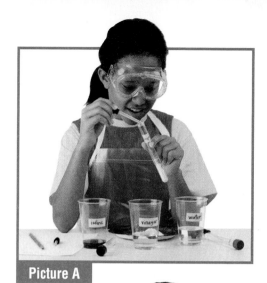
Picture A

6 Wash the test tubes with soap and water. Repeat Steps 3–5 three more times using cornstarch, talcum powder, and baking powder in the test tubes instead of baking soda. Be sure to wash the test tubes between tests. **Observe** and **record** what happens each time. (Picture B)

7 Get an "unknown" sample from your teacher. It will be one of the substances you have already tested. Test it with water, vinegar, and iodine solution, just as you did before. **Observe** and **record** what happens when you add each of the liquids. What is your unknown substance?

Picture B

Draw Conclusions

1. How did you find out what your unknown sample was?

2. Vinegar is one of a group of substances called *acids*. Acids react with substances called *bases*. Of the substances you tested, which are bases? How can you tell?

3. Baking powder is not a pure substance. It is a mixture of two of the other substances you tested. Based on your results, what do you **infer** are the two substances in baking powder?

4. **Scientists at Work** Scientists **experiment** to find out if two substances react. What signs of reactions did your experiments produce? What **variables** did you **control**?

Investigate Further Suppose you wanted to discover some of the chemical properties of chalk. **Predict** whether chalk is an acid or a base. Then **experiment** to test your prediction.

Process Skill Tip

When you **experiment**, it is important to vary only one factor at a time. This helps make clear which factor is the cause of the results you observe. Varying one factor at a time is called **controlling variables**.

Changes in Matter

Physical and Chemical Changes

FIND OUT

- about physical and chemical changes

- how physical and chemical changes can be used to identify substances and to separate mixtures

- about the law of conservation of matter

VOCABULARY

reactivity
combustibility

When ice melts, it changes into liquid water. When liquid water boils, it changes into water vapor. But through all the changes, it is still water. Changes in which no new substances are formed are physical changes. All changes in state are physical changes.

When you shape clay on a potter's wheel, you change its form. This is a physical change. Cutting up a piece of paper is also a physical change. Gases such as hydrogen and oxygen can be cooled and squeezed until they become liquids. When this happens, the gases go through changes in state, volume, and density. These are all physical changes!

But if an electric current is sent through water, a different kind of change takes place. Gases are produced, but the gases are not water. They are oxygen and hydrogen, the substances that make up water. In the space shuttle's main engines, liquid oxygen and liquid hydrogen are mixed and burned as a fuel. Water—a new substance—is produced. Changes in which one or more new substances are formed are called chemical changes, or *chemical reactions*.

A marshmallow melting is an example of a physical change. A marshmallow burning is an example of a chemical change. ▼

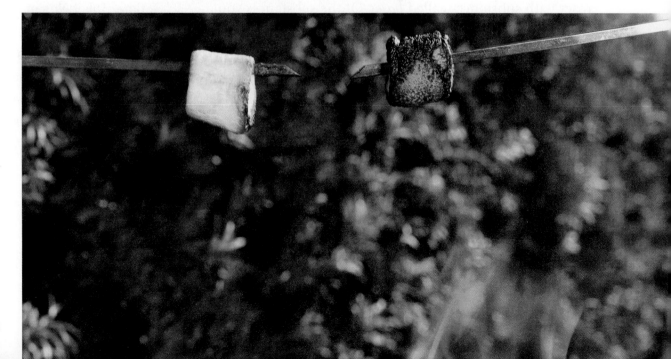

Burning is one kind of chemical reaction. When charcoal burns, for example, carbon reacts with oxygen to produce carbon dioxide. Carbon and oxygen are *reactants*, the starting substances in a chemical reaction. Carbon dioxide is a *product* of the reaction. It is a new substance.

Some substances are more likely than others to react. Chlorine gas reacts chemically with many different substances. But neon gas does not. The ability of a substance to react chemically is called **reactivity**.

There are some clues that can help you identify chemical reactions. They include a change in color or the production of light, heat, or a gas. Paper turns black as it burns, for example. When baking soda is mixed with vinegar, it bubbles. This shows that carbon dioxide has been produced. A candle produces heat and light as it burns.

However, it's sometimes hard to tell the difference between a physical change and a chemical reaction. Cherry-flavored drink powder is pale pink. When you mix it with water, it turns bright red. But the powder has only dissolved. It has gone through a physical change, not a chemical reaction. When you open a cold soft drink, bubbles are produced. But a chemical reaction has not taken place. The carbon dioxide has simply come out of solution. And if you rub your hands quickly back and forth across a surface, they become hot. But the heat is due to friction, not a chemical reaction.

✔ **What is the difference between a physical change and a chemical reaction?**

▲ Production of a different kind of gas shows that a chemical reaction has taken place. When hydrogen peroxide is used to clean a wound, it reacts with a substance in blood, forming oxygen and water.

◄ When sodium combines with chlorine to make sodium chloride (salt), light is produced. This new product shows that a chemical reaction has occurred.

Steel wool burns, but only in pure oxygen, not in air. Steel wool is not as reactive as charcoal, which does burn in air. ▼

Using Physical and Chemical Properties

Chemical reactions often form products with properties that are different from those of the reactants. So observing the chemical and physical properties of a substance can help you decide whether a chemical change or a physical change has taken place.

For example, when iron rusts, it turns red or brown. But is this a chemical reaction or a physical change? Is rust a new substance, or is it still iron?

If you examine rust carefully, you will find that it is no longer shiny like iron. Rust is powdery, while iron bends and is easily formed into other shapes. Iron can conduct electricity, but rust cannot. Iron melts at 1535°C (about 2795°F), and rust at 1594°C (about 2901°F). The density of rust is 5.18 g/cm^3 (about 323 lb/ft^3), while the density of iron is 7.86 g/cm^3 (about 491 lb/ft^3). And rust does not react with oxygen as iron does. A new substance has definitely been formed. A chemical reaction has taken place.

Chemical properties alone can sometimes be used to identify substances. Since charcoal burns, it has the chemical property of **combustibility** (kuhm•buhs•tuh•BIL•uh•tee). Some substances can be identified by certain characteristics of their combustibility. Flame tests can be used to identify substances based on the color of the flame they produce when burned. Barium, for example, produces a green flame. Sodium produces a yellow flame, and potassium produces a violet flame.

Chemical properties are also important in deciding how certain substances can be used. For example, many solutions are either acids or bases. Acids are sour, and weak acids can be used to flavor foods. Weak bases can be used in cleaning products. However, strong acids and strong bases are dangerous. Therefore, it's important to be able to measure their strengths. The strengths of acids and bases are measured using dyes called *indicators*. Indicators react chemically with acids and bases and turn different colors depending on their strengths.

Physical and chemical properties can also be used to separate mixtures or to identify substances in mixtures. Remember that the

Gold can be separated from sand by panning, because gold is more dense than sand.

substances that make up mixtures keep their physical properties. They also keep their chemical properties.

One industry that uses physical and chemical properties to separate mixtures is the mining industry. Metals must be separated from their ores before they can be made into useful products. An *ore* is a combination of a metal and other substances, such as oxygen, sulfur, carbon, or silicon. Several methods can be used to separate metals from their ores. Some impurities, or unwanted substances, are less dense than water, so they float in water and can be washed away. Others, like sulfur, can be burned away.

If a mixture contains a substance that is magnetic, a magnet can be used to separate the mixture. For example, a magnet can be used to separate steel from a mixture of car parts containing steel, aluminum, and plastics. The steel can then be recycled into new car parts.

Some liquid mixtures can be separated by spinning at very high speeds—up to 80,000 turns per minute. The force of the spinning pushes solids and other dense substances to the bottom of the container. This process can be used to separate heavy blood cells from the liquid, called plasma. It can also be used to separate the lighter cream from the heavier milk. This produces skim milk.

A solution of a solid and a liquid can be separated by boiling away the liquid, leaving the solid behind. When salt water is boiled, the water boils away and the salt is left as crystals in the container. The water can be recovered by collecting the water vapor and condensing it. This process is called *distillation*. Distillation is used to separate petroleum into products such as gasoline, motor oil, and asphalt.

Sometimes both a physical change and a chemical reaction are used to recover a substance from a mixture. For example, suppose you wanted to recover some copper from a mixture of copper, sugar, and charcoal. Since sugar is the only substance of the three that is soluble in water, water can be added to dissolve the sugar. The sugar water can be removed from the mixture by pouring it through filter paper. Sugar water will pass through the filter paper, but the large particles of copper and charcoal won't. After the charcoal-and-copper mixture dries, the charcoal can be burned away, leaving only copper.

✔ **What physical and chemical properties are used to separate metals from their ores?**

Conservation of Matter

Physical changes and chemical reactions cause matter to look different. But neither can change the amount of matter present. Matter is neither created nor destroyed during a physical change or a chemical change. Scientists call this the *law of conservation of matter.*

This law is easier to prove for some changes than it is for others. If you cut a piece of paper into tiny pieces, you have more pieces of paper, but you have not made more paper. However, when water changes from a liquid to a gas, there may appear to be more matter because the volume of water vapor is greater. But no new matter has been produced. The density of the water is less, so the same mass of water takes up more space. If you measured carefully, you would discover that the mass of the water before the change of state is equal to the mass of water vapor produced.

It may be harder to believe that matter is not produced or destroyed during a chemical change. The reactants seem to disappear and the products seem to appear. However, in the 1700s, Antoine Lavoisier (lah•vwah•ZYAY), a French chemist, was among the first scientists to carefully measure chemical reactions. He found that during a chemical change, the mass of the products equals the mass of the reactants. Because there is no change in mass after a chemical reaction, there is no more and no less matter than there was before the reaction.

Sometimes the masses involved in a chemical change may be harder to measure than those in a physical change. For example, one of the reactants of combustion reactions is oxygen from the air. If the oxygen is not included in the mass of the reactants, then the mass of the products appears to be greater than the mass of the reactants. It looks as if matter has been produced!

✔ **Give an example of a physical change, and explain how matter was neither created nor destroyed.**

When vinegar reacts with baking soda, the mass of the reactants before the reaction is equal to the mass of the products after the reaction.

Summary

Physical changes do not result in the formation of new substances. However, new substances are formed during chemical changes. Physical and chemical properties can be used to identify substances and to separate mixtures. Matter is neither produced nor destroyed during physical and chemical reactions.

Review

1. Give an example of a physical change and a chemical change for iron.
2. Give an example of a chemical change that produces light and heat.
3. Does distillation produce a chemical change or a physical change in petroleum? Explain your answer.
4. **Critical Thinking** Describe how to use physical properties to separate a mixture of ice cubes and nails.
5. **Test Prep** The law which says that matter is neither produced nor destroyed in a physical or chemical reaction is the law of —
   A conservation of matter
   B metallurgy
   C chemical properties
   D physical changes

LINKS

MATH LINK

Conservation of Mass Sometimes it is easier to calculate the mass of a gas involved in a chemical reaction than it is to measure it. If 56 g of iron react with oxygen gas to produce 80 g of rust, calculate the mass of the oxygen that reacted.

WRITING LINK

Persuasive Writing—Opinion Scientists sometimes don't agree whether a certain change is physical or chemical. They use data from experiments to support their positions. Choose an example that you think is a physical or chemical change, and then write a persuasive paragraph for your teacher using experimental data to support your opinion.

SOCIAL STUDIES LINK

History The progress of science is often affected by politics. Research the life of Antoine Lavoisier to find out how the politics in France during the late 1700s may have affected the progress of science.

TECHNOLOGY LINK

Learn more about physical and chemical changes by investigating *Matter Mania* on the **Harcourt Science Explorations CD-ROM.**

Self-Healing Asphalt

The tissue of many living organisms heals itself. Trim away branches of a tree, for example, and it quickly produces new shoots. Can nonliving things also repair themselves? Some asphalt seems to.

Tired Pavement

Asphalt is the sticky, black stuff used to pave roads and parking lots. It is made from petroleum and crushed rock. After it dries, fresh asphalt feels smooth under the wheels of a car. As it gets old, however, asphalt cracks and crumbles from the weight of many vehicles rolling over it.

It's hard to repair roads that are busy all day.

Highway repair takes a lot of time, money, and machinery.

This cracking and crumbling is called fatigue. If the cracks widen and deepen, potholes appear. Eventually the road falls apart. In some places, however, asphalt cracks just seem to disappear. Researchers have conducted tests to find out why some asphalt repairs itself.

In one test a heavy machine imitates traffic on test pavement. Then engineers measure how much cracking has occurred. A day later they measure the pavement again. Remarkably, the cracks in some of the test pavement "heal" overnight. Somehow resting gives some kinds of asphalt a chance to recover.

Cracking the Mystery

Why does some asphalt heal itself? Molecules in any material—asphalt, glass, or anything else—bond with molecules around them. When a material cracks, the bonds between molecules break. Why do molecules in some kinds of asphalt reconnect after the asphalt rests, but the bonds in other asphalt do not? Scientists are studying the ingredi-

ents in different asphalts. They hope to find out which ones produce healing.

Some researchers hypothesize they can speed up asphalt healing with microwaves. Heating the asphalt causes more molecules to reconnect. But it would be impractical to do this on a large scale. Engineers suggest building wider roads. During the day, driving lanes could alternate, giving each lane a rest period. Whichever process is used, self-healing roads could save taxpayers millions of dollars in repairs each year.

THINK ABOUT IT

1. What are some ways the healing process in roads could be speeded up?

2. Why do you think asphalt gets more "rest" in some locations than others?

WEB LINK:
For science and technology updates, visit The Learning Site.
www.harcourtschool.com

Careers Highway Engineer

What They Do
Highway engineers plan, design, construct, and inspect highways, tunnels, and other structures. They analyze speed limits, study the soil, and work with asphalt mixtures.

Education and Training To become a highway engineer, a person needs to study civil and environmental engineering. Math, chemistry, physics, and computer studies are also important.

Theophilus Leapheart

CHEMIST

"No one can put the whole puzzle together alone. Chemists, engineers, mathematicians, and physicists all need to work together to solve problems and to develop new products. To be successful, you have to know how to work with others."

Theophilus Leapheart is the leader of a group of chemists who make new chemical compounds. An important part of this job is finding out the structures of the compounds being made. To do this, Mr. Leapheart's team uses the technology of NMR spectroscopy. The letters *NMR* stand for *n*uclear *m*agnetic *r*esonance.

When the team is ready to test a new compound, they take a sample and dissolve it in a solvent. Then they place the sample in the NMR machine, which produces a strong magnetic field. The magnetic field causes molecules of the sample compound to line up in a certain way, just as Earth's magnetic field causes a compass needle to point north.

The NMR spectrum of a compound is like its fingerprint—no two compounds produce exactly the same spectrum. By looking at an NMR spectrum, Mr. Leapheart can tell which atoms are present and how many are present. In this way he can determine the structure of even the most complicated molecules.

THINK ABOUT IT

1. How does an NMR spectrum help identify a compound?
2. Why is it important for chemists to communicate the processes they use and the results of their work?

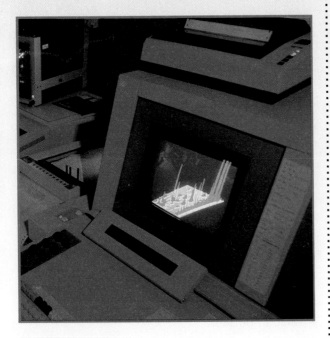

An NMR spectrum

Density Column

Why do some liquids separate?

Materials

- 250-mL graduate
- 50 mL cooking oil
- 50 mL water
- blue food coloring
- 50 mL corn syrup
- 50 mL alcohol
- small cork
- glass marble
- small rock
- wood cube
- metal nut

Procedure

1. Add the food coloring to the water.

2. Pour the liquids into the graduate in order: corn syrup, colored water, oil, and alcohol.

3. Predict in which layers the cork, marble, rock, wood, and metal will end up.

4. Gently drop in the cork, marble, rock, wood, and metal and observe.

Draw Conclusions

Why do the liquids separate into four layers? In which liquid does each of the objects end up? How does this match your predictions? Why do some of the objects sink, while others float?

Mix It Up

How can some mixtures be separated?

Materials

- coffee filter
- scissors
- 3 different-colored water-soluble markers
- small paper cups
- water

Procedure

1. Cut the coffee filter into three strips, each 3 cm X 10 cm.

2. Touch a different-colored marker near one end of each of the pieces of filter paper.

3. Put the bottom edge of each piece of filter paper in a paper cup containing a small amount of water.

4. Observe what happens.

Draw Conclusions

Most inks are mixtures of different-colored pigments. As water traveled up the filter papers, the pigments separated. Which pigments made up the colors you tested? Why do you think some of the pigments traveled farther up the paper than others?

Chapter 1 Review and Test Preparation

Vocabulary Review

Use the terms below to complete the sentences. The page numbers in ( ) tell you where to look in the chapter if you need help.

matter (E6)
physical
    properties (E6)
mass (E7)
weight (E7)
volume (E8)
density (E9)
solubility (E10)

solid (E14)
liquid (E14)
gas (E14)
evaporation (E16)
condensation (E17)
reactivity (E23)
combustibility (E24)

1. ____ is a measure of the amount of matter in an object.

2. ____ is the amount of space that an object takes up.

3. A substance's ability to be dissolved is its ____.

4. A measure of the pull of gravity on an object is ____.

5. ____ are properties that can be observed or measured without changing a substance into a new substance.

6. The concentration of matter in an object is its ____.

7. Particles escape from a nonboiling liquid and become a gas during ____. ____ is a change in state from a gas to a liquid.

8. ____ is anything that has mass and takes up space.

9. Three states of matter are ____, ____, and ____.

10. ____ is a kind of ____ that refers to a substance's ability to burn.

Connect Concepts

Diagrams that stand for three states of matter are shown below. Fill in the blanks (11–13) to identify each state shown. Describe how changes in state take place by labeling the arrows between the diagrams (14–19). The mass of a substance in one state is given. Give the mass of the substance in the other two states by filling in the blanks (20, 21). Add arrowheads to the lines labeled *volume* and *density* to show the direction in which they increase (22, 23).

_____ (11)   _____ (12)   _____ (13)

_____ (14)   _____ (16)
_____ (15)   _____ (17)
                                   _____ (18)

_____ (19)

mass = ____ (20)   mass = 20g   mass = ____ (21)

volume (22)

density (23)

Check Understanding

Write the letter of the best choice.

24. Which of the following is **NOT** a physical property of an iron nail?
    A It rusts.   C It bends.
    B It's shiny.   D It's a solid.

25. Bill weighs 135 lb and Rodney weighs 175 lb. Bill's mass is _____ Rodney's mass.
    F more than   H the same as
    G less than   J unknown

26. If solid copper sulfate is mixed with water, _____ is formed.
    A a mixture   C a solvent
    B a solution   D both **A** and **B**

27. A substance seems to completely fill a container, but more can be forced in. The substance is a —
    F solid   H liquid
    G gas   J none of these

28. A liquid is usually _____ a gas.
    A denser than
    B less dense than
    C the same density as
    D lighter than

29. Nitrogen can be compressed and cooled into a liquid at a very low temperature. So, nitrogen normally exists as a —
    A solid   C gas
    B liquid   D none of these

30. The melting point of gold is 1064°C. The freezing point of gold —
    F is 1064°C
    G is greater than 1064°C
    H is less than 1064°C
    J cannot be determined from the information given

31. Because paper will burn, it has the property of —
    A combustibility   C evaporation
    B condensation   D sublimation

Critical Thinking

32. Choose an object in the room, and describe some of its physical and chemical properties.

33. Explain a possible way to separate a mixture of water, ethanol, and sand.

Process Skills Review

34. What properties of your apple were you able to **observe**? What properties of your apple were you able to **measure**?

35. What change of state can you **infer** when you **observe** that the water level in a pan is lower after the water has boiled for ten minutes?

36. In your **experiment** with baking powder, which substance did you vary?

Performance Assessment

Matter Models

   Work with two other students. Use marbles and boxes of different sizes to make models that show the density and behavior of particles in solids, liquids, and gases.

Chapter

2

Atoms and Elements

The Statue of Liberty has stood in New York Harbor for more than one hundred years—but it has never been completely still. Every particle of the statue is constantly in motion. These particles are so small that they can barely be seen with the most powerful microscopes.

Vocabulary Preview

nucleus
proton
neutron
electron
element
atom
molecule
periodic table
compound

FAST FACT

The copper skin of the Statue of Liberty was once shiny, like a new penny. A chemical change produced a *patina*, or covering, that protects the copper from the salt air of New York Harbor.

Oxygen makes up about half of the mass of Earth's water, soil, and rocky crust. However, it's not the most common substance in Earth's atmosphere.

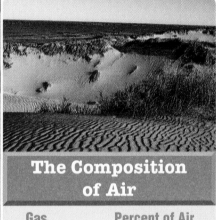

The Composition of Air

Gas	Percent of Air
Nitrogen	78.00
Oxygen	20.90
Argon	0.93
Carbon dioxide	0.03
All other gases	0.14

FAST FACT

Diamonds, graphite, and coal are all made of carbon. They have different properties because the particles of each material are arranged in different ways.

LESSON 1

What Are Atoms and Elements?

In this lesson, you can . . .

INVESTIGATE objects you cannot see or touch.

LEARN ABOUT atoms and elements.

LINK to math, writing, technology, and other areas.

Many of the treasures in this chest are metals and other natural materials. ▽

Mystery Boxes

Activity Purpose It's easy to study the characteristics of an object you can see and touch. You can **observe** them directly. You can pick up the object to see patterns and feel textures. You can also **measure** its mass, volume, and dimensions. In this investigation you will study characteristics of an object you can't see or touch. You will have to **infer** information from indirect observations.

Materials

- sealed box provided by your teacher
- ruler
- balance
- magnet

Activity Procedure

1 With a partner, **observe** the sealed box your teacher gave you. **Record** any observations you think might help you learn about what's inside the box.

2 Use the ruler to **measure** the outside of the box. Use the balance to find the mass of the box. **Record** your results. (Picture A)

3 Carefully tilt and shake the box. How many objects do you **infer** are in the box? How big do you infer the objects are? **Record** your inferences and the reasons for them.

4 Hold the magnet to the surface of the box. Then tilt the box. Are any of the objects in the box attracted to the magnet? Repeat this at several places on the surface of the box. (Picture B)

Picture A

Picture B

5 What objects do you **infer** are inside the box? Base your inferences on your measurements and observations.

6 What do you **infer** about the inside of the box? Draw a picture of what you think the inside of the box looks like.

7 Now open the box. **Compare** your inferences about the objects in the box with the objects the box really contains. Also compare your inferences about what the box looks like inside with what it really looks like.

Draw Conclusions

1. How did what you **inferred** about the objects inside the box **compare** with what was really inside?

2. How did what you **inferred** about the inside of the box **compare** with the way it really looked inside?

3. **Scientists at Work** Different scientists may **infer** different things about objects they can't **observe** directly. Compare your inferences about the contents and the inside of the box with the inferences of other pairs. How were your inferences similar? How were they different?

Investigate Further Construct your own mystery box, and place various objects inside it. Give your box to a classmate. Your classmate will **observe** the box and **infer** things about its contents and how it looks inside.

> **Process Skill Tip**
>
> When you can't **observe** something directly, you may be able to **infer** some of its characteristics. To do this, you might observe how the object reacts under certain conditions.

Atoms and Elements

The Atomic Theory

In the investigation you probably found it difficult to identify an object you couldn't see. Early scientists had the same difficulty in trying to understand what matter was made of.

The theory that matter is made of tiny particles that can't be divided was first proposed by a Greek philosopher, Democritus (di•MAHK•ruh•tuhs), in 400 B.C. The particles Democritus proposed were too small to be seen. Aristotle (AIR•is•taht•uhl), a Greek philosopher who lived after Democritus, believed that matter was not made of particles. This theory was widely accepted for 2000 years. However, neither of these theories was based on experimental evidence.

By the early 1800s, scientists had begun to measure chemical reactions. The measurements made it possible for John Dalton, an English chemist, to propose an atomic theory of matter that was based on experimental evidence. Dalton's atomic theory is that all matter is made up of tiny particles called *atoms*.

✔ **What is the atomic theory?**

FIND OUT

- what matter is made of
- what atoms are made of
- about elements and metals

VOCABULARY

nucleus
proton
neutron
electron
element
atom
molecule

The helium in these ballons is one of more than a hundred different kinds of atoms. ▼

The Structure of an Atom

How small is an atom? About 5 million atoms could be lined up across the period at the end of this sentence. When Dalton proposed his theory, it was thought that atoms were the smallest particles of matter. There was no evidence of smaller particles.

Scientists now know that atoms are made up of even smaller particles called *subatomic particles.* The **nucleus** (NOO•klee•uhs) is the very tiny center of an atom. The nucleus is made up of protons and neutrons. A **proton** (PROH•tahn) is a subatomic particle with a positive charge. A **neutron** (NOO•trahn) is a subatomic particle with no charge. The rest of an atom is made up of electrons, which surround the nucleus. An **electron** (ee•LEK•trahn) is a subatomic particle with a negative charge.

In 1913, Niels Bohr proposed a model of the structure of an atom. In his model, electrons circle the nucleus at fixed distances from it. The paths in which the electrons move are called *orbits.* They are also referred to as *energy levels,* because their distance from the nucleus depends on the energy of the electrons in them. Low-energy electrons orbit close to the nucleus. High-energy electrons orbit farther away.

Although the nucleus is very tiny, almost all of an atom's mass is in its nucleus. The mass of a proton is nearly 2000 times the mass of an electron. Protons and neutrons have about the same mass.

Although their masses are very different, electrons and protons have charges that are equally strong. Part of what holds atoms together is the attraction between the positive protons and the negative electrons. If an atom has more protons than electrons, it has a positive charge. If it has more electrons than protons, it has a negative charge. An atom with the same number of protons and electrons is called a *neutral atom,* because the positive and negative charges cancel each other.

✔ **What subatomic particles make up an atom?**

The Bohr model of a helium atom shows electrons orbiting the nucleus, much as planets orbit the sun.

The modern atomic model shows spherical orbitals instead of circular orbits. Orbitals (blue haze) are areas where electrons are likely to be found.

Elements

An **element** (EL•uh•muhnt) is a substance made up of only one kind of atom. For example, gold is an element. If a single atom is taken from a nugget of gold, that single atom is still gold. An **atom** is the smallest unit of an element that has all the properties of that element.

Each element has an *atomic number,* which is the number of protons in one atom of that element. There are more than 100 elements. An atom of each element has a specific number of protons in its nucleus. The nucleus of a hydrogen atom, for example, has only one proton. So the atomic number of hydrogen is 1. The atomic number of plutonium is 94. All atoms that have 94 protons are plutonium atoms.

In their pure form, most elements are solids at room temperature. A few elements, such as oxygen, nitrogen, and helium, are gases. Only mercury and bromine are liquids.

The atoms of most elements do not occur alone. Instead, they are linked together. Two or more atoms linked together form a **molecule**. When atoms are linked only to atoms of the same kind, they are in a pure state. Oxygen gas, for example, is made up of oxygen molecules. Oxygen molecules are made up of two oxygen atoms linked together.

✔ **What is an element?**

Diamond

Graphite

Anthracite

Diamond, graphite, and anthracite are all made up of carbon atoms, which have six protons. These materials have different properties because their carbon atoms are arranged differently. ▼

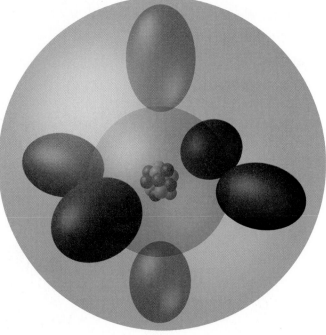

Common Elements

NAME	NUCLEUS MODEL	USES
Oxygen Oxygen is a colorless gas. It makes up about 20 percent of Earth's atmosphere. Oxygen is the most common element in Earth's crust. It is combined with other elements in many metal ores and minerals.	**Atomic number 8**	The mask supplies oxygen for the pilot.
Sodium Sodium is a soft, silver-colored metal. It is a waxlike solid at room temperature, but it becomes brittle as the temperature falls. Sodium combines easily with nonmetals to form salts such as sodium chloride—table salt.	**Atomic number 11**	The sodium vapor in this light glows when electricity passes through it.
Aluminum Aluminum is a silver-colored metal solid. Because it combines easily with oxygen, it is never pure in nature. Aluminum is the third most common element in Earth's crust.	**Atomic number 13**	Most baseball bats are now made of aluminum, instead of wood.
Silicon Silicon is a dark nonmetal solid. It is the second most common element in Earth's crust. Silicon combines mainly with oxygen to form a mineral that is found in many beach sands.	**Atomic number 14**	Electric circuits are printed on thin pieces of silicon.
Chlorine Chlorine is a greenish yellow gas with a sharp odor. It is 2.5 times as dense as air, and it forms a pale yellow solution in water. Chlorine combines easily with metals to form salts, such as sodium chloride—table salt.	**Atomic number 17**	Chlorine bleach is a solution of chlorine gas in water.
Iron Iron is a silver-white metal solid. There are large amounts of minerals containing iron in Earth's crust. Many useful materials, such as steel, are made from iron. Iron is also found in blood. It carries oxygen to cells.	**Atomic number 26**	Iron can be shaped more easily if it is red hot.

Metals

Elements are classified by their properties. About one-fourth of all elements are classified as nonmetals. The rest are metals. All metals except mercury are solid at room temperature.

Metals have many familiar properties. Gold is used in jewelry because of its high *luster,* or shininess. Most metals, like silver and nickel, have a gray or silver luster.

Most metals are said to be *malleable* (MAL•ee•uh•buhl). They can be hammered or rolled into thin sheets. The foil used to cover and store food is a thin sheet of aluminum. Metals are also *ductile* (DUHK•til). They can be formed into wires. Copper and aluminum are used in electric wiring.

Copper and aluminum are used in electric wiring because of another property. Metals *conduct,* or transfer, electricity. The electrons farthest from the nucleus of a metal atom are not held by just that atom. They are free to move to other metal atoms. This freedom of electrons allows metals to conduct electricity.

Electrons in materials such as glass, plastic, and rubber are bound tightly to their atoms. These materials conduct hardly any electricity. They are *insulators.*

Metals also conduct heat. Have you ever noticed that when a car has been sitting in the sun, its metal parts are much hotter than its plastic parts? Metal conducts heat better than plastic does. For this reason the

▼ Metal can be rolled into very thin sheets, called foil, that can be used to decorate buildings.

▼ Copper is often used on the bottom of pans because it conducts heat easily.

Metals such as aluminum and copper are good conductors of electricity. Most electric wiring is made of these metals.

handles of pots and pans are often made of plastic.

Some substances we think of as metals are not pure metal elements. They are actually *alloys*, or mixtures of metals. Bronze is an alloy of copper and tin. Steel is an alloy of iron and carbon. Brass is an alloy of copper and zinc.

✔ **What are five properties of metals?**

Summary

Matter is made up of tiny particles called atoms. Atoms are made of smaller, subatomic particles called protons, neutrons, and electrons. Elements are substances made up of only one kind of atom. Metals are elements that have luster, are malleable and ductile, and conduct electricity and heat.

Review

1. If you were to add all the missing elements to the table on page E41, how many would there be between silicon and chlorine? What would their atomic numbers be?

2. What subatomic particles make up the nucleus of an atom?

3. How do atoms with different atomic numbers differ from each other?

4. **Critical Thinking** Choose a metal you know, and list three uses that illustrate three properties of metals.

5. **Test Prep** Which are **NOT** a part of atoms?

   A protons

   B electrons

   C neutrons

   D elements

LINKS

MATH LINK

Relative Mass Units Twelve atomic mass units (abbreviated as *amu*) is equal to the mass of one carbon atom. Calculate how many amu there are in 20 atoms of carbon and in 200 atoms of carbon.

WRITING LINK

Informative Writing—Report The development of the atomic theory is central to the development of chemistry. Suppose you are a newspaper reporter, and John Dalton has just published his atomic theory. Research the history of the development of the atomic theory, and write an article for your school newspaper announcing John Dalton's new theory.

HEALTH LINK

Essential Minerals Many elements, such as iron, are minerals needed for human health. Find out which ones are in multivitamin tablets. How much of each element does a vitamin tablet contain? Report your findings to your class.

TECHNOLOGY LINK

Learn more about metals by viewing *Intermetallics* on the **Harcourt Science Newsroom Video.**

What Are Compounds?

In this lesson, you can . . .

INVESTIGATE how elements are grouped.

LEARN ABOUT the periodic table and compounds.

LINK to math, writing, technology, and other areas.

Mixing chemicals often produces unexpected results. ▽

INVESTIGATE

Grouping Elements

Activity Purpose Suppose you have 100 baseball cards, and you want to know whether the players at certain positions have anything in common. If you group the cards by player position, you will be able to **infer** common characteristics about each group more quickly. Scientists have grouped elements by their properties. In this investigation you will learn how elements can be grouped.

Materials

- aluminum foil
- copper wire
- steel (iron) paper clip
- sulfur
- graphite pencil "lead"
- lead solder
- helium-filled balloon

CAUTION

Activity Procedure

1 Copy the chart on page E45. You will use it to **record** the properties of the elements you **observe**.

2 What elements do the objects represent? **Record** your answers in the second column of the chart.

3 **Observe** each element. Is it a solid, a liquid, or a gas at room temperature? **Record** your observations in the column labeled "Phase" of the chart.

4 What is the color of each element? (Carefully release some of the helium from the balloon.) **Record** what you **observe** in the chart. (Picture A)

5 Which elements have luster? (Which are shiny?) **Record** what you **observe** in the fifth column of the chart.

Picture A

Picture B

Object	Element	Phase	Color	Luster	Malleability
foil					
wire					
paper clip					
sulfur					
graphite					
solder					
balloon					

6 Which elements bend easily? **Record** what you **observe** in the column labeled "Malleability." **CAUTION** **Wash your hands after handling the objects in this investigation.** (Picture B)

Draw Conclusions

1. What similar properties did you **observe** in different elements?

2. Consider the properties you **observed** to form groups. Which elements could you group together? Explain.

3. **Scientists at Work** Scientists have made a periodic table, in which elements are grouped by their properties. Using your observations, **predict** which elements from the activity are near each other in the periodic table.

Investigate Further Think of other properties that could be used to group elements. Are there any you could test? **Plan and conduct a simple investigation** of one group of elements from this activity using these new tests.

Process Skill Tip

Using your observations of different elements you can **predict** relationships among those elements.

Elements and Compounds

The Periodic Table

FIND OUT

- how elements are grouped in the periodic table
- how compounds form

VOCABULARY

periodic table
compound

As you learned in the investigation, some elements can be grouped together because they have similar properties. In 1869 a Russian chemist named Dmitri Mendeleev (duh•MEE•tree men•duh•LAY•uhf) organized elements by their atomic masses. Mendeleev noticed that if elements were put in order of atomic mass, some properties appeared in predictable patterns.

Scientists later found that using an order based on the number of protons in one atom of an element—atomic number—is better than one based on atomic mass.

THE INSIDE STORY

The Periodic Table

In the modern **periodic table**, elements are arranged in order of atomic number. They are also arranged so that elements with similar properties are in the same column. The elements in a column are part of a *group*. Elements in the same group often have the same number of electrons in the outer energy levels of their atoms. The arrangement of electrons gives elements their chemical properties.

All the elements on the left side of the periodic table, except hydrogen, are metals. All the elements on the far right are nonmetals. A change of color separates metals from nonmetals. Some elements have properties of both metals and nonmetals. These elements are called *metalloids*.

Notice that every element in the table has an abbreviation, called a *chemical symbol*.

When the periodic table was first set up, it had empty spaces. The spaces were for elements that had not yet been discovered. As new elements were found, scientists filled in the spaces. Using the periodic table, Mendeleev correctly predicted that three new elements with certain properties would be discovered. Even today, new elements are being added to the table. However, now most new elements are made artificially.

✔ **Which two things determine the arrangement of elements in the periodic table?**

Compounds

In nature most elements are joined with other elements in compounds. A **compound** is a substance made of the atoms of two or more elements. Water is one of the most common compounds. It contains hydrogen and oxygen atoms. Table salt, sodium chloride, contains sodium and chlorine atoms.

A *chemical formula* shows which elements and how many atoms of each are in a compound. The chemical formula for water is H_2O. The small 2 next to the H means that there are 2 hydrogen atoms in every water molecule. Each water molecule also has 1 atom of oxygen. The chemical formula for

table salt is NaCl. A salt molecule has 1 sodium atom and 1 chlorine atom. The chemical formula for glucose, a simple sugar, is $C_6H_{12}O_6$. In each molecule of glucose, there are 6 carbon atoms, 12 hydrogen atoms, and 6 oxygen atoms.

When atoms join to form a compound, they undergo a chemical change. The properties of the compound are different from those of the elements in it. Hydrogen and oxygen, both gases, combine to form water, a liquid compound. Compounds can also react with each other. When compounds react, they change, and form new products. For example, hydrochloric acid contains hydrogen and chlorine atoms. It reacts with

Two chemical reactions are happening here. In one, iron combines with oxygen to form iron oxide (rust). In the other, gasoline burns to form carbon dioxide and water. Burning gasoline also produces a lot of energy, which is used to move the truck. ▼

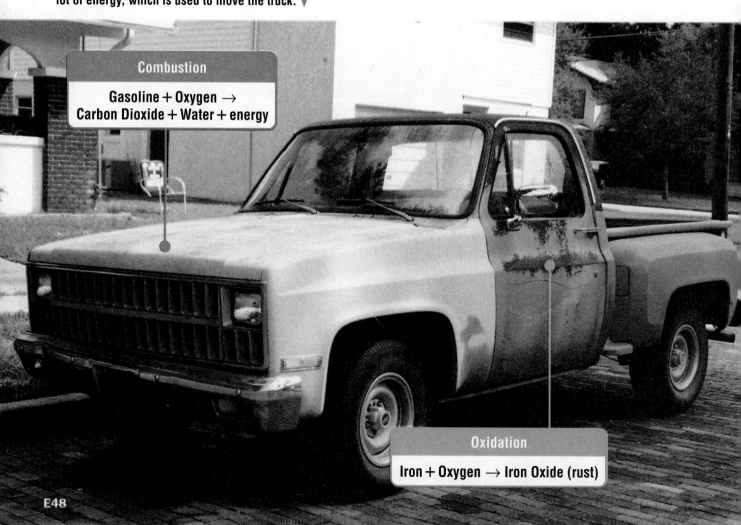

Combustion

Gasoline + Oxygen → Carbon Dioxide + Water + energy

Oxidation

Iron + Oxygen → Iron Oxide (rust)

sodium hydroxide, which contains sodium, oxygen, and hydrogen atoms. The products are sodium chloride, which contains sodium and chlorine atoms, and water, which contains hydrogen and oxygen atoms.

✓ **What does a chemical formula show?**

Summary

In the periodic table, elements are arranged by atomic number and properties. The table shows names, chemical symbols, and atomic numbers for all the known elements. A compound is a combination of two or more different elements. A chemical formula shows the number of atoms of each element in one molecule of a compound.

Review

1. Using the periodic table on pages E46 and E47, find the name of the element that has 36 protons.

2. In what form are most elements in nature? What does this mean?

3. What information is shown in a chemical formula?

4. **Critical Thinking** Using their placement in the periodic table, classify these elements as metals or nonmetals: iron, cobalt, sodium, oxygen, chlorine, and helium.

5. **Test Prep** Which of these is **NOT** found in the periodic table?
   A name
   B atomic number
   C luster
   D chemical symbol

LINKS

MATH LINK

Ratios and Fractions Chemical formulas give the ratios of atoms in compounds. From this information you can calculate what fraction of the atoms in a compound are atoms of one element. For example, the chemical formula for ammonia is NH_3. What is the ratio of nitrogen atoms to hydrogen atoms? What fraction of the atoms in ammonia are nitrogen atoms?

WRITING LINK

Informative Writing—Description From the periodic table, choose an element. Research the element, and write a description for your teacher. Include the element's properties and uses.

LANGUAGE ARTS LINK

Word Origins The chemical symbols for some elements don't seem to make sense. Many, such as Au for gold, are based on the Latin name of the element. Use a dictionary of word origins to look up other elements with strange symbols. Make a list of these elements and the origins of their symbols.

TECHNOLOGY LINK

Learn more about molecules and compounds by visiting the National Museum of American History Internet site. **www.si.edu/harcourt/science**

 Smithsonian Institution®

Discovering Elements

Ancient cultures believed that matter was made up of just four or five elements. The Greeks believed these elements were water, fire, earth, and air. The Chinese added wood as a fifth element. These beliefs continued to be held for many centuries.

About 2000 years ago, the practice of alchemy (AL•kuh•mee) began in Egypt. Although the goal of alchemy—changing one substance into another—was not possible, it led to the discovery of new chemical substances. It also marked the beginning of a new science—chemistry.

Atoms and Elements

Alchemy continued for the next 1600 years. Then in 1661, Robert Boyle, a British scientist, stated that matter is made up of tiny particles. He later proposed that all matter could be broken down into elements but that elements could not be broken down into simpler substances. Within the next century, oxygen and hydrogen were both identified as elements. Scientists also discovered that elements could combine to form compounds, such as water.

In 1808 John Dalton published his atomic theory, in which he stated that every element is made up of atoms and that each element has a unique arrangement of atoms. Dalton also showed that each element has a specific mass.

The Periodic Table

After the First International Chemical Congress met in 1860, chemists began grouping elements by atomic mass. Dmitri Mendeleev was the first to publish his

The History of Elements

350 B.C.
Aristotle suggests that all substances are made of fire, water, wind, or earth.

400
The term *chemistry* is first used by Egyptian alchemists to describe the practice of changing matter.

1808
Dalton states his atomic theory.

400 B.C. — A.D. 500 — A.D. 1000 — A.D. 1600 — A.D. 1700 — A.D. 1800

100
Gold, silver, copper, lead, iron, tin, and mercury are known.

880
A Muslim chemist, al-Razi, classifies chemical substances into mineral, vegetable, animal, and derivative.

1661
Boyle's book, *The Sceptical Chymist*, proves the ancient "four elements" theory wrong.

1869
The periodic table of the elements is published.

groupings. The chart, known as the periodic table of the elements, showed each element's symbol and atomic mass in a clear, orderly arrangement.

More Elements

In 1911 the atomic nucleus was discovered. Protons and neutrons were discovered soon after. These discoveries led scientists to define elements not only by atomic mass but also by atomic number—the number of protons in each atom. Grouping atoms by atomic number became a feature of the periodic table.

During the rest of the 1900s, many elements were added to the periodic table. Scientists continue to find new elements.

Knowledge of chemistry and atomic structure has even allowed scientists to make elements that don't occur in nature. And equipment such as the scanning tunneling microscope has made it possible to photograph the structure of some elements, revealing their ordered arrays of atoms.

THINK ABOUT IT

1. How were alchemists different from chemists?
2. Why is the number of elements in the periodic table not fixed?

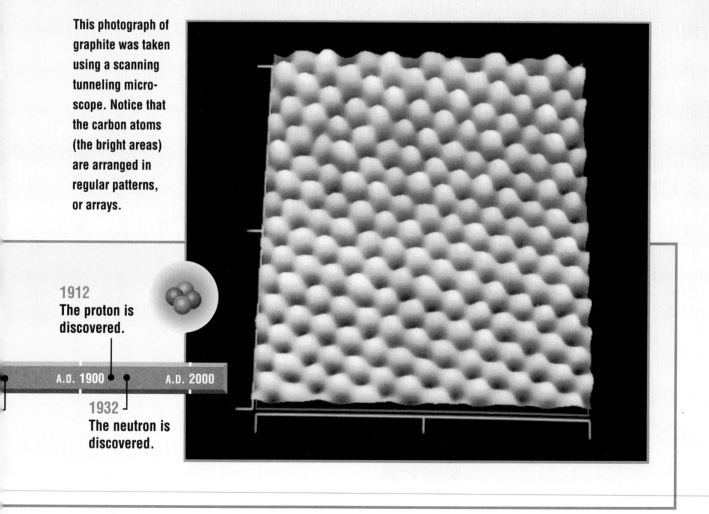

This photograph of graphite was taken using a scanning tunneling microscope. Notice that the carbon atoms (the bright areas) are arranged in regular patterns, or arrays.

1912
The proton is discovered.

A.D. 1900   A.D. 2000

1932
The neutron is discovered.

Lise Meitner

NUCLEAR PHYSICIST

"I am not important; why is everyone making a fuss over me?"

Lise Meitner was a shy, quiet woman whose love of science made her go against the accepted ideas of her day. First, she insisted on going to college at a time when most women didn't even go to high school. Second, she chose to study physics, a subject that at the time was studied only by men. Third, she earned a doctoral degree, which had been given to only 13 other women in 541 years.

Born in Vienna, Austria, in 1878, Dr. Meitner grew up dreaming of becoming a scientist like Marie Curie. After finishing her doctoral studies at the University of Vienna, she went to Germany, where she worked as a researcher at the Kaiser-Wilhelm Institute in Berlin. While working there, she and chemist Otto Hahn discovered the element with atomic number 91, protactinium. After leaving Germany in 1938, Dr. Meitner continued her research in Sweden with her nephew, Otto Frisch. It was while working with Frisch that Dr. Meitner made her most famous discovery—that the splitting of a uranium nucleus produces energy. This process is called nuclear fission and is the basis of nuclear energy.

Although Dr. Meitner's work on nuclear fission led in time to the development of the nuclear bomb, she refused to work on it. A peaceful person who had been forced to flee Germany just before World War II, she didn't want to see her discovery used to make a weapon. The development of nuclear-energy stations was more what she wanted her research to lead to.

THINK ABOUT IT

1. Why did Dr. Meitner go against the customs of her time?
2. Do you think a scientist can control the way his or her research is used? Explain.

Inside a nuclear reactor

Speedy Reactions

How can you speed up a reaction?

Materials

- 250-mL beaker
- 200 mL carbonated soft drink
- 1 teaspoon sugar

Procedure

1 Pour the carbonated drink into the beaker.

2 Add the sugar.

3 Observe what happens.

4 Repeat the procedure with different brands of soft drinks.

Draw Conclusions

Carbonated soft drinks contain flavorings, colorings, water, and dissolved carbon dioxide gas. You probably heard some of the gas escape when you opened the can or bottle the soft drink came in. The remainder of the carbon dioxide comes out of the soft drink slowly over time. What happened when you added sugar to the drink? What do you think the foam is made of? Did different carbonated drinks behave differently when the sugar was added? Explain.

Periodic Table

Where are various elements found?

Materials

- a copy of the periodic table
- poster board
- tape
- string
- various objects, such as a helium-filled balloon, a piece of charcoal, an aluminum can, a glass bottle, garden fertilizer, an eggshell, a steel nail, an old penny, a fishing weight

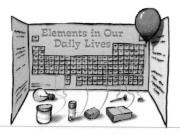

Procedure

1 Mount the periodic table on the poster board.

2 Tape one end of a piece of string to the balloon, and the other end to *He* (helium) on the periodic table.

3 Tape string to all the objects.

4 Tape the other end of each string to the correct element on the periodic table.

Draw Conclusions

Which elements are found in these common objects? Why can't you find objects for all the elements on the periodic table?

Chapter 2 Review and Test Preparation

Vocabulary Review

Use the terms below to complete the following passage. The page numbers in ( ) tell you where to look in the chapter if you need help.

nucleus (E39)   **atom** (E40)

proton (E39)   **molecule** (E40)

neutron (E39)   **Periodic Table** (E47)

electron (E39)   **compound** (E48)

element (E40)

The atomic theory states that matter is made up of tiny particles. One of these particles is called a(n) __1.__ . At the center of an atom is a tiny __2.__ . A(n) __3.__ , a positively charged subatomic particle, and a(n) __4.__ , a subatomic particle with no charge, are in the nucleus. A(n) __5.__ is a subatomic particle with a negative charge. It is found outside the nucleus. If an atom has a different number of protons from another atom, it is an atom of a different __6.__ . The elements are arranged in the __7.__ by atomic number. In nature, most elements are joined together in a(n) __8.__ . Two or more atoms joined together form a(n) __9.__ .

Connect Concepts

Using the Periodic Table, complete the table below.

Common Elements

Element	Chemical Symbol	Atomic Number	Number of Protons	Number of Electrons	Metal or Nonmetal	Example Compound
oxygen	(10)	8	(11)	(12)	(13)	(14), water
(15)	Ba	56	56	(16)	metal	$BaSO_4$, barium sulfate
(17)	S	16	(18)	(19)	nonmetal	(20), sulfur dioxide
sodium	(21)	(22)	(23)	11	(24)	(25), sodium chloride
(26)	C	(27)	(28)	(29)	nonmetal	CH_4, methane
iron	Fe	(30)	26	(31)	metal	FeO, iron oxide
(32)	(33)	(34)	1	(35)	nonmetal	(36), water
nitrogen	N	7	7	7	(37)	NH_3, ammonia
(38)	(39)	(40)	17	(41)	(42)	NaCl, sodium chloride
lead	(43)	82	(44)	82	metal	$PbSO_4$, lead sulfate

Check Understanding

Write the letter of the best choice.

45. Theories in science —
- **A** are based on philosophy
- **B** are based on experimental evidence
- **C** are never proved wrong
- **D** never change

46. The atomic theory states that matter is made up of —
- **F** atoms
- **G** earth and air
- **H** elements
- **J** earth, air, fire, and water

47. If an element has a gray luster and can be drawn into a wire, it is probably a —
- **A** nonmetal   **C** metal
- **B** gas   **D** alloy

48. What elements does the compound $MgCl_2$, magnesium chloride, contain?
- **A** chloride only
- **B** magnesium only
- **C** magnesium and calcium
- **D** magnesium and chlorine

Process Skills Review

49. What did you **observe** about the sealed box in the Lesson 1 investigation?

50. What did you **infer** about the contents and the inside shape of the sealed box?

51. What properties of elements can you **observe**?

Critical Thinking

Use the following information to answer the questions below.

- Fluorine is a pale yellow, poisonous gas. It does not conduct electricity. It has an atomic number of 9.

- Oxygen is a colorless gas. It does not conduct electricity. It has an atomic number of 8.

- Iron is a solid with a gray luster at room temperature. It is malleable and conducts electricity. It reacts with oxygen. It has an atomic number of 26.

- Sulfur is a bright yellow solid at room temperature. It is brittle and does not conduct electricity. It reacts with oxygen. It has an atomic number of 16.

- Gold is a yellow solid with a luster. It is malleable and conducts electricity. It has an atomic number of 79.

- Phosphorus can be a white solid at room temperature. It does not conduct electricity. It reacts with oxygen. It has an atomic number of 15.

52. Divide the elements into groups based on their properties. Explain how you grouped them.

53. Which of the elements are metals?

54. Which of the elements are nonmetals?

Performance Assessment

Element Detective

Divide into teams of five. Your teacher will give each student an element clue card. Using your clue, decide the name of your element. Discuss your reasoning with other members of your team. Then line up in order of atomic number.

Unit Project Wrap Up

Here are some ideas for ways to wrap up your unit project.

Make a Chart

Use a computer and word processing software to make a chart comparing cereals. Which do you think is most healthful? Which do you think is the best buy?

Write an Ad

Write and illustrate an ad for a real food product. Tell how you are sure the claims you make for the product are true.

Make a Scrapbook

Cut pictures from newspapers and magazines that show changes in matter. Mount the pictures on sheets of paper and put the paper together to make a book. Write on the pages how matter changed in each picture.

Investigate Further

How could you make your project better? What other questions do you have about matter? Plan ways to find answers to your questions. Use the Science Handbook on pages R2-R9 for help.

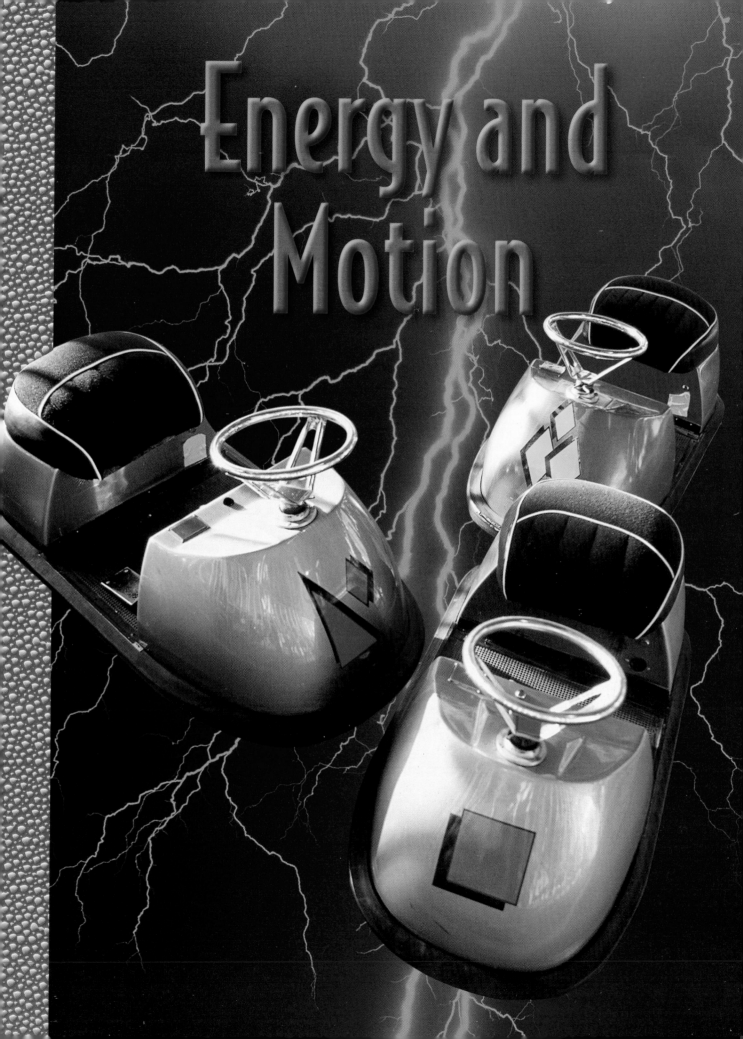

Energy and
Motion

UNIT F

PHYSICAL SCIENCE

Energy and Motion

Unit Project   Amusement Park

Design and build a model amusement park. Use craft sticks, marbles, wood scraps, rulers, clay, cardboard, and other materials to build the rides in the park. The rides should be able to move, or allow a rider to move. Demonstrate the rides in your park, and tell how forces move objects.

Forces

Have you ever wondered why things fall down instead of up? Or why you can't just keep going when you jump up? In fact, nothing really falls. Instead, everything is pulled toward the center of Earth.

Vocabulary Preview

force
friction
magnetism
gravitation
balanced forces
unbalanced forces
acceleration
net force
work
power
machine

FAST FACT

The biggest problem in traveling to the moon is breaking free of Earth's gravity. A spacecraft such as this Apollo/Saturn rocket must reach a speed of about 40,000 km/hr (25,000 mi/hr) to leave Earth.

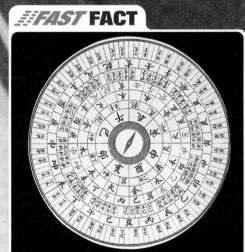

What Forces Affect Objects on Earth Every Day?

In this lesson, you can . . .

INVESTIGATE magnetism.

LEARN ABOUT the forces of friction, magnetism, and gravity.

LINK to math, writing, social studies, and technology.

△ When a magnet pulls objects to it, it exerts a force on the objects.

INVESTIGATE

Magnetism

Activity Purpose Earth and everything on it are affected by forces. One of the forces that affects your life every day is magnetism. Cassette tapes, computer disks, electric motors, and televisions are just some of the things that work because of magnetism. A magnet produces a force field, called a *magnetic field*, around itself. This magnetic field affects certain objects. In this investigation you will **experiment** to find out what types of objects are affected by magnetic fields.

Materials

- test objects
- compass
- 2 bar magnets

Activity Procedure

1. Make a chart that has three columns. Label the columns *Object*, *Prediction*, and *Test Result*.

2. From the group of objects, choose one to test. Write the name of the object on your chart. **Predict** whether this object will be attracted, or pulled, by one of the magnets. **Record** your prediction on your chart. (Picture A)

3. Place the object on a desk. Slide a magnet slowly toward the object until the magnet touches it. In your chart, **record** whether the object is attracted to the magnet or not.

4. Repeat Steps 2 and 3 for each of the test objects.

5. Bar magnets have two different ends, called poles. One is labeled *N* for north seeking, and the other is labeled *S* for south seeking.

Observe what happens when you bring the north-seeking pole of one magnet near the south-seeking pole of another magnet. Then observe what happens when you bring two north-seeking poles or two south-seeking poles together. **Record** your observations.

6 Now place the compass on the desk. Slowly slide one of the magnets toward the compass. **Observe** what happens to the compass needle. Now move the magnet around the compass and observe what happens. **Record** your observations. (Picture B)

Picture A

Picture B

Draw Conclusions

1. What characteristic of an object determines whether or not it is attracted by a magnet?

2. **Infer** what characteristic of a compass needle accounts for your observations of the compass and the magnet.

3. **Scientists at Work** Scientists often **hypothesize** about why things happen. Then they **plan and conduct investigations** to test their hypotheses. Form a hypothesis about why unlike magnetic poles attract each other while like magnetic poles repel, or push away, each other. Then plan and conduct an investigation to test your hypothesis.

Investigate Further Research to find out why a compass needle always points to the north.

Process Skill Tip

After you **hypothesize** about why something happens, you can **plan and conduct an investigation** to test your hypothesis.

Everyday Forces

Forces

FIND OUT

• what forces are and what they do

• how the forces of friction, magnetism, and gravity act in our everyday lives

VOCABULARY

force
friction
magnetism
gravitation

In the investigation you experimented with magnetic force. A **force** is any push or pull that causes an object to move, stop, or change direction. An object starts to move, stops moving, or changes direction *only* when a force acts on it.

Some forces act on objects directly. When you push on a door, you directly apply the force that makes the door open. Other forces, such as gravity and magnetism, act on objects at a distance. In the investigation you saw objects move toward the magnet even if the magnet wasn't touching them. The force of the magnetic field attracted objects to the magnet.

✔ **What is a force?**

Friction, Magnetism, and Gravity

Three of the forces that affect objects on Earth every day are friction, magnetism, and gravity. **Friction** is a force that opposes, or acts against, motion when two surfaces rub against each other. Rough surfaces produce more friction than smooth surfaces do. When a baseball player slides into second base, the friction of his or her legs rubbing on the dirt

The luge (LOOZH) is a type of sled. The rider exerts a force with her arms to get the luge moving. ▼

There is little friction between the luge's runners and the ice. The force of gravity pulls the luge downhill. ▼

When the rider wants to stop, he pulls up on the runners and puts his feet down. The increased friction stops the luge. ▼

The force of Earth's magnetic field is strong enough to protect us by repelling most of the dangerous radiation moving through space.

Magnetic forces act along field lines. Iron filings align themselves along these lines, as shown in these photographs. When like poles are brought together (top), the lines bend away from each other. When unlike, or opposite, poles are brought together (bottom), the lines join. Lines of magnetic force never cross each other.

provides enough force to stop the slide. However, a sled on ice keeps on moving for quite a while. There is very little friction from ice.

Another force that affects us every day is magnetic force, or magnetism. **Magnetism** is the force of repulsion (pushing) or attraction (pulling) between poles of magnets.

Every magnet has two poles. A bar magnet hanging from a string will turn so that one end points north and one points south. The end that points north is the magnet's north-seeking pole. The end that points south is the magnet's south-seeking pole.

Every magnet has a magnetic field around it. You can think of a magnetic field as lines of force that run from the north-seeking pole to the south-seeking pole of the magnet.

Why do a magnet's poles point north and south? It's because Earth is a huge magnet. On Earth the magnetic north and south poles are about 1500 km (930 mi) from the geographic North and South Poles. Earth's

magnetic field causes the needle of a compass to point north and south.

The north- and south-seeking poles of two magnets attract each other—magnetic force pulls them together. But if you try to bring like poles (two north-seeking poles or two south-seeking poles) of two magnets together, they will repel each other. Magnetic force pushes them apart.

How does an object become a magnet? An iron magnet that has been broken in half becomes two magnets. This is because every piece of iron magnet has groups of atoms that produce magnetic fields. Each group has its own north and south poles. In iron that isn't a magnet, each group of atoms has a different magnetic field. These magnetic fields cancel each other out. In an iron magnet, the magnetic fields are lined up. The north-seeking poles all point in the same direction. The south-seeking poles all point in the opposite direction. So each piece of magnetized iron becomes a magnet.

▲ A scale measures the force of gravity pulling you and Earth toward each other. Saturn has more mass than Earth. On Saturn the force of gravity would be much greater, and you would be much heavier.

A third force that affects objects on Earth all the time is gravity. This is the force that holds things to the surface of Earth. Gravity is a special case of gravitation. **Gravitation** is the force that pulls all objects in the universe toward one another.

Even two Ping Pong balls sitting side by side on a table pull on each other with gravitation. The force acting on them is very small, however, so the balls don't move toward each other.

Earth and a Ping Pong ball pull on each other with a much stronger force, so they stay together. This is because the strength of the gravitation between two objects depends on the mass of the objects. The total mass of two Ping Pong balls is small, so the force between them is small. The total mass of a Ping Pong ball and Earth is very large, so the force between them is much larger.

The strength of gravitation between two objects also depends on the distance between the objects. When two objects are close to each other, they are pulled together by a greater force than if they were far apart. The greater the distance between two objects, the less the force of gravitation acts on them.

Earth and the moon have a lot of mass. The moon is kept in orbit around Earth by gravity. However, if Earth and the moon were much farther apart, gravity would not be enough to keep the moon in orbit around Earth.

Keep in mind that the force of gravitation between two objects pulls on *both* objects. When you toss a ball into the air, gravity pulls the ball toward

Gravitation pulls objects toward each other's centers. So the meteors both fall toward the center of Earth. ▼

Earth. Gravity also pulls Earth toward the ball. Earth, however, has so much mass that its movement toward the ball is not enough to be measured. So even though a gravitational force pulls on both objects, the smaller object does most of the moving.

✔ **What three forces affect Earth and objects on Earth every day?**

Summary

A force is a push or a pull that can make an object move, stop, or change direction. Some forces are direct, while others act at a distance. Where two surfaces rub against each other, the force of friction opposes motion. Magnetism pulls the poles of magnets together or pushes them apart. Gravitation pulls objects toward each other. The strength of gravitation depends on the masses of the objects and how far apart the objects are.

Review

1. What starts an object moving or stops it if it is already moving?
2. Name three forces that affect you every day.
3. What force keeps the moon in orbit around Earth?
4. **Critical Thinking** Suppose you push a cart toward the west. In what direction does the force of friction push on the cart's wheels?
5. **Test Prep** The force of gravitation between two objects is less when —
   A the total of their masses is greater
   B friction between them is greater
   C the force of magnetism is greater
   D the distance between them is greater

LINKS

MATH LINK

Newtons In the United States, we measure weight in pounds. However, scientists everywhere measure weight in newtons. Gravity pulls on a 1-lb object with a force of about 4.5 newtons. Make a table that shows the weights of several objects in pounds and in newtons.

WRITING LINK

Informative Writing—Classification Every day you are affected by the forces of gravitation, friction, and magnetism. These forces start objects moving, stop objects that are already moving, and change the speed or direction of moving objects. For one day, keep a journal for your own use. Record and classify the forces you see in action.

SOCIAL STUDIES LINK

Magnetic North Earth's magnetic north pole is about 1500 km from its geographic North Pole (the point through which Earth's imaginary axis passes). Research the location of the magnetic north pole, and make a map that shows that location.

TECHNOLOGY LINK

Learn more about the effects of gravity by viewing *Microgravity* on the **Harcourt Science Newsroom Video.**

F9

2

What Are Balanced and Unbalanced Forces?

In this lesson, you can . . .

INVESTIGATE
how forces interact.

LEARN ABOUT
forces that act
together.

LINK to math,
writing, physical
education,
and
technology.

Balanced forces
are at work in this
pyramid. ›

INVESTIGATE

Forces That Interact

Activity Purpose In Lesson 1 you learned about three forces that affect objects on Earth: gravitation, friction, and magnetism. Two or more of these forces often interact or act at the same time. In this investigation you will **experiment** with two opposing forces—the force of gravity pulling down on an object and the force of a spring pulling up on the same object.

Materials

- clipboard
- graph paper
- tape
- ring stand
- spring
- weight
- marker

Activity Procedure

1. Tape the graph paper to the clipboard. Across the bottom of the graph paper, draw a line and label it *Seconds*. Starting at one end of the line, make a mark every 2.5 cm.

2. Attach the spring to the ring stand. Then attach the weight to the free end of the spring. Tape the marker to the bottom of the weight so that its tip points toward the back of the setup.

3. Have a partner hold the clipboard with the graph paper taped to it behind the weight. The marker point should just touch the graph paper. Pull the weight until the spring is fully stretched. (Picture A)

Picture A

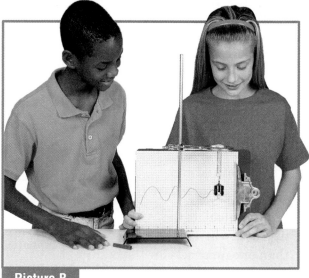

Picture B

4 Have your partner slide the clipboard across a table at a steady rate of about 2.5 cm/sec. As soon as the clipboard starts to move, drop the weight. As it bounces, it traces its movements on the graph paper. (Picture B)

5 **Interpret the data** on your graph. Identify and mark the points where the weight was not moving up or down for an instant. Identify and mark the direction (up or down) the weight was moving along each sloping line. Identify and mark the places where the weight was moving most rapidly.

Draw Conclusions

1. At what points was the weight not moving?

2. At what point was the weight moving most rapidly?

3. From your graph, **infer** the point at which the force of the spring was the greatest.

4. **Scientists at Work** Scientists often **draw conclusions** after they **interpret data** they have collected. After studying your graph, draw conclusions to answer the following questions:
   • During which part of each cycle was the force of gravity greater than the force of the spring?
   • During which part of each cycle was the force of the spring greater than the force of gravity?

Investigate Further **Hypothesize** how your graph would look if you repeated the activity with a heavier weight. **Plan and conduct a simple investigation** to test your hypothesis.

Forces That Act Together

Balanced and Unbalanced Forces

VOCABULARY

balanced forces
unbalanced forces
acceleration
net force

In the investigation you made a graph of two forces acting on an object. Most of the time, forces act together. Imagine a car moving along a highway. Many forces are interacting in this situation. The force of the ground is holding up the car. The force of gravity is pulling the car down. The force of the engine is turning the wheels to make the car move forward. And the force of friction with the road and with the air around the car is holding the car back.

Sometimes the forces acting on an object balance each other. **Balanced forces** are equal in size and opposite in direction. As a result, they cancel each other out. When balanced forces act on an object, they do not change the object's motion or direction. If the object is stopped, it will remain stopped. If it is moving, it will keep moving at the same speed and in the same direction. Because balanced forces are equal in size and opposite in direction, it seems as if no force is acting on the object.

Suppose you exert a force by pushing on a very heavy object, such as a sturdy wall. The wall doesn't move because it is exerting an opposite force that exactly balances the force you exert while pushing against it. Even though the wall doesn't move, you are still exerting a force.

The force of friction and the wheelchair's inertia are smaller than the force the boy exerts on the wheelchair. The forces are unbalanced, so the wheelchair moves. ▼

The force of the woman pushing against the railroad car is balanced by the force of friction and the car's large mass. So the car doesn't move. ▼

A bulldozer pushing against the same wall might exert a force large enough to overcome the force exerted by the wall. In this case, the forces are unbalanced. **Unbalanced forces** occur when one force is greater than its opposite force. When unbalanced forces act on an object, the object's motion changes. When the bulldozer pushes against the wall, unbalanced forces make the wall fall down.

Unbalanced forces can stop a moving object. When you catch a ball, you stop it from moving by using a stopping force greater than the force the ball had while moving.

Unbalanced forces can also speed up or slow down a moving object. A person riding a bicycle up a hill may be slowed by the force of gravity even though he or she applies a strong force to the pedals of the bicycle. If the hill is steep enough, the force of gravity becomes the greater force. The forces are unbalanced, and the cyclist slows down. Once the cyclist gets to the top of the hill and starts down the other side, the unbalanced force of gravity may cause the bicycle to speed up.

When unbalanced forces act on an object, the object starts to move, speeds up, slows down, stops, or changes direction. This change of motion is called **acceleration**.

✓ **What happens to an object's motion when unbalanced forces act on it?**

Forces Act in Pairs

The change in motion of an object is always caused by a force or forces. One place to see forces in action is in games such as marbles, billiards, or croquet.

Suppose you are playing a game with a blue marble and a red marble. The blue marble is moving, and the red marble is not. When the blue marble hits the red marble, the red marble moves. The force needed to move the red marble came from the blue marble. But what happens to the blue marble after it hits the red one? It slows down, changes direction, or stops. A force must have acted on the blue marble as well. The force that acts on the blue marble comes from the red marble it hit.

One of the basic laws of science is this: *Forces always act in pairs.* When one object acts on a second object, the second object also acts on the first object. When you walk, your feet push against the floor. The floor also pushes against your feet, partly through the force of friction. On ice, which has little friction to push back against your feet, walking is harder.

✓ **If you see an object change its motion, what has happened to it?**

▲ Both players push with the same amount of force but in opposite directions. Their forces exactly cancel each other out, so neither player moves.

▲ The players push in opposite directions, but the player on the left pushes with greater force. The players move to the right.

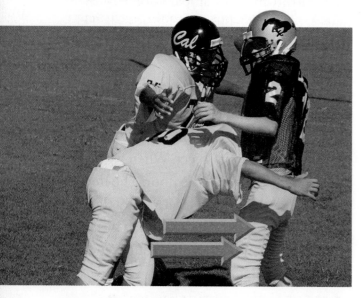

▲ The combined forces are acting in the same direction. In an instant, these forces will move the quarterback.

Net Force

When two forces act on an object at the same time, the forces may be balanced or unbalanced. Adding or subtracting the individual forces gives a value, called the **net force**, of the combined forces.

If two forces act on an object in the same direction, you add the forces to get the net force. For example, suppose two people who are moving a refrigerator push on the same side. Each pushes with a force of 120 newtons (N) toward the right.

$$120 \, \text{N} \rightarrow + 120 \, \text{N} \rightarrow = 240 \, \text{N} \rightarrow$$

The net force on the refrigerator equals 240 newtons to the right.

If two forces act on an object in opposite directions, you subtract the smaller force from the larger force to get the net force. The net force acts in the direction of the larger force.

In the case of the refrigerator, suppose the force of friction resisting the movement of the refrigerator is 100 newtons. This force acts in a direction opposite to the force acting to the right on the refrigerator.

$$240 \, \text{N} \rightarrow - 100 \, \text{N} \leftarrow = 140 \, \text{N} \rightarrow$$

The net force on the refrigerator equals 140 newtons to the right.

If two equal forces act on an object in opposite directions, the net force will be balanced and the object's motion will not change. To review the concept of net force, study the series of photographs at the left.

✔ **What is the net force when a force of 100 newtons pushes against a force of friction of 80 newtons?**

Summary

Balanced forces occur when two forces acting on an object are equal in size and opposite in direction. Unbalanced forces occur when forces acting on the same object are not opposite and equal. A net force occurs when forces are unbalanced, causing acceleration. When you calculate the net force on an object, you must account for both the size and the direction of the forces.

Review

1. What happens to an object when balanced forces act on it?
2. A moving object speeds up. Are the forces acting on the object balanced? Explain.
3. Suppose you ride a bike along a flat, straight road at a constant speed. Are the forces acting on the bike balanced or unbalanced?
4. **Critical Thinking** Two bumper cars collide. Both cars stop. How do you know that a force has acted on both cars?
5. **Test Prep** Suppose a book weighs 35 newtons and you apply a force of 50 newtons to lift it. The net force acting on the book is —
   A 85 newtons, up
   B 50 newtons, up
   C 15 newtons, up
   D 35 newtons, down

LINKS

MATH LINK

Net Force Suppose two teams have a tug of war. The four players on Team A pull with these forces: 80 newtons (N), 120 N, 130 N, and 90 N. The four players on Team B pull with these forces: 100 N, 100 N, 90 N, and 90 N. Which team will win the tug of war?

WRITING LINK

Informative Writing—Explanation Have you ever heard the phrase "caught between a rock and a hard place"? Or "an unstoppable force meets an immovable object"? Both of these figures of speech refer to forces. What does each mean? Write a paragraph for a classmate that explains these phrases.

PHYSICAL EDUCATION LINK

Balanced Forces One type of exercise involves exerting a force against something that does not move. Press your palms together in front of your chest. Observe how balanced forces are exerted by the muscles in your arms. Design other exercises in which you exert balanced forces.

TECHNOLOGY LINK

Learn more about forces by visiting the National Air and Space Museum Internet site.
www.si.edu/harcourt/science

Smithsonian Institution®

What Is Work and How Is It Measured?

In this lesson, you can . . .

INVESTIGATE how to measure work.

LEARN ABOUT work and how machines make work easier.

LINK to math, writing, and technology.

◄ How much force does it take to lift a car?

INVESTIGATE

Measuring Work

Activity Purpose In Lesson 2 you learned that unbalanced forces affect the motion of an object. We say that an unbalanced force does *work* on the object it moves. In this investigation you will **measure** the amount of work done when you move objects in a certain way.

Materials

- heavy object
- spring scale
- meterstick
- flight of stairs
- calculator

Activity Procedure

1 Copy the table below.

Work

Trial	Weight (newtons)	Height (meters)	Work (joules)
1			
2			
3			
4			

2 Weigh the object using the spring scale and **record** its weight in the table, next to *Trial 1*. (Picture A)

3 **Measure** the total height of the stairs in meters. **Record** the measurement in the table, also next to *Trial 1*. (Picture B)

④ Work can be **measured** as the product of force (in newtons) and distance (in meters). **Calculate** the number of newton-meters, or *joules,* of work you would do if you carried the object up the flight of stairs. **Record** the product in the table.

⑤ Suppose you carried the object up two flights of stairs. Beside *Trial 2* on the table, **record** the new height and **calculate** the work done.

⑥ For *Trial 3,* **calculate** how much work you would do if you carried the object up three flights every day for a week.

⑦ For *Trial 4,* suppose your weight is 300 newtons. **Record** this new data and **calculate** the work you do climbing the stairs without carrying the object.

Picture A

Picture B

Draw Conclusions

1. **Compare** the amount of work a person weighing 300 newtons does climbing one flight of stairs to the total amount of work the same person does climbing three flights of stairs every day for a week.

2. **Interpret** your **data,** and **draw conclusions** about how work is related to force and distance.

3. **Scientists at Work** When scientists **interpret data**, they often **draw conclusions** based on the data they collected. What can you conclude about the amount of work done by people who weigh more than 300 newtons?

Investigate Further *Power* is the measure of how quickly work is done. You can measure power in *joules per second.* **Plan and conduct a simple investigation** to calculate how much power you use walking up a flight of stairs compared to running up a flight of stairs.

Process Skill Tip

When you **interpret data**, you should look for patterns in the results. You can then **draw conclusions** based on those patterns.

Work and Power

FIND OUT

- how work is defined and measured
- how power is defined and measured
- what machines do

VOCABULARY

work
power
machine

Work and Effort

How was work today? Have you finished your homework? You've probably heard questions like these before, but to a scientist, work may be somewhat different than what you're familiar with. To understand how scientists define *work*, think about the following situation.

Suppose a gardener is trying to pull an old tree stump out of the ground. He pulls and pulls until his face is red and he is soaked in sweat. But the stump doesn't move. Nearby a little girl on a tricycle rides from one corner of the block to the next, passing the gardener along the way. Who is exerting more effort? Who is doing work?

The gardener is clearly exerting more effort than the girl, because he is applying a much larger force. But according to the way scientists define *work*, he has done no work. **Work** is the use of a force to move an object through a distance. The girl, on the other hand, moves herself and her tricycle along the sidewalk. According to the definition, she has done work.

✔ **What is work?**

It takes the same amount of work to lift one piano two floors as it does to lift two pianos one floor. The table below shows how much work is done moving a piano in different situations.

Work Needed to Lift Pianos

Object to Be Moved	Force Needed (Weight of Object)	Distance to Be Moved	Work Done (Force × Distance)
1 piano	1000 N	1 floor (4 m)	1000 × 4 = 4000 J
1 piano	1000 N	2 floors (8 m)	1000 × 8 = 8000 J
2 pianos	2000 N	1 floor (4 m)	2000 × 4 = 8000 J
2 pianos	2000 N	2 floors (8 m)	2000 × 8 = 16,000 J

Calculating Work and Power

In the investigation you used a scale to measure force and you used a meterstick to measure distance. From these measurements you calculated the amount of work done. To calculate the amount of work done, multiply the force used to move an object by the distance the object moves.

The metric unit of work is the *joule* (JOOL). One joule is equal to a force of 1 newton exerted over a distance of 1 meter. For example, 1 joule is the amount of work it takes to lift a 1-newton weight 1 meter off the ground.

An average fifth grader does about 200 joules of work getting out of bed in the morning. When a 1000-newton (N) (about 225-lb) basketball star jumps 1 m (about 3 ft) to slam-dunk the ball, he or she does about 1000 joules (J) of work.

1000 N × 1 m = 1000 J

An average adult could probably push a small car along a flat road. The car's engine could also move the car along the same road. Even though the person and the engine do the same amount of work, the engine can do the work much more quickly. The engine has more power than a person. **Power** is the amount of work done for each unit of time. It is a measure of how quickly someone or something does work.

The metric unit of power is the *watt*. One watt is equal to doing 1 joule of work in 1 second. For example, lifting an apple

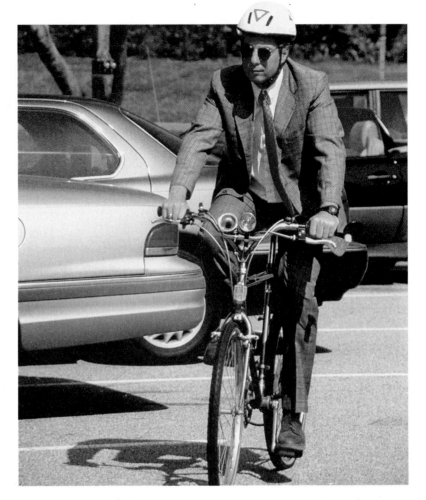

▲ The car's engine can produce about 100,000 watts of power. A well-trained bicycle racer can produce about 400 watts of power for a few seconds. A relaxed bicycle ride might take only 100 watts of power for the same period of time.

1 m requires about 1 joule of work. To lift that apple 1 m in 1 second takes about 1 watt (W) of power.

A person who weighs about 400 newtons (90 lb) does about 1200 joules of work climbing a 3-m (about 10-ft) flight of stairs.

400 N × 3 m = 1200 J

To run up the stairs in 3 seconds takes about 400 watts of power.

1200 J ÷ 3 sec = 400 J/sec = 400 W

✔ **Which requires more power, walking up a flight of stairs or running up the same flight of stairs? Explain.**

Machines and Work

The movers do a lot of work lifting a piano. But they can make this work easier for themselves by using a machine. A **machine** is something that makes work seem easier by changing the size or the direction of a force. There are six simple machines: pulley, lever, inclined plane, wedge, screw, and wheel and axle.

A machine makes work seem easier by changing force into distance or distance into force. Using pulleys, for example, a person can lift a 1000-newton piano using only 100 newtons of force. But to lift the piano 1 m with the pulleys, that person would need to have a rope 10 m long.

$$1000 \text{ N} \times 1 \text{ m} = 1000 \text{ J}$$

$$100 \text{ N} \times 10 \text{ m} = 1000 \text{ J}$$

Pulleys, like all machines, do *not* reduce the amount of work to be done. The amount of work needed to lift the 1000-newton piano 1 m is still 1000 joules. Instead, a machine allows a person to do the same amount of work by exerting a smaller force over a longer distance. Other machines, such as a lever, allow a person to exert a larger force over a shorter distance. A lever increases the force, rather than the distance as the pulley did. Machines can also change the direction of a force. A wheel and axle, for example, can change a twisting force into a downward force.

✓ **A certain machine reduces the amount of force needed to move an object. What must it do to the distance through which the force is exerted?**

This strange machine makes use of many simple machines. Some of these are labeled and described.

A pulley doesn't increase force or distance. Instead, it changes the direction of the force.

This wedge takes a downward force and changes it to an outward force to crack the egg.

A wheel and axle is a special type of lever. This one increases the force the cat exerts.

An inclined plane reduces the force necessary for the chicken to get back into the coop.

A screw changes a force's direction. This one changes a turning motion into a side-to-side motion.

This lever increases the force but decreases the distance through which it can move.

Everyday Machines

Most of the machines people use are compound machines. That is, they are made up of two or more simple machines. For example, a shovel is a wedge at the end of a lever. A hand-cranked pencil sharpener uses a wheel and axle to turn a set of wedges that cut.

Even a water faucet is made up of several simple machines. When you turn a faucet on or off, you are turning a wheel and axle that is attached to a metal screw. The metal screw is, in turn, attached to a rubber wedge.

Turning on a faucet lifts the rubber wedge, called a *washer*, and allows the water to flow. The more you turn the handle, the larger the opening becomes, allowing more water to flow.

When you turn the faucet off, the force of your hand turning the wheel and axle is moved along the screw threads. This presses the rubber wedge back down into its seat, stopping the flow of water.

✔ **What simple machines are part of a water faucet?**

THE INSIDE STORY

A Not-So-Simple Machine

The handle of the faucet is a wheel and axle—a type of lever. The larger the handle, the easier it is to turn.

The screw inside the faucet changes the turning force of the handle into a downward force. It also increases the force.

The rubber washer is a kind of wedge. It changes the downward force of the screw into an outward force that presses the rubber against the metal seat.

Summary

Work is the force applied to an object times the distance the object is moved. Work is measured in joules. Power is a measure of the speed at which work is done. Power is measured in watts. Machines are devices that make work seem easier by changing the size or direction of a force. Pulleys, levers, wheels and axles, inclined planes, wedges, and screws are simple machines.

Review

1. How much work is done if you lift a 20-newton weight 10 meters?

2. Which involves speed—work or power?

3. Look at the table on page F18. How much power is needed to lift 1 piano 1 floor in 10 seconds?

4. **Critical Thinking** Explain how a set of pulleys could help the gardener mentioned on page F18 remove the tree stump.

5. **Test Prep** The amount of power needed to do 10 joules of work in 1 second is —
   A 1 watt
   B 10 joules
   C 10 watts
   D 1000 watts

LINKS

MATH LINK

Climbing to the Top The top of the Washington Monument is about 150 m above the ground. Gravity pulls on each pound of your body with a force of about 4.5 newtons. Calculate the amount of work you would do in climbing the stairs to the top of the Washington Monument. About how much power would you use if you climbed those stairs in 5 minutes?

WRITING LINK

Informative Writing—Compare and Contrast Write out definitions of *work* and *power* as you learned them in this lesson. Use each word in a sentence that clearly shows what the word means. Then look up the common meanings of these words in a dictionary. Write a paragraph for each word, comparing its everyday meaning with its scientific meaning. Then read the paragraph to your family.

TECHNOLOGY LINK

Learn more about simple machines by visiting the Harcourt Learning Site. **www.harcourtschool.com**

WELCOME TO THE LEARNING SITE

WEIGHTLESS WORK

The third law of motion states that when you apply a force to an object, an equally strong force is applied to you, but in the opposite direction. However, nature has a hard time "enforcing" that law in space.

In Space, the Force Is Still With You

In space, a simple job—like loosening or tightening a screw—becomes a difficult task because your body tends to twist. On Earth, gravity keeps you firmly on the ground, so it's easy to resist the twisting. But in space, there is almost no gravity to hold you in place. Astronauts working in microgravity, as it is called, must use their arms or legs to brace themselves against something solid.

To build structures in space, engineers and scientists have developed new ways of working and new tools to work with. Working in space poses other problems, too. Joe Allen, who has spent more time working in space than any other American astronaut, says the pressurized space suits that astronauts wear squeeze you. "Every movement takes a lot of energy. The best way to get used to working in space," Allen says, "is to practice on Earth."

Astronauts train for space by working under water.

Floating is the easiest way to travel in space.

Practice in a Pool

Where do astronauts find a microgravity environment on Earth? In the Neutral Buoyancy Laboratory (NBL), the world's biggest swimming pool, located at the Johnson Space Center in Houston, Texas.

Six meters (about 20 ft) under water in the NBL, astronauts wearing space suits float as if they were in space. The NBL is big enough to hold a full-size model of the space shuttle cargo bay, so astronauts can spend several hours every day working in microgravity.

Working with Waldos

Astronauts need more than just practice to work in space. They need special tools, too. One of the most useful tools is the Remote Manipulator System, or RMS. Sometimes called the shuttle "arm," it was built for NASA by Canadian engineers. The RMS looks like the cranes used on construction sites on Earth, but it is much more than a crane. The RMS has a large grasping

"hand" and joints that act like human wrist, elbow, and shoulder joints. The RMS can be operated remotely. That means an astronaut inside a space shuttle can use simple hand controls (like joy sticks) to maneuver bulky cargo, such as satellites or parts of the International Space Station. Using cameras to guide the RMS, astronauts can make the fine movements needed to line up and connect huge pieces of the space station.

THINK ABOUT IT

1. Why are simple jobs, such as tightening or loosening screws, difficult in space?
2. Astronauts practicing in the Neutral Buoyancy Laboratory wear space suits filled with air. Why do you think they wear space suits in the water?

WEB LINK:
For science and technology updates, visit The Learning Site.
www.harcourtschool.com

Careers   Mission Specialist

What They Do
Mission specialists perform the scientific experiments and construction projects on space shuttle flights.

Education and Training Most astronauts have advanced degrees in sciences such as physics, chemistry, engineering, and medicine. Mission specialists also go through months or years of training for the specialized tasks they will perform in space.

Ephraim Fischbach

PHYSICIST

"On the whole, the recent experiments do not point to the existence of a new force, although a number of the existing anomalies [unusual things] remain to be explained."

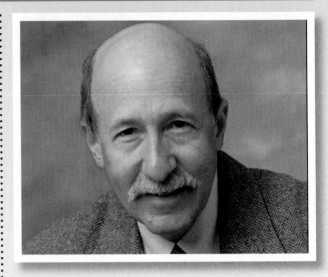

Among the most important ideas of modern science are the laws of motion. Although these laws were formulated in the 1600s, they are still used to calculate orbits for satellites and flight paths for space probes. The first three laws describe motion, and the fourth law describes gravity.

Is it possible that, in some cases, the fourth law might be wrong? Physics professor Ephraim Fischbach and a group of researchers at Purdue University have tried to answer that question for years. The scientists studied the idea that a force other than gravity might be at work in certain situations. Predictions based on the law of universal gravitation may not be accurate over all distances. So far, Dr. Fischbach's group has not found enough evidence to support the existence of what they hypothesize as a "fifth force." But they have discovered exceptions to the fourth law that no one can explain yet.

In addition to being a professor and research scientist, Dr. Fischbach has also worked to develop the Physics Funfest, a physics show put on every year for people who live near the university. The shows have been so popular that they are now being taken to schools throughout Indiana. Dr. Fischbach has also worked on a project to establish a science and technology center at Purdue University, which will include a hands-on museum.

THINK ABOUT IT

1. What does the fourth law of motion describe?
2. Why is it important for scientists to continue testing ideas that are considered to be "laws" of science?

The laws of motion in action

Making Magnets

How does an object become a magnet?

Materials
- compass
- sewing needle
- small piece of thin Styrofoam
- shallow bowl of water
- bar magnet

Procedure
1 Put the compass on the table. Observe the direction the north-seeking end points to.

2 Put the needle on the piece of Styrofoam, and float it in the bowl of water. Observe which way the needle points.

3 Now stroke the needle with the bar magnet.

4 Put the needle back on the floating Styrofoam. Which way does the needle point?

Draw Conclusions
Does the needle act like a compass in Step 2? Does it act like a compass in Step 4? How did you turn the needle into a magnet?

Center of Gravity

How can you find an object's center of gravity?

Materials
- 10-cm square of paper
- flat toothpick
- 30 cm of 24-gauge wire
- cardboard cutout of your state

Procedure
1 Fold the paper in half, and then in half again. Balance the paper on your finger.

2 Balance the toothpick on your finger.

3 Straighten out the wire. Then fold the wire in half. Wrap the midpoint of the wire tightly around the toothpick. Now balance the toothpick on your finger.

4 Using the cardboard cutout and what you have learned about balancing objects, find the geographic center of your state.

Draw Conclusions
An object's center of gravity is the point at which the force of gravity is evenly balanced. Where is the center of gravity of the toothpick? When you added weight (the wire) to the toothpick, what happened to its center of gravity? How did the cardboard cutout's center of gravity help you find the geographic center of your state?

Vocabulary Review

Use the terms below to complete the sentences. The page numbers in ( ) tell you where to look in the chapter if you need help.

force (F6)　　　　　**acceleration** (F13)
friction (F6)　　　　**net force** (F14)
magnetism (F7)　　　**work** (F18)
gravitation (F8)　　　**power** (F19)
balanced forces (F12)　**machine** (F20)
unbalanced
　　forces (F13)

1. A ＿＿＿ is a push or a pull and can make an object speed up, slow down, or change direction. This change in movement is called ＿＿＿.

2. The force of ＿＿＿ attracts all objects toward each other.

3. When an object's motion changes, you know that the forces acting on it are ＿＿＿.

4. A ＿＿＿ makes work easier by trading force for distance.

5. A force that acts on an object does ＿＿＿ only when the object moves.

6. ＿＿＿ act on an object without causing a change in the object's motion.

7. The watt is a unit of ＿＿＿, which is a measure of how quickly work is done.

8. ＿＿＿ is a force of repulsion or attraction between objects with two poles.

9. When you slide one object over another, the force of ＿＿＿ acts in the opposite direction.

10. Adding or subtracting individual forces gives a combined force called a ＿＿＿.

Connect Concepts

Write the vocabulary terms or units that complete the concept map.

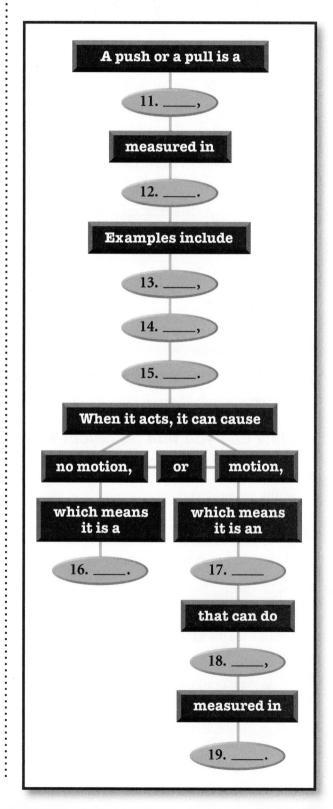

A push or a pull is a

11. ＿＿＿,

measured in

12. ＿＿＿.

Examples include

13. ＿＿＿,

14. ＿＿＿,

15. ＿＿＿.

When it acts, it can cause

no motion,　　or　　motion,

which means it is a

which means it is an

16. ＿＿＿.

17. ＿＿＿

that can do

18. ＿＿＿,

measured in

19. ＿＿＿.

Check Understanding

Write the letter of the best choice.

20. When a leaf falls from a tree, the force acting on the leaf is —
    A friction   C magnetism
    B gravitation   D balanced

21. You can exert a force on an object, but only if the object moves do you —
    F make an effort   H do work
    G feel gravity   J exert power

22. When two forces act on an object in opposite directions and the object moves, it moves in the direction of the —
    A friction   C magnetic field
    B smaller force   D greater force

23. If you lift a 200-newton crate 1 meter off the floor, how much work do you do?
    F 100 joules   H 2000 joules
    G 200 joules   J 600 joules

24. The north and south poles of two magnets —
    A repel each other
    B magnetize each other
    C align with each other
    D attract each other

Critical Thinking

25. An object is not moving. Can you conclude that no forces are acting on it? Explain.

26. A dog chases a cat up a flight of stairs. The cat runs faster than the dog and gets away. Can you conclude that the cat is more powerful than the dog? Explain.

Process Skills Review

27. **Compare** the forces of gravitation and magnetism.

28. **Hypothesize** about whether your weight would be greater or less on top of Mount Everest than at sea level.

29. A line graph shows the speed of a race car during a short race. The horizontal axis shows time. The vertical axis shows speed. How would you **interpret the data** to identify the points at which the brakes were exerting the greatest force on the car's wheels?

30. Jamal and Janet climbed Mount Equinox together. Jamal weighs 120 newtons more than Janet. What can you **conclude** about who did more work?

Performance Assessment

Forces at Work

Slide a brick down an inclined plane. Analyze the forces that act on the brick as it slides and after it stops at the bottom of the ramp. Include as much detail as possible about the forces and the work they do. You may want to draw a diagram to help you communicate your findings.

Vocabulary Preview

position
speed
velocity
acceleration
momentum
inertia
action force
reaction force
orbit
law of universal gravitation

Motion

Moving objects tend to keep moving, and objects that are not moving tend to remain not moving. This is one of the laws of motion. What other scientific laws have you heard about?

FAST FACT

The sun moves through space at about 899,462 km/hr (558,900 mi/hr). At the same time, Earth is revolving around the sun at about 107,240 km/hr (66,636 mi/hr). The table shows the speed of some of the other planets in their paths around the sun.

How Fast?	
Planet	**Speed Around Sun** (kilometers per hour)
Mercury	172,324
Venus	126,043
Jupiter	47,034
Pluto	17,088

Jupiter from one
of its moons

If a rifle is fired horizontally and a bullet is
dropped from the same height at the same
time, they will hit the ground at the same
time. The force of gravity is the same
for both.

A hovercraft floats on a cushion of air.
The lack of friction means there are no
brakes. The only way to stop it is to turn
off the engine—or run into something.

How Are Motion and Speed Related?

In this lesson, you can . . .

INVESTIGATE the effects of changes in motion.

LEARN ABOUT speed, velocity, acceleration, and momentum.

LINK to math, writing, social studies, and technology.

The cheetah is the fastest land animal. Unlike most animals, it can change direction while running at top speed. ▼

INVESTIGATE

Changes in Motion

Activity Purpose Have you ever had to stand on a moving train or bus? It's hard to keep your balance when the vehicle starts, stops, speeds up, slows down, or turns. While standing on the moving train or bus, your body senses changes in direction and speed. In this investigation you will build and use a simple device to help you **observe** changes in motion.

Materials

- clear plastic bottle with cap
- water
- small piece of soap

Activity Procedure

1. Fill the bottle nearly to the top with water. Leave only enough space for a small air bubble. Add a small piece of soap to the water. This will keep the air bubble from sticking to the side of the bottle. Put the cap tightly on the bottle.

2. Lay the bottle on its side on a flat surface. You should see one small bubble in the bottle. Hold the bottle steady until the bubble moves to the center of the bottle and stays there. (Picture A)

3. **Predict** what will happen to the air bubble if you turn the bottle to the left or right. Turn the bottle and **observe** what happens. **Record** your observations.

Picture A

Picture B

4 Now **predict** what will happen to the air bubble if you move the bottle straight ahead at a steady speed. Move the bottle and **observe** what happens. **Record** your observations. (Picture B)

5 Repeat Step 4, but this time slowly increase the bottle's speed. **Observe** what happens to the air bubble. **Record** your observations.

Draw Conclusions

1. **Compare** your predictions and your observations. What happened when you turned the bottle to the left or right, or moved it forward?

2. From what you **observed**, how did a change in speed affect the bubble?

3. **Scientists at Work** Were you surprised by the way the air bubble moved? When scientists get surprising results, they often **hypothesize** about the cause of those results. Form a hypothesis about why the bubble moves the way it does.

Investigate Further **Predict** what will happen to the air bubble if the bottle is moving at a steady speed and its direction changes. **Plan and conduct a simple investigation** to test your prediction.

F33

Motion and Speed

Position and Motion

In the investigation you built a device that detected changes in motion. To observe motion, you must first determine an object's position. **Position** is an object's place, or location. If an object's position is changing, the object is in motion. However, whether you observe the motion depends on your *frame of reference.* That is, you must be able to observe the motion against a background that is *not* moving. For example, if you see a roller coaster moving, your frame of reference includes the track and the background, which are not moving.

For some objects in motion, several different frames of reference are possible. Suppose a person is sitting in a chair, reading a book. To the person reading, the book is not moving. But if the person reading the book is on a train, a person outside the train sees the book moving. The two people have different frames of reference. Suppose a third person is on a train going in the opposite direction. That person sees the book from yet another frame of reference. The motion of any object depends on your motion when you observe the object.

✔ **Why does motion need a frame of reference?**

FIND OUT

- the relationships among speed, velocity, acceleration, and momentum
- how speed, velocity, acceleration, and momentum are measured

VOCABULARY

position
speed
velocity
acceleration
momentum

Suppose you're observing this hiker. To decide whether she's moving or not, you need to compare her positions on the ground at two different times. ▶

Speed				
Interval	0–6 m	6–16 m	16–22 m	22–30 m
Distance	6 m	10 m	6 m	8 m
Time	12 sec	5 sec	9 sec	32 sec
Speed (D/T)	0.5 m/sec	2 m/sec	0.67 m/sec	0.25 m/sec

As she moves down the hill, her speed increases. Her speed changes again when she reaches the bottom of the hill. It changes once more when she starts up the next hill.

1 meter

Speed and Velocity

One way to describe the motion of an object is to describe its speed. **Speed** is a measure of the distance an object moves in a given amount of time. Suppose you roll a ball along a sidewalk. If it travels 3 m in 1 sec, its speed is 3 m/sec.

In 5 sec, the ball's speed will probably vary. The ball starts fast and then slows down. *Average speed* is the total distance an object moves divided by the total amount of time. If the ball rolls 10 m in 5 sec, its average speed is calculated as follows:

10 m ÷ 5 sec = 2 m/sec.

The motions of two cars going east at the same speed are the same. But if one car is going east and the other is going west, their motions are different. For two objects to have the same motion, they must be moving at the same speed *and* in the same direction. An object's speed in a particular direction is its **velocity** (vuh•LAHS•uh•tee).

✔ **If two bicyclists ride north at the same speed, do they have the same velocity? Explain.**

Acceleration

When an object starts, stops, speeds up, slows down, or turns left or right, it changes velocity. Any change in velocity is called **acceleration** (ak•sel•er•AY•shuhn).

Suppose that you are riding a bicycle. When you start pedaling, you accelerate. When you speed up going down a hill, you accelerate. And when you slow down going up a hill, you also accelerate. Slowing down is also known as *deceleration*. When you turn a corner, you accelerate, because you change direction. Finally, when you stop the bike, you accelerate, because your speed changes once again. The only time you are not accelerating is when you ride in a straight line at a constant speed.

✔ **If a car is driven along a curved stretch of road at a constant speed, is it accelerating? Explain.**

▲ The bicyclists are on a curve. Their velocities are constantly changing because their directions are constantly changing.

Momentum

When a car crashes, it stops almost instantly. Without seat belts or air bags, the passengers may be seriously hurt. A seat belt or an air bag must stop a person who has a lot of momentum. **Momentum** (moh•MEN•tuhm) is a measure of how hard it is to slow down or stop an object. It is the product of an object's velocity and its mass.

If two objects have the same velocity, the one with the greater mass has more momentum. Which would be harder to stop—a toy truck moving in a straight line at 50 km/hr or a real truck with the same velocity? Obviously the real truck would be harder to stop, because its greater mass gives it more momentum than the toy truck.

If two objects have the same mass, the one with the greater velocity has more momentum. Which would be harder to stop—a baseball thrown gently or a hard line drive hit by a batter? The line drive would be harder to stop because of its greater velocity. The greater the velocity of an object, the greater its momentum.

High-speed crashes tend to cause more serious injuries than low-speed crashes. That's because high speed produces greater momentum. Velocity can give even small objects a lot of momentum. A bullet fired from a gun is dangerous because of its velocity.

✔ **Which has more momentum—a big car moving at 100 km/hr or a small car moving at the same speed?**

A large ship is hard to stop or turn because of its momentum. A personal watercraft may move at a higher speed, but it has much less mass. So it has less momentum than the ship.

Summary

Motion is a change in an object's position. Speed is a measure of the distance an object moves in a given amount of time. Velocity is speed in a particular direction. Acceleration is a change in velocity, either in direction or in speed. Momentum is a measure of how hard it is to slow down or stop an object. It is the product of an object's velocity and its mass.

Review

1. Two objects move for the same amount of time. Object A moves farther than Object B. Which object moved at a greater average speed?
2. Explain how velocity differs from speed.
3. An object speeds up. Then it slows down. Then it changes direction. Which of these are examples of acceleration?
4. **Critical Thinking** Use the idea of momentum to explain why a football coach might choose a large, fast runner to carry the ball.
5. **Test Prep** If you observe a change in an object's speed or direction, you are observing a change in its —

   A frame of reference

   B velocity

   C position

   D momentum

L I N K S

MATH LINK

Using a Formula This is the formula for average speed:

$$\text{Average speed} = \text{total distance} \div \text{total time}$$

Light from the sun travels at 300,000 km/sec. The distance from the sun to Earth is 150,000,000 km. How long does it take sunlight to reach Earth?

WRITING LINK

Informative Writing—Classification Keep track of your movements as you go from class to class, from home to school, or from school to home. In a journal, record and classify any changes in velocity you made. Then write a paragraph summarizing the changes.

SOCIAL STUDIES LINK

History The *Titanic* sank in the North Atlantic after hitting an iceberg. Research the events of the sinking. Then decide whether the collision was unavoidable because of the ship's momentum. Back up your conclusion with facts.

TECHNOLOGY LINK

Learn more about motion and speed by visiting this Internet site.
www.scilinks.org/harcourt

What Are the Three Laws of Motion?

In this lesson, you can . . .

INVESTIGATE how mass and velocity affect momentum.

LEARN ABOUT the laws of motion.

LINK to math, writing, technology, and other areas.

When the ball collides with the pins, the momentum it loses is equal to the momentum the pins gain. ▼

INVESTIGATE

How Mass and Velocity Affect Momentum

Activity Purpose In Lesson 1 you read that mass is related to momentum. A moving object with a lot of mass has a lot of momentum. You also read that velocity is related to momentum. An object with a high velocity also has a lot of momentum. In this investigation you will **experiment** to see for yourself how mass and velocity affect momentum.

Materials

- gameboard
- several books
- meterstick
- small toy car
- dime
- quarter

Activity Procedure

1. Make a ramp by setting one end of the gameboard on a stack of books about 15 cm high. Place another book as a barrier about 10–15 cm from the bottom of the ramp. (Picture A)

2. Position the car at the top of the ramp. Put the dime on one end of the car. Let the car roll down the ramp and strike the barrier. **Observe** what happens to the dime. **Measure** and **record** its distance from the barrier. (Picture B)

3. Repeat Step 2, this time placing the quarter on the car instead of the dime. **Observe** what happens to the quarter. **Measure** and **record** its distance from the barrier.

Picture A

Picture B

4 Repeat Steps 2 and 3 several times. **Measure** and **record** the distance for each trial.

5 **Predict** how the results would differ if the ramp were steeper. Add another book to the stack under the ramp, and repeat Steps 2 and 3 several times. **Measure** and **record** the distances for each trial.

Draw Conclusions

1. Make a table to organize your data. **Compare** the results for the dime with the results for the quarter. **Infer** how the mass of the coin is related to the distance it travels.

2. What happened to the distances the coins traveled when you made the ramp steeper? Explain the results.

3. **Scientists at Work** While **gathering data**, scientists try to **identify and control variables**, or conditions, that may affect the results. In this investigation, what variables did you control in Steps 2 and 3? What variable did you test?

Investigate Further **Plan and conduct a simple investigation** to test various methods of keeping the coin on the car when it strikes the barrier. Carefully select the equipment you will need, and conduct several trials for each method you test.

The Laws of Motion

Newton's Ideas

FIND OUT

- how the laws of motion explain the actions of forces on objects
- how momentum is transferred from one object to another

VOCABULARY

inertia
action force
reaction force

Isaac Newton was born in England in 1642. He introduced new ideas about forces and motion. By the time of his death in 1727, his ideas had changed the way scientists observe the natural world.

Before Newton, Aristotle, a Greek philosopher, described four basic "elements": earth, air, water, and fire. He believed that everything was made of one or more of these elements. It seemed reasonable to Aristotle that an object would try to move toward objects made of the same element. For example, Aristotle believed that smoke belonged to the air. He believed that smoke naturally rose to rejoin the air.

At the age of 23, Newton developed three laws of motion. These laws were the first to describe the movement of objects in terms of forces. For example, Newton didn't say that an apple falls from a tree because it is made of earth. He said that a force (gravitation) causes Earth and the apple to attract each other. The laws of motion describe the movement of objects on Earth. They also describe the movement of planets and moons.

✔ **According to Newton, why does a meteor fall to Earth?**

Newton once said that ideas did not just come to him suddenly. For example, the story of the apple falling on his head isn't true. Instead, he thought long and hard about problems until he worked them out.

The two Voyager spacecraft, launched in the 1970s, have left our solar system. They will continue moving through space for thousands of years.

The First Law of Motion

Before Newton's time, scientists hypothesized that any moving object would stop moving unless something continued to push it. Newton saw things differently. He realized that a moving object would continue to move in a straight line until a force interfered with it. He also decided that an object that was not moving would remain motionless unless a force acted on it. These ideas became the first law of motion:

An object at rest will remain at rest, and an object in motion will continue moving in a straight line at a constant speed until an outside force acts on it.

Because of its great mass, this train has a lot of inertia. It takes a long time to get it moving and a long time to stop it.

According to this law, a ball rolling down a sidewalk stops because a force (friction) acts on it. In space there is very little friction. A spacecraft will continue moving at the same speed and in the same direction practically forever. Its motion will change only if forces from a nearby star or planet act on it.

The other part of this law states that an object at rest will remain at rest. This is easy to see if you place a ball on a flat, level surface. Unless you push the ball or tilt the surface, the ball will stay where it is.

The property of matter that keeps it moving in a straight line or keeps it at rest is called **inertia** (in•ER•shuh). An object's inertia resists any change in its motion.

Have you ever seen a performer pull a tablecloth from under a table setting? The items remain in place on the table, amazing the audience. How does the trick work? If the performer pulls the tablecloth quickly enough, the inertia of the objects on the table keeps them in place. If the objects are heavy, it is easier to pull the tablecloth off without disturbing them. This is because the amount of inertia in an object is related to its mass. The greater the mass, the greater the object's inertia.

✔ **What is the first law of motion?**

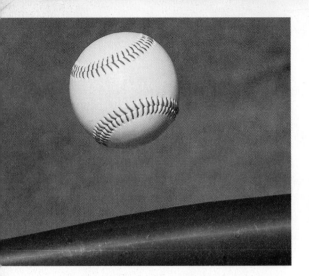

▲ As the ball approaches the bat, the ball and the bat exert forces in different directions. The bat exerts a greater force.

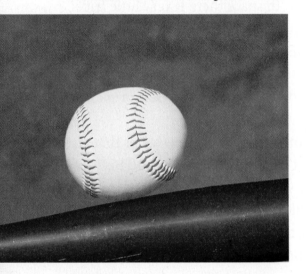

▲ When the ball and the bat meet, forces are transferred between the two.

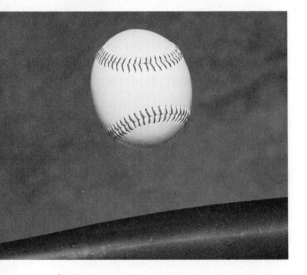

▲ The force of the bat accelerates the ball— it changes direction. The more force the batter uses, the faster the ball accelerates.

The Second Law of Motion

In Lesson 1 you read that acceleration is a change in an object's velocity—its speed or its direction. According to the laws of motion, the only thing that can cause acceleration is a force. The amount of acceleration depends on the size of the force *and* on the mass of the object. This is the second law of motion:

An object's acceleration depends on the size and direction of the force acting on it and on the mass of the object.

The size of the force A large force acting on an object will cause more acceleration than a small force. The harder a tennis player hits a ball, the more the ball's motion will change and the faster the ball will go.

The second law helps explain why race car drivers put the most powerful engines possible in their cars. A more powerful engine provides more force. It causes greater acceleration. So the car speeds up or changes direction more quickly.

The direction of the force A force that acts on an object may cause it to speed up, slow down, stop, or change direction. A rolling soccer ball, for example, will speed up if it's kicked from behind. If the goalie blocks it from the front, it may slow down, stop, or change direction. If kicked from the side, the ball will change direction.

The mass of the object A force has more effect on an object with less mass than it has on an object with more mass. Cars that are used for drag racing are very light because a car with less mass accelerates faster.

To think about what this means, consider a model rocket and a space shuttle. The model rocket has much less mass than the shuttle. So a much smaller force is needed to lift it off the ground. Could the model rocket's engine lift the shuttle? What would the engine of the shuttle do to the model rocket?

✔ **What happens to an object's acceleration as the size of the force acting on the object increases?**

The Third Law of Motion

According to the laws of motion, if you push against a wall, there is an equal force that pushes back. For the wall to stop your push, there must be a force pushing against you. Forces always occur in pairs. Whenever an object (you) exerts a force on a second object (the wall), the second object also exerts a force on the first object. This is the third law of motion:

For every action, there is an equal and opposite reaction.

This law also applies to forces that produce motion. Think about an in-line skater holding a basketball. If the skater throws the ball really hard, the ball goes forward and the skater rolls backward.

The third law is also stated this way: For every action force, there is an equal and opposite reaction force. The first force is the **action force**. The force that pushes or pulls back is the **reaction force**.

The skater exerts an action force on the basketball by throwing it. The thrown ball exerts an equal reaction force on the skater, but in the opposite direction. The result is that the basketball moves in one direction and the skater moves in the other direction. These movements are a sure sign that forces have acted on both of them.

You can see the third law in action in many situations. When you run, your feet push against the ground. And the ground pushes back against your feet. If it didn't, you wouldn't go anywhere.

Space travel depends on the third law as well. A rocket engine pushes burning gases out the back of the rocket. The gases provide the force that moves the rocket forward. The

▲ The rowers' oars exert an action force on the water. The water exerts an equal reaction force on the oars, but in the opposite direction. This pushes the boat forward.

rocket provides the force that sends the gases backward. These two forces are equal in size and opposite in direction.

✔ **While sitting in a chair, you exert a force on the seat of the chair. What are the size and direction of the force the chair exerts on you?**

Conservation of Momentum

Curling is a game played on ice with large, rounded stones. A player from one team slides a stone toward a target on the ice. If the stone stops on or near the target, a player from the opposing team tries to knock it off the target by hitting it with a second stone.

If the second stone hits the first stone directly, it pushes the first stone away, and the second stone stops on the target. Why does the second stone stop, and the first stone start moving?

In Lesson 1 you read that the momentum of a moving object is equal to its mass times its velocity. When a moving object exerts a force on another object, the total momentum of the two objects remains the same. No momentum is produced, and none is lost. Scientists call this *conservation of momentum*. The second stone stops because its momentum is transferred to the first stone.

✔ **A moving car hits the back of a car stopped at a traffic light. The moving car stops, and the stopped car moves. What has happened to the momentum of the cars?**

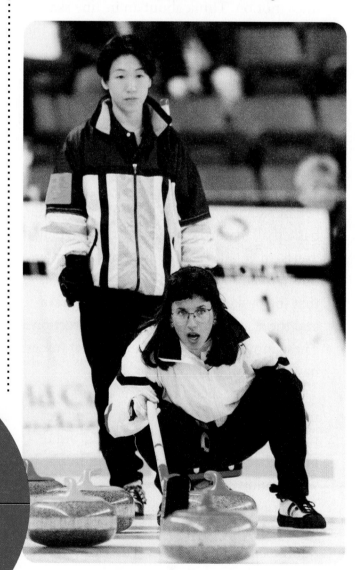

Conservation of Momentum

Mass	Speed			Mass	Speed
18 kg	2 m/sec			18 kg	2 m/sec
9 kg	2 m/sec			18 kg	1 m/sec
18 kg	2 m/sec			9 kg	4 m/sec

▲ The table shows that the red stone transfers all of its momentum to the blue stone, setting it in motion. Since momentum equals mass times velocity, the momentum of the two stones together remains the same. Only the velocities of the stones change.

▲ Curling is a popular winter sport in many northern countries.

Summary

Isaac Newton stated three laws that describe the motion of objects. The first law of motion is that an object at rest tends to remain at rest, and an object in motion tends to move in a straight line at a constant speed unless an outside force acts on it. The second law is that an object's acceleration depends on the mass of the object and on the size and direction of the force acting on it. The third law is that for every action, there is an equal and opposite reaction.

Review

1. If an astronaut throws an object into space, what happens to the object?
2. A truck and a falling leaf collide. The leaf accelerates rapidly. Why doesn't the truck?
3. Explain what happens when a person pushes on a stuck door.
4. **Critical Thinking** Suppose a golf ball and a bowling ball are rolled toward each other. When they collide, the bowling ball stops. How did the golf ball's speed compare with the bowling ball's speed?
5. **Test Prep** What is the property of matter that keeps it moving in a straight line at the same speed?
   A inertia
   B mass
   C momentum
   D velocity

LINKS

MATH LINK

Computing Momentum Carl's mass is 35 kg. He is running north at 3 m/sec. What is his momentum?

WRITING LINK

Narrative Writing—Personal Story You have probably seen pictures of astronauts floating in space. Picture yourself "walking" in space outside an orbiting shuttle. Floating next to you is a satellite. You need to move the satellite into the shuttle's cargo bay. Write a story for your class describing what happens when you try to move the satellite.

HEALTH LINK

Buckle Up Use what you've learned about momentum and the laws of motion to explain why a car crash is dangerous to a person not wearing a seat belt.

LITERATURE LINK

Isaac Newton: The Greatest Scientist of All Time Read this book by Margaret J. Anderson to learn more about the life, work, and goals of Isaac Newton.

TECHNOLOGY LINK

Learn more about forces and motion by viewing *Baseball Physics* and *Egg Drop* on the **Harcourt Science Newsroom Video.**

Why Do the Planets Stay in Orbit?

In this lesson, you can . . .

INVESTIGATE orbits and inertia.

LEARN ABOUT the orbits of planets and moons.

LINK to math, writing, social studies, and technology.

This mechanical model, known as an *orrery* (OHR•er•ee), shows the solar system as it was known in the 1800s.

INVESTIGATE

Orbits and Inertia

Activity Purpose In Lesson 2 you learned about the laws of motion. The first law states that an object in motion will continue moving in a straight line at a constant speed until an outside force acts on it. In this investigation you will **make a model** to see how the first law helps explain why moons and planets stay in orbit.

Materials
- 2 m string
- metal washers
- safety goggles

CAUTION

Activity Procedure

1 Tie three or four metal washers securely to one end of the string.

2 **CAUTION** **Take the string with the washers outside to an open area. Be sure that you are far from any buildings or objects and that no one is standing close to you. Put on the safety goggles.** Hold the loose end of the string. Slowly swing the string and washers in a circle above your head. **Observe** the motion of the washers. (Picture A)

3 **Predict** what will happen if you let go of the string while swinging it in a circle.

4. **CAUTION** Again, make sure that there are no people, buildings, or other objects near you. Swing the string and washers in a circle again. Let the string slip through your fingers. **Observe** the motion of the washers. How does it **compare** with your prediction? (Picture B)

5. Using a drawing, **record** the motion of the washers in Steps 2 and 4. Be sure to show the forces acting in each situation. Now make a drawing of the moon orbiting Earth. **Compare** the two drawings.

Picture A

Draw Conclusions

1. **Compare** the path of the washers while you were swinging them with their path once you let go of the string.

2. The string and washers can be used to **model** the moon orbiting Earth. **Compare** the motion of the washers circling your head with the motion of the moon orbiting Earth.

Picture B

3. **Scientists at Work** When scientists **experiment,** they must **communicate** their results to others. One way of doing this is with diagrams. Look at the drawing you made of the washers. What motions and forces does it show?

Investigate Further **Hypothesize** about the effect the length of the string has on the time the washers take to complete one revolution. Then **experiment** to test your hypothesis.

Process Skill Tip

After you **experiment,** you need to **communicate** your results by using a graph, a chart, a table, a written summary, or a drawing.

The Orbits of Planets and Moons

FIND OUT

- how inertia and gravity interact to make an orbit

- what the law of universal gravitation is

VOCABULARY

orbit

law of universal gravitation

Orbits

In the investigation you made a model of an orbit. An **orbit** is the path one body in space takes as it revolves around another body. All of the planets in our solar system are in orbit around the sun. The moon orbits Earth. The orbit you modeled in the investigation was like the moon's orbit in two ways. First, the moon moves around Earth in much the same way as the washers moved around your head. Second, forces acted on the washers to keep them circling in the same way that forces act on the moon to keep it in orbit.

Think about what happened to the washers when you let go of the string. They flew away from you instead of continuing in a circle. This is an example of the first law of motion. A moving object will continue to move in a straight line until an outside force acts on it. The inertia of the washers made them fly away when you let go. In the

The shuttle's inertia tries to keep it moving in a straight line while gravity tries to pull it toward Earth. The result is that the shuttle orbits Earth.

same way, inertia would make the moon fly off in a straight line unless another force was acting on it.

What is the other force? In your model it was the force exerted by the string, which pulled the washers toward your hand. In the moon's orbit, the other force is gravitation

After launch, the shuttle separates from its booster rockets and then from its fuel tank. Inertia tries to keep the objects moving forward, but gravity pulls them back to Earth.

between Earth and the moon. The moon's orbit is the path that results when inertia and gravitation act together.

✔ **What keeps the moon in orbit around Earth?**

Universal Gravitation

In addition to three laws of motion, Isaac Newton stated a law of gravitation. The **law of universal gravitation** is that all objects in the universe are attracted to all other objects. This attraction is observable only when the masses of the objects are huge. The masses of Earth and the moon produce a strong gravitational pull between them. The gravitational pull between two paperclips on a table isn't enough to pull them together because their masses are small.

The law of universal gravitation, when combined with the property of inertia, also explains why planets orbit the sun. The size of a planet's orbit is related to the planet's speed and its mass. Earth moves around the sun at an average speed of about 30 km/sec. The outer planets move in much longer, slower orbits.

✔ **Why is gravitation between small objects not observed?**

In *Principia Mathematica,* Isaac Newton presented three laws of motion and the law of universal gravitation. ▼

Earth and the Moon

A moon is a body that orbits a planet. Earth has one moon. Some planets have no moons, while Jupiter has 17.

As a planet orbits the sun, the planet's moons orbit with it. In the same way, the planets move with the sun as it orbits the center of the Milky Way Galaxy.

Earth and the moon move together around the sun. Because the moon is always orbiting Earth while the Earth-moon system orbits the sun, the moon's path around the sun is a series of loops.

Inertia and the pull of gravity keep the moon in a nearly circular orbit around Earth.

Newton saw the universe as a giant machine. This model of the solar system, built in 1712, reflects that view. Turning the crank, like winding a clock, sets the planets in motion. ▶

Summary

The moon circles Earth in a path called an orbit. Gravitation between Earth and the moon keeps the moon from flying off into space because of its inertia. The balance between inertia and gravitation keeps Earth in orbit around the sun. It also keeps other planets and moons in their orbits.

Review

1. What is an orbit?
2. What keeps Earth in orbit around the sun?
3. What is the law of universal gravitation?
4. **Critical Thinking** Suppose the gravitation between Earth and the sun suddenly stopped. What path would Earth follow?
5. **Test Prep** Gravitation between Earth and the moon pulls on the moon as the moon orbits. What property of the moon keeps it from crashing into the Earth?

   A gravitation

   B inertia

   C mass

   D momentum

MATH LINK

Calculate For a certain satellite to remain in orbit around Earth, it must move forward at about 8 km/sec. This satellite takes about 90 minutes to make one orbit. About how far does it travel in one orbit?

WRITING LINK

Informative Writing—Explanation Some people say that to learn something really well, you should teach it. Write a short lesson for a younger student. Explain why Earth stays in orbit around the sun. Make diagrams to go with your lesson.

SOCIAL STUDIES LINK

History of Astronomy Two important astronomers before Newton were Tycho Brahe and Johannes Kepler. Find out more about them and their contributions to the study of the solar system. Report to your class on your research.

TECHNOLOGY LINK

Learn more about orbits by visiting the National Air and Space Museum Internet site.
www.si.edu/harcourt/science

 Smithsonian Institution®

SKIPPING THROUGH SPACE

Engineers have designed a new aircraft called the HyperSoar. It will be part rocket and part airplane. It will skip along the edge of space, like a flat stone on a smooth pond. When it becomes operational, the HyperSoar will take passengers anywhere on Earth in less than two hours.

No More Gas-Guzzlers

Rocket engines need oxygen to burn their fuel. When the space shuttle roars into orbit, it must carry its own oxygen because there isn't any in outer space. And every kilogram of oxygen means more fuel is needed. The space shuttle uses 50 kilograms of fuel to lift every kilogram of cargo (including oxygen) on board.

The HyperSoar will use what scientists call rocket-based combined cycle (RBCC) engines to get to the edge of space with a lot less fuel. The HyperSoar will fly in a skip-along style that will get people and packages from Chicago to Tokyo in 90 minutes instead of today's 10 hours.

The HyperSoar's RBCC engines won't need to carry oxygen because they will use

The HyperSoar could fly vacationers to Hawai'i from any city on the mainland in less than an hour.

You may soon travel to the edge of space in the Hypersoar.

air. The engines will be powerful enough to get the HyperSoar moving at speeds of more than 10,500 km/hr (about 6500 mi/hr). The HyperSoar will fly at nearly 40,000 m (about 130,000 ft) above Earth's surface. Then the engines will shut down because there is not enough air at that altitude for them to operate. The HyperSoar will then drift back into the upper atmosphere, restart its engines, and fly back up into space.

High-Speed Hopper

For a trip from Chicago to Tokyo, the HyperSoar would make two dozen of these skips into and out of space. Although friction will make the HyperSoar heat up when it's flying through the atmosphere, it will cool off again when it's in space.

As the HyperSoar leaves the atmosphere, passengers will feel nearly weightless. And with each skip into the atmosphere, they will feel as if they are accelerating from the bottom of a gentle roller coaster ride. After rocketing and gliding along at more than ten times the speed of sound, the HyperSoar will land just like a regular airplane.

Because its RBCC engines will breath air, the HyperSoar will need only 3 kilograms of fuel for each kilogram of cargo. This will make it much less expensive to operate than a rocket-powered aircraft. And because it will go so fast, the HyperSoar will carry a lot more cargo and people around the world each day than a jet airplane. According to one of the HyperSoar's engineers, "Hyper-Soar has the potential of opening the space frontier to ordinary people."

THINK ABOUT IT

1. All engines need oxygen. Where will the HyperSoar get its oxygen?
2. Why will the HyperSoar be less expensive to operate than a rocket?

 WEB LINK:
For science and technology updates, visit The Learning Site.
www.harcourtschool.com

Careers — Aeronautical Engineer

What They Do
Aeronautical engineers design the engines and wings that power and lift aircraft. They also design and build aircraft that are as light as possible so that they can carry a lot of passengers or cargo without using too much fuel.

Education and Training People wishing to become aeronautical engineers should study subjects such as aerodynamics and engine design in college and graduate school.

Patricia Cowings
PSYCHOPHYSIOLOGIST

Astronauts in space often experience physical problems, such as nausea and swelling of the legs and feet. The nausea, or "space sickness," is similar to the motion sickness some people feel while riding on an amusement park ride. One scientist trying to cut down on these problems or prevent them is Patricia Cowings. She is the director of psychophysiological research at NASA's Ames Research Center in California. As a psychophysiologist, she studies the science of mind and behavior.

In order to study the problems that astronauts experience, Dr. Cowings produces conditions on Earth that are similar to conditions in space. For example, to study nausea, she straps an astronaut into a seat that spins very rapidly. By observing the changes that occur in the astronaut's body just before he or she becomes nauseated, Dr. Cowings can teach the astronaut to use biofeedback to prevent the nausea. Biofeedback is a technique that allows a person to control certain body functions, such as heart rate, blood pressure, and breathing rate. If, for example, an astronaut's breathing rate increases just before the feeling of nausea, he or she can learn to slow the breathing rate and perhaps prevent the nausea.

THINK ABOUT IT

1. Why is it important to know how an astronaut's body changes just before he or she feels nauseated?

2. Why do you think astronauts experience nausea in space?

Simulating space flight

It's the Law

How does a rocket demonstrate the third law of motion?

Materials

- 5 m of string
- drinking straw
- rubber balloon
- double-backed tape

Procedure

1. Thread the string through the straw. Then hold the ends of the string or tie them to stationary objects.

2. Blow up the balloon and pinch the end.

3. While you hold the balloon, have a partner tape the balloon to the straw.

4. When the balloon is taped to the straw, release the balloon. Observe the balloon.

Draw Conclusions

What is the third law of motion? What is the action force in your balloon rocket? What is the reaction force? Do you think the action force and the reaction force are equal? In what direction did the air push out? How could you make a more powerful balloon rocket?

Spin Factor

What forces act on a spinning object?

Materials

- fishing weight
- string
- paper-towel tube

Procedure

CAUTION Do this activity in an open area, away from buildings and other people.

1. Tie the weight to the string. Then thread the string through the paper-towel tube.

2. Holding the paper-towel tube with one hand and the end of the string with your other hand, carefully spin the weight in a circle over your head.

3. As you spin the weight, slowly pull the end of the string through the tube.

4. Observe what happens to the motion of the weight.

Draw Conclusions

The variables you are experimenting with are momentum, velocity, and mass of the weight and the radius of the orbiting weight. When you pulled the string through the tube, which variable changed? How did changing that variable change the forces acting on the weight?

Chapter 2 Review and Test Preparation

Vocabulary Review

Use the terms below to complete the sentences. The page numbers in ( ) tell you where to look in the chapter if you need help.

position (F34)

speed (F35)

velocity (F35)

acceleration (F35)

momentum (F36)

inertia (F41)

action force (F43)

reaction force (F43)

orbit (F48)

law of universal gravitation (F49)

1. A statement of the ____ might be this: Everything is attracted to everything else.

2. An object's ____ is the product of its velocity and its mass.

3. How far an object moves in a given amount of time is a measure of its ____.

4. When an object undergoes ____, it speeds up, slows down, stops, or changes direction.

5. Newton's third law of motion can be stated this way: For every ____, there is an equal and opposite ____.

6. The property of matter that resists any change in an object's motion is ____.

7. Speed in a particular direction is ____.

8. An object's place or location is called its ____.

9. An ____ is the path a body in space takes as it revolves around another body.

Connect Concepts

This Venn diagram shows how some of the measurements from this chapter are related. Copy the Venn diagram. Write each term from the Word Bank in its proper place in the diagram.

velocity   speed

acceleration   inertia

average speed   momentum

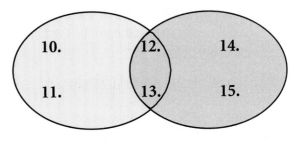

10.
11.
12.
13.
14.
15.

Check Understanding

Write the letter of the best choice.

16. The property of matter that makes it difficult to push a stopped car is —
   A acceleration
   B action forces
   C reaction forces
   D inertia

17. Unlike speed, velocity includes —
   F direction
   G acceleration
   H mass
   J time

18. A golf ball hits a tennis ball. The golf ball stops, but the tennis ball rolls away. This is an example of —
   A gravitation
   B conservation of momentum
   C equal and opposite forces
   D velocity

19. A person driving a car and a person walking have different views of the motion of an object. Each person has a different —
   F acceleration
   G position
   H frame of reference
   J orbit

20. If gravitation suddenly stopped, Earth would move —
   A in the same orbit
   B in the opposite direction
   C nowhere
   D in a straight line

21. If you throw a ball in a straight line, it moves in a straight line until gravity pulls it back to Earth. This is an example of —
   F the first law of motion
   G the second law of motion
   H the third law of motion
   J the law of universal gravitation

Critical Thinking

22. Two ice skaters stand facing each other. One pushes the other, and both move in opposite directions. Explain why both skaters move instead of just the skater who is pushed.

23. If gravitation attracts all objects in the universe toward each other, why don't all of the clothes hanging in a closet cling together?

24. If Earth pulls on a grapefruit with a force of 1 newton, the grapefruit also exerts a force of 1 newton on Earth. Explain why this is true.

Process Skills Review

25. You roll a basketball and a bowling ball directly toward each other at the same speed. **Predict** what will happen to each after the two collide. Use what you know about momentum and Newton's laws of motion.

26. Two cars are driven next to each other along 1 km of straight road. **Compare** the cars' velocities.

27. An engineer wants to compare the damage low-speed collisions do to three cars. Which **variable** should she **control** in her experiment?

28. Which would be more useful to **communicate** how an object's velocity changes—a drawing with arrows, or a table? Explain.

Performance Assessment

Demonstrating the Laws of Motion

Your teacher will give you two balls. Use them to demonstrate each of Newton's three laws of motion. You may refer to pages F41–F43 in Lesson 2 of this chapter.

Chapter 3

Forms of Energy

What do a flashlight battery, snow on a mountainside, and a match have in common? Each has a form of stored energy. What do a beam of light, an avalanche, and a fire have in common? Each is energy in action.

Vocabulary Preview

energy	insulator
kinetic	resistor
energy	electromagnet
potential	reflection
energy	refraction
electric	lens
charge	pitch
electric	volume
force	temperature
electric	heat
current	conduction
conductor	convection
electric	radiation
circuit	

FAST FACT

An avalanche is a mass of snow that breaks loose and falls rapidly down a mountainside. Wind, skiers, or even loud noises can start an avalanche. Some avalanches reach speeds of 160 km/hr (about 100 mi/hr).

Using Food Energy	
Activity	**Calories per Hour**
Sleeping	less than 1
Sitting	60
Doing Housework	120
Bicycling (slowly)	140
Shoveling Snow	300
Playing Football	320
Jogging	300–500

F59

What Are Kinetic and Potential Energy?

In this lesson, you can . . .

INVESTIGATE how energy is changed from one form to another.

LEARN ABOUT kinetic and potential energy.

LINK to math, writing, social studies, and technology.

Changing Energy Forms

Activity Purpose There are two major kinds of energy. For example, a bowling ball rolling down an alley has one kind of energy, and a diver standing on the edge of a platform has another kind of energy. In this investigation you will **experiment** with these two kinds of energy and **observe** how one kind can be changed into the other.

Materials

- graph paper, 8 sheets
- tape
- meterstick
- tennis ball
- colored markers
- computer (optional)

Activity Procedure

1. Tape four sheets of graph paper vertically to a wall as shown. Starting at the floor, use a meterstick to mark off 10-cm intervals on the left edge of the paper to a height of 100 cm. (Picture A)

2. Work with a partner. One person sits on the floor about 0.5 m from the graph paper. The other person holds the tennis ball a few centimeters from the wall at the 50-cm mark. Then he or she drops the ball.

3. The seated person **observes** the ball as it bounces, and uses a colored marker to **record** the height of each bounce on the graph paper. **Count** and record the number of times the ball bounces. (Picture B)

◀ This "balanced" rock has a lot of potential energy.

④ Repeat Steps 2 and 3 several times. Use a different-colored marker to **record** each trial.

⑤ Replace the paper and repeat Steps 1–4, but this time drop the ball from a height of 100 cm.

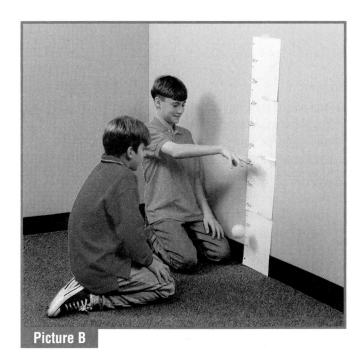

Picture A

Draw Conclusions

1. **Compare** the drop height to the bounce height for each trial in the experiment. How are the heights related?

2. When you hold the ball in the air before dropping it, it has *potential energy* because of its position and because of gravitation. When you let go of the ball, it has *kinetic energy* because of its movement. **Infer** the point at which the ball has the most kinetic energy.

3. **Draw a conclusion** about how potential energy and kinetic energy are related in the bouncing ball.

4. **Scientists at Work** Scientists often use computers to help them **interpret data** and **communicate** the results of an experiment. Use a computer graphing program, such as *Graph Links,* to **compare** the height of each bounce and the number of bounces from one trial of 50-cm drops and one trial of 100-cm drops. Make a different-colored line graph for each trial.

Picture B

Investigate Further Analyze the data you graphed in Step 4, and **predict** how high and how many times a ball dropped from a height of 200 cm will bounce. Then **experiment**, and **compare** your results to your predictions.

> **Process Skill Tip**
>
> Using a computer to help you **compare** and **interpret data** is one way to **communicate** the results of an experiment to others.

Energy

Kinetic and Potential Energy

Have you ever heard someone say that a person has a lot of energy? What is energy? **Energy** is the ability to cause changes in matter. In the investigation energy caused matter (the tennis ball) to move. Energy can also change matter in other ways. For example, heat, which is a form of energy, can change solid ice into liquid water.

There are two basic kinds of energy—the energy of motion and the energy of position or condition. The energy of motion, or energy in use, is **kinetic energy**. Any matter in motion has kinetic energy. When you let go of the tennis ball, it gained kinetic energy as it moved faster and faster toward the floor. It also had kinetic energy after it bounced back up from the floor. When the ball reached the top of each bounce, it stopped for an instant between rising and falling again. At this point its kinetic energy was zero.

While bouncing up, the ball gained energy of position. When the ball stopped at the top of a bounce, it had potential energy. **Potential energy** is the energy an object has because of where it is or because of its condition. Once the ball reached the top of its bounce, it fell again, changing more and more of its potential energy back into kinetic energy. If you caught the ball at the top of a bounce, it would keep that potential energy until you dropped it again.

FIND OUT

- **what kinetic and potential energy are**
- **about different forms of energy**

VOCABULARY

energy
kinetic energy
potential energy

① The potential energy of food is changed into kinetic energy by the pole vaulter's muscles as he runs toward the bar.

② When the vaulter sticks his pole in the ground, much of this kinetic energy is changed to potential energy in the bent pole.

③ As the pole straightens, it releases that potential energy as kinetic energy to lift him up toward the bar.

The snow that has fallen high in the mountains has a lot of potential energy. During an avalanche, that potential energy is suddenly changed to kinetic energy, and the fast-moving snow can cause a lot of damage.

The change of the ball's energy back and forth between kinetic energy and potential energy is called the *transformation of energy.* Although energy often is transformed, or changed, from one form to another, the total amount of energy doesn't change. Energy can't be created or destroyed. This is the *law of conservation of energy.*

Energy can change forms several times during one activity. Look at the series of photographs of the pole vaulter. According to the law of conservation of energy, the amount of energy is always the same, but its form keeps changing.

Both the tennis ball in the investigation and the pole vaulter eventually stopped. However, it wasn't because energy was destroyed. With each bounce some of the ball's energy was lost as sound and heat. The heat caused by the friction of the ball hitting the floor warmed the air and the floor slightly. Eventually, the results of bouncing turned all of the ball's energy into other forms.

✓ **At what point in the process does the pole vaulter have his greatest kinetic energy?**

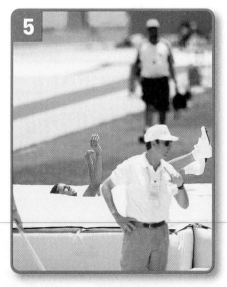

❹ At the instant the vaulter goes over the bar, kinetic energy is changed back to potential energy.

❺ As he falls, potential energy becomes kinetic energy until he hits the ground. At that instant he has neither kinetic energy nor potential energy.

Forms of Energy

The kinetic energy that moving objects have is also called *mechanical energy*. A spinning top, a rolling bicycle, a flying airplane, and flowing water all have mechanical energy. But mechanical energy isn't the only form of kinetic energy. Kinetic energy can have many different forms.

Thermal energy is another form of kinetic energy. The movement of molecules of matter produces heat. Another form of kinetic energy, *electric energy,* is caused by the movement of electrons. Electric energy can be felt in a shock. It also produces the picture and sound on a television. *Light energy* from the picture moves to your eyes in waves. Your ears receive vibrations produced by the television speakers as *sound energy*.

Potential energy also takes several forms. *Elastic potential energy* is the energy stored in compressed springs, stretched rubber bands, and bent vaulting poles. In fact, any object that can be forced into a shape that's different from its natural shape can store elastic potential energy—if it has the ability to return to its natural shape.

Gravitational potential energy is the energy an object has when it's in an elevated position. The tennis ball in the investigation had gravitational potential energy at the top of its bounce and elastic potential energy at the bottom of its bounce. Water behind a dam, a "balanced" rock, or any object that can fall has gravitational potential energy.

Most of Earth's energy comes from the sun. Plants absorb light energy and store it as *chemical energy* in the food they make. When a pole vaulter starts running, chemical energy stored in his muscles is changed into *thermal energy* and *mechanical energy*.

✔ **Name three forms of energy.**

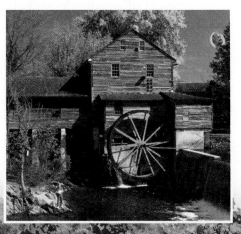

Energy is the ability to do work. In a water-powered mill, the mechanical energy of falling water turns the mill wheel. This mechanical energy is carried throughout the mill and is used by machines to do work.

The flashlight's dry cells (also called batteries) store chemical energy. When you flip the switch, chemical energy is changed to electric energy that moves through the light bulb. In the light bulb's filament, electric energy becomes thermal energy and light energy.

Summary

Energy is the ability to cause changes in matter. There are two basic types of energy—kinetic energy and potential energy. Electric energy, thermal energy, mechanical energy, light energy, and sound energy are all forms of kinetic energy. Chemical energy, gravitational potential energy, and elastic potential energy are forms of potential energy. The law of conservation of energy says energy can change form, but it can't be created or destroyed.

Review

1. What is energy?
2. What is kinetic energy?
3. You use mechanical energy to walk around. What form did this energy have before your body changed it to mechanical energy?
4. **Critical Thinking** If you toss a ball in the air, at what point does it have the most potential energy?
5. **Test Prep** Which law states that energy can't be created or destroyed?
   A the law of mechanical energy
   B the law of conservation of energy
   C the law of kinetic energy
   D the law of potential energy

LINKS

MATH LINK

Energy To calculate kinetic energy, you can use the following formula:

Energy = (mass × speed × speed) ÷ 2

Suppose a 1-kg object is moving at 10 m/sec. If the object speeds up to 20 m/sec, does its energy double?

WRITING LINK

Expressive Writing—Poem Brainstorm a list of words related to forms of kinetic and potential energy, such as *rush, shining,* and *loud.* Then use your favorite words to write a poem about using energy, such as in pole vaulting. Read your poem to a classmate.

SOCIAL STUDIES LINK

Energy Crisis In the 1970s the United States had an "energy crisis." There were fears that there would not be enough energy to run our cars, light and heat our homes, and meet other needs. Learn more about what caused this energy crisis. Report on your findings to your classmates.

TECHNOLOGY LINK

Learn more about kinetic and potential energy by visiting this Internet site. **www.scilinks.org/harcourt**

SCI**LINKS**
THE WORLD'S A CLICK AWAY

What Is Electric Energy?

In this lesson, you can . . .

INVESTIGATE electric circuits.

LEARN ABOUT electric charges, currents, and circuits and electromagnets.

LINK to math, writing, art, and technology.

Electric Circuits

Activity Purpose Electricity is one form of energy. It results from the force of electrons being attracted or repelled. To use this energy, you need to make an *electric circuit*—a path of wires and devices that electrons can follow back to their source. In this investigation you will **make a model** of two different electric circuits and **compare** them.

Materials

- 4 lengths of insulated wire with bare ends
- 2 light-bulb holders
- battery holder
- 2 light bulbs
- batteries

Activity Procedure

1. To make electricity flow between the terminals, or charged ends, of a dry cell or battery, you need to connect the terminals in some way, such as with a wire. Electricity will then flow through any device you put along this path. Connect the wires, bulb holders, and battery holder as shown. (Picture A)

2. Insert the light bulbs and batteries. **Observe** what happens and **record** your observations.

3. Remove one of the bulbs from its holder. **Observe** and **record** what happens to the other bulb.

4. Now reconnect the wires, bulb holders, and battery holder as shown. **Observe** what happens and **record** your observations. (Picture B)

◀ Van de Graaff generators use friction to rub off electrons and build up electric charges on the spheres. These are the "lightning machines" used in old science-fiction movies.

Picture A

Picture B

5 Again remove one of the bulbs from its holder. **Observe** and **record** what happens to the other bulb.

6 Draw diagrams of both of the circuits you built. Use arrows to **compare** the path of the electric current in each circuit.

Draw Conclusions

1. What happened to the other bulb when one bulb was removed from the first circuit?

2. What happened to the other bulb when one bulb was removed from the second circuit?

3. **Scientists at Work** Scientists often **compare** results before they **draw a conclusion**. Cross out one bulb in each of your drawings. Then diagram the path the electric current must take if it can't pass through the bulb you crossed out. Compare your diagrams, and then draw a conclusion about which type of circuit would be better to use for a string of lights.

Investigate Further In the investigation you demonstrated that electricity flowing through a circuit produces light and heat (the glowing bulbs were warm). Now **plan and conduct a simple investigation** to demonstrate that electricity flowing through a circuit can also produce sound and magnetism. Decide what equipment you will need to use in your investigation.

Electric Energy

Electric Charges

Electric energy runs computers, televisions, radios, and appliances, and it lights homes and streets. It is also the energy that produces lightning. Electric energy is produced by the movement of electrons.

You may recall that within an atom, electrons have a negative charge and protons have a positive charge. So the two types of particles attract each other. Most objects have equal numbers of protons and electrons. Sometimes, however, electrons are attracted to the protons of another object and rub off. When an object gains or loses electrons, it has an **electric charge**. An object that has gained electrons has a negative electric charge. An object that has lost electrons has a positive electric charge.

For example, when you drag your feet across a carpet on a dry day, electrons rub off your shoes and onto the carpet. The loss of these electrons produces a positive charge on your body, which makes it attract more electrons. When you reach for an object such as a doorknob, your body attracts electrons from that object. When this attraction is great enough, the electrons jump from the doorknob to your hand. You feel a shock and may even see a small spark.

✔ **What causes an electric charge?**

FIND OUT

- what electric energy is
- how static electricity differs from current electricity
- what an electric circuit is
- how electromagnets work

VOCABULARY

electric charge
electric force
electric current
conductor
electric circuit
insulator
resistor
electromagnet

When the boy rubs the balloon on his hair, electrons rub off the balloon and it becomes positively charged. Opposite charges on the balloon and the boy's sweater make the two objects attract each other.

Electric Force

Most objects have no charge because most objects have about the same numbers of protons and electrons. If an object has a charge, it attracts objects with the opposite charge. Similar to magnetic force, unlike charges attract each other, and like charges repel each other. This attraction or repulsion is called **electric force**. If two objects have large electric charges, they produce a large electric force. Like gravitational force, electric force depends on distance. Two charged objects produce a larger electric force when they are close together.

Charged objects have potential electric energy. This is sometimes called *static electricity,* because the electrons aren't moving. When charged objects are close to each other, potential energy can become kinetic energy. If the charges on the objects are the same, the objects repel each other. If the charges are opposite, the objects are drawn together. If the objects touch or come very close to each other, electrons may flow from one object to the other.

Electrons flow from negatively charged objects to positively charged objects. The

The Van de Graaff generator produces a large static charge by building up electrons on the sphere. The girl touching the sphere is also charged. You can see the effect of this charge in her hair. Since electrons all have the same charge, they repel each other, causing the girl's hairs to separate.

flow of electrons is called **electric current**. Once electrons have moved from one object to the other, the attraction between the objects is gone. The charges are balanced, and there is no electric force.

✔ **How do charges interact?**

◀ As updrafts in a thunderstorm carry rain along, friction rubs electrons off the drops. The bottom of the thundercloud has extra electrons. The top has extra protons. There is potential electric energy between the top and bottom of the cloud.

When the attraction between positive and negative charges becomes great enough, electrons move rapidly through the air between these areas. The potential electric energy becomes electric current. The cloud then gives off its energy in a flash of lightning. ▶

◄ **A wall socket is an extension of the terminals of a generator.**

Electric Current

Unlike static electricity, which does not move, an electric current is a flow of electrons. The shock you get by touching a doorknob is a small electric current. A lightning bolt is a brief but strong electric current.

To light a light bulb or run a computer, a continuous electric current must be produced. This requires a constant electric force, so a source of electrons is needed. A dry cell, a battery, or a generator can be the source of electrons.

In a dry cell or a battery, two different metals in a chemical bath build up opposite charges. In a generator, some outside force turns coils of wires between two magnets to produce opposite charges. Opposite charges build up on the terminals of a battery or generator.

Electrons are attracted from one terminal to the other. Connecting the two terminals allows an electric current to flow between them. Electric current flows through many kinds of matter if the electric force is strong enough. But some kinds of matter conduct, or carry, electrons more easily than others. Material that conducts electrons easily is called a **conductor**.

✔ **What is a conductor?**

THE INSIDE STORY

Comparing Circuits

For electrons to flow, a circuit has to complete a path between two terminals of opposite charges. Strings of lights can be wired between these terminals in series circuits or in parallel circuits.

In a *series circuit*, there is only one path for the electrons. If one of the bulbs burns out, all the other bulbs go out because the circuit is broken, and the electric current stops flowing.

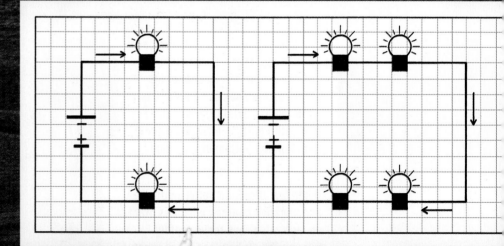

Electric Circuits

A conductor is used in the wire that makes an electric circuit. An **electric circuit** is any path along which electrons can flow. Copper and aluminum are often used as conductors. Metals are good conductors of electric current because their atoms don't hold electrons tightly. This allows electrons to move along from one atom to the next. An electric current flows through good conductors with little resistance.

The conductor in a circuit is wrapped with a material called an insulator (IN•suh•layt•er). An **insulator** is a material that doesn't carry electrons. Rubber, plastic, glass, and air are good insulators. They resist the flow of electrons through them. Insulation keeps wires from touching each other and completing an electrical circuit before

the electrons can reach a device. When this happens, it is called a *short circuit.*

Some materials are neither conductors nor insulators. Inside many appliances are materials that don't completely stop the flow of electrons. However, they resist the flow in some way. These materials are called **resistors** (rih•ZIS•terz). Materials that resist electric current are important because they allow electric energy to be changed into other forms.

The filament in a light bulb, for example, resists the flow of electrons. This resistance produces heat. The filament gets hot enough to glow. Electrons flowing in an electric circuit can produce heat, light, sound, or movement. People use all these results in electric devices.

✔ **What materials make good conductors?**

In a *parallel circuit*, each bulb is on a separate path. If one of the bulbs burns out, the others stay lighted because the electric current continues to flow.

Magnets and Electricity

Magnets are used to generate, or produce, electricity. Spinning a coil of wire inside a magnetic field produces an electric force between the ends of the coil. In a similar way, an electric current produces a magnetic field around it. A compass placed next to a wire carrying an electric current will point to the wire.

A current-carrying wire wrapped in a coil of more wire makes a strong magnet. A coil of current-conducting wire wrapped around an iron bar makes an even stronger magnet. Around the coil is a magnetic field much like the one around a bar magnet. But a bar magnet is always magnetized, while a coil wrapped around an iron bar is a magnet only when electric current flows through the coil. For this reason it is called an **electromagnet** (ee•LEK•troh•MAG•nit).

This link between electricity and magnetism allows motion to be produced from

▲ A junkyard is one place to see an electromagnet in action. This huge one picks up scrap metal when current flows through it. When the crane operator wants to drop the scrap, he or she will simply shut off current to the electromagnet.

Current moving through coils of wire inside a fan motor makes the coils electromagnets. Changing the direction of the current at just the right times makes the magnetic poles switch back and forth. Magnetic attraction and repulsion work together to turn the motor's shaft, to which the fan's blades are attached.

electric energy. An electric motor uses electromagnets. By changing the direction of the electric current back and forth, these electromagnets alternately attract and repel each other. This causes the motor to turn.

✔ **What forms around a wire carrying an electric current?**

Summary

Electric energy is the movement of electrons between areas that have opposite charges. When objects with opposite charges are close enough together, or when the charges are very large, electrons move between the objects. Electric current moves through an electric circuit. When electric current flows through a conductor, it produces a magnetic field, turning the conductor into an electromagnet.

Review

1. How do like electric charges react to each other?
2. Why are insulators placed around electric conductors?
3. What are resistors, and why are they important?
4. **Critical Thinking** Are the lights in your school connected in series circuits or parallel circuits? Explain.
5. **Test Prep** A coil that is magnetized only when an electric current flows through it is —
   A a battery
   B a generator
   C a conductor
   D an electromagnet

LINKS

MATH LINK

Power Power is measured in *watts*. A 60-watt light bulb uses 60 watts of power every second. Use a calculator to determine how much power a 60-watt light bulb would use in a year if it were never turned off.

WRITING LINK

Informative Writing—Narration
Alessandro Volta, Michael Faraday, Georg Simon Ohm, Charles Coulomb, Joseph Henry, and Nikola Tesla all added to our understanding of electricity and magnetism. Learn more about one of these scientists, and write a short biography to share with your class.

ART LINK

Wiring Diagrams Electrical engineers use a set of symbols to stand for electric devices when they draw circuits. Learn more about these symbols, including the symbols for a battery, a light bulb, a resistor, and a switch. Use these symbols to redraw the circuit diagrams you did in the investigation.

TECHNOLOGY LINK

Learn more about electricity by visiting the Smithsonian Institution Internet site.
www.si.edu/harcourt/science

 Smithsonian Institution®

What Are Light and Sound Energy?

In this lesson, you can . . .

INVESTIGATE how light is reflected.

LEARN ABOUT light waves and sound waves and how they travel.

LINK to math, writing, social studies, and technology.

The Path of Reflected Light

Activity Purpose   You probably use a mirror every day. But looking at a reflection as a scientist would can help you learn something about light. In this investigation you will **observe** and **measure** the angle at which light is reflected by a mirror.

Materials
- piece of corrugated cardboard, 10 cm × 10 cm
- small mirror
- masking tape
- ruler
- 3 pushpins of different colors
- protractor

Activity Procedure

1. Lay the cardboard flat. Use tape to attach the mirror vertically to one end of the cardboard. Push two of the pins into the cardboard, about 5 cm from the mirror. (Picture A)

2. Position yourself at eye level with the mirror. Align yourself so that your view of one pin lines up with the reflection of the other pin. Push a third pin into the cardboard at the edge of the mirror, right in front of where you see the reflection of the second pin. The first pin, the third pin, and the reflection of the second pin should appear to be in a straight line.

3. Draw lines on the cardboard to connect the three pins. These lines show how the reflected light from the first pin traveled to your eye. (Picture B)

◀ This one-person band can send both sound energy and light energy your way. Your ears and eyes receive this energy, and your brain turns it into an image and sound.

Picture A

Picture B

4. Using the protractor, **measure** the angle between each line and the edge of the mirror. You will probably have to trace the edge of the mirror and then move it out of your way to make this measurement. **Record** your results.

5. Now remove the original pins and place two of them 10 cm from the mirror. Repeat Steps 2–4 with this new arrangement of pins. **Measure** the angles of the new lines, and **record** your results.

6. Now draw diagrams to **communicate** the results of the two experiments. Each diagram should show the locations of the pins and the mirror and the path of the reflected light.

Draw Conclusions

1. **Compare** the two angles you **measured** in each experiment.

2. The angle at which light strikes a mirror is the *angle of incidence*. The angle at which it reflects from the mirror is the *angle of reflection*. **Draw a conclusion** about the angle of incidence and the angle of reflection from a flat surface.

3. **Scientists at Work** When scientists **observe** a pattern that seems to always be true, they try to come up with a clear, simple rule. This helps them **predict** what will happen in the future. Predict what the angle of incidence and the angle of reflection would be if the pins were 20 cm from the mirror.

Investigate Further **Hypothesize** how light would be reflected from a mirror that was not flat. Then **plan and conduct a simple investigation** to test your hypothesis.

> **Process Skill Tip**
>
> If you **observe** that something always happens the same way under the same conditions, you will be able to **predict** what will happen in the future if the conditions are the same.

Light and Sound Energy

FIND OUT

- the characteristics of light energy and sound energy
- the wave characteristics of light and sound

VOCABULARY

reflection
refraction
lens
pitch
volume

Light Energy

We usually think about light as rays that start at a source, such as the sun, and travel in a straight line until they strike something, such as Earth. Light rays are a form of energy that can travel through empty space or through some kinds of matter. For example, light passes easily through gases in the atmosphere and through clear glass windows.

Sometimes light energy is absorbed when it strikes matter. Most objects absorb some colors of light. Other colors bounce off objects as a **reflection**. The colors of light that objects reflect are the colors we see.

A green leaf, for example, absorbs much of the sunlight that strikes it. The rest of the light—the green part—reflects off the leaf. That's why a leaf looks green to us. A mirror, however, reflects all colors.

In space, light energy from the sun travels at about 300,000 km/sec (186,000 mi/sec). When light passes through a glass window, it slows down. This change in speed causes light rays to bend. This bending of light rays is called **refraction**.

Light often refracts when it moves from one substance to another. For example, a pencil in a glass of water appears to bend at the water's surface. This is because light rays traveling from the pencil to your eyes bend as they move from the water, through the glass, and into the air.

✔ **What is reflection?**

A mirror reflects all the light that strikes it. ▼

Light rays bend when passing through clear objects. ▼

Some objects absorb all colors of light, producing a shadow. ▼

Lenses

Many people wear corrective lenses—glasses or contacts—to improve their vision. A **lens** is a piece of clear material that bends, or refracts, light rays passing through it. There are two kinds of lenses. A *convex lens* is thicker in the middle than at the edges. When light passes through a convex lens, the rays bend toward each other. The hand lens you use for investigations is a convex lens. It makes nearby objects look larger.

People who are farsighted have trouble seeing things that are close to them, like print on a page. Glasses or contacts with convex lenses magnify the print, allowing these people to read more easily.

Movie projectors and slide projectors also use convex lenses. As light from the bulb shines through the film, light rays spread apart. As these rays pass through the projector lens, they bend toward each other again.

The other type of lens is a *concave lens.* This lens is thicker around the edges than in the middle. When light rays pass through a concave lens, they bend away from each other. This makes distant objects seem nearer and smaller. Some cameras have a concave lens in their viewfinders. When you look through the viewfinder, you see a small version of what the final photograph will look like.

Concave lenses help people who are nearsighted. These people have trouble seeing distant objects. Concave lenses bend light rays outward just enough to make distant objects seem closer.

✔ **Compare the shapes of convex lenses and concave lenses.**

◀ The concave lens in a camera viewfinder bends light rays outward. The rays then appear to be coming from an image that is smaller and closer to the camera than it really is.

◀ The light rays bent by a convex lens all meet at one point and then cross, making the image on the screen appear upside-down. So slides or movie film must be put into a projector upside down.

F77

Light Waves

When waves move across the ocean, the water doesn't actually move with the wave. Only the energy of the wave form moves. Light energy also moves as waves. These waves, called *electromagnetic waves*, are produced when vibrating electrons inside atoms give off energy.

Visible light waves—those we can see—are just a small part of the electromagnetic waves produced in the universe. Radio waves, microwaves, infrared waves, ultraviolet waves, and X rays are also types of electromagnetic waves. Unlike water waves, electromagnetic waves don't need a substance to move through. They move fastest, in fact, when there is no matter to slow them down, such as in space.

Within the range of visible light waves are different wave patterns that humans sense as different colors of light. We sense long wave patterns as red, and short wave patterns as violet. Between red and violet are all the colors of the rainbow.

✔ **How are electromagnetic waves produced?**

◀ When sunlight passes through a raindrop, the different waves that make up visible light move at slightly different speeds. This separates the white light into different colors.

Light and Sound

Your eyes gather light waves, and your ears gather sound waves. In these organs the energy waves are changed into nerve impulses. Your brain interprets these impulses, and you see images and hear sounds.

Lens Light passes through the clear *lens*, which can thicken to help focus light from nearby objects.

Iris The colored *iris* widens in darkness and narrows in bright light to control the amount of light that enters through the *pupil*.

Cornea Light enters through the clear *cornea*, which acts as a convex lens and bends light rays.

Retina An upside-down image falls on the *retina*, where cells change light energy to electrical and chemical energy in the form of nerve impulses.

Sound Waves

Sound also moves as waves. However, in the case of sound, these waves are carried by vibrating matter.

Most of the sound waves we hear travel through air. But sound waves also travel through liquids, such as water, and even through solids. If you click two stones together while underwater, you can hear the sound more clearly than you can in air.

As a sound wave travels through matter, molecules in the matter move back and forth in the direction the sound wave is moving. As the sound moves forward, the molecules are squeezed together. This is called *compression*. After the first compression passes, pressure on the molecules drops. This is called *rarefaction* (rer•uh•FAK•shuhn). If a sound is continuous, both compression and rarefaction are repeated again and again.

The speed with which sound waves move determines the **pitch** of the sound. The

As the harp string vibrates, it moves quickly from side to side. When the string moves to the right, air to the right is compressed. When the string moves to the left, air to the right is rarefied.

faster the waves, the higher the pitch. In music, pitch is labeled with letters called notes. As you move from left to right on a piano keyboard, pitch increases.

Another way of measuring sound waves is to measure their strength. The more the molecules are squeezed during compression, the louder the sound is. The loudness of a sound is called **volume**.

✔ **How are sound waves carried?**

Hair cells When hair cells in the cochlea move, they change their mechanical energy to electrical energy—nerve impulses that are sent along the *cochlear nerve* to the brain.

Hammer, anvil, and stirrup The vibrating eardrum starts these three tiny bones—the *hammer*, *anvil*, and *stirrup*—moving.

Cochlea The stirrup transfers vibrations to the fluid in the *cochlea*, a coiled canal. The vibrating fluid moves hair cells that line the cochlea.

Eardrum The air pressure changes cause the *eardrum* to vibrate in and out at the same rate as the pitch of the sound.

Ear canal Sound waves enter the *ear canal* as air pressure changes.

Sound Energy

Like water waves, sound waves are waves of energy moving through matter. And like water waves, sound waves move molecules back and forth without carrying them along with the wave.

Because sound waves are vibrations of molecules, molecules must be present for sound to travel. Where there is no matter, such as in outer space, sound cannot travel.

The sounds we hear travel mostly as vibrations of the gas molecules in the air around us. When sound waves move through air, they travel about 340 m/sec (1100 ft/sec). When sound waves move through denser materials, such as liquids and solids, they move faster. You can compare some of these speeds by using the table below.

Denser objects carry sound energy farther as well as faster than less dense objects. Whales, for example, produce sounds that travel underwater for hundreds of kilometers. Only very loud sounds can travel that far through air.

Sound energy travels even better through most solids. The rich sounds made by a cello or a guitar are due partly to the vibrations of the wood in the instruments. Try putting a ticking watch on one end of a table and

Humans see objects when light waves reflect off them. Animals such as dolphins and bats can use the reflection of sound waves to form "pictures" of objects around them. This sense is similar to humans using sonar to "see" objects on the ocean floor.

observing how clearly you can hear the ticking if you put your ear against the other end of the table.

However, not all solids carry sound vibrations. Materials that carry sound waves are called sound *conductors*. Materials that don't carry sound are called sound *insulators*. Materials with a lot of air spaces in them, such as fabrics and plastic foam, are good sound insulators.

✓ **About how fast does sound travel through air?**

Speed of Sound Waves Through Different Materials

Material	Speed of Sound in Material
Air	340 m/sec (about 1100 ft/sec)
Water	1500 m/sec (about 4900 ft/sec)
Steel	5000 m/sec (about 16,400 ft/sec)
Silver	2650 m/sec (about 8700 ft/sec)
Granite	3950 m/sec (about 13,000 ft/sec)

Summary

Light energy is electro-magnetic energy that travels through space and through certain materials. When light waves strike an obstacle, they are absorbed, reflected, or refracted. Lenses are curved pieces of transparent matter that refract light rays. Sound energy is vibrations that travel through matter. Solids and liquids conduct sound better than gases.

Review

1. What is refraction?
2. What type of lens would you use to magnify your view of a butterfly?
3. What is a sound wave?
4. **Critical Thinking** If a bright, loud explosion took place in space, would it be seen or heard on Earth?
5. **Test Prep** Which part of the eye has cells that change light energy to nerve impulses?
   A the iris
   B the blind spot
   C the lens
   D the retina

LINKS

MATH LINK

Lightning and Thunder Suppose a thunderstorm is coming. First you see a flash of lightning. You hear the thunder 22 seconds later. Knowing the speed of sound in air, estimate how far away the storm is.

WRITING LINK

Informative Writing—Classification Make a list of all the uses of lenses you can think of. Classify the lens in each case as *concave* or *convex*. Exchange lists with a classmate, and talk about any differences between your lists.

SOCIAL STUDIES LINK

Law of Refraction The Egyptian astronomer Ptolemy stated the first law of refraction. But it was Willebrord Snell who finalized the law now known as Snell's law. Research these men, and write a short report about Snell's law of refraction.

TECHNOLOGY LINK

Learn more about light energy by viewing *Psychologams* on the **Harcourt Science Newsroom Video.**

What Are Thermal and Chemical Energy?

In this lesson, you can . . .

INVESTIGATE the way heat moves through different materials.

LEARN ABOUT how thermal energy is transferred and how chemical energy is stored.

LINK to math, writing, social studies, and technology.

INVESTIGATE

Heat Flow

Activity Purpose In this lesson you will learn about thermal energy, or heat. In this investigation you will **experiment** to help you understand the ways heat moves through different materials.

Materials

- margarine
- metal butter knife
- Styrofoam cup
- hot water
- clock
- plastic knife

Activity Procedure

1 Place a dab of cold margarine near the middle of the metal knife. Place another dab of margarine the same size near the tip of the knife's blade.

2 **CAUTION** **Be careful when pouring the hot water.** Half-fill the cup with hot water. Put the metal knife's handle into the water. The dabs of margarine should be above the level of the water. (Picture A)

3 **Predict** which dab of margarine will melt first—the one near the middle of the knife or the one near the end of the knife.

◄ This is a *thermogram*, a photo that records thermal energy. The purple, red, and orange areas are warmer than the blue and green areas.

Picture A

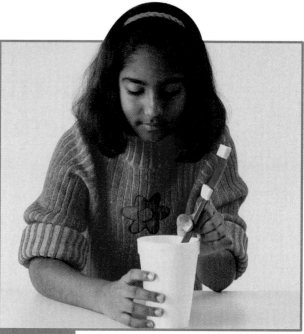

Picture B

4 **Observe** the metal knife for ten minutes, and **record** your observations.

5 Repeat Steps 1–4, using the plastic knife. (Picture B)

6 **Experiment** to find out which material transfers heat faster—metal or plastic. Be sure to **identify and control variables** that might affect the results.

Draw Conclusions

1. **Draw conclusions** about how heat moves through the metal knife.

2. **Draw conclusions** about which material transfers heat faster.

3. **Scientists at Work** Scientists **identify and control variables** in an experiment to see how changing one variable affects the results. What variables did you control in your experiment? What variable did you test?

Investigate Further **Experiment** to find out which knife cools faster. Decide what equipment you will need.

Process Skill Tip

To be sure that the results of an experiment are valid, you must **identify and control** all **variables** that might affect the results.

Thermal Energy and Chemical Energy

Thermal Energy

FIND OUT

• what thermal energy is and how it moves

• what chemical energy is

VOCABULARY

temperature
heat
conduction
convection
radiation

You may recall that kinetic energy is the energy of motion. Kinetic energy is present in the movement of molecules. In liquids and gases, molecules bounce off one another at high speeds. Even in solid matter, molecules vibrate constantly. This kinetic energy of molecules is *thermal energy.*

The average kinetic energy of all the molecules in an object is the object's **temperature**. The higher the average kinetic energy, or the faster the molecules move, the higher the temperature. It's important to note that temperature and thermal energy aren't the same. For example, a large pot of boiling water and a small pot of boiling water have the same temperature, but the large pot has more thermal energy because it has more molecules.

When rapidly moving molecules (those in a hot substance) bump into slowly moving molecules (those in a cold substance), they transfer, or give off, some of their thermal energy to the slower molecules. The transfer of thermal energy from one substance to another is called **heat**. Heat always flows in the same direction—from the warmer substance to the cooler substance. As you observed in the investigation, heat warms the cooler substance, raising its temperature. Heat can also change the state of a substance, making a solid melt or a liquid evaporate.

✔ **What is heat?**

The molecules in the milk are moving slowly. Their thermal energy is low, so the liquid feels cold. ▼

The molecules in the hot cocoa are moving quickly. Their thermal energy is high, so the liquid feels hot. ▼

The foods in this hot breakfast were cooked by three methods of transferring heat.

▲ Radiation from the glowing coils in the toaster transfers heat to the surface of the bread.

Conduction transfers heat from the stove burner through the metal frying pan to the ham. ▼

◀ Convection currents transfer heat from the bottom of the pan all through the boiling water to the egg.

Transferring Thermal Energy

Thermal energy can be transferred, or moved, between objects in three ways: conduction, convection, and radiation.

Conduction (kuhn•DUHK•shuhn) is the direct transfer of heat between objects that touch. A frying pan in direct contact with an electric-stove burner gets hot because the burner is hot.

When solids transfer heat to other solids, it is usually by conduction. Materials that conduct heat easily are called *conductors*. Metals are good heat conductors. Materials that do a poor job of conducting heat are called *insulators*. Air is a good heat insulator. For example, double-paned windows have a layer of air between two layers of glass. This air slows down the rate at which heat can be conducted into or out of a building.

Convection (kuhn•VEK•shuhn) is heat transfer as a result of the mixing of a liquid

or a gas. When you heat a pan of water on a stove, the water at the bottom of the pan heats up first. The hot water becomes less dense, and cold water from the top of the pan sinks below it. As the hot water rises, it cools and sinks. This movement of hot water rising, cooling, sinking, being reheated, and rising again transfers thermal energy throughout the pan.

Radiation (ray•dee•AY•shuhn) is the transfer of thermal energy by electromagnetic waves. Energy from the sun is transferred to Earth by electromagnetic waves. Some of that energy is thermal energy. Conduction and convection can transfer heat through matter, but only radiation can transfer heat through space.

✔ **What are the three ways thermal energy can be transferred?**

Chemical Energy

Chemical energy is the energy stored in the bonds between atoms when they join together to form molecules. Some chemical reactions give off thermal energy. Others take in thermal energy. This thermal energy is stored as a form of potential energy called *chemical energy*. Chemical energy can be released as kinetic energy when molecules break apart.

Chemical energy can be released as several forms of kinetic energy. Batteries, for example, contain chemical energy that can be used to produce electricity. During cellular respiration, your body changes chemical energy stored in the food you eat into mechanical energy that allows you to carry on your daily activities.

Other body processes change chemical energy into thermal energy. Some of that thermal energy is used to keep your body temperature at about 37°C (98.6°F). The table shows the amount of chemical energy stored in some of the foods you eat. The potential energy of foods is measured in units called Calories (C). A Calorie is the amount of heat needed to raise the temperature of 1000 g of water by 1°C.

Chemical energy can also be released as light and heat when wood and other fuels are burned. You will learn more about the release of chemical energy from fuels in Chapter 4.

✔ **What is chemical energy?**

Potential Energy in Foods

Food (1 serving)	Energy (in Calories)	Food (1 serving)	Energy (in Calories)
Fruits		**Dairy Products**	
Apple	80	Ice cream	270
Banana	105	Cheese	110
Orange	80	Yogurt	230
Meats		**Vegetables**	
Chicken, roasted	140	Carrots	30
Hot dog	145	Corn	85
Pork chop	275	French fries	220
Roast beef, lean	175	Green beans	35
Salmon, baked	140	Lettuce	5
Shrimp, fried	240	Tomato	25
Bread and Cereal		**Snacks**	
Bread, white	65	Peanut butter	95
Macaroni and cheese	430	Pizza, cheese	290
Oatmeal	105	Popcorn, plain	30
Rice, white	180	Pretzel sticks	10

Grass stores energy from sunlight as chemical energy. By eating grass, the cow takes in this stored energy. Some of it becomes thermal energy, and some becomes mechanical energy. Some of it is stored as chemical energy in the cow's milk. ▼

Summary

Thermal energy is the kinetic energy of molecules. The average kinetic energy of the molecules in an object is the object's temperature. Heat is the transfer of thermal energy from one object to another. Conduction is the direct transfer of heat between objects that touch. Convection is the transfer of heat through currents in a gas or a liquid. Radiation is the transfer of energy by electromagnetic waves. When atoms join to form molecules, thermal energy can be stored as chemical energy. Chemical energy can be released as kinetic energy.

Review

1. What is convection?

2. What type of heat transfer takes place when you burn your hand on a stove?

3. Two atoms absorb thermal energy when joining together to form a molecule. What happens to that thermal energy?

4. **Critical Thinking** Suppose you drop an ice cube into a warm drink, and it melts. How is thermal energy transferred?

5. **Test Prep** Which form of energy transfer allows you to feel the warmth of the sun on your face?

      A radiation

      B conduction

      C convection

      D chemical energy

LINKS

MATH LINK

Thermal Energy Which has a higher temperature, a 100-g ice cube or 10 g of water at 1°C? Which has more thermal energy?

WRITING LINK

Informative Writing—Explanation Write two or three paragraphs for your teacher explaining how the transfer of energy from the sun provides most of Earth's energy.

SOCIAL STUDIES LINK

History of Calories Scientists once thought of heat as a fluid, called *caloric*, that flowed from one object to another. Benjamin Thompson, also known as Count Rumford, came up with the idea that, because heat could be caused by motion, heat and motion must be different forms of the same thing (energy). Research Count Rumford's experiments and his ideas about heat, and report to your class.

TECHNOLOGY LINK

Learn more about thermal and chemical energy by visiting the Harcourt Learning Site. **www.harcourtschool.com**

WELCOME TO THE LEARNING SITE

Developing Sources of ENERGY

Archaeologists estimate that humans burned wood as a fuel as much as 14,000 years ago. For thousands of years, wood was just about the only source of fuel people had.

Fossil Fuels and Steam

During the Middle Ages, Europeans began mining coal. As centuries passed, coal was used more and more, since the growing population was rapidly cutting down the few remaining forests. In areas along rivers or streams, mills for grinding grain were powered by flowing water, and in Spain and Holland, wind power was used. In the mid-1600s, machines were invented that were powered by steam. Many of these machines were used to pump water out of coal mines.

In 1765 James Watt, a pioneer in the development of steam engines, was repairing a broken engine when he discovered a way to improve it. By 1800 Watt had made a condenser steam engine. It was more efficient than the old engines because it changed water vapor back into liquid water, which could be reheated to make more steam.

By 1830 a steam-powered train was running regularly in the United States. And by 1838 a steam-powered ship had crossed the Atlantic Ocean. Coal was the most widely used fuel for steam engines, especially in Europe. In the United States, many early steam engines used wood for fuel because the supply there seemed endless.

The History of Energy Sources

60 B.C.
Hero of Alexandria invents a simple steam engine.

1592
First wind-powered sawmill is in operation.

1883
The internal combustion engine is invented.

100 B.C.　　A.D. 1500　　A.D. 1600　　A.D. 1700　　A.D. 1800

400–1400
People use wood, peat, and coal as fuel.

1699
The steam-powered pump is invented.

Internal Combustion and Electricity

In 1883 a high-speed engine was invented that ignited gasoline mixed with air inside metal cylinders. Improvements in this internal combustion engine, as it was called, led to the development of the automobile. Gasoline, kerosene, and other petroleum products are still used as fuel for most forms of transportation.

In 1888 the first turbine-powered electric energy station was built. In the turbine, large blades, driven by steam, turned a shaft connected to an electric generator. Later, flowing water from hydroelectric dams was used as a source of energy to drive the turbines. Today coal is the most commonly used fuel for generating electricity.

New Fuels

Obtaining and using fossil fuels often harms the environment. For this reason, scientists and engineers have begun developing alternative energy sources, including solar energy, wind, and geothermal energy. Solar cells can capture the sun's energy and change it directly into electricity. In some desert areas, huge solar panels generate large amounts of electricity for use in homes and businesses. In California, Britain, the Netherlands, and other places, high-tech windmills generate electricity for many homes. In Hawai'i and Iceland, intense heat from inside of Earth, called geothermal energy, is used to heat buildings and to generate electricity.

THINK ABOUT IT

1. Why did coal replace wood as a fuel source in Europe?
2. Today's electric generating stations use turbines that are similar to what older devices?

In the 1960s, nuclear energy stations were built in many countries.

1960s
Nuclear fission energy stations are built.

1980s
Alternative energy sources, such as solar and wind, are developed.

A.D. 1900

A.D. 2000

1950s
Many hydroelectric dams are built.

1990s
Work on nuclear fusion and other new sources of energy continues.

Jean M. Bennett

PHYSICIST

Jean M. Bennett is a physicist who has done a great deal of work in the study of light scattering. Light scattering occurs when a beam of light strikes an uneven surface and is reflected in many different directions. This scattering is not at all like the parallel rays of light that are reflected by a smooth surface.

Dr. Bennett's work has many real-life uses, especially for optical equipment such as lenses. Most lenses used in optical equipment are polished to a very smooth finish. Then the lenses are treated with a thin coating to help prevent "ghost" reflections. If you have ever seen a faint double image on a television screen instead of one sharp image, you have an idea of what a ghost reflection is. However, the thin coating also gives a lens a surface that is not perfectly smooth, which causes the light to scatter. Dr. Bennett has worked with lens manufacturers to make lenses with smoother surfaces and coatings that scatter less light. This research helps people who wear glasses to be able to see better, especially at night.

In addition to working on light scattering, Dr. Bennett has also done research on the physics of Earth's atmosphere. She is currently an important member of the research department of the Naval Air Warfare Center at China Lake, California.

THINK ABOUT IT

1. Why is it important to develop better coatings as lenses also get better?

2. Can you think of another situation in which doing something to solve one problem caused another problem? Describe the situation and the problem.

Grinding lenses

Sound Waves

How do sound waves travel?

Materials

- glass pie pan with 200 mL water
- overhead projector
- tin can
- tuning fork
- uncooked rice
- balloon
- Slinky

Procedure

1. Put the pie pan with water on the projector. Turn the projector on.

2. Tap the tuning fork on a solid object. Place the end of the fork in the water. Observe the waves on the screen.

3. Now stretch the balloon over the tin can.

4. Sprinkle rice on top of the stretched balloon.

5. Tap the tuning fork, and gently touch the end of the fork to the balloon. Observe the action of the rice.

6. Stretch the Slinky out on a smooth surface. Gather some coils at one end. Then let them go. Observe how the compression waves travel.

Draw Conclusions

In Step 2, how did the sound waves travel from the tuning fork? How did Step 5 show that sound waves are energy waves? Sound waves travel as compression waves, like those you made with the Slinky. Describe the movement of compression waves.

The Eyes Have It

How does the brain receive images?

Materials

- flashlight
- small, round fishbowl
- small toy car
- sheet of white paper
- hand lens

Procedure

1. Line up the materials in the order shown.

2. Darken the room. Turn on the flashlight.

3. Shine the light on the toy car.

4. Focus the shadow through the lens and the fishbowl, and onto the white paper. Observe the image formed on the paper.

Draw Conclusions

What organ does this model represent? What parts of that organ does each part of the model represent? What happens to the shadow of the toy car projected onto the paper? When an image is received on the retina and sent to the brain, what does the brain do with this image?

Vocabulary Review

Use the terms below to answer Questions 1 through 12. The page numbers in ( ) tell you where to look in the chapter if you need help.

energy (F62)	**reflection** (F76)
kinetic energy (F62)	**refraction** (F76)
potential energy (F62)	**lens** (F77)
electric charge (F68)	**pitch** (F79)
electric force (F69)	**volume** (F79)
electric current (F69)	**temperature** (F84)
conductor (F70)	**heat** (F84)
electric circuit (F71)	**conduction** (F85)
insulator (F71)	**convection** (F85)
resistor (F71)	**radiation** (F85)
electromagnet (F72)	

1. The three ways in which heat is transferred are ____, ____, and ____.

2. A ____ is a clear material that bends light rays.

3. ____ causes changes in matter.

4. A ____ carries electric current easily, while an ____ does not.

5. A sound's ____ is determined by the speed of its energy waves, while ____ is determined by the strength of the waves.

6. When an ____ flows through a coil of wire wrapped around a bar of iron, it makes an ____.

7. When a piece of wood burns, it releases ____.

8. The energy of motion is called ____, while the energy of position is called ____.

9. The bouncing of light rays off an object is called ____. The bending of light rays by an object is called ____.

10. A path for electricity, called an ____, may include a ____ that changes electric energy into other forms of energy.

11. The attraction or repulsion of an ____ is called an ____.

12. The average kinetic energy of all the molecules in an object is the object's ____.

Connect Concepts

Write the terms from the Word Bank that belong in the concept map.

potential	kinetic	static	thermal
radiation	sound	light	convection
chemical	electric	current	conduction

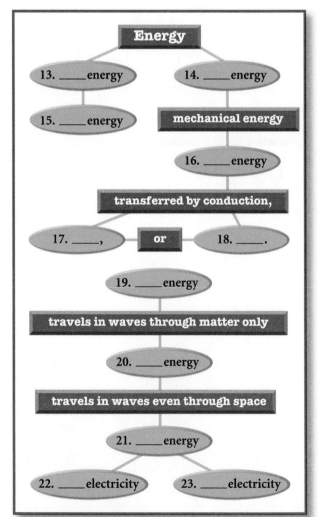

Energy

13. ____ energy

14. ____ energy

15. ____ energy

mechanical energy

16. ____ energy

transferred by conduction,

17. ____,   or   18. ____.

19. ____ energy

travels in waves through matter only

20. ____ energy

travels in waves even through space

21. ____ energy

22. ____ electricity

23. ____ electricity

Check Understanding

Write the letter of the best choice.

24. Metals and other materials that transfer heat and electricity easily are called —
    A insulators   C radiators
    B resistors   D conductors

25. The color you see in an object is the color of light the object —
    F absorbs   H refracts
    G reflects   J conducts

26. Because there is no matter in space, thermal energy moves from the sun to Earth by —
    A radiation   C insulation
    B convection   D conduction

27. Lightning and the spark you may see when you touch a doorknob on a dry day are both caused by —
    F thermal energy
    G static electricity
    H electromagnetism
    J resistors

28. An object with a positive charge will attract another object with —
    A a negative charge
    B a positive charge
    C a positive or a negative charge
    D no charge

Critical Thinking

29. Suppose you throw a ball high into the air and then it falls to the ground. Describe where the ball has the greatest potential energy and where it has the greatest kinetic energy.

30. If energy can be neither created nor destroyed, what happens to the sunlight that falls on Earth?

Process Skills Review

31. You touch a lamp cord and get a shock. **Draw a conclusion** about the insulation on the cord.

32. You record the temperature in a pan of water as it heats. You want to **make a graph** to display your results. What type of graph should you use?

33. You conduct an experiment with parallel and series electric circuits. What is one way you could **communicate** about the circuits you built?

34. You want to **compare** two materials to see which is the better conductor of thermal energy. Name two quantities you will measure.

35. You want to **plan and conduct an experiment** to show convection. Name two items you could use in your experiment.

36. You experiment to compare the colors of light reflected by different substances. Name one **variable** you must **control**.

Performance Assessment

Energy Audit

Take ten minutes to identify as many forms of energy around you right now as possible. Make a list of these forms and of how they are being transferred or changed from one form to another during those ten minutes.

How People Use Energy

Early humans used energy mostly for heating and for cooking. When they learned how to work with metal, their energy use increased. Each new technology led them to use more energy. This is still true today. Every year people use about two percent more energy than they did the year before.

Vocabulary Preview

chemical bonds
hydroelectric energy
tidal energy
biomass
nuclear energy
geothermal energy
solar energy
fusion energy

FAST FACT

Most of the world's energy is used by a small number of countries. The United States, for example, uses one-fourth of all the energy in the world.

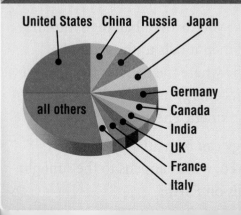

Energy Use

United States   China   Russia   Japan

Germany
Canada
India
UK
France
Italy

all others

Less than one-billionth of the sun's energy reaches the surface of Earth. Yet one hour's worth of solar energy is more energy than everyone on Earth uses in an entire year.

≡FAST FACT

ENIAC, the first electronic digital computer, required huge amounts of electricity. Fifty years later, some hand-held computers use less energy than a portable radio.

How Do People Use Fossil Fuels?

In this lesson, you can . . .

INVESTIGATE
how stored energy is released from chemical compounds.

LEARN ABOUT
how fossil fuels are used.

LINK to math, writing, health, and technology.

INVESTIGATE

How Stored Energy Is Released

Activity Purpose In a previous chapter you learned about the law of conservation of energy. It states that energy can change forms but cannot be created or destroyed. One of the forms that potential energy takes is the chemical energy stored in fossil fuels and other compounds. In this investigation you will release chemical energy stored in a compound called calcium chloride. You will **observe** and **compare** liquids to determine what form of energy is released.

Materials

- water
- measuring cup
- Styrofoam cup
- thermometer
- clock with second hand
- safety goggles
- calcium chloride
- spoon

CAUTION

Activity Procedure

1. Make a table like the one on page F97. Measure 50 mL of water in the measuring cup, and pour it into the Styrofoam cup. Put the thermometer in the water. After 30 seconds, **measure** the temperature of the water and **record** it in the table.

2. **CAUTION** **Put on the safety goggles.** Add 2 spoonfuls of calcium chloride to the cup of water. Stir the water with the spoon until the calcium chloride dissolves. Wait 30 seconds. Then **measure** and **record** the temperature. (Picture A)

◄ In 1859 E. L. Drake drilled the first producing oil well, at Oil Creek in Titusville, Pennsylvania. Most of the oil was used to produce kerosene for lamps.

Substance	Temperature
Water without chemical	
Water with chemical after 30 seconds	
Water with chemical after 60 seconds	
Water with chemical after 120 seconds	

3 **Measure** and **record** the temperature of the water two more times, after 60 seconds and again after 120 seconds. Then **compare** the temperature of the water before and after you added calcium chloride. (Picture B)

Picture A

Draw Conclusions

1. How did the temperature of the water change when you added calcium chloride?

2. **Infer** whether the calcium chloride gives off heat or absorbs heat as it dissolves in water.

3. What do you **infer** might have caused the water temperature to change?

4. **Scientists at Work** Scientists **observe** and **measure** to gather as much data as they can from an experiment. What did you learn from this experiment about how the chemical energy in some compounds can be released?

Picture B

Investigate Further **Hypothesize** what will happen when a different chemical, such as magnesium sulfate (Epsom salts), is placed in water. Then **plan and conduct a simple investigation** to test your hypothesis.

Process Skill Tip

When you **observe** and **measure** carefully, the data you gather will be more useful.

Fossil Fuel Use

Burning Fuels Produce Thermal Energy

As a tree grows, it uses energy from sunlight to build the chemical compounds it needs. Solar energy is stored in the tree's molecules. If molecules are broken apart, energy is released. In the investigation you observed that much of that energy is thermal energy, or heat. Burning wood or fossil fuels also breaks apart molecules and releases heat.

Stored solar energy, or chemical energy, exists in all living organisms. Most of it is stored in the **chemical bonds** that join atoms of carbon to each other and to atoms of other elements, such as hydrogen. When living matter from forests, swamps, and shallow seas is buried under sediments for long periods of time, the chemical energy is buried as well. When fossil fuels are taken from the ground, their chemical energy can be converted to thermal energy by burning.

✓ **How is the chemical energy stored in fossil fuels released?**

Solar energy is stored as chemical energy in living organisms. This energy can be released by burning. Wood was used as a fuel for heating and for cooking during much of America's history, but it doesn't really release much heat. The table shows the amount of thermal energy released by burning different fuels.

Heat Released Burning 1 kg of Fuel

Fuel	Heat (in millions of joules)
Hard coal	1,935,000
Gasoline	2,540,000
Hardwood	786,000
Propane gas	2,843,000

Heat (in millions of joules)

This generator is a smaller version of what you might find at an energy station. It changes the energy of burning fuel into mechanical energy (for turning the generator) and then into electric energy. ▽

Using Fossil Fuels

Fossil fuels are the main source of energy for industrial nations like the United States. Coal is taken from Earth's crust by strip mining or by deep mining. Wells are drilled into the crust to obtain natural gas or petroleum.

As the graph on page F98 shows, fossil fuels release large amounts of thermal energy when they're burned. People use this energy in many ways. In homes, offices, and schools, thermal energy is used to heat water or the air. On cold days the heat that comes from your classroom's radiators or air vents was probably produced by burning coal, oil, or natural gas.

In a gas stove, natural gas or bottled gas, such as propane, is burned to provide heat for cooking food. Natural gas is usually distributed through underground pipelines. Bottled gas is brought in by truck to fill local storage tanks.

Petroleum is the main source of energy for transportation. Cars, trucks, buses, trains, and planes have engines that burn fuel made from petroleum, such as gasoline or diesel fuel. As gasoline burns, it expands rapidly. The resulting force turns the engine's crankshaft. Through a series of gears, this movement turns the wheels that push the vehicle.

Similar engines are used in electric energy stations. As you learned in an earlier chapter, when these engines run, they turn electric generators.

Much of the energy for generating electricity in the United States comes from burning fossil fuels, especially coal. Fossil fuels are also used for purposes other than thermal energy production. Plastics, fertilizers, chemicals, and some medicines are made partly from petroleum and coal. Even your shoes and clothes may be made partly from petroleum.

✓ **Name four uses of fossil fuels.**

Fossil fuels are used for plastics, such as the ones in this kayak, paddle, and helmet. ▽

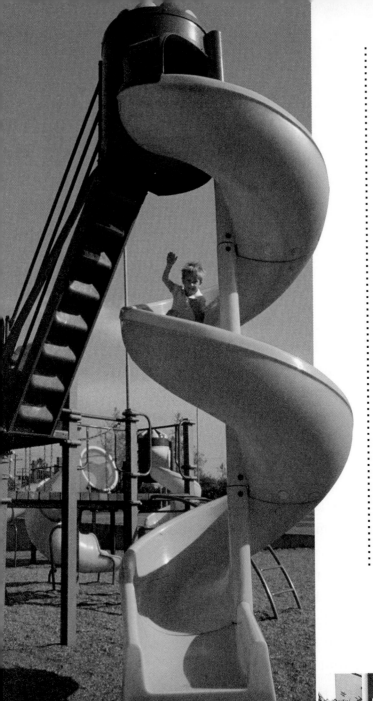

Alternatives to Fossil Fuels

Experts disagree about how much fossil fuel is still buried in the Earth, but the supply is limited. The remains of living organisms take millions of years to become petroleum or coal. However, in just a few years, a geologist can find a fossil-fuel deposit, a company can sell the fuel, and users can burn it. Since fossil fuels form so slowly but are used so quickly, they are *nonrenewable resources.*

Scientists don't know how small the supplies of fossil fuels are, but there are good reasons to use other sources of energy. One reason is that fossil fuels are needed more and more to make things, such as new types of plastics. Fossil fuels may also turn out to have uses not yet discovered.

Another reason for using other sources of energy is that burning fossil fuels releases large amounts of carbon dioxide into the air. Some scientists are concerned that the carbon dioxide may trap heat in Earth's

An electric car produces no carbon dioxide itself. But the electricity to charge the car's battery may be produced by burning fossil fuels. ▼

▲ This playground equipment is made of recycled soft drink bottles and other plastic items. Recycling plastics can reduce the use of fossil fuels.

atmosphere and cause environmental changes such as global warming.

To reduce the use of fossil fuels, many companies are developing alternative sources of energy. These include wind energy and geothermal energy (heat from within the Earth). In California and other places, some utility companies generate large amounts of electricity from these inexhaustible energy sources. Another method of using less fossil fuels is to recycle plastics and oils, such as the oil from car engines.

✓ **Why are fossil fuels considered nonrenewable resources?**

Summary

Coal, natural gas, and petroleum are fossil fuels formed from once-living matter that has been buried for millions of years. Fossil fuels are used to heat homes, move vehicles, and generate electricity. Because fossil fuels take millions of years to form, they are nonrenewable.

Review

1. Name three types of fossil fuels.
2. How is the chemical energy in fossil fuels changed to electric energy?
3. In what way does the energy in fossil fuels come from sunlight?
4. **Critical Thinking** Why isn't it correct to say that fossil fuels *make* thermal energy?
5. **Test Prep** Gasoline is produced from —

   A coal   **C** kerosene

   B natural gas   **D** petroleum

LINKS

MATH LINK

Calories A *calorie* is a unit of heat. One calorie is the amount of heat needed to raise the temperature of 1 g of water by 1°C. Suppose you fill a kettle with 1000 g of water at 20°C. Then you heat the water until it reaches 100°C. How many calories are needed to do this?

WRITING LINK

Expressive Writing—Friendly Letter Send e-mail to a friend. In the e-mail, describe all the energy changes that have occurred over millions of years to produce the electricity to send the e-mail.

HEALTH LINK

Comparing Calorie Content When you read on a food label that a snack has a certain number of Calories, you are learning about the chemical energy stored in that food. Each food Calorie (*Calorie* with a capital *C*) is the amount of energy needed to raise the temperature of 1 kg of water 1°C. Make a table that compares the energy stored in equal amounts of different foods.

TECHNOLOGY LINK

Learn more about generating electricity by visiting the National Museum of American History Internet site. **www.si.edu/harcourt/science**

 Smithsonian Institution®

How Can Moving Water Generate Electricity?

In this lesson, you can . . .

INVESTIGATE the power of falling water.

LEARN ABOUT how the energy of falling water is changed to electric energy.

LINK to math, writing, social studies, and technology.

INVESTIGATE

Water Power

Activity Purpose To produce electricity, an energy station must change some other form of energy. In some cases, the mechanical energy of falling water is used. In this investigation you will **make a model** of a water wheel. Then you will **plan and conduct an investigation** to determine the amount of energy in falling water.

Materials
- two 10-cm plastic disks
- stapler
- scissors
- pencil sharpened at both ends
- 0.5-m length of string
- 30-g mass
- basin
- 1-L plastic bottle filled with water
- meterstick
- stopwatch

CAUTION

Activity Procedure

1 **CAUTION** **Be careful when using scissors.** Staple the plastic disks together near their centers. Using the scissors, cut four 3-cm slits into the disks as shown. At each slit, fold the disks in opposite directions to form a vane. (Picture A)

2 Again using the scissors, punch a 0.5-cm hole at the center of the disks. Insert the pencil. It will serve as the axle on which the water wheel rotates.

3 Use the scissors to make a smaller hole next to the pencil hole. Insert one end of the string into the hole, and tie a knot in the string to keep it in place. Tie the mass to the other end of the string.

◀ The water behind Hoover Dam has a lot of potential energy. The dam's hydroelectric plant will change this potential energy to kinetic energy and then to electric energy.

4 Place the basin near the edge of the desk. Hold your water wheel over the basin. Your fingertips should hold the pencil points so the pencil can turn. The mass on the string should hang over the edge of the desk. (Picture B)

5 Have a partner slowly pour water over the wheel from a height of about 10 cm. Using the stopwatch, **measure** and **record** the time it takes for the mass to reach the level of the desk. Repeat this step several times.

6 Now repeat Steps 4 and 5, but have your partner pour the water from a height of about 20 cm. Again, **measure** and **record** the time it takes for the mass to reach the level of the desk.

Picture A

Picture B

Draw Conclusions

1. What **variables** did you **control** in your investigation? What variable did you change?

2. Recall that the greater the power, the more quickly work is done. Which of your trials produced more power? Why?

3. **Scientists at Work** Scientists often look beyond the results of an investigation. For example, how does the height from which the water is poured affect the speed at which the water wheel turns? **Plan and conduct a simple investigation** to find out. Be sure to **identify and control variables,** changing only the height from which the water falls.

Investigate Further **Hypothesize** about the rate of flow and the speed at which the water wheel turns. Then **plan and conduct a simple investigation** to test your hypothesis. Be sure to **identify and control variables,** changing only the rate of flow of the water.

Process Skill Tip

Scientists **plan and conduct simple investigations** to gather data. To gather accurate data, **identify and control variables,** allowing only one to change.

Electricity and Moving Water

FIND OUT

- how electric energy is produced from the mechanical energy of moving water

- how tidal energy stations work

VOCABULARY

hydroelectric energy

tidal energy

Hydroelectric dams often produce large lakes, which can be used for recreation. ▼

Hydroelectric Energy

Recall that energy cannot be created or destroyed, but that it can change forms. An electric generator works by changing mechanical energy into electric energy. Generators can be connected to any source of mechanical energy that makes their parts spin. One of these sources is falling water. Electricity generated from the force of falling water is called **hydroelectric energy**. *Hydro* means "water."

For thousands of years, people have used the energy of falling water to turn wheels along streams and rivers. The first water wheels probably powered mills that ground grain. During the

Fish swimming upstream can't get past a hydroelectric dam, so many dams have small rivers around them. Other dams have "fish ladders"—stepped waterfalls that fish can jump up, step by step, to get past the dam.

The water that moves through the dam (above) flows through turbines (at the right), setting them spinning. The turbines turn the electric generators.

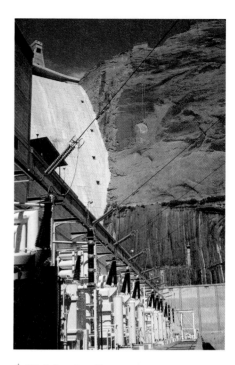

▲ High-tension lines carry electricity produced at the energy station to places where it is needed.

Industrial Revolution of the 1700s and 1800s, water wheels provided the energy that turned the machines in many factories. Today about one-fifth of the world's energy is hydroelectric energy.

Hydroelectric energy stations use the energy of falling water to spin turbines. A *turbine* is an improved form of the water wheel you made in the investigation. Water strikes the blades of a turbine and makes it spin. The rotating turbine then spins the shaft of an electric generator. The electricity produced by the generator is then sent over power lines to homes, schools, and factories.

The energy that spins a hydroelectric turbine comes from the potential energy of water under pressure. Water near the surface of a lake exerts a force on the water below it. The greater the depth of the water, the greater the energy the water has due to this pressure. So people build dams across rivers to increase the depth of the water. The dam has openings, or gates, at the bottom that allow water to flow through. As water flows through a gate, it spins the vanes of the turbine.

Like almost all energy on Earth, hydroelectric energy can be traced back to the sun. The sun provides the energy that evaporates water from lakes and oceans and carries water vapor high into the air. When this water vapor condenses, it falls back to Earth as rain or snow. As runoff water flows into lakes, it compresses the water beneath it, passing on its potential energy. Rivers below the turbines carry the water back to the oceans. The water cycle is complete, and people have an inexhaustible source of energy.

✔ **What form of energy goes into a hydroelectric energy station? What form comes out?**

Tidal Energy

Along much of Earth's coastlines, tides rise and fall twice a day. In some places these changes in water level are especially large. There the mechanical energy of the moving water can be used to produce electricity. This is a form of hydroelectric energy called **tidal energy**.

Tidal energy plants depend on the difference in water height between high tide and low tide. They produce electricity by holding back water at high tide and letting it fall through turbines at low tide. For a tidal energy station to be efficient, the difference between water level at high tide and low tide must be large.

One place that is famous for its tides—sometimes called *supertides*—is the Bay of Fundy, in Canada. Supertides occur where

The world's first commercial tidal energy station was built at the mouth of the Rance River in Brittany, France. The station produces enough electricity for a city of 300,000 people. ▼

THE INSIDE STORY

A Tidal Energy Station

Tidal energy stations have turbines that are turned by tidal currents. The turbines are usually reversible so that they can operate on both incoming and outgoing tides.

When the tide comes in, water levels rise on one side of the station. Once the difference in water level is 3 m (about 10 ft) or more, the force of the water is great enough to spin turbines connected to electric generators.

When water is at the same level on both sides of the station, the gates are closed. The tide goes out, leaving higher water behind the station. Then the gates are opened and water again flows through the turbines, this time spinning them in the opposite direction.

an incoming tide is funneled into a narrow bay or river channel. As the bay narrows, the water level rises. Tides in the Bay of Fundy can rise and fall more than 15 m (50 ft). Several tidal energy plants have been proposed for this bay, and one is already working.

✔ **Why are tidal energy plants most efficient in places with supertides?**

Summary

An electric generator changes mechanical energy to electric energy. One source of this mechanical energy is moving water. Hydroelectric energy stations use the energy of falling water to spin turbines that generate electricity. The mechanical energy present in ocean tides can also generate electric energy.

Review

1. What is hydroelectric energy?
2. What is the name of a device that turns mechanical energy into electricity?
3. Why do tidal energy stations depend on large differences in water height between high tide and low tide?
4. **Critical Thinking** Compare tidal energy with the hydroelectric energy generated by a dam.
5. **Test Prep** Raising the level of water behind a dam improves the efficiency of a hydroelectric plant by increasing —

   A the water's weight

   B the water's potential energy

   C the water's temperature

   D the water's mass

LINKS

MATH LINK

Estimation In 1990, hydroelectric stations in the United States generated about 264 billion kilowatt hours of energy. This was less than $\frac{1}{10}$ of the total electric energy produced in the United States that year. Estimate the total electric energy production in the United States in 1990.

WRITING LINK

Informative Writing—Report You flip a switch and light floods the room. Electric energy produces that light. Write a short report for your teacher describing the source of electricity in your area. Where is the generator that produces the electric energy? What sort of energy station produces it? What kind of energy is changed to produce the electric energy?

SOCIAL STUDIES LINK

History of Water Wheels Learn more about the early history and uses of water wheels in other parts of the world. Report your findings to your class.

TECHNOLOGY LINK

Learn more about hydroelectric and other forms of energy by investigating *Energy and You* on the **Harcourt Science Explorations CD-ROM.**

3

What Other Sources of Energy Do People Use?

In this lesson, you can . . .

INVESTIGATE how steam can turn a turbine.

LEARN ABOUT alternative energy sources.

LINK to math, writing, literature, and technology.

People have used windmills for hundreds of years to capture the energy of the wind. ▶

INVESTIGATE

A Steam-Powered Turbine

Activity Purpose A turbine is a type of rotating engine powered by water, wind, or steam. It is often part of an electric energy station. In Lesson 2 you saw how water can turn a turbine. But wind or steam can also turn a turbine. In this investigation you will **make a model** of a steam-powered turbine.

Materials

- two 10-cm plastic disks
- stapler
- scissors
- pencil
- ring stand
- 2 paper clips
- flask
- water
- one-hole stopper with bent-glass tube
- hot plate
- safety goggles

CAUTION

Activity Procedure

1. You can modify the water wheel you made in the last investigation by adding 12 more vanes to the wheel and enlarging the hole. Or you can follow Steps 2 and 3 to make your turbine.

2. **CAUTION** **Be careful when using the scissors.** Staple the plastic disks together near their centers. Using the scissors, cut sixteen 3-cm slits into the disks as shown. At each slit, fold the disks in opposite directions to form a vane. (Picture A)

3. Again using the scissors, cut a 0.5-cm round hole in the center of the disks. Make the hole as round as possible. Insert the pencil. It will serve as the axle on which the turbine rotates. The turbine should

spin freely on its axle. Now suspend the axle and turbine from the ring stand arm with two bent paper clips.

4 Fill the flask with water. Put the stopper with the bent glass tube in the flask. Set the flask on the hot plate. Point the open end of the glass tube toward the vanes on the bottom of the turbine. (Picture B)

5 **CAUTION** **Put on the safety goggles, and use caution around the steam.** Turn on the hot plate. **Observe** and **record** your observations of the turbine as the water begins to boil. Draw a diagram of your turbine to **communicate** your results. Be sure to include labels and arrows to show what happens.

Picture A

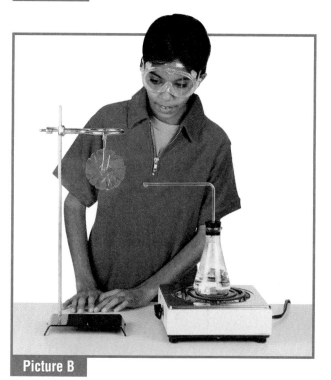
Picture B

Draw Conclusions

1. **Infer** the source of energy for turning the turbine.

2. **Communicate** in a short paragraph how the energy from the source was changed to turn the turbine.

3. **Scientists at Work** When scientists **communicate,** they try to show clearly or describe what is happening. In what two ways did you communicate the results of this investigation? Which way was clearer?

Investigate Further **Plan and conduct a simple investigation** to determine how much work your turbine can do. Decide what questions you will need to answer and what equipment you will need to use.

Process Skill Tip

Including arrows on a diagram can be a clear way to **communicate** information about motion and direction.

Other Energy Sources

Energy for Today

FIND OUT

- what other energy sources are used in the United States
- what energy sources we may rely on in the future

VOCABULARY

biomass
nuclear energy
geothermal energy
solar energy
fusion energy

Fossil fuels and hydroelectric energy are major energy sources in much of the world. Other energy sources may be less common, but they are still important. These include biomass, nuclear, wind, geothermal, and solar energy.

Biomass In some parts of the world, biomass is an important source of energy. **Biomass** is organic matter, such as wood, that is living or was recently alive. Biomass is often burned directly. However, as you saw in the graph on page F98, burning wood doesn't release much energy. In the United States, a major source of biomass is garbage. Burning garbage doesn't release much energy either, but it is basically a free energy source. Heat from burning biomass is used to boil water. The steam then turns turbines that run electric generators.

Wood, a type of biomass, is still used as a source of energy in some places. ▼

Nuclear energy is released in a pool of water. This helps keep dangerous materials from getting too hot. ▼

Biomass can also be made into liquid fuels. Alcohol made from wood or corn is mixed with gasoline to produce a fuel called gasohol. Other plants produce oils that can be burned in modified gasoline or diesel engines.

Nuclear Energy Energy is released when the nucleus of an atom is split apart. This energy is called **nuclear energy**. Splitting nuclei releases a large amount of thermal energy. A nuclear energy station uses this thermal energy to boil water. The resulting steam is directed through turbines and electric generators.

A nuclear energy station produces a large amount of energy from a small amount of fuel. However, the fuel and the waste products of the nuclear reactions are very dangerous to living organisms.

Wind Energy Wind energy is one of the oldest forms of energy used by people. Wind is still used all over the world. In the United States, for example, many farmers use windmills to pump water from below the ground for irrigation. Some windmills on farms also generate small amounts of electricity.

A different kind of farm—a wind farm—uses modern windmills, or wind turbines, connected to electric generators. A wind farm can produce electricity wherever there is a steady wind. To get as much energy from the wind as possible, the blades of some wind turbines are 100 m (about 330 ft) across.

The advantage of using windmills or wind turbines to generate electricity is that the fuel—the wind—is free, nonpolluting, and inexhaustible. However, wind turbines are expensive, and the strength of the wind usually isn't constant.

Geothermal Energy In some parts of the world, people use heat from inside the Earth, called **geothermal energy**, to heat homes and produce electricity. Geothermal energy occurs where underground water lies close to hot magma. The water boils, and the steam forces its way to the surface. There it is used to turn turbines to generate electric energy. Sometimes steam or very hot water is piped directly to buildings to provide heat. In the United States, there are several geothermal energy stations near San Francisco, California.

▲ At The Geysers, north of San Francisco, underground water is heated by nearby magma. The escaping steam is directed to turbines to generate electricity.

▲ Solar panels change light energy directly into electricity.

Solar Energy The energy of sunlight is called **solar energy**. There are several ways to use solar energy. Solar collectors absorb and focus the sun's energy to heat water. Solar-heated water is often used to heat

This wind farm at Altmont Pass in California relies on a strong, steady wind to drive a set of 300 wind turbines.

swimming pools. In some homes and businesses, the hot water is piped to faucets throughout the building.

Some solar energy stations heat water until it boils. The steam is then used to spin turbines connected to electric generators.

Solar energy can also be changed directly into electricity by *solar cells*. These cells, arranged in flat panels, are made in layers. Sunlight frees electrons from one layer. They are attracted to the other layer. This produces an electric potential that can turn on lights or run motors. Large panels of solar cells are used to power satellites and space stations. Strips containing just a few cells provide the small amount of electricity needed to run a calculator.

Although solar energy is free, solar collectors and cells can be expensive. And many places do not have enough sunny days to make it possible to use solar energy.

✔ **What are the advantages and disadvantages of each source of energy?**

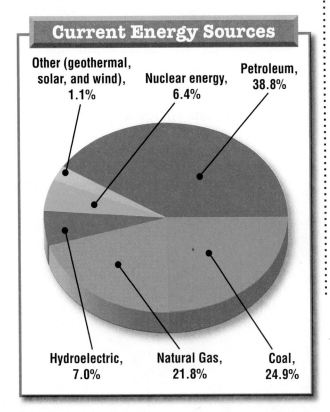

Current Energy Sources

Other (geothermal, solar, and wind), 1.1%

Nuclear energy, 6.4%

Petroleum, 38.8%

Hydroelectric, 7.0%

Natural Gas, 21.8%

Coal, 24.9%

▲ Ocean thermal energy conversion (OTEC) uses thermal energy from the ocean to produce electricity. This experimental system uses differences in temperature between warm upper layers and cold lower layers of ocean water.

Energy for Tomorrow

New sources of energy are always being developed. Scientists look for sources low in cost and low in risk to humans and to the environment.

One of these future sources is fusion. **Fusion energy** is released when the nuclei of two small atoms are forced together to form a larger nucleus. This is the same process that happens in the core of the sun. The heat you feel on a sunny day has fusion energy as its source.

Unfortunately, the heat needed to start fusion is so high that no known material can contain it. Success with fusion has so far been limited to small experiments using force fields to hold the atoms.

◄ Energy sources such as wind, geothermal, and solar make up a larger percent of world energy production today than in the past. In the future they will probably be even more important.

Another promising source of energy for the future is hydrogen, which can be burned like fossil fuels. Ocean water could provide an almost limitless source of hydrogen. Today the best way to separate hydrogen from water is by using electricity. However, using electricity to produce another energy source is expensive.

Scientists are also working on ways to release thermal energy from water to produce electricity. This process is called ocean thermal energy conversion, or OTEC.

✓ **What is the biggest problem with developing fusion power?**

Summary

In addition to fossil fuels and hydroelectric energy, the United States uses small amounts of energy from other sources. These sources include biomass, nuclear energy, wind, geothermal energy, and solar energy. Researchers continue to work on new sources of energy, such as fusion.

Review

1. What is the disadvantage of nuclear energy?

2. Why is geothermal energy not an energy source that can be used in all areas?

3. In what ways are wind and solar energy similar?

4. **Critical Thinking** · How is the nuclear energy now in use different from fusion energy?

5. **Test Prep** Many forms of energy are used to heat water, producing —

   A fuel   **C** hydrogen

   B wind   **D** steam

LINKS

MATH LINK

Comparing Wind Speeds For a windmill to produce electric energy, the wind speed should be at least 13 km/hr. The wind should also be constant. Research the wind conditions in your area by using the weather station from an earlier chapter or by looking at the weather page of a local newspaper. Decide whether wind energy is a possible source for producing electricity where you live.

WRITING LINK

Persuasive Writing—Business Letter Write a letter to your electric company. Ask for information on your area's use of alternative sources of energy, such as biomass, nuclear energy, wind energy, geothermal energy, or solar energy. Be sure to ask clearly, to explain why you are asking, and to thank the person for his or her time.

LITERATURE LINK

Poem: "The Wind" Read "The Wind," a poem by Robert Louis Stevenson. What words does the poet use to describe the wind's energy?

TECHNOLOGY LINK

Learn more about alternatives to using fossil fuels by viewing *Wind Power and Electric Cars* on the **Harcourt Science Newsroom Video.**

Canola Motor Oil

What can you do with vegetable oil, besides making a salad or frying something for supper? Soon you can put it in your family's car! At least that's the hope of the scientists developing vegetable motor oil.

Did You Say Vegetable Oil?

The engine of a car has many moving parts. To reduce the friction produced when those parts rub together, oil lubricates them, or keeps them slippery. Motor oil helps a car work by keeping the engine running smoothly. The oil now used for this purpose is a petroleum product. Petroleum oil works well in engines. Why replace it with something different? Why use vegetable oil?

Duane Johnson, an agronomist, or crop scientist, wanted to help Colorado farmers. He was looking for a crop they could grow to make money for themselves and their communities. He realized that canola might be that crop. For years people had grown canola plants, crushed their seeds to extract the oil, and used it for cooking. Colorado farmers could raise canola, and the oil could be processed in nearby towns.

But all the canola needed for cooking oil was already being grown. Growing more

A field of canola

Canola oil can be used in place of petroleum-based oil in most vehicles.

canola would simply drive down the price. So Johnson started thinking about other ways to use canola oil. For example, would it work in an engine?

The Advantages of Canola Motor Oil

After several years of research, he developed a canola-based motor oil and tested it in various cars. It worked! As word of his invention spread, mechanics from as far away as New Zealand wanted to buy canola motor oil.

People were eager to try it because they recognized its advantages. One advantage is that it helps protect the environment. Engines using petroleum-based motor oils make a lot of pollution. Switching to canola motor oil reduces the amount of pollution from car engines by up to 40 percent. Also, canola oil spills aren't harmful to organisms as petroleum spills are. Still another advantage is that after the oil has been used in car engines, drivers can dispose of it easily, since it isn't a hazardous waste. Like recycled petroleum oils, it can be made into chain oils and other lubricants, or it can be burned as a low-grade fuel oil. But unlike recycled

petroleum oil, recycled canola oil doesn't cause pollution.

Perhaps the biggest advantage is that canola is a renewable resource. It can be grown year after year. Scientists hope that growing canola and other renewable energy sources will help meet future needs now filled by petroleum products. Some European buses have been using seed-oil fuels. Think about exhaust fumes that smell like popping corn!

THINK ABOUT IT

1. What are some advantages of using canola motor oil?
2. Why are crop fuels renewable resources, but fossil fuels are not?

 WEB LINK:
For science and technology updates, visit The Learning Site.
www.harcourtschool.com

Careers   Auto Mechanic

What They Do Auto mechanics repair and maintain cars, buses, and trucks. They work at service stations, garages, auto centers, and public transportation agencies.

Education and Training Many mechanics get their start by taking old cars apart and putting them back together. High schools, community colleges, and automobile manufacturers have auto mechanic classes and training seminars. On-the-job training at a service station is also possible.

Meredith Gourdine
PHYSICIST, ENGINEER

"We believe there are many uses for this discovery in everyday life—an improved source of power for heat and light in homes, making sea water drinkable by taking the salt out of it, making painting and coating processes easier, and reducing the amount of pollutants in smoke."

As an undergraduate at Cornell University, Meredith Gourdine majored in engineering physics and served as captain of the track team. His performance as an athlete was so outstanding that he won a silver medal at the 1952 Olympic Games. Then he went on to earn a doctorate at the California Institute of Technology.

Over the next 30 years, Dr. Gourdine developed a career as a pioneer researcher and inventor in the field known as electrogasdynamics.

Electrogasdynamics is the generation of energy from the motion of gas molecules that have been electrically charged under high pressure. Dr. Gourdine holds about 30 patents for inventions, such as a system for removing smoke from burning buildings and a method for removing fog from airport runways. Both of these inventions work by giving particles in the air a negative charge. The charged particles are then attracted to the ground by electromagnets.

Currently, Dr. Gourdine is working to perfect a generator that uses moving gas particles to convert low-voltage electricity into high-voltage electricity. Dr. Gourdine's generator may provide a much-needed new source of energy.

THINK ABOUT IT

1. Why is it important to give airborne particles such as smoke and fog a negative charge?
2. Why do you think Dr. Gourdine's generator might be important in the future?

A smoky fire

Saving Energy

What materials make good heat insulators?

Materials

- 4 tin cans
- 4 thermometers
- cotton batting
- newspaper
- Styrofoam peanuts

Procedure

1. Put a thermometer in each can. Record the temperature of each can.

2. Pack cotton batting around one thermometer, shredded newspaper around another,

and Styrofoam peanuts around a third. The control can will have a thermometer only.

3. Predict which item will be the best heat insulator.

4. Put all four cans in a sunny window.

5. Record the temperature of each can every minute for 10 min.

Draw Conclusions

In this experiment you tested three items that could help conserve energy. Which material was the best insulator? Home builders try to build energy-efficient homes. Design an energy-efficient house for an outdoor pet. Remember that the house may need to protect the pet from cold weather as well as hot weather.

Clean It Up

What materials can be used to contain and clean up an oil spill?

Materials

- small bowl of water
- 20 mL vegetable oil
- rubber bands
- string
- cotton batting
- paper towels

Procedure

1. Carefully pour a small amount of oil on top of the water in the bowl.

2. Brainstorm different ways to use the materials to contain the spill or clean up the oil.

3. Try out your ideas.

Draw Conclusions

To protect the environment from damage, an oil spill must be contained quickly. Then the oil must be removed from the water. Which of the items you tested were most helpful in containing the oil spill? Which of the items were most helpful in cleaning up the oil spill? Research to find out what materials are actually used.

Vocabulary Review

Use the terms below to complete the sentences. The page numbers in ( ) tell you where to look in the chapter if you need help.

chemical bonds (F98)

hydroelectric energy (F104)

tidal energy (F106)

biomass (F110)

nuclear energy (F110)

geothermal energy (F111)

solar energy (F111)

fusion energy (F112)

1. One alternative energy source is ____, organic matter that is burned or may be turned into liquid fuel.

2. One future energy source is ____, which is the same process the sun uses.

3. One of the biggest disadvantages of ____ is that the fuel used and the waste produced are dangerous to organisms.

4. The energy in fossil fuels is stored in ____ that join atoms of carbon together.

5. A ____ station produces energy by holding water at high tide and releasing it through turbines at low tide.

6. In some areas people use ____ from water heated by hot magma.

7. A solar cell turns ____ directly into electricity.

8. A ____ station produces electricity from the energy of falling water.

Connect Concepts

Write the terms from the Word Bank below in the correct column of the concept map.

nuclear energy   wind   fossil fuels

geothermal   hydroelectric   ocean thermal
  energy   energy   energy conversion
                                               (OTEC)
tidal energy   solar energy

fusion energy   biomass

Energy Sources			
Energy from Sunlight	**Energy from Atoms**	**Energy from Earth**	**Energy from Forces in Space**
9. ____	15. ____	17. ____	18. ____
10. ____	16. ____		
11. ____			
12. ____			
13. ____			
14. ____			

Check Understanding

Write the letter of the best choice.

19. The energy in fossil fuels that is turned into thermal energy when it burns is —

A chemical   C heat

B electric   D mechanical

20. The energy at the bottom of a waterfall is the same energy that is turned into electric energy in a —

F hydroelectric energy station

G nuclear energy station

H solar energy station

J coal energy station

21. Solar cells are dependent on the weather from day to day, as are —

A hydroelectric energy stations

B nuclear energy stations

C geothermal energy stations

D wind farms

22. The thermal energy from many sources is turned into —

F chemical energy

G electric energy

H solar energy

J mechanical energy

Critical Thinking

23. Fossil fuels form from once-living matter. Why are they considered *nonrenewable* sources of energy?

24. Suppose you are an engineer designing a hydroelectric energy station. You can build the dam 10 m high or 25 m high. Which would you choose? Explain.

25. Suppose you are going to build a wind farm. What decisions will you need to make about its location? Explain.

Process Skills Review

26. Your family is going to build a new house. What three features might you **compare** in choosing an energy source for heating the house?

27. You plan to **measure** the thermal energy released during a chemical reaction. What tool would you use?

28. You decide to **plan and carry out a simple investigation** to decide the best place for a solar collector at your home. What are two factors you should test for in each area you investigate?

29. You want to **compare** the amounts of heat released by gasoline and kerosene. What **variables** should you **identify and control** when you experiment?

30. For a report on fossil fuels, you plan to **communicate** the steps necessary to produce electricity from coal. Choose a type of display—a table, a chart, a diagram, or a graph. Explain why this is the best way to communicate the steps.

Performance Assessment

Producing Light Energy

Draw a diagram that traces the energy in this light back through the steps it took in getting to you. Show the different forms the energy took on its journey.

UNIT F

Unit Project Wrap Up

Here are some ideas for ways to wrap up your unit project.

Make a Map

Use a computer and mapping software to make a map of the amusement park grounds. Include a map key and a scale of miles.

Report on Tape

Pretend you are a news reporter, and have someone record your news report on audiotape or videotape. Tell about the rides in the amusement park and how they move.

Display at a Science Fair

Display your amusement park in a school science fair. Label the rides to show how forces enable the riders to move. Write directions about how the rides work.

Investigate Further

How could you make your project better? What other questions do you have about energy and motion? Plan ways to find answers to your questions. Use the Science Handbook on pages R2-R9 for help.

References

Science Handbook

Planning an Investigation

When scientists observe something they want to study, they use the method of scientific inquiry to plan and conduct their study. They use science process skills as tools to help them gather, organize, analyze, and present their information. This plan will help you use scientific inquiry and process skills to work like a scientist.

Step 1—Observe and ask questions.

I wonder which design of paper airplane will fly the greatest distance?

- Use your senses to make observations.
- Record a question you would like to answer.

Step 2—Make a hypothesis.

My hypothesis: This airplane with the narrow wings will fly the greatest distance.

- Choose one possible answer, or hypothesis, to your question.
- Write your hypothesis in a complete sentence.
- Think about what investigation you can do to test your answer.

Step 3—Plan your test.

I'll launch each airplane three times from the same spot, with the same amount of force.

- Write down the steps you will follow to do your test. Decide how to conduct a fair test by controlling variables.
- Decide what equipment you will need.
- Decide how you will gather and record your data.

Step 4—Conduct your test.

I'll record each distance, then find the average distance each airplane traveled.

- Follow the steps you wrote.
- Observe and measure carefully.
- Record everything that happens.
- Organize your data so that you can study it carefully.

Step 5—Draw conclusions and share results.

My hypothesis was correct. The airplane with the narrow wings flew the greatest distance.

- Analyze the data you gathered.
- Make charts, graphs, or tables to show your data.
- Write a conclusion. Describe the evidence you used to determine whether your test supported your hypothesis.
- Decide whether your hypothesis was true.

Investigate Further

I wonder which airplane will fly for the longest time?

Using Science Tools

Using a Hand Lens

A hand lens magnifies objects, or makes them look larger than they are.

1. Hold the hand lens about 12 centimeters (5 in.) from your eye.

2. Bring the object toward you until it comes into focus.

Using a Thermometer

A thermometer measures the temperature of air and most liquids.

1. Place the thermometer in the liquid. Don't touch the thermometer any more than you need to. Never stir the liquid with the thermometer. If you are measuring the temperature of the air, make sure that the thermometer is not in line with a direct light source.

2. Move so that your eyes are even with the liquid in the thermometer.

3. If you are measuring a material that is not being heated or cooled, wait about two minutes for the reading to become stable. Find the scale line that meets the top of the liquid in the thermometer, and read the temperature.

4. If the material you are measuring is being heated or cooled, you will not be able to wait before taking your measurements. Measure as quickly as you can.

Caring for and Using a Microscope

A microscope is another tool that magnifies objects. A microscope can increase the detail you see by increasing the number of times an object is magnified.

Caring for a Microscope

• Always use two hands when you carry a microscope.

• Never touch any of the lenses of a microscope with your fingers.

Using a Microscope

1. Raise the eyepiece as far as you can using the coarse-adjustment knob. Place your slide on the stage.

2. Always start by using the lowest power. The lowest-power lens is usually the shortest. Start with the lens in the lowest position it can go without touching the slide.

3. Look through the eyepiece, and begin adjusting it upward with the coarse-adjustment knob. When the slide is close to being in focus, use the fine-adjustment knob.

4. When you want to use a higher-power lens, first focus the slide under low power. Then, watching carefully to make sure that the lens will not hit the slide, turn the higher-power lens into place. Use only the fine-adjustment knob when looking through the higher-power lens.

You may use a Brock microscope. This is a sturdy microscope that has only one lens.

1. Place the object to be viewed on the stage.

2. Look through the eyepiece, and begin raising the tube until the object comes into focus.

A Light Microscope

A Brock Microscope

Pans

Middle mark

Standard masses

Using a Balance

Use a balance to measure an object's mass. Mass is the amount of matter an object has.

1. Look at the pointer on the base to make sure the empty pans are balanced.

2. Place the object you wish to measure in the left pan.

3. Add the standard masses to the other pan. As you add masses, you should see the pointer move. When the pointer is at the middle mark, the pans are balanced.

4. Add the numbers on the masses you used. The total is the mass in grams of the object you measured.

Using a Spring Scale

Use a spring scale to measure forces such as the pull of gravity on objects. You measure weight and other forces in units called newtons (N).

Measuring the Weight of an Object

1. Hook the spring scale to the object.

2. Lift the scale and object with a smooth motion. Do not jerk them upward.

3. Wait until any motion of the spring comes to a stop. Then read the number of newtons from the scale.

Measuring the Force to Move an Object

1. With the object resting on a table, hook the spring scale to it.

2. Pull the object smoothly across the table. Do not jerk the object.

3. As you pull, read the number of newtons you are using to pull the object.

Beaker   **Graduate**

Measuring Liquids

Use a beaker, a measuring cup, or a graduate to measure liquids accurately.

1. Pour the liquid you want to measure into a measuring container. Put your measuring container on a flat surface, with the measuring scale facing you.

2. Look at the liquid through the container. Move so that your eyes are even with the surface of the liquid in the container.

3. To read the volume of the liquid, find the scale line that is even with the surface of the liquid.

4. If the surface of the liquid is not exactly even with a line, estimate the volume of the liquid. Decide which line the liquid is closer to, and use that number.

Using a Ruler or Meterstick

Use a ruler or meterstick to measure distances and to find lengths of objects.

1. Place the zero mark or end of the ruler or meterstick next to one end of the distance or object you want to measure.

2. On the ruler or meterstick, find the place next to the other end of the distance or object.

3. Look at the scale on the ruler or meterstick. This will show the distance you want or the length of the object.

Using a Timing Device

Use a timing device such as a stopwatch to measure time.

1. Reset the stopwatch to zero.

2. When you are ready to begin timing, press start.

3. As soon as you are ready to stop timing, press stop.

4. The numbers on the dial or display show how many minutes, seconds, and parts of seconds have passed.

Using a Computer

A computer can help you communicate with others and can help you get information. It is a tool you can use to write reports, make graphs and charts, and do research.

Writing Reports

To write a report with a computer, use a word processing software program. After you are in the program, type your report. By using certain keys and the mouse, you can control how the words look, move words, delete or add words and copy them, check your spelling, and print your report.

Save your work to the desktop or hard disk of the computer, or to a floppy disk. You can go back to your saved work later if you want to revise it.

There are many reasons for revising your work. You may find new information to add or mistakes you want to correct. You may want to change the way you report your information because of who will read it. Computers make revising easy. You delete what you don't want, add the new parts, and then save. You can save different versions of your work if you want to.

For a science lab report, it is important to show the same kinds of information each time. With a computer, you can make a general format for a lab report, save the format, and then use it again and again.

Making Graphs and Charts

You can make a graph or chart with most word processing software programs. Or, you can use special software programs such as Data ToolKit or Graph Links. With Graph Links you can make pictographs and circle, bar, line, and double-line graphs.

First, decide what kind of graph or chart will best communicate your data. Sometimes it's easiest to do this by sketching your ideas on paper. Then you can decide what format and categories you need for your graph or chart. Choose that format for the program. Then type your information. Most software programs include a tutor that gives you step-by-step directions for making a graph or chart.

Doing Research

Computers can help you find current information from all over the world through the Internet. The Internet connects thousands of computer sites that have been set up by schools, libraries, museums, and many other organizations.

Get permission from an adult before you log on to the Internet. Find out the rules for Internet use at school or at home. Then log on and go to a search engine, which will help you find what you need. Type in keywords, words that tell the subject of your search. If you get too much information that isn't exactly about the topic, make your keywords more specific. When you find the information you need, save it or print it.

Harcourt Science tells you about many Internet sites related to what you are studying. To find out about these sites, called Web sites, look for Technology Links in the lessons in this book.

If you need to contact other people to help in your research, you can use e-mail. Log into your e-mail program, type the address of the person you want to reach, type your message, and send it. Be sure to have adult permission before sending or receiving e-mail.

Another way to use a computer for research is to access CD-ROMs. These are discs that look like music CDs. CD-ROMs can hold huge amounts of data, including words, still pictures, audio, and video. Encyclopedias, dictionaries, almanacs, and other sources of information are available on CD-ROMs. These computer discs are valuable resources for your research.

Measurement Systems

SI Measures (Metric)

Temperature
Ice melts at 0 degrees Celsius (°C)
Water freezes at 0°C
Water boils at 100°C

Length and Distance
1000 meters (m) = 1 kilometer (km)
100 centimeters (cm) = 1 m
10 millimeters (mm) = 1 cm

Force
1 newton (N) = 1 kilogram $\times$
   1 meter/second/second (kg-m/s^2)

Volume
1 cubic meter (m^3) = 1m $\times$ 1m $\times$ 1m
1 cubic centimeter (cm^3) =
   1 cm $\times$ 1 cm $\times$ 1 cm
1 liter (L) = 1000 milliliters (mL)
1 cm^3 = 1 mL

Area
1 square kilometer (km^2) =
   1 km $\times$ 1 km
1 hectare = 10,000 m^2

Mass
1000 grams (g) = 1 kilogram (kg)
1000 milligrams (mg) = 1 g

Rates (Metric and Customary)
kmh = kilometers per hour
m/s = meters per second
mph = miles per hour

Customary Measures

Volume of Fluids
8 fluid ounces (fl oz) = 1 cup (c)
2 c = 1 pint (pt)
2 pt = 1 quart (qt)
4 qt = 1 gallon (gal)

Temperature
Ice melts at 32 degrees
   Fahrenheit (°F)
Water freezes at 32°F
Water boils at 212°F

Length and Distance
12 inches (in.) = 1 foot (ft)
3 ft = 1 yard (yd)
5280 ft = 1 mile (mi)

Weight
16 ounces (oz) = 1 pound (lb)
2000 pounds = 1 ton (T)

Health Handbook

Good Nutrition

The Food Guide Pyramid

No one food or food group supplies all the nutrients you need. That's why it's important to eat a variety of foods from all the food groups. The Food Guide Pyramid can help you choose healthful foods in the right amounts. By choosing more foods from the groups at the bottom of the pyramid, and few foods from the group at the top, you will eat nutrient-rich foods that provide your body with energy to grow and develop.

Fats, oils, and sweets
Eat sparingly.

Meat, poultry, fish, dried beans, eggs, and nuts
2–3 servings

Milk, yogurt, and cheese 2–3 servings

Fruits
2–4 servings

Vegetables
3–5 servings

Breads, cereals, rice, and pasta 6–11 servings

Understanding Serving Size

The Food Guide Pyramid suggests a number of servings to eat each day from each group. But a serving isn't necessarily the amount you eat at a meal. A plate full of macaroni and cheese may contain three or four servings of pasta (macaroni) and three servings of cheese. That's about half your bread group servings and all your milk servings at one sitting! The table below can help you estimate the number of servings you are eating.

Food Group	Amount of Food in One Serving	Easy Ways to Estimate Serving Size
Bread, Cereal, Rice, and Pasta Group	$\frac{1}{2}$ cup cooked pasta, rice, or cereal 1 ounce ready-to-eat (dry) cereal 1 slice bread, $\frac{1}{2}$ bagel	ice-cream scoop large handful of plain cereal or a small handful of cereal with raisins and nuts
Vegetable Group	1 cup of raw, leafy vegetables $\frac{1}{2}$ cup other vegetables, cooked or chopped raw $\frac{3}{4}$ cup vegetable juice $\frac{1}{2}$ cup tomato sauce	about the size of a fist ice-cream scoop
Fruit Group	medium apple, pear, or orange $\frac{1}{2}$ large banana, or one medium banana $\frac{1}{2}$ cup chopped or cooked fruit $\frac{3}{4}$ cup of fruit juice	about the size of a baseball
Milk, Yogurt, and Cheese Group	$1\frac{1}{2}$ ounces of natural cheese 2 ounces of processed cheese 1 cup of milk or yogurt	about the size of two dominoes $1\frac{1}{2}$ slices of packaged cheese
Meat, Poultry, Fish, Dried Beans, Eggs, and Nuts Group	3 ounces of lean meat, chicken, or fish 2 tablespoons peanut butter $\frac{1}{2}$ cup of cooked dried beans	about the size of your palm
Fats, Oils, and Sweets Group	1 teaspoon of margarine or butter	about the size of the tip of your thumb

Preparing Foods Safely

Fight Bacteria

You probably already know to throw away food that smells bad or looks moldy. But food doesn't have to look or smell bad to make you ill. To keep your food safe and yourself from becoming ill, follow the procedures shown in the picture below. And remember—when in doubt, throw it out!

Food Safety Tips

Tips for Preparing Food

- Wash hands in hot, soapy water before preparing food. It's also a good idea to wash hands after preparing each dish.
- Defrost meat in the microwave or the refrigerator. Do NOT defrost meat on the kitchen counter.
- Keep raw meat, poultry, fish, and their juices away from other food.
- Wash cutting boards, knives, and countertops immediately after cutting up meat, poultry, or fish. Never use the same cutting board for meats and vegetables without thoroughly washing the board first.

Tips for Cooking Food

- Cook all food thoroughly, especially meat. Cooking food completely kills bacteria that can make you ill.
  - Red meats should be cooked to a temperature of 160°F. Poultry should be cooked to 180°F. When done, fish flakes easily with a fork.
  - Eggs should be cooked until the yolks are firm. Never eat food that contains raw eggs. Never eat cookie dough made with raw eggs.

Tips for Cleaning Up the Kitchen

- Wash all dishes, utensils, and countertops with hot, soapy water. Use a disinfectant soap, if possible.
- Store leftovers in small containers that will cool quickly in the refrigerator. Don't leave leftovers on the counter to cool.

Being Physically Active

Planning Your Weekly Activities

Being active every day is important for your overall health. Physical activity strengthens your body systems and helps you manage stress and maintain a healthful weight. The Activity Pyramid, like the Food Guide Pyramid, can help you choose a variety of activities in the right amounts to keep your body strong and healthy.

The Activity Pyramid

Sitting for more than thirty minutes at a time: Only Once in a While

Flexibility and Strength: Two to Three Times a Week

Light Exercise: Two to Three Times a Week

Twenty-plus minutes of continuous aerobic activity: Three to Five Times a Week

Stay active: Every Day

Guidelines for a Good Workout

There are three things you should do every time you are going to exercise—warm up, workout, and cool down.

Warm-Up When you warm up, your heart rate, respiration rate, and body temperature gradually increase and more blood begins to flow to your muscles. As your body warms up, your flexibility increases, helping you avoid muscle stiffness after exercising. People who warm up are also less prone to exercise-related injuries. Your warm-up should include five minutes of stretching, and five minutes of a low-level form of your workout exercise. For example, if you are going to run for your primary exercise, you should spend five minutes stretching, concentrating on your legs and lower back, and five minutes walking before you start running.

Workout The main part of your exercise routine should be an aerobic exercise that lasts twenty to thirty minutes. Some common aerobic exercises include walking, bicycling, jogging, swimming, cross-country skiing, jumping rope, dancing, and playing racket sports. You should choose an activity that is fun for you and that you will enjoy doing over a long period of time. You may want to mix up the types of activities you do. This helps you work different muscle groups, and provides a better overall workout.

Cool-Down When you finish your aerobic exercise, you need to give your body time to return to normal. You also need to stretch again. This portion of your workout is called a cool-down. Start your cool-down with three to five minutes of low-level activity. For example, if you have been running, you may want to jog and then walk during this time. Then do stretching exercises to prevent soreness and stiffness.

Warm-Up and Cool-Down Stretches

Before you exercise, you should always warm up your muscles. The warm-up stretches shown here should be held for at least fifteen to twenty seconds and repeated at least three times. At the end of your workout, spend about two minutes repeating some of these stretches.

▶ **Hurdler's Stretch** HINT—Keep the toes of your extended leg pointed up.

▼ **Sit-and-Reach Stretch** HINT—Remember to bend at the waist. Keep your eyes on your toes!

▲ **Shoulder and Chest Stretch** HINT—Pulling your hands slowly toward the floor makes this stretch more effective. Keep your elbows straight, but not locked!

▲ **Upper Back and Shoulder Stretch**
HINT—Try to stretch your hand down
so that it lies flat against your back.

▼ **Thigh Stretch** HINT—Keep both
hands flat on the floor. Try to lean
as far forward as you can.

▲ **Calf Stretch** HINT—Remember to keep both
feet on the floor during this stretch. Try
changing the distance between your feet. Is
the stretch better for you when your legs
are closer together or farther apart?

Tips for Stretching

- Never bounce when stretching.
- Remember to hold each stretch for fifteen to twenty seconds.
- Breathe normally. This helps your body get the oxygen it needs.
- Stretch only until you feel a slight pull, NOT until it hurts.

Being Physically Active

Building a Strong Heart and Lungs

Aerobic activities, those that cause deep breathing and a fast heart rate for at least twenty minutes, help both your heart and your lungs. Because your heart is a muscle, it gets stronger with exercise. A strong heart doesn't have to work as hard to pump blood to the rest of your body. Exercise also allows your lungs to hold more air. With a strong heart and lungs, your cells get oxygen faster and your body works more efficiently.

◀ **Swimming** Swimming may provide the best overall body workout of any sport. It uses all the major muscle groups, and improves flexibility. The risk of injury is low, because the water supports your weight, greatly reducing stress on the joints. Just be sure to swim only when a lifeguard is present.

▶ **In-Line Skating** In-line skating gives your heart and lungs a great workout. Remember to always wear a helmet when skating. Always wear protective pads on your elbows and knees, and guards on your wrists, too. Learning how to skate, stop, and fall correctly will make you less prone to injuries.

▶ **Tennis** To get the best aerobic workout from tennis, you should run as fast, far, and hard as you can during the game. Move away from the ball so that you can step into it as you hit it. Finally, try to involve your entire body in every move.

▲ **Bicycling** Bicycling provides good aerobic activity that places little stress on the joints. It's also a great way to see the countryside. Be sure to use a bike that fits and to learn and follow the rules of the road. And *always* wear your helmet!

▶ **Walking** A fast-paced walk is a terrific way to build your endurance. The only equipment you need is a good pair of shoes and clothes appropriate for the weather. Walking with a friend can make this exercise a lot of fun.

Fire Safety

Fires cause more deaths than any other type of disaster. But a fire doesn't have to be deadly if you prepare your home and follow some basic safety rules.

- Install smoke detectors outside sleeping areas and on any additional floors of your home. Be sure to test the smoke detectors once a month and change the batteries in each detector twice a year.

- Keep a fire extinguisher on each floor of your home. Check monthly to make sure each is properly charged.

- Work with your family to make a fire escape plan for each room of your home. Ideally, there should be two routes out of each room. Sleeping areas are most important, because most fires happen at night. Plan to use stairs only; elevators can be dangerous in a fire.

- Pick a place outside for everyone to meet. Designate one person to call the fire department or 911 from a neighbor's home.

- Practice crawling low to avoid smoke. If your clothes catch fire, follow the three steps listed below.

1. STOP

2. DROP

3. ROLL

Earthquake Safety

An earthquake is a strong shaking of the ground. The tips below can help you and your family stay safe in an earthquake.

Before an Earthquake	During an Earthquake	After an Earthquake
• Secure tall, heavy furniture, such as bookcases, to the wall. Store the heaviest items on the lowest shelves. • Check for potential fire risks. Bolt down gas appliances, and use flexible hosing and connections for both gas and water utilities. • Reinforce and anchor overhead light fixtures to help keep them from falling.	• If you are outdoors, stay outdoors and move away from buildings and utility wires. • If you are indoors, take cover under a heavy desk or table or in a doorway. Stay away from glass doors and windows and heavy objects that might fall. • If you are in a car, drive to an open area away from buildings and overpasses.	• Continue to watch for falling objects as aftershocks shake the area. • Adults should have the building checked for hidden structural problems. • Check for broken gas, electric, and water lines. If you smell gas, an adult should shut off the gas main and leave the area. Report the leak.

Thunderstorm Safety

Thunderstorms are severe storms. Lightning associated with thunderstorms can injure or kill people, cause fires, and damage property. Here are some thunderstorm safety tips.

• **If you are inside, stay there.** The best place to take cover is inside a building.

• **If you are outside, try to take shelter.** If possible, get into a closed car or truck. If you can't take shelter, get into a ditch or low area, if possible.

• **If you are outside, stay away from tall objects.** Don't stand under a lone tree, in an open field, on a beach, or on a hilltop. Find a low place to stay.

• **Stay away from water.** Lightning is attracted to water, and water conducts electricity.

• **Listen for weather bulletins and updates.** The storms that produce lightning may also produce tornadoes. Be ready to take shelter in a basement or interior hallway away from windows and doors.

First Aid

The tips on the next few pages can help you provide simple first aid to others or yourself. Always tell an adult about any injuries that occur.

For Choking . . .

If someone else is choking . . .

1. Recognize the Universal Choking Sign—grasping the throat with both hands. This sign means a person is choking and needs help.

2. Stand behind the choking person, and put your arms around his or her waist. Place your fist above the person's belly button.
Grab your fist with your other hand.

3. Pull your hands toward yourself, and give five quick, hard, upward thrusts on the person's stomach.

If you are choking when alone . . .

1. Make a fist, and place it above your belly button. Grab your fist with your other hand. Pull your hands up with a quick, hard thrust.

2. Or, keep your hands on your belly, lean your body over the back of a chair or over a counter, and shove your fist in and up.

For Bleeding . . .

If someone else is bleeding . . .

Wash your hands with soap, if possible.

Put on protective gloves, if available.

Wash small wounds with soap and water. Do *not* wash serious wounds.

Place a clean gauze pad or cloth over the wound. Press firmly for ten minutes. Don't lift the gauze during this time.

If you don't have gloves, have the injured person hold the gauze or cloth in place with his or her hand for ten minutes.

If after ten minutes the bleeding has stopped, bandage the wound. If the bleeding has not stopped, continue pressing on the wound and get help.

If you are bleeding . . .

- Wash your wound if it is a small cut. If it is a serious wound, do *not* wash it.
- Place a gauze pad or clean cloth over the wound, and hold it firmly in place for ten minutes. Don't lift the gauze or cloth until ten minutes has passed.
- If you have no gauze or cloth, apply pressure with your hand.
- If after ten minutes the bleeding has stopped, bandage the wound. If the bleeding has not stopped, continue pressing on the wound and get help.

Sense Organs

Eyes

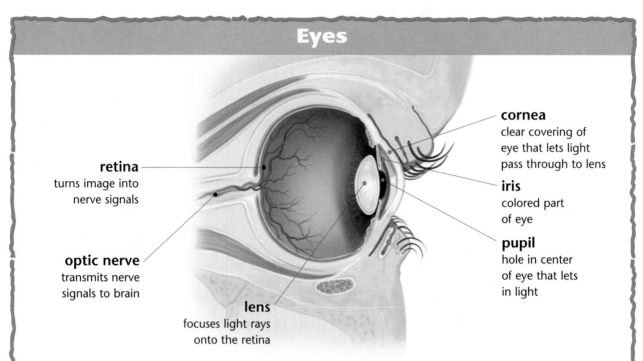

retina
turns image into
nerve signals

optic nerve
transmits nerve
signals to brain

lens
focuses light rays
onto the retina

cornea
clear covering of
eye that lets light
pass through to lens

iris
colored part
of eye

pupil
hole in center
of eye that lets
in light

Light rays bounce off objects and enter your eye through your pupil. A lens inside your eye focuses the light rays, and the image of the object is projected onto the retina at the back of your eye. In the retina the image is turned into nerve signals. Your brain analyzes the signals to tell you what you're seeing.

Ears

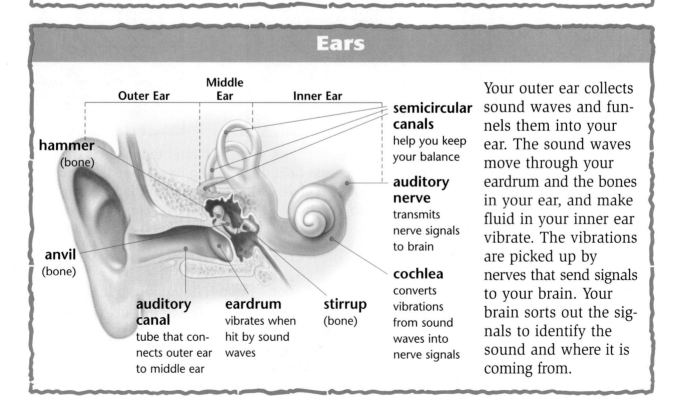

Outer Ear

Middle
Ear

Inner Ear

hammer
(bone)

anvil
(bone)

**auditory
canal**
tube that con-
nects outer ear
to middle ear

eardrum
vibrates when
hit by sound
waves

stirrup
(bone)

**semicircular
canals**
help you keep
your balance

**auditory
nerve**
transmits
nerve signals
to brain

cochlea
converts
vibrations
from sound
waves into
nerve signals

Your outer ear collects sound waves and funnels them into your ear. The sound waves move through your eardrum and the bones in your ear, and make fluid in your inner ear vibrate. The vibrations are picked up by nerves that send signals to your brain. Your brain sorts out the signals to identify the sound and where it is coming from.

Nose

skull

nasal bone

olfactory (sense of smell) bulb
group of nerves that carry information to olfactory tract

nostrils
openings to nose

olfactory tract
carries information from olfactory bulb to brain

mucous membrane
warms and moistens air you breathe in

nasal cavity
main opening inside nose

When you breathe in, air is swept upward to nerve cells in your nasal cavity. Your nasal cavity is the upper part of your nose inside your skull. Different nerve cells respond to different odors in the air and send signals to your brain.

Skin

The skin is made of three layers, the outer epidermis, the middle dermis, and the lower subcutaneous layer. Nerve cells in your skin signal your brain about stimuli (conditions around you) that affect your skin.

Merkel's endings
respond to medium pressure

epidermis

dermis

subcutaneous layer

Krause's endings
cold and mechanoreceptors

Pacini's endings
react to heavy pressure

free nerve endings
react to painful stimuli

Meissner's endings
respond to light pressure and small, fast vibration

Ruffini's endings
sense changes in temperature and pressure

Caring for Your Senses

Injuries to your brain can affect your senses. Protect your brain by wearing safety belts in the car and helmets when playing sports or riding your bike.

Tongue

Your tongue is covered with about 10,000 tiny nerve cells, or taste buds, that pick out tastes in the things you eat and drink. Different taste buds respond to different tastes and send signals to your brain.

taste buds

Activity

With a partner, toss a table tennis ball back and forth 15 times. Then put a patch over one eye and toss the ball again. Was it easier to catch the ball when you had both eyes open or only one eye open?

Skeletal System

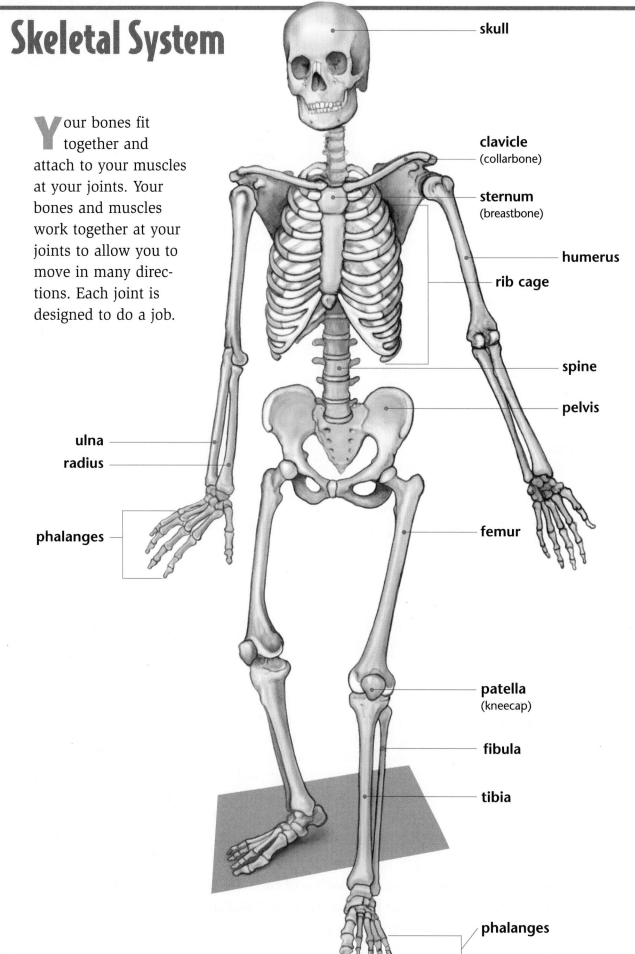

Your bones fit together and attach to your muscles at your joints. Your bones and muscles work together at your joints to allow you to move in many directions. Each joint is designed to do a job.

skull

clavicle
(collarbone)

sternum
(breastbone)

humerus

rib cage

spine

pelvis

ulna

radius

phalanges

femur

patella
(kneecap)

fibula

tibia

phalanges

Bones and Joints

Kinds of Bones Bones come in four basic shapes: long, short, flat, and irregular. Long bones, such as those in your legs, arms, and fingers, are narrow with large ends and are slightly curved. These bones can support the most weight. Short bones, found in your wrists and ankles, are chunky and wide. These bones allow maximum movement around a joint. Flat bones, such as your skull and ribs, are platelike. They provide protection for especially delicate parts of your body. Irregular bones, such as those in your spine and your ears, have unique shapes that don't fit into any other category.

flat bone (rib)

irregular bone
(vertebra)

short bone
(wrist)

muscle

tendons

long bone
(femur)

BACK

FRONT

bone

ligament

bone

Parts of a Joint A joint has several parts. Ligaments are tough, elastic bands that attach one bone to another. Ligaments give flexibility for bending and stretching. Cartilage is a cushioning material at the ends of bones that meet in a joint. Cartilage helps the bones move smoothly and absorbs some of the impact when you move. Tendons are dense cords that connect bones to muscles.

Caring for Your Skeletal System

- Move and flex your joints regularly through exercise. If you don't, they might get injured or become stiff and sore. Be sure to warm up and cool down whenever you exercise.

- You can injure a joint by using it too much or moving it in a way it is not designed to move.

- Calcium is necessary for healthy bones. You can get calcium from milk, dairy products like yogurt and cheese, or some dark green, leafy vegetables.

Activities

1. **Build a model of a long bone and a short bone. Use a sheet of construction paper. Cut off a strip about 1 inch (2.5 cm) wide. Roll the strip and the remainder of the sheet into tight cylinders. Test their strength by putting objects on top of them.**

2. **Make a model of a joint. Cut out two strips of cardboard and join them together using a round metal fastener. What does the fastener represent?**

Muscular System

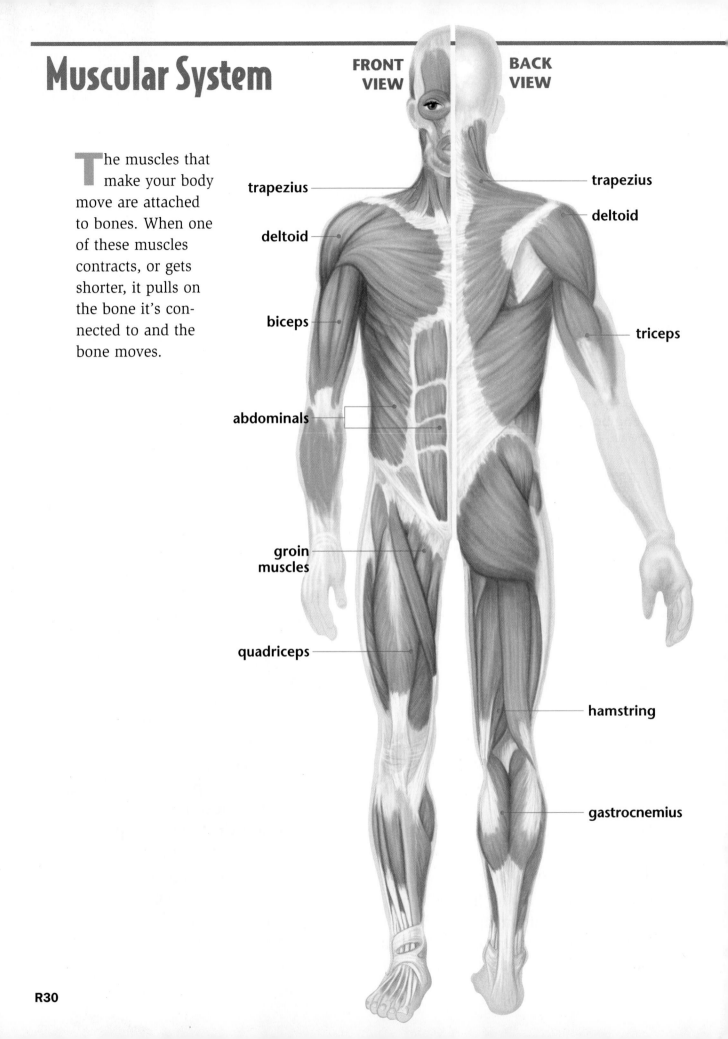

FRONT VIEW

BACK VIEW

The muscles that make your body move are attached to bones. When one of these muscles contracts, or gets shorter, it pulls on the bone it's connected to and the bone moves.

trapezius

deltoid

biceps

abdominals

groin muscles

quadriceps

trapezius

deltoid

triceps

hamstring

gastrocnemius

Muscles and Bones

How a Muscle Connects to a Bone A muscle has a bulging middle and narrow ends called tendons. The tendons attach the muscle to a bone.

Muscles Work in Pairs Your muscles can only pull your bones. They cannot push them. So, many muscles make your body move by working in pairs. One muscle pulls one way and another muscle pulls the opposite way. For example, when the large muscle in the back of your thigh contracts, it pulls on the back of your tibia ("shin" bone) and your knee bends. When the muscle in the front of your thigh contracts, it pulls on the front of your tibia and your leg straightens again.

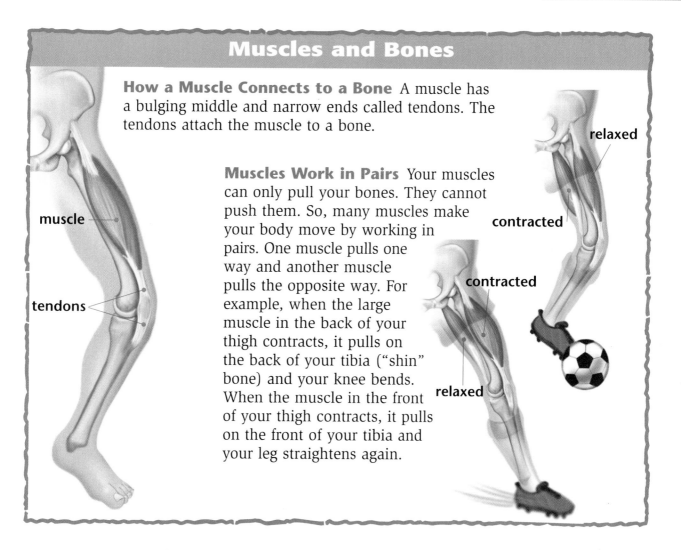

muscle

tendons

relaxed

contracted

contracted

relaxed

Caring for Your Muscular System

- Take a brisk five-minute walk and do gentle stretches before you start to play a sport to loosen your tendons, ligaments, and muscles and help prevent injuries.

- You should ease out of exercise too. Because your muscles contract during exercise, they need to be stretched when you finish.

Activities

1. Wrap your fingers around your upper arm, so you can feel both the top and bottom of your arm. Slowly bend and straighten your arm several times. Which muscles are working as a pair?

2. Write a paragraph about which muscles work in pairs when you play your favorite sport.

Digestive System

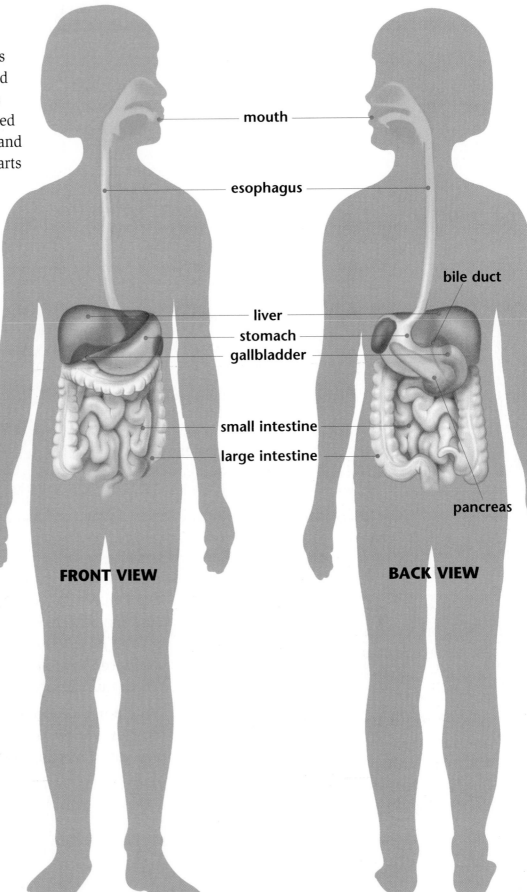

igestion is the process of breaking food into tiny pieces that are absorbed by your blood and carried to all parts of your body. Each part of your digestive system does a different job.

mouth

esophagus

liver

stomach

gallbladder

small intestine

large intestine

FRONT VIEW

bile duct

pancreas

BACK VIEW

Some Digestive Organs

Esophagus When you swallow, the chewed and moistened food goes down a tube to your stomach. This tube, called the esophagus, is about 10 inches (25.4 cm) long. The food is pushed down the esophagus by a squeezing muscle action, similar to squeezing a tube of toothpaste. When you swallow, your airway is protected by the epiglottis and your vocal cords. If you try to talk and swallow, you cough or choke.

esophagus

stomach

salivary glands

Stomach The walls of your stomach are made of very strong muscles. Once food reaches the stomach, more chemicals are added that digest the food more thoroughly. At the same time, the stomach muscles squeeze the liquid food mixture.

Salivary Glands When you chew your food, it is moistened with saliva. The saliva comes from three sets of glands: one set under your tongue, one on each side of your head in front of your ear, and one on each side of your head under your jaw.

Food leaves your stomach in two stages. First, the top of your stomach squeezes the liquid food mixture into the small intestine. Second, the solid particles are pushed into the small intestine by the muscles in the lower part of your stomach.

Saliva is mostly water, but it does contain a chemical called *amylase* that helps digest starches. Saliva also helps keep your mouth clean and helps control infection.

Caring for Your Digestive System

- Try to drink at least six to eight glasses of water a day. Water helps food move through your digestive system.

- Chew your food thoroughly. Large pieces of food are more difficult to digest, and the large pieces might cause you to choke.

Activities

1. Chew a cracker and then hold it in your mouth for about a minute. Move it around. How has the taste changed?

2. Record the amount of water you drink every day for three days. Are you drinking at least six glasses of water every day?

Circulatory System

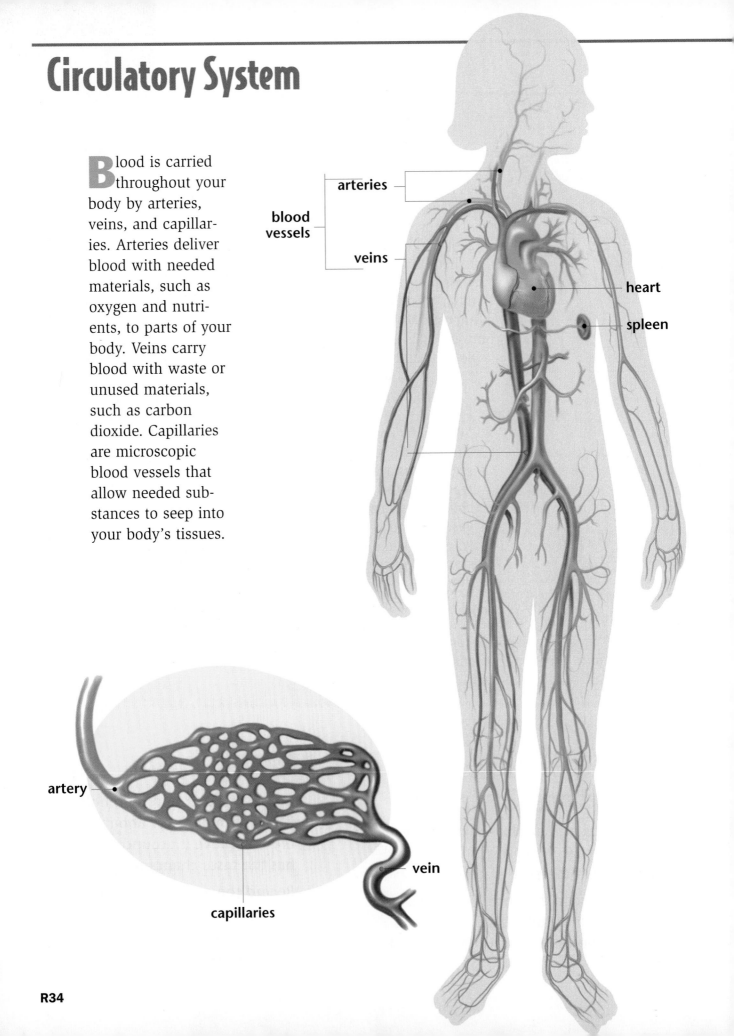

Blood is carried throughout your body by arteries, veins, and capillaries. Arteries deliver blood with needed materials, such as oxygen and nutrients, to parts of your body. Veins carry blood with waste or unused materials, such as carbon dioxide. Capillaries are microscopic blood vessels that allow needed substances to seep into your body's tissues.

blood vessels

arteries

veins

heart

spleen

artery

capillaries

vein

How Blood Moves in Your Heart

Your heart has four chambers. The upper chambers are called atria. The lower chambers are called ventricles. Here is how blood moves through the heart.

1. Blood comes from your body into the right atrium. Blood comes from your lungs into the left atrium. The atria squeeze.

2. Two valves open, and the blood moves into the ventricles. When both ventricles have filled with blood, the valves shut. The ventricles squeeze.

3. Two different valves then open. The right ventricle sends blood through one valve to the lungs. The left ventricle sends blood through the other valve to the body. The "lub-dub" of your heartbeat is the sound of valves slamming shut.

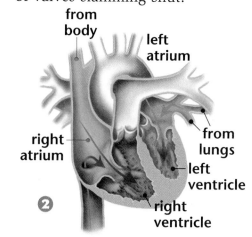

Caring for Your Circulatory System

- Don't ever smoke. Smoking narrows blood vessels and can cause high blood pressure.

- Remember, your heart is a constantly working muscle. Exercise strengthens your heart by making it beat harder, which makes the heart muscles larger and able to push more blood with each "squeeze" or "beat."

Activities

1. Take your pulse for ten seconds. Multiply that number by six to find how many times your heart beats in a minute. How many times does your heart beat in a day?

2. Feel your pulse in various places—your wrist, your neck, behind your knee. Where is it easiest to feel?

Respiratory System

Your lungs are filled with air tubes, air sacs, and blood vessels. The air tubes and blood vessels in your lungs divide until they are very small. At the ends of the tiny air tubes are air sacs called alveoli. The smallest blood vessels, capillaries, surround the alveoli.

Blood coming from your body (blue) delivers waste gases to your lungs. It then picks up oxygen (red) and takes it to your body.

nose

mouth

trachea
(windpipe)

air tubes

lungs

blood vessels

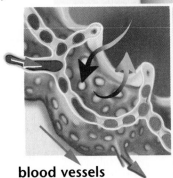

blood vessels
surrounding alveoli

alveoli
(air sacs)

How Oxygen Travels to Your Body Parts

Your heart and lungs are connected by veins and arteries. The blood your heart pumps out to the rest of your body comes directly from your lungs, where it is filled with oxygen. The blood delivers the oxygen and picks up carbon dioxide. When the blood returns to your heart, it needs oxygen. Your heart sends the blood to your lungs, where oxygen is added and carbon dioxide is removed.

Tiny blood vessels in your lungs release carbon dioxide into the alveoli and absorb oxygen from the air inside the alveoli. The replenished blood returns to the heart, and the process starts over.

It takes just one minute for blood to circulate around your entire body.

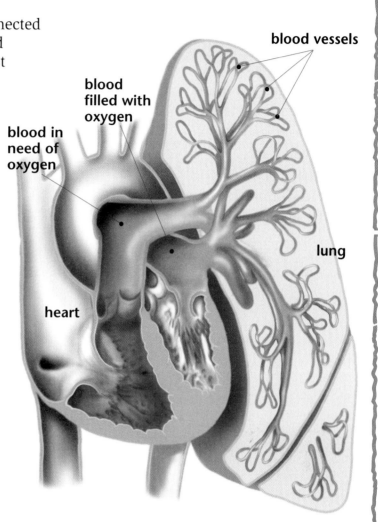

blood vessels

blood filled with oxygen

blood in need of oxygen

lung

heart

Caring for Your Respiratory System

- Don't ever smoke. The tar in cigarettes damages the lungs. Avoid environmental tobacco smoke too. Inhaling someone else's smoke can be as dangerous as smoking a cigarette yourself, especially for people with asthma.

- If you exercise so hard that you can't talk or you feel dizzy, your body is not getting enough oxygen. Slow down.

Activities

1. List three sports you think would exercise your respiratory system the most and three sports you think would exercise it the least.

2. Survey people you know about their thoughts on cigarettes and health. Record their answers.

3. Write the words to a jingle for an anti-smoking commercial.

Nervous System

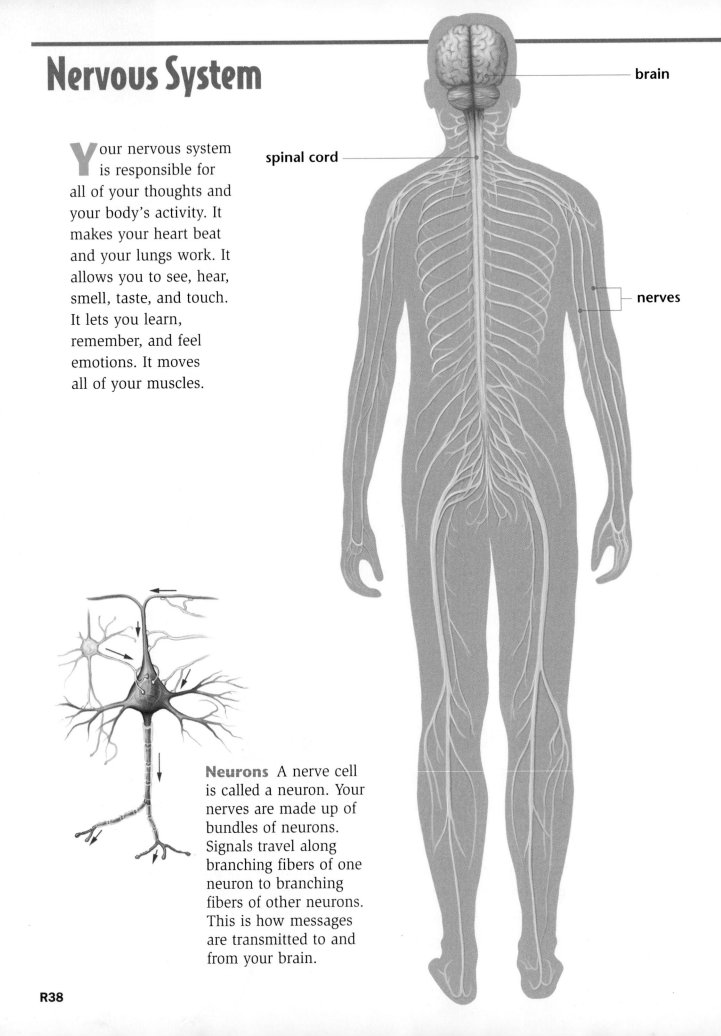

Your nervous system is responsible for all of your thoughts and your body's activity. It makes your heart beat and your lungs work. It allows you to see, hear, smell, taste, and touch. It lets you learn, remember, and feel emotions. It moves all of your muscles.

brain

spinal cord

nerves

Neurons A nerve cell is called a neuron. Your nerves are made up of bundles of neurons. Signals travel along branching fibers of one neuron to branching fibers of other neurons. This is how messages are transmitted to and from your brain.

Your Nervous System

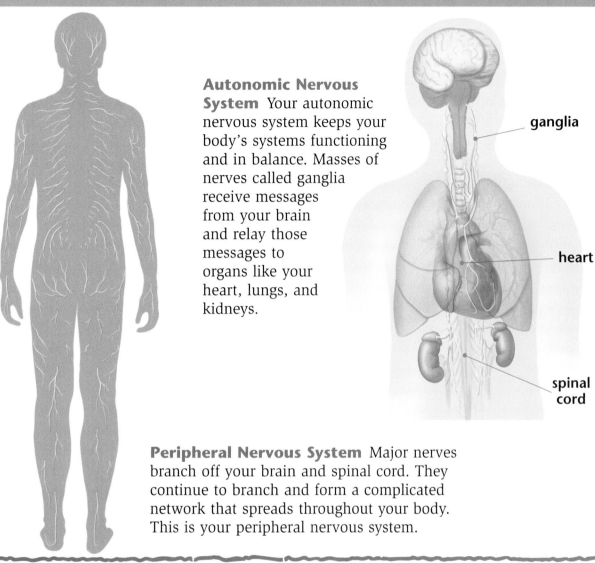

Autonomic Nervous System Your autonomic nervous system keeps your body's systems functioning and in balance. Masses of nerves called ganglia receive messages from your brain and relay those messages to organs like your heart, lungs, and kidneys.

ganglia

heart

spinal cord

Peripheral Nervous System Major nerves branch off your brain and spinal cord. They continue to branch and form a complicated network that spreads throughout your body. This is your peripheral nervous system.

Caring for Your Nervous System

- Do not take any drugs unless given by your parents or guardian or a doctor. Some drugs can affect your brain cells.

- Eat a well-balanced diet. Your nervous system cannot work properly without certain nutrients.

- Learning new skills builds new nerve connections in your brain.

Activities

1. Put one hand in a bowl of very warm water and one hand in a bowl of cold water. Then put both hands in a bowl of warm water. How does each hand feel?

2. Blindfold a friend. Touch your friend's back with two fingers and your friend's palm with two fingers. Can your friend tell how many fingers you used in each place?

Immune System and Endocrine System

Your immune system defends your body from harmful invaders, such as organisms that cause infection. White blood cells, which are your immune system's primary infection fighters, are produced in your bone marrow, thymus, lymph nodes, and spleen.

Tonsils Your tonsils are also lymph tissue. They produce white blood cells. When your body has an infection, lymph nodes can become infected. Infected lymph nodes become swollen and painful.

tonsils

thymus

lymph nodes

spleen

long bone marrow

Macrophage A macrophage is a type of white blood cell that eats harmful invader cells.

Caring for Your Immune System

One way to help your body fight disease is through immunization (shots that protect you from certain diseases). You were required to have some immunizations as an infant and "boosters" before you started school.

Activity

Find out what immunizations are recommended at various ages. What will you need next?

Your endocrine system works with your nervous system to help your body grow normally and work and react as it should. The endocrine system does this by releasing hormones into your bloodstream. Hormones are chemicals that deliver instructions to various organs and tissues.

pituitary gland
controls body's day-to-day functioning, long-term growth, and reproduction

thyroid gland
helps set the pace at which your body functions

parathyroid glands
control level of calcium in your blood

thymus gland

adrenal glands
produce a sudden, remarkable burst of energy in response to stress or danger

pancreas
helps regulate the amount of sugar in your bloodstream

Caring for Your Endocrine System

Some drugs, such as steroids, can harm your endocrine system. Avoid these drugs.

Activity

The next time you are startled, feel your heartbeat. How is it different from normal?

Glossary

This Glossary contains important science words and their definitions. Each word is respelled as it would be in a dictionary. When you see the ′ mark after a syllable, pronounce that syllable with more force than the other syllables. The page number at the end of the definition tells where to find the word in your book. The boldfaced letters in the examples in the Pronunciation Key that follows show how these letters are pronounced in the respellings after each glossary word.

PRONUNCIATION KEY

a	**a**dd, m**a**p	m	**m**ove, see**m**	u	**u**p, d**o**ne
ā	**a**ce, r**a**te	n	**n**ice, ti**n**	û(r)	b**ur**n, t**er**m
â(r)	c**are**, **air**	ng	ri**ng**, so**ng**	yo͞o	f**u**se, f**ew**
ä	p**a**lm, f**a**ther	o	**o**dd, h**o**t	v	**v**ain, e**v**e
b	**b**at, ru**b**	ō	**o**pen, s**o**	w	**w**in, a**w**ay
ch	**ch**eck, cat**ch**	ô	**o**rder, j**aw**	y	**y**et, **y**earn
d	**d**og, ro**d**	oi	**oi**l, b**oy**	z	**z**est, mu**s**e
e	**e**nd, p**e**t	ou	p**ou**t, n**ow**	zh	vi**s**ion, plea**s**ure
ē	**e**qual, tr**ee**	o͝o	t**oo**k, f**u**ll	ə	the schwa, an
f	**f**it, hal**f**	o͞o	p**oo**l, f**oo**d		unstressed vowel
g	**g**o, lo**g**	p	**p**it, sto**p**		representing the sound
h	**h**ope, **h**ate	r	**r**un, poo**r**		spelled
i	**i**t, g**i**ve	s	**s**ee, pa**ss**		*a* in **a**bove
ī	**i**ce, wr**i**te	sh	**s**ure, ru**sh**		*e* in sick**e**n
j	**j**oy, le**dg**e	t	**t**alk, si**t**		*i* in poss**i**ble
k	**c**ool, ta**k**e	th	**th**in, bo**th**		*o* in mel**o**n
l	**l**ook, ru**l**e	th	**th**is, ba**th**e		*u* in circ**u**s

Other symbols:
- • separates words into syllables
- ′ indicates heavier stress on a syllable
- ′ indicates light stress on a syllable

acceleration [ak•sel′ər•ā′shən] A change in motion caused by unbalanced forces or a change in velocity **(F13, F35)**

acid rain [as′id rān′] Precipitation resulting from pollution condensing into clouds and falling to Earth **(B99)**

action force [ak′shən fôrs′] The first force in the third law of motion **(F43)**

air pressure [âr′ presh′ər] The weight of air **(C65)**

alveoli [al•vē′ə•lē] Tiny air sacs located at the ends of bronchi in the lungs **(A18)**

angiosperm [an′jē•ō•spûrm′] A flowering plant **(A77)**

anthracite [an′thrə•sīt′] A hard, black rock; the fourth stage of coal formation **(C45)**

asexual reproduction [ā•sek′shōō•əl rē′prə•duk′shən] Reproduction by simple cell division **(A41)**

atmosphere [at′məs•fir] The layer of air that surrounds Earth **(C64)**

atom [at′əm] The smallest unit of an element that has all the properties of that element **(E40)**

axis [ak′sis] An imaginary line that passes through Earth's center and its North and South Poles **(D7)**

balanced forces [bal′ənst fôrs′əz] The forces acting on an object that are equal in size and opposite in direction, canceling each other out **(F12)**

biomass [bī′ō•mas′] Organic matter, such as wood, that is living or was recently alive **(F110)**

biome [bī′ōm′] A large-scale ecosystem **(B64)**

bitumen [bi•tōō′mən] A fairly hard, dark brown or black rock; the third stage of coal formation **(C45)**

bone marrow [bōn′ mar′ō] A connective tissue that produces red and white blood cells **(A24)**

capillaries [kap′ə•ler′ēz] The smallest blood vessels **(A17)**

carbon dioxide–oxygen cycle [kär′bən dī•ok′sīd′ ok′sə•jən sī′kəl] The process by which carbon and oxygen cycle among plants, animals, and the environment **(B8)**

cell [sel] The basic unit of structure and function of all living things **(A6)**

cell membrane [sel′ mem′brān′] The thin covering that encloses a cell and holds its parts together **(A8)**

cellular respiration [sel′yōō•lər res′pə•rā′shən] The process by which cells release the energy in food to carry on life processes **(A100)**

chemical bonds [kem′i•kəl bondz′] The forces that join atoms to each other **(F98)**

chlorophyll [klôr′ə•fil′] A pigment, or coloring matter, that helps plants use light energy to produce sugars **(A70)**

chromosome [krō′mə•sōm′] A threadlike strand inside the nucleus that is made up of DNA **(A39)**

climate [klī′mit] The average of all weather conditions through all seasons over a period of time **(C78)**

climate zone [klī′mit zōn′] A region throughout which yearly patterns of temperature, rainfall, and amount of sunlight are similar **(B64)**

climax community [klī′maks′ kə•myoo′nə•tē] The last stage of succession **(B93)**

combustibility [kəm•bus′tə•bil′ə•tē] The chemical property of being able to burn **(E24)**

community [kə•myoo′nə•tē] All the populations of organisms living together in an environment **(B28)**

competition [kom′pə•tish′ən] The contest among organisms for the limited resources of an ecosystem **(B42)**

compound [kom′pound] A substance made of the atoms of two or more different elements **(E48)**

condensation [kon′dən•sā′shən] The process by which a gas changes back into a liquid **(B14, C67, E17)**

conduction [kən•duk′shən] The direct transfer of heat between objects that touch **(F85)**

conductor [kən•duk′tər] A material that conducts electrons easily **(F70)**

conserving [kən•sûrv′ing] The saving or protecting of resources **(B104)**

consumer [kən•soo′mər] An organism in a community that must eat to get the energy it needs **(B34)**

continental drift [kon′tə•nen′təl drift′] A theory of how Earth's continents move over its surface **(C22)**

convection [kən•vek′shən] The transfer of heat as a result of the mixing of a liquid or a gas **(F85)**

core [kôr] The center of the Earth **(C15)**

corona [kə•rō′nə] The sun's atmosphere **(D33)**

cotyledons [kot′ə•lēd′ənz] The structures where food is stored in seeds **(A116)**

crust [krust] The thin, outer layer of Earth **(C14)**

current [kur′ənt] A stream of water that flows like a river through the ocean **(C96)**

cytoplasm [sīt′ō•plaz′əm] A jellylike substance containing many chemicals that keep a cell functioning **(A9)**

decomposer [dē′kəm•pōz′ər] Consumer that breaks down the tissues of dead organisms **(B35)**

density [den′sə•tē] The concentration of matter in an object **(E9)**

deposition [dep′ə•zish′ən] The process of dropping, or depositing, sediment in a new location **(C7)**

desalination [dē•sal′ə•nā′shən] The process of removing salt from sea water **(C112)**

diffusion [di•fyoo′zhən] The process by which many materials move in and out of cells **(A10)**

direct development [də•rekt′ di•vel′əp•mənt] A kind of growth where organisms keep the same body features as they grow larger **(A46)**

dominant trait [dom′ə•nənt trāt′] A strong trait **(A53)**

earthquake [ûrth′ kwāk′] A shaking of the ground caused by the sudden release of energy in Earth's crust **(C18)**

eclipse [i•klips′] The passing of one object through the shadow of another **(D8)**

ecosystem [ek′ō•sis′təm] A community and its physical environment together **(B28)**

electric charge [i•lek′trik chärj′] The charge obtained by an object when it gains or loses electrons **(F68)**

electric circuit [i•lek′trik sûr′kit] The path along which electrons can flow **(F71)**

electric current [i•lek′trik kûr′ənt] The flow of electrons from negatively charged objects to positively charged objects **(F69)**

electric force [i•lek′trik fôrs′] The attraction or repulsion of objects due to their charges **(F69)**

electromagnet [i•lek′trō•mag′nit] A temporary magnet made by passing electric current through a wire coiled around an iron bar **(F72)**

electron [ē•lek′tron′] A subatomic particle with a negative charge **(E39)**

element [el′ə•mənt] A substance made up of only one kind of atom **(E40)**

El Niño [el nēn′yō] A short-term climate change that occurs every two to ten years **(C81)**

embryo [em′brē•ō] The tiny plant inside a seed **(A116)**

endangered [en•dān′jərd] A term describing a population of organisms that is likely to become extinct if steps are not taken to save it **(B51)**

energy [en′ər•jē] The ability to cause changes in matter **(F62)**

energy pyramid [en′ər•jē pir′ə•mid] Shows the amount of energy available to pass from one level of a food chain to the next **(B38)**

epidermis [ep′ə•dûr′mis] The outer layer of cells of a leaf **(A96)**

erosion [i•rō′zhən] The process of moving sediment from one place to another **(C7)**

estuary [es′chōo•er′ē] The place where a freshwater river empties into an ocean **(B80, C102)**

evaporation [ē•vap′ə•rā′shən] The process by which a liquid changes into a gas **(B14, C67, E16)**

exotic [ik•sä′•tic] An imported or nonnative organism. **(B50)**

extinct [ik•stingkt′] No longer in existence; describes a species when the last individual of a population dies and that organism is gone forever **(B51)**

fault [fôlt] A break or place where pieces of Earth's crust move **(C18)**

fertilization [fûr′təl•ə•zā′shən] The joining of a male reproductive cell with a female reproductive cell **(A110)**

fiber [fī′bər] Any material that can be separated into threads **(A84)**

food chain [fōōd′ chān′] The ways in which the organisms in an ecosystem interact with one another according to what they eat **(B35)**

food web [fōōd′ web′] Shows the interactions among many different food chains in a single ecosystem **(B36)**

force [fôrs] A push or pull that causes an object to move, stop, or change direction **(F6)**

fossil [fos′əl] The remains or traces of past life found in sedimentary rock **(C23)**

fossil fuel [fos′əl fyōō′əl] A fuel formed from the remains of once-living organisms **(C42)**

friction [frik′shən] A force that opposes, or acts against, motion when two surfaces rub against each other **(F6)**

fusion energy [fyo͞o′zhən en′ər•jē] The energy released when the nuclei of two atoms are forced together to form a larger nucleus **(F112)**

galaxy [gal′ək•sē] A group of stars, gas, and dust **(D46)**

gas [gas] The state of matter that does not have a definite shape or volume **(E14)**

gene [jēn] Structures on a chromosome that contain the DNA code for a trait an organism inherits **(A54)**

geothermal energy [jē′ō•thûr′məl en′ər•jē] Heat from inside the Earth **(F111)**

germinate [jûr′mə•nāt′] To sprout as a seed does **(A118)**

global warming [glō′bəl wôrm′ing] The hypothesized rise in Earth's average temperature from excess carbon dioxide **(C82)**

grafting [graft′ing] A form of artificial reproduction that can produce desirable characteristics in woody plants **(A120)**

grain [grān] The seed of certain plants **(A82)**

gravitation [grav′i•tā′shən] The force that pulls all objects in the universe toward one another **(F8)**

gravitropism [grav′i•trō′piz•əm] A plant's response to gravity **(A105)**

greenhouse effect [grēn′hous′ i•fekt′] process by which the Earth's atmosphere absorbs heat **(C82)**

gymnosperm [jim′nə•spûrm′] Plant with unprotected seeds; conifer or cone-bearing plant **(A76)**

habitat [hab′ə•tat′] A place in an ecosystem where a population lives **(B29)**

headland [hed′land′] A hard, rocky point of land left when softer rock is washed away by the sea **(C103)**

heat [hēt] The transfer of thermal energy from one substance to another **(F84)**

humidity [hyo͞o•mid′ə•tē] A measure of the amount of water in the air **(C65)**

hydroelectric energy [hī′drō•ē•lek′trik en′ər•jē] Electricity generated from the force of moving water **(F104)**

individual [in′də•vij′o͞o•əl] A single organism in an environment **(B28)**

inertia [in•ûr′shə] The property of matter that keeps it moving in a straight line or keeps it at rest **(F41)**

inherited trait [in•her′it•əd trāt′] A characteristic that is passed from parent to offspring **(A52)**

instinct [in′stingkt] A behavior that an organism inherits **(B46)**

insulator [in′sə•lāt′ər] A material that does not carry electrons **(F71)**

intertidal zone [in′tər•tīd′əl zōn′] An area where the tide and churning waves provide a constant supply of oxygen and nutrients to living organisms **(B77)**

jetty [jet′ē] A wall-like structure made of rocks that sticks out into the ocean **(C104)**

joint [joint] A place where bones meet and are attached to each other and to muscles **(A24)**

kinetic energy [ki•net′ik en′ər•jē] The energy of motion, or energy in use **(F62)**

landform [land′fôrm′] A physical feature on Earth's surface **(C6)**

law of universal gravitation [lô′ uv yo͞on′ə•vûr′səl grav′i•tā′shən] Law that states that all objects in the universe are attracted to all other objects **(F49)**

learned behavior [lûrnd′ bē•hāv′yər] A behavior an animal learns from its parents **(B46)**

lens [lenz] A piece of clear material that bends, or refracts, light rays passing through it **(F77)**

life cycle [līf′ sī′kəl] The series of distinct stages of life that most organisms grow and mature through **(A46)**

ligament [lig′ə•mənt] One of the bands of connective tissue that hold a skeleton together **(A25)**

light-year [līt′yir′] The distance light travels in one Earth year; about 9.5 trillion km **(D47)**

lignite [lig′nīt′] A soft, brown rock; the second stage of coal formation **(C44)**

liquid [lik′wid] The state of matter that has a definite volume but no definite shape **(E14)**

local winds [lō′kəl windz′] The winds dependent upon local changes in temperature **(C73)**

machine [mə•shēn′] Something that makes work easier by changing the size or the direction of a force **(F20)**

magma [mag′mə] A hot, soft rock from Earth's lower mantle **(C16)**

magnetism [mag′nə•tiz′əm] The force of repulsion (pushing) or attraction (pulling) between poles of magnets **(F7)**

magnitude [mag′nə•to͞od] Brightness of stars **(D38)**

main sequence [mān′ sē′kwəns] A band of stars that includes most stars of average color, size, magnitude, and temperature **(D39)**

mantle [man′təl] The layer of rock beneath Earth's crust **(C14)**

mass [mas] The amount of matter in an object **(E7)**

mass movement [mas′ mo͞ov′mənt] The downhill movement of rock and soil because of gravity **(C9)**

matter [mat′ər] Anything that has mass and takes up space **(E6)**

meiosis [mī•ō′sis] The process that reduces the number of chromosomes in reproductive cells **(A42)**

metamorphosis [met′ə•môr′fə•sis] A change in the shape or characteristics of an organism's body as it grows **(A47)**

microclimate [mī′krō•klī′mit] The climate of a very small area **(C78)**

mitosis [mī•tō′sis] The process of cell division **(A39)**

molecule [mol′ə•kyo͞ol′] A grouping of two or more atoms joined together **(E40)**

momentum [mō•men′təm] A measure of how hard it is to slow down or stop an object **(F36)**

natural gas [nach′ər•əl gas′] A gas, methane, usually found with petroleum **(C43)**

natural resource [nach′ər•əl rē′sôrs′] Any of the useful minerals and other materials that people take from the Earth **(C36)**

near-shore zone [nir′shôr′ zōn′] The area beyond the breaking waves that extends to waters that are about 180 m deep **(B77)**

nephrons [nef′ronz′] Tubes inside the kidneys where urea and water diffuse from the blood **(A20)**

net force [net′ fôrs′] The result of two or more forces acting together on an object **(F14)**

neuron [noŏr′on′] A specialized cell that can receive information and transmit it to other cells **(A26)**

neutron [noō′tron′] A subatomic particle with no charge **(E39)**

niche [nich] The role each population has in its habitat **(B29)**

nitrogen cycle [nī′trə•jən sī′kəl] The cycle in which nitrogen gas is changed into forms of nitrogen that plants can use **(B7)**

nonrenewable resource [non′ri•noō′ə•bəl rē′sôrs′] A resource that cannot be readily replaced once it is used **(C36)**

nonvascular [non•vas′kyə•lər] Not having xylem and phloem; said of some plants **(A74)**

nuclear energy [noō′klē•ər en′ər•jē] The energy released when the nucleus of an atom is split apart **(F110)**

nucleus [noō′klē•əs] **1** *(cell)* The organelle that controls all of a cell's activities. **2** *(atom)* The center of an atom. **(A8, E39)**

open-ocean zone [ō′pən•ō′shən zōn′] The area that includes most deep ocean waters; most organisms live near the surface **(B77)**

orbit [ôr′bit] The path one body in space takes as it revolves around another body; such as that of Earth as it revolves around the sun **(D7, F48)**

organ [ôr′gən] Tissues that work together to perform a specific function **(A12)**

osmosis [os•mō′sis] The diffusion of water and dissolved materials through cell membranes **(A10)**

ovary [ō′və•rē] The portion of a flower, at the base of the pistil, that contains the eggs **(A111)**

palisade layer [pal′ə•sād′ lā′ər] The layer of cells in a leaf where most photosynthesis occurs **(A97)**

Pangea [pan•jē′ə] A supercontinent containing all of Earth's land that existed about 225 million years ago **(C22)**

peat [pēt] A soft, brown material made up of partly decayed plants; first stage of coal formation **(C44)**

periodic table [pir′ē•od′ik tā′bəl] The table of elements in order of increasing atomic number; grouped by similar properties **(E47)**

phloem [flō′em] The tubes that transport food in the vascular plants **(A69)**

photosphere [fōt′ə•sfir′] The visible surface of the sun **(D33)**

photosynthesis [fōt′ō•sin′thə•sis] The process by which plants make food **(A96)**

phototropism [fō•tō•trō′piz•əm] A plant's response to light **(A104)**

physical properties [fiz′i•kəl prop′ər•tēz] The characteristics of a substance that can be observed or measured without changing the substance **(E6)**

pioneer plants [pī′ə•nir′ plantz′] The first plants to invade a bare area **(B92)**

pistil [pis′təl] The female part of a flower **(A110)**

pitch [pich] An element of sound determined by the speed which sound waves move **(F79)**

plate [plāt] The rigid blocks of crust and upper mantle rock **(C15)**

pollen [pol′ən] Flower structures that contain the male reproductive cells **(A76)**

pollution [pə•lōō′shən] Waste products that damage an ecosystem **(B99)**

population [pop•yə•lā′shən] All the individuals of the same kind living in the same environment **(B28)**

position [pə•zish′ən] An object's place, or location **(F34)**

potential energy [pō•ten′shəl en′ər•jē] The energy an object has because of its place or its condition **(F62)**

power [pou′ər] The amount of work done for each unit of time **(F19)**

precipitation [pri•sip′ə•tā′shən] Any form of water that falls from clouds, such as rain or snow **(B14, C65)**

prevailing winds [prē•vāl′ing windz′] The global winds that blow constantly from the same direction **(C73)**

producer [prə•dōōs′ər] An organism that makes its own food **(B34)**

proton [prō′ton′] A subatomic particle with a positive charge **(E39)**

radiation [rā′dē•ā′shən] The transfer of thermal energy by electromagnetic waves **(F85)**

reaction force [rē•ak′shən fôrs′] The force that pushes or pulls back in the third law of motion **(F43)**

reactivity [rē′ak•tiv′ə•tē] The ability of a substance to go through a chemical change **(E23)**

receptors [ri•sep′tərz] Nerve cells that detect conditions in the body's environment **(A26)**

recessive trait [ri•ses′iv trāt′] A weak trait **(A53)**

reclamation [rek′lə•mā′shən] The process of restoring a damaged ecosystem **(B110)**

recycle [rē•sī′kəl] To recover a resource from an item and use the recovered resource to make a new item **(B105)**

recycling [rē•sī′kling] The process of taking a resource from a product and making it into a new product **(C52)**

reduce [ri•dōōs′] To cut down on the use of resources **(B104)**

reflection [ri•flek′shən] The light energy that bounces off objects **(F76)**

refraction [ri•frak′shən] The bending of light rays when they pass through a substance **(F76)**

renewable resource [ri•nōō′ə•bəl rē′sôrs] A resource that is replaced as it is used **(C38)**

resistor [ri•zis′tər] A material that resists the flow of electrons in some way **(F71)**

reusable resource [rē•yōō′zə•bəl rē′sôrs] A natural resource that is renewed by natural cycles and can be used more than once; an inexhaustible resource **(C38)**

reuse [ri´yōōz´] To use items again; sometimes for a different purpose **(B105)**

revolve [ri•volv´] To travel in a closed path around an object such as Earth does as it moves around the sun **(D6)**

rotate [rō´tāt] The spinning of Earth on its axis **(D7)**

satellite [sat´ə•līt´] A natural body, like the moon, or an artificial object that orbits another object **(D15)**

scuba [skōō´bə] Underwater breathing equipment; the letters stand for **s**elf-**c**ontained **u**nderwater **b**reathing **a**pparatus **(C109)**

seedling [sēd´ling] The stage when a germinated seed begins growing and making its own food **(A118)**

sexual reproduction [sek´shōō•əl rē´prə•duk´shən] The form of reproduction in which cells from two parents unite to form a zygote **(A42)**

shore [shôr] The area where the ocean and land meet and interact **(C102)**

solar energy [sō´lər en´ər•jē] The energy of sunlight **(F111)**

solar flare [sō´lər flâr´] A brief burst of energy from the sun's photosphere **(D34)**

solar wind [sō´lər wind´] A fast-moving stream of particles thrown into space by solar flares **(D34)**

solid [sol´id] The state of matter that has a definite shape and a definite volume **(E14)**

solubility [sol´yə•bil´ə•tē] The ability of one substance to be dissolved in another substance **(E10)**

sonar [sō´när´] A device that uses sound waves to determine water depth **(C109)**

space probe [spās´ prōb´] A robot vehicle used to explore deep space **(D16)**

speed [spēd] A measure of the distance an object moves in a given amount of time **(F35)**

spore [spôr] A single reproductive cell that grows into a new plant **(A75)**

stamen [stā´mən] The male part of a flower **(A110)**

submersible [sub•mur´sə•bəl] An underwater vehicle **(C109)**

succession [sək•sesh´ən] A gradual change in an ecosystem, sometimes occurring over hundreds of years **(B92)**

sunspot [sun´spot´] A dark spot on the photosphere of the sun **(D34)**

symbiosis [sim´bē•ō´sis] A long-term relationship between different kinds of organisms **(B45)**

system [sis´təm] Organs that work together to perform a function **(A12)**

telescope [tel´ə•skōp´] An instrument that magnifies distant objects, or makes them appear larger **(D15)**

temperature [tem´pər•ə•chər] The average kinetic energy of all the molecules in an object **(F84)**

tendons [ten´dənz] Tough bands of connective tissue that attach muscles to bones **(A25)**

threatened [thret´ənd] Describes a population of organisms that are likely to become endangered if they are not protected **(B51)**

tidal energy [tīd´əl en´ər•jē] A form of hydroelectric energy that produces electricity from the rising and falling of tides **(F106)**

tide [tīd] The repeated rise and fall in the level of the ocean **(C98)**

tide pool [tīd′ pōōl′] A pool of sea water found along a rocky shoreline **(C103)**

tissue [tish′ōō] Cells that work together to perform a specific function **(A12)**

tissue culture [tish′ōō kul′chər] Process that grows plants artificially in laboratories **(A120)**

transpiration [tran′spə•rā′shən] The process in which plants give off water through their stomata **(B15)**

tropism [trō′piz′əm] A plant's response to a stimulus **(A104)**

unbalanced forces [un•bal′ənst fôrs′əz] Forces that are not equal **(F13)**

universe [yōōn′ə•vûrs′] Everything that exists—planets, stars, dust, gases, and energy **(D46)**

vascular [vas′kyə•lər] Term that decribes a plant with xylem and phloem **(A74)**

vegetative propagation [vej′ə•tāt′iv prop′ə•gā′shən] A form of asexual reproduction without seeds **(A119)**

velocity [və•los′ə•tē] An object's speed in a particular direction **(F35)**

villi [vil′ī] The tiny tubes sticking into the small intestine **(A19)**

volcano [vol•kā′nō] A mountain formed by lava and ash **(C16)**

volume [vol′yōōm] **1** *(measurement)* The amount of space that an object takes up. **2** *(sound)* The loudness of a sound **(E8, F79)**

W

water cycle [wôt′ər sī′kəl] The cycle in which Earth's water moves through the environment **(B14)**

wave [wāv] The up-and-down movement of surface water **(C94)**

weathering [weth′ər•ing] The process of breaking rock into soil, sand, and other tiny pieces **(C7)**

weight [wāt] A measure of the pull of gravity on an object **(E7)**

wetlands [wet′landz′] The water ecosystems that include saltwater marshes, mangrove swamps, and mud flats **(B111)**

work [wûrk] The use of a force to move an object through a distance **(F18)**

X

xylem [zī′ləm] The tubes that transport water and minerals in vascular plants **(A69)**

A

Abdominal muscles, R30
Absolute magnitude, D38
Acceleration, F35, F42
Acid(s), E24
Acid rain, C38, E25
    (map), B99
Acorns, A117
Action force, F43
Active transport, A11
Activity pyramid,
    weekly planning, R16
Adaptations, B43
    in desert, B69
    in estuaries, B80
    in freshwater ecosystem, B79
Adrenal glands, R41
Adult, insect, A47, A48
Aerobic activities, R20–21
A4 ballistic rocket, D20
African plate, C16
Agriculture, saltwater, C114–115
Agronomist, A123
Air, gases in, E10
Air pollution, B99, C51
Air pressure, C65, C66, C73,
    D30–31
Air tubes, lung, R36
Alchemy, E50
Algae bloom, B98
Allen, Joe, F25
Aluminum, C36
Aluminum (element), E41
Alveoli (air sacs), A18, R36
Alvin, C109
Ammonia, A20, B7
Amylase, R33
Anacapa Island, CA, C103
Anchorage, AK, C18
Anemometer, C65
Angiosperm(s), A77, A110, A116
Ant(s), B45
Anther, A111
Anthracite, C45, E40
Anvil, F79, R26
Aphids, B45

Apollo 11, D21
Apparent magnitude, D38
Aqua-lung, C109
Arcata, CA, wetlands, B111
Aristotle, C84, E38, E50, F40
Armstrong, Neil, D15, D20, D21
Arp, Alissa J., B94
Arrazi, E50
Arteries, A17, R34
Asexual reproduction, A41, A119
Ash, C16, C17
Asphalt, self-healing, E28–29
Aspirin, A84
Astronaut(s), D12
Astronautical engineer, F53
Astrophysicist, D51
Atacama Desert, Chile, A72
Athabasca Glacier, C8
Atmosphere, C64, D31
Atmospheric conditions,
    measuring, C65–67
Atom(s), E38, E40, E50, F86
    iron, F7
    structure of, E39
Atomic mass, E51
Atomic number, E40, E51
Atomic theory, E38
Auditory canal, R26
Auditory nerve, R26
Aurora(s), D34
Aurora borealis, D21
Autonomic nervous system, R39
Auto mechanic, A115
Avalanche, F58, F63
Axis, D7
Axon, A26

B

Bacteria, A7
    fighting, R14
    and nitrogen, B7
    in nodules, B7
Balance, E7
    using, R6
Balanced forces, B12–13
Bald eagles, B52, B115
Ball-and-socket joints, A24

Ballard, Robert, C111, C116
Baptist, Kia K., C28
Bark, A69
Barometer, C65, C66, C84–85
Barrier island, C105
Basalt, D9
Bases, E24
Bat(s), A113
Battery, F70
Bauxite, C36, C51
Bay of Fundy, Canada, F106
Bay of Fundy tides, C98
Beach crossovers, B102
Behaviors, changing, C51
Bennett, Jean M., F90
Biceps, R30
Biomass, F110
Biome(s), B64–65
    comparing, B72–73
    differences within, B65
    land, B64–73
    world, B64–65
Biosphere 2 (AZ), B62
Bitumen, C45
Bjerknes, Jacob, C85
Bladder, A20
Blood, A16, A17
Blood vessels, A16, R34, R36
Bluebonnet, B112
Body organization, A12
Body system, A12
Bohr, Niels, E39
Boiling, E16–17
Boiling point, E18
Bone(s), A24–25
    kinds of, R29
Bone marrow, A24, R40
Boyko, Hugo and Elizabeth, C114
Boyle, Robert, E50
B-protein, A86, A87
Brackish-water ecosystem, B76,
    B80–81
Brain, A26, R38
Branches, A69
Breathing, A18
Brock microscope, R5
Bronchi, A18
Bud, A111

Cornfield, A96
Corn kernel, A116
Corona, D32–33
Cotyledons, A116, A118
Cousteau, Jacques, C109
Cowings, Patricia, F54
Creep, C9
Creosote, B69
Crocuses, A66
Crossbreeding, A53
Cross-pollination, A112
Crust, Earth's, C14
Cumulonimbus clouds, C68
Cumulus clouds, C15, C68
Curling, F44
Currents
    and Earth's rotation, C99
    ocean, C80, C96–97
    and shoreline, C103
Cuticle, leaf, A97
Cuttings, A120
Cytoplasm, A8, A9, A11, A39

D

Dalton, John, E38, E50
Dandelions, A67
Day-neutral plants, A106
DDT, B52
Decay, B9
Deceleration, F35
Deciduous forests, B64–65, B67
Decomposers, B35
Decomposition, A122
Deep-ocean currents, C97
Deer, B42
Delta(s), C7
Deltoid, R30
Democritus, E38
Dendrites, A26
Density, E9
Deposition, C7
Dermis, R27
Desalination, C112–113
Desert, B65, B69
    growth of, worldwide, B89
Desert zone, C80

Diamond(s), E40
    density of, E9
Diapers, from corn, D123
Dicots, A116
Diesel fuel, F99
Diet, healthful, A82
Diffusion, A10
Digestive system, A16, A19,
    R32–33
Digitalis, A84
Direct development, A46
Displacement, E8
Distillation, E25
Diversity, B66
Diving bell, C109
DNA code, A28, A29, A39, A54
Dominant trait(s), A53, A54
Donne, John, B24
Doppler radar, C85
Douglas, Marjory Stoneman, B20
Drake, E.L., F96
Drop of Water, A (Wick), B17
Dry cell, F70
Ductility, E42
Dunes, C8

E

E. coli, A87
Ear(s), R26
Ear canal, F79
Eardrum, F79, R26
Earth
    gravity of, E7, F2, F8
    growth in population of, B61
    interior of, C14–15
    as magnet, F7
    and moon compared, D6–11
    revolution of, F30
    rotation of, D7
Earth Day, B107
    first, B114
*Earthmaker's Tales: North
American Indian Stories*
    (Mayo), C83
Earthquake(s), C15, C18–19
    major, C18
    safety, R23

Earth's surface, C6–25
    uneven heating of, C72–75
Ear tubes, C74
Eastwood, Alice, A88
Ecologist, B83
Ecosystem(s), B28–32
    human effect on, B98–101
    limiting factors in, B43
    restoring, B110–113
    water, B76–81
Egg(s), A47, A48, A110, A112
Elastic potential energy, F64
Electric charge, F68
Electric circuits, F71
Electric current, F69, F70
Electric energy, F64, F68–73,
    F99
Electric energy station, F89
Electric force, F69
Electric generators, F99, F105
Electricity, C43, F89
    production of, C42
Electric motor, F73
Electromagnet, F72
Electromagnetic waves, F78
Electrons, E39, F68, F70
Element(s), E40, E50–51
    basic, F40
    common (chart), E41
    grouping, E46–47
    history of, E50
El Niño, C81, C85
Elodea, B5
Embryo, A78, A79
    seed, A116
Endangered organisms, B51
Endangered species, in U.S., B24
Endangered Species Act, B115
Endocrine system, R41
Energy, F62–65
    developing sources of, F88–89
    forms of, F64
    kinetic, F62
    potential, F62
    transferral of, B34–39
    transformation of, F63
    worldwide use of (chart), F94
Energy levels, E39